International Management

A CULTURAL APPROACH

Second Edition

Carl Rodrigues

Montclair State University

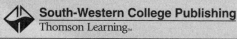

South-Western College Publishing
Thomson Learning™

Australia • Canada • Mexico • Singapore • Spain • United Kingdom • United States

International Management: A Cultural Approach, 2e
by Carl Rodrigues

Vice President/Publisher: Jack W. Calhoun
Executive Editor: John Szilagyi
Marketing Manager: Rob Bloom
Development Editor: Ohlinger Publishing Services
Production Editor: Elizabeth A. Shipp
Media Production Editor: Kristen Meere
Manufacturing Coordinator: Sandee Milewski
Internal Design: Carolyn Deacy Design, San Francisco
Cover Design: Carolyn Deacy Design, San Francisco
Cover Illustration: © Campbell Laird/Stock Illustration Source
Production House: Mazer Corporation
Printer: Westgroup

This book is printed on acid-free paper.

For more information contact South-Western College Publishing
5101 Madison Road
Cincinnati, Ohio 45227
or find us on the Internet at http://www.swcollege.com

For permission to use material from this text or product, contact us by
➤ telephone: 1-800-730-2214
➤ fax: 1-800-730-2215
➤ web: http://www.thomsonrights.com

Printed in the United States of America

1 2 3 4 5 03 02 01 00

Library of Congress Cataloging-in-Publication Data
Rodrigues, Carl.
    International management: a cultural approach / Carl Rodrig[u]es.--2nd ed.
        p.   cm.
    Includes bibliographical references and index.
    ISBN 0-324-04150-0
        1. International business enterprises--Management--Social aspects. 2. Strategic planning--Social aspects. 3. International business enterprises--Management--Case studies. 4. Intercultural communication. I. Title.
HD62.4.R645 2001
658'.049--dc21

                                                                    00-034441

Dedication

To my children, Robert, Carole, and Christopher;
and to Eva Nicholas, Lynn Block, and Helen Beland

Brief Contents

Contents

CHAPTER 2

Cross-National Ethics and Social Responsibility 39

Learning Objectives of the Chapter 39

CROSS-NATIONAL ETHICS 40

BRIBERY AND PAYOFFS ABROAD 42
Forms of Bribery 43
Extortion 44
To Bribe or Not to Bribe? 44
The U.S. Foreign Corrupt Practices Act of 1977 45
An Alternative Payoff Approach 50

CROSS-NATIONAL SOCIAL RESPONSIBILITY 50
Cultural Relativism 51
Universalism 54

TOWARD THE GLOBALIZATION OF BUSINESS ETHICS 55
The Impact of Culture on the Business Ethics Visibility Gap 57
Business Ethics and the Internet 57

SUMMARY 59
Key Terms and Concepts 60
Discussion Questions and Exercises 60
Assignment 60

Part II THE INTERNATIONAL PLANNING PROCESS 69

CHAPTER 3

The Global Environment 71

Learning Objectives of the Chapter 71

C H A P T E R 4

International Strategy 111

C H A P T E R   5

International Strategy: The Four Ps 151

Part VI CROSS-CULTURAL COORDINATION 393

C H A P T E R   1 1

Cross-Cultural Decision Making 395

Learning Objectives of the Chapter 395

CHAPTER 1 2

Cross-Cultural Leadership and Motivation 427

Part VII INTERNATIONAL CONTROL 473

C H A P T E R   1 3

Headquarters–Foreign Subsidiary Control Relationships 475
Learning Objectives of the Chapter 475

GLOBAL CONTROLS: CENTRALIZATION AND DECENTRALIZATION 476

HEADQUARTERS–FOREIGN SUBSIDIARY GOVERNANCE MECHANISMS 479
The National Culture Scheme 482
The Situational Scheme 487
Information Technology: Communication Costs 493
International Managers Must Consider Both Schemes 494

A FRAMEWORK FOR ATTAINING A BALANCED HSR 494
Due Process as a Means of Attaining Balanced HSRs 495
Global Corporate Culture and Core Values as a Means of Attaining Balance 497
Nurturing Balance 499

SUMMARY 501
Key Terms and Concepts 501
Discussion Questions and Exercises 501
Assignment 502

Preface

TO THE STUDENT

Text Objective

The purpose of *International Management: A Cultural Approach* is to teach, in a comprehensive, "user friendly" style, the managerial process (planning, organizing, staffing, coordinating, and controlling) in a global context to upper undergraduate and MBA students who will take a course on international management. Ideally, students who enroll in this course will have completed a generic management course, such as Introduction to Management, Principles of Management, Management Process, Organizational Behavior, or Introduction to International Business.

In the past, in some nations, the United States for example, most business enterprises were able to maintain a steady growth rate—or at least survive—in their home-country market. However, since costs have steadily increased in those nations and foreign competitors with lower costs have rapidly emerged, many of those businesses lost that market stability and have been or are now being forced to compete in the international market arena. And, as technologies continue to transfer across countries, businesses in more and more nations are becoming active and competitive participants in the global economy. These developments will continue to generate not only new global competitors but new business opportunities in foreign markets as well. This means that more firms will have to, or choose to, become involved in international business. It also means that more companies will need managers with the ability to apply the managerial process across countries and cultures with differing characteristics. A good starting point toward the development of such managers is at the college/university level (and even at the pre-college level). Thus, there is a need for a college/university text of this nature.

Text Organization
The text describes how varying national cultures affect the application of the managerial process. For example:

➤ Individuals in some cultures commit to plans more readily than individuals in others.

➤ Strategies are affected by the varying cross-cultural preference for products and services and marketing techniques.

➤ People in some cultures require more organizational structure than people in others.

➤ Executives sent abroad to manage a firm's foreign subsidiary adapt more readily to some cultures than to others. Many executives have great difficulty adapting to any foreign culture.

➤ Individuals in some cultures want to participate more in the decision-making process and have a lower tolerance for authoritarian managers than individuals in other cultures.

➤ The business practices and negotiation styles that work in one culture usually do not succeed in another culture.

➤ Most nations have their own unique language, both verbal and non-verbal, which affects the application of the communication process across cultures.

➤ Employee motivation and work values vary from country to country. Thus, the motivational technique that works in one culture might not necessarily work in another culture.

➤ Managers in some cultures want more control over an international corporation's local subsidiary than do managers in other cultures.

➤ The practice of business ethics is affected by the country's culture, as is a corporation's social responsibility.

Chapter 1 gives an overview of how culture affects the managerial process. Chapter 2 discusses cross-cultural business ethics and corporate social responsibility. Chapter 3 describes how other country factors, such as the legal, political/governmental, economic, and technological systems, affect the managerial process. Chapters 4 and 5 discuss strategies for internationalizing business operations. Chapter 6 presents various international organizational structures. Chapters 7 and 8 discuss options for staffing international operations and training and developing global managers. Chapters 9 and 10 discuss cross-cultural communication, business practices, and negotiations. Chapters 11 and 12 discuss cross-cultural decision making, leadership, and motivation. Chapter 13 discusses controlling global organizations. And Chapter 14 presents some of the managerial challenges executives may face in the future in managing global business enterprises, especially the difficulties of applying total quality management (TQM) across cultures. In addition, each chapter contains at least one section describing how current information technology affects the international management process.

TO THE INSTRUCTOR

Text Flexibility

Some of the chapters in *International Management: A Cultural Approach* can be adapted to an instructor's preference for sequencing topics. For example, an instructor may prefer to cover certain topics, such as cross-cultural business ethics and corporate social responsibility (Chapter 2) later in the course. Some instructors may prefer to cover international organizational structures (Chapter 6) and international controls (Chapter 13) sequentially. And others may see fit to cover parts of chapters out of sequence.

Pedagogy

The text provides the following features.

Practical Chapter Opening Quotation
Each chapter begins with a practical international management opening quotation intended to pique students' interest in the material contained in the chapter.

Learning Objectives of the Chapter
Following the opening quotation, all chapters offer a brief background of the substance of the chapter and its objectives.

Practical Perspectives and Anecdotes
All chapters contain numerous practical perspectives inserted in toned form. (Two practical perspectives in Chapter 10 are long and are thus presented as appendices at the end of the chapter.) The chapters also contain short practical anecdotes throughout the body. The aim of these practical perspectives and anecdotes is to help students understand the theoretical aspects of the chapter.

Figures, Tables, and Graphs
To make reading the chapters more interesting, many of the processes, concepts, and theories are presented in figure, table, or graphic form. For classroom discussion, these can generally be displayed via overhead transparencies (or through a PowerPoint presentation).

Key Terms and Concepts, Discussion Questions and Exercises, Chapter Assignment, and Case Studies
At the end of each chapter there is a set of key terms and concepts, followed by discussion questions and exercises, an assignment, and case studies. All

of these tie to the body of the chapter and help students develop an integrative understanding of the essence of the chapter.

Textbook Integrative Cases

Nine textbook integrative cases are presented after the final chapter (Chapter 14). These are to be assigned just before the end of the semester, after students have completed the key terms and concepts, discussion questions and exercises, assignment, and case studies in all chapters.

Glossary and Combined Index

A glossary section and a combined index are contained at the end of the text.

The Supplement Package For Instructors

An *Instructor's Manual and Test Bank* provides lecture assistance. The manual includes the purpose of each chapter, teaching notes, and the answers to the questions, exercises, and chapter integrative cases. It also includes the purpose of the nine text integrative cases, how they should be used, the questions that should be posed to students, and the answers. The Test Bank portion of the manual includes multiple-choice, true-false, and suggested essay questions, and the answers.

NEW TO THIS EDITION

The second edition of *International Management: A Cultural Approach* has been updated and revised to reflect the most recent research, laws, cases, and examples. Specific changes and new material include:

Organizational Changes

We have reorganized the sequence of the chapters within the overall structure of the book in order to enhance its continuity for the student. In order to accomplish this, Chapter 13 (Ethics and Social Responsibility) has been moved to follow Chapter 1, and Chapter 2 (The Global Environment) has been moved into Part II (The International Planning Process).

Additional Material

Each chapter includes updated research findings, new textual examples, and Practical Perspectives where appropriate. In addition, each chapter uses a more varied representation of countries and regions as examples to more accurately reflect the global focus of the book. Furthermore, current information technology, such as the Internet, the Web, e-mail, videoconferencing, and cellular phones, is a new topic added to each chapter of this edition of the textbook. Each chapter now contains a section describing how current information technology affects the chapter's focus, such as international planning, organizing, staffing, coordinating, and controlling. These comprehensive revisions and expansions were designed to allow greater depth into specific issues in International Management and to enhance chapter readability and relevance for all students. Revisions to specific chapters and parts are as follows:

➤ Part II includes major revisions to Chapters 4 and 5, "International Strategy" and "International Strategy: The Four Ps." These chapters were extensively rewritten to strengthen the clarity and treatment of International Strategy. In addition, feedback from the first edition recommended that these chapters focus more on implementation strategies, and appropriate revisions reflect this suggestion.

➤ New material has been added to Chapter 14 (TQM and Implementation Challenges) to include new quality assurance standards.

Pedagogy

International Management: A Cultural Approach is a text designed to accomplish many goals, including, but not limited to, a multidimensional approach designed to enhance and fortify student comprehension and retention of the information. Thus, the text and ancillaries are a complete package with a balance of concepts, examples, and practical applications. In order to promote understanding of International Management, the following changes have been made to the text and ancillaries:

➤ Practical Perspectives have been modified to reflect the most up-to-date perspectives on International Management issues and concepts. It is our belief that these Practical Perspectives reflect the most cutting edge information available in International Management today.

➤ Key Terms have been expanded to include Key Terms and Concepts to accurately reflect and draw attention to the most important points in the text.

➤ Many Chapter Cases and Integrative Cases have been updated and replaced with informative, thought-provoking, and current cases in order to accurately reveal to students the issues and challenges facing international business and managers today. These cases were selected with the student of the twenty-first century in mind.

➤ Due to their popularity among both students and professors, the Integrative Cases have been expanded to include two additional cases, bringing the total number of Integrative Cases to nine. This expansion allows a greater depth of exploration into key concepts and processes in the chapters.

➤ This edition also includes a Power Point presentation with 140 full-color slides. The presentation is varied and is designed to hold students' interest while reinforcing each of the chapters' main points.

Acknowledgments

Sheila A. Adams
University of North Carolina at Wilmington

Douglas Allen
University of Denver

Fritz E. Bachli
Lesley College

Richard Baldwin
Cedarville College

B.R. Baliga
Wake Forest University

Charles Byles
Virginia Commonwealth University

Warnock Davies
Golden Gate University

Raffaele DeVito
Emporia State University

Richard E. Dutton
University of South Florida

David Flynn
Hofstra University

Manton C. Gibbs, Jr.
Indiana University of Pennsylvania

George Gore
University of Cincinnati

Santiago Ibarreche
University of Texas at El Paso

Sara L. Keck
Pace University

Franz T. Lohrke
Louisiana State University

Robert C. Losik
New Hampshire College

Ray Montagno
Ball State University

Francine Newth
Providence College

John N. Orife
Indiana University of Pennsylvania

Steven K. Paulson
University of North Florida

Joseph A. Petrick
Wright State University

S. Benjamin Prasad
Central Michigan University

Abdul Rasheed
University of Texas at Arlington

Rajib N. Sanyal
Trenton State College

C. Richard Scott
Metropolitan State College of Denver

John A.C. Stanbury
Indiana University at Kokomo

Gregory K. Stephens
Texas Christian University

Arthur Whatley
New Mexico State University

A deep debt of gratitude is owed to the reviewers for their expert assistance. Each comment and suggestion was thoroughly evaluated, and served to improve the final product. To each of the above reviewers, I give my most sincere thanks.

I especially wish to thank Nailin Bu, my colleague at Queen's University, Canada, for providing me with numerous materials that were very useful in the development of the text as well as for her willingness to help whenever I needed it. For the second edition, I wish to thank the reviewers for their valuable suggestions on how to improve the textbook. I also wish to thank Theresa and Kelly Curtis of Ohlinger Publishing Services for their very valuable ideas on how to improve the textbook and for their skillful management of the project. Many thanks also to Libby Shipp, the production editor, and Debbie Cress, the project manager. And I wish to thank John R. Szilagyi, Executive Editor, South-Western/Thomson Learning for believing in the project.

I

Introduction To International Management

The term *management* is defined in many Western, and particularly U.S., textbooks as the process of completing activities efficiently with and through other individuals. The process consists of the functions or main activities engaged in by managers. These functions or activities are usually labeled planning, organizing, staffing, coordinating (leading and motivating), and controlling. The management process is affected by the organization's home country environment, which includes the shareholders, creditors, customers, employees, government, and community, as well as technological, demographic, and geographic factors. *International management* is applied by managers of enterprises that attain their goals and objectives across unique multicultural, multinational boundaries. These business enterprises are generally referred to as international corporations, multinational corporations (MNCs), or global corporations, which are discussed in Chapter 1. This means that the process is affected by the environment where the organization is based, as well as by the unique culture, including views on ethics and social responsibility, existing in the country or countries where it conducts its business activities. Chapter 1 discusses the impact of culture on the managerial process, and Chapter 2 describes the views on ethics and social responsibility that have an impact on international management.

1

The International Management Process: An Overview

"Why do some international managers succeed while nearly half of their counterparts fail? The answer is culture shock—the failure to adjust to people with different motivations, behaviors, and ways of making decisions."[1]

Learning Objectives of the Chapter

Since the environment differs across countries, the managerial approach that works in one country does not necessarily work in another. This suggests that, to manage effectively across cultures, managers require skills beyond those required to manage in the home country. For example, managers would know that in the U.S. it is the individual who counts. In Japan, it is the group. Things get done not by nonconforming lone rangers but by group consensus. The consensus is possible only through cultivation of relationships. Relationships help define the essence of Japanese society, including the conduct of business. After studying this chapter, you should be able to:

1. Describe culture.
2. Briefly describe the impact of culture on international planning, international organization, international staffing, international coordinating, and international controlling.
3. Describe the skills international/global managers require.
4. Discuss why it is important to study international management.

THE INTERNATIONAL MANAGEMENT PROCESS

The **international management process** is heavily affected by the culture (as well as other factors) of the country where enterprises pursue their goals and objectives. (For a description of how culture affects the international management process in Asia, read Practical Perspective 1-1.)

Culture

Culture comprises an entire set of social norms and responses that condition people's behavior; it is acquired and inculcated, a set of rules and

PRACTICAL PERSPECTIVE 1-1

Managing Cultural Diversity in Asia

Cultural elements can affect business behavior in Asia in several ways. Western companies may find that differences occur in areas such as commitment to the organization, work ethic, the drive to achieve and succeed, acceptance of responsibility; the relationship with seniors, the way in which subordinates are motivated, or handling discipline and control. The Confucian cultures hold a secret to success. [The author cites Gordon Redding, a professor at Hong Kong University.]

From the huge monolithic networks of Japan (*keiretsu*) and Korea (*chaebol*) to the small family-owned businesses of overseas Chinese that dominate Taiwan, Hong Kong, and Southeast Asia, "patterns replicate like successful recipes," he [Professor Redding] says. The common denominator is paternalism. It is difficult to generalize, but it has been argued that the hierarchical, vertical, familial, highly status-differentiated structures that permeate Asia show marked contrast to the more egalitarian, horizontal institutions of the West.

Social relationships tend to be more authoritarian, paternalistic, and personal in Asia, nurturing autocratic or unilateral decision-making processes and interpersonal relationships that are based on collectivism and group welfare. Corresponding parameters in the West include more consultative decision making but an emphasis on individualism, self-interest, and impersonal or aggressive relations. Words such as *loyalty*, *trust*, and *cooperation* enjoy high rating in motivating and controlling Asian employees, whereas *competency* and *individual performance* are strong motivators in the West.

Western multinationals planning to gear up their businesses in Asia may have to adapt their corporate cultures to embrace elements more familiar to Asian businesses. This could include profit sharing, a highly disciplined structure, a more humanistic corporate culture, increased nonindividualistic reward, a greater sense of corporate pride, or a stronger cementing-in of workers by use of fringe benefits.

Source: Excerpted from Lyn Tattum, "Managing Cultural Diversity in Asia," *Chemical Week* (February 3, 1993): 14. Reprinted with permission.

behavior patterns that an individual learns but does not inherit at birth.[2] It enables people to make sense of their world, and it is foreign only to those outside. Knowledge of the concept of culture is imperative for understanding human behavior throughout the world, including in one's own country. Fundamentally, groups of individuals develop a social environment as an adaptation to their physical environment, and they pass down their customs, practices, and traditions from generation to generation.[3]

For a brief account of how cultures differ across countries, see Practical Perspective 1-2. For an illustration of how culture affects international business practices, read Practical Perspective 1-3.

How Culture Is Learned

According to the well-known anthropologist Edward T. Hall, culture is learned through formal, informal, and technical means.

In **formal learning,** "formal activities are taught by precept and admonition. The adult mentor molds the young according to patterns he [or she] himself [herself] has never questioned."[4]

In **informal learning,** "the principal agent is a model used for imitations. Whole clusters of related activities are learned at a time, in many cases without the knowledge that they are being learned at all or that there are patterns or rules governing them."[5]

Technical learning, in its pure form, "is close to being a one-way street. It is usually transmitted in explicit terms from the teacher to the student, either orally or in writing."[6]

PRACTICAL PERSPECTIVE 1-2

Different Cultures, Different Meanings

Never touch the head of a Thai or pass an object over it, as the head is considered sacred in Thailand. Likewise, never point the bottoms of the feet in the direction of another person in Thailand or cross your legs while sitting, especially in the presence of an older person. Avoid using triangular shapes in Hong Kong, Korea, or Taiwan, as a triangle is considered a negative shape in those countries. Remember that the number 7 is considered bad luck in Kenya, good luck in Czechoslovakia [now Czech Republic and Slovakia Republic], and has magical connotations in Benin. Red is a positive color in Denmark but represents witchcraft and death in many African countries. A nod means "no" in Bulgaria, and shaking the head side-to-side means "yes."

Source: Excerpted from M. Katharine Glover, "*Do*'s and Taboos: Cultural Aspects of International Business," *Business America* (August 13, 1990): 2. Reprinted with permission.

Culture in the Arab World

Most managers in the U.S. and other Western countries say that culture consists of beliefs, values, ways of thinking, and language. But most Arab managers—like their Japanese counterparts—think of culture as history, tradition, and a way of life. Clearly, culture is a behavioral norm that a group of people have agreed upon in order to survive. These norms vary by time and place and are constantly adapted to the changing environment.

Within each culture, there are many subcultures of which we are simultaneously members. An Egyptian-born executive of a Cairo computer company belongs to the subcultures of Egypt, his company, his sales department, product group, family, and so forth. Every sort of normal, day-to-day business activity is affected by these cultural identities—including personal introductions, meetings, presentations, training, motivation, and written communication.

One way of looking at culture is to consider what values are most important: competition, formality, group harmony, risk-taking, or authority. Among Americans, emphasis is usually placed on independence, competition, and individual success. In the Arab world, however, primacy is given to family security, compromise, and personal reputation. Let's consider a few situations in which dramatic differences in behavior can generate conflict, or at least misunderstanding:

An American attending a business conference is likely to introduce himself to an Arab businessman then quickly walk off to talk to other Arab executives, declining invitations to have some coffee during the break. The American doesn't have enough time for more

than a brief chat with anyone; his objective is to make as many contacts as possible. The Arab businessmen are put off by this behavior because Arabs place a high value on building personal relationships; they want to get to know someone fairly well before discussing business matters.... Like the Japanese, Arabs hold a much longer-term view of time; they don't shun spending months or years building personal relationships and trust....

Friction is likely to occur when there is disagreement in the workplace since Arabs take a very different view of how to manage conflict than do Americans. If an American worker disagrees with his [her] manager, he [or she] is most likely to discuss the matter directly with the manager. This is because Americans value social equality and believe that frank discussion can solve many difficult problems. In the Arab countries, however, an employee who has a disagreement with his or her immediate supervisor (American or otherwise) may well decide to appeal to a higher authority— the manager's boss. If the immediate supervisor is American, this surprise can generate even greater ill will.

Even the "simple" subject of physical distance can create misunderstandings. An Arab executive may well stand closer to you than would an American or Japanese. While this is a way of expressing personal warmth and hospitality most Westerners—and Japanese—will retreat, because they feel their comfort zone of personal space has been invaded.

Source: Excerpted from Farid Elashmawi, "Managing Culture in the Arab World," *Trade & Culture* (September–October 1994): 48–49. Farid Elashmawi, Ph.D., a native of Cairo, Egypt, is president of Tech-Trans/Global Success, a consultancy that specializes in issues of global cultural diversity. Copyright © 1994, *Trade and Culture* Inc. Reprinted with permission. All rights reserved.

Sources of Cultural Learning

Sources of cultural learning include the family, educational institutions, and religion.

The Family

The most fundamental unit to the development of culture is the family.[7] The construction of family households varies across cultures. For example, in America, the nuclear family has been a fairly independent unit. However, in many cultures, such as that of Italy, the family unit is made up of the mother, father, children, grandparents, aunts, and uncles.

Educational Institutions

Another fundamental source of cultural development is educational institutions, which differ from society to society. Some societies, such as Germany, heavily emphasize organized, structured forms of learning that stress logic, while others, including Great Britain and America, take a more abstract, conceptual approach.[8]

Religion

Different societies develop different religions, which are the major causes of cultural differences in many societies. Basically, religious systems "provide a means of motivation and meaning beyond the material aspects of life."[9] For example, the United States, to a great extent, reflects the Protestant work ethic. Protestantism, as does Catholicism, derives from Christianity. On the other hand, many Asian cultures, such as Japan and China, are heavily influenced by Buddhism and the practical aspects of Confucianism. (It should be noted that, as will be discussed below, Confucianism is not a religion; it is a practical philosophy.)

There are many religions throughout the world, but four dominate: Christianity, Islam, Hinduism, and Buddhism.

Christianity. Most Christians live in Europe and the Americas, but Christianity is growing rapidly in Africa. The major symbol of Christianity, which emerged from Judaism, is Jesus Christ. Like Judaism, Christianity is a monotheistic (belief in one god) religion. The two major Christian organizations are the Roman Catholic Church and the Eastern Orthodox Church. The Roman Catholic Church is dominant in Southern Europe and Latin America, and the Eastern Orthodox Church is dominant in numerous countries, including Greece and Russia.

The Reformation in the 16th century led to a split in the Catholic Church and to the formation of Protestantism by Martin Luther. Subsequently, numerous denominations, including Baptist, Methodist, and Calvinist, emerged under the umbrella of Protestantism. The famous

German sociologist, Max Weber, once noted that, in Western Europe, "business leaders and owners of capital, as well as the higher grades of skilled labor, and even more the higher technically trained personnel of modern enterprises, are overwhelmingly Protestant."[10]

Islam. Islam, which dates back to about A.D. 600, was started by the prophet Muhammad. Those who adhere to Islam are referred to as Muslims. Islam is the major religion in many African and Middle Eastern countries and in some parts of China, Malaysia, and some other Far East countries. Islam has some roots in both Judaism and Christianity—it accepts Jesus Christ as one of God's prophets. The major principles of Islam (similar to Judaism and Christianity) are honor and respect parents, respect the rights of others, be generous but do not squander, avoid killing when no justifiable cause is present, do not commit adultery, be just and equitable with others, have a pure heart and mind, safeguard the possessions of orphans, and be humble and nonpretentious.[11] Religion is paramount in all aspects of Muslims' lives—for example, Muslim ritual necessitates prayer five times a day, and women dress in a certain way and must be subordinate to men.

Hinduism. Hinduism is dominant in the Indian subcontinent, where it began about 4,000 years ago. Hindus adhere to the belief that there exists a moral force in society that requires the acceptance of certain responsibilities, referred to as dharma. They believe in reincarnation and karma—the spiritual progression of each individual's soul. One's karma is affected by the way he or she lives, and it determines the challenges the individual will be confronted with in his or her next life. Hindus believe that by making their soul more perfect in each new life, they can eventually attain nirvana—a state of total spiritual perfection that makes reincarnation no longer necessary. They also believe that nirvana is attained through a lifestyle of material and physical self-denial—by devoting one's life to spiritual, rather than material, attainment.

Buddhism. Buddhism also has roots in India. It was founded in about 600 B.C. by Siddhartha Gautama. Gautama, who later became known as Buddha ("the awakened one"), was an Indian prince who renounced his wealth to pursue an austere lifestyle and spiritual perfection. He believed he had achieved nirvana but decided to stay on earth to teach his followers. According to Buddhism, misery and suffering derives from people's desires for pleasure. These desires can be repressed by following the Noble Eightfold Path: right views, right intention, right speech, right action, right livelihood, right effort, right awareness, and right concentration. Hinduism supports the caste systems; Buddhism does not. And Buddhism does not advocate the type of extreme ascetic behavior that is encouraged by Hinduism. Most of the world's followers of Buddhism reside in central and southeast Asia, China, Korea, and Japan.

The Effects of Religion on International Management. It is apparent that religion is closely associated with the development of cultural values and that it affects people's day-to-day activities, such as a business's opening and closing times, employees' days off, ceremonies, work habits, and foods. For example, most businesses in Christian-dominated societies close on Christmas Day and often during the week before Christmas Day because of festivities; output slows down enormously. Muslim ritual requires prayer five times a day, work is often interrupted. For instance, Muslim workers at Whirlpool Corporation's Nashville, Tennessee, plant demand time off from the assembly line for daily prayers.[12] Managers of international corporations must therefore be sensitive to employees' religious needs and corporate policies must be flexible and accommodating to the varying needs existing around the globe—otherwise there may be high employee absenteeism and many disappearances from work to satisfy these needs.

Religion also affects international management with respect to employee motivation. For example, the principles of Hinduism and Buddhism do not focus on the practice of working to accumulate wealth; Hindus value spiritual achievements more than they value material achievements.

The Impact of Culture on International Planning

Planning entails defining the organization's mission and establishing goals and objectives and an overall strategy to achieve them. It means being more proactive than reactive. Instead of just responding to a situation, planning allows an organization to create and influence its environment, to exert some degree of control over its destiny. International planning is affected by the various ideas on which normative cultural concepts are based, including the master-of-destiny versus the fatalistic viewpoint and the never-ending-quest-for-improvement viewpoint.[13]

The **master-of-destiny** viewpoint is prominent in numerous cultures, including those of America, Britain, and Australia. Individuals holding this viewpoint believe that they can substantially influence the future, that they can control their destiny, and that through work they can make things happen. Planning in such cultures is feasible because individuals are willing to work to achieve objectives.[14]

In contrast, in many societies, including numerous Middle East cultures, and those of the Muslim faith in Malaysia and Indonesia, the **fatalistic** viewpoint, or "determinism,"[15] is part of the cultural fabric. Individuals influenced by this viewpoint believe that they cannot control their destiny, that God has predetermined their existence and willed what they are to do during their lives. International managers are therefore likely to encounter more difficulty in obtaining a commitment to their plans in fatalistic cultures than they would in master-of-destiny cultures.

Furthermore, some societies, such as those of Native Americans, are dominated by **antiplanning** beliefs. Antiplanners believe that "any attempt to lay out specific and 'rational' plans is either foolish or dangerous or downright evil. The correct approach is to live in them [existing systems], react in terms of one's experience, and not to try to change them by means of some grandiose scheme or mathematical model."[16] Implementing managerial plans in these cultures is therefore difficult.

The international planning function is also affected by the concept of never-ending quest for improvement. Managers in some cultures, such as America, adhere to this view: a belief that change is normal and necessary and that no aspects of an enterprise are above improvement. Organizations' current practices, therefore, are constantly evaluated in hopes that improvements can be made. In contrast, in many other cultures, managers' power arises not from change but from the maintenance of stability in the status quo. These managers will interpret a suggestion for improvement as a threat and an implication that they have failed.[17] Planned change may be difficult to implement in these cultures as well.

The Impact of Culture on International Organizing

Organizing involves designing an organizational structure that best enables the enterprise to attain its goals and objectives. This includes determining what tasks need to be done, by whom, how tasks should be grouped, who is responsible for what, and how authority should be delegated. Organizing across countries is affected by the cultural views held by the society, such as the cultural viewpoint of the independent enterprise as an instrument of social action.

The concept of independent enterprise as an instrument of social action is widely accepted in some cultures, such as the American. Here a corporation is viewed as an entity that has rules and a continuous existence, a separate and important social institution that must be protected and developed. As a result, individuals develop strong feelings of obligation to serve the company, and the enterprise can take priority over their personal preferences and social obligations, including family, friends, and other activities. American managers, for example, assume that each member of the organization will give primary effort to carrying out assigned tasks in the interests of the firm, that they will be loyal and conforming to the enterprise's managerial systems. In contrast, individuals in many cultures, including some South American cultures, consider personal relationships more important than the enterprise.[18] The organizing approach applied in the two cultures would thus be different—for example, there is likely to be less delegation of authority in the personal relationships culture than in the independent enterprise culture.

The Impact of Culture on International Staffing

Staffing means finding, training, and developing the people necessary to accomplish tasks. It is obvious from the previous discussion that the cultural views held by a society have an enormous impact on international staffing strategies and policies. One cultural viewpoint is the concept of personnel selection based on merit.

That personnel selection is based on merit is a managerial view dominant in some cultures, including that of the United States. Managers holding this view select or promote the best qualified people for jobs and keep them as long as their performance standards meet the firm's expectations. In contrast, in many cultures, including some South American cultures, friends and family are considered more important than the enterprise's vitality; organizations expand to accommodate the maximum number of friends and relatives. For example, a Mexican's first priority is often his family, and since employers view it as an obligation that they take care of the people who work for them, nepotism is a natural part of the working world in Mexico. In Venezuela, most companies are family-owned and decisions are made to please family members more than to increase productivity.[19] Individuals who are not members of the family or in the circle of friends may therefore be less motivated to work hard or may work harder to make themselves indispensable, and family members may not work as hard since their jobs are guaranteed.[20]

The staffing function is also affected by individuals' views of wealth. In most cultures, such as Australia, wealth is generally considered desirable, and the prospect of tangible gains serves as a substantial motivator. However, the practice in some cultures, such as Mexico and Malaysia, is to work only until one earns a desired amount of money and then not return to work until the money has been spent.[21] Offering rewards in these cultures will thus not obtain high commitment to organizational goals.

The Impact of Culture on International Coordinating

Coordinating refers to the function of directing the people in the organization. It includes inspiring, appealing to individual motivations, communicating, and resolving conflicts. In their leading roles, some managers make all the decisions, and some managers allow their subordinates to make decisions. Culture also affects this managerial function. For example, the cultural viewpoint of wide sharing in decision making has an impact on the coordination of organizations across cultures.

In some cultures, such as America, managers adhere to the viewpoint of wide sharing in decision making. They believe that personnel in an organization need the responsibility of making decisions for ongoing development, and they give employees the opportunity to grow and to prove their ability, decentralizing decision making as they grow. On the other hand, managers in many cultures, such as France, believe that only a few people in the organization have the right to make decisions, and they offer no such opportunities; they centralize decision making.[22]

Culture also impairs international communication. As was suggested earlier, societies possess unique social norms and responses that condition their members' behavior. The behavior includes the tendency to block out practices that are not congruent with one's own cultural beliefs. As a result, many groups tend to reject prospective change, and dissimilar groups tend to misjudge one another. When an individual from one group interacts with an individual from another group, there is the tendency to make certain assumptions about the precepts, judgments, and thought processes of the other person. When these assumptions are inaccurate, misunderstanding and miscommunication occur.[23]

This means that international managers must be aware of countries' local practices with respect to leadership style and communication approaches and adapt accordingly to them. For example, an international manager from a culture in which employee participation or consultation in decision making is the norm would not do well applying the same practice in cultures in which employees expect authoritarian leadership, and vice versa. And an international manager who is frank in communicating with people because it is a valued practice in his or her culture (American, for example) would not be respected by people in a culture in which frankness is unacceptable and face-saving is valued (Japan, for instance). Also, in some cultures, including American, an individual feels uneasy when the person with whom he or she is communicating becomes silent (pauses to think). Americans find silence clumsy and like to plug any conversational pauses, and they measure people who respond directly as being trustworthy. On the other hand, the Japanese distrust a person who responds directly; they value a person who pauses (becomes silent) to give careful thought to a question before responding.[24]

The Impact of Culture on International Controlling

Controlling is the act of evaluating performance; it is monitoring the results of the goals and objectives previously established and implemented, including measuring individual and organizational performance and taking corrective action when required. Establishing controlling mechanisms across countries is also affected by the cultural views held by the society's members, such as making decisions based on objective analysis.

A belief in making decisions based on objective analysis is widely held by managers in numerous cultures, including the American culture. Managers who practice this belief make decisions based on accurate and relevant information, and they are prompt in reporting accurate data to all levels in the organization. On the other hand, in many cultures managers do not place much value on factual and rational support for decisions, and the reporting of details is unimportant. These decision makers do not seek out facts; they often rely on emotional and mystical considerations rather than on objective analysis; when they are asked to explain the rationale for their decisions, they will interpret the question as a lack of respect or confidence in their judgment.[25] The international manager has to address this problem when establishing controls.

Hofstede's Cultural Dimensions Model

Currently one of the most popular theories addressing the impact of culture on the management process is that developed by Geert Hofstede, a researcher from the Netherlands.[26] He proposed a paradigm to study the impact of national culture on individual behavior and examined the values and beliefs of 116,000 IBM employees based in forty nations throughout the world. (He subsequently conducted the study in ten other countries.) Hofstede developed a typology consisting of four national, cultural dimensions by which a society can be classified: **power distance, uncertainty avoidance, individualism,** and **masculinity.** The characteristics of these cultural dimensions are depicted in Figures 1-1, 1-2, 1-3, and 1-4. Figures 1-5

FIGURE 1-1	The Power Distance Dimension

Small Power Distance	Large Power Distance
Inequality in society should be minimized.	There should be an order of inequality in this world in which everybody has a rightful place; high and low are protected by this order.
All people should be independent.	A few people should be independent; most should be dependent.
Hierarchy means inequality of the roles, established for convenience.	Hierarchy means existential inequality.
Superiors consider subordinates to be "people like me."	Superiors consider subordinates to be a different kind of people.
Superiors are accessible.	Superiors are inaccessible.
The use of power should be legitimate and is subject to the judgment as to whether it is good or evil.	Power is a basic fact of society that antedates good or evil. Its legitimacy is irrelevant.
All should have equal rights.	Power holders are entitled to privileges.
Those in power should try to look less powerful than they are.	Those in power should try to look as powerful as possible.
The system is to blame.	The underdog is to blame.
The way to change a social system is to redistribute power.	The way to change a social system is to dethrone those in power.
People at various power levels feel less threatened and more prepared to trust people.	Other people are a potential threat to one's power and can rarely be trusted.
Latent harmony exists between the powerful and the powerless.	Latent conflict exists between the powerful and the powerless.
Cooperation among the powerless can be based on solidarity.	Cooperation among the powerless is difficult to attain because of their low-faith-in-people norm.

Source: Geert Hofstede, "Motivation, Leadership, and Organization: Do American Theories Apply Abroad?" *Organizational Dynamics* (Summer 1980): 46. Copyright © Geert Hofstede. Reprinted with permission.

FIGURE 1-2	The Uncertainty Avoidance Dimension
Weak Uncertainty Avoidance	**Strong Uncertainty Avoidance**
The uncertainty inherent in life is more easily accepted and each day is taken as it comes.	The uncertainty inherent in life is felt as a continuous threat that must be fought.
Ease and lower stress are experienced.	Higher anxiety and stress are experienced.
Time is free.	Time is money.
Hard work, as such, is not a virtue.	There is an inner urge to work hard.
Aggressive behavior is frowned upon.	Aggressive behavior of self and others is accepted.
Less showing of emotions is preferred.	More showing of emotions is preferred.
Conflict and competition can be contained on the level of fair play and can be used constructively.	Conflict and competition can unleash aggression and should therefore be avoided.
More acceptance of dissent is entailed.	A strong need for consensus is involved.
Deviation is not considered threatening; greater tolerance is shown.	Deviant persons and ideas are dangerous; intolerance holds sway.
The ambience is one of less nationalism.	Nationalism is pervasive.
More positive feelings toward younger people are seen.	Younger people are suspect.
There is more willingness to take risks in life.	There is great concern with security in life.
The accent is on relativism, empiricism.	The search is for ultimate, absolute truths and values.
There should be as few rules as possible.	There is a need for written rules and regulations.
If rules cannot be kept, we should change them.	If rules cannot be kept, we are sinners and should repent.
Belief is placed in generalists and common sense.	Belief is placed in experts and their knowledge.
The authorities are there to serve the citizens.	Ordinary citizens are incompetent compared with the authorities.

Source: Geert Hofstede, "Motivation, Leadership, and Organization: Do American Theories Apply Abroad?" *Organizational Dynamics* (Summer 1980): 47. Copyright © Geert Hofstede. Reprinted with permission.

and 1-6 show Hofstede's classification of the fifty countries and three regions on a range of moderate-to-low or moderate-to-high for each dimension. Figure 1-7 shows the index and the ranking for the fifty countries and three regions.

These cultural dimensions have an impact on international management in many ways (as will be demonstrated throughout the book). For example, people in large power distance cultures prefer stronger leadership than do people in small power distance cultures, and people in strong uncertainty avoidance cultures take fewer risks than individuals in weak uncertainty avoidance cultures. This would affect international coordinating and planning functions. For instance, the current buzzword in management is empowerment—higher levels transferring responsibilities to

FIGURE 1-3	The Individualism Dimension
Collectivist	**Individualist**
In society, people are born into extended families or clans who protect them in exchange for loyalty.	In society, everybody is supposed to take care of himself/herself and his/her immediate family.
"We" consciousness holds sway.	"I" consciousness holds sway.
Identity is based on the social system.	Identity is based in the individual.
There is emotional dependence of the individual on organizations and institutions.	There is emotional independence of the individual from organizations or institutions.
The involvement with organizations is moral.	The involvement with organizations is calculative.
The emphasis is on belonging to organizations; membership is the ideal.	The emphasis is on individual initiative and achievement; leadership is ideal.
Private life is invaded by organizations and clans to which one belongs; opinions are predetermined.	Everybody has the right to a private life and opinion.
Expertise, order, duty, and security are provided by the organization or clan.	Autonomy, variety, pleasure, and individual financial security are sought in the system.
Friendships are predetermined by stable social relationships, but there is need for prestige within these relationships.	The need is for specific friendships.
Belief is placed in group decisions.	Belief is placed in individual decisions.
Value standards differ for in-groups and out-groups (particularism).	Value standards should apply to all (universalism).

Source: Geert Hofstede, "Motivation, Leadership, and Organization: Do American Theories Apply Abroad?" *Organizational Dynamics* (Summer 1980): 48. Copyright © Geert Hofstede. Reprinted with permission.

lower levels. However, people in large power distance and strong uncertainty avoidance cultures may not be able to cope with the increased responsibility that empowerment brings.

The Confucian Dynamism Dimension

Subsequent to his study that identified the cultural dimensions of power distance, individualism, masculinity, and uncertainty avoidance, Hofstede, in collaboration with Michael Bond, a professor and researcher currently at the Chinese University of Hong Kong, identified an additional cultural dimension by which nations can be classified, the *Confucian Dynamism*. This fifth dimension was identified through a questionnaire (labeled the Chinese Value Survey) developed on the basis of traditional Confucian values that are believed to influence East Asian countries (including the People's Republic of China, South Korea, Japan, Hong Kong [now part of China], and Singapore).[27]

This survey included twenty-two countries. Eighteen of these countries and two regions were included in Hofstede's earlier study. The scores for

FIGURE 1-4	The Masculine Dimension

Feminine	Masculine
Men needn't be assertive but can also assume nurturing roles.	Men should be assertive. Women should be nurturing.
Sex roles in society are more fluid.	Sex roles in society are clearly differentiated.
There should be equality between the sexes.	Men should dominate in society.
Quality of life is important.	Performance is what counts.
You work in order to live.	You live in order to work.
People and environment are important.	Money and things are important.
Interdependence is the ideal.	Independence is the ideal.
One sympathizes with the unfortunate.	One admires the successful achiever.
Small and slow are beautiful.	Big and fast are beautiful.
Unisex and androgyny are ideal.	Ostentatious manliness ("machismo") is appreciated.

Source: Geert Hofstede, "Motivation, Leadership, and Organization: Do American Theories Apply Abroad?" *Organizational Dynamics* (Summer 1980): 49. Copyright © Geert Hofstede. Reprinted with permission.

Country Abbreviations For Figures 1-5 and 1-6

ARA	Arab countries	GBR	Great Britain	PAN	Panama
	(Egypt, Lebanon,	GER	Germany	PER	Peru
	Libya, Kuwait, Iraq,	GRE	Greece	PHI	Philippines
	Saudi Arabia, U.A.E.)	GUA	Guatemala	POR	Portugal
ARG	Argentina	HOK	Hong Kong	SAF	South Africa
AUL	Australia	IDO	Indonesia	SAL	(El) Salvador
AUT	Austria	IND	India	SIN	Singapore
BEL	Belgium	IRA	Iran	SPA	Spain
BRA	Brazil	IRE	Ireland	SWE	Sweden
CAN	Canada	ISR	Israel	SWI	Switzerland
CHL	Chile	ITA	Italy	TAI	Taiwan
COL	Colombia	JAM	Jamaica	THA	Thailand
COS	Costa Rica	JPN	Japan	TUR	Turkey
DEN	Denmark	KOR	South Korea	URU	Uruguay
EAF	East Africa	MAL	Malaysia	USA	United States
	(Kenya, Ethiopia,	MEX	Mexico	VEN	Venezuela
	Zambia)	NET	Netherlands	WAF	West Africa
ECA	Ecuador	NOR	Norway		(Nigeria, Ghana,
FIN	Finland	NZL	New Zealand		Sierra Leone)
FRA	France	PAK	Pakistan	YUG	Yugoslavia

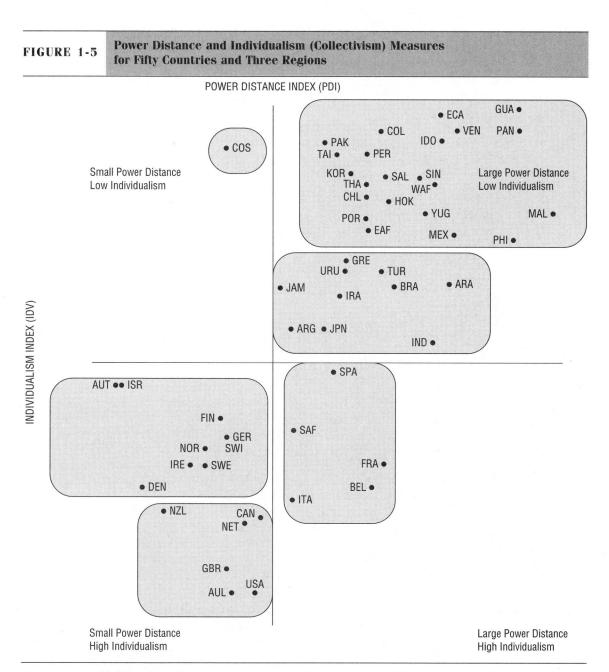

FIGURE 1-5 **Power Distance and Individualism (Collectivism) Measures for Fifty Countries and Three Regions**

POWER DISTANCE INDEX (PDI)

INDIVIDUALISM INDEX (IDV)

Small Power Distance
Low Individualism

Large Power Distance
Low Individualism

Small Power Distance
High Individualism

Large Power Distance
High Individualism

Source: Geert Hofstede, "The Cultural Relativity of the Quality of Life Concept," *Academy of Management Review 9*, no. 3 (1984): 391, 392. Reprinted with permission by the Academy of Management.

FIGURE 1-6 | **Masculinity and Uncertainty Avoidance Measures for Fifty Countries and Three Regions**

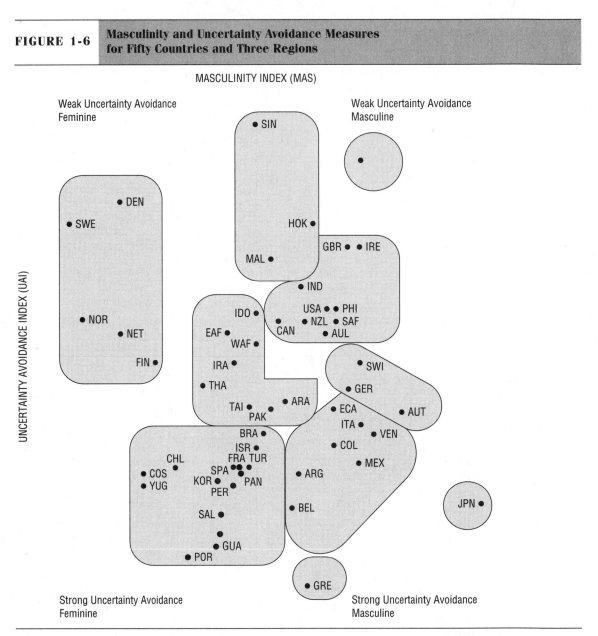

MASCULINITY INDEX (MAS)

Weak Uncertainty Avoidance Feminine

Weak Uncertainty Avoidance Masculine

UNCERTAINTY AVOIDANCE INDEX (UAI)

• SIN

• DEN
• SWE

HOK •

GBR • • IRE

MAL •

• IND

IDO •

USA • • PHI
• NZL • SAF

CAN •
• AUL

EAF •
WAF •

• NOR
• NET

• SWI

IRA •

• GER

FIN •

• THA

TAI •

• ARA

• ECA
ITA •

• AUT

PAK

• VEN

BRA •

• COL

ISR •

CHL

FRA TUR

• MEX

• COS

SPA •

KOR •

• PAN

• ARG

• YUG

PER

SAL •

• BEL

• JPN

• GUA

• POR

• GRE

Strong Uncertainty Avoidance Feminine

Strong Uncertainty Avoidance Masculine

Source: Geert Hofstede, "The Cultural Relativity of the Quality of Life Concept," *Academy of Management Review 9,* no. 3 (1984): 393. Reprinted with permission by the Academy of Management.

FIGURE 1-7	Scores on Five Dimensions for Fifty Countries and Three Regions in IBM's International Employee Attitude Survey									
Country	Power Distance		Individualism		Masculinity		Uncertainty Avoidance		Confucian Dynamism	
	Index	*Rank*	*Index*	*Rank*	*Index*	*Rank*	*Index*	*Rank*	*Index*	*Rank*
Argentina	49	35–36	46	22–23	56	20–21	86	10–15		
Australia	36	41	90	2	61	16	51	37	31	11–12
Austria	11	53	55	18	79	2	10	24–25		
Belgium	65	20	75	8	54	22	94	5–6		
Brazil	69	14	38	26–27	49	27	76	21–22	65	5
Canada	39	39	80	4–5	52	24	48	41–42	23	17
Chile	63	24–25	23	38	28	46	86	10–15		
Colombia	67	17	13	49	64	11–12	80	20		
Costa Rica	35	42–44	15	46	21	48–49	86	10–15		
Denmark	18	51	74	9	16	50	23	51		
Ecuador	78	8–9	8	52	63	13–14	67	28		
Finland	33	46	63	17	26	47	59	31–32		
France	68	15–16	71	10–11	43	35–36	86	10–15		
Germany	35	42–44	67	15	66	9–10	65	29	31	11–12
Great Britain	35	42–44	89	3	66	9–10	35	47–48	25	15–16
Greece	60	27–28	35	30	57	18–19	112	1		
Guatemala	95	2–3	6	53	37	43	101	3		
Hong Kong	68	15–16	24	37	57	18–19	29	49–50	96	1
Indonesia	78	8–9	14	47–48	46	30–31	48	41–42		
India	77	10–11	48	21	56	20–21	40	45	61	6
Iran	58	19–20	41	24	43	35–36	59	31–32		
Ireland	28	49	70	12	68	7–8	35	47–48		
Israel	13	52	54	19	47	29	81	19		
Italy	50	34	76	7	70	4–5	75	23		
Jamaica	45	37	39	25	68	7–8	13	52		
Japan	54	33	46	22–23	95	1	92	7	80	3
Korea (S)	60	27–28	18	43	39	41	85	16–17	75	4
Malaysia	104	1	26	36	50	25–26	36	46		
Mexico	81	5–6	30	32	69	6	82	18		
Netherlands	38	40	80	4–5	14	51	53	35	44	9
Norway	31	47–48	69	13	8	52	50	38		
New Zealand	22	50	79	6	58	17	49	39–40	30	13
Pakistan	55	32	14	47–48	50	25–26	70	24–25	0	20
Panama	95	2–3	11	51	44	34	86	10–15		
Peru	64	21–23	16	45	42	37–38	87	9		
Philippines	94	4	32	31	64	11–12	44	44	19	18
Portugal	63	24–25	27	33-35	31	45	104	2		
South Africa	49	35–36	65	16	63	13–14	49	39–40		
Salvador	66	18–19	19	42	40	40	94	5–6		
Singapore	74	13	20	39–41	48	28	8	53	48	8
Spain	57	31	51	20	42	37–38	86	10–15		
Sweden	31	47–48	71	10–11	5	53	29	49–50	33	10

(continued)

| FIGURE 1-7 | Scores on Five Dimensions for Fifty Countries and Three Regions in IBM's International Employee Attitude Survey, *continued* |

Country	Power Distance		Individualism		Masculinity		Uncertainty Avoidance		Confucian Dynamism	
	Index	*Rank*	*Index*	*Rank*	*Index*	*Rank*	*Index*	*Rank*	*Index*	*Rank*
Switzerland	34	45	68	14	70	4–5	58	33		
Taiwan	58	29–30	17	44	45	32–33	69	26	87	2
Thailand	64	21–23	20	39–41	34	44	64	30	56	7
Turkey	66	18–19	37	28	45	32–33	85	16–17		
Uruguay	61	26	36	29	38	42	100	4		
United States	40	38	91	1	62	15	46	43	29	14
Venezuela	81	5–6	12	50	73	3	76	21–22		
Yugoslavia	76	12	27	33–35	21	48–49	88	8		
Regions:										
East Africa	64	21–23	27	33–35	41	39	52	36	25	15–16
West Africa	77	10–11	20	39–41	46	30–31	54	34	16	19
Arab Ctrs.	80	7	38	26–27	53	23	68	27		

The distance between the lowest- and the highest-scoring country is about 100 points.
Rank Numbers: 1=Highest; 53=Lowest (For Confucian Dynamism: 20=Lowest)

Source: Geert Hofstede and Michael H. Bond, "The Confucius Connection: From Cultural Roots to Economic Growth," *Organizational Dynamics* (Spring 1988), pp.12–13. Copyright © Geert Hofstede. Reprinted with permission.

Confucian Dynamism for the eighteen countries and two regions are listed in the last column of Figure 1-7. As shown, Hong Kong, with an index score of 96, ranked number one on the Confucian Dynamism dimension, and Pakistan, with an index score of zero, ranked number twenty. As Figure 1-7 also depicts, East Asian countries measure high on the Confucian Dynamism dimension, while non-East Asian countries, with the exception of Brazil, tend to measure low.

Confucianism. Confucianism is not a religion but a system of practical ethics; it is based on a set of pragmatic rules for daily life derived from experience. The key tenet of Confucian teachings is that unequal relationships between people create stability in society. The five basic relationships are ruler–subject, father–son, older brother–younger brother, husband–wife, and older friend–younger friend. The junior owes the senior respect, and the senior owes the junior protection and consideration. The prototype for all social institutions is the family. A person is mainly a member of a family, as opposed to being just an individual.

Harmony in the family must be preserved, and harmony is the maintenance of one's *face*, that is, one's dignity, self-respect, and prestige. Treating others as one would like to be treated oneself is virtuous behavior. *Virtue* with respect to one's tasks consists of attempting to obtain skills and education, working hard, not spending more than necessary, being patient, and persevering. It should be noted that individuals may have inner thoughts that differ from the group's norms and values; however, individuals may not act on those thoughts because group harmony and not shaming the group are of paramount importance.[28] (For an illustration of how Confucianism affects international management, refer again to Practical Perspective 1-1. Practical Perspective 1-4 illustrates the self versus group orientation.

The African Thought System *(Ubuntu)*[29]

Just as there is no totally homogeneous thought in other regions of the world, such as Europe and South America, there is no totally homogeneous thought in Africa. There is in fact a diverse sociocultural, linguistic, and historical composition among the African nations. However, as is the case in the other regions throughout the globe, there is an underlying pan-African character that results from a unique geographical, historical, cultural, and political experience. Therefore, Africans can be identified by certain common characteristics in their daily lives. Just as there is an Asian thought system *(Confucianism)*, for example, there is an African thought system—*Ubuntu*. One important characteristic of *Ubuntu* is a high degree of harmony—unity of the whole rather than its distinct parts is emphasized. Thus, similar to *Confucianism*, the individual is strongly connected to the group. Hence, *Ubuntu*, too, emphasizes suppression of the self-interest for the sake of the group's needs. Figure 1-8 presents a comparison of African and Western systems. Therefore, in general, managing people in organizations in Africa is likely to require a substantially different managerial approach from the one used in many of the organizations in America, Sweden, and Denmark, for example. This means that, in many organizational situations in Africa, a reward system emphasizing group achievement is often more effective than a reward system emphasizing individual achievement.

Other Factors That Affect the Management Process

(The above shows how the management process is affected across cultures. Figure 1-9 provides a broad outline). However, besides culture, different societies also develop distinct economic and technological systems by which they produce and distribute goods and wealth; distinct political systems, such as tribal, democratic, or communistic systems; and distinct legal systems.[30] Societies also develop distinct written, verbal, and nonverbal means of communication, and are at differing stages of economic development. These factors affect international management in many ways. For example, differences in language make cross-country business negotiations difficult to conduct. And the stage of the country's economic development affects product/service strategies. For instance, economically poor countries

PRACTICAL PERSPECTIVE 1-4

The Self Versus The Group

Upon leaving the United States for several months of study at a Japanese university, Leo got a crash course in culture shock. Activities that the undergraduate had enjoyed in his native land, such as playing a match of volleyball with friends, suddenly felt strange and unnatural. Casual volleyball games back at home featured a relaxed, cheerful atmosphere and good-humored competitiveness. In Japan, players adopted a grim, no-nonsense manner suited to the application of *ganbaru*, a dogged determination to persevere and keep trying until the end of a task.

Leo's Japanese volleyball experience was, to use a culinary analogy, like biting into a cheeseburger and getting a mouthful of sushi. Something about Japanese life changed the flavor of even the most innocuous items on his menu of customary pursuits. Leo quickly learned to put on a Japanese-style "game face" when he played volleyball, but he did not feel like himself.

Culture clashes such as this accentuate the fact that largely unspoken, collective assumptions about appropriate social behavior vary greatly from one country or geographic region to another, says Japanese psychologist Shinobu Kitayama of Kyoto University. Moreover, the goals, values, ideas, and behaviors that a person learns and uses as a member of a cultural group have far-reaching effects on mental life, Kitayama argues.

The cherished Western concept of a sovereign self provides a case in point. Consider Leo, whose passport to Japan probably should have been stamped with this brief warning: Bearer comes from a culture that treats individuals as independent operators, each of whom must emphasize personal strengths and pump up self-esteem to succeed in life.

In contrast, Japanese culture views individuals as part of an interconnected social web, Kitayama contends. A sense of self develops as a person discerns the expectations of others concerning right and wrong behavior in particular situations. Self-improvement requires an unflagging commitment to confronting one's shortcomings and mistakes; their correction fosters harmony in one's family, at work, and in other pivotal social groups.

This cultural perspective appears in various forms throughout East Asia. Its adherents tend to write off the European-American pursuit of self-esteen as an immature disregard for the relationships that nurture self-identity, Kitayama says.

Source: Excerpted from Bruce Bower, "My Culture, My Self," *Science News* 152 (October 18, 1997): 248. Reprinted with permission from *Science News,* the weekly newsmagazine of science. Copyright © 1997 by Science Service Inc.

usually cannot afford the expensive products manufactured in economically richer countries. The quality of the product may have to be reduced to make it affordable in poorer countries. Or the enterprise may have to move manufacturing to a country where labor is cheaper as a means of making the product affordable in poorer countries. These factors will be discussed more thoroughly in Chapter 3 and in subsequent chapters. Figure 1-9 provides a broad overview of how culture impacts the management process. Figure 1-10 presents an overview of the book's content.

FIGURE 1-8	A Comparison of African and Western Systems	
Element	African	Western
Other people	Treat others as human beings; your child is my child is the community's child. Strangers are regarded as part of extended family.	Relations are instrumental, contractual. Strangers are kept at a distance. Children are taught "Don't talk to strangers."
Focus of benefits	Center of focus is the collective community or society at large. Individual drives are subjugated to the collective.	Individual is the center of focus.
Decision making	Decisions arrived at by consensus. The process is circular. Vision tends to be polyocular. Dissenters compensated for at some future time.	Usually by majority. Winner takes all. The process is linear. Unity of vision is typical. Monocular.
Time	Not a finite commodity, it is the healer. Allow enough of it for important issues before arriving at a decision.	Time is money. It is a strategic commodity to be used frugally.
Age	An ongoing process of maturing and acquiring wisdom. Gray hairs are respected.	Age beyond a certain point become's a negative. Senior citizens regarded as "dead wood."
Familial ties	Extended family ties are central. Family connectedness is important.	Nuclear
Dispute resolution	Aims to restore harmony rather than justice. Good of the collective is preeminent.	Justice takes precedence over harmony. Individual rights are preeminent.

Source: M.P. Mangaliso, N.A. Mangaliso, and J.H. Bruton, "Management in Africa, or Africa in Management? The African Philosophical Thought in Organizational Discourse." Paper presented at the International Management Division, Academy of Management Meetings, San Diego, CA, August 6, 1998, p. 27. Reprinted with permission. Permission conveyed through Copyright Clearance Center, Inc.

GLOBAL MANAGEMENT: A FUTURE PERSPECTIVE

Because more and more nations are developing economically, interdependence among countries is increasing, the competition confronting firms is intensifying, and the opportunities for business growth and expansion are increasing. The increased interdependence, the intensified competition, and the increased opportunities mean that more and more domestic enterprises (those whose revenues derive totally from sales in their home markets) will develop strategies to internationalize their operations. It also means that those enterprises whose current revenues from international business is only a small percentage of their total revenues will develop strategies to increase and restructure their international business operations.

FIGURE 1-9	Cultural Classifications and Some of Their Influences on Management

Cultural Classifications	Managerial Influences
Master-of-destiny	With the right rewards, there is likely to be high employee commitment to plans.
Fatalism	There is likely to be low commitment to plans; strong formal controls may be required; greater use of expatriates may be needed.
Quest for improvement	Planning and implementing change may be feasible.
Maintaining status quo	Planning and implementing change may not be feasible, and strong motivational incentives and control mechanisms may be required.
Enterprise is important	Managers may be able to delegate a high degree of authority to subordinates.
Relationships are important	Managers may be able to delegate only a low degree of authority to subordinates, and strong control mechanisms may be required; greater use of expatriates may be required.
Selection based on merit	Employees may be highly motivated to work.
Selection based on relationships	Employees in outer circle may be less motivated to work, and so may family members and members of the inner circle; strong work incentives and controls may be needed; greater use of expatriates may be required.
Accumulation of wealth	A higher commitment to the organization's goals and objectives may be obtained.
"Just enough"	There may be a lower commitment to the organization's goals and objectives; strong controls may be needed; greater use of expatriates may be needed.
Sharing in decision making	Participative decision-making and leadership styles may work best, and substantial authority may have to be delegated to subordinates.
Few people make decisions	Authoritative decision-making and leadership styles may work best.
Decisions based on data	Looser control mechanisms can be applied.
Decisions based on emotions	Stronger control mechanisms may have to be applied; greater use of expatriates may be required.
High-context cultures	Business transactions and negotiations may have to be slow paced.
Low-context cultures	Business transactions and negotiations may have to be fast paced.
Large power distance	Authoritative decision-making and leadership styles may work best.
Small power distance	Participative/consultative decision-making and leadership styles may work best.
Collectivism	Heavy reliance on informal controls; team approach highly applicable.
Individualism	Heavy reliance on formal controls; team approach not very applicable.
Strong uncertainty avoidance	Mechanistic organization may work best.
Weak uncertainty avoidance	Organic organizational structures may work best.
Masculinity	Equal employment opportunity programs may be resisted by males.
Femininity	Equal employment opportunity programs may be resisted relatively less by males.
Confucianism	Organizations may rely more on informal than on formal controls; individuals prefer authoritative decision making and leadership.

Source: Carl Rodrigues, "Cultural Classifications of Societies and How They Affect Cross-Cultural Management," *Cross-Cultural Management: An International Journal 5,* no. 3 (1998): 31–41.

FIGURE 1-10   International Management

The Management Process	Varying Country Factors That Impact the Management Process

Planning *(discussed in Chapters 4 and 5)*
Product/Service
   Price
   Promotion
   Distribution/Entry Mode
	Culture *(discussed throughout book)*
	
	Other Factors
	
	(discussed in Chapter 10)
	Business Practices
	Negotiating Styles

Organizing *(discussed in Chapter 6)*
   Centralization
   Decentralization
	(discussed in Chapter 2)
	Business Ethics

Staffing *(discussed in Chapters 7 and 8)*
   Expatriate
   Host-Country
   Training/Development
   Compensation
	(discussed in Chapter 9)
	Language
	
	(discussed in Chapter 3)
	Legal Systems
	Labor Laws

Coordinating
   Leadership/Motivation Style
    (discussed in Chapter 12)
   Decision-Making Style
    (discussed in Chapter 11)
   Communication
    (discussed in Chapter 9)
	Political System
	Government Policies
	Competitive Forces
	Economic Forces
	Trade Barriers

Control *(discussed in Chapter 13)*
   Formal/Informal
   Loose/Tight	

For example, an American business enterprise may currently obtain 100 percent of its revenues from its home market operations, or it may obtain 90 percent, for instance, from sales at home and 10 percent from sales in foreign markets. But when more competitive firms (perhaps those that have access to cheaper labor) from foreign countries penetrate its home market and it loses market share, to survive, it must either "get out of the old business" and get into a new one, look for new customers in foreign markets, or transfer manufacturing operations to a foreign site where labor is cheaper. (This will be discussed more thoroughly in Chapter 4.) Below are some other examples of the globalization of business enterprises:

➤ The sequel to *Gone with the Wind*, published by Warner Books in 1991, was released simultaneously in 40 countries.[31]

➤ New technologies in state-of-the-art Ford Motor Company plants are set up in Mexico.[32]

➤ Five of the six giant corporations that dominate the U.S. music industry are foreign. Warner Music is the American one. Bertelsmann now owns the RCA label; Sony owns CBS Records, Columbia

Pictures, and Radio City Music Hall; and Matsushita owns MCA. Bertelsmann also owns Bantam, Doubleday, and Dell book publishers.[33]

➤ Mattel now produces African American, Hispanic, and Asian Barbie dolls for the world market.[34]

➤ The number-one baker of Girl Scout cookies in the United States is President Enterprises, a Taiwanese company.[35]

➤ The official major-league baseball, that most American of icons, is made exclusively in Costa Rica.[36]

➤ U.S.'s Ford Motor Company gained control of Japan's Mazda Motor Corporation in 1996.[37]

➤ In 1999, Carrefour in France acquired Planalto, a Brazilian super-market chain; Promodès and Exxcel expanded their presence in Argentina by purchasing stores from Unimarc, a Chilean supermarket chain; Wal-Mart got the approval from the EC in Brussels to acquire the Asada Group for some U.S. $10.6 billion.[38]

➤ Starbucks Corporation acquired Seattle Coffee Co. of Britain in a stock swap worth about U.S. $83 million.[39]

➤ German conglomerate Bertelsmann purchased Random House and became the largest American publisher.[40]

➤ Freightliner, of Portland, Oregon, America's largest manufacturer of heavy-duty trucks, is owned by Germany's Daimler-Benz (now DaimlerChrysler), maker of the Mercedes-Benz.[41]

➤ Kellogg, of Battle Creek, Michigan, sells over 50 percent of the cold cereal consumed outside the United States.[42]

➤ In 1992, Honda exported 55,000 of its Ohio-made cars to eighteen countries, Japan included.[43]

These are just a few examples that help demonstrate the increasing trend of companies investing more and more in foreign countries. Figure 1-11 depicts the enormous amount of trade taking place between nations.

Global Corporations

Another increasing trend is the emergence of the global corporation. (Refer to Practical Perspective 1-5.) Enterprises involved in international business are usually referred to as international corporations, multinational corporations (MNCs), or global corporations. Some people use the **international corporation** label to mean firms that export their products to other countries and the **multinational corporation** label to mean companies that establish subsidiaries in foreign countries. Other people use the two labels interchangeably; both labels refer to companies that have expanded their business activities beyond their home-country market. These enterprises are therefore, for example, Japanese, American, German, or Dutch companies

FIGURE 1-11	Ranked by Exports	
1997 Total	**Exports***	**Imports***
United States	$688.7	$899.0
Germany	511.7	441.5
Japan	421.0	338.8
France	289.5	268.4
Britain	281.6	308.2
Italy	238.2	208.1
Canada	214.4	200.9
The Netherlands	193.8	177.2
Hong Kong	188.2	213.3
China	182.7	142.4
Belgium/Luxembourg	168.2	155.8
South Korea	136.2	144.6
(*billions of U.S. dollars)		

Source: Michael M. Weinstein, "Limits of Economic Diplomacy," *The New York Times*, April 8, 1999, p. C1. Copyright © 1998 by The New York Times Company. Reprinted by permission.

that do business in multiple nations—usually their own and at least one other. There appears to be, however, a clear difference between the global corporation label and the other two labels.

Global corporations view themselves as "world corporations" (sometimes referred to as *stateless corporations*); they view the world as their marketplace. In other words, these corporations do not promote any overall national label; instead, they integrate themselves into the environment in which they happen to be doing business. For example, Honda, a Japanese global corporation, established operations in the United States. Through the media, Honda has tried to convince the American public that it is, in reality, an American company—not a Japanese company. Other global corporations include Bertelsmann, Coca-Cola, Ford, Citicorp, and Asea Brown Boveri.

Another distinct difference is that global corporations, because of their size, scope, and power, are able to make decisions with little regard to national boundaries, and they are able to move factories and laboratories around the world freely. On the other hand, MNCs make decisions with much regard to national boundaries. Some observers believe that the power of global corporations transcends the power of national governments. Some observers also believe that global corporations are forming even more powerful strategic alliances in response to the threats presented by the emergence of regional trading blocks in Europe, North America, and East Asia.[44]

PRACTICAL PERSPECTIVE 1-5

The Stateless Corporation

Percy Barnevik, the Swedish chief executive of Asea Brown Boveri, heads to his British Aerospace 128 jet for a quick hop to Rome.... Barnevik's enterprise is at the forefront of one of the most significant business and economic trends of the late 20th century. As cross-border trade and investment flows reach new heights, big global companies are effectively making decisions with little regard to national boundaries. Though few companies are totally untethered from their home countries, the trend toward a form of "stateless" corporation is unmistakable. The European, American, and Japanese giants heading in this direction are learning how to juggle multiple identities and multiple loyalties. Worried by the emergence of regional trading blocs in Europe, North America, and East Asia, these world corporations are developing chameleon-like abilities to resemble insiders no matter where they operate. At the same time, they move factories and labs "around the world without particular reference to national borders," says Unisys Corporation Chairman W. Michael Blumenthal. World corporations represent a dramatic evolution from the U.S. multinational alternately feared and courted since the 1960s.

These giants treated foreign operations as distant appendages for producing products designed and engineered back home. The chain of command and nationality of the company were clear. Not today. With the U.S. no longer dominating the world economy or holding a monopoly on innovation, new technologies, capital, and talents flow in many different directions. The most sophisticated manufacturing companies are making breakthroughs in foreign labs, seeking to place shares with foreign investors and putting foreigners on the fast track to the top. A wave of mergers, acquisitions, and strategic alliances has further clouded the question of national control....

Today, dozens of America's top manufacturing names, including IBM, Gillette, Xerox, Dow Chemical, and Hewlett-Packard, sell more of their products outside the U.S. than they do at home, and U.S. service companies are close behind.... The trend is even more pronounced in terms of profits. As companies begin to reap half or more of their sales and earnings from abroad, they are blending into the foreign landscape to win acceptance and avoid political hassles.... At the same time, foreign-based multinationals are arriving on American shores with greater strength than ever before.... Sweden's ABB, the Netherlands' Philips, France's Thomson, and Japan's Fujitsu are waging campaigns to be identified as American companies that employ Americans, transfer technology, and help the U.S. trade balance and overall economic health....

Source: Excerpted from W.J. Holstein et al., "The Stateless Corporation," *Business Week* (May 14, 1990): 98–99. Copyright 1990, McGraw-Hill. Used with permission. All rights reserved. Reprinted with permission.

Although these corporations view themselves as stateless, at this time many of them still maintain their corporate headquarters in the nation where they were first established—Honda is headquartered in Japan and Citicorp is headquartered in the United States. Thus, realistically, these corporations still maintain their original nationality. Therefore, whether an international business enterprise is an international corporation, an MNC, or a global corporation is a matter of perception and definition. For the most part, this book uses the three labels interchangeably.

Technological Advancements and Cultural Change

Technological advances, such as the Internet, satellite television, and video-conferencing, along with the globalization of business, are spreading cultural traits across cultures at a very rapid rate. As these traits are absorbed by a culture, cultural changes are likely to occur. Critics in some cultures have accused American companies of **cultural imperialism** (as an illustration, read Practical Perspective 1-6). This suggests that there may be a growing uniformity of cultures throughout the globe. Uniformity, however, will evolve at a very slow pace. International managers may thus deal with the accusation of cultural imperialism by being more adaptable to the needs of cultures where they are conducting business.[45]

Of course, these advancements are also revolutionizing international management. The Internet and electronic commerce are reshaping how business thinks about managing its employees. Distance—geographic, political, and cultural—has been a factor that shaped how companies organized and managed their global operations. The Internet's compression of time and distance has forced multinational organizations to rethink these patterns—for example, employees located throughout the globe can now work in teams.

Characteristics of the Global Manager

These trends mean that more and more business firms must now develop managers with global management and multicultural capabilities. (Refer to Practical Perspective 1-7.) The managerial skills that are effective in managing enterprises at home will not be effective in managing enterprises across the globe. What type of skills do **global managers** need? According to Ed Dunn, corporate vice president of Whirlpool Corporation, "The top twenty-first-century manager should have multienvironment, multicountry, multifunctional, multicompany, and multi-industry experience."[46]

Cecil G. Howard, a consultant and professor of management at Howard University, Washington, D.C., has proposed that the twenty-first-century global managers will possess multidimensional skills and knowledge. He grouped the skills and knowledge into two categories: core skills and augmented skills. These are depicted in Figure 1-12. According to

---

PRACTICAL PERSPECTIVE 1-6

A Battle Against Globalization

Fist raised, mustache bristling, José Bové looked defiant as he handed himself in to French police in the southern town on Montpellier a few days ago. "My struggle remains the same," this farmer declared to an appreciative crowd, "the battle against globalization and for the right of people to feed themselves as they choose."

A Parisian-turned-sheep-farmer who moved to southwest France 20 years ago, Mr. Bové emerged this month as a sort of Subcomandante Marcos of the French countryside, the leader of a self-styled, anti-imperialist revolt over food. His crime, committed on August 12, was to lead the ransacking and demolition of a McDonald's restaurant nearing completion in the southwestern town of Millau.

It was only the most conspicuous of a rash of recent protests against McDonald's, targeted not so much for anything the company has done but as a symbol of the United States and of what Mr. Bové has called "the multinationals of foul food." His efforts have struck a chord. French labor unions, ecologists, communists,

and farmers have joined to demand his immediate release, burying other differences in a shared politico-gastronomic outcry.

An army, Napoleon noted, marches on its stomach, and the European forces gathering this summer in protest against what is seen as American-led globalization have abruptly focused on food. Where it was once the deployment of American nuclear missiles that caused alarm, it is now McDonald's, Coca-Cola, genetically modified American corn, and American beef fattened with growth hormones that have Europeans up in arms.

"Behind all this lies a rejection of cultural and culinary dispossession," said Alain Duhamel, a French political analyst. "There is a certain allergy in Europe to the extent of American power accumulated since the cold war's end, and the most virulent expression of that allergy today seems to be food."

Source: Excerpted from Roger Cohen, "Fearful Over the Future, Europe Seizes on Food," *The New York Times*, August 29, 1999, Section 4, p. 1. Copyright © 1999 by The New York Times Company. Reprinted by permission.

Howard, the core skills are a must for the expatriate manager to succeed in the foreign assignment, but the augmented skills help facilitate managing in a foreign country.[47]

WHY STUDY INTERNATIONAL MANAGEMENT?

The discussion above shows that the transfer of business activities across nations is growing at a rapid rate. Furthermore, the collapse of communism in the Soviet Union and Eastern Europe, the emergence of market economies in Latin America and Asia, and emerging democracy in Africa has led to placing a nation's economic destiny in the hands of its people. To set the stage for economic boom, these countries are making themselves attractive places for foreign enterprises to invest. This means that in the

PRACTICAL PERSPECTIVE 1-7

The Multicultural Manager

You cannot motivate anyone, especially someone of another culture, until you have been accepted by that person. A multilingual salesperson can explain the advantages of a product in other languages, but a multicultural salesperson can motivate foreigners to buy it. That's a critical difference.

A buyer will not like a foreigner who is arrogant about his own culture. He will find reasons not to buy from such monocultural saleperson. The trouble is most people are arrogantly monocultural without being aware of it. Even those who have become aware of it cannot hide it. Foreigners sense this at once and set up their own cultural barrier, effectively blocking any attempt by the monocultural person to motivate them.

Ironically, that multicultural requirement has been neglected too often in hiring managers for international positions. Worse, it has mostly been neglected when sending fast-track managers on international assignments, pointing to almost certain failure. And it is affecting every industry. Even if you do not work for a multinational company, you may be in touch with foreign customers, distributors, suppliers, licensers or licensees. Do you have the right employee forging these relations?

For more than 20 years, I [Gunnar Beeth] have run a PanEuropean executive-search firm from Brussels. When clients ask us to find the right person for a sales or management position, they usually ask for the same qualities as for a domestic position but in addition require the new manager to speak English, German, and French.

After discussion, we usually specify something like:

The new manager must be able to motivate throughout Europe. That requires

An ability to be accepted throughout Europe. Thus, the new manager should be multicultural.

Source: Excerpted from Gunnar Beeth, "Multicultural Managers Wanted," *Management Review* (May 1997): 17, 19. Copyright © 1997 American Management Association International. Reprinted by permission of American Management Association International, New York, NY. All rights reserved. http://www.amanet.org.

years ahead, the globalization of business activities is likely to increase enormously and global competition is likely to intensify even more than in recent years. It also means that, in order to remain competitive in the global marketplace, firms must employ people who possess international business skills. (Refer again to Figure 1-12 and Practical Perspective 1-7).

SUMMARY

A major thrust of this chapter has been to point out that the managerial approach that works in one country may be ineffective in another. This is because the managerial process is affected by unique national factors,

FIGURE 1-12	Characteristics of the Twenty-First-Century Expatriate Manager

Core Skills	Managerial Implications
Multidimensional perspective	Extensive multiproduct, multi-industry, multifunctional, multicompany, multi-country, and multienvironment experience.
Proficiency in line management	Track record in successfully operating a strategic business unit(s) and/or a series of major overseas projects.
Prudent decision-making skills	Competence and proven track record in making the right strategic decisions.
Resourcefulness	Skillful in getting himself or herself known and accepted in the host country's political hierarchy.
Cultural sensitivity	Quick and easy adaptability into the foreign culture. An individual with as much cultural mix, diversity, and experience as possible.
Ability as a team builder	Effective people skills in dealing with a variety of cultures, races, nationalities, genders, religions. Also sensitive to cultural differences.
Physical fitness and mental maturity	Endurance for the rigorous demands of an overseas assignment.

Augmented Skills	Managerial Implications
Computer literacy	Comfortable exchanging strategic information electronically.
Prudent negotiating skills	Proven track record in conducting successful strategic business negotiations in multicultural environment.
Ability as a change agent	Proven track record in successfully initiating and implementing strategic organizational changes.
Visionary skills	Quick to recognize and respond to strategic business opportunities and potential political and economic upheavals in the host country.
Effective delegatory skills	Proven track record in participative management style and ability to delegate.

Source: Cecil G. Howard, "Profile of the 21st-Century Expatriate Manager," *HR Magazine* (June 1992): 96. Reprinted with the permission of *HR Magazine,* published by the Society for Human Resource Management, Alexandria, VA. All rights reserved.

including culture and religion. Some cultures view change positively; others view it negatively. Organizations are viewed in some cultures as entities to be protected and developed; in many cultures, they are viewed simply as a place to socialize. In some cultures, employees are selected and promoted on the basis of merit; in others, promotion is on the basis of friendship and family affiliations. Managers in some cultures make decisions participatively; in many cultures, decisions are made authoritatively. Organizational controls in some cultures are based on objective data and information; in others, they are based on subjective means. People in some cultures, such as weak uncertainty avoidance cultures, take higher risks than people in other cultures, such as strong uncertainty avoidance cultures.

Another major thrust has been to point out that, because business opportunities in foreign nations are increasing rapidly and because enterprises from foreign countries are increasingly presenting threats to many businesses, more and more domestic firms will enter the international business arena, and more and more firms will become global corporations. This suggests that in the future more and more managers with the ability to manage in multinational, multicultural environments will be required. The study of international management is thus becoming increasingly important.

Key Terms and Concepts

1. The international management process
2. Culture
3. Formal, informal, and technical cultural learning
4. Religion
5. master of destiny; fatalistic; never-ending quest for improvement; independent enterprise as an instrument of social action; personal selection based on merit; wide sharing of decision making; the concepts of decisions based on objective analysis

6. Antiplanning
7. The cultural dimensions of power distance; uncertainty avoidance; individualism; masculinity; and Confucian Dynamism
8. *Ubuntu*
9. Domestic enterprises
10. International corporations, multinational corporations, and global corporations
11. Cultural imperialism
12. The global manager

Discussion Questions and Exercises

1. Differentiate between management and international management.
2. What is culture? How is it learned? What are the sources of learning it?
3. Discuss how the following cultural viewpoints affect international planning, international organization, international staffing, international coordinating, and international controlling: decisions based on objective analysis, independent enterprise as an instrument of social action, master of destiny, fatalistic, never-ending quest for improvement, personnel selection based on merit, and wide sharing of decision making.
4. How does religion affect international management?
5. You are the personnel director of an American international corporation and are interviewing an American executive for assignment in the firm's subsidiary in

Japan. You notice that the executive is quite frank and direct in communication. What will you advise the executive to do?

6. How do the large power distance and strong uncertainty avoidance cultural dimensions affect international management?
7. What is Confucianism? What is the key tenet of Confucianism? What are the five basic relationships of Confucianism? In Confucianism, what does virtue mean?
8. What is *Ubuntu*? What is its key tenet?
9. Besides culture, what are some of the other factors that affect international management?
10. What are some of the characteristics of the effective global manager?
11. Differentiate between the international corporation, the multinational corporation, and the global corporation.

12. Why is it important to train global managers?

13. You are the cross-cultural trainer for an American global corporation. You are preparing a group of American executives for assignment in China. What will you point out to these executives?

14. How are technological advancements affecting international management?

15. Why is it important to study international management?

Assignment

Go to the library. Peruse business periodicals, such as *The Wall Street Journal*, *Business Week*, and *Fortune*. Select an article that discusses an international management topic, and prepare a short summary to be shared with your peers.

CASE 1-1

Globalizing Yourself

Kelly O'Dea used to think of himself as a Lone Ranger, living and working in countries where only a select breed of American businesspeople had gone before. As president of worldwide client services for Ogilvy & Mather Advertising, O'Dea commutes between London and New York. He's outside the United States about 70 percent of the time; for the past 15 years he's handled assignments in dozens of countries on five continents.

Six months ago, on a layover in the Bangkok airport, O'Dea realized that the Lone Ranger wasn't alone. He struck up a conversation with the woman sitting next to him, an investment banker who was also making the 25-hour flight from Sydney to London. As the two of them talked about their companies' urgent emphasis on global operations, two others chimed in with similar stories. The four of them soon realized that they represented a completely new kind of business leader: one who is multicultural and multiskilled, who doesn't regard an overseas assignment as either exotic or traumatic. It occurred to O'Dea that people, just like brands must be "globalized" if they're to compete successfully in rapidly changing international markets.

"International work experience is no longer just an option—it's mandatory for anyone in business," says O'Dea. "Five years ago, only 6 of our 15 largest clients were actively marketing brands across borders; now all 15 are. So it's no longer adequate to think about only your domestic market. You need to have a firm understanding of how business gets done in different countries."

Before you rush off for parts unknown, a few words of caution: an overseas assignment helps only if you do it right.

Questions

1. Discuss what O'Dea means by "an overseas assignment helps only if you do it right."

2. Describe some of the key determinants of the effective international manager.

Source: Excerpted from Eric Matson, "How to Globalize Yourself." Reprinted from the April–May 1997 issue of *Fast Company* magazine. All rights reserved. To subscribe, please call 800-688-1545.

CASE 1-2

Managing in the Constantly Changing Global Environment

How do we manage in this constantly changing global and regional environment? Change is certainly not new. But I [Paul Allaire, Chairman and CEO of Xerox Corporation] think there are two aspects of change that are different and worth focusing on. First is the speed of change. It is clearly faster and, in my view, it is accelerating. And that acceleration is going to continue. The second difference is that change is much less predictable. And in addition to global and regional issues, there are a number of other changes that complicate our jobs of managing global enterprises in this environment. I'll just mention a couple of those.

The first is that our traditional sources of competitive advantage are now short-lived. Capital is becoming a global commodity moving very easily across borders. Technology also is being very quickly dispersed. And in almost all of the markets in which we operate, we're also finding very fine skills that previously existed only in the developed countries, generally our home markets. . . .

So, the question is: How do we manage in this new environment? Rather than trying to give you a prescription, let me briefly tell you about some principles that Xerox has used to change our corporation in order to manage in this new environment that we foresee continuing at least through the 90s and into the twenty-first century.

The first principle in which I believe very strongly is that the old command-and-control system of management will no longer work. It is too slow and cumbersome, our environment is too complex, and our customers are too demanding. As we move away from this command-and-control approach, we must focus on speed. Our organizations must have

the capability of making decisions much more quickly, and, more importantly, implementing those decisions much more quickly. So what we are trying to do is to maintain the advantages of a large global enterprise and still have the speed of a small local company.

Another key principle around which we've organized is empowerment: pushing responsibility and accountability down to the people who really have the knowledge—first, to do what is right for the customer, and second, to bring capabilities to the customer in a value-added manner. This includes allowing the individuals down in the organizations to define the management process that they will use to best achieve that.

Questions

1. CEO Allaire's ideas certainly have substance. However, there are bound to be cultural barriers. Discuss some of the barriers culture may present.

2. What are the technological changes which have taken place in the past few decades that have helped improve international organizations' capability of making decisions more quickly than was the case prior to these changes?

3. How is the implementation of empowerment programs hindered by culture? Give some examples.

Source: Excerpted from "Decentralization for Competitive Advantage," *Across the Board 31* (January 1994): 24–25. Copyright © 1994, Conference Board Inc., New York. All rights reserved. Used by permission of publisher.

Notes

1. Elizabeth Marx, *Breaking Through Culture Shock: What You Need to Succeed in International Business* (London: Nicholas Brealey Publishing, 1999).
2. A.L. Roeber and C. Kluckhohn, "Culture: A Critical Review of Concepts and Definitions," *Papers of the Peabody Museum of American Archaeology and Ethnology* (Cambridge, MA: Harvard University, 1952), no. 1.
3. P.H. Harris and R.T. Moran, *Managing Cultural Differences* (Houston, TX: Gulf Publishing, 1979).
4. E.T. Hall, *The Silent Language* (Garden City, NY: Anchor Press/Doubleday, 1973), p. 68.
5. Ibid., p. 69.
6. Ibid., p. 71.
7. Harris and Moran, *Managing Cultural Differences.*
8. Ibid.
9. Ibid., p. 63.
10. Max Weber, *The Protestant Ethic and the Spirit of Capitalism* (New York: Scribner's Sons, 1958, originally 1904–1905).
11. S.M. Abbasi, K.W. Hollman, and J.H. Murray, "Islamic Economics: Foundations and Practices," *International Journal of Social Economics 16*, no. 5 (1990): 5–17.
12. Glenn Burkins, "Work Week," *The Wall Street Journal*, March 24, 1998, p. A1.
13. A descriptive discussion of these concepts appears in W.H. Newman, C.E. Summer, and E.K. Warren, *The Process of Management* (Englewood Cliffs, NJ: Prentice-Hall, 1977).
14. N.J. Adler, *International Dimensions of Organizational Behavior* (Cincinnati, OH: South-Western College Publishing, 1997).
15. G. Renwick and E.J.Witham, *Managing in Malaysia: Cultural Insights and Guidelines for Americans* unpublished manuscript, 1997.
16. C. West Churchman, *The System's Approach* (New York: Dell Books, 1968), p. 14.
17. Newman, Summer, and Warren, *Process of Management.*
18. Ibid.
19. Valerie Frazee, "Getting Started in Mexico," *Workforce 2*, no. 1 (January 1997) 16–17; and Mike Johnson, "Untrapped in Latin America," *Management Review* (July 1996): 32.
20. Newman, Summer, and Warren, *Process of Management.*
21. R.N. Farmer and B.M. Richman, *Comparative Management and Economic Progress* (Homewood, IL: Richard D. Irwin, 1965), pp. 177–189; Adler,

no. 14 (1997).
22. Newman, Summer, and Warren, *Process of Management.*
23. Harris and Moran, *Managing Cultural Differences*, p. 63.
24. "Go Along and Get Along," *The Economist* (November 24, 1990): 76.
25. Newman, Summer, and Warren, *Process of Management.*
26. Geert Hofstede, "The Cultural Relativity of the Quality of Life Concept," *Academy of Management Review 9*, no. 3 (1984): 389–398; and Geert Hofstede, "Motivation, Leadership, and Organization: Do American Theories Apply Abroad?" *Organizational Dynamics* (Summer 1980): 42–63.
27. G. Hofstede and Michael H. Bond, "The Confucius Connection: From Cultural Roots to Economic Growth," *Organizational Dynamics* (Spring 1988): 5–21.
28. Ibid.
29. This discussion draws from M.P. Mangaliso, N.A. Mangaliso, and J.M. Bruton, "Management in Africa, or Africa in Management? The African Philosophical Thought in Organizational Discourse," a paper presented at the International Management Division, Academy of Management Annual Meetings, San Diego, CA, August 6, 1998.
30. Hofstede and Bond, "The Confucius Connection."
31. Cited in Robert Mamis, "Who's in Control of the New World Order," *Profiles* (February 1994): 50.
32. Ibid.
33. Ibid., p. 51.
34. Ibid., p. 53.
35. See Rhonda Richards, "Famous Amos Goes to Taiwan," *USA Today*, September 18, 1992, p. 1B.
36. Mark Starr, "Kiss That Baby Goodbye," *Newsweek* (May 10, 1993): 72.
37. S. Strom and K. Bradsher, "Wedding or Wipeout," *The New York Times*, May 23, 1999, Section 3, p. 1.
38. Len Lewis, "Growing Global," *Progressive Grocer 78*, no. 9 (1999): 23.
39. "Starbucks Coffee Begins European Expansion," *Business Journal* (April 29, 1998).
40. Edmund L. Andrews, "American Pop-Culture, Foreign Owned," *The New York Times*, March 29, 1998, Week in Review, p. 16.
41. See Dori Jones Yang, "How Freightliner Put the Pedal on the Metal," *Business Week* (September 6, 1993): 86.

42. Gary Belsky, "The 12 Best Investments in the World Today," *Money 22* (April 1993): 102–110.

43. Alex Taylor III, "The Dangers of Running Too Lean," *Fortune* (June 14, 1993): 113–116; and Warren Brown, "The Humbling of Honda," *The Washington Post National Weekly Edition*, October 11–17, 1993, p. 18.

44. See Richard J. Barnet and John Cavanagh, *Global Dreams* (New York: Simon & Schuster, 1994); and W. J. Holstein et al., "The Stateless Corporation," *Business Week* (May 14, 1990): 98–106.

45. William B. Werther, Jr., "Toward Global Convergence," *Business Horizons* (January–February 1996): 3–9.

46. Cecil G. Howard, "Profile of the 21st-Century Expatriate Manager," *HR Magazine* (June 1992): 96.

47. Ibid.

2

Cross-National Ethics and Social Responsibility

In the Third World, many nations—and their bribe-takers—have never known life without bribery. Countries such as Indonesia, Malaysia, China, India, Nigeria, and Thailand are known for having government officials who are easily bribable. "In the U.S., the social lubricant is alcohol," says [A. Rushdi] Siddiqui [an international trade lawyer]. "In many Third World nations, it's gifts." Sometimes these gifts can be as much as 10 percent of the cost of the project.[1]

Learning Objectives of the Chapter

When managers of corporations begin to formulate strategy to conduct business across nations, they must possess a thorough understanding of their firms' views on business ethics and social responsibility, as well as the views of each nation in which the firm wishes to transact business. Views on what is ethical or unethical in business transactions vary from company to company, as well as from country to country. For example, the practice of bribery in business transactions is acceptable in many countries, and in many situations it is expected and needed to supplement a low-wage structure, while in other countries it is unacceptable and illegal. And in the United States, managers must understand that, under the U.S. Foreign Corrupt Practices Act (FCPA) of 1977, it is illegal to practice the act of bribery not only in the U.S. but in other countries as well, even if it is an acceptable business practice there.

Views on what actions denote corporate social responsibility also vary from company to company, as well as from country to country. For example, some executives believe that they must not be judgmental and should adhere to countries' varying views. Following this view, an executive of a U.S. multinational corporation (MNC) would hire female managers at home because it is the right thing to do but would not do so for the firm's operations in Saudi Arabia. This is because it is not an acceptable practice in Saudi Arabia to hire female managers for most jobs.[2] Others believe that there should be a universal guideline: MNCs should apply one view on social responsibility in all nations. Therefore, adhering to this view, the executive of the U.S. MNC *would* hire female managers in Saudi Arabia—which conflicts with Saudi Arabia's views. Dealing with conflicting ethical norms between home and host country, as well as defining and applying social responsibility in cross-national settings, is thus a huge problem confronting the managers of MNCs. After studying this chapter, you should be able to:

1. Describe what ethics are, including legality and social acceptability.
2. Examine the considerations and complications in complying with foreign ethical practices.
3. Examine some of the events leading to the passage of the FCPA.
4. Examine the impact of the FCPA on MNCs.
5. Discuss social responsibility in a cross-national context.

CROSS-NATIONAL ETHICS

Some businesspeople believe that what is **ethical or unethical** is governed by the legality of the situation and by the social aspects of the situation (what members of the society generally accept as being "right" or "wrong"). For example, if it is illegal to practice the act of bribery in a country and a firm's manager bribes someone there to obtain a favor, it would be unethical, and the violator could be prosecuted under the law. And if **bribery** is not illegal in a country, but it is known to be generally **socially unacceptable**, it would be unethical to practice it; the violator would be punished not by formal law but by informal means, such as by negative publicity and/or by customers boycotting the firm's product or service.

Regarding the social aspects of the situation, many cultures establish informal ethical principles or moral standards that define "right" and "wrong" conduct. However, what is right or wrong is difficult to define conclusively and agree upon in any culture. For example, in the U.S., some Americans believe legal abortion is right; others think it is wrong. And what is right or wrong is far more difficult to define conclusively and agree upon among the different cultural environments around the globe. This is because different societies are confronted with different opportunities and constraints, and to cope, each society develops a unique culture and standard of ethics. As a result, what is right and wrong may differ dramatically from one culture to another. This means that managers of MNCs will often find themselves with **conflicting ethical responsibilities**; that is, one's own nation's standard of ethics often collides with those of other nations. For example, the practice of bribery in business transactions is acceptable in Thailand but not in the United States. An American executive transacting business in Thailand would thus be confronted with conflicting ethical responsibilities.

In part because of these conflicting ethical responsibilities, the actions of many U.S. MNCs have been subjected to considerable criticism, which in turn has led to a wide range of negative consequences, such as bad publicity, consumer boycotts, lawsuits, and government intervention, such as the passage of the Foreign Corrupt Practices Act (to be discussed later in this chapter). Practical Perspective 2-1 presents the case of Lockheed's involvement in bribery in Egypt and the negative consequences.

PRACTICAL PERSPECTIVE 2-1

A Violation of the Foreign Corrupt Practices Act

Several years ago, Lockheed hired a consultant and promised her a sizable commission for each plane sold to the Egyptian government. The consultant was later elected to the Egyptian Parliament, becoming—under the U.S. Foreign Corrupt Practices Act—a foreign government official. Before taking office, she turned over the consulting responsibilities to a company her husband headed. Two years later Lockheed sold three C-130 transport aircraft to the Egyptian government, and Lockheed allegedly paid the local consulting company a termination fee in lieu of the commissions, keeping the payment confidential through code names and other means.

A federal grand jury in Georgia subsequently indicted Lockheed and two of its officers for conspiracy to violate the Foreign Corrupt Practices Act, even though there was no factual allegation that the Parliament member had taken a single step to misuse her official position on Lockheed's behalf. The prosecutors successfully argued that it was Lockheed's intent, not the recipient's actions, that mattered, and that one indication of corrupt intent was the secrecy surrounding the commission payment.

Lockheed pleaded guilty to a negotiated single count and agreed to pay the maximum fine of $24.8 million. The Lockheed executives pleaded guilty to false information charges or bribery charges and were fined $20,000 and $125,000, respectively, and sentenced to three years' probation in one case and eighteen months in prison in the other.

Source: Excerpted from Margaret M. Ayres, "Staying Above Board Overseas," *Financial Executive* (March–April 1996): 38.

BRIBERY AND PAYOFFS ABROAD

An investigation in the early 1970s by the U.S. Securities and Exchange Commission (SEC) into illegal corporate contributions to President Nixon's campaign fund discovered that many corporations had made substantial illegal contributions during the 1972 presidential election campaign. Subsequent investigations in 1976 and 1977 by the SEC revealed that instances of undisclosed, questionable, or illegal corporate payments, both domestic and foreign, were widespread—major MNCs regularly made **"payoffs"** abroad to foreign government officials and politicians in the course of conducting business.[3] The SEC investigation generated other investigations by the Senate Foreign Relations Committee, the Internal Revenue Service (IRS), and the departments of Defense and State. (Department of Defense corporations had been a major source of payoffs abroad.) These investigations, too, revealed that many U.S. MNCs regularly made questionable or illegal payments to foreign government officials and politicians in order to secure business.

The difficulties and pressures MNCs face in conducting business with foreign government officials and politicians were presented in testimony before a U.S. Senate Foreign Relations Subcommittee by then-chairman of Gulf Oil Corporation, Bob R. Dorsey. Dorsey described his dealings with then-finance chairman of South Korea's Democratic Republican Party, S.K. Kim: "He [S.K. Kim] happens to be as tough a man as I've ever met. I have never been subjected to that kind of abuse."[4] When Kim first approached Dorsey, his demand was $1 million. Later, Kim demanded $10 million from Dorsey in the form of a campaign contribution to his political party. Dorsey said, "He [Kim] left little to the imagination as to what would happen to Gulf's $300 million investment, most of it in refining and petrochemicals, if the company would choose to turn its back on the request."[5] Dorsey haggled the $10 million extortion demand by Kim down to $3 million, making it a total of $4 million to save $300 million in assets in South Korea.[6]

Another case that helps illustrate the difficulties and pressures MNCs face in transacting officials and politicians involved Exxon in Italy. Italy is noted for a government and political system in which approvals, permits, and licenses are issued extremely slowly, and perhaps disapproved, when payments (called *bustarella*) are not made to the proper officials. Exxon had large refineries in Italy producing oil products for sale in Italy and in the entire European Union. Between 1963 and 1972, Exxon admitted making payments of more than $29 million to Italian political parties. In the wake of the ongoing SEC investigation into such foreign payments, Exxon suspended any further payments to Italian political parties. Subsequently, rate increases requested by Exxon during the period when OPEC was drastically raising the price of crude oil were ignored. As a result, the once profitable Exxon subsidiaries in Italy generated large losses.[7]

The investigations caused many board members of MNCs to become concerned about their exposure and liability to lawsuits brought by stockholders. U.S. Internal Revenue Service officials were concerned about the apparent laxity of independent auditing firms in pointing out such questionable and often sizable payments. And the SEC believed that "when a company receives substantial benefits as a result of a payoff or, if its continued operations are subject to extortion, investors are entitled to know."[8] Assertions were made at the time that "the SEC had embarked on a typical American exercise in ethnocentrism—imposing its own moral judgments on foreign governments and U.S. international corporations."[9]

Forms of Bribery

Basically, a **bribe** can be defined as *a payment in any form (cash or gift) for the purpose of influencing action by a government official in order to obtain or retain business*. Bribes can be classified as "whitemail bribes" or as "lubrication bribes."

Whitemail Bribes

Whitemail bribery refers to payments made to induce an official in a position of power to give favorable treatment where such treatment is either illegal or not warranted on an efficiency, economic benefit scale. Fundamentally, a key point in this type of bribery is that the payment be intended to induce the official "to do or omit doing something in violation of his lawful duty, or to exercise his [or her] discretion in favor of the payor's request for a contract, concession, or privilege on some basis other than merit."[10] These payments, when exposed, can lead to scandals, fines, and so on. Payments of this nature have historically been "buried" in the books of MNCs or concealed in some other way. (Practical Perspective 2-2 presents some illustrations of whitemail bribes.)

Lubrication Bribes

This type of bribe is typically described as payment to facilitate, expedite, or speed up routine government approvals or other actions to which the firm would legally be entitled. Such payments are generally made to minor officials like custom agents or licensing clerks. Another trait of **lubrication bribes** is that the amounts are generally smaller than whitemail bribes although there have been cases where large lubrication-type payments were made. The number and acceptability of the practice of lubrication bribes is much greater than that of whitemail bribes. Officials in many Third World countries are especially noted for requiring "grease" to make their political and administrative wheels turn. Somewhat similar to waiters or waitresses in the United States who receive a low salary and rely on customers' tips to supplement their income, in many countries, numerous officials receive a low salary and rely on "grease" payments to supplement their income.

PRACTICAL PERSPECTIVE 2-2

Wandering into Ethical No-Man's Land

When American businesspeople venture abroad, a common view is that they're wandering into an ethical no-man's land, where each encounter holds forth a fresh demand for a "gratuity," or *baksheesh*. William C. Norris, who founded and for many years headed Control Data Corporation, says, "No question about it. We were constantly in the position of saying how much we were willing to pay" to have a routine service performed overseas. Norris recalls frequently facing situations such as this: "The computer is on the dock, it's raining, and you have to pay $100 to get it picked up...."

In South America, firms often face a "closed bidding system" when dealing with that region's large, nationalized companies, says John Swanson, a senior consultant of communications and business conduct at Dow Corning Corporation. He says that his company has been locked out of the South American market at times because it refused to pay the bribes necessary to get that business.

In Japan, bids for government construction jobs are routinely rigged—a result of Japanese firms purchasing "influence" from politicians, according to one former U.S. government official who asked to remain anonymous. Donald E. Peterson, former chairman and chief executive officer of the Ford Motor Company, cites ethical challenges in much of the developing world. "Give me a military dictator with absolute power, and it doesn't matter if he's South American or African or Asian—you've got problems."

Source: Excerpted from Andrew W. Singer, "Ethics: Are Standards Lower Overseas?" *Across The Board* (September 1991): 31. Copyright © 1991, Conference Board, Inc., New York. Reprinted with permission. All rights reserved.

Extortion

A distinction can be made between bribery and extortion. Bribery is offered by an individual or a corporation seeking an unlawful advantage, while extortion is force exerted in the other direction—an official seeking payment from an individual or corporation for an action to which the individual or corporation may lawfully be entitled. Gulf Oil's dilemma in South Korea is an example of extortion.

To Bribe or Not to Bribe?

Bribery and corruption top the list of global ethics issues. According to former U.S. Commerce Secretary Mickey Cantor, bribery and corruption cost U.S. firms $64 billion in lost business in 1996.[11] Thus, when a manager crosses a nation's borders to conduct or negotiate business, he or she will sometimes be confronted with the need to decide whether or not to practice the act of bribery. Figure 2-1 presents some questions whose answers can help international executives make such a decision. Figure 2-2 presents a perspective on how to conduct business legally in foreign countries.

FIGURE 2-1	**Questions to Determine Whether to Bribe**

Legal Questions

1. What are the legal consequences in the parent country?
2. How comprehensive is the law of the host country? What is the enforceability of its law?
3. Will the corporation be liable to its competitors for financial damages (such as unfair practice or restraint of trade)?
4. Will the company be held liable by stockholders in the host or parent country?

Moral Questions

1. What is the company's policy regarding overseas payoffs? Will it cause any deviation from standard practice?
2. If the questionable payment is disclosed, will it damage the public image of the company in the parent country?
3. Will the payoff activity affect employee morale of the company at home or overseas?
4. What is the custom in the host country?
5. Does the public opinion of the host country carry the same weight as it does in the parent country?

Economic Questions

1. How does the expected gain compare with the company's total earnings?
2. What is the cost of payoff as a percentage of total revenue? Is it a one-time payment or a periodic contribution?
3. Is the company diversified in many countries?
4. Will the payoff trigger other host countries to make the same demand?
5. Will the payoff action cause retaliation from competitors?

Personal Questions

1. Will top management find out about the payoff? If so, am I subject to censure?
2. Am I likely to be held personally liable for such action?
3. Does the company carry insurance to pay my legal fees if I am found guilty of violating a law?
4. Will disclosure of payoff harm my reputation and make it difficult to obtain or retain a management position in the future?
5. How would my family and friends react to disclosure of such activity?

Source: G.W. Gruenberg and Y. Kugel, "Criteria and Guidelines for Decision Making: The Special Case of International Payoffs," *Columbia Journal of World Business* (Fall 1977): 120. Copyright © 1977, JAI Press Inc. Used with permission of JAI Press Inc. All rights reserved.

The U.S. Foreign Corrupt Practices Act of 1977

The revelations by the SEC and Senate Foreign Relations subcommittee investigations of U.S. MNCs' "whitemail bribery" practices abroad, and the concern for the negative image such practices generated for the U.S., helped plant the seed that eventually produced U.S. Senate Bill 305, the

➤ Rigorously learn about the culture, the business practices, and the laws of your host country—not just the customs and niceties. Talk with others who have done business there and with local lawyers. Contact the area group that represents American and indigenous interests, often a local chamber of commerce with a joint agreement with the U.S. Chamber of Commerce. Seek out the commercial attaché in the U.S. embassy.

➤ Hire a local journalist to do a comprehensive local media search. Do not rely solely on the U.S. business press. You need to know how much attention is being paid to corruption and whether criminal charges have ever been brought—in short, how seriously bribery and corruption are regarded in your host country.

➤ Perform a due diligence investigation of everyone who will work for the company as an agent, representative, distributor, licensee, or joint venture partner. Examine the reputation, especially with regard to honesty. Enter into a specific contract delineating the person's responsibilities as they pertain to company policies and the Foreign Corrupt Practices Act. The person must sign a detailed statement promising not to engage in bribery. This prudent step could lessen both your company's liability and your personal liability.

➤ For all managers: Clearly enunciate your corporate policies regarding bribery and U.S. law to your employees with direct and indirect sales responsibilities overseas. Restate them often—annually, at least. Each time, employees should complete and sign a detailed worksheet and a declaration that they have read and understood the policies; they know these papers go into their dossiers.

Foreign Corrupt Practices Act (FCPA). (See Practical Perspective 2-3.) The FCPA was passed and signed into law in 1977. Its purpose was twofold:

1. to establish a worldwide code of conduct for any kind of payment by United States businesses to foreign government officials, political parties, and political candidates; and

2. to require appropriate accounting controls for full disclosure of firms' transactions.

The law applies even if such payments are common practice (viewed as an ethical practice) in the country where they are made. Some of the basic provisions of the FCPA are as follows:

➤ It is a criminal offense for a firm to make payments to a foreign government official, political party, party official, or candidate for political office in order to secure or retain business in another nation.

➤ Sales commissions to independent agents are illegal if the business has knowledge that any part of the commission is being passed to foreign officials.

➤ Government employees whose duties are essentially ministerial or clerical are excluded, so expediting payments to persons such as customs agents and bureaucrats are permitted. (Thus, the FCPA does not apply to small "lubrication" bribes.)

➤ In addition to the antibribery provisions that apply to all businesses, all publicly held corporations that are subject to the SEC are required to establish internal accounting controls to ensure that all payments abroad are authorized and properly recorded.[12]

The penalty levied on the business enterprise for not complying with the FCPA was set at $1 million for each count. The penalty levied on individual members of the corporation found guilty of making the illegal payment is a fine of up to a $10,000 and/or five years imprisonment, with the added provision that the firm may not pay or reimburse the employees for the fines levied on them. Thus, the FCPA calls for both civil and criminal penalties.

Enforcement of the FCPA was assigned to two federal agencies: the SEC and the Department of Justice. The SEC's responsibility included enforcement of the record keeping and accounting control provisions of the FCPA and civil authority to enforce the prohibitions against foreign bribery by U.S. publicly held corporations. The Department of Justice was given the responsibility to enforce the criminal penalties for corporate bribery of foreign officials and the authority to bring civil actions against domestic concerns whose securities are not registered with the SEC.

PRACTICAL PERSPECTIVE 2-3

The Murky Land of the FCPA

The Foreign Corrupt Practices Act (FCPA) became law in 1977, in the wake of foreign bribery scandals involving U.S. companies that shook the governments of Belgium, the Netherlands, Honduras, Italy, and Japan. One of the most notorious incidents involved an estimated $25 million in concealed payments made overseas by Lockheed Corporation in connection with sales of its Tristar L-1011 aircraft in Japan. This culminated in the resignation and subsequent criminal conviction of Japanese Prime Minister Kankuie Tanaka.

The FCPA, which makes it a crime for U.S. corporations to bribe officials of foreign governments to obtain or increase business, is controversial, in part, because it seeks to forge a distinction between "bribes" (which it deems illegal) and "gratuities" (which the FCPA permits). The difference is murky, according to the FCPA's critics.

"The law marked the difference between gratuities paid to low-level officials and payments made to authorities," writes Duane Windsor in his book, *The Foreign Corrupt Practices Act: Anatomy of a Statute*. "In many countries a payment to a customs official is a matter of course and a matter of economic necessity. A customs official may backlog an order or hinder a shipment by elaborately checking each imported item. The detrimental effect to the shipment is obvious. In response, lawmakers sought to delineate gratuities and bribes very clearly. But in reality the delineation of gratuities was so vague that some people felt it had a chilling effect [on business]."

Source: Excerpted from Andrew W. Singer, "Ethics: Are Standards Lower Overseas?" *Across The Board* (September 1991): 33. Copyright © 1991, Conference Board, Inc., New York. Reprinted with permission. All rights reserved.

Over the years, numerous companies have been fined. For example, in the late 1980s, Young & Rubicam Inc., the New York-based advertising agency, and three of its executives were indicted on a conspiracy charge under the FCPA. The U.S. government contended that the firm had "reason to know" that one of its Jamaican agents was paying off that country's Minister of Tourism to obtain advertising business. In order to avert a lengthy trial, the corporation paid a $500,000 penalty, says R. John Cooper, executive vice president and general counsel of Young & Rubicam. And in the 1970s, Control Data Corporation was prosecuted by the U.S. government under the FCPA for making payments in Iran. In 1978, Control Data Corporation pleaded guilty to three criminal charges that it made improper payments to unnamed foreign officials. It was fined $1,381,000 by the U.S. Customs Services.[13] Practical Perspective 2-1 describes the fines imposed on Lockheed.

Complaints from MNCs Over the FCPA

The major areas of concern communicated by U.S. multinational corporations over the FCPA were as follows:

➤ The FCPA placed them at a competitive disadvantage because companies from other countries, as well as from the host country, were not bound by the FCPA laws and could continue making whitemail payments to secure business, thus putting them at a competitive advantage. (See Practical Perspective 2-4.)

➤ The accounting burden of internal controls, along with the vagueness of this section of the law, makes the MNCs' duty and liability difficult to assess.

➤ MNCs complain that the FCPA forces them to become political tools of the U.S. government because they have to exert its will in the world through their economic power.

Furthermore, a report issued in 1978 by the Export Disincentives Task Force, created by the White House to find ways of improving the negative balance of trade between the U.S. and other nations, pointed to the FCPA as being potentially harmful. This statement, which was made one year after passage of the FCPA, was based on interviews with executives of U.S. MNCs who claimed that their firms lost export business because of compliance with the FCPA.

Yet another problem with the FCPA was that it was not clear enough with respect to the use of foreign subsidiaries to transact business. For example, Boeing Corporation sold its planes abroad through a distributorship, Overseas International Distributors Company, which was registered as a Netherlands company, but doing business out of Geneva. Overseas International Distributors bought planes from Boeing after obtaining orders for the aircraft from officials in the Middle East. Finally, many MNCs saw

PRACTICAL PERSPECTIVE 2-4

Can We Litigate Morality?

Passed in the late '70s in the wake of Watergate [the investigation that led to President Richard M. Nixon's resignation] and the overseas bribery scandals, the Foreign Corrupt Practices Act (FCPA) made it a felony for U.S. companies to obtain business by paying off foreign government officials. From its inception, the FCPA has been controversial. "Managers in other countries often chuckle at the United States hoping to export its morality in the form of the Foreign Corrupt Practices Act," says Gene Laczniak, management professor at Marquette University in Milwaukee.

"It's anachronistic in today's world," says William Norris, the former Control Data [Corporation] chief. "It's like the antitrust laws in many ways. The world has passed it by." [The antitrust laws] worked fine as long as the U.S. economy was an isolated system, say critics. But now antitrust laws may be inhibiting large U.S. firms from competing in the international arena. In any case, says Norris, most U.S. companies don't want to become involved in activities such as bribing foreign officials.

R. John Cooper, executive vice president and general counsel of Young & Rubicam Inc., makes a similar argument. The FCPA was enacted at a time when the competitive position of U.S. companies in the world was stronger than it is today, Cooper points out. In 1970, the United States was the source of 60 percent of the world's direct foreign investment. By 1984, according to the United Nations, that figure dropped to 12 percent. Japanese, European, and East Asian firms have picked up much of the slack, launching economic forays even into America's own backyard. The United States risks becoming economically hamstrung by statutes such as the Foreign Corrupt Practices Act, suggests Cooper. "We have to reexamine some of these high-toned notions." According to Cooper, with increasingly heated international competition, the act is out of date. It puts too much of a burden on U.S. corporations to know everything about their foreign agents—a burden not shouldered by foreign competitors.

Source: Excerpted from Andrew W. Singer, "Ethics: Are Standards Lower Overseas?" *Across The Board* (September 1991): 33. Copyright © 1991, Conference Board, Inc., New York. Reprinted with permission. All rights reserved.

the FCPA as landmark legislation that could beget more legislation, thus hindering the ability of the U.S. MNCs to deal effectively in the global marketplace. Overall, many U.S. MNCs saw the FCPA as another stumbling block to an already complex challenge of competing in the global arena.

1988 Amendments to the FCPA

In early 1981 and again in early 1983, the U.S Senate attempted to repair some of the uncertainties associated with the FCPA. The Senate's proposed amendments were rejected by the House of Representatives. The amendment finally passed as a section of the Omnibus Trade and Competitiveness Act of 1988. The amendment clarifies various provisions of the FCPA, consolidates most of the enforcement responsibilities for bribery violations into the U.S. Department of Justice, and increases the civil and criminal penalties for violating the FCPA. Relative to the accounting aspects of the FCPA, the amendment limits future criminal liability to intentional actions to circumvent the internal accounting control system or falsify the corporation's books. With respect to payments made through third parties, the amendment eliminates the "reason to know" standard and modified the "knowing" standard. Under the act, "knowing" is defined to entail the substantial certainty or conscious disregard of a high probability that the third-party payment will become a bribe.[14]

Relative to enforcement of the FCPA, the amendment increased the civil and criminal penalties for violations. Criminal penalties were increased from $1 million to $2 million for corporations and from $10,000 to $100,000 for individuals. The maximum imprisonment remained five years. A civil penalty of $10,000 for individuals was established and may not be paid by the corporation. All jurisdictions for enforcing the antibribery provisions of the FCPA were consolidated within the Department of Justice. The SEC remained responsible for civil enforcement of the records and internal accounting control provisions of the FCPA.[15]

An Alternative Payoff Approach

Many international executives do not view the FCPA as hindering their competitiveness in the global marketplace. (See Practical Perspective 2-5.) These executives enhance their competitiveness by improving their enterprises' technical expertise, their customer service, and their responsibility to the customer through quality. Furthermore, there are indications that the practice of bribery is not as widespread as it once was; it seems to be waning. (See Practical Perspective 2-9.) And when these executives must make some sort of payment to obtain a favor, they do not pay "private individuals"; instead, they make payments to institutions, such as contributions to build schools, hospitals, medical clinics, or agricultural projects.[16] Payments of this nature obtain favors and goodwill for the MNC; they also improve the local situation, such as by increasing local employment. This payment approach, thus, does not improve only one person's bank account; instead, the payment is shared with the community.

CROSS-NATIONAL SOCIAL RESPONSIBILITY

Social responsibility has been defined as "the notion that corporations have an obligation to constituent groups in society other than stockholders and beyond that prescribed by law or union contract."[17] Corporate social responsibility therefore means that a firm's actions must take into account

PRACTICAL PERSPECTIVE 2-5

Keeping the Cutting Edge Sharp

Because the Foreign Corrupt Practices Act has been such an entrenched influence, many U.S. companies have ceased to regard it as a stumbling block. "I've never had a manager say, 'We can't do business because we're limited by the Foreign Corrupt Practices Act,'" says Raymond V. Gilmartin, [former] chairman, president, and CEO of Becton Dickinson and Company and board chairman of the Ethics Resource Center. "We are not at a competitive disadvantage at all."...

Gilmartin says foreign sales are growing twice as fast as domestic. But Gilmartin is the first to say that any company doing business beyond U. S. borders has to keep sharply focused on doing the lawful thing.

Before, echoing the thoughts of many U.S. companies, Becton Dickinson thought it was "an ethical company with ethical employees," Gilmartin says. "We said we wanted to do the right thing, but it became clear that we must use training and reinforcement." Accordingly, Becton Dickinson is using interactive workshops for the first time—small group exercises

and case studies that train employees to recognize ethical dilemmas and to work them through. The company is also revising its written code of conduct, making it more "understandable, readable, and practical," says Gilmartin. "I've also made it clear in speeches that in no way do we want you, the employee, to compromise your personal integrity. But we are going beyond that. We are serious. We are giving recognizable managerial support."

When doing business abroad, Gilmartin says, an aggressive approach works best. A company should "make it clear right upfront" to any prospective foreign client that it doesn't give payoffs. "If our principles seem to preclude us from certain business, we'll forego this opportunity—but we won't give up," he states. "We will try other avenues."

Source: Excerpted from Barbara Ettorre, "Why Overseas Bribery Won't Last," *Management Review* (June 1994): 22. Copyright © 1994 American Management Association International. Reprinted by permission of American Management Association International, New York, NY. All rights reserved. http://www.amanet.org.

not only the well-being of the stockholders but also the well-being of the community, the employees, and the customers. Figure 2-3 presents the **ten commandments of corporate social responsibility**. With respect to MNCs' **cross-national social responsibility,** many international business executives condone the concept of cultural relativism, while others condone the concept of universalism.

Cultural Relativism

Cultural relativism holds that "no culture's ethics are any better than any other's."[18] Under this standard there are no international "rights" or "wrongs." Thus, if Thailand tolerates the bribery of public officials, then Thai tolerance is no worse than American or German intolerance. If

FIGURE 2-3	The Ten Commandments of Social Responsibility

I. Thou Shall Take Corrective Action Before It Is Required.

II. Thou Shall Work with Affected Constituents to Resolve Mutual Problems.

III. Thou Shall Work to Establish Industrywide Standards and Self-Regulation.

IV. Thou Shall Publicly Admit Thy Mistakes.

V. Thou Shall Get Involved in Appropriate Social Programs.

VI. Thou Shall Help Correct Environmental Problems.

VII. Thou Shall Monitor the Changing Social Environment.

VIII. Thou Shall Establish and Enforce a Corporate Code of Conduct.

IX. Thou Shall Take Needed Public Stands on Social Issues.

X. Thou Shall Strive to Make Profits on an Ongoing Basis.

Source: Larry D. Alexander and William F. Matthews, "The Ten Commandments of Corporate Social Responsibility," *Business and Society Review* 50 (Summer 1984): 62–66.

Switzerland is liberal with respect to insider trading, then Swiss liberalism is no worse than American restrictiveness.[19] These executives would therefore not support the FCPA.

But the concept of cultural relativism can backfire. For example, suppose a U.S. corporation invents a product and patents it. Patent piracy is wrong (and illegal) in the U.S., but it is not wrong in some nations (and if it is illegal, culturally, it is not enforced). What if a company in one of these countries pirated the patent? Would the executives in the company from which the patent was pirated simply write the loss off as, "Oh well, that's culture"? As illustration, some enterprises in China readily pirate U.S. firms' copyrighted computer software, movies, and music and put phony American labels on consumer products. (See Practical Perspective 2-6.) If the American pirated firms' executives adhered to the cultural relativism concept, they would not complain about the Chinese firms' pirating practices because they are not viewed as being unethical in China. However, U.S. trade representatives are currently applying strong pressure on Chinese government officials to implement and enforce policies that preclude Chinese enterprises from undertaking such activities.[20] Suppose also that a U.S. MNC is manufacturing in Bangladesh using cheap child labor. Use of child labor in such a way is not tolerable in the United States, but it is tolerable in Bangladesh. What happens to the MNC when the U.S. press gets hold of the information and promulgates it among the U.S. public? Will it result in a boycott? (Practical Perspective 2-7 illustrates this problem.) It therefore seems that the concept of cultural relativism is often not very practical.

PRACTICAL PERSPECTIVE 2-6

The Risks Are Rising in China

China's flagrant piracy of American pop music, movies, and computer software is more than the biggest rip-off in global commerce. It's also the latest evidence of the growing and increasingly visible risks confronting Western and Asian companies doing business in the People's Republic....

Nowhere are the stakes bigger—or less amenable to a quick, lasting solution—than the current U.S.-China dispute over heisted copyrights. More than a trade war, think of this fight as a clash of civilizations. The new U.S. economy, with its edge in handling information technology, confronts an ambitious Asian giant with a voracious appetite for capital, know-how, and export markets—and a primitive legal system that lacks almost any concept of the Western notion of intellectual property. Says Kenneth DeWoskin, a University of Michigan business school professor and China specialist, "Most Chinese do not understand the notion of intangible assets like brands or copyrighted material. We're in for a long siege on these issues."

Beijing would have a hard time fixing the situation if it wanted to: It has devolved economic power upon the provinces, which control the pirate factories and the courts. Further complicating matters, senior politicians, military men, and their families are often involved in the pirating industries. Says Howard Lincoln, chairman of Nintendo of America, "We have evidence that government officials have ownership stakes in companies doing the counterfeiting...."

Showbiz products such as Madonna recordings and Mickey Mouse films grab the spotlight, but intellectual property of corporations with manufacturing plants in China is equally at risk. To get into the PRC, companies must disclose to authorities details of their products and processes. Says DeWoskin, "Chinese research and design institutes look for the best technology in the country and spread it around. They also examine plans and specifications of new ventures, so there's bound to be some leakage."

Protecting a brand name in the China market often resembles a mission impossible. A bogus Chinese breakfast cereal product called Kongalu Cornstrips has a trademark and packaging identical to that of Kellogg's cornflakes. A small Chinese computer manufacturer, Mr. Sun, has appropriated the trademark of Sun Microsystems for its machines. And mineral water drinkers in China can enjoy Pabst Blue Ribbon Water. As for videos, movies, compact discs, and computer software, virtually the entire Chinese market is a pirate's den because Beijing denies market access to most of the legal products. Nor is there much shame about the grand larceny, which costs U.S. companies more than $1 billion a year. According to a report issued by the U.S. Trade Representative's office, "Anyone can walk into a store in Beijing and buy a pirated copy of Microsoft's popular Windows software package. The store simply copies it onto a few blank floppy disks while you wait."

The crisis atmosphere has at least sent everyone back to the bargaining table.... Can a solution emerge? Optimists point to Taiwan. Only a dozen years ago that island nation harbored a vigorous underground export industry that skillfully copied leading global brands. A visitor could buy good-looking knockoffs of

(continued)

Rolex watches in the back streets of Taipei. The counterfeiting abated once Taiwanese companies developed their own intellectual property and thus a deeper appreciation of its value. Given time and a few more knocks in the game of global trade, the Chinese too should eventually come to see piracy as more expensive than it's worth. Until then, expect it to remain one more reason to cast a cautious eye on China's red-hot but risky market.

Source: Louis Kraar, "The Risks Are Rising in China," *Fortune* (March 6, 1995): 179–180. Copyright © 1995, Times, Inc. New York. Reprinted with permission. All rights reserved.

Universalism

On the other hand, the concept of **universalism**, a rigid global yardstick by which to measure all moral issues (for example, the FCPA), is often not very practical either. This is because its application would show disrespect for valid cultural differences and different economic needs. For example, people in the U.S. do not tolerate manufacturing facilities that disperse health-damaging smog. Under the concept of universalism, it would be unethical to transfer such manufacturing facilities to another country. But in countries where people are starving, economic development may be more important than health, and such manufacturing facilities would thus be welcome. A manager guided by the cultural relativism view would export such manufacturing facilities to the starving country. But, as mentioned above, it is likely to backfire.

For example, U.S.-based Union Carbide established gas production facilities in Bhopal, India. In its U.S. plants, Union Carbide was required by the government to install expensive accident-prevention systems. The government of India did not require such systems. In the 1980s an accident at the Bhopal plant killed more than 3,000 people and injured thousands of others.[21] The press coverage of the Union Carbide incident was very negative. Many Americans felt that Union Carbide, knowing the dangers of not taking preventive measures, had a moral obligation to have taken them in India, even if India did not require them and could not afford them. These Americans thus adhere to the concept of universalism. On the other hand, many Americans adopted the concept of cultural relativism—they believed that Union Carbide did not have the right to interfere with Indian government matters.

Thus, developing, implementing, and controlling cross-cultural business ethics and social responsibility programs is an enormous challenge confronting the managers of MNCs. The problem is enlarged by the press sometimes persuading MNCs to impose their social responsibility on their manufacturing subcontractors. For example, Starbucks Coffee has agreed to adopt a "code of conduct" that must be adhered to by its coffee suppliers and may help workers in Guatemala and other Third World nations. Starbucks' management made the decision after stores in British Columbia,

PRACTICAL PERSPECTIVE 2-7

How Multinational Corporations Export Human Rights

In 1996 Kathie Lee Gifford made front-page news. The well-liked television personality had lent her name to a discount line of women's clothing that, it was discovered, had been made by underage Central American workers. That same year the Walt Disney Company was exposed contracting with Haitian suppliers who paid their workers less than Haiti's minimum wage of $2.40 a day. Nike and Reebok, makers of perhaps the world's most popular athletic footwear, were similarly and repeatedly exposed.

In all these cases, the companies accused were U.S. manufacturers of consumer products. They were being targeted for human rights violations committed abroad not by their own managers or in their own plants but by the subcontractors who produced their products in overseas facilities. Traditionally, the corporate response to this subcontractor problem has been predictable, if unfortunate. U.S. firms have argued that they cannot realistically or financially be held responsible for the labor practices of their foreign suppliers. "The problem is, we don't own the factories," a Disney spokesperson protested. "We are dealing with a licensee."

Recently, though, this attitude has started to change. As a direct result of heightened human rights activism, sharper media scrutiny, and the increased communication facilitated by the Internet, U.S. corporations are finding it difficult to sustain their old hands-off policy. Under pressure, they are beginning to accept responsibility for the labor practices and human rights abuses of their foreign subcontractors.

Source: Excerpted from Debora L. Spar, "The Spotlight and the Bottom Line," *Foreign Affairs* 77, no. 2 (March–April 1998): 7. Reprinted with permission.

Canada, and the U.S. were targeted in a February 1995 leafletting blitz. The protesters were concerned about "harsh working conditions, paltry pay, and human rights violations on Guatemalan coffee plantations."[22] (As an illustration, read Practical Perspectives 2-7 and 2-8.) The press therefore often asks MNCs to reject the concept of cultural relativism and apply the concept of universalism.

TOWARD THE GLOBALIZATION OF BUSINESS ETHICS

The U.S. approach to business ethics is unique. In comparison with other capitalistic societies, it is more individualistic, legalistic, and universalistic.[23] In other words, issues of business ethics are far more visible in the United States than they are in other capitalistic societies. This may be because there

PRACTICAL PERSPECTIVE 2-8

The Supply Police

The Christmas-week NBC show asserting that Wal-Mart's "Buy American" program misleads consumers also leveled a more sinister charge: that children as young as nine churn out clothes for the nation's largest retailer in Bangladeshi sweatshops. Other big-name U.S importers aren't waiting to see whether the public buys Wal-Mart's denials. Instead they're making sure their own suppliers are free of environmental, human rights, or other potential embarrassments. The supplier police had better hurry. Jeff Fiedler, the AFL-CIO official who helped NBC mug Wal-Mart, says that he's drawing beads on a dozen new targets, including apparel and dress-shoe companies.

Suddenly, "going global" invites a hazard nobody mentioned back in B-school. Activists pushing a variety of causes have discovered that exposing corporate exploitation will accomplish what tamer strategies, such as leafletting annual meetings, have not. Scrutiny by labor unions, activists, and socially conscious investors is forcing importers to monitor not just their foreign subsidiaries but their far-flung network of independent suppliers—and their suppliers' as well. Says Donna Katzin of the Interfaith Center on Corporate Responsibility, "Just because companies don't make a product themselves doesn't relieve them of all obligations...."

Is it fair to hold Third World suppliers to U.S. standards of conduct? Even many of those who say it is admit to ambivalence about imposing their values on countries and companies halfway around the world. "It's easy to take cynical views of American corporations," says Northwestern University business ethicist David Messick. "But what gives us the right to decide at what age people in Bangladesh should work?"...To which image-conscious executives might respond: Why take risks? As the Wal-Mart case demonstrates, even perceived transgressions can lead to big embarrassment...

Several companies have made pre-emptive strikes to avoid similar pratfalls. Last March, Sears said it wouldn't import forced-labor products from China. Phillips-Van Heusen explicitly threatens to terminate orders to apparel suppliers that violate its broad ethical, environmental, and human rights code. And Dow Chemical asks suppliers to conform not just to local pollution and safety laws but to the often tougher U.S. standards. At least one major U.S. company acted merely to stamp out falsehoods: Persistent rumors that McDonald's suppliers grazed their cattle on cleared rainforest land finally led it to ban the practice in writing....

Separating right from wrong overseas doesn't guarantee a company high praise at home. Just ask Nike, which ran afoul of cultural relativism late in 1992. *Harper's* magazine printed a U.S. labor activist's dissection of a pay stub for an Indonesian woman; she netted the equivalent of $37.46 a month for making sneakers. Later, an article in the *Far Eastern Economic Review* reported that Indonesians who make Nikes earn far more than most workers lucky enough to get jobs in the impoverished country. "Americans focus on wages paid, not what standard of living those wages relate to," says Nike's Dusty Kidd. But such arguments miss the point. When it comes to social responsibility, it's not enough for a company to be right. It also has to convince its increasingly touchy customers.

Source: Excerpted from John McCormick and Marc Levinson, "The Supply Police," *Newsweek* (February 15, 1993): 48–49. Copyright © 1993, Newsweek, Inc. All rights reserved. Reprinted with permission.

are far more laws regulating business in the U.S. than there are in other capitalistic countries. Therefore, the American public reads and hears far more about business misconduct than do people in other countries. Hence, the "**ethics gap**" between the United States and the rest of the developed world is considerably large.[24]

Until recently, minor strides toward closing the ethics gap had been made in Europe and, on a much smaller scale, in Japan. In 1987, a group of 75 European business executives and academics established the European Business Ethics Network (EBEN), and the first European business journal, *Ethica Degli Affari*, was published in Italy. Since the mid-1980s, ethics research centers have been established in Britain, Belgium, Spain, Germany, and Switzerland. In 1989 and 1991, the Institute of Moralogy sponsored international ethics conferences in Kashiwa City, Chiba Ken, Japan.[25] Notwithstanding, as pointed out above, a considerably large ethics gap between the U.S. and other advanced nations still exists. However, as discussed in Practical Perspective 2-9, major strides were recently made to close the ethics gap.

The Impact of Culture on the Business Ethics Visibility Gap

The United States is one of the most individualistic cultures in the world. As indicated in the first chapter, people's decisions in individualistic cultures tend to be guided by self-interests, as opposed to group interests. On the other hand, managers in group-oriented cultures tend to reflect less their personal moral guidance and more their shared understanding of the nature and scope of the corporation's responsibilities—and the enterprise's moral expectations are shaped by the norms of the community, not the personal values and reflections of the individual.[26] This helps explain why there are far more laws regulating business in the U.S. than there are in other advanced nations, and it helps explain why there is such a large business ethics gap between the U.S. and other nations.

This suggests that globalization of business ethics (application of the concept of universalism) is distant and that the concept of cultural relativism still prevails. Thus, as the integration of the global economy increases, effective international managers develop a "better appreciation of the differences in the legal and cultural context of business ethics between the United States and other capitalist nations and between Western and Asian economies as well."[27]

Business Ethics and the Internet

The **World Wide Web**, an area of the Internet, is a virtual, global, open-ended organization of interconnected information sources. It is now a quick

A Tough Act to Follow

For most major multinationals, bribery has long ceased to be good business practice. There's never been any guarantee it would work. And now, thanks to years of international negotiation, it will no longer be legal either. Last November, 34 nations signed the first Convention on Combating Bribery of Foreign Public Officials in International Business Transactions in Paris. The signatories comprised the 29 member-nations of the Organization for Economic Cooperation and Development (OECD), in addition to Argentina, Brazil, Bulgaria, Chile, and Slovakia. The OECD includes all major exporting nations except China.

Each nation participating in the convention pledged to submit an act criminalizing bribery in that country to its legislature by April 1. The treaty will enter into force once five of the ten largest of the OECD exporting countries have ratified it.... To the treaty's negotiators, this is a mere technicality. They believe the concept of banning international bribery as a means of doing business is one whose time has finally come.

In fact, the pressure for change is coming from all quarters. From the sellers' perspective, bribery has become an increasingly expensive and dangerous way to do business. From the buyers' side, it has added more costs to expensive international acquisitions at a time when a country's scarce resources should be used to develop its economy and infrastructure, not to pad the foreign bank accounts of bureaucrats and officials. As for international financial institutions and distributors of development assistance, bribes divert desperately needed resources from their intended purposes.

"In the last few years, countries have begun to wake up and say the costs of this kind of corruption are unacceptably high," says Thomas White, deputy director of the State Department's office of investment affairs and the chief U.S. negotiator of the treaty. "That's what has enabled us to take this out of the arena of being a simple competitive issue and place it in the area of good governance and economic efficiency. That's the argument that has won over other governments; we can no longer devote scarce resources to development while at the same time permitting governments to distort and pervert the development process. We can't undermine our own efforts to promote more stable governments while at the same time permitting our companies to undertake the kinds of bribery that destabilize political systems and discourage the development of democratic institutions."

For more than 20 years, the United States has held the moral high ground almost single-handedly in this area in the form of the Foreign Corrupt Practices Act. Over time, U.S. companies have come to grips with this law and learned to live with its constraints. "I don't think we can expect things to change overnight," says GE's Heimann. "I would expect it would take a five- to ten-year time frame for things really to change."

Source: Excerpted from David A. Andelman, "Bribery: The New Global Outlaw," *Management Review* (April 1998): 49. Copyright © 1998 American Management Association International. Reprinted by permission of American Management Association International, New York, NY. All rights reserved. http://www.amanet.org.

way for companies, large or small, to market products or services globally to people who access the Internet. However, managers of such a global network are faced with the challenge of addressing the concerns of its constituents with respect to confidentiality, authenticity, and integrity, balancing security against responsiveness and performance. The system needs to be secure against malicious use, misuse, and data corruption while protecting the privacy of its users and the intellectual property of the vendors. For example, providing copyright protection for knowledge providers on the Internet is quite different from providing it to their counterparts in hardcopy publication. However, as was demonstrated in this chapter, hardcopy publications do not have much protection in numerous countries. The Internet may thus be a great challenge in this respect.[28]

SUMMARY

This chapter has discussed cross-national ethics and social responsibility. It has proposed that certain business practices, such as bribery, are viewed as unethical in some cultures but ethical in others. The practice of bribery and "payoffs" by numerous U.S. MNCs led to the passage of the Foreign Corrupt Practices Act of 1977. Managers of many MNCs have complained that the act, because it precluded them from bribing or "paying off" officials in foreign countries to obtain "favors," even if it was an acceptable practice in the country, put them at a competitive disadvantage with foreign competitors who were not bound by the act. The chapter has also discussed cross-national corporate social responsibility. It has proposed that some international executives condone the concept of "cultural relativism," which holds that no culture's ethics are any better than any other's; that there are no international "rights" or "wrongs." It was suggested that the practice of cultural relativism often backfires. Some international executives condone the concept of "universalism," which holds that there should be a global yardstick by which to measure all moral issues. This approach often leads to a show of disrespect for valid cultural differences. The media often influence MNCs to reject cultural relativism and apply the concept of universalism. There is a large business ethics gap between the U.S. and other advanced nations; Americans are exposed to far more business misconduct issues than are people in other advanced countries.

Key Terms and Concepts

1. Ethical or unethical
2. Bribery
3. Socially acceptable or unacceptable
4. Conflicting ethical responsibilities
5. "Payoffs"
6. *Bustarella*
7. Whitemail bribes; lubrication bribes
8. Extortion
9. The Foreign Corrupt Practices Act
10. The ten commandments of corporate social responsibility
11. Cross-cultural social responsibility
12. Cultural relativism; universalism
13. Business ethics gap
14. Business ethics visibility gap
15. World Wide Web

Discussion Questions and Exercises

1. How do some businesspeople determine what is ethical or unethical?

2. Why is it difficult to define what is ethical or unethical across cultures?

3. What is meant by "conflicting responsibilities"?

4. Differentiate between "whitemail" and "lubrication" bribes, and extortion.

5. Why do so many international businesspeople pay lubrication bribes?

6. What was the major purpose of the Foreign Corrupt Practices Act?

7. What were some of the major complaints from U.S. international executives against the Foreign Corrupt Practices Act?

8. The top management of a U.S. MNC has decided to build a manufacturing facility in a city in country X. A city bureaucrat in country X has approached the executive responsible for implementing top management's decision. The bureaucrat has informed the executive that a permit to build in the city is extremely difficult to obtain and it is a very lengthy process; that he has "a friend" on the city council who, for U.S. $200,000, would be able to get the council to issue the permit immediately. It is important to the top management that the permit be issued, and, for competitive reasons, that it be issued as fast as possible. Time is thus very important to the MNC. You are the executive. What will you do?

9. With respect to cross-national social responsibility, what are the potential negative consequences of the practice of cultural relativism and universalism?

10. From a social responsibility perspective, what are the potential negative consequences associated with home-country corporations using manufacturing subcontractors abroad?

11. Why is there a relatively large business ethics gap between the U.S. and other advanced nations?

12. Discuss the challenges with which managers of the Wide Web World are confronted.

Assignment

Contact an international executive in a MNC, and ask him or her to describe the company's policy pertaining to cross-national ethics and social responsibility. Prepare a short report to be shared with the class.

C A S E   2 - 1

Bribery and Extortion in International Business

The following cases have been disguised but reflect actual events with which I [Louis T. Wells, Jr.] am familiar or which have been reported in the press.

1. You are in charge of trying to secure a contract for the sale of U.S. telecommunications equipment worth about $40 million to the communications and transport ministry of a Latin American country with a military government. European firms are also eager for the contract. Quality differences in the products of the various suppliers are not important. A local accountant, who has helped you with government negotiating in the past, suggests to you that the company might receive the contract if it were to be willing to deposit $2 million in the Swiss bank account of the general in charge of the ministry.

2. You are responsible for negotiating with an African government the terms under which your company would build and operate a battery plant in the country. You have U.S. counsel and know a local law firm with two Harvard-trained principals. However, other Americans who have successful investments in the country suggest that you hire the local Speaker of the House, who is a lawyer, to help represent you in the negotiations. You are aware that the House must eventually approve the agreement you negotiate.

3. Your U.S. company has a major petroleum investment in a non-Arab oil country. All foreign investors have been notified that their contracts (covering taxes, royalties, and so on) will be reviewed in the light of events in other countries. A lawyer, who is the brother of the vice president, offers his services to your firm in the upcoming renegotiations. The proposed fees are about 25 percent higher than those that might be asked by a U.S. law firm.

4. You have just been put in charge of a U.S. subsidiary in a developing country and have discovered that the previous manager has been paying $40 to immigration officials each time the residence permit of U.S. employees is to be extended. There is no official basis for the charge and it has been paid each time in cash. You are told other foreign companies and even private U.S. foundations pay similar fees.

5. You are a vice president for international operations of a U.S. company. One of your new managers of a rapidly expanding subsidiary in a developing country reports the following experience: A tax collector visited the firm with a bill for the firm's annual income tax. Although the bill seemed a bit high, based on the accounts earlier submitted to the government, the manager told the collector that he would authorize a check to the Treasury. The collector pointed out that the total due could be discussed and he was sure that some less costly arrangement could be worked out. The manager replied that he preferred to accept the Treasury's calculation and had a check made out. Two weeks later, the manager receives a registered letter from the collector saying that an error had been made and that the company owed about 35 percent more. A bill was enclosed, but the letter mentioned that the tax collector would be happy to discuss the matter further.

6. You are the U.S. manager of a local subsidiary in a developing country. As you are

leaving the country for a brief visit to head-quarters, the clerk at the counter for the local airline you are using points out that you have overweight luggage. (This was not a surprise to you, since you are carrying home Christmas presents for your and your wife's families, but you know some international airlines have dropped the weight limit or would simply overlook the small amount of excess weight.) You ask the charge and hear that it is $75. When you look hesitant, the clerk suggests that $5 might actually take care of the matter.

7. You are on a consulting trip to a Latin American country and discover a very fine suit in a smart downtown shop. You ask about the price and discover that it is 9000 pesos. The clerk explains that that would be $75, if you will pay in dollars. You realize that it is $300 at the official rate of exchange that you encountered at the airport and at banks.

8. The American manager of one of your Latin American subsidiaries has been kidnapped by a leftist political group. You are informed that he will be released unharmed if you will have your company run an ad in the local newspaper presenting the group's criticism of the government in power, if you will provide $100,000 of food for distribution to the poor, and if you will pay $1 million in ransom to the group. You discover that the ransom payment would be illegal in that country.

Questions

1. What would you do in each of the above cases?

2. Why?

Source: Louis T. Wells, Jr., Harvard Business School, Harvard University. Used with permission.

CASE 2-2

America's New Merchants of Death

In Germany three women in black miniskirts set up a display table beside a Cadillac in the center of Dresden. In exchange for an empty pack of local cigarettes, they offer passersby a pack of Lucky Strikes and a leaflet that reads: "You just got hold of a nice piece of America. Lucky Strike is the original...a real classic." Says German physician Bernhard Humberger, who monitors youth smoking: "Adolescents time and again receive cigarettes at such promotions."

➤ A Jeep decorated with the yellow Camel logo pulls up in front of a high school in Buenos Aires. The driver, a blond woman wearing khaki safari gear, begins handing out free cigarettes to 15- and 16-year-olds on their lunch recess.

➤ In Malaysia a man responds to a television commercial for "Salem High Country Holidays." When he tries to book a trip, he is refused by the office manager, who later admits that the $2.5 million-a-year operation exists only to advertise Salem on TV. This promotes Salem cigarettes without technically breaking the law.

➤ At a video arcade in Taipei, free American

cigarettes are strewn atop each game. "As long as they're here, I may as well try one," says a ponytailed high-school girl in a Chicago Bears T-shirt. Before the United States entered the Taiwanese cigarette market, such giveaways were uncommon at spots frequented by adolescents.

A *Reader's Digest* investigation covering 20 countries on four continents has revealed that millions of children are being lured into nicotine addiction by American cigarette makers. In several nations, U.S. tobacco companies have been fighting legislation that curtails cigarette use by minors and are cleverly violating the spirit of curbs on advertising. Their activities clearly show a cynical disregard for public health. But the most shocking finding is that children are being seduced into smoking in the name of America itself. In some countries tobacco companies never would have gained a foothold without the help of a powerful ally: the U.S. government.

Although sales in the United States have dropped for eight years straight, and by the year 2000, only one in seven Americans will likely smoke, sales elsewhere have more than tripled since 1985. Smoking rates in the Third World are climbing by more than 2 percent a year. Most alarming is the rise in youth smoking. In the Philippines, 22.7 percent of people under 18 now smoke. In some Latin American cities, the teenage rate is an astonishing 50 percent. In Hong Kong, children as young as seven are smoking. Why are the young so important? Because millions of adult smokers either kick their habit or die each year, the cigarette industry depends on attracting new customers. Most smokers begin between ages 12 and 16; if a young person hasn't begun by 18, he or she is unlikely to ever smoke.

"Tobacco is a growth industry, and we are gaining in volume and share in markets around the world," Philip Morris assured stockholders in its 1991 annual report. "Growth prospects internationally have never

been better," gushed Dale Sisel, chief executive officer of R.J. Reynolds (RJR) Tobacco International, at last summer's international tobacco conference in Raleigh, N.C. "We all produce and sell a legal product that more than one billion consumers around the world use every single day."

Unmentioned at the conference was the fact that smoking is one of the leading causes of premature death, linked to cancers of the mouth, lung, esophagus, kidney, pancreas, bladder, and cervix, as well as to heart disease. Or that according to the World Health Organization, tobacco will prematurely kill 200 million who are now children and eventually wipe out 10 percent of the world's population. This grim prospect is due in no small part to the spectacular U.S. invasion of overseas markets. More than 50,000 medical studies have demonstrated these hazards. Yet the tobacco gurus assembled at Raleigh referred to the "debate" and "controversy" over smoking.

"People need to know precisely how American companies and their government are promoting smoking among the world's children," says Dr. Carlos Ferreyra Nuñez, president of the Argentine Association of Public Health. "If they knew the full story, I believe they would stop this outrage."

Here is that story.

Pervasive Influence

Developing countries are unusually vulnerable to cigarette advertising. Until recently some of them sold tobacco only through government monopolies, with little or no attempt at persuasion. And because most of these countries don't have effective antismoking campaigns, many of their people are surprisingly innocent of the link between tobacco and disease. In Manila we even found cigarettes sold at a snack bar operated by the local Boy Scouts. Many governments, moreover, are reluctant to wage antismoking wars because they're addicted to tobacco taxes. Argentina gets 22.5 percent of its tax revenue from tobacco; Malawi, 16.7 percent.

Into this climate of naiveté and neglect, U.S. tobacco companies have unleashed not only the marketing wizardry that most Americans take for granted but other tactics they wouldn't dare use in the U.S. market.

In Malaysia, *Gila-Gila*, a comic book popular with elementary-school students, carried a Lucky Strike ad. Teenagers going to rock concerts or discos in Budapest are regularly met by attractive women in cowboy outfits who hand them Marlboros. Those who accept a light on the spot also receive Marlboro sunglasses.

Tobacco advertising is more pervasive in many other parts of the world than in the United States. African merchants can get their shops painted to look like a pack of Marlboros. The Camel logo adorns taxis and store awnings in Warsaw. Christmas trees in Malaysian discos are trimmed free by Kent—with balls and stars bearing the Kent logo. In Mexico one in five TV commercials is for cigarettes. On an average day, 60 spots for American brands appear on Japanese TV, many of them during programs watched by teens.

Although their marketing budgets are secret, tobacco companies have bolstered their spending for international advertising, adding substantially to the $4 billion allocated yearly for the United States. "It's crucial for them," says Richard Pollary, professor of marketing at the University of British Columbia. "Familiarity in advertising breeds trust." Tobacco spokespeople insist that cigarette advertising draws only people who already smoke. But an ad executive who worked until recently on the Philip Morris account, speaking on condition of anonymity, disagrees. "You don't have to be a brain surgeon to figure out what's going on. It's ludicrous for them to deny that a cartoon character like Joe Camel is attractive to kids."

Dr. John L. Clowe, president of the American Medical Association, says: "It is clear that advertising fosters tobacco use among children. And despite tobacco-industry denials, ads like Joe Camel are especially appealing to adolescents, equating smoking with sexual prowess, athleticism, even success." Numerous independent studies support this view. They show that cigarette advertising creates an environment in which young people are more likely to smoke. That may explain why the U.S. Centers for Disease Control found that smokers between ages 12 and 18 prefer Marlboro, Newport, and Camel—three of the most advertised brands.

"Brand Stretching"

Like the United States and Canada, some of the progressive developing countries have banned cigarette commercials on TV and radio. This doesn't stop the tobacco companies, however. To keep their logos before the public, they resort to "brand stretching"—advertising nontobacco products and services named after their brands. Most of these items have special appeal to young people: Marlboro jeans and jackets, for example. In Malaysia a music store called Salem Power Station wraps customers' tapes and CDs in plastic bags bearing the Salem logo, and television carries a rock-video show called "Salem Powerhits." A Budapest radio station broadcasts a rock program called the "Marlboro Hit Parade," and in China, Philip Morris sponsors the "Marlboro American Music Hour."

Rock concerts are especially effective. One of the live performances under tobacco sponsorship (Sales in Seoul) was by Paula Abdul, who is popular among teens. Stars who have appeared in televised concerts underwritten by the industry include Madonna (Sales in Hong Kong) and Dire Straits (Kents in Malaysia). Sports sponsorship is even more insidious, for it implies that smoking and fitness go together.

Tobacco logos are blazoned on events of every description, from cycling in Morocco to badminton in Indonesia. There are the Salem Open Tennis Tournament in Hong Kong and the Kent International Sailing Regatta, to name just a couple. American tobacco companies spent $100 million sponsoring sports in 1992—double the 1985 total.

Tobacco companies regularly skirt laws against TV commercials. In Shanghai, Philip Morris airs spots for "The World of Marlboro" at the end of American sitcom reruns. Except that cigarettes aren't mentioned, the ad is identical to a Marlboro commercial: The Marlboro man and his horse splash across a stream, the man dismounts and gazes towards mountains that look like the Rockies. One of the most misleading forms of brand stretching is the "travel" ad. In Thailand, where all cigarette advertising is forbidden, an ad appeared in the Bangkok *Post* for "Kent Leisure Holidays." It showed the company's logo and offered "A Pleasure Trip." A Thai doctor phoned to book the trip but was turned down. He was told the cruise ship was in the Caribbean and wouldn't be in Bangkok for at least two years.

Unfortunately many of the children who succumb to brand stretching find habits that begin as cobwebs end as steel cables. At a McDonald's in Malaysia, Sunil Ramanathan, 16, finishes off a Big Mac, lights a Marlboro, and inhales deeply. He says he's smoked since he was ten. "I know smoking is bad for me, but I can't stop. I try to quit, but after one day I start again."

Easy Access

Just off Taipei's bustling Keelung Road, high-school students begin filing into the Whisky A Go-Go disco about 9 p.m., and soon the room is a sea of denim. On each table are free packs of Salems. Before long, overhead fans are fighting a losing battle with the smoke.

"American tobacco companies spend more than a quarter of a billion dollars every year giving away cigarettes, many of which are smoked by children and teenagers," says Joe Tye, editor of the newsletter *Tobacco Free Youth Reporter*. "If they can get a youngster to smoke a few packs, chances are he'll [or she'll] be a customer for life."

The companies say adult establishments such as discos cannot legally admit minors. The industry insists it instructs distributors of free samples to screen out the underaged. "It doesn't work," says Cecilia Sepulveda, a tobacco expert with Chile's Ministry of Public Health. "We estimate that 40 percent of 13-year-olds in Santiago smoke." Of seven under-18 students assembled at the Beltram High School in Buenos Aires, five say they have been offered free Camels. None was asked his [or her] age. One, Ruben Paz, 16, said he got his from a "blond, American-looking girl" handing out cigarettes from "the Camel Jeep" at the school door.

Young black-marketers hawk single cigarettes to their peers. Ten-year-olds in the tin-roofed *kampongs* of the Malaysian jungle can buy a Salem for eight cents. Students at the St. Ignatius School in Santiago buy cigarettes for ten cents at *carritos*, handcarts that also sell candy and soft drinks near the school. Although increasingly controlled in the United States, vending machines are used widely abroad. They were rare in East Germany, but since reunification U.S. and British companies have installed tens of thousands. In parts of Japan, machines sit on almost every corner.

Sell America

"Many African children have two hopes," says Paul Wangai, a physician in Nairobi, Kenya. "One is to go to heaven, the other to America. U.S. tobacco companies capitalize on this by associating smoking with affluence. It's not uncommon to hear children say they start because of the glamorous lifestyle associated with smoking." Cigarette advertising outside the United States focuses heavily on U.S. lifestyles; indeed, the ads are seen as a way of learning about America itself. A letter from secretarial students in China appeared in the Petaluma, California, *Argus-Courier*: "Every day we listen to the 'Marlboro American Music Hour.' We enjoy Elvis Presley and Michael Jackson. We smoke American cigarettes and wear American clothes. We are eager to gain more information about American life."

To hear the children of the rest of the world tell it, everyone in the United States smokes. The truth is, the United States has one of the lowest smoking rates—25.5 percent of the population. Yet because of U.S. advertising, American cigarettes are considered a gauge of style and panache. In Bangkok, Thai youths sew Marlboro logos on their jackets and jeans to boost their status. At the city's Wat Nai Rong High School, 17-year-old Wasana Warathongchai says smoking makes her feel "sophisticated and cosmopolitan, like America." She lumps Marlboros with "jeans and denim jackets, Pizza Hut, everything we like about America."

Friends in High Places

The theme of last summer's Raleigh conference was "The Tobacco Industry to the Year 2000," and on hand were two experts from the U.S. Department of Agriculture to help the industry sell tobacco overseas.... Wait a minute. Didn't the American government decide in 1964 that cigarettes are a major cause of death and disease, and doesn't the U.S. government discourage its own citizens from smoking? Then how can it encourage people of other nations to smoke? For many years Japan, Korea, Taiwan, and Thailand imposed stern trade restrictions on imported cigarettes. But in the early 1980s, American

tobacco companies joined forces with the Office of the U.S. Trade Representative (USTR) to crack these Asian markets.

The weapon Washington wielded was Section 301 of the Trade Act of 1974. It empowers the USTR to retaliate—with punitive tariffs—against any nation thought to have imposed unfair barriers on American products. In September 1985 the USTR began an investigation of Japanese trading practices. Senator Jesse Helms, from the tobacco-growing state of North Carolina, then stepped in on behalf of the tobacco industry. Helms dispatched a letter to Prime Minister Yasuhiro Nakasone, intimating he could not support a substantial U.S. defense presence in the Pacific or help stem the tide of anti-Japanese trade sentiment in Congress unless Japan opened its cigarette market.

"I urge that you establish a timetable for allowing U.S. cigarettes a specific share of your market," Helms wrote. "I suggest a total of 20 percent within 18 months." Three months later the Japanese government agreed to open its markets more. During this same period, tobacco companies enlisted two former aides to President Ronald Reagan—Michael Deaver and Richard Allen—as lobbyists. Deaver received $250,000 for pressing Philip Morris's case in South Korea and in a meeting with President Chun Doo Hwan. That country yielded to a Section 301 action in May 1988. By 1990 tobacco-industry clout had opened markets in Taiwan and Thailand.

The results have been devastating. Before the Americans arrived, smoking rates were declining slightly in Japan, but since 1987, cigarette consumption by minors has increased 16 percent. Among Taiwanese high school students, the smoking rate climbed from 19.5 percent in 1985 to 32.2 percent in 1987. Between 1988 and 1991, the number of Thai smokers ages 15 to 19 increased 24 percent, with similar increases for Korean high-school boys. "We were making headway in discouraging smoking, but all has been washed away by the flood of American advertising," says David D. Yen, chairman of an antismoking group in Taiwan. "We want your friendship, but not your tobacco."

The U.S. cigarette business is booming. Exports are soaring, factories are being built. And at the end of the rainbow lies China, with 300 million smokers—30 percent of the world market. "This vastly larger marketplace means a whole new world of opportunities," RJR's Dale Sisel told the Raleigh conference. Expansion abroad, he continued, would "pave the way for a bigger and brighter future." That kind of talk makes Argentina's Dr. Ferreyra Nuñez quake with anger. "American tobacco companies know their product causes death. Yet they promote smoking among children. What must these people think? Don't they have children of their own?"

Questions

1. Are the cigarette companies behaving ethically?

2. Would you consider the free samples of cigarettes these companies give to teenagers in foreign countries a form of bribery? Please explain your answer.

3. Based on what you have learned in this chapter regarding cross-national social responsibility, are these MNCs behaving in a socially responsible fashion?

4. Do you believe this problem can be solved? What are your thoughts?

Source: William Ecenbarger, "America's New Merchants of Death," *Reader's Digest* (Canadian version) (April 1993): 85–92. Reprinted with permission from the April 1993 *Reader's Digest*. Copyright © 1993 by the Reader's Digest Assn., Inc.

Notes

1. John Kimelman, "The Lonely Boy Scout," *FW* (Fall 1994): 50.
2. Thomas Donaldson, "Global Business Must Mind Its Morals," *The New York Times*, February 13, 1994, p. F11.
3. O. Ronald Gray, "The Foreign Corrupt Practices Act: Revisited and Amended," *Business and Society* (Spring 1990): 11.
4. P. Nehemkis, "Business Payoffs Abroad: Rhetoric or Reality?" *California Management Review* (Winter 1975): 13.
5. Ibid.
6. Ibid.
7. Ibid.
8. Ibid., p. 6.
9. Ibid.
10. W.A. Label and J. Kaikati, "Foreign Antibribery Law: Friend or Foe?" *Columbia Journal of World Business* (Spring 1980): 46.
11. Patricia Digh, "Shades of Gray in the Global Marketplace," *HR Magazine* (April 1997): 93.
12. Gray, "The Foreign Corrupt Practices Act," p. 14.
13. Andrew W. Singer, "Ethics: Are Standards Lower Overseas?" *Across the Board* (September 1991): 33.
14. Ibid., pp. 15–16.
15. Ibid., p. 16.
16. Kent Hodgson, "Adapting Ethical Decisions to a Marketplace," *Management Review* (May 1992): 56–57.
17. Donna J. Wood, "Corporate Social Performance Revisited," *Academy of Management Review* 16 (October 1991): 691–718.
18. Donaldson, "Global Business Must Mind Its Morals"; Thomas Donaldson, "Values in Tension: Ethics Away from Home," *Harvard Business Review* (September–October 1996): 48–62.
19. Donaldson, "Global Business Must Mind Its Morals."
20. David E. Rosenbaum, "China Trade Rift with U.S. Deepens," *The New York Times*, January 29, 1995, p. 1.
21. R.C. Trotter, S.G. Day, and A.E. Love, "Bhopal, India and Union Carbide: The Second Tragedy," *Journal of Business Ethics* 8 (1989): 439–454.
22. Sarah Cox, "Starbucks Pours One for Coffee Workers," *Monday Magazine* (Victoria, B.C.)

(March 16–22, 1995): 6

23.David Vogel, "The Globalization of Business Ethics: Why America Remains Distinctive," *California Management Review 35*, no. 1 (Fall 1992): 30.

24.Ibid., pp. 35–37.

25.Ibid., p. 35.

26.Ibid., pp. 46–47.

27.Ibid., p. 49.

28.N.A. Adam, B. Slonim, J. Wagner, P. Yesha, Yelena, "Globalizing Business, Education, Culture, Through the Internet," *Communications of the ACM 40*, no. 2 (February 1997): 115–121.

II

The International Planning Process

P laning means monitoring the enterprise's external environment to ascertain where there are business opportunities and/or threats and to become familiar with the internal aspects of the organization, including knowledge of its resources and business strengths. When the external environment presents opportunities and/or threats, planning involves preparing a strategy to mobilize the firm's resources and strengths to seize the opportunities or combat the threats. The global environment is discussed in Chapter 3. The reasons why firms establish strategy to penetrate the international business arena, as well as the types of international strategies and objectives, are discussed in Chapter 4. International product/service, place/entry, price, and promotion strategies are discussed in Chapter 5.

3

The Global Environment

Every company is looking to reduce its costs, raise its market share. or generate more value for the money it spends. When contemplating a project, you can't afford to look only at your home market. Instead, you evaluate the whole world. You look at what countries offer in terms of infrastructure, tax structure, intellectual property protection, technical capabilities, and markets, and you evaluate the trade-offs.

—Robert Ackerman, an advisor to Mitsubishi International[1]

Learning Objectives of the Chapter

Effective managers are constantly aware of the changes taking place at home and around the globe; they scan their environment on an ongoing basis, and when they detect opportunities and/or threats, they transform their organization to seize the opportunities and/or combat the threats.[2] This means that, to make effective decisions, managers must gather information from their domestic (home country) environment, as well as from the international and foreign environments. After studying this chapter, you should be able to:

1. Briefly discuss the nature of the firm's home country environment.

2. Describe the international environment, such as groupings of nations that have an impact on international business—the European Union, for example.

3. Discuss the nature of countries' cultural, economic, legal and political,

and competitive environments, as well as trade barriers, exchange rates, and labor relations.

4. Point out some sources of this information.

THE DOMESTIC ENVIRONMENT

At the domestic (home country) level, international business enterprises are affected by numerous factors, including the political, competitive, economic, legal, and governmental climates.

Domestic Political Climate

International managers must remain informed about the political climate in their home country; based on the information, they must ascertain whether the climate can now or in the future have an impact on their enterprises' industry. For example, for economic and other reasons, interest groups sometimes persuade their government to attach tariffs (taxes) or place quotas (number limits) on certain imports. Tariffs can have a direct, as well as an indirect, effect on businesses. For illustration purposes, suppose that the managers of a corporation manufacturing tractors in country X are considering exporting to country Y, that companies in country Y export wheat to country X, and that wheat growers at home (country X) are attempting to persuade their government to apply a quota or a tariff to wheat imports. It is possible that if a tariff or a quota is imposed, country Y's wheat exporters, in retaliation, might persuade their government to attach a tariff or quota on tractor imports. (As history shows, one tariff usually begets another.) The tariff or quota would affect the tractor exporters' business.

International business managers thus need to be thoroughly familiar with nations' tariffs and quotas practices. In the United States, an aid is *The National Trade Estimate Report on Foreign Trade Barriers*, generated by the Office of the U.S. Trade Representatives (U.S.T.R.), which had a new purpose bestowed upon it by the 1988 Trade Act. The act requires the U.S.T.R. to submit the report to Congress by the end of April and point out the trade barriers that cost the U.S. the most exports. Recalcitrants will be open to retaliatory tariffs or bans.[3] (For illustration purposes, read Practical Perspective 3-1.)

Domestic Competitive Climate

Managers also need information about domestic competitors' objectives. Domestic competitors may be developing similar strategies to penetrate foreign markets, and they may be introducing a newer product that would give them a competitive edge. Or they may be planning to manufacture their

PRACTICAL PERSPECTIVE 3-1

U.S. Hikes Tariffs on Imports

WASHINGTON—A bitter trade battle between the United States and Europe over bananas turned even nastier yesterday as the United States began notifying importers that they are now liable for hefty penalty tariffs on $520 million worth of European goods.

If allowed to stand, the tariffs of 100 percent on items such as German coffee makers and French handbags effectively would double their price, putting them out of reach for most U.S. consumers.

The administration is seeking to penalize European producers by an amount equal to the damages U.S.-based banana companies say they are suffering in lost sales because of unfair European trade barriers.

The U.S. action, which caught European officials by surprise, was immediately denounced by the 15-nation European Union.

The move came only a day after the World Trade Organization asked for more information before ruling on the legality of the U.S. trade sanctions. The WTO had requested both sides to provide that information by March 15.

"The United States decided to defy the WTO system by introducing a form of sanctions that has no WTO authorization whatsoever," said Leon Brittan, EU's trade minister,

said in a statement issued in Brussels. "What the United States has done is therefore unacceptable and unlawful."

The United States said it would not collect any punitive tariffs until the WTO rules on the appropriate size of the sanctions.

But starting yesterday, importers of those products must post bonds and assume liability for paying the higher tariffs if the WTO rules in the U.S.'s favor.

The United States contends that American banana companies are losing $520 million annually in lost sales to Europe because of illegal trade barriers that favor bananas imported from former European colonies in the Caribbean and Africa.

Chiquita Brands, Inc. and Dole Food Company, Inc., the major American companies involved, grow their bananas on plantations in South America.

While the United States won a WTO case on this issue, the EU argued that the matter needed further review because it has changed some banana import rules. The U.S. side says the changes do not satisfy American objections.

Source: Excerpted from Martin Crutsinger, "U.S. Hikes Tariffs on Imports," *The Star Ledger* (March 4, 1999): 43. Reprinted with permission. Copyright by the Associated Press.

products in a foreign country where labor is cheaper, which would also give them a competitive edge. This would have an impact on the enterprise's promotional, product, pricing, and place (channels of distribution) strategies (discussed in Chapter 5).

Domestic Economic Climate

Information is also needed about the domestic economic climate. If it is deteriorating, the government may place constraints on foreign investments in order to strengthen the domestic economy. On the other hand, if a firm's sales are declining because the local economy is in recession and there are no governmental constraints, entering prosperous foreign countries may be a viable survival strategy. (This will be discussed more thoroughly in Chapter 4.)

Domestic Legal System and Government Policies

Managers must be thoroughly familiar with their home country's legal system and government policies. For security and for political reasons, governments sometimes prohibit the export of certain technologies. For example, managers of several American high-tech industries, such as machine tools, telecommunications, and supercomputers, have complained about contradictions in U.S. government policies. They claim that while the government helped them develop technology for military reasons, it used the same national security concerns to impose export controls on high technology, hence keeping America's most dynamic corporations from competing in global commercial markets. Machine tool manufacturers, for instance, were deterred from exporting advanced machines for producing soda cans to Hungary. U.S. West was prohibited from assisting the former U.S.S.R. in laying modern optical fiber cable. And Cray Research Corporation, a maker of supercomputers subsidized by the military, has had difficulty getting government clearance to sell products in India and Brazil.[4]

THE INTERNATIONAL ENVIRONMENT

Managers must remain informed about the **international environment**, which consists of groupings of nations (such as the European Union), of worldwide bodies (such as the World Bank and the International Monetary Fund), and of organizations of nations by industry agreements (such as OPEC—the Organization of Petroleum Exporting Countries). It seems as if the consolidation of nations into free trade blocks is going to continue. (For illustration purposes, read Practical Perspective 3-2.) Such organizations also have an impact on firms' international strategies. For example, the economic unification of the European Union (EU) will have a strong impact on international business. The unification, which officially took place on December 31, 1992, is the result of the Single European Act of July 1, 1987. The act aimed to commit the then–twelve member EU nations to an economically standardized/harmonized single market of about 320 million people—which is expected to be the industrialized world's largest single market.[5] The twelve nations are Belgium, Denmark, France, Germany, Great Britain, Greece, Ireland, Italy, Luxembourg, the Netherlands, Portugal, and Spain, and in January 1995, Austria, Finland, and Sweden also became members. This change will generate many opportunities and threats for external firms, both small and large.

PRACTICAL PERSPECTIVE 3-2

The Road to Santiago

When in December 1994 Bill Clinton welcomed to Miami the leaders of 33 other countries in the Americas, their meeting was widely seen as the start of a new chapter in the often troubled relations between the United States and Latin America. With the Cold War over, with elected governments in power except (uninvited) Cuba, and with market reforms and freer trade supplanting statist protectionism, many old sources of tension seemed to have been replaced by shared ideas and new opportunities for cooperation.

Chief among these was the notion, mooted earlier by President George Bush in 1990, of a "free-trade area of the Americas" (FTAA), stretching from Alaska to Cape Horn. In Miami, Latin America's leaders embraced the idea with surprising enthusiasm. A target date of 2005 was set for its achievement, with "concrete progress" to be made by 2000. Alongside this, the 34 summiteers put their names to a long list of collective virtues, 150 "action items" concerned with topics ranging from health services through women's rights to the environment.

On April 18 and 19 in the Chilean capital, Santiago, the 34 countries' leaders [were scheduled to] meet again...[to] formally launch the FTAA negotiations. After three years of hard talking, at a final preparatory meeting in Costa Rica last month, their trade ministers agreed to a detailed agenda of what to negotiate, how, where, and when. Their ambitious dream might seem, at first glance, to be steadily becoming a reality.

True, the FTAA concept faces criticism. Some economists argue that regional preferences divert more trade than they create. Some Latin Americans fear that the cost of adjusting to free trade with the world's most powerful economy will far outweigh the benefits, especially in smaller and less developed countries.

Source: Excerpted from "The Road to Santiago," *The Economist* (April 11, 1998): 25. Reprinted with permission.

Opportunities Presented by the EU

The harmonization aims to replace the existing patchwork of standards, which vary from country to country, region to region within countries, and even city to city within regions. This means that external firms can realize greater profits because they will need to produce only one version of a product as opposed to their current practice of producing dozens. Furthermore, the EU intends to establish mutual recognition among member countries. Under the mutual recognition directive, goods and services legitimately produced in one member country can be marketed without hindrance anywhere in the EU.[6] This also helps firms attain greater economies of scale as they will no longer need to make expensive modifications and prepare the 100 or so customs forms now required to meet different EU regulations.[7]

The EU also aims to establish the means for capital, including cash and bank transfers, to move freely between member countries. This, too, is likely to provide new opportunities to many external firms, as will the EU's deregulation of transportation. Previously, trucks entering one EU country could make only one stop in the nation. Now trucks will be permitted to make several stops and will not be required to stop for border checks.[8] This will decrease transportation costs and make transportation more efficient. For example, U.S.'s Federal Express, which is likely to benefit from this change, has been purchasing companies in the EU that hold national trucking licenses.[9]

The EU also has proposed a directive permitting cross-border transmission of television signals. This will enable firms to advertise more efficiently. As a result, many new cable and satellite stations have already been started. 3M Corporation, for example, is taking a pan-European approach to advertising and expects to reach a vast audience at far less cost.[10] The EU also is committed to fair competition. The cartels that monopolize certain EU industries are to be dismantled to provide competition and opportunities to new businesses.[11]

Threats Presented by the EU

The objective of the EU unification is to make its members' firms more competitive in the global marketplace, not to offer external enterprises a large market to exploit. This threatens many external firms. For example, some external firms that plan to start operating in the EU fear that they will not have direct contact with the EU's standard-setting body. To combat this, some American companies already in the EU are trying to secure fair treatment in tenders for public contracts and to avert being handicapped when the EU sets product and safety standards. In order to have input, IBM has been attempting to join JESSI, a government-backed European research project on semiconductors.[12]

External companies also fear that a "Fortress Europe," which allows protectionism and preferential treatment, may evolve. For example, the EU has indicated that it may continue imposing quantitative restrictions on some imported products—such as automobiles—to enable EU companies to adjust to their internal market. Its directive on telecommunications proposes that bids must be rejected unless 50 percent or more of their value is derived from EU sources and that EU companies be preferred even when the 50 percent condition is met. Furthermore, the harmonization of the EU is expected to lead to the fall of prices across Europe.[13] This is likely to provide threats to many external firms who depend on the prices they are currently charging in the EU but may have to lower them to compete with EU enterprises.

It should be noted that the North American Free Trade Agreement (NAFTA), a union consisting of Canada, Mexico, and the United States, presents opportunities and threats similar to those presented by the European Union.

THE FOREIGN ENVIRONMENT

Foreign (individual nations') **environmental** factors can have a dramatic impact on international business. The factors include the cultural environment, the economic environment, the legal and political environment, as well as the competition, trade barriers, fluctuating monetary exchange rates, and labor relations. These factors differ in many respects from country to country, and in some cases from region to region within each nation. In order to develop an effective strategic plan for doing business in a foreign country, enterprises' managers must first become thoroughly familiar with the foreign factors and how they differ from their home country factors.[14] And they must make the necessary adaptations—otherwise, failure is almost inevitable. The ensuing sections briefly explain the above factors.

Culture

Culture is the total of humankind's knowledge, beliefs, arts, morals, laws, customs, and other capabilities and habits adapted by individuals as members of society.[15] As pointed out in Chapter 1, societies around the globe develop differing cultures. In order to develop an effective international business strategy, the critical aspects of culture must be identified. (As an illustration of how culture affects international strategies, read Practical

---

PRACTICAL PERSPECTIVE 3-3

The Case of the Sacred Ground

A civil engineer in a U.S. construction firm was given the responsibility of selecting a site for, designing, and constructing a fish-processing plant in a West African nation. The engineer identified viable sites on the basis of availability of reliable power, closeness to transportation means and to the river which accesses fishing boats from the Atlantic Ocean, nearness to major markets, and the availability of housing and human resources.

Following the analysis of the viable sites, the optimum site was selected. Just before obtaining bids from contractors for site

preparation, the engineer happened to learn that the site was located on ground considered by local people to be sacred—where their gods resided. The local people on whom the engineer was counting to "man" the operation would thus not work there. The engineer therefore chose another site.

Source: Excerpted from H.W. Lane and J.J. DiStefano, *International Management Behavior*, 2d ed. (Boston: PWS-Kent, 1992): 27. Reproduced with permission of South-Western College Publishing, a division of Thomson Learning. Fax 800-730-2215.

PRACTICAL PERSPECTIVE 3-4

The Impatient North Americans

Numerous North American government officials and businesspeople were sent on a
trade mission to Brazil. They returned two
weeks later after having toured several Brazilian
cities. Upon their return, one of the businesspeople commented that the trip had been a flop
since no orders had been obtained during the
entire trip. In contrast, a Japanese firm sent a
business manager to Rio de Janeiro with
instructions to "Get to know the people and
learn Portuguese during your first year there,
then concern yourself with conducting
business."

Source: Excerpted from H.W. Lane and J.J. DiStefano,
International Management Behavior, 2d ed. (Boston: PWS-Kent,
1992): 27. Reproduced with permission of South-Western
College Publishing, a division of Thomson Learning. Fax 800-
730-2215.

Perspective 3-3.) Practical Perspective 3-4 suggests that Japanese international business managers tend to make greater efforts to learn foreign cultures than do U.S. international managers.

The **cultural environment**, as demonstrated in Chapter 1, affects the
international management process. For example, for many managers of
U.S. organizations, the highest priority is profit maximization. However, for
many managers of Japanese organizations, the highest priority has always
been, and remains, increasing market share and keeping people employed.[16]
Therefore, American managers' practice would not fit well in Japanese
organizations. The cultural environment also dictates what a product or
service should look like or be able to do, what people will consume, as well
as promotional strategies. For example, the British like dry cakes with their
tea; Americans, on the other hand, tend to favor fancy, iced cakes. Similar
issues were at stake when United Airlines entered the Pacific market.
During the inauguration of its concierge services for first-class passengers
from Hong Kong, each concierge proudly wore a white carnation. This was
not well received by the Chinese, for whom the white carnation is a symbol
of death.[17]

Culture also affects how business and negotiations are conducted. For
instance, in Mexico and most of South America as well as in many other
cultures, personal relationships must be established before business negotiations can begin. Furthermore, culture affects a country's human resources
management practices. For example, in China, employees expect their
enterprises to watch out for their welfare, ranging from the provision of pay
and bonuses, to housing, health care, child education, meal services, and
recreation. Chinese managers are expected to become involved in their
employees' personal family matters. And, although divorce is rare in China,

when a couple divorces, the enterprise is often expected to provide housing for the departing spouse. However, as China heads toward a market economy, these practices are likely to become less and less common.

As was also pointed out in Chapter 1, closely related to culture is religion. The religious aspects of culture are of great importance in consumption patterns. For example, Judaism and Islam prohibit the consumption of pork. In essence, religion influences people's habits, the products they buy, and their perception of life. Sex in advertising, for example, which is widely used in the United States, may not be acceptable in some cultures as a result of religious beliefs; it may be viewed as immoral or demeaning. And some religions have a negative view of profits earned by investors who do not work for the business. (Practical Perspective 3-5 presents an illustration of how religion affects the banking system in the Muslim world.)

Economic Environment

Economics is the way people manage their material wealth and the results of their management. The **economic environment** includes the production of goods and services, their distribution and consumption, means of exchange, and income derived from them. In the search for new markets, international business managers will find that nations differ in their stage of economic development. A nation's stage of economic development will have a dramatic effect on the types of products and services needed, the price, the promotional strategies, and the distribution system. It will also have a dramatic effect on the type of financial concessions a foreign government is willing to make to attract technologies that will aid the country in its economic development efforts. Nations in earlier stages of development tend to subsidize foreign investments more than countries in a later stage of development. (For illustration purposes, read Practical Perspective 3-6.)

Nations' Technological Needs as They Develop

Walt W. Rostow, a professor in the U.S., developed a theory that can aid managers in assessing a foreign country's technological needs.[18] The theory concludes that societies pass through **five stages of economic development**, described in Figure 3-1. In general, the goods and services required by a country in an earlier stage of economic development are different from the goods and services required in a later stage. For example, residents in a country where electricity is scarce would have little use for electric refrigerators. A **less-developed country** may need to import industrial machinery and equipment to explore its raw materials and to produce agricultural products as well as specialized construction equipment in order to develop a transportation system.[19] It may need management consulting, accounting systems, and training and development services. These services are needed because nations seldom possess the systems and skilled personnel required to manage the new technologies.

PRACTICAL PERSPECTIVE 3-5

Turning the Prophet's Profits

According to Islamic tradition, overturned wine jars stained the streets of Medina red when Allah revealed to the prophet Muhammad that Muslims should be forbidden alcohol. He banned interest payments too, but bankers have had better luck than vintners. Most banks across the Muslim world still earn their money in the time-honored way, rewarding savers with some interest and charging borrowers a little more. Some, however, claim to offer a truly "Islamic" alternative. These are proving popular as well as pious. But in order to keep growing, they are having to explore more adventurous ways to invest their depositors' cash.

There are now more than 100 specialized institutions that invest money according to strict Islamic principles, ranging from mass-market savings banks in Jordan to pukka private banks in Geneva. Even some western banks are embracing the concept: last month the U.S.'s Citibank opened the first western-owned Islamic bank. Based in Bahrain, Citi Islamic Investment Bank has a start-up capital of $20 million.

Islamic banks are still puny by international standards. Taken together, their assets of somewhere between $25 billion and $100 billion (depending on whom you believe) are equal only to those of a middling American or European bank. But they are growing fast. Some of the biggest, such as Kuwait Finance House and Pakistan's Muslim Commercial Bank, are growing their assets by about 10 percent a year. The potential market—one billion or so Muslims—is huge.

Islam's religious revival is the industry's motor. True believers obey *sharia*, Islam's holy law. This places several demands on Muslim savers. They must not finance activities prohibited by the Koran, such as gambling and the consumption of alcohol. Nor are they allowed to receive interest. ("Those who benefit from interest," warns the Koran, "shall be raised like those driven mad by the touch of the devil.")

To abide by these strictures, Islamic banks have developed alternative financial contracts. The most common of these is *murabaha*, a form of so-called "cost-plus" financing. This works as follows: Say a company wants to purchase $100 million of equipment. Instead of lending it the money for three months at 2 percent interest, an Islamic bank will buy the equipment itself. It will then sell it to the firm for $102 million, with payment deferred for three months. The bank can then claim that it is charging a profit mark-up rather than an interest rate.

Source: Excerpted from "Turning the Prophet's Profits," *The Economist* (September 9, 1996): 32. Reprinted with permission.

When a country begins to process its raw materials and resources for export, the demand may be for other kinds of machinery and industrialized goods. Entering the stage in which investment and manufacturing become a leading growth sector, a country may need products necessary to operate entire manufacturing facilities. When the country becomes fairly well industrialized, producing capital and consumer goods such as machinery, automobiles, and refrigerators, it may need more specialized and heavy capital

PRACTICAL PERSPECTIVE 3-6

Singer's Internationalization Strategy

The Singer Company developed itself into an international enterprise, conducting business in more than 30 countries, including the U.S., soon after it was founded in Europe in the late 1800s by Sir Isaac Singer. The firm primarily produced sewing machines. Early in the twentieth century, Singer applied techniques for assessing entry into foreign markets that are widely applied by many corporations today. It analyzed foreign country variables, such as geography, labor costs, economic environment, financial stability, market support for the product, export potential, and the country's repatriation of profits policies. Singer consid-

ered foreign government subsidies, such as tax breaks and land and factories provided for free or at reduced rates, important factors in deciding whether or not to start operations in a foreign nation. Foreign governments were willing to make many concessions to Singer because they needed the technology for economic development reasons. Singer thus became a pioneer in entering markets in less-developed countries and developed excellent skills in negotiating foreign government subsidies.

Source: Excerpted from an unpublished term paper by M.B.A. student William Werner for the course "Issues in International Management," Montclair State University, Spring 1992.

FIGURE 3-1	The Stages of Economic Development of Nations
Stage One	In the first stage, agriculture usually comprises the largest part of the country's resources. The society operates on past societal precepts, technology is essentially static, occupations are passed down from one generation to the next, and the social and economic systems remain essentially closed to change.
Stage Two	In the second stage, government and entrepreneurs establish the preconditions for takeoff. The government must be dedicated to modernization and must be willing to spend public monies on education and infrastructure to service industry (roads, communication, electricity, etc.). A leading sector, such as agriculture, mining, petroleum, etc., is essential.
Stage Three	In stage three, takeoff begins. Investment rises; manufacturing becomes a leading growth sector; political, social, and institutional structures are transformed to help maintain a steady rate of growth. This period lasts 20 to 30 years.
Stage Four	Stage four is the drive to maturity. The most advanced technology available is used. This period lasts about 60 years.
Stage Five	In stage five, high mass consumption occurs. Emphasis is given to consumer durables and services that allow the majority of a country's population to attain a relatively high standard of living.

Source: Excerpted from Walt W. Rostow, *The Stages of Economic Development* (New York: Cambridge University Press, 1971).

equipment not yet manufactured there. For example, a country producing automobiles may need more modern equipment, such as wheel alignment indicators. In the fifth stage, a country reaches complete industrialization and usually assumes world leadership in the production of a variety of goods. Even though a country may be totally industrialized, a demand for goods from another country still exists, because highly industrialized countries tend to specialize in the production of certain goods. For example, U.S. enterprises are highly skilled in producing communications and sophisticated computer technologies, and Japanese enterprises are highly skilled in producing process technologies.

It should be noted that Rostow's theory has received several criticisms. First, in practice the stages are not clearly distinguishable from each other. Second, they do not display characteristics that can be tested empirically. Third, the characteristics that tend to cause movement from one stage to another are not identifiable. Fourth, the time periods Rostow suggests do not apply to all industrialized nations. And fifth, the model is more applicable to some nations than others.[20] Nevertheless, the theory can be useful as a concept or framework for strategic analysis. For example, the theory tells the international manager that people in countries in an earlier stage of development may possess a different perspective from those in countries in a later stage with respect to the aesthetic values of a product/service and preference for managerial styles. For instance, people in less-developed countries may place relatively little value on electric toothbrushes, and they may not value participative management as much as do people in the more developed nations. As demonstrated in Chapter 1, most of the less-developed countries tend to be governed by the large power distance cultural dimension.

Legal and Political Systems

A nation's legal and political systems have an enormous impact on international business management. As Joseph Conner, chairman of Price Waterhouse World Firm, has indicated, "Multinational corporations start by looking at the stability of government, the legal structure regarding expropriation and how strongly private property is protected, and they look at how easy it is to move capital in and out of the country."[21] (Practical Perspective 3-7 discuss the instability in Mexico.)

Legal Systems

Laws vary widely in the world's societies. The following are some common issues of the **legal environment** that must be given special attention when planning to transact business in a foreign country:

1. Rules of competition on (a) collusion, (b) discrimination against certain buyers, (c) promotional methods, (d) variable pricing, and (e) exclusive territory agreements

2. Retail price maintenance laws

3. Cancellation of distributor or wholesaler agreements

4. Product quality regulations and controls

5. Packaging laws

6. Warranty and after-sales exposure

7. Price controls, limitations on markups or markdowns

8. Patents, trademarks, and copyright laws and practices[22]

Labor laws, foreign investment, and contract enforcement must also be given special attention. For example, foreign moviemakers are not allowed to distribute movies in mainland China or even own copyrights. They can, however, share in the profits by setting up co-productions with Chinese companies, provided they give the government final cut.[23] And, besides imposing steep taxes on cars, the Thai government unofficially controls their price. Car manufacturers must file the prices of new cars three weeks before they go on sale. In 1996, government officials decreed that the $15,000 Honda City was overpriced by 16,000 baht ($625) because of too much corporate overhead. In addition to lowering prices, Honda was required to pay rebates to 150 customers.[24]

Labor Laws. Wages may be low in a nation, but its legal authority may require that high fringe benefits, such as profit sharing, health and dental, and retirement benefits be given to workers. **Labor laws** in many countries provide extensive security for workers and make it extremely expensive to terminate an employee. For example, China has had a 100 percent employment policy. Many companies in China are therefore overstaffed. Furthermore, the laws in many countires mandate long vacations—for example, there is a six-week mandatory vacation in Germany.

Foreign Investment. Many countries' laws often dictate that **foreign investments** in their nation must be in the form of a joint venture with local partners and that the local partners must be majority owners. For example, in the past, IBM's policy was that their foreign subsidiaries had to be wholly owned (100 percent ownership). IBM became confronted with a problem when many countries' governments began to mandate joint ventures with local partners. For instance, IBM was operating in India on a wholly owned basis. The Indian government subsequently issued a mandate requiring that foreign investments in India be on a joint-venture basis, with the local partners owning 70 percent. Not wanting to take on partners, IBM elected to pull its operations out of India.

Also, the legal systems in some countries mandate that top management of foreign-owned enterprises must consist of locals. This can lead to problems when capable managers are not available in the foreign country. For example, when Russia began to shift from a communistic to a market-like

PRACTICAL PERSPECTIVE 3-7

Troubles in Mexico

In Mexico, the path to progress has some enormous obstacles along its way. True, the economic reforms of the 1980s and 1990s were impressive, even if the government badly mismanaged its currency devaluation at the end of 1994. Today the country appears to be on the road to recovery from the peso crisis: forecasters estimate growth in the range of 4 to 5 percent for 1997, and the nation's export economy is flourishing. But the current-account deficit is rising again. Mexico's external debt has grown from 35 percent of GDP in 1992 to more than 60 percent in 1996. High interest rates and taxes are strangling the middle class. The banking system borders on insolvency. In the recession of the past two years, 5 million Mexicans have been added to the 22 million citizens (one-fourth of the population) who already live in extreme poverty. And the government estimates that an annual growth rate of 6 percent is necessary to absorb the 1 million new entrants into the labor force each year—a rate that does not appear to be attainable anytime soon.

Mexico's ability to deal with those daunting problems depends on an effective government. The country has been ruled by the iron fist of the Institutional Revolutionary Party for more than 60 years, but the party has become arthritic and corrupt. It is incapable of acting as a safety valve for the wellspring of popular discontent in Mexico, let alone as a vehicle for implementing critical new policies necessary for a rapidly changing economy. The party is in fact resisting change, having recently overturned President Ernesto Zedillio's far-reaching proposal to open and modernize Mexico's political process.

Nevertheless, political change will come—if not peacefully then violently. Already, crime, kidnapping, assassinations, and guerilla activity are on the rise, signaling both a mounting level of dissatisfaction and the inability of the public sector to maintain order. But even if a more open and representative government emerges, it will lack the experience and the underlying institutions—such as honest courts—to govern effectively in the short run. Initially, that government may be besieged by the accumulated demands of tens of millions of Mexican citizens who have felt disenfranchised. It also will have its hands full cleaning up the old system— getting a grip on widespread criminality and creating a rule of law that all segments of the population can respect.

In light of those pressures, future governments may put off liberalizing the economy and instead concentrate on the immediate welfare of ordinary citizens. A democratic administration could become more nationalistic and more protectionist than the existing oligarchy. It could take many years before Mexico restores its current trajectory, at least in the eyes of foreign companies and governments.

Source: Excerpted from Jeffrey E. Garten, "Troubles Ahead in Emerging Markets," *Harvard Business Review* (May–June 1997): 39–40. Reprinted with permission.

economy in the mid-1980s and began to draw foreign investments, its laws required that top management of foreign-owned enterprises be Russian. However, since Russians lacked experience in managing market-like enterprises, they were not very effective. By the late 1980s, the Russian government repealed the law, allowing foreigners to manage foreign-owned operations.

Contract Enforcement. Contract enforcement can sometimes be a problem. For example, if there is a default in a contract entered into by firms from different nations, which nation's law is applied? Usually, the contract stipulates whose law is applied in the event of default. However, some countries' legal systems mandate that the laws of the nation where the contract was signed shall be applied. Other legal systems mandate that the laws of the country where the contract was executed shall be applied.

Political Systems

Awareness of the foreign country's political thinking and activities is absolutely essential. Before investing in a foreign country, a manager must learn about the country's type of government and what effect it could have on business operations. (Practical Perspective 3-8 describes the climate in Romania.) Is the **political system** primarily a democracy, dictatorship, monarchy, a socialist or communist system, or does it seem to be moving in any of these directions? The **political environment**, if it is extreme or headed toward extremes, would greatly influence an investment decision. If a country's radical party is likely to be dominant, investment may be too risky. International companies have had their foreign subsidiaries confiscated when a radical political party in the country suddenly assumed power. Extreme social and economic turbulence are sometimes omens that foreshadow the emergence of extremist parties.

Types of Political Systems. Some nations, such as the U.S. and Britain, function with a two-party system. Change from one party to another does not cause great changes in the business realm. Other nations, such as Germany and France, are not dominated by any one party; theirs is a multiparty system, and the government may be controlled by a coalition of parties. Still other nations, such as Mexico, have a multiparty system, but only the candidates of one party have a real chance of being elected and controlling the government. This one-party control provides some degree of stability in Mexico's governmental policies. The most extreme type is the one-party political system, such as in China and in the former U.S.S.R., where opposition is repressed. The one-party system can, however, also provide stability.

Regardless of the political system, firms can generally do business in any nation and with any party as long as there is stability in policy. For

PRACTICAL PERSPECTIVE 3-8

Dwindling Investment

Sadly, the current business climate in Romania is discouraging. Long the country of perpetual promise for investors, Romania today is more a nation of perpetual problems, almost all of which are self-imposed and almost always avoidable. The continuous change in Romania's investment, tax, and privatization laws, and the government's perceived indifference to their impact upon investors, have created an unstable and unfair climate for business. This situation has been further exploited by bureaucratic incompetence, red tape, and corruption, all combining to drive foreign investment away from Romania.

Unfortunately, we cannot avoid mentioning the pall cast upon Romania by the perception that corruption flourishes in the country. Investors are not unaware that Transparency International ranks Romania among the most corrupt countries in the world. This unfortunate distinction, whether true or not, casts a further shadow upon an already bleak business environment. So, like the little boy in the Hans Christian Andersen story "The Emperor's New Clothes," one must reluctantly point out the perception that justice is for sale in Romania and the failure to meaningfully address the problem has caused foreign investors to openly question the security of their investments. Moreover, the perceived political clout of local "barons" and the influence of the local Mafias have allowed dishonest businesspeople to openly flout the law in unfair competition with honest investors.

Source: Excerpted from "Crisis of Confidence," *The Romanian Digest 4*, no. 8 (August 1999). Reprinted with permission.

example, some American firms, such as Pepsi-Cola, conducted business effectively in the former U.S.S.R. and many foreign firms are currently conducting business effectively in China. If policies change gradually, as they do in most nations, the firm has time to adjust its business strategies accordingly. The danger occurs when a country's dominant party makes radical changes in its policy. In this case, the firm would not have sufficient time to adapt, thus placing it in a difficult situation.

Government Policies. Extreme social and economic conditions may sometimes force a political party into radical policy changes. Generally, however, **government policies** change gradually; governments implement new policies to attract the foreign investments needed by the nation to attain its economic development objectives. William Stoever, a professor of international business at Seton Hall University, has developed a schema linking the stages of a country's economic development described in Rostow's theory to the country's policy changes toward foreign investment.[25] This model can be helpful to international managers in predicting and understanding a nation's policy changes.

According to Stoever, countries at stage one of economic development are usually unattractive to foreign investment, though government subsidies may attract some "show" factories. Stage two countries tend to attract low-technology investments; they attract labor-intensive technology for assembling or producing for the local market or for assembling for export. In moving to stage three, Stoever proposes, policy makers begin to be more selective in the type of investments they import, and their policies aim to take over part or full ownership of foreign-owned facilities. In order to move to stage four, the country's economy must strengthen and diversify to the point where it can rely more on market mechanisms. The country's policies are therefore those that guide the nation to a "free market" system. The more productive capabilities now existing in these countries make it an attractive investment for multinational corporations, and firms are usually more willing to supply their advanced technologies to these countries.

The Government's Attitude Toward the Product. International business managers also need to learn about the foreign **government's attitude toward investment and products.** Some investments and products are more politically vulnerable than others. Some receive favorable consideration by a nation, such as lower tariffs and higher quotas, while others receive unfavorable impositions. Product vulnerability is influenced by political philosophies, economic variations, and cultural differences. By obtaining accurate answers to the questions in Figure 3-2, an international manager may discover whether a product will face a favorable or a hostile environment. Generally, a firm may expect to receive favorable consideration if its product/service contributes to the achievement of the import nation's goals, and it will receive unfavorable attention if, in view of the nation's current needs, the product/service is nonessential. Figure 3-3 presents a framework that helps international firms improve the political considerations they will receive in a foreign country.

As a case illustration, Honda Motor Company of Japan applies a strategy of localizing profits and production.[26] Honda reinvests as much of its profits as possible in the local market. It regards itself as a local company and aims to prosper together with the host nation. For example, in 1959 Honda established a wholly owned marketing subsidiary, American Honda, in California with a capital investment of $250,000. By 1999, this sum had grown to $200 million through reinvestment of American Honda's profits. Honda has invested in the construction and expansion of motorcycle, automobile, and engine manufacturing plants in Ohio and Canada. Relative to localization of production, Honda does not merely make profits by exporting completed products to a foreign market; it produces where major markets exist, therefore contributing to the development of the host country and achieving mutual prosperity. For example, in 1990, Honda produced about 470,000 automobiles in its North American plants, in 1994 it produced about 520,000, and it planned to produce 610,000 in 1995—an indication that Honda continues to invest locally (*Source*: Honda

---

FIGURE 3-2   A Process for Assessing the Political Vulnerability of a Product

1. Is the availability of the product ever going to be subject to political debate? (sugar, salt, gasoline, public utilities, medicines, foodstuffs)

2. Do other industries depend upon the production of the product? (cement, power machine tools, construction machinery, steel)

3. Is the product considered socially or economically essential? (key drugs, laboratory equipment, medicines)

4. Is the product essential to agricultural industries? (farm tools and machinery, crops, fertilizers, seed)

5. Does the product affect national defense capabilities?

6. Does the product require important resources that are available from local sources? (labor, skills, materials)

7. Is there local competition or potential local competition from manufacturers in the near future? (small, low investment manufacturing)

8. Does the product relate to channels of mass communication media? (newsprint, radio equipment)

9. Is the product primarily a service?

10. Does the use of this product or its design depend upon legal requirements?

11. Is the product potentially dangerous to the user? (explosives, drugs)

12. Does the product induce a net drain on scarce foreign exchange?

Source: Adapted from Richard D. Robinson, "The Challenge of the Underdeveloped National Market," *The Journal of Marketing* (October 1961): 24–25. Used with permission of publisher. © 1961 American Marketing Association, Chicago, IL. All rights reserved.

Motor Corp. Ltd. Annual Report [March 31, 1995]: 13). As of October 1999, Honda's investment was $2.562 billion in the U.S., $800 million in Canada, and $92 million in Mexico.[27] Practical Perspective 3-9 presents a time line of some of Honda's expansion activities in the U.S. through October 1999.

Scarce Foreign Exchange. International managers must understand the dynamics of hard versus soft currencies. **Hard currencies** are those readily accepted as payment in international business transactions. The currencies of most of the industrialized nations, such as Japan, the U.S., Germany, France, and Britain, are hard currencies. The currencies of most less-developed countries, and of countries with government-controlled economies (Cuba and China, for example), are generally classified as **soft currencies**. These are normally not accepted as payment in international business transactions.

The government of countries whose money is classified as soft currency usually accumulates hard currencies. These countries' government uses the hard currencies to pay for foreign goods and services, which in its view are needed to accomplish national goals. If the product or service is viewed as being needed, the government may authorize payment in hard currency; if not, the government usually will not authorize such payment.

FIGURE 3-3	How to Make Friends in Foreign Countries

Remember that:

1. The company is a guest in the country and its managers should act accordingly.

2. The profits of an enterprise do not belong solely to the company—the local "national" employees and the economy of the purchasing country should also benefit.

3. It is not wise to try to win over new customers by trying to completely "Americanize" them.

4. Although English is an accepted language overseas, a fluency in the language of the international customer goes further in making sales and cementing good public relations.

5. The international company should try to contribute to the host country's economy and culture with worthwhile public projects.

6. It should train its executives, and their families, to act appropriately overseas.

7. It is best not to conduct business from headquarters but to staff foreign offices with competent foreign nationals and supervise the operation from headquarters.

Source: Adapted from "Making Friends and Customers in Foreign Lands," *Printer's Ink* (June 3, 1960): 59. Reprinted with permission.

PRACTICAL PERSPECTIVE 3-9

American Honda—Time Line

1959 American Honda Motor Co. was established with a small motorcycle store in Los Angeles.

1970 Honda introduced its first car, the N600 Sedan, to the U.S.

1979 Production began at the Honda Motorcycle Plant in Marysville, Ohio.

1982 A new auto plant began producing the Accord, making Honda the first Japanese automobile company to manufacture in the U.S.

1985 Honda began production at an engine plant in Anna, Ohio, to manufacture both motorcycle and automobile engines.

1988 The first American-made Accord was exported to Japan.

1989 Honda began production of the Civic Sedan and Coupe at its new plant in East Liberty, Ohio.

1991 Honda began exporting the Accord Wagon to Europe and Japan. It was designed, engineered, and produced exclusively in the U.S.

1994 Honda sold its 10-millionth car in the U.S.

1999 In September, Honda sold 91,054 units, and for the nine-month period, it sold 1,067,468 units in the U.S.

Source: http://www.honda.com

(Figure 3-2 aids the international manager in assessing the situation.) Payment in hard currency usually must be negotiated with authorized government officials. If the officials do not authorize payment in hard currency, international managers who have decided to do business in the country must seek alternative ways, such as barter trade; payment is made in goods or services that can be sold for a profit in another market. For example, the U.S.'s PepsiCola sells its product to Russia for vodka, which it sells in other markets for a profit.

Political Risk Insurance. Many industrial nations offer some form of political risk insurance when investments are made in foreign countries. The U.S., for example, provides coverage through the Overseas Private Investment Corporation (OPIC). OPIC insures new investments in qualified projects, in less-developed but friendly countries, against losses owing to certain political risks. OPIC is authorized to provide insurance against three specific types of risks:

1. Inability to convert into dollars currencies received by the investor as profits of earnings or return on the original investment
2. Loss of investments resulting from expropriation, nationalization, or confiscation by action of a foreign government
3. Loss due to war, revolution, civil strife, or insurrection. Civil strife, coverage for which is optional, would encompass damage resulting from politically motivated violent acts, including terrorism and sabotage.[28]

The Multilateral Investment Guarantee Agency (MIGA), an affiliate of the World Bank, offers quite similar insurance.[29]

Expropriation is the seizure by a government of foreign-owned assets. This does not violate international law if it is followed by prompt, adequate, and effective compensation.

Nationalization occurs when a government takes over private property. Reasonable compensation is usually paid by the government.

Confiscation occurs when a government seizes foreign-owned assets and does not make prompt, effective, and adequate compensation.

Competition

Throughout the twentieth century, most nations tried to avoid competition. The major exception has been the United States. However, as the world heads toward a single marketplace, a more aggressive international **competitive environment** seems to be evolving. Japanese culture considers competition a wasteful practice, but the Japanese behave very competitively in the global arena. Numerous factors restrict international competition, including cartels, bribery, economic conditions, government-owned enterprises, and a short-range versus long-range managerial orientation.

Cartels

Cartels consist of groups of private businesses that agree to set prices, share markets, and control production. (OPEC is a prime example.) Cartels restrict competition. In Japan, *keiretsu* links (giant industrial groups linked by cross-ownership, such as Mitsubishi or Sumitomo), bidding cartels, and old-boy networks present external firms with formidable obstacles that Japanese corporations do not face in some markets, such as the U.S. market.[30]

Bribery

Bribery as a means of obtaining a competitive edge is an accepted business practice in some nations. As pointed out in Chapter 2, the U.S. Foreign Corrupt Practices Act of 1977 makes it illegal for U.S. businesspeople to engage in bribery in any country, even if it is an accepted practice there. Many U.S. business people have complained that this law has made their firms less competitive, because competitors from other nations are not bound by such laws. Numerous U.S. business people, however, have said that the law has not impeded their competitive position, and that what really makes some U.S. firms less competitive in the international arena is the high-cost, low-quality products they are trying to market.

Economic Conditions

Competition can also be weakened by a nation's economic conditions. During difficult economic times, many governments apply protectionist policies, such as tariffs and quotas, to restrict or diminish foreign competition.

Government-Owned Enterprises

Competition is further weakened by government-owned enterprises competing with private firms. Governments do not necessarily have to realize profits and therefore can afford to cut prices. These government-owned enterprises can also get cheaper financing, can easily win government contracts, and, with government assistance, can even hold down wages in their country. Government-owned firms thus have a competitive advantage over private enterprises. The Japanese, for example, through the Ministry of International Trade and Industry (MITI), target certain industries, help them reduce the risk of developing new technologies, and assist them in achieving large-scale production to reduce costs. These practices enable Japanese firms to compete more effectively in international markets.[31] By conducting research, which is made available to businesses for commercialization, the U.S. government also aids firms in reducing risk and in obtaining a competitive edge. The NASA program, for example, has generated many ideas that were subsequently commercialized by business entrepreneurs. Furthermore, the U.S. government awards grants to less-developed nations to aid them in their development objectives. Some of these grants stipulate that certain goods and services necessary to carry out the program must be procured from U.S.-based enterprises. Such practices also restrict competition.

Long-Range Versus Short-Range Orientation

Firms holding a short-range managerial orientation (for example, many U.S. firms) often find it difficult to compete with firms holding a long-range managerial orientation (for example, many Japanese firms). For instance, one of Japan's top computer manufacturers won a contract over a U.S. firm to design a computer system in Hiroshima by bidding $1. Its strategy was to give away the design job in order to gain the inside advantage for the city's equipment purchase. This exemplifies a common Japanese strategy of forgoing short-range profits for long-term profits. Japanese firms project that once they have established a business relationship, they will obtain life-time orders. Firms that cannot wait for possible profits down the road will therefore encounter difficulties in competing with Japanese companies.

It should be noted that some Japanese MNCs have been accused of "dumping," which, under GATT (the General Agreement on Tariffs and Trade), is illegal. (GATT will be discussed further in the "Trade Barriers" section.) **Dumping** is practiced when an MNC sells a product in a foreign market at a price lower than the one it sells the product for in its own market and/or at below production cost. For example, the U.S. Department of Commerce issued a preliminary finding that South Korean chip makers Hyundai Electronics Company and LG Semicon Company [now merged and known as Hyundai Electronics Industries Company, Ltd.] dumped memory chips in the U.S. If upheld, the ruling would potentially subject the companies to several hundred million dollars in fines. The Commerce Department found that, in an attempt to drive out competitors, Hyundai and LG dumped memory chips, or sold them below costs, in the U.S. market from May 1, 1996 to April 30, 1997.[32]

The intent of dumping is to sell the product at a price much lower than the competitors' price, thus putting the competition out of business. Once the competition is out of the way, the MNC raises the price. These accusations are debatable and Japanese managers refute them. Many international business managers and scholars view managers of Japanese MNCs not as "dumpers," but as effective customer- and quality-oriented strategists.

A Theory That Aids in Predicting Foreign Competition

Raymond Vernon and Louis T. Wells, Jr., professors at Harvard Business School, developed a theory labeled the **International Product Life Cycle** (IPLC), which can be used to assess which products are in danger of international competition.[33] According to this theory, many products pass through four phases.

Phase One. As a result of competition, large market size, strong market expertise, and openness to innovation in the society, firms in advanced countries, through research and development (R&D), create new products. In this phase, many firms eventually sell the product in foreign markets. In the twentieth century, U.S. firms were the leaders in this phase.

Phase Two. Demand in some of these foreign markets grows large enough to justify local production, and many firms make direct investment in manufacturing facilities in those markets. Eventually, locals in some of the overseas markets learn the manufacturing process and gain control of domestic production. The original manufacturers' sales thus begin to decline.

Phase Three. Some of the early foreign producers become experienced in marketing and manufacturing the product, and their costs lessen. As their markets become saturated, they look for customers in foreign markets. For example, in the 1960s Japan and West Germany (now Germany) began competing with U.S. firms in many industries, including the automobile industry. Japan, for instance, had only one industrial corporation in the top 50 of the world's largest industrial corporations in 1970; by 1980 it had six.[34] As of 1993, Japan had 128 companies on *Fortune*'s Global 500 list; the U.S. had 161; Great Britain, 40; Germany, 32; and France, 30. U.S. firms held 10 of the 15 major industries in 1960; the number was reduced to 9 in 1970, and to 3 in 1980.[35] At this point, according to the IPLC theory, foreign producers are competing in the original producer's foreign markets. The original producers' sales continue to decline. Of the top 50 corporations listed on the 1999 Fortune 500 list (http://www.fortune.com), 16 are U.S.-based, 16 Japanese-based, and 7 German-based. The German car manufacturer Daimler-Benz recently merged with U.S. car manufacturer Chrysler—the headquarters for the merger is in Germany. And as indicated in Practical Perspective 3-9, Honda, a Japanese car manufacturer, now builds cars in the U.S., sells them locally, and exports them to Europe and Japan as well.

Phase Four. Production to meet the wants of both domestic and foreign consumers may be large enough to allow the foreign manufacturers to reach economies of scale similar to those of the original producers. Since foreign producers began later, they possess newer plants, which may result in a cost advantage. At this point, the original manufacturers' exports dwindle, and sales in their domestic market by the foreign producers accelerate. Such competition may become so severe that the original manufacturers close production completely. For example, in the late 1960s, there were as many as 18 American television set manufacturers; today most brands (for example, RCA, GE, Magnavox) are made by Japanese and European companies.[36] German steel and Japanese radios and automobiles compete with U.S. industries in the domestic market. A great many of the automobiles sold in the U.S. market are imported from Japan. By 1979, the Japanese, unchallenged, were flooding the American market with videocassette recorders.[37] (For a case illustration of the automobile industry, read Practical Perspective 3-9.)

The U.S. television, steel, and automobile industries are cases that help substantiate the IPLC theory. These industries seem to be in phase four, and to remain "alive," they have tried to push the U.S. government to take protective measures;[38] that is, through tariffs and quotas (discussed in the next section), the government keeps out or limits foreign competition. It should be noted that it is not a necessary condition that the original producers go out of business. They often, as indicated above, make direct investment in foreign markets to enjoy the same advantages foreign producers enjoy. The large increases in U.S. direct foreign investment and the huge U.S. trade deficits in recent years indicate that many U.S. firms are doing this. Many U.S. firms are producing goods in foreign markets and shipping them back to the U.S. domestic market.

Trade Barriers

In an effort to limit or restrict competition, nations often take protective measures by imposing **trade barriers**. (As an illustration, read Practical Perspective 3-10.) Some of the reasons for protectionist activities include:

➤ protection of an infant industry.

➤ protection of the home market.

➤ the need to keep money at home.

➤ the encouragement of capital accumulation.

➤ maintenance of the standard of living and real wages.

➤ conservation of natural resources.

➤ industrialization of a low-wage nation.

➤ maintenance of employment and reduction of unemployment.

➤ national defense.

➤ increase of business size.

➤ retaliation and bargaining.[39]

Tariffs and Quotas

Tariffs and quotas are often employed by governments to restrict trade. **Tariffs** are a form of tax imposed on incoming products. **Quotas** specify the number of foreign units allowed to enter the country. The tax added to the incoming products will increase prices on imported goods, thus reducing competition for domestic manufacturers. Quotas also tend to reduce competition and increase the price domestic manufacturers charge their home-country customers. For example, for a period of three years in the early

PRACTICAL PERSPECTIVE 3-10

WTO's Kodak Ruling Heightens Trade Tensions

The World Trade Organization's resounding rejection of U.S. claims of Japanese protectionism in photographic film promises to heighten trade tensions and increase competitive pressures on Eastman Kodak Company.

The WTO's verdict brought calls by Kodak for consideration of new tariffs or other unilateral sanctions against Japan. Set against the backdrop of a widening trade deficit with Japan and a strong dollar that is fettering U.S. exports and making imports from Japan cheaper, it also stands to set back efforts by the Clinton administration to convince congressional skeptics and voters that the international trade system is fair and open.

The WTO ruling "raises serious questions about the credibility of this international body and of the U.S. trade representatives' capacity to secure and defend free-trade agreements," said Sen. John Ashcroft, a Missouri Republican, in a statement.

While the U.S. does have the right to challenge the decision, it could be awkward. The U.S. doesn't want to be seen as undercutting an organization it worked hard to create. Also, it doesn't want to turn up the heat too high on Japan while Tokyo is trying to deal with its economic problems. But the U.S. believes Japan can only deal with economic stagnation if it opens up its economy—exactly what it was calling for in its complaint.

Setback for Kodak CEO

The decision was also a setback for Kodak Chief Executive George Fisher, who has billed the case as critical not just for Kodak but for all U.S. industries seeking to break down alleged "internal barriers" to trade in Japan—

such as the locked-up film-distribution system that Kodak portrayed in the WTO case.

Fisher called the decision "totally unacceptable" and called for the administration to develop a "concrete plan to open the Japanese market."

Photography analysts say that Japan's Fuji Photo Film Company, relieved of some of the political pressure by the WTO's verdict, will feel even freer to attack Kodak in the U.S., where the two have been waging a price war that has gained Fuji substantial market share. Kodak has a stagnant 10 percent share of Japan's film business; Fuji has about 15 to 16 percent of the dollars spent in the U.S. market, up from 11 percent a year ago.

Thomas A. Shay, a spokesman for Fuji's American subsidiary, praised the ruling as "a complete win before a worldwide, neutral umpire."

Some Viewed Kodak's Case as Weak

Kodak had called the film case one of the best-documented ever at the Geneva-based WTO, a multilateral body created in 1995 to be chief arbiter of trade disputes. But many trade experts, including some U.S. officials, had viewed the case as weak, partly because it relied on old evidence and attacked vertical distribution alliances common in many countries.

A three-member WTO panel agreed with them. The U.S., Kodak, and Fuji—which have viewed the otherwise unreleased decision—said the panel rejected all 21 claims of Japanese government measures that allegedly violated multilateral trade agreements. Partly because of

(continued)

these measures, Kodak says none of the four main film distributors who control Japanese retail channels will buy large amounts of Kodak film.

The 21 claims were made in support of three main Kodak legal claims, the central one of which was that Japanese regulations and business practices had deprived Kodak of fair access to the market and therefore negated trade benefits granted to the U.S. in reduced tariffs over many years. But the WTO panel ruled that the Japanese regulations predated any lowered tariffs and therefore couldn't have negated them.

Call for Tariffs on Fuji Film

The decision is a preliminary one, but a reversal is seen as highly unlikely before he final decision in January.

In the wake of the decision, Kodak's chief trade official, Christopher Padilla, suggested the U.S. might consider imposing tariffs on Fuji's imported film, as well as on the chemicals that Fuji must import from Japan to a new manufacturing facility it has built in South Carolina.

The company might also ask the Commerce Department to impose antidumping penalties on Fuji, which he said unfairly sells film in Japan for about 170 percent of the cost of the same film it sells in the U.S. The Clinton administration said it is considering "the broad range of options."

The somewhat technical nature of the film ruling allowed the WTO to sidestep the thorny issue of internal barriers and avoid what might have become an endless stream of disputes had it ruled in Kodak's favor. Prior to film, the U.S. had won outright victories or concessions in all 14 of the other cases it brought to the WTO.

Source: Excerpted from K.S. Greenberger, L. Johannes, and R. Kerber, "WTO's Kodak Ruling Heightens Trade Tensions," *The Wall Street Journal,* December 8, 1997, pp. A3, A14. Permission conveyed through Copyright Clearance Center, Inc.

1980s, Japanese car manufacturers could export only an established number of cars to the U.S. per year. The quota was established by the Japanese government—which was encouraged by the U.S. government. This measure was taken so that U.S. car manufacturers could earn higher profits, which they would use to invest in retooling strategies. General Motors, for instance, diversified into other manufacturing fields, such as robotics and artificial intelligence.

Tariffs tend to

➤ increase   inflationary pressures, special interests' privileges, govern ment control and political considerations in economic matters, and the number of tariffs (because tariffs beget other tariffs). (As an illustration, refer again to Practical Perspective 3-1.)

➤ weaken   balance of payment positions, supply and demand patterns, and international understanding—they can start trade wars.

➤ restrict   manufacturers' supply sources, choices available to consumers, and competition.[40]

GATT/WTO

The imposition of tariffs has in the past been governed (although not very effectively) by **GATT**—the 124-nation General Agreement on Tariffs and Trade. GATT provided the conditions under which a nation could impose tariffs—for example, a nation could impose a tariff to protect its infant industry. GATT also prohibited a nation from imposing tariffs on selected countries; that is, if the tariff was legally imposed, it had to be applicable to all nations.

There is a current movement among nations to make GATT a more forceful regulatory organization. To accomplish this, a new organization, the World Trade Organization (**WTO**) has been established to replace the old GATT organization. The three main goals of the WTO are to aid in the free flow of trade, to help negotiate further opening of the markets, and to settle trade disputes between its members. In 1999, the WTO recognized 133 member nations and 35 observer members, of which 31 have applied for membership. In recent years, there has been wide media coverage of China's efforts to become a member. The new organization intends to slash tariffs by an average of 38 percent worldwide; and for some products, such as beer, tariffs are eliminated altogether. The WTO, based in Geneva, also settles trade disputes. (Refer again to Practical Perspectives 3-1 and 3-10.)

Monetary Barriers

Monetary barriers are another form of protection imposed by governments. Using this approach, the government creates a trade barrier by imposing exchange restrictions. Three methods used are blocked currency, differential exchange rate, and governmental approval requirements. *Blocked currency* is a method used for cutting off all importing above a certain level. In using this approach, a government refuses to redeem national currencies in the world financial marketplace for specified imports or above specified amounts on certain imports. With *differential exchange rates*, a government encourages the importation of certain goods and discourages the importation of others. The government accomplishes this by requiring the importer to pay a higher amount of domestic currency for the foreign currency needed to pay for the imported product being discouraged and a lower amount for the foreign currency needed to pay for the imported product being encouraged. Using *governmental approval requirements* for securing foreign exchange, a government can create a barrier by not approving the acquisition of foreign exchange needed by importers for the purchase of specific foreign products.

Nontariff Protection

Nontariff barriers are used by many governments. Using this approach, a government can discourage imports by creating administrative barriers, such as by making importing a complex, frustrating, and expensive process. Japan offers a prime example. Because of administrative barriers, many foreign firms refuse to export to Japan. There are also cultural barriers. For example, Americans with an individualistic cultural perspective (discussed in Chapter 1) often do not transact business well in Japan's collectivistic culture. In other words, Americans' "spirit of competitiveness" culture does not integrate well into the Japanese "spirit of cooperation" culture, and many Americans would thus have difficulty when attempting to penetrate Japan's market.

Consequences of Trade Barriers

The added costs that result from trade barriers have an impact on a product's price as well as on the channels of distribution. The higher the tariffs, the higher the costs, and therefore the higher the prices. To avoid tariffs, instead of exporting, a firm may decide to manufacture or at least assemble the product in the foreign market. Many countries have a much higher tariff rate on products brought in assembled than on products brought in unassembled because assembling the products locally helps create jobs, which in turn helps the nation's economy. On the other hand, the exporting country will encounter a loss of jobs. Furthermore, tariffs keep out competition. Lack of competition leads to higher prices being charged to consumers. For example, in 1989, Japan's virtual ban on rice imports was costing Japanese consumers an estimated $28 billion a year. The U.S. Rice Millers' Association claimed that "if even 10 percent of the Japanese market were opened to imports, the resulting lower prices would have saved the Japanese $6 billion annually."[41]

Fluctuating Exchange Rates

Countries' currency exchange rates, just like the selling value of a company's stock, can fluctuate. For example, one U.S. dollar can equal 100 Japanese yen today, and change to 95 yen or to 105 yen next month. Fluctuations can be "dirty" or "clean." *Dirty fluctuations* are the result of a government, for economic and/or other reasons, adjusting the exchange rate up or down. *Clean fluctuations* are the result of supply and demand, just like a company's stock. If there is an abundance of a nation's currency for sale in international financial markets, its sale value is likely to decline, and if it is scarce and there is a demand for it, it is likely to appreciate.

The fluctuation can have an enormous impact on international business transactions. And the impact can be positive or negative depending on the direction of the fluctuation. International business managers must thus be skilled, or employ skilled people, in this area. The case of Laker Airways serves as a good example of what can happen to an international enterprise when exchange rates fluctuate and its managers had not taken that possibility into account.

Laker Airways, a British firm, was gravely affected by fluctuating exchange and interest rates and by fixed prices.[42] In 1980, Fred Laker borrowed $240 million from banks in the U.S. to finance its growing fleet of airplanes. At the time it seemed like a wise transaction because British interest rates were far above the U.S. levels. Laker sold advance tickets to British travelers with fares fixed in British pounds. Subsequently, U.S. interest rates rose and the value of the U.S. dollar also began rising rapidly. The fares had been fixed late in 1980 when one British pound equaled U.S. $2.40. Laker's U.S. bank loans had to be repaid in dollars in August 1981 when one British pound equalled U.S. $1.93.

When Laker borrowed the $240 million, it was the equivalent of 100 million British pounds (240 million divided by $2.40). When the loans were to be paid, however, Laker had to pay back approximately 124 million British pounds ($240 million divided by $1.93). In other words, to purchase the 240 million U.S. dollars it owed the U.S. banks, Laker Airways now had to spend 124 million British pounds, which is far more than the 100 million it would have spent had the exchange rate remained stable. Since Laker had sold tickets at a fixed rate, it could not adjust its prices to compensate for the change in the exchange rates. As a result of this and the refusal of the banks to postpone payment or grant more loans, Laker went bankrupt in early 1982. Another illustration is the case of Coca-Cola. In 1998, Coca-Cola reported a 13.2 percent drop in its first-quarter earnings, sending its stock down. The company attributed the decline to devalued currencies in many countries where it did business.[43]

Of course, if the fluctuation had gone the other way, the firms would have realized unexpected profits. Although there are businesses that realize profits solely by buying and selling foreign currencies, like Laker Airways, most companies are in the business of realizing profits from sales of goods and/or services—not from buying and selling foreign currencies. As a result, such businesses often attempt to protect against negative fluctuations by contracting for a fixed exchange rate; by contracting for payment with a nation's currency that has a history of being relatively stable, for example, the U.S. dollar; or by contracting for a choice of payment by one of several nations' currencies, for instance, German marks, British pounds, French francs (whichever is the most advantageous at the time of payment is selected).

Labor Relations

Labor relations, also referred to as *industrial relations*, has been defined as the "totality of the interactions between an organization's management and organized labor."[44] The term **international labor relations** can be misleading when applied within the context of the MNC. *Webster's New Collegiate Dictionary* defines "international" as: "1. of, relating to, or constituting a group or association having members in two or more nations. 2. affecting or involving two or more nations. 3. of or relating to one whose activities extend across national boundaries." Even though some labor unions contain the word "international" in their title, they are not really international. This is because their domain does not really cut across multiple nations. International labor relations in the context of the MNC thus means management interacting with organized labor units in each country. It should be noted, however, that in the early 1980s some U.S. unions began seeking transnational bargaining and standardization of labor conditions among MNC operations.[45]

Furthermore, it is difficult to compare labor (or industrial) relations systems and behavior across nations. For example, *collective bargaining* in the U.S. means negotiations between the firm's management and the labor union local, but in Germany and Sweden it means negotiations between an employer's organization and a trade union at the industry level. Also, the objective of collective bargaining is viewed differently across nations. For example, in the U.S. it is viewed mostly in economic terms, but in Europe it is viewed as a form of "class struggle." And workers' actions also differ across countries. For instance, dissatisfied workers in U.S. unionized firms may disrupt output as a way of protesting, but in Japan, dissatisfied workers may protest during their work breaks, thus not disrupting output.

Differences in Labor Relations Across Nations

Labor relations across nations have their roots in two fundamental ideological themes: the pluralist/systems approach and the class approach.[46] *The pluralist/systems approach*, which is the prevalent ideology in, for example, the United States and the United Kingdom, tends to focus on procedural and institutional methods in labor-relations problem solving. *The class (Marxist) approach* places greater emphasis on politics, political action, and tensions between employers and employees than it does on procedures and practices related to labor relations. This type of system is dominant in Italy. Japan melds the two approaches. Different societies have thus developed their labor-relations systems differently. It should be noted that governments also play an increasingly significant role in collective bargaining. In "varying ways, countries have developed income policies, or wage and price guidelines, for the purpose of controlling the outcomes of the collective bargaining process."[47]

Labor Unions' Impact on MNCs' Strategies

Labor unions affect MNCs' strategies in three ways: by influencing wage levels; by limiting MNCs' employment level variation; and by hindering global integration.[48]

Influencing Wage Levels. Unions can influence wages to a cost level that puts MNCs at a disadvantage. This makes them less competitive.

Limiting Employment Level Variation. Redundancy legislation in many nations often specifies that enterprises must compensate involuntarily terminated employees on the basis of a specified formula, such as one week's pay for each year of service, and in some countries it may even be more. For example, if an employer in Mexico decides to terminate an employee who has been with the company for six months, the employee could create a back pay issue of as much as an additional six weeks, plus prorated vacation and bonuses.[49] Labor unions influence this process by lobbying for such legislation.

Hindering Global Integration. As Chapter 5 will discuss, many MNCs rationalize production and pricing across a number of nations to optimize their investments. Powerful unions, however, can force MNCs not to undertake such activities or force them to make suboptimal investments in their nation.

SOURCES OF INFORMATION

The above discussion of the global environment suggests that effective international business managers require an abundance of information. How is the information obtained? Information can be obtained through primary research and/or secondary research. **Primary research** is carried out to obtain first hand information about the environment. Generally only larger, wealthier corporations can afford to gather primary information, and only a few can afford to establish information sources around the globe. General Electric Corporation, for example, a huge multinational corporation, has established its own global scanning system. Less wealthy enterprises usually depend on information obtained through secondary research, which is less costly. Basically, secondary research means obtaining information that was gathered through primary research by other organizations. There are many sources of secondary data. Some of these include

➤ *corporations.* Some large multinational enterprises, such as General Electric, and banks, such as Citicorp, gather primary information. These corporations make much of the information available to other organizations.

➤ *governments.* Many governments have established agencies to gather and compile information to aid managers in making international business decisions. For instance, the United States Department of Commerce has established agencies that gather information relative to worldwide economic, social, political, and technological developments. This information is available at nominal cost.

➤ *the United Nations.* The U.N. also gathers and disseminates an abundance of information about global economic, political, social, and technological developments.

➤ *international organizations.* Organizations such as the Organization for Economic Cooperation and Development, the European Union, the Pan American Union, the World Bank, and the International Monetary Fund gather and compile information that is useful in international business decisions.

➤ *chambers of commerce and trade organizations.* National and international chambers of commerce and foreign trade associations also gather and disseminate useful information.

➤ *research universities.* Many professors at universities conduct empirical research relevant to global economic, social, political, and technological developments. Their findings are made available in published practical (and academic) journals, books, and professional conference papers.

➤ *business periodicals.* There is an abundance of business periodicals. In the U.S., to mention just a few, there are *The Wall Street Journal, Business Week, Fortune, Business International,* and *Business America.*

The Internet as a Source of Information

The Internet is generating rapid changes in homes, businesses, and organizations of all kinds. Using the Internet on a laptop computer, it is possible, while sipping coffee in bed, to order products from anywhere in the world. Technologies of this nature have within the past decade generated rising expectations in consumers and business for value, choice, and innovation. These expectations have encouraged governments, regulatory agencies, and industry-leading companies to provide more diversity, openness, and competition in the marketplace.[50] (Practical Perspective 3-11 presents the views of C. Michael Armstrong, AT&T's chairman and CEO, on the new technology.)

Such changes are likely to force governments and international organizations to change their policies toward international trade, investment, intellectual property, and financial transactions. They will have to find ways to deal with the new issues of privacy, consumer protection, taxation, and the like. For example, a company publishing a magazine in Country A exports it to Country B and pays a tax for crossing the border. What if the publisher decides to transmit the magazine via electronic means to Country B for production and sale there? Is the tax avoided?

Therefore, to be effective, international managers must continuously scan their environment for changes taking place around the globe. The Internet, a global web of more than 25,000 computer networks,[51] provides a quick and inexpensive means of global communication and access to information about the external environment. The search tools found on the Internet include:[52]

➤ Yahoo (http://www.yahoo.com)

➤ Magellan (http://www.magellan.mckinley.com)

➤ Galaxy (http://www.galaxy.einet.net)

➤ Alta Vista (http://www.altavista.digital.com)

PRACTICAL PERSPECTIVE 3-11

It's All Coming Together

Now technology and competition will redefine communications between countries. They will slip the constraints of national borders to make the very concept of "place" irrelevant.

That, in essence, is what multinational businesses have long wanted: seamless communications services that operate the same way in New York, New Delhi, and New Zealand. Multimedia capabilities that make it possible to hold virtual meetings wherever an executive finds herself. Toll-free calling that crosses borders....

Use of global communications by the world's largest companies is growing by 19 percent a year. Use by small and medium-sized companies is growing even faster—about 25 percent. And consumer demand for international voice and data services is increasing by 20 percent a year. In fact, traffic between countries is increasing almost twice as fast as traffic within the countries themselves. Overall, what is now a $40 billion market will grow to $200 billion in a few years.

Communications companies are racing to make the Internet a reliable business tool. They are using wireless technology to extend advanced services to less-developed nations.

They are increasing networking intelligence to give their customers greater control over communications, making them reachable whenever and wherever they want, on their own terms.

Sometime in 1999, data [was expected to] overtake voice traffic on the majority of the world's communication networks. In fact, global communications traffic is rapidly becoming global data transfer. Technology's ability to digitalize and transmit every form of information, combined with the ubiquity of the Internet, is redefining what the industry delivers to customers.

A number of giant mergers within the industry, with a market capital of some $194 billion, are up for regulatory approval in 1999. These reflect the fact that technology could remove the boundaries between markets: wired and wireless services, local and long distance, cable television and telephone, information and entertainment. Technology could bring these services together and so the market is bringing together companies that want to make customers an expanded offer.

Source: Excerpted from C. Michael Armstrong, Chairman and CEO, AT&T, "It's All Coming Together," *The World in 1999* (*The Economist* Publications): 90. Reprinted with permission.

➤ Excite (http://www.excite.com)

➤ Infoseek (http://www.infoseek.com)

➤ Open Text (http://www.opentext.com)

Most organizations around the globe now offer information about their activities on the Web. For example:

➤ Nike (http://www.nike.com)

➤ Reebok (http://www.reebok.com)

➤ Adidas (http://www.adidas.com)

➤ Toyota (http://www.toyota.co.jp)

➤ Sony (http://www.sony.com)

➤ Hoechst AG (http://www.hoechst.com)

Caveat

Before they use information, managers first must analyze carefully its sources and its age. They must obtain answers to the following questions:

➤ Who collected the information? Would there be any reason for deliberately misrepresenting the facts? (National pride and politics sometimes persuade the gatherers of information to inflate or deflate the data. For example, around election time politicians like to create optimism or establish a positive image of their past performance; they sometimes do this by manipulating economic data.)

➤ For what purpose were the data collected?

➤ How were they collected (methodology)?

➤ Are the data internally consistent and logical in light of known data sources or market factors?[53]

The age of data must also be considered. Information about nations now changes very rapidly. For example, not too long ago, the idea of a McDonald's in Paris, France, was absurd. They are popular there now. Also, many countries are rapidly growing economically. The national totals of income and income distribution are therefore quickly invalidated. And, while primary and secondary data are of vital importance to international managers for decision-making purposes, it is also very important that they make on-site visits to intuitively assess the situation before they make final decisions.

SUMMARY

The major thrust of this chapter was that managers of effective international businesses must be aware of the changes taking place in their home country and throughout the globe. At home, they remain informed about changes that can affect their organization, including legal, political, economic, and competitive changes. They also remain informed about changes taking place in international organizations, such as the European Union, and in individual foreign nations. When the changes present opportunities and/or threats, managers develop strategies to seize the opportunities and/ or combat the threats. These managers also recognize that different countries present different cultural, economic, legal, political, and competitive environments, as well as trade barriers, monetary exchanges, and labor relations. When they develop international strategies, these managers consider the differing factors and make the necessary adaptations. Therefore, effective international business managers do their "homework"; they gather the information needed to make effective decisions.

Key Terms and Concepts

1. Domestic environment
2. International environment
3. Foreign environment
4. Cultural environment
5. Economic, legal, and political environments
6. The five stages of economic development
7. A less-developed country
8. Labor laws; foreign investment; contract enforcement
9. Political systems; government policies
10. Government's attitudes toward products/services
11. Hard and soft currencies
12. Expropriation, nationalization, and confiscation
13. Competitive environment
14. Cartels, *keiretsu*
15. Dumping
16. The international product life cycle (IPLC)
17. Trade barriers; tariffs and quotas
18. GATT/WTO
19. Monetary barriers
20. Nontarriff barriers
21. Currency exchange rates
22. International labor relations
23. Primary and secondary research
24. The Internet as a source of information

Discussion Questions and Exercises

1. Discuss how the domestic environment affects international business strategies.

2. What is meant by the term *international environment*? How does the international environment affect international business strategies?

3. What is meant by the term *foreign environment*?

4. How does culture affect international business?

5. You are an international business consultant who has been employed by a domestic company involved in selling beef and pork products. The firm wants to expand its business activities into foreign markets. What would be the primary advice you would give your client?

6. How does a nation's economic environment affect international business?

7. The theory of the stages of economic development has been criticized. What are the criticisms? Notwithstanding the criticisms, how is the theory useful to international business managers?

8. How do labor laws, foreign investment laws, and contract enforcement laws affect international business management?

9. Political systems differ from country to country. Should a nation's political system be a factor in an international corporation's decision on whether or not to do business there? Why or why not?

10. How can an international firm reduce its political vulnerability?

11. You are an international business consultant employed by a domestic firm seeking to conduct business in a less-developed country. The chapter discusses hard

and soft currencies. In this context, what advice would you give your client?

12. How do cartels, bribery practices, the state of a nation's economic conditions, government-owned enterprises, and long-range versus short-range managerial orientations affect competition?

13. Discuss the international product life cycle (IPLC) theory. How is it useful to international business managers?

14. Discuss the reasons for a nation's protectionist activities (tariffs and quotas).

15. What is nontariff protection?

16. What are the negative aspects of tariffs?

17. What is the role of GATT in international business?

18. What are monetary barriers?

19. How do fluctuating monetary exchange rates affect international business?

20. What are "clean" and "dirty" exchange fluctuations?

21. Discuss how labor relations differ across nations.

22. How do labor relations affect international business strategies?

23. You are an international consultant employed by a firm seeking to establish a subsidiary in China. What would you tell your client to expect?

24. Discuss the major sources of information available to international managers.

25. What are the major concerns about information?

Assignment

Interview a student or an acquaintance who is from another country. Ask him or her to describe the ways some of the factors discussed in this chapter differ between his or her country and your country.

CASE 3-1

Protecting the Pepsi Taste

When PepsiCo, Inc. was obliged to begin producing concentrate within China for its Chinese bottling plants, the company decided a wholly owned venture would be the only viable option. Only a WFOE [wholly foreign-owned enterprise] could adequately protect patented soft-drink formulas—but Chinese central government officials drove a hard bargain before approving the project.

While PepsiCo chose the WFOE option to protect formulas, there was another compelling reason for opening a new plant—pressure from the Chinese government to reduce imports of soft-drink concentrates. The company currently imports concentrates and sells them in hard currency to four joint-venture bottling plants—producing Pepsi Cola, 7 Up, and Mirinda Orange—in which it has equity stakes of up to 15–20 percent. PepsiCo balances foreign exchange through various countertrade and production ventures, such as its joint venture with McCormick & Co. Inc. in Shanghai, which processes spices sourced in China and sells them to the United States. Even though PepsiCo was not a net user of foreign exchange, China expressed dissatisfaction with the use of scarce hard currency to buy soft-drink concentrate. China views soda as a luxury item and refuses to let PepsiCo open any new bottling facilities before localizing concentrate production. Thus, PepsiCo agreed it would produce concentrate within China, selling in renminbi (RMB) to domestic factories and exporting part of the production—expected to average 20–50 percent—to bottling plants in Asia to balance foreign exchange. "This puts the monkey on our back to balance our foreign-exchange requirements," says Peter M.R. Kendall, regional vice president for PepsiCo/North Asia. PepsiCo hopes eventually to source most of the citrus extracts, essential oils, caramel, and other ingredients within China, but finding suppliers that meet international standards is expected to be a problem. Negotiations for the 20-year, $10 million venture began in 1988, and construction was to be completed in June 1990.

"What's in It for China?"

PepsiCo chose the WFOE site in the Huangpu Economic and Technological Development Zone (ETDZ), about 20 miles from the center of Guangzhou. Near Hong Kong, the site offers proximity to shipping lines and convenience for expatriate staff. Perhaps more important, PepsiCo had developed good working relationships with local Guangzhou and Guangdong authorities through its bottling plants in Guangzhou and Shenzhen, and that local support proved important in selling the project in Beijing. As "very visible signs of foreign presence," soft drink production ventures must receive central approval regardless of the size of investment, says Kendall. Huangpu ETDZ authorities acted, in effect, as consultants to PepsiCo in shepherding the project through the approval process involving the central Ministry of Light Industry (MLI), the Ministry of Foreign Economic Relations and Trade (MOFERT), and the State Planning Commission.

MLI proved to be the toughest sell. "The ministry was saying, 'What's in it for China?'" Kendall says. "They put pressure on PepsiCo to give a better deal," in part by initially refusing permission for a WFOE that would sell its products domestically on grounds that WFOEs must produce exclusively for export.

In order to win WFOE approval and demonstrate their long-term commitment to China, PepsiCo agreed to build a neighboring joint-venture plant in partnership with the Chinese soda giant Asia Soft Drinks, which will produce concentrate for new, local soft-drink brands and a product-development lab and training facility to help China develop high-quality soft drinks. The two facilities, which will together employ around 40 people (the same number as planned to staff the WFOE), will also provide training in water treatment, packaging, and the development of new flavors.

Government authorities stipulated that the joint-venture plant use the most modern equipment and made specific demands about staffing, management, expatriate compensation, and training. At the WFOE, however, PepsiCo will have a free hand in staffing and compensation. In the later stages of negotiation, government authorities concerned themselves only with holding PepsiCo to a capital-commitment schedule and negotiating foreign-exchange arrangements. Authorities have promised PepsiCo the WFOE plant will receive "high-technology enterprise" status, providing lower land-use fees and possibly some reduction in taxes. Under Chinese law, PepsiCo would not receive notification of its legal status until the plant's opening in fall 1990.

Soda Market Going Flat

Construction was already underway at the WFOE plant in June 1989, when political upheaval devastated China's tourist trade. Not only were tourists avoiding China, but the domestic austerity campaign had reduced spending power and helped discourage official banquets, which formerly provided much business to companies selling international-name beverages. In addition, tightening restrictions on the import and production of aluminum cans had severe impact on PepsiCo's domestic can business, which accounted for 20 percent of total volume. With plastic-bottle (PET) sales also reduced by austerity, the plants saw a rising volume of returnable-bottle sales, necessitating a bigger truck fleet and glass investment by PepsiCo and associated bottlers. And while before austerity PepsiCo's joint venture plants made some of their sales in foreign-exchange certificates (FEC), sales became almost exclusively in RMB.

Since its initial feasibility study for the WFOE, PepsiCo has lowered sales projections by about 20 percent and is keeping a cautious eye on China's political situation. However, in China's enormous market, PepsiCo believes that even severe constrictions in the short term leave ample room for sales. One sign of encouragement may be the strong support PepsiCo has continued to receive from local Guangzhou officials, despite attempts by Beijing to curtail Guangdong's authority over foreign investment. PepsiCo is confident

China will continue to support its sales, Kendall says. "A bottle of Pepsi produced in the PRC is almost entirely a Chinese product. It contributes to the country's economic development."

Questions

1. Based on what you have learned in this chapter, do you believe PepsiCo's managers effectively analyzed China's environment? Why?

2. Based on what you have learned in the chapter, discuss the problems China's systems present for foreign companies planning to invest in China.

3. What did PepsiCo do to establish a more positive relationship with the Chinese government?

4. What draws foreign investors to China?

Source: Excerpted from Anne Stevenson-Yany, "Protecting the Pepsi Taste," *The China Business Review* (January–February 1990): 32–33. Reprinted with the permission of The U.S.–China Business Council, Washington, D.C.

Notes

1. Cited by Stephen Kindel, "Staying Competitive in a Shrinking World," *FinancialWorld 160*, no. 21 (October 15, 1991): 22.

2. E.J. Miller and A.K. Rice, *Systems of Organization* (London: Tavistock, 1967).

3. Rahul Jacob, "Export Barriers the U.S. Hates Most," *Fortune* (February 27, 1989): 88.

4. R. Kuttner, "Facing Up to Industrial Policy," *The New York Times Magazine* (April 19, 1992): 22, 26, 27, 42.

5. *Europe in the 1990s* (State of New Jersey Department of Commerce and Economic Development, KPMG Peat Marwick, 1990).

6. R.E. Gut, "The Impact of the European Community's 1992 Project," *Vital Speeches of the Day* (November 1988): 34–37.

7. *Europe in the 1990s.*

8. R. Straetz, "U.S. Exporters Should Find the Benefits of Europe 1992: Program Will Outweigh Problems," *Business America* (May 1989): 10–11.

9. L.C. White, "Bold Strategies for a Brave New Market: Federal Express," *Business Month* (August 1989): 32–34.

10. T. Murray, "Bold Strategies for a Brave New Market: 3M," *Business Month* (August 1989): 35–37.

11. *Europe in the 1990s.*

12. "American Firms in Europe," *The Economist 311* (May 13, 1989): 70–71.

13. Ibid.

14. P.R. Cateora and J.M Hess, *International Marketing*, 4th ed. (Homewood, Il: Richard D. Irwin, 1979), p. 262.

15. P.H. Harris and R.T. Moran, *Managing Cultural Differences* (Houston, TX: Gulf Publishing Co., 1979).

16. "Japan on the Brink," *The Economist* (April 11, 1998): 16.

17. J.R. Zeeman, "Service—The Cutting Edge of Global Competition: What United Airlines Is Learning in the Pacific" (remarks before the annual meeting of the Academy of International Business, Chicago, November 14, 1987).

18. W.W. Rostow, *The Stages of Economic Development* (New York: Cambridge University Press, 1971).

19. This discussion draws on Cateora and Hess, *International Marketing*, pp. 263–266.

20. W.A. Stoever, "The Stages of Developing Country Policy Toward Foreign Investment," *The Columbia Journal of World Business 20*, no. 3 (Fall 1985): 6–8.

21. Cited by Kindel, "Staying Competitive," pp. 22–24.

22. "151 Checklists—Decision Making in International Operations," *Business International* (1974): 84.

23. Frank Rose, "Think Globally, Script Locally," *Fortune* (November 8, 1999): 160.

24. Alex Taylor III, "Danger: Rough Road Ahead," *Fortune* (March 17, 1997): 116.

25. Stoever, "The Stages of Developing Country Policy."

26. This case illustration draws from Hideo Sugiura, "How Honda Localizes Its Global Strategy," *Sloan Management Review 32*, no. 1 (Fall 1990): 77–82.

27. http://www.honda.com

28. Overseas Private Investment Corporation, *Investment Insurance Handbook*, p. 4, cited in M.C. Schnitzer, M.L. Liebrenz, and K.W. Kubin, *International Business* (Cincinnati, OH: South-Western Publishing Co., 1985), p. 253.

29. L.T. Wells and E.S. Gleason, "Is Infrastructure Investment Still Risky?," *Harvard Business Review* (September–October 1995): 54.

30. Edmund Faltermayer, "Does Japan Play Fair?" *Fortune* (September 7, 1992): 41.

31. Lionel H. Olmer, "Japan Trip Report: Japan's Drive for Technological Preeminence Challenges U.S.," *Business America* (January 24, 1983): 6–10.

32. Dan Takahashi, "U.S. in a Preliminary Ruling, Finds South Korea Companies Dumped Chips," *The Wall Street Journal*, April 16, 1998, p. A1.

33. R. Vernon and L.T. Wells, Jr., *Manager in the International Economy* (Englewood Cliffs, NJ: Prentice-Hall, 1976).

34. U.S. Congress, Office of Technology Assessment, *U.S. Industrial Competitiveness: A Comparison of Steel, Electronics, and Automobiles* (Washington, DC: U.S. Government Printing Office, 1981), pp. 11–17.

35. M.A. Hitt, R.E. Hoskisson, and J.S. Harrison, "Strategic Competitiveness in the 1990s: Challenges and Opportunities," *Academy of Management Executive 5*, no. 2 (May 1991): 8.

36. Ibid., p. 1.

37. C. Christopher, *The Japanese Mind* (New York: Linden Press, 1983).

38. See R.B. Reich, *The Next American Frontier* (New York: Times Books, 1983).

39. Cateora and Hess, *International Marketing*, p. 63.

40. Ibid., p. 64.

41. Rahul Jacob, "Export Barriers the U.S. Hates the Most," p. 88.

42. The information on Laker Airways is drawn from Frederick Gluck, "Global Competition in the 1980's," *Journal of Business Strategy* (Spring 1983): 223–27.

43. Constance L. Hays, "13.% Fall in Coca-Cola's Net Tied to Devalued Currencies," *The Wall Street Journal*, April 16, 1998, p. A1.

44. Jay Shafriz, *Directory of Personnel Management and Labor Relations* (Oak Park, IL: Moore Publishing Co., 1980), p. 188.

45. Roy B. Helfgott, "American Unions and Multinational Companies: A Case of Misplaced Emphasis," *Columbia Journal of World Business 18*, no. 2 (1983): 81–86.

46. The source of this discussion is Peter Doeringer, *Industrial Relations in International Perspective* (New York: Holmes and Meier Publishers, 1981).

47. Albert Blum, *International Handbook of Industrial Relations Contemporary Developments and Research* (Westport, CT: Greenwood Press, 1981), p.674.

48. This discussion draws from P.J. Dowling and R.S. Schuler, *International Dimensions of Human Resource Management* (Boston: PWS-Kent Publishing 1990), pp.145–147.

49. Jeff Stinson, "Maquiladoras Challenge Human Resources," *Personnel Journal* (November 1989): 92.

50. *Northern Telecom's Transformation 1985–1995*, pp. 7–8.

51. M.A. Hitt, R.D. Ireland, and R.E. Hoskisson, *Strategic Management* (Cincinnati: South-Western College Publishing, 1999), p. 57.

52. For an in-depth discussion on this topic matter refer to Cynthia B. Leshin, *Management on the World Wide Web* (Upper Saddle River, NJ: Prentice-Hall, Inc., 1997).

53. Cateora and Hess, *International Marketing*, p. 255.

4

International Strategy

To U.S. automakers, Asia looks like...a place to strike it rich. Weary of competing in the slow-growing, overcrowded markets of North America and Western Europe, they cheer at the thought of millions of potential customers who have yet to buy their first Cavalier, Explorer, or Jeep. General Motors, Ford, and Chrysler executives are streaming into cities like Shanghai, Manila, and Kuala Lumpur to negotiate with government officials, meet with potential dealers, and scout locations for parts depots and assembly plants. "There will be ten million units of worldwide automotive growth in the next ten years," says Ford's international boss, W. Wayne Booker, "and the vast majority of that growth will be in Asia."... U.S. automakers are planning a huge sales offensive and their first local production in half a century. Each company is pursuing a separate strategy. GM, the most ambitious, is setting up an integrated Asian production system that utilizes its vast parts-making operations as well as its affiliation with Japanese automakers Isuzu and Suzuki. Ford, meanwhile, is pursuing what it calls a "reasoned approach" that relies on alliances with local partners in select markets like Vietnam and India. Chrysler wants to manufacture in only a few countries; its primary focus is exporting vehicles built in North America.[1]

Learning Objectives of the Chapter

The changes taking place throughout the globe are creating many opportunities and threats for business enterprises. These opportunities and threats will lure many domestic enterprises into the international business arena; they will entice those firms that rely only slightly on revenues derived from international business into expanding and relying more on their international operations. This means that more and more corporations will have to develop strategies and establish objectives to internationalize their domestic business operations or to expand their current international business operations. After studying this chapter, you should be able to discuss:

1. The opportunities and threats that cause firms to internationalize their operations.
2. The strategic approaches used by international corporations.
3. The internal factors managers must understand before they attempt to internationalize their enterprises' business operations.
4. International strategic and tactical objectives.
5. The areas in which international objectives should be established.

WHY FIRMS INTERNATIONALIZE THEIR OPERATIONS

Historically, domestic enterprises have **internationalized their business operations** either to seize **opportunities** or to deal with **threats,** or both.[2] For example, as was pointed out in Chapter 3, the European Union's (EU) current efforts to become more unified are expected to present both opportunities and threats for non-EU business enterprises. Practical Perspective 4-1 lists some of the corporations that developed strategies to seize the opportunities and/or combat the threats anticipated by the EU unification. The advent of the Internet as a means of conducting international business also presents opportunities and threats. The ensuing sections discuss the opportunities and threats that cause domestic enterprises to internationalize their operations.

Opportunity Reasons

The opportunity reasons for internationalizing operations include greater profits, appearance of new markets, faster growth in new markets, obtaining new products for the domestic market, and globalization of financial markets.

Greater Profits

Many domestic firms have internationalized their operations because their managers saw the opportunity to earn greater profits by charging higher prices in a higher per capita income foreign country where a high demand

PRACTICAL PERSPECTIVE 4-1

Examples of Firms That Have Reacted to the EC's Unification Aims

The popular press reports many cases of external firms acting to take advantage of the opportunities and/or to combat the threats presented by the EC-92 [when the EC member nations were to become officially unified]. The Whirlpool Corporation has entered into a $2 billion joint venture in order to penetrate the European appliance market. The International Paper Company has made a $350 million bid for a French paper maker. Shearson Lehman Hutton Inc. has expanded its investment banking offices in Milan and Madrid. Coca-Cola has started construction of one of the world's largest canning plants in France and has revamped its organizational chart to put greater emphasis on the EC. Citicorp, already the most prominent non-European bank in Europe, has purchased banks in Belgium, Italy, and Spain.

AT&T has built a $220 million semiconductor plant in Spain. Connecticut Mutual has set up a Luxembourg-based company, CM Transnational, to sell life insurance. American International Group is restructuring its $500 million European property and casualty insurance operations. AIG is merging most of its operations into one new company, UNAT

Europe, replacing 13 different national companies. The U.S.-based Scott Paper Company started planning for EC-92 because it expected to benefit from simplified border restrictions and the deregulation of trucking, grocery distribution, and retailing. Federal Express has established regional counsels in Belgium and the United Kingdom in order to stay close to EC political developments at all times. To adapt to the anticipated fierce competition in the EC, 3M has formed European Management Action Teams consisting of representatives from management, R&D, sales and marketing, and finance. These teams aim to integrate individual units' business plans and blend them into a Europe-wide strategy in order to compete on a pan-European basis.

Source: Adapted from S. Greenhouse, "U.S. Corporations Expand in Europe for '92 Prospects," *The New York Times*, March 13, 1989, pp. 1, 6; R.W. King, S.J. Dryden, and J. Kapstein, "Who Is That Knocking on Foreign Doors? U.S. Insurance Salesmen," *Business Week* (March 6, 1989): 84–85; H. Lampert, "Bold Strategies for a Brave New Market: Scott Paper Company," *Business Month* (August 1989): 39–41; L.C. White, "Bold Strategies for a Brave New Market: Federal Express," *Business Month* (August 1989): 32–34; T. Murray, "Bold New Strategies for a Brave New Market: 3M," *Business Month* (August 1989): 35–37.

for the product or service existed or where there was less competition. Enterprises have also internationalized their operations because their managers determined that they could earn higher profits by attaining greater *economies of scale* with foreign expansion. Additionally, many enterprises have been able to earn greater profits by producing in a country where labor was cheaper and/or where materials cost less than at home.

Selling the Product at Higher Prices. Companies in many countries, especially in less-developed countries, can often sell their products at a higher price in the more advanced countries. For example, in China one can purchase a bottle of Tsingtao beer for about U.S. $0.30. The same bottle of beer sells for about U.S. $1.30 in the United States.

For illustration purposes, imagine the following scenario: A company's annual domestic market share is 110,000 units, its sales price per unit is $100, its variable costs per unit amount to $70, and its fixed costs total $3 million annually. This enterprise's before-tax earnings would be $300,000, computed as follows:

Number of units sold	110,000
Profit margin per unit ($100 – $70)	$30
Income before fixed costs and taxes	$3,300,000
Fixed costs	$3,000,000
Earnings before taxes	$300,000

Assume the firm determined that if it exported to a certain foreign market, it could increase the unit sales price there to $110; that the foreign market share would be 20,000 units; and that it would incur additional costs of $20 per unit to modify those units to fit the specific market's needs and to ship them overseas. In this situation the company would earn, before taxes, an additional $400,000, computed as follows:

Additional units sold	20,000
Before tax profit margin ($110 – $70 – $20)	$20
Additional earnings before taxes	$400,000

Greater Economies of Scale. To demonstrate the case in which the firm can obtain larger profits by attaining greater economies of scale, assume the company determined that due to market and/or other conditions (such as foreign government restrictions), it could not increase the price to $110 as illustrated above that it could sell the unit in the foreign market for only the same $100 domestic price. In this situation, due to the attainment of greater economies of scale, the company would still realize an additional $200,000 before tax earnings, computed as follows:

Additional units sold	20,000
Profit margin ($100 – $70 – $20)	$10
Additional earnings before taxes	$200,000

For example, Korea's five automobile manufacturers have plans to increase their worldwide vehicle-making capacity by 60 percent by 2002. Their aim is to develop additional capacity to gain the economies of scale required to become more competitive in the global marketplace.[3]

Cheaper Labor and/or Materials. The cost of labor and materials varies among countries. Many less-developed nations, to attract foreign investments, have developed a **capable workforce**. The cheaper costs and the capable workforce in a country will sometimes enable foreign firms to realize greater profits if they transfer their manufacturing operations there.

To illustrate the instance where **cheaper labor and/or cheaper materials** in foreign markets contribute to greater profits, suppose a corporation determined that if it established operations in a foreign country, it would incur an additional $800,000 in fixed costs, the variable costs for the units produced abroad would be reduced by 50 percent to $35 per unit, and the $20 per unit exporting costs would be reduced to $2. In this scenario, the firm would earn, before tax, an additional $460,000, computed as follows:

Additional units sold	20,000
Before tax profit margin ($100 – $35 – $2)	$63
Earnings before fixed costs/taxes	$1,260,000
Less additional fixed costs	$800,000
Additional earnings before taxes	$460,000

Clothing, electronics, watchmaking, and numerous other industries have transferred portions of their operations to foreign locations in pursuit of lower costs. For instance, to help enhance its competitiveness in the 1990s, General Electric continued shifting some of its appliance manufacturing operations to various parts of the world where labor was cheaper—its gas ranges are now made in Mexico.[4]

Appearance of New Markets

Population expansion, income growth, and technological advancements around the globe have created **new markets** and demands and thus new business opportunities. Many domestic firms have internationalized their operations to meet those new demands. For example, Motorola, Inc. reorganized its operations to tap into the huge market for chips used by Japanese companies to manufacture consumer goods.[5] Xircom, Inc., which manufactures pocket-size adapters for portable notebook computers, targeted the European Union (EU) in 1991 because of the increased popularity of portable computers there. They expect even greater success when the EU completes its market integration process.[6] Kobs & Draft, a U.S. direct marketer, has been expanding into foreign markets at a rapid pace because common U.S. technologies are now reaching the rest of the world, therefore creating a demand for its services.[7] Automobile executives around the globe are drooling at the vision of hundreds of millions of potential drivers in China. For example, W. Wayne Booker, Ford Motor Co.'s executive vice-president for international operations [and who became vice chairman in 1996] indicated that his first priority for the 1990s was China.[8]

In addition, new car sales in China have been rising rapidly since 1990, up from about 300,000 to a projected over 2 million by 2002.[9] Microsoft said that its new PC technology, known as the Venus project (the box) would be rolled out at the end of October 1999. The box, with TV-customized software, lets users read e-mail, surf the Internet, and do simple word processing while sitting in front of a television with a remote keyboard. Microsoft's plan is to sell the box in China, where more than 300 million households own a television, but only 2 million own PCs.[10] For a manufacturer such as Emerson Electric, China offers enormous potential. Rural villages in China need and can afford Emerson's small electric generators. Emerson also has opportunities in the rest of Asia, where newly affluent populations are demanding increasing numbers of air conditioners and refrigerators.[11]

Faster Growth in New Markets

Many domestic organizations have a strong growth orientation. These firms often enter foreign markets because they can grow at a faster rate there than they can in the established domestic market. For instance, Asian and European computer markets are stronger than the U.S. market partly because they lag behind the U.S. in computer installations. This enables U.S. computer companies to grow much faster in Asia and Europe than at home. As an example, in 1989, Intel Corporation's European sales were growing twice as fast as they were in the U.S. market.[12] Fusion Systems, now a division of Eaton Corporation of Maryland, which makes sophisticated industrial equipment, began penetrating foreign markets in 1975. At that time, Fusion had 15 employees and $450,000 in annual sales; in 1989, it had 320 employees and $33 million in sales—35 percent from overseas—from 1985 to 1990. It grew at the rate of 25 percent.[13] In 1996, Guess Inc., the U.S. jeans maker, targeted expansion into Europe for aggressive growth.[14] Frito-Lay plans to continue its rapid growth by seizing international business opportunities—for example, to improve its European market position, it purchased United Biscuits Holdings PLC (headquartered in the U.K.).[15]

Obtaining New Products for the Domestic Market

Many individuals from the home market travel abroad and develop a desire for a product that they would like to have available in their home market. For example, English ales, German beers, and French wines sell well in the U.S. market. Domestic enterprises therefore internationalize their operations to obtain products for domestic consumers. If they do not, their competitors will.

Globalization of Financial Markets

In recent decades, there has been an expansion in the ways by which international business can be financed. This growth in **financial options** has been the catalyst for the expansion of international business. These new tools include the International Monetary Fund, created in 1945 by the United Nations to encourage and aid world trade, and the World Bank, created by the United Nations for the purpose of encouraging the extension of loans to less-developed countries. Banks such as Citicorp, Dai-ichiKangyo Bank, and Bank Nationale de Paris have grown into international organizations that draw on a variety of investors from many parts of the world.[16]

Threat Reasons

The threat reasons for internationalizing operations include protection from **declining demand in the home market,** acquisition of raw materials, acquisition of managerial know-how and capital, protection of the home market, and protection from imports.

Protection from Declining Demand in Home Market

Demand for a firm's product or service may be low in the home market due to recessionary conditions, a saturated market, or a declining product life cycle. Many firms have been able to hedge against recessions at home and maintain their growth by expanding into foreign markets. For example, in the late 1980s, many U.S. technology corporations found themselves headed for a slump in domestic sales. To offset the slump, many of these companies entered the European and Asian markets. For instance, the market for chips in the U.S. went flat in the 1980s, but U.S. firms such as International CMOS Technology Inc. and Microsoft Corporation have done well as a result of booming sales in Europe and Asia. Microsoft's senior vice president for international operations, Jeremy Butler [now retired], has said that a firm with overseas sales has a much better chance of surviving because it does not put all its eggs in one basket.[17]

By 1989, several U.S. semiconductor-equipment makers, such as PerkinElmer Corporation, were dropping out of the business. Applied Materials, Inc., however, was doing 40 percent of its sales in Japan. Applied Materials is doing well now, in part because it got its foot in the door early; it established its own subsidiaries in Japan in the 1970s. It has gained experience in dealing with Japanese customers, therefore eliminating dependency on Japanese representatives, third parties that increase costs.[18]

Because the American market is saturated, dozens of U.S. insurance companies, including Prudential, Equitable Life, and Connecticut Mutual Life, have been aggressively penetrating new global markets.[19] Philip Morris Company realized that the domestic cigarette market would shrink because of Americans' evolving health consciousness. It thus expanded into foreign markets.[20] Even though Anheuser-Busch, the beer brewing company, controled 43 percent of the U.S. beer market, its domestic sales growth was slowing dramatically. Analyst Emanuel Goldman of PaineWebber Inc. had estimated that Busch's profits would grow less than 1 percent in 1993 to $1 billion, as sales had risen by a mere 2 percent, to $11.6 billion. "That forced the brewer to tap into thirstier regions abroad."[21] (Anheuser-Busch's recent globalization strategies are discussed in subsequent chapters.) And more recently, recognizing that the U.S. market is close to a saturation point, Merrill Lynch, a U.S. financial services provider, looked outside its own borders to capture more customers. According to its CEO, David Komansky, it intends to make non-U.S. revenues account for 50 percent of its business within five years.[22]

Furthermore, emerging markets, such as Argentina, Brazil, India, Mexico, Poland, South Africa, South Korea, Turkey, the ANSEAN region (Indonesia, Malaysia, Singapore, Thailand, and Vietnam), and the Chinese Economic Area (China, Hong Kong, and Taiwan), have opened their markets to foreign investment and trade, thus providing many commercial opportunities for foreign businesses.[23]

To illustrate this aspect mathematically, assume the same conditions used to demonstrate the attainment of greater profits. Suppose that the company's market share declined from 110,000 units annually to 104,000. If this happened, the enterprise's before-tax earnings would decline from $300,000 to $120,000, computed as follows:

Number of units sold	104,000
Profit margin	$30
Income before fixed costs and taxes	$3,120,000
Fixed costs	$3,000,000
Earnings before taxes	$120,000

If the corporation internationalized its operations, as illustrated in the greater profits discussion above, it could maintain its profit margin or even increase it.

Acquisition of Raw Materials

Many domestic manufacturers depend on and import raw materials available in foreign countries. To be assured of the necessary raw materials, numerous enterprises have set up operations overseas. For example, rubber, which is required by numerous U.S. manufacturers, is not available in the continental U.S. Tire-producing firms must acquire rubber from other countries—those in Southeast Asia, for instance. Likewise, oil companies search the world for new petroleum reserves.

Acquisition of Managerial Know-How and Capital

Enterprises sometimes must go abroad to obtain the **managerial know-how and capital** that they lack but need to improve their operations. For example, in recent years, there has been a booming demand for travel in Russia. The Russian airline, Aeroflot, was one of the least efficient airlines in the world. To deal with this problem, the Russian carrier's management shopped around for Western partners who could bring the managerial know-how and capital it needed to meet its expansion demands.[24]

Protection of Home Market

Many firms have internationalized their operations to protect their home market. For example, a firm services a domestic manufacturer which, for its own reasons, decides to set up subsidiary operations abroad. The service enterprise would be wise to follow and provide the services required by the manufacturer's foreign subsidiaries. Otherwise, an aggressive competitor that gets its "foot in the door" through the manufacturer's foreign subsidiary may soon take over the service activities in the domestic market as well.

PRACTICAL PERSPECTIVE 4-2

Applied Digital Data Systems Transfers Manufacturing Abroad

Applied Digital Data Systems (ADDS) was a wholly owned subsidiary of NCR Corporation [NCR sold ADDS in the mid-1990s], which produced terminals for both its parent company and for other computer OEMs. Founded in 1969 and acquired by NCR in 1981, the firm put heavy emphasis on a flexible assembly operation that offers quick response—and reliable just-in-time (JIT) delivery—to its customers. The "flex" system was devised as part of ADDS' overall strategy for achieving competitive advantage in returning to U.S. soil. Not many years ago, however, that notion might have seemed a bit paradoxical. In the early 1980s, the company found itself at a distinct cost disadvantage with respect to its chief competitors. Most of them had already shifted manufacturing operations to the Far East—which today dominates many of the core technologies for producing TV and display-terminal components.

It wasn't so much a question of labor costs. "The thing that defeated us in those days was material costs," says David G. Laws, president and CEO of ADDS. "We were buying materials in the U.S. at U.S. prices; and our competitors were buying materials—and consuming them—in East Asia at East Asian prices. We found that we were paying in excess of a 30 percent premium for parts compared with our competitors. And we couldn't crack that problem." So in 1985 ADDS made the difficult decision to shut down its assembly operation in Hauppauge, N.Y., and have its product built by an offshore contract manufacturer that would be able to take advantage of East Asian component prices. In some respects, it was a smart decision. The immediate impact was a 23 percent reduction in product cost—even after adding shipping costs back to the U.S. (More than half of ADDS' business volume is with U.S.-based customers.)

Source: Excerpted from John Sheridan, "ADDS Finds 'There's No Place Like Home'," *Industry Week* (June 17, 1991): 12–13. Reprinted with permission from *Industry Week*. Copyright © Penton Publishing, Inc., Cleveland, Ohio.

Protection from Imports

Foreign competitors often hold an advantage over domestic firms because they have access to cheaper labor and/or materials in a foreign country. To remain competitive, domestic firms must often transfer their production activities to a foreign country to obtain the same cost advantages the foreign competitors enjoy. For example, many of the parts used to manufacture U.S.-produced automobiles are actually manufactured abroad. Practical Perspective 4-2 presents the case of Applied Digital Data Services, which transferred its manufacturing operations from the U.S. abroad because its chief competitors who had already gone abroad had access to much cheaper material costs.

Why Do Firms Internationalize?

It is not always clear whether firms' internationalization strategies are to seize opportunities or to combat threats. For example, a few years ago PepsiCo's management recognized that its U.S. markets were mature and that it was unlikely to realize profits attempting to capture market share in cola drinks from the formidable Coca-Cola Company. To deal with the situation, PepsiCo's management developed a strategy to cash in on changing eating and drinking habits in the rapidly industrializing parts of the world.[25] Was PepsiCo's strategy stimulated by the threatening situation in its home market or by its desire to seize the new opportunities that arose in foreign markets? In other words, if there had been no threats in its home market, would PepsiCo's management still have developed a strategy to seize the new opportunities in the foreign markets?

THE INTERNAL AUDIT

As suggested above, environmental changes, which are detected through an **external audit** of the global environment (covered in Chapter 3), often require that firms develop international strategies. To help them develop effective international strategies, along with total familiarity with the external environment, managers must examine their enterprises' internal conditions; they must conduct an internal audit to become familiar with the company's internal situation. Knowledge of their firm's internal factors will help its managers develop wise strategies for penetrating a foreign market or for coping with environmental changes. Basically, managers need to determine how much money the firm has access to, including cash on hand, borrowing power, and ability to sell stock, which can be used to finance the strategy; the nature of its physical assets; its personnel capabilities; and its strengths.

Foreign Sources of Finance

Even if an enterprise has access to the funds required to finance the expansion, managers should inquire about the availability of **financial assistance in the foreign market**. The governments of many foreign countries make special concessions to foreign firms that bring them the technologies they believe will aid their nations' development efforts. For example, the government of Morocco was actively seeking foreign investment in its tourism sector. To attract investment, it offered several incentives, such as the possibility of 100 percent foreign ownership; tax exemptions of up to ten years, depending on the location of investment; and the availability of long-term, low-interest financing.[26] (For another illustration, read Practical Perspective 4-3.)

PRACTICAL PERSPECTIVE 4-3

Bangkok's Strategies to Draw Foreign Investments

Bangkok, famed for its tourist attractions and warm hospitality, is now attracting more businesspeople than sightseers.... Thailand wavers on the brink of becoming an important international business hub, and opportunity knocks for those who understand this country's native culture and its business and economic climate.... One of the reasons why many multinationals have decided to do business in Thailand is that the Thai government is favorable to foreign trade.... Thai government development policies, stated under the Sixth Five-Year Development Plan (1987–92), restrict the public sector to a supporting, coordinating, and advisory role, while fostering activity and growth in the private sector.

The Office of the Board of Investments (OBI) encourages development in key industrial segments such as telecommunications, building supplies, medical supplies, and electronics and other technologies by offering privileges and incentives for businesses that support governmental policy.... Encouragement is offered in a number of forms, including holidays or reductions in corporate income taxes, exemptions or reductions on import duty, and exclusion of dividends from taxation.... The Thai government also offers guarantees against price controls, state competition, nationalization, the formation of state monopolies, or the granting of special privileges to government agencies or enterprises.

Source: Excerpted from Bill Bruce, "Thailand: The Next NIC?" *The International Executive* (November–December 1990): 35–37. Copyright © 1990. John Wiley & Sons, Inc., New York. All rights reserved. Reprinted by permission of publisher.

Nature of the Firm's Physical Assets and Personnel Competencies

Managers also need to obtain information about the enterprise's physical assets and their current state. Is their manufacturing capacity capable of producing for the foreign market? Or are new manufacturing means needed? Furthermore, managers must obtain information about their firm's **personnel competencies** in relation to the company's international strategy. Does the enterprise have the personnel capable of producing for the foreign market(s)? Does it have personnel with the ability to manage the international operations? Again, the governments of many foreign countries will help foreign firms finance machinery and factories and will provide trained personnel, or assist in training personnel, as a means of attracting technologies to aid in accomplishing the nation's developmental objectives.

The firm's internal conditions also affect how it enters a foreign market. Two fundamental approaches to conducting business abroad are by exporting to it or by manufacturing in it. Exporting involves manufacturing at home and shipping the goods to the foreign market. Exporting generally requires less investment than manufacturing abroad. If the firm is cash-short, has idle equipment, and its personnel is not highly competent in international business, the firm may prefer to export. However, by producing abroad, the company can often save on transportation, labor, and materials costs, as well as on tariffs. Therefore, if an enterprise has adequate cash to invest, has international managerial know-how, the foreign demand justifies the investment, and the foreign environment is conducive to the investment, it may want to produce abroad.

Lead from Strength

The internal audit should also include an assessment of the enterprise's strengths. A business should always **"lead from strength"**; that is, it should focus on doing what it can do better than its competitors. For example, a firm's strength may be engineering and design. Instead of manufacturing, it may be more efficient for the firm to farm it out to a company whose strength is manufacturing. For instance, Apple's [former] vice president Al Eisenstat said that "If I can loop off one area of activity and say, 'Gee, I can join with such and such company,' then I can focus my resources on what I do best."[27] Firms such as Apple, Nike, and IBM have established themselves as design, engineering, and marketing companies, farming out much of their manufacturing to those who are able to do it cheaper and better. Maatschappij Van Berkel's Patent N.V., a Dutch-based multinational supplier of weighing and food processing equipment, met competitive cost pressures by outsourcing its manufacturing and engineering activities and transforming itself into a sales and service company.[28]

Furthermore, a firm may be strong in production, but weak in conducting foreign business. This firm may therefore have to form a joint venture or enter into a strategic alliance with an enterprise that is strong in conducting foreign business. (Joint ventures and strategic alliances will be discussed more thoroughly in Chapter 5.) Basically, organizations enter into joint ventures or strategic alliances to share costs and risks, to gain additional technical and market knowledge, to complement each other, to serve an international market, to strengthen themselves against other competitors, and to develop industry standards together.[29] As Jack Welch of GE put it, "tomorrow's organization will be boundaryless. It will work with out-

---

PRACTICAL PERSPECTIVE 4-4

Bury Thy Teacher

In October [1992], Chicago's 97-year-old Schwinn Bicycle Co., the grand name in American bicycles, filed for bankruptcy. On the other side of the world, Antony Lo took a breather from promoting his high-priced mountain bikes at the Tokyo International Cycle Show to deliver an eloquent eulogy for Schwinn, the company that Lo helped bury. "Without Schwinn, we never would have grown to where we are today," said Lo, the polished president of Taiwan's Giant Manufacturing Co., now the world's largest bike exporter. "We learned many basic things from them: quality, value, service." Down in Hong Kong, in his office in a converted factory near the colony's mammoth container port, Jerome Sze, the managing director and a large shareholder of Shenzhen, China's publicly traded China Bicycles Co., also pays his respects to the American company that helped him grow. "Schwinn," says Sze, "helped to promote our products in the U.S."...

[The] great American company lost its way and, through management blunders, created powerful competitors that ultimately did it in. Says Scott Montgomery, president of Cannondale Japan, a wholly owned unit of the successful Georgetown, Connecticut high-end bike company: "After Schwinn built them up (Giant and China Bicycles), they ate Schwinn." ...

Going overseas in the 1970s, Schwinn was more concerned with moving production out of the U.S. than with selling abroad. "Schwinn was obsessed with cutting costs," says Cannondale Japan's Montgomery, "instead of innovation." Schwinn began its foreign campaign by sourcing many of its bicycles from Japan....

As part of its new partnership with Giant, Schwinn handed over everything—technology, engineering, volume—that Giant needed to become a dominant bikemaker.... Says an executive of a U.S. competitor. "Schwinn gave the franchise to Giant on a silver platter."...

Dazed by Giant's aggressive brand-name push, Schwinn tried to protect itself by forging a new alliance, this time with Jerome Sze's China Bicycle Co. It began buying CBC's bikes and selling them under the Schwinn name.... Until Schwinn went into business with China Bicycles, CBC's main business in the U.S. was supplying commodity house-brand bikes to Sears and other mass merchandisers from its low-cost factory in Shenzhen, in the heart of southern China's capitalist revolution. ... But Schwinn taught CBC about the U.S. specialty dealer market, raised the Chinese factory's quality standards and lent it credibility. "CBC came light-years in a short period of time because of a lot of technology transfer from

(continued)

Schwinn," says *Bicycling's* [editor and publisher J.C.] McCullagh. Sze subsequently used all the knowledge he gleaned from Schwinn to help bolster his business supplying bicycles to the European operations of bike companies such as Scott and France's MBK (owned by Japan's Yamaha).

Burned once by Giant, Schwinn tried to dissuade China Bicycles from developing its own brand-name business in the U.S. But that didn't stop Sze. In 1990, despite Schwinn's opposition, Sze and his Shenzhen partner together acquired a medium-size U.S. bicycle importer and distributor, which owned the Diamond Back name. That gave CBC its own U.S. brand name and distribution channels. Diamond Back competed directly with Schwinn and was particularly strong on the West Coast. With Giant, China Bicycles, and other competitors taking big bites out of its market share, Schwinn was finally forced to file for bankruptcy in October. It still imports bikes from its two former students and sells them under the Schwinn name. But production of its own bikes in the U.S. is down to under 10,000 units a year, sold under the Paramount name of high-priced racing bikes.

Source: Excerpted from Andrew Tanzer, "Bury Thy Teacher," *Forbes* (December 21, 1992): 90–95. Reprinted by permission of *Forbes* magazine © 1999. Forbes 1992.

siders as closely as if they were insiders."[30] Managers should be aware, however, that joint ventures and strategic alliances can backfire, especially when one of the partners becomes stronger by learning more than the other(s). The stronger partner may break up the alliance and go on its own, which may harm the weaker partner. (For an illustration, read Practical Perspective 4-4, the case of Schwinn Bicycle Co.)

It should be noted that foreign countries' environments generally have an effect on a firm's strengths and weaknesses. For example, an organization may possess a strong ability to distribute a product in one nation because it is capable of dealing with that country's distribution laws and practices. At the same time it may possess a weak capability to distribute in another country because it lacks the ability to deal with that nation's distribution laws and practices. For instance, international business transactions are either in cash or in barter trade (to be discussed in Chapter 5). Many enterprises have experience in cash transactions but not in barter trade transactions. In the latter case, if the enterprise wishes to penetrate a foreign market where barter trade is required, it may have to form a partnership with a firm that has experience in barter trade.

Also, an enterprise may possess the ability to differentiate a product to fit the needs of a specific country's culture, and at the same time lack the ability to differentiate to fit another country's cultural needs. U.S. car manufacturers, for example, have historically possessed the capability of differentiating their automobiles to fit the needs of many countries, but not the needs of some countries, such as England, where the steering wheel is located on the right-hand side of the automobile. In this case, if a U.S. car manufacturer wanted to penetrate the British car market, it might have to form a partnership with a car manufacturer that has the capability of producing cars with the steering wheel on the right-hand side.

Firms also form strategic alliances to acquire knowledge. That is, each partner is to learn about the other's or others' strengths. But some firms learn more and faster than others—as in the case of Schwinn Bicycle Company, presented in Practical Perspective 4-4. It seems as if Schwinn's partners learned faster and much more than it did. Furthermore, learning through alliances can be a difficult, frustrating, and often misunderstood process, and, it has been argued on the basis of observation, creating a successful alliance learning environment is the exception rather than the rule.[31] The reasons for failure include

➤ the alliance knowledge was undervalued;

➤ the necessary "connections" were not put into place;

➤ the nature of the knowledge made learning difficult; and

➤ the present corporate culture did not support learning.[32]

TYPES OF INTERNATIONAL STRATEGIES

International firms typically develop their core strategy for the home country first. Subsequently, they internationalize their core strategy through international expansion of activities and through adaptation. Eventually, they globalize their strategy by integrating operations across nations.[33] These steps translate into four distinct types of strategies applied by international enterprises: ethnocentric, multidomestic, global, and transnational.

Ethnocentric Strategy

Following World War II, U.S. enterprises operated mainly from an **ethnocentric** perspective. These companies produced unique goods and services, which they offered primarily to the domestic market. The lack of international competition offset their need to be sensitive to cultural differences. When these firms exported goods, they did not alter them for foreign consumption—the costs of alterations for cultural differences were assumed by the foreign buyers. In effect, this type of company has one strategy for all markets.

Dean Foods, a $2 billion dairy and vegetable-processing company based in Illinois, uses this strategy. It exports non-dairy powdered creamer and canned and frozen vegetables to Europe and Asia. Its strategy does not provide for operating production facilities abroad. The firm's managers decided that they do not want to take on the problems of setting up complicated distribution systems in underdeveloped countries.[34]

Multidomestic Strategy

The multidomestic firm (discussed as an MNC in Chapter 1) has a different strategy for each of its foreign markets. In this type of strategy, "a company's management tries to operate effectively across a series of worldwide positions with diverse product requirements, growth rates, competitive environments, and political risks. The company prefers that local man-

PRACTICAL PERSPECTIVE 4-5

Aldus's International Strategy

At Aldus [established in 1984 and now known as Adobe], entering foreign markets was not a strategy pursued after its products had been successfully marketed in the U.S. Aldus President Paul Brainerd set out from the beginning to build products that could be quickly adapted to local markets.... The firm's major product is a computer program known as PageMaker which allows individuals to design, edit, and produce printed documents using microcomputer systems available to most businesses. The firm's potential market includes both businesses that generate documents and the publishing industry itself....

The first U.S. version of Aldus PageMaker was shipped in July 1985. But even before the end of 1984, Brainerd had made a trip to Europe to set up channels of distribution. He was determined to introduce Aldus products almost simultaneously in the U.S. and Europe. But the firm was small and had very little capital at the time. (An initial public offering of common stock would raise approximately $30 million in June 1987.) "We had to build a step-by-step progression of just what we could afford to do at any given point in the development of the company," Brainerd says. So Aldus developed a strategy to penetrate foreign markets quickly and at minimal cost.... The first phase of the plan was to engineer PageMaker

in such a way that the computer program could be readily and quickly adapted to different national markets. "Localization" is the term employed by Aldus executives. Since Page-Maker and similar programs are oriented to text and design considerations, the same program can hardly be sold in different countries. Software must be modified to conform to local languages and design idioms....

Localization projects have ranged from international English (distinct from American usage) to European languages with their different hyphenation requirements, to Asian languages with thousands of characters as well as vertical headlines and right to left orientation.... Although PageMaker was designed to be adopted to foreign requirements, the capital constraints remained. Brainerd describes the Aldus solution: "We worked out a strategy where the distributors who wished to carry our products would essentially do the work for us. They would front end the investment for localization, and we would pay them back on a per-unit basis as they sold the software."

Source: Excerpted from Warren Kalbacker, "At Aldus, Globalization Wasn't an Afterthought," *The International Executive* (January–February 1990): 8–9. Copyright © 1990, John Wiley & Sons, Inc., New York. All rights reserved. Reprinted with permission.

agers do what is necessary to succeed in R&D, production, marketing, and distribution, but holds them responsible for results."[35] In essence, this type of corporation competes with local competitors on a market-by-market basis. A multitude of American corporations use this strategy, for example, Procter & Gamble in household products, Honeywell in controls, Alcoa in aluminum, and General Foods in consumer goods. Japanese car manufacturer Toyota also follows this strategy. Practical Perspective 4-5 presents Aldus's international localization strategy.

Global Strategy

The **global corporation** (discussed in Chapter 1) uses all of its resources against its competition in a very integrated fashion. All of its foreign subsidiaries and divisions are highly interdependent in both operations and strategy. As Thomas Hout, et al., said:

> *In a global business, management competes worldwide against a small number of other multinationals in the world market. Strategy is centralized, and various aspects of operations are decentralized or centralized as economics and effectiveness dictate. The company seeks to respond to particular local market needs, while avoiding a compromise of efficiency of the overall global system.*[36]

Therefore, whereas in a multidomestic strategy the managers in each country react to competition without considering what is taking place in other countries, in a global strategy, competitive moves are integrated across nations. The same kind of move is made in different countries at the same time or in a systematic fashion. For example, a competitor is attacked in one nation in order to exhaust its resources for another country, or a competitive attack in one nation is countered in a different country—for instance, the counterattack in a competitor's home market as a parry to an attack on one's home market.[37] For an illustration, read Practical Perspective 4-6, the case of Wal-Mart and Carrefour.

Numerous MNCs are applying the global strategy, including IBM in computers; Caterpillar in large construction equipment; Timex, Seiko, and Citizen in watches; and General Electric, Siemens, and Mitsubishi in heavy electrical equipment. The reasons this strategy can work include "growing similarity of what citizens of different countries want to buy, the reduction of tariff and nontariff barriers, technology investments that are becoming too expensive to amortize in one market only, and competitors that are globalizing the rules of the game."[38] Whirlpool, which was mainly a North American corporation, now applies a global strategy. It manufactures in eleven nations with facilities in the U.S., Europe, and Latin America, and markets products in more than 120 locations as diverse as Thailand, Hungary, and Argentina.[39] Practical Perspective 4-7 describes Whirlpool's global strategy.

PRACTICAL PERSPECTIVE 4-6

Retail Rival Carrefour Bulks Up

All right, so it's not quite as good as winning the World Cup. But the French, dispirited after months of fruitless haggling to create Europe's largest bank, have bounced back by creating Europe's No. 1 retailer with the merger of homegrown chains Carrefour and Promodès Group. Carrefour's $16.5 billion acquisition of Promodès, announced on August 30 [1999], does far more than give France a national champion, though: The merger creates a much tougher playing field for Wal-Mart Stores Inc. in its drive to expand internationally.

With 8,800 stores in 26 countries and combined revenues of $65 billion, Carrefour is set to challenge Wal-Mart around the globe. As Europe's new top dog, Carrefour can use its buying clout to extract deeper discounts from suppliers, undercutting rivals and accelerating a push toward consolidation in the industry. The Promodès deal also widens Carrefour's impressive lead in several Latin American and Asian countries. What's more, Promodès brings to the union a reputation for solid inventory and distribution systems, an area where Carrefour has long lagged behind Wal-Mart. "We're cre-ating a worldwide retail leader," says Carrefour Chief Executive Daniel Bernard, who will head the merged company.

Critical Mass

In Europe, the deal puts pressure on Wal-Mart to make another acquisition. The retailer already has holdings in Britain and Germany. But if it doesn't grab another partner soon, it could be left without the critical mass to become a major European player. Its biggest European holding, Britain's Asda Group PLC, is only one-fifth the size of the bulked-up Carrefour. Likewise, Wal-Mart needs to counter Carrefour's expansion in emerging markets. Only hours after unveiling the Promodès deal, Carrefour announced the acquisition of three Brazilian chains, boosting its market share there above 20 percent, vs. 1.4 percent for Wal-Mart.

Source: Excerpted from C. Matlack, I. Resch, and W. Zellner, "En Garde, Wal-Mart," *Business Week* (September 13, 1999): 54. Copyright © 1999, McGraw-Hill. All rights reserved. Used with permission.

Advantages and Disadvantages of the Global Strategy

Outlined below are the advantages and disadvantages of the global strategy.[40] The advantages of the global strategy would negate the disadvantages of the multidomestic strategy, and the disadvantages of the global strategy would be negated by the advantages of the multidomestic strategy.

Advantages (Multidomestic strategy does not provide these advantages.)

➤ By pooling production or other activities for two or more nations, a firm can increase the benefits derived from economies of scale.

➤ A company can cut costs by moving manufacturing or other activities to low-cost countries.

PRACTICAL PERSPECTIVE 4-7

Whirlpool's Views on Global Strategy

The only way to gain lasting competitive advantage is to leverage your capabilities around the world so that the company as a whole is greater than the sum of its parts. Being an international company—selling globally, having global brands or operations in different countries—isn't enough. In fact, most international manufacturers aren't truly global. They're what I [Whirlpool CEO David R. Whitwam] call flag planters. They may have acquired or established businesses all over the world, but their regional and national divisions still operate as autonomous entities. In this day and age, you can't run a business that way and expect to gain a long-range competitive advantage.

To me, "competitive advantage" means having the best technologies and processes for designing, manufacturing, selling, and servicing your products at the lowest possible costs. Our vision at Whirlpool is to integrate our geographical businesses wherever possible, so that our most advanced expertise in any given area—whether it's refrigeration technology, financial reporting systems, or distribution strategy—isn't confined to one location or division. We want to be able to take the best capabilities we have and leverage them in all our operations worldwide.

In the major-appliance industry, both the size of our products and varying consumer preferences require us to have regional manufacturing centers. But even though the features, dimensions, and configurations of machines like refrigerators, washing machines, and ovens vary from market to market, much of the technology and manufacturing processes involved are similar. In other words, while a company may need plants in Europe, the United States, Latin America, and Asia to make products that meet the special needs of local markets, it's still possible and desirable for those plants to share the best available product technologies and manufacturing processes.... [Before you can develop common technologies and processes,] you must create an organization whose people are adept at exchanging ideas, processes, and systems across borders, people who are absolutely free of the "not-invented-here" syndrome, people who are constantly working together to identify the best global opportunities and the biggest global problems facing the organization. If you're going to ask people to work together in pursuing global ends across organizational and geographic boundaries, you have to give them a vision of what they're striving to achieve as well as a unifying philosophy to guide their efforts.

That's why we've worked so hard at Whirlpool to define and communicate our vision, objectives, and the market philosophy that represents our unifying focus. Our vision is to be one company worldwide. Our overarching objective is to drive this company to world-class performance in terms of delivering shareholder value.... Our market philosophy suggests that the only way to deliver this value over a long term is by focusing on the customer. Only prolonged, intensive effort to understand and respond to genuine customer needs can lead to the breakthrough products and services that earn long-term customer loyalty....

Before 1987, we didn't see the potential power our existing capabilities could give us in the global market because we had been limiting our definition of the appliance market to the United States. Obviously, this also limited our

(continued)

definition of the industry itself and the opportunity it offered. Our eight months of analysis turned up a great deal of evidence that, over time, our industry could become global, whether we chose to become global or not. With that said, we had three choices. We could ignore the inevitable—a decision that would have condemned Whirlpool to a slow death. We could wait for globalization to begin and then try to react, which would have put us in the catch-up mode, technologically and organizationally. Or we could control our own destiny and try to shape the very nature of globalization in our industry. In short, we could force our competition to respond to us.

Before we began making moves on the global stage, Electrolux was out in front of us. It had bought White Consolidated and had acquired several appliance makers in Europe. But Electrolux appeared to be taking advantage of individual opportunities rather than following a coordinated plan. After our Philips acquisition, we also saw General Electric take some opportunistic steps. Today, however, Whirlpool is the front-runner when it comes to implementing a pan-European strategy and leveraging global resources. By expanding our strategic horizon, not just our geographic reach, we've been able to build global management capability that provides us with what we feel is a distinct competitive advantage. Clearly, this should enable us to improve returns to our shareholders significantly.

➤ A firm that is able to switch production among different nations can reduce costs by increasing its bargaining power over suppliers, workers, and host governments.

➤ By focusing on a smaller number of products and programs than under a multidomestic strategy, a corporation is able to improve both product and program quality.

➤ Worldwide availability, serviceability, and recognition can increase preference through reinforcement.

➤ The company is provided with more points from which to attack and counterattack competition.

Disadvantages (Multidomestic strategy can reduce these disadvantages.)

➤ Through increased coordination, reporting requirements, and added staff, substantial management costs can be incurred.

➤ Overcentralization can harm local motivation and morale, therefore reducing the firm's effectiveness.

➤ Standardization can result in a product that does not really satisfy any customers.

➤ Incurring costs and revenues in multiple countries increases currency risk.

➤ Integrated competitive moves can lead to the sacrificing of revenues, profits, or competitive positions in individual countries—especially when the subsidiary in one country is told to attack a global competitor in order to convey a signal or divert that competitor's resources from another nation.

Transnational Strategy

The **transnational strategy** provides for global coordination (like the global strategy) and at the same time it allows local autonomy (like the multidomestic strategy). Nestlé, the world's largest food company, headquarted in Switzerland, follows this strategy.[41] The challenges managers of transnational corporations face are to identify and exploit cross-border synergies and to balance local demands with the global vision for the corporation. Building an effective transnational organization requires a corporate culture that values global dissimilarities across cultures and markets.[42]

INTERNATIONAL STRATEGIC AND TACTICAL OBJECTIVES

Organizations generally establish two kinds of measurable objectives: strategic and tactical. **Strategic objectives,** which are guided by the enterprise's mission or purpose and deal with long-term issues, associate the enterprise to its external environment and provide management with a basis for comparing performance with that of its competitors and in relation to environmental demands. (Refer again to the Whirlpool case, Practical Perspective 4-7.) Examples of strategic objectives include to increase sales, to increase market share, to increase profits, and to lower prices by becoming an international firm. Tactical objectives, which are guided by the enterprise's strategic objectives and deal with shorter term issues, identify the key result areas in which specific performance is essential for the success of the enterprise and aim to attain internal efficiency. They identify specifically how, for example, to lower costs, to lower prices, to increase output, to capture a larger portion of the market, and to penetrate an international market.

Areas in Which Objectives Should Be Established

Peter Drucker, the globally known management authority, has indicated that objectives should be established in at least eight areas of organizational performance: market standing, innovations, productivity, physical and financial resources, profitability, manager performance and responsibility, worker performance and attitude, and social responsibility.[43]

Market Standing

In general, *market standing* objectives measure performance relating to products/service, markets, distribution, and customer service. In an international context, a firm's strategic objective may be to increase market share by entering foreign markets. Tactical objectives established to enter foreign markets may include refocusing advertising, product/service, and pricing to fit each foreign market's environment. (As indicated in Practical Perspective 4-8, Whirlpool Corporation did not attain its objectives.) Performance measures must therefore be developed for each foreign market. Overall, international firms need to measure performance relating to worldwide, region, and country sales volume.

Innovations

A strategic *innovation* objective may be to lead the industry in introducing new products; a tactical objective may be to spend a specific percentage of revenues from sales for research and development (R&D). Innovation

---

PRACTICAL PERSPECTIVE 4-8

Tough Target

Nine years ago, Whirlpool Corporation came to Europe in a big way, believing that the Continent's appliance business, then a $20 billion market with dozens of marginally profitable companies, was becoming more American. The industry had no choice, Whirlpool thought, but to consolidate into a handful of companies. And America's biggest appliance maker wanted to be one of them.

But the market didn't change; only the competition did. It got tougher. Whirlpool's two biggest rivals, Sweden's AB Electrolux and Germany's Bosch-Siemens Hausgeraete GmbH, improved efficiency step-for-step with Whirlpool. And smaller competitors managed to hold on.

The result for Whirlpool, which earlier had had only a minor presence in Europe, is disappointment. Instead of winning an anticipated

20 percent of the market, it has about 12 percent. Its European profits also are less than expected. In the U.S., the Benton Harbor, Michigan, company makes $10 on every $100 of sales; in Europe, it earns about $2.30 on that amount of revenue.

Now, Whirlpool is struggling through its second European restructuring. The goals remain the same, but the company concedes it will take longer to reach them. "We see Europe as being in the fifth year of a 10-year restructuring," says Jeff Fettig, who runs Whirlpool's European operation from his Comerio headquarters. He acknowledges that the company "underestimated the competition."

Source: Excerpted from G. Steinmetz and C. Quintanilla, "Whirlpool Expected Easy Going in Europe and It Got a Big Shock," *The Wall Street Journal*, April 10, 1998, pp. A1, A6. Permission conveyed through Copyright Clearance Center, Inc.

objectives are based on a clear vision of where a firm wants to be ten, fifteen, and twenty years from now. R&D may aim at innovation of patentable products and/or production technology—U.S. firms tend to focus on the former and Japanese firms on the latter. It is generally believed that the global and competitive battles of the 2000s will be won by enterprises that are able to get out of the traditional and declining product markets by building and dominating basically new markets. Many believe that Japanese firms' **production technology superiority**, coupled with the fact that they are rapidly catching up to the U.S. in the ability to innovate in new products, will put them at a competitive advantage in the global market. (Practical Perspective 4-9 presents Honda's efforts to attain a competitive advantage through innovation.). Managers must also establish tactical objectives concerning the redesigning of products/services to fit the needs of

PRACTICAL PERSPECTIVE 4-9

Accord's Flexible Design

Honda president Nobuhiko Kawamoto realized years ago that Honda's long-term success was threatened if the automaker couldn't make the company's most important car more successful outside the U.S. At the same time, to keep up with the needs of its aging baby-boomer buyers, Honda executives say they needed to substantially enlarge the new U.S. version. The obvious solution to the Accord's woes—designing a different model for each market—was out of the question. Honda may have big brand presence in the U.S., but it ranks only 13th among the world's automakers. That means it can't afford to spend as much as its bigger rivals—not even on the all-important Accord. While General Motors budgets a generous $9 billion a year for research and development, Honda gets by with a mere $2.1 billion.

Now, however, Honda may have found a way to customize the Accord for world markets without breaking the bank. The completely overhauled 1998 Honda Accord that will hit U.S. showrooms on September 25 [1997] will look and feel nothing like the Accord being simultaneously introduced in Japan or the one that will debut in Europe next spring. The U.S. Accord will be a big, staid family car, matching the Ford Taurus in interior roominess. The European version will be short and narrow and is expected to feature the stiff and sporty ride Old World drivers prefer.

Honda's secret lies in an ingenious frame that allows the automaker to shrink or expand the overlying car without starting from the ground up. By coming up with a platform—by far the most expensive part of a new car—that can be bent and stretched into markedly different vehicles, Honda has saved hundreds of millions of dollars in development costs. Analysts estimate that Honda developed the Accord for a relatively modest $600 million. In comparison, Ford Motor Company spent $2.8 billion redesigning the 1996 Taurus.

Source: Excerpted from K. Naughton, E. Thorton, K. Kerwin, and H. Dawl, "Can Honda Build a World Car?" *Business Week* (September 8, 1997): 101–102. © 1997, McGraw-Hill. All rights reserved. Used with permission.

PRACTICAL PERSPECTIVE 4-10

Think Globally, Script Locally

William Pfeiffer [the executive who launched a Hindi-language channel for Sony] can remember when there was no McDonald's in Katmandu. That was 16 years ago, when he'd just moved to Tokyo after B-school at Stanford. He was working for Disney at the time; then, in 1992, Sony hired him to scout business opportunities for Columbia Tri-Star, its then-floundering Hollywood studio. The biggest opportunity was in India, where there was little competition and a newly liberalized foreign investment policy. From modest beginnings—a dirt-floored Bombay office lit by a single bulb that went dark whenever a monsoon hit—Sony has become a powerhouse, producing 33 hours of Hindi-language programming a week and beaming it not just to India but also to Africa, Britain, North America, and the Middle East. Reif Cohen notwithstanding, Pfeiffer maintains that Sony Entertainment Television, the Hindi-language television channel he launched in 1995, actually makes money.

After getting established in India, Sony launched the mostly English-language AXN Action satellite channel across Asia. Last winter it became sole owner of Super TV, a Mandarin-language channel that reaches 77 percent of the 5.1 million homes in Taiwan. Sony also produces or co-produces some 35 hours of Mandarin-language programming a week, much of it for Super TV—from *City of Love*, a prime-time Taiwan soap, to a revivified *Charlie's Angels* starring a trio of willowy Chinese babes who chopsock it to bad guys from Shanghai to Kuala Lumpur. (Recently cancelled, alas, is *Feng Shui Talk*, an hour devoted to proper management of energy flow.) But the real news is that Super TV gives Sony the potential to go after the mainland's 305 million television households via satellite, instead of just selling shows like *Chinese Restaurant* to existing terrestrial stations. "China is a market we're very respectful of," says Pfeiffer. "We're certainly interested, if we're allowed in, in entertaining the people."

Source: Excerpted from Frank Rose, "Think Globally, Script Locally," *Fortune* (November 8, 1999): 158. Reprinted with permission.

each specific foreign market their firms wish to penetrate. (Practical Perspective 4-10 discusses Sony's TV programming adaptations in China and India.) And they must develop strategies related to the type of technology to be transferred abroad.

Classification of Technology. The term *technology* has been defined as machinery, blueprints, process designs, equipment, products, patents, licenses, trademarks, and other techniques such as marketing and advertising, accounting, personnel management, and general management.[44] It should be noted that old technology in the home market may sometimes be innovative technology in a foreign market. Technology has been classified as hard and soft, proprietary and nonproprietary, bundled and unbundled, and front-end and obsolete technology.[45]

Hard technology includes hard goods, blueprints, technical specifications, and knowledge and assistance necessary for the efficient use of such hardware. *Soft technology* includes management, marketing, financial organization, and administrative techniques. *Proprietary technology* is technology that is owned by particular individuals or organizations. *Nonproprietary technology* includes knowledge that can be imitated or reproduced by observation or reverse engineering without infringement on proprietary rights. **Reverse engineering** means learning to reproduce technology by taking it apart to determine how it works and then copying it. *Bundled technology* is controlled technology that the owner is willing to transfer as part of a package. The owner maintains an ownership interest in the overseas affiliate using the technology. *Unbundled technology* is technology that is transferred independent of the supplier's total package of resources. *Front-end technology* is the most advanced technology available. *Obsolete technology* is usually older technology.

Export Older or Advanced Technology? Historically, some less-developed countries (LDCs) have sought to import **advanced technologies** from developed countries and others have pursued the importation of **older technology**. A survey has addressed the question of whether LDCs should import the most advanced technology available or older technology that may be obsolete in the developed countries.[46] Some international executives feel that LDCs with low capital and an abundance of labor should import older technology. They believe that many LDCs in this situation lack the infrastructure, both material and in human resources, "to support, feed, operate, and gainfully exploit advanced technology."[47] Other international executives suggest that LDCs should import technology that promotes employment, that is, they should import labor-intensive older technology, especially in those countries where unemployment or underemployment is a severe problem.

A number of executives disagree. They feel that in most situations, LDCs should import the most advanced technology available. One reason for this perspective is that in the long range, older technology produces inferior products and the country thus becomes less competitive in world markets. Another reason is that, regardless of social effects on employment, the most modern technology will contribute more to a country's national income. It is also felt that if countries import the obsolete technology of advanced countries, they will always remain LDCs. Some international executives feel that the sophistication of technology should be based on the destination of the product. If the product manufactured by the imported technology is for local consumption, then older technology would be more appropriate; if, however, the product produced is for exporting, advanced technology would work better.[48] Another view is that the approach a country uses is contingent upon such factors as its economic situation, its leaders, and its people. For example, an oil-rich LDC may be able to afford the acquisition of advanced technology. On the other hand, a very poor

LDC may be better off importing older, labor-intensive technology, which is often obsolete in the advanced countries and thus less costly. Some leaders have greater ability than others in implementing new technologies, and people in some cultures are more open to innovation than people in others.

Tactical objectives relative to the type of technology—old or new—a firm transfers are therefore influenced by nations' perceived needs as well as by the extent to which the enterprise's management protects its intellectual property rights. High-technology industries are generally very concerned with intellectual property rights. The laws protecting such rights, however, vary considerably around the globe. It was estimated by the U.S. International Trade Commission that in 1984 infringement of intellectual property throughout the world cost $8 billion in lost U.S. sales. The loss could be even greater today. It was reported in 1997 that $1.409 billion of illegal copies of entertainment software were sold in China in the past year, and the total in ten reported countries (including China) amounted to $5.190 billion (including $2.780 billion in the U.S.); illegal sales of CDs and cassettes in ten reported countries (not including the U.S.) amounted to $924 million; and illegal sales of copies of videos in ten reported countries (not including the U.S.) amounted to $1.034 billion.[49] Further, it is alleged that U.S. enterprises have suffered from a "lack of rigorous and uniform international standards for intellectual property rights."[50] U.S. Senator John J. Rockefeller has communicated some concerns in this respect. He stated that "Once the technology is developed and the resulting product is commercialized, it is vital that patent rights be protected. If a company cannot sell its products and recoup its development costs, the next product will not be developed."[51] The problem is now enlarged by the advent of Internet commerce. As was pointed out in Chapter 2, providing copyright protection for knowledge sources on the Internet is quite different from providing it to their counterparts in hardcopy publication.

Productivity

Productivity is usually measured by the ratio of output to input, for example, ratio of output to labor costs, ratio of output to capital costs, ratio of value added to sales, and ratio of value added to profit. In an international context, the manager is concerned with the ratio of foreign to domestic production volume and the economies of scale by means of international production integration. A strategic objective may be to reduce production costs. Tactical objectives based on this strategic objective may include replacing equipment, enhancing plant utilization rates, improving quality control, and transferring production overseas where labor and/or material costs are lower. (Refer again to Practical Perspective 4-2.) Tactical objectives may also include the development of a system for forecasting, monitoring, and interpreting costs. Japan's cost-management system is much more sophisticated than the United States'. For example, U.S. enterprises developing a new product normally design it first and then compute

---

FIGURE 4-1   How the Japanese Keep Costs Low

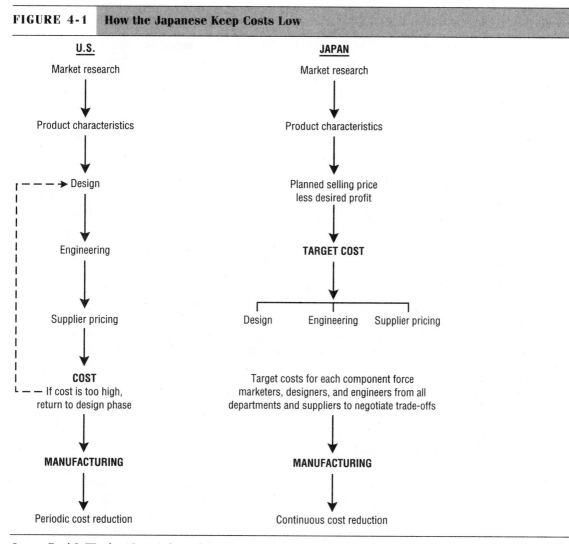

Source: Ford S. Worthy, "Japan's Smart Secret Weapon," *Fortune* (August 12, 1991): 73. Copyright © 1991 Time Inc., New York. All rights reserved. Reprinted by permission.

the cost. If it is too much, the product is returned to the drawing board—or the firm accepts a lower profit. On the other hand, the Japanese begin with a target cost estimated on the price the market is likely to accept. Subsequently, they instruct designers and engineers to meet the target. (See Figure 4-1.) The Japanese system also encourages managers to be concerned less about a product's cost than about the role it could play in gaining market share. This approach is a large reason Japanese firms often generate winning products the accountants would have killed in a U.S. firm.[52]

Physical and Financial Resources

Physical and financial measures include current ratio, working-capital turnover, the acid test ratio, debt to equity ratio, accounts receivable, and inventory turnover. In an international dimension, managers are concerned with how foreign affiliates are to be financed (for example, by retained earnings, franchising, borrowing, or forming joint ventures), with minimizing the tax burden globally, and with foreign exchange management that seeks to minimize losses from monetary exchange fluctuations.

Profitability

Profitability measures include the ratios of profits to sales, profits to total assets, and profits to net worth. A strategic objective may be to increase profits. Tactical objectives may be to reduce costs by consolidating functions, or, as discussed earlier in this chapter, by transferring operations overseas where costs and/or materials are lower.

Manager Performance and Responsibility

Managers' international performance and responsibility are based on their skills. A strategic objective may be to identify and upgrade critical areas of international management depth and succession. A tactical objective may be to establish programs aimed at developing managers with a **global outlook** (refer again to Chapter 1), at developing host country nationals for managerial positions, and at initiating programs that prepare employees for foreign assignments. (This will be discussed more thoroughly in Chapters 7and 8.)

Worker Performance and Attitude

A strategic objective to improve worker performance and attitude may be to maintain levels of employee satisfaction consistent with the firm's industry and with similar industries since this is part of an organization's stability and durability. Tactical objectives in this aspect may include bonus plans, pay increases, and application of participative management. In an international context, equipment transfers to a foreign country, in comparison with transferring technical skills, is relatively easy. The problem occurs when there is a **shortage of trained personnel** in the country and/or workers do not maintain the proper attitude and are low producers. When this is the case, the firm must develop and implement training programs.

For example, after nearly half a century of communism, China has recently begun to shift to a market economy. The vastness of China's market potential and low labor costs makes it attractive for foreign corporations to invest there. Under the communist regime, a system evolved of paying employees the same whether they worked hard or not. Therefore, the skills and efficiency of China's workforce do not yet compare to those of the advanced nations' workforces. Thus, foreign corporations establishing subsidiaries in China may need to implement appropriate training programs. For instance, Motorola, Inc. sponsors a technical university and provides hundreds of scholarships to support its new plant in China established to produce paging devices. Panasonic implemented a military-like boot camp for workers at its Beijing television tube plant. Xian-Jenssen Pharmaceutical Ltd., a China-U.S. joint venture, spends several thousand dollars to train each local employee; it offers in-house courses in sales, accounting, English, and computer usage.[53]

Other strategic objectives may be to control excessive absenteeism and lateness. It should be noted that individuals in some cultures object to too much control. They believe that it is none of the corporation's business as to why an employee is absent, and any attempt to control absenteeism is viewed as corporate exploitation of individuals. Therefore, rather than attempting to control absenteeism in some cultures, a flexible work system may sometimes be more appropriate.

Social Responsibility

A *social responsibility* objective would be to respond appropriately everywhere possible to societal expectations and environmental needs. For example, Canon Corporation's "spiritual" basis for its activities and the behavioral norms for employees are based on the following managerial philosophy:

> *1. To manufacture the best products in the world and thereby contribute to advancement of international development, and 2. to build an ideal corporation that will enjoy continuous prosperity.*[54]

Corporate social responsibility is built into the Japanese system—more and more Japanese enterprises are giving a percentage of their profits to promote education, social welfare, and culture.

Furthermore, all businesses have the responsibility to correct the environmental problems they create in attaining their goals and objectives. Most nations are concerned with environmental problems and have laws mandating corrective and/or preventive action. (In the U.S., the Environmental Protection Agency enforces these laws.) Also, companies that employ child labor are viewed as socially irresponsible in many nations. International corporations must develop objectives in this respect, otherwise there can be negative consequences. (This topic was discussed more thoroughly in Chapter 2.)

TECHNOLOGY AND GLOBAL STRATEGY

Technology has been the root of the most dramatic changes occurring in commerce today. It now enables organizations to integrate their systems, where changes in one part ripple throughout the system, causing shifts in the other parts. Therefore, no strategy has been left untouched. It has leveled the playing field for small firms, allowing them to compete successfully with large corporations in the same markets. With e-mail, teleconferencing, multimedia CD-ROMs, and networked databases, small businesses can emulate the marketing tactics of much larger companies—they can set up a home page on the World Wide Web right next door to Wal-Mart. And electronic networks and the Internet have enabled organizations to decentralize business activities and to outsource activities to other organizations.

From a strategic viewpoint, technology impacted international strategy in several ways:[55]

➤ Emphasis has moved from products to information and solutions.

➤ Products can be launched from commercialization tactics based on identifying specific customer needs.

➤ Relationships with customers have been made easier, which enhances product acceptance and minimizes costs due to redesign.

➤ Firms can now target specific products and services to specific customers.

➤ Technology supports the integration of engineering and commercialization to get the product to the customer in the least amount of time.

➤ Technology helps prevent midcourse corrections in product design, which usually result in higher costs and longer time to commercialize.

From a tactical viewpoint, current technology aids businesses in the commercialization of their products and services in numerous ways:

➤ E-mail enables firms to communicate rapidly and easily with customers, strategic partners, suppliers, distributors, and others around the globe. This lowers the costs of travel and speeds up response time.

➤ Teleconferencing allows enterprises to hold international strategic meetings without getting on an airplane.

➤ Networked databases provide organizations with on-line access to research and development information existing around the globe.

➤ Modems and laptop computers let employees work from virtually anywhere in the world, increasing efficiency and bringing the organization closer to the customer.

➤ Voice mail lets organizations record telephone messages when no one is available to receive them.

➤ Satellite systems, which a firm can lease from a provider, allow organizations to receive broadcast messages from chain manufacturers that help move the product.

➤ Laser color printers let enterprises quickly produce signs, banners, cards, price tags, and so on, that look as good as those printed by a professional.

➤ Some industries have CD-ROM services that businesses can tie into on a regular basis to receive updated information of things such as equipment and supplies. This also makes it easier for a firm to quickly locate customer items that it normally does not carry in stock.

➤ The World Wide Web as a commercial tool is enabling smaller businesses to be on the same playing field as larger businesses.

➤ On-line databases have put information at the hands of anyone who chooses to access them.

One must bear in mind that **technology is a tool used by strategists to improve business** activities. It is not intended to replace personal contact with the customer, nor is it intended to replace a manager's unique ability to take vast amounts of information and make sense of it in terms of strategy for the organization. It does make it easier for the manager to integrate all activities of the firm, to automate routine tasks, and generally free up more time to focus on the firm's strategy.

Business Opportunities Being Seized Via the Internet

➤ Buy wine on-line? One of the first and most successful enterprises in this market is Virtual Vineyards. The five-year-old company is positioning itself for a growth spurt owing to a fresh infusion of venture capital funding secured in June 1999. Peter Granoff and Robert Olson founded the company in 1994 and opened its Web site (VirtualVineyard.com) the following January. Today the firm operates in 40 U.S. states and internationally.[56]

➤ Sea-Land Service, a Charlotte, N.C.-based global ocean transportation provider and a subsidiary of CSX Corporation, has enhanced its logistics capapbilities by using Web-based technology to manage customer information throughout the supply chain and throughout the customer service process. In conjunction with RockPort Trade Systems, a software vendor that specializes in supply chain management on a global scale, Sea-Land and CSX Corporation developed a comprehensive global supply chain management systems for Buyers and Shippers Enterprises, the logistics arm of their business. The custom-designed system is used to track goods from the time they are ordered all the way through to delivery at retail sites.[57]

➤ Deere & Company, the parent company for John Deere equipment and a host of related manufacturing and financial services companies with headquarters in Moline, Illinois, has operations in 160 countries. The corporation is making a strong push to expand its overseas business activities. Like other global companies, Deere faces the challenges of global information storage requiring support for various languages and databases, uneven network services and technology implementations from one country to another, and a corporate culture of diverse and generally autonomous business units. Deere manages to balance the conflicting demands of central data control and business autonomy by employing a single worldwide database created from individual databases maintained by local business units. The corporation's DataJoiner project, implemented with IBM technologies, links these worldwide databases into a logical warehouse, allowing business units to access information throughout the Deere corporate network and across companies as easily and seamlessly as they access data on a local server. Deere is moving toward a completely borderless environment in terms of data access.[58]

➤ The number of Internet users in Latin American will grow from 4.8 million in 1998 to 7.5 million in 1999 and 19 million by 2003, according to U.S.-based International Data Corporation. Latin American Internet users average 8.2 hours of on-line time per week, compared to 7.1 hours in the U.S. E-commerce sales are expected to soar from $167 million in 1998 to $8 billion within five years. In August 1999, Microsoft Corporation paid $126 million for an 11.5 percent stake in Globo Cabo, Brazil's largest cable-TV operator. The two plan to introduce cable-modem Internet access and a joint portal in the coming months. A few weeks earlier, AT&T shelled out $300 million for Brazil's Netstream, which provides high-speed Internet hookups to business. And a $200 million joint venture between AOL and Venezuela's Cisneros Group was expected to launch an on-line service in Brazil by the end of 1999 and in Mexico and Argentina in 2000.[59]

Internet Shortcomings

Today most electronic commerce transactions are done via dedicated lines and value-added networks. The Internet supports open access, involves more than 30 million users worldwide, and is, as the above examples demonstrate, experiencing an enormous growth rate. And it does generate many opportunities for international businesses. However, the Internet in its current state also has some shortcomings, including insecure transactions, though secure protocols are being considered; protocols that provide minimal or nonexistent guarantees of service; no mechanisms for protecting intellectual property; and no support for interoperation or data interchange standards.[60]

SUMMARY

This chapter has proposed that domestic business enterprises internationalize their operations in response to opportunities and threats generated by changes that have taken place in foreign markets. They develop international strategies to seize the opportunities or to combat the threats.

To develop effective international strategies, managers must be totally familiar with the firm's external environment as well as with its internal resources and capabilities. If a firm does not possess the ability to manage international operations, it may have to form a partnership with a firm that does. The chapter has also described four types of international strategies: ethnocentric, multidomestic, global, and transnational, and it has presented the advantages and disadvantages of the multidomestic and the global strategies. It has concluded that the international enterprise must establish strategic and tactical objectives in at least eight areas of organizational performance: market standing, innovations, productivity, physical and financial resources, profitability, manager performance and responsibility, worker performance and attitude, and social responsibility. The chapter has also discussed how the Internet is affecting global commerce.

Key Terms and Concepts

1. Internationalization of operations
2. Opportunites and threats
3. Capable workforce in foreign country
4. Cheaper labor and/or materials
5. Appearance of new markets
6. Globalization of financial systems; financial options
7. Declining demand in home market
8. Acquisition of managerial know-how and capital
9. External and internal audit
10. Foreign sources of finance
11. Personnel competencies
12. Lead from strength
13. Joint venture; strategic alliance
14. International strategies: ethnocentric, multidomestic, global, and transnational strategy
15. International strategic and tactical objectives
16. Production technology superiority
17. Classification of technology
18. Reverse engineering
19. Older and advanced technology
20. A global outlook
21. Shortage of trained personnel in foreign country
22. Corporate social responsibility
23. The Internet as a tool for improving global business

Discussion Questions and Exercises

1. Why do domestic enterprises internationalize their business operations?
2. You are an international management consultant hired by a firm that sells computers only in the U.S. market. The firm's growth rate has been steadily declining over the past few years. The firm's management is seeking a solution to the problem. What will you advise the management to do? Why? Where?
3. How are greater profits realized in the global market?
4. Discuss the "globalization of financial systems" opportunity.
5. You are an international management consultant hired by a firm that manufactures and sells textiles in the U.S. Competition from Hong Kong is rapidly taking away the firm's market share. The firm's management is seeking a solution. What will

you advise the management to do? Why? Where?

6. List some of the U.S. insurance companies that have internationalized their operations. Why did they do so?

7. You are an international management consultant hired by a domestic firm that has decided to internationalize its operations. An internal audit reveals that the firm has strong production capabilities but lacks personnel with international management capabilities. What will you advise the management to do?

8. Discuss some of the major ideas contained in Practical Perspectives 4-1 to 4-10.

9. Discuss the four types of international strategy.

10. What are the advantages and disadvantages of multidomestic strategy and global strategy? What is the major difficulty in applying the transnational stratedgy?

11. Differentiate between international strategic and tactical objectives.

12. Briefly describe the areas in which international objectives should be established.

13. Describe the classification of technology.

14. You are an international management consultant hired by the government of a less-developed country wishing to begin industrializing. The country is relatively poor economically and has an abundance of untrained labor. The government needs your advice on establishing policy relating to technology imports. What advice will you give to the government?

15. Discuss the major concern of international corporations that transfer technology to a foreign country.

16. Discuss how, from a strategic viewpoint, current technology affects international strategy.

17. Discuss how, from a tactical viewpoint, current technology affects international strategy.

Assignment

Scan business periodicals. Select an article describing a company's international strategy. (The Practical Perspectives should help you in this respect.) Provide a brief summary of the major themes contained in the article for class discussion.

CASE 4-1

Levi's International Strategies

As the U.S. denim jeans market continues to shrink, foreign sales are driving Levi's growth. In the nine months ended in August [1990], about 39 percent of the company's total revenues and 60 percent of its pretax profit before interest and corporate expenses came from abroad.... Ironically, it wasn't that long ago that Levi's stumbled around overseas like a clumsy American tourist. Back in 1984 and 1985, its international operations were losing money. A strong dollar clobbered foreign sales, and the designer-jeans craze made Levi's basic five-pocket model look rather déclassé.... By the mid-1980s, Chief Executive Robert D. Haas recognized that Levi's was squandering its brand identity in jeans. So, he dumped the fashion businesses and focused anew on blue jeans, at home and abroad.

Then, in 1985, the great-great-grand-nephew of company founder Levi Strauss, a Bavarian immigrant who sold canvas pants to California gold seekers, took Levi's private in a leveraged buyout. The restructuring paid off: Operating income hit $589 million in fiscal 1989, up 50 percent since 1986. Sales rose 31 percent, to $3.63 billion.... Since then, Levi's foreign ads have played up the company's American roots. An Indonesian television commercial shows Levi's-clad teenagers cruising around Dubuque, Iowa, in 1960s convertibles. In Japan James Dean serves as the centerpiece in virtually all Levi's advertising. And in most foreign ads for Levi's 501 buttonfly jeans, the dialogue usually is in English. Says John G. Johnson, president of VF International: "The positioning of the 501 has really set them apart." In more ways than one. Overseas, Levi's has cultivated a top-drawer image that would surprise most Americans, and the company is pricing accordingly. A pair of 501 jeans sells for $30 in the U.S. but fetches up to $63 in Tokyo and $88 in Paris.

To protect that tony image, Levi's eschews mass merchants and discounters abroad. Levi's snob appeal has meant lush profit margins. The company's international operation has the highest profit per unit of the company's seven operating divisions. Levi's garners gross margins of 45 percent on 501s sold outside the U.S., compared with less than 30 percent domestically, figures Bernard Duflos, chairman of the North American unit of London-based Pepe Clothing Inc., a jeans marketer.... To provide merchandise for its foreign subsidiaries, Levi's stitched together a global manufacturing network. With a mix of its own 11 sewing plants and contract manufacturers, Levi's can supply foreign customers from nearby factories. And by shortening shipping times, Levi's can react speedily to fads in denim shading.... Technology is also helping

Levi's stay on top of global fashion trends. Through its Levi-Link system, retailers can transfer sales and inventory data from barcoded clothing direct to Levi's computers....

Levi's innovative approach overseas has allowed it to penetrate one of the world's toughest markets—Japan. The company set up its Japanese subsidiary in 1971. "That was a very important strategic decision—not to go the joint-venture or licensing route," says David E. Schmidt, a Canadian who runs Levi Strauss Japan, where only 4 out of 400 workers today are non-Japanese. "We brought over our own people and hired and trained Japanese."... Today, Levi's holds the No. 2 position in Japan behind domestic rival Edwin Co., up from No. 5 four years ago. Earnings for fiscal 1990 were expected to jump 38 percent, to $23.2 million, on $224 million in sales, a 30 percent gain. To gain a stronger local identity and raise cash, Levi's sold 15 percent of its Japanese subsidiary to the public in 1989....

In Brazil, Levi's prospers by letting local managers call the shots on distribution. For instance, Levi's penetrated the huge, fragmented Brazilian market by launching a chain of 400 Levi's Only stores, some of them in tiny, rural towns. The stores now pull in 65 percent of Levi's $100 million-a-year Brazilian women sales.... Levi's also is sensitive to local tastes in Brazil, where it developed the Feminina line of jeans exclusively for women there. Brazilian women traditionally favor ultra tight jeans, and the curvaceous cut provides a better fit. What Levi's learns in one market can often be translated into another. Take the Dockers line of chino pants and casual wear. The name originated in Levi's Argentinean unit and was applied to a loosely cut pair of pants designed by Levi's Japanese subsidiary. The company's U.S. operations adopted both in 1986, and the line now generates $550 million a year in North American revenues.

Questions

1. Is Levi's seizing opportunities, or combatting threats, or both? Explain your answer.

2. Did Levi's "lead from strength"? Explain.

3. Is Levi's strategy ethnocentric, multidomestic, global, or transnational, or a combination? Explain your answer.

4. Relative to "market standing," "innovation," "productivity," and "profitability," discuss Levi's' tactical objectives.

Source: Excerpted from M. Shao, R. Neff, and J. Ryser, "For Levi's, a Flattering Fit Overseas," *Business Week* (November 5, 1990): 76–77. Copyright © 1990, McGraw-Hill. All rights reserved. Used with permission.

CASE 4-2

This E-biz Early Bird Didn't Get the Worm

Lots of companies claim to be pioneers in e-business, but few can match the bona fides of Open Market, Inc. Founded in May 1994—one month before Netscape Communications Corporation—Open Market spotted back in the early days the critical need for software that lets companies offer their wares on the Internet. It attracted an A-list of strategic partners, including AT&T Corporation and Time Warner, Inc. And with the dawn on Internet commerce being widely anticipated, the company's initial public offering in May 1996 was a spectacular hit, placing a market cap of $1.2 billion on a company with only $1.8 million in revenues the previous year.

Now, three years later, Open Market's lead has all but disappeared. Although the company is still the No. 1 seller of consumer e-commerce software, its market share fell to 22 percent in 1998, down from 31 percent the year before, even as competitors such as BroadVision, Inc. and Intershop Communications, Inc. gained ground, according to Dataquest. Four of the company's top managers have defected in the past six months, including Robert Weinberger, vice president for marketing. Worse yet, all of this is happening when the e-commerce software market is finally exploding. It's expected to top $580

million this year [1999] and hit $3.7 billion in 2002. "The market for commerce software is taking off. Open Market isn't," according to analyst Greg P. Vogel at Banc of America Securities.

Easy Errors

What went wrong? The Burlington (Mass.) company's executives made a series of fundamental mistakes—which serve as valuable lessons for other e-biz entrepreneurs. For starters, they chose the wrong market initially, investing $50 million in complex software plumbing best suited to large Web sites. The real hot spot was supplying easy-to-build electronic storefronts. Then they branched out into the lesser market of electronic catalogues instead. And they stumbled when it came to acquisitions. An ill-conceived merger with Folio Corporation saddled Open Market with a money-losing business that stalled its annual revenue growth at around 12 percent. That's a disaster in a business where growth rates of 100 percent are common.

The formidable advantages that Open Market started out with just melted away—in spite of its promising technology and a ready-made market. Its struggles show just how difficult it is to make smart choices in the chaotic e-business environment, where conventional business logic goes out the window. Normally, seeking out the largest customers, acquiring companies to fill in gaps in a production line, and building up a broad portfolio of proprietary technology are considered wise moves. In Open Market's case, they were blunders.

Just now there are glimmers that Open Market may finally be turning itself around. Financial results for the fiscal third quarter, due out on October 18 [1999], were expected to show a 20 percent gain in revenue, to $17 million, while the company's net loss was narrowed to about $1.2 million, compared with $6.6 million a year ago, according to analysts. [Former] CEO Gary B. Eichhorn, who was hired in 1995, promises to deliver a new suite of products before the end of the year [1999] that includes less expensive versions of its software, with simpler tools for setting up electronic storefronts. "They're providing a very robust product," says James. R. Preissler, an analyst at PaineWebber, Inc., who believes the company will eventually recover.

For now, though, Open Market finds itself in a sort of purgatory. In most industries, the rank of various players can change over time. But e-business enforces a harsh discipline: The leading companies tend to get big quickly, and they snap up the lion's share of the market. That leaves precious little room for players who don't execute crisply. "Very few Internet companies occupy the middle, like Open Market," says Shikhar Ghosh, the company's founder and chairman. "The vast majority are either in the high stratosphere of market valuations, or they've died."

Open Market may still be alive—but it's none too healthy. Ghosh and Eichhorn's first mistake was aiming too high. They focused on developing complex systems to help companies such as AT&T and Time Warner build on-line shopping malls. The price, including services: $1 million and up. Meanwhile, competitors

such as BroadVision were building simple products for individual businesses. They focused on creating a satisfying shopping experience. Open Market paid less attention to shoppers—and got left behind.

When Ghosh and Eichhorn finally decided to branch out, they picked the wrong target. Instead of going after the storefront business, they added an electronic product catalog to their lineup. And they acquired a company to do it—Folio in Provo, Utah. Open Market's strategy was to increase sales quickly by introducing its e-commerce software to Folio's customers. But they weren't interested. Worse, integrating Folio's operations proved hugely distracting. "What we lost in focus, we didn't gain back in business," admits Eichhorn.

Inflexible

At the same time, Open Market was wasting precious cash by investing needlessly in technologies that weren't absolutely vital. When it started, it had to build its own Web application server software—which makes e-commerce Web sites run faster. Later, after Netscape and other companies started specializing in such software, Open Market continued to pour money into the project. Partly it was misdirected pride. "We considered ours to be better than Netscape's," says Ghosh. When he finally realized he was wasting money on something that wasn't strategic, switching over to Netscape's Web server "was very expensive."

Another costly blunder was spreading resources too thin by expanding overseas. After only one year of business, Open Market was offering its software in 25 countries. That played to the strengths of its software, developed from the ground up to have the capacity to handle e-commerce transactions in multiple currencies and different tax regimes. But updating software for all those companies was expensive—and didn't pay off. "There is usually one customer in each country who wants this stuff," says Ghosh. "It's very seductive.""

Now, Open Market is behind—and, what's more, it's having real trouble winning over new customers. In some cases, it because the company isn't flexible enough. Kirk Sanders, CEO of Professional Golf Commerce Inc., which sells golfing gear on the Web to 17,000 pro shops, found Interworld Corporation to be more willing to modify its software to his requirements. "Open Market thought they were the only solution," he says. Other times, Open Market was said to be a technology laggard. Cozone.com, CompUSA Inc.'s on-line computer retail store, chose BroadVision over Open Market. . . Open Market "is on the right track," says R. Stephen Polley, cozone.com's CEO. "But BroadVision is six to eight months ahead. We wanted someone geared to staying ahead, who can work with us to push the envelope."

Eichhorn is pushing hard to catch up with rivals. He believes the company will ultimately regain momentum, thanks to the powerful sales-transaction technology that Ghosh started investing in five years ago. He's betting that it will become vital to thousands of Web sites as they grow up and that the competition won't be able to match Open Market's capabilities. "In two years people might look at us and think it was a brilliant strategy," he says.

Open Market has a second chance—rare for startups that make this many mistakes. Now it has to do much more to deliver on all of its early promise.

Questions

1. Discuss this case in the context of "lead from strength."

2. What are Open Market's strengths and weaknesses?

3. How should Open Market have handled its overseas expansion?

Source: Paul C. Judge, "Where Is It Now: Open Market's Fall," *Business Week* (November 1, 1999): EB76, EQ78. Copyright © 1999, McGraw-Hill. All rights reserved. Used with permission.

Notes

1. Alex Taylor III, "Rough Road Ahead," *Fortune* (March 17, 1997): 114.
2. Part of this discussion draws from S. Rose, "Why the Multinational Is Ebbing," *Fortune* (August 1977): 111–120. Rose uses the labels "aggressive" and "defensive" reasons.
3. M. Schuman and V. Reitman, "A Worldwide Glut Doesn't Sway Samsung from Auto Business," *The Wall Street Journal* (August 25, 1997): A1, A11.
4. A. Bernstein, S. Jackson, and J. Byrne, "Jack Cracks the Whip Again," *Business Week* (December 15, 1997): 34–35.
5. S.K. Yoder, "U.S. Technology Firms Go Global to Offset Weak Domestic Market," *The Wall Street Journal* (November 14, 1989): A1.
6. A.G. Holzinger, "Selling in the New Europe," *Nation's Business* (December 1991): 18.
7. I. Teinowitz, "Kobs Looks to Growth Overseas," *Advertising Age* (February 27, 1989): 70.
8. J.B. Treece et al., "New Worlds to Conquer," *Business Week* (February 28, 1994): 50
9. Taylor, p. 116.
10. Dexter Roberts, "A Hard Sell for Microsoft," *Business Week* (November 1, 1999): 60.
11. The editors of *Fortune* and Joe McGowan, *Fortune Advertiser* (1998): 84.
12. S. K. Yoder, "U.S. Technology Firms Go Global."
13. E.D. Welles, "Being There," *INC* (September 1990): 143.
14. J.R. Emshwiller and F. Rose, "Guess' Ambitious Design for Global Expansion Falters," *The Wall Street Journal*, November 26, 1997, p. B4.
15. M. Halkias, "Frito-Lay to Buy Snack Brands Abroad," *Dallas Morning News*, November 18, 1997, pp. D1, D10.
16. D.C. Shanks, "Strategic Planning for Global Competition," *Journal of Business Strategy 5*, no. 3 (Winter 1985): 80.

17. S.K. Yoder, "U.S. Technology Firms Go Global."
18. Ibid.
19. K.H. Hammonds and J. Friedman, "Who's That Knocking on Foreign Doors? U.S. Insurance Salesmen," *Business Week* (March 6, 1984): 8.
20. "Spain Puffs On," *Economist 305* (December 19, 1987): 47.
21. R.A. Melcher, J. Flynn, and R. Neff, "Anheuser-Busch Says Skoal, Salude, Prosit," *Business Week* (September 20, 1993): 76.
22. M. Bernstein and M. Weinstein, "Globalshakeout: The Changing Landscape of Financial Services," *Prudential Leader 3*, no. 2 (February 1998): 9.
23. Jeffrey E. Garten, "Troubles Ahead in Emerging Markets," *Harvard Business Review* (May–June 1997): 38.
24. R. Brady, M. Maremont, and P. Galuszka, "Aeroflot Takes Off for Joint-Ventureland," *Business Week* (October 30, 1989): 48–49.
25. Seth Lubove, "We Have a Big Pond to Play In," *Forbes* (September 13, 1993): 216.
26. Frank E. Bair, (Ed.) *International Marketing Handbook* 2nd Edition (Detroit: Michigan: Gale Research Company, 1985), p. 1582.
27. B. Dumaine, "The Bureaucracy Busters," *Fortune* (June 17, 1991): 46.
28. J. Dupuy, "Learning to Manage World-Class Strategy," *Management Review* (October 1991): 40.
29. J.G. Wissema and L. Euser, "Successful Innovation Through Inter-Company Networks," *Long-Range Planning 24* (December 1991): 33–39.
30. B. Dumaine, "The Bureaucracy Busters," p. 46.
31. Andrew C. Inkpen, "Learning and Knowledge Acquisition Through International Strategic Alliances," *Academy of Management Executive 12*, no. 4 (1998): 70.
32. Ibid.
33. Thomas Hout, Michael E. Porter, and Eileen Rudden, "How Global Companies Win Out," *Harvard Business Review* (September–October 1982): 103.
34. Fred L. Steingraber, "How to Succeed in the Global Marketplace," *USA Today Magazine* (November 1997): 32.
35. Hout, et al., "How Global Companies Win Out."
36. Ibid.
37. George S. Yip, "Global Strategy...in a World of Nations?" *Sloan Management Review* (Fall 1989): 29.
38. Ibid.
39. Regina Fazio Maruca, "The Right Way to Go Global: An Interview with Whirlpool CEO David Whitwam," *Harvard Business Review* (March–April 1994): 136.
40. Yip, "Global Strategy...in a World of Nations?"
41. Nestle Home Page, February 8, 1998 (http://www.nestle.com).
42. M.A. Hitt, B.W. Keats, and S.M. DeMario, "Navigating in the New Competitive Landscape: Building Strategic Flexibility and Competitive Advantage in the 21st Century," *Academy of Management Executive 12*, no. 4 (November 1998): 23.
43. Peter Drucker, *The Practice of Management* (New York: Harper and Row, 1954).
44. J.R. Basch, Jr. and M.G. Duerr, *International Transfer of Technology: A Worldwide Survey of Executives* (New York: The Conference Board, Inc., 1975), p. 1.
45. S.H. Robock and K. Simmonds, *International Business and Multinational Enterprises* (Homewood, IL: Richard D. Irwin, Inc., 1983), p. 461.
46. Basch and Duerr, *International Transfer of Technology*.
47. Ibid., p. 8.
48. Ibid., pp. 10–11.
49. John Tagliabue, "Fakes Blot a Nation's Good Names," *The New York Times* (July 3, 1997): D1, D2.
50. Masaaki Kotabe, "A Comparative Study of U.S. and Japanese Patent Systems," *Journal of International Business Studies 23*, no. 1 (First Quarter 1992): 148.
51. Ibid., p. 149.
52. Ford S. Worthy, "Japan's Smart Secret Weapon," *Fortune* (August 12, 1991): 72.
53. John R. Engen, "Getting Your Chinese Workforce Up to Speed," *International Business* (August 1994): 48.
54. Toshio Nakahara and Yutaka Isono, "Strategic Planning For Canon: The Crisis and the New Vision," *Long Range Planning 25* (February 1992): 63.
55. Charles K. Kao, *A Choice Fulfilled: The Business of High Technology* (New York: St. Martin's Press, 1991).
56. Ann Saccomano, "Time for Wine Online," *Traffic World 259*, no. 8 (August 23, 1999): 14.
57. Sunny Baker, "Global E-Commerce, Local Problems," *Journal of Business Strategy 20*, no. 4 (July–August 1999): 32–38.
58. Ibid.
59. I. Katz and E. Malkin, "Battle for the Latin American Net," *Business Week* (November 1, 1999): 194–195.
60. N.A. Adam, Baruch Slonim, Jacob Wagner, Peter Yesha, Y. Yesha, "Globalizing Business, Education, Culture through the Internet," *Communications of the ACM 40*, no. 2 (February 1997): 115–121.

5

International Strategy: The Four Ps

SÃO BERNARDO, Brazil – Wal-Mart Stores, Inc. is finding out that what plays in Peoria isn't necessarily a hit in suburban Sao Paulo.

Tanks of live trout are out; sushi is in. American footballs have been replaced by soccer balls. The fixings for feijoadas, a medley of beef and pork in black bean stew, are now displayed on the deli counter. American style jeans priced at $19.99 have been dropped in favor for $9.99 knockoffs.

But adapting to local tastes may have been the easy part. Three years after embarking on a blitz to bring "everyday low prices" to the emerging markets of Brazil and Argentina, Wal-Mart is finding the going tougher than expected.

Brutal competition, market conditions that don't play to Wal-Mart's ability to achieve efficiency through economies of scale, and some of its own mistakes have produced red ink. Moreover, the company's insistence on doing things "the Wal-Mart way" has apparently alienated local suppliers and employees.[1]

Learning Objectives of the Chapter

Because of changes taking place around the globe, to remain competitive and to increase their opportunities, domestic enterprises will need to develop strategies for entering the international business arena. Effective internationalization of business operations relies on managers' ability to develop international product/service, place/entry, price, and promotion strategies in light of the enterprise's external environment (discussed in Chapter 3), as well as in light of the firm's internal situation (discussed in Chapter 4). After studying this chapter you should be able to discuss:

1. International product/service strategy.
2. International place/entry strategy.
3. International pricing strategy.
4. International promotion strategy.

PRODUCT/SERVICE STRATEGY

In developing **product/service strategy,** managers are typically concerned with what the product or service should look like and what it should be able to do. In conducting this assessment for foreign markets, managers must overcome the *self-reference criterion* (SRC). They must determine whether their product or service can be sold in standard form or whether it must be customized to fit differing foreign market needs. They must understand that many products or services do not immediately sell well in foreign markets but that they must undergo a diffusion process.

The Self-Reference Criterion (SRC)

The **self-reference criterion** (SRC) is the unconscious reference to one's own cultural values. This unconscious reference is the root of many international business problems.[2] Huge problems can occur when the SRC leads a manager to assume that a product or service that sells well in the home market will sell well in foreign markets. In many cases it does not because the needs for products and services differ among societies. Managers can eliminate the SRC by first defining the problem in terms of the home society's cultural traits, values, habits, and norms, and then redefining the problem, without value judgments, in terms of the foreign market's cultural traits, values, habits, and norms. The difference represents the cultural influence on the problem. The manager subsequently restates and solves the problem in the context of both cultures.

For example, Americans like moist, creamy cakes for dessert, purchased already baked in grocery stores. However, attempting to market moist, creamy cakes in grocery stores in England may result in failure because the English generally like dry cakes that can be eaten with their fingers while having tea, and when the occasion calls for moist, creamy cakes, they like to bake their own. General Mills ran into this problem when it took Betty Crocker to England many years ago.[3] J.C. Penney made a mistake when it put up a store in the affluent Santiago neighborhood of Las Condes in 1996. It misread Chilean taste, which favors simple clothes, and offered expensive lines in the flashy colors popular in tropical markets such Miami and Mexico.[4] From the start (1985), IKEA's U.S. foray has run into problems—starting with its failure to tailor its European products to U.S. tastes.

IKEA sold European size sheets and curtains that did not fit American beds and windows.[5] Americans have in recent years developed a liking for commodious cupholders in their cars. Mercedes-Benz and BMW, the European car manufacturers, rejected the notion of installing cupholders in their socially prestigious automobiles. Now they are bowing to the American driver's wants; they are installing cupholders.[6] (For another example, read Practical Perspective 5-1, the case of Disney's expansion to France. Notice that Disney's management had to repackage some of the original Disney characters.)

It should be noted that the assessment may sometimes reveal that the firm's product or service, because of cultural or other factors, cannot be customized for a foreign market. For example, in the 1970s, Kentucky Fried Chicken (KFC), the popular U.S.-based fast-food chain, expanded its operations to Brazil. The expansion was a failure. A Brazilian marketing executive believes that KFC failed because Brazilians do not much care to eat chicken outside of their homes.[7] KFC however tried again, this time targeting only specific market groups—for example, Brazilians of Italian descent, who do like to eat chicken at restaurants and at home. Campbell's soups also had little success in Brazil, where most housewives felt a need to do more preparation than merely heat up an already-finished soup.[8] But Campbell's soup, as Practical Perspective 5-2 indicates, seems to have learned.

PRACTICAL PERSPECTIVE 5-1

Disney Goes to France

A few years ago, an amazed Japanese girl asked an American visitor, "Is there really a Disneyland in America?" That should be music to the mouse ears of Euro Disneyland's management, beleaguered by charges that they are defining the Frenchness of France. Ah, to convince the French that Mickey and Donald belong as much to Marne-la-Vallee as they do to Anaheim, Orlando, and Tokyo. Sensitive to the charge that Euro Disneyland amounts to what theater director Ariane Mnouchkine, in a widely quoted assessment, called a "cultural Chernobyl," the company tried for months to persuade Europeans that, in the words of a Disney spokesperson, "It's not America, it's

Disney." On opening day last month [April 1992], Disney's chairman Michael Eisner stressed, like a guest too eager to please, that the company had repackaged original European characters: the French Cinderella, the Italian Pinocchio, the German Snow White. More truculently, a Euro Disneyland spokesperson said: "Who are these Frenchmen, anyway? We offer them the dream of a lifetime and lots of jobs. They treat us like invaders."

Source: Excerpted from Todd Gitlin, "World Leaders: Mickey, et al.," *The New York Times,* Section 2, May 3, 1992, p. 1. Copyright © 1992 by The New York Times Company. Reprinted by permission.

Therefore, international strategists should seek answers to four basic questions:[9]

1. *Who in the foreign market uses the product?* In what way(s) are the targeted foreign buyers similar to or different from domestic buyers? How can this product be incorporated into foreign market's lifestyle?

2. *What are the values of the people in the foreign market?* Is their value based on timeliness, quality, service, or price? What changes in the products/services need to be made to meet the foreign customers' needs?

3. *What are the signals that indicate change in the market?* Does the market accept foreign ideas? Are there cross-cultural trends?

4. *How can the firm increase market share?* Who are the local competitors? Who are the foreign competitors? How much disposable income do consumers have?

PRACTICAL PERSPECTIVE 5-2

Campbell's Soup: Expanding an International Presence

By the year 2000, Campbell's hopes to generate half its revenue from outside the U.S. Gaining global share is not going to be easy, however, as its major competitors, CPC International and H.J. Heinz, are well-entrenched and generate a significant portion of their sales outside the U.S. market.

A key component of Campbell's strategy is to develop products suited to local tastes in various foreign markets. In Poland, where soup consumption is three times higher than in the U.S., they have developed varieties of condensed soup, including chicken noodle and flaki, a peppery tripe soup. For China, Campbell kitchens in the U.S. and Hong Kong have developed an extensive array of exotic soups, including duck gizzards, watercress, and scallop broth, and radish-and-carrot, pork, fig, and date soup. In Mexico, they have developed Crema de Chile Poblano, and in the Argentine market, split pea with ham has proven popular.

Developing varieties that suit local tastes is not the only challenge that Campbell faces. In Argentina there is a strong preference for powered soups and CPC's Korr brand controls 80 percent of the market. Campbell has enjoyed some success by stressing the fresh ingredients in Sopa de Campbell. In Poland, where 98 percent of the soup is homemade, Campbell has targeted working mothers while stressing the convenience of its product. Here again, however, they face competition from CPC, owner of the Polish soup market, Amino. Campbell and others in the food industry have recognized the need to develop new products and brand extensions that are geared to local market tastes.

Source: Excerpted from G.S. Graig and S.P. Douglas, "Developing Strategies for Global Markets: An Evolutionary Perspective," *The Columbia Journal of World Business* (Spring 1996): 73. Reprinted with permission.

Customization versus Standardization

Fundamentally, there are three viable alternatives when entering a foreign market: (1) market the same product or service everywhere (**standardization**), (2) adapt the product or service for foreign markets (**customization**), and (3) develop a totally new product or service. By combining these three alternatives with promotional efforts, five different product strategies can be developed.[10]

1. **Standardize product/standardize message.** Using this strategy, a firm sells the same product and uses the same promotional appeals in all markets. In other words, product and promotional appeals are globally standardized. Coca-Cola, Pepsi-Cola, Avon, McDonald's, Sony Walkman, Levi's, and Maidenform follow this strategy.

2. **Standardize product/customize message.** Enterprises using this approach customize only the promotional message. For example, a bicycle may be sold in the U.S. market as a pleasure vehicle. In an economically poor country, however, the promotional message may have to be customized to stress economy; that is, the bicycle would be promoted as a means of relatively inexpensive basic transportation.

3. **Customize product/standardize message.** Using this strategy, the company customizes the product to meet the needs of the specific foreign market, but promotes the same use as it does in the domestic market. For example, electric sewing machines manufactured for the U.S. market would not sell well in a market where few residents have access to electricity. The manufacturer could, however, customize the machine to sell in that market by producing hand- or foot-cranked sewing machines. The hand- or foot-cranked machine would be promoted in the foreign market in the same way it is in the U.S. market—to sew clothes.

4. **Customize product/customize message.** Manufacturers applying this strategy customize the product to meet different use patterns in the foreign market and customize the promotional message attached to it as well. For example, bicycles in the U.S. are usually lightweight and are generally promoted for use in leisure activities. In many less-developed countries, however, because of rough roads, the need may be for a stronger bicycle, and the bicycle is often used as a major form of transportation. China is one example of a country where bicycles are heavyweight and are used as a major means of transportation.

5. **Different product.** Using this approach, rather than adapting an existing product, the manufacturer invests in the development of a totally new one to fit the needs of specific foreign markets. For example, Coca-Cola's and Pepsi's diet sodas do not sell well in Asia and Europe because consumers there prefer the creamy sweetness of regular Coke or Pepsi and consider sugar-free sodas as drinks of diabetics and the obese, not of the young and vital. To deal with this

problem, Pepsi designed a new diet cola, called Pepsi Max, specifically for these and other markets. Pepsi Max uses a sweetener that makes it close to the regular colas in taste.[11]

American marketing professor Theodore Levitt contends that in an era of global competition, the product strategy of successful firms is evolving from offering customized products (a multidomestic strategy) to offering globally standardized ones (a global strategy). Such a product strategy requires the development of universal products or products that require no more than a cosmetic change for adaptation to different local needs and use conditions.[12] As was pointed out in Practical Perspective 4-9, Japanese automobile manufacturer Honda has a strategy to build a global car. The strategy entails using a new standardized manufacturing system with flexibility to build cars customized to fit specific market needs. Using this new

---

PRACTICAL PERSPECTIVE 5-3

Script Locally

Sony last year [1998]became the first global company to go into foreign-language film production when Columbia TriStar set up shop in Germany at Babelsberg, the long-dormant Potsdam studio where Fritz Lang shot *Metropolis*. Sony execs figure English-language pictures still command nearly 80 percent of the world's box office—but for how long? "When you've got that kind of market share," worries Columbia TriStar film chief Ken Lemberger, "you can only go down."

In television, that's happening already: For two years running, the big news at Mipcom, the global television sales fest at Cannes, has been American series being pushed out of prime time by the local stuff. Network hits like *ER* are still big, but the fledgling satellite and cable companies that bought American shows wholesale a few years ago, outfits like Canal Plus in France, are now billion-dollar enterprises with the resources to fill their evenings with local programming. "As the European marketplace continues to mature, you won't find a lot of American series in prime time, "says Andy Kaplan of Columbia TriStar Television.

This is bad news for Hollywood studios, which have been relying on international sales to make up the difference between the $1.5 million or so that it costs to produce an hour-long drama episode and the $1 million a U.S. network will typically pay for it. But in the emerging markets of Asia and Latin America, where the big media conglomerates own channels instead of just selling to them, they have even more at stake. Sony Entertainment Television in India, Time Warner's HBO Olé and HBO Brasil partnerships in Latin America, News Corporation's Star TV in Asia—these companies have sunk billions into pipelines for delivering entertainment, partly to exploit the millions of hours of American movies and television shows they own. Blockbuster Hollywood movies are still a huge draw worldwide, but most audiences prefer local TV shows—and if that's what they want, that's what they'll get.

Source: Excerpted from Frank Rose, "Think Globally, Script Locally," *Fortune* (November 8, 1999): 157–158.

manufacturing system, the costs of customization are far lower than when using the older systems. U.S.'s Ford Motor Company and General Motors have a similar strategy.[13] Strategies 1 and 2 discussed above fit this mode (the global strategy). Strategy 5, however, can fit both the global and the multidomestic strategy modes. For example, Hollywood can make a film which, with some minor customization, such as dubbing in the local language, can be distributed globally, or it can make a film specifically for one market. (Refer to Practical Perspective 5-3.) Practical Perspective 5-4 presents Microsoft's strategy to develop a product for the Chinese market.

As was discussed in Chapter 4, both the multidomestic and the global strategy approaches have advantages and disadvantages. The global strategy may be appropriate for some products and services and for some nations, but not for many other products and services and nations. For example, Japan is a difficult market for many foreign companies—especially American companies—to penetrate because of **cultural barriers.** To penetrate Japan's market, most products and services require customization. For instance, when Kentucky Fried Chicken entered the Japanese market, it had to make adaptations to local taste buds, including taking the mashed potatoes and gravy off the menu and substituting french fries, and halving the sugar in the slaw recipe.[14] Furthermore, some products and services have global appeal

PRACTICAL PERSPECTIVE 5-4

A Hard Sell For Microsoft

Meet Wu Yanbin, a 21 year-old college student checking out the new computers at the Xidan Department Store in western Beijing. He's a devoted techie who surfs the Internet every day. So ask him what he thinks about Microsoft Corporation's key China strategy: promoting set-top boxes with its WinCE software that allows anyone with a TV Set to go on-line. "Microsoft is a giant. I really admire it," he says. But would he buy one of their set-top boxes? No way. Says Wu: "Their functions are too limited for me."

Both blessing and curse—that refrains seems to run through Microsoft's attempts to do business in China. After months of setbacks, Microsoft says that its new technology, known as the Venus project, will be rolled out at the end of October. The box, with TV-customized software, lets users read e-mail, surf the Internet, and do simple word processing while sitting in front of the tube with a remote keyboard.

The plan certainly has potential: More than 300 million households in China own a television. And Chinese so far own just 2 million PCs. So Microsoft wants to "stake a claim in the living room," says Sean Zhang, managing director of the Microsoft (China) Research & Development Center and initiator of the project. Analysts say the set-top-box market could be worth several hundred million dollars.

Source: Excerpted from Dexter Roberts, "A Hard Sell For Microsoft," *Business Week* (November 1, 1999): 60. Reprinted with permission.

only by age groups. For example, teenagers are the most global market of all age groups. Teenagers almost everywhere purchase a common gallery of products: Reebok sports shoes, Procter & Gamble Cover Girl makeup, Sega and Nintendo video games, Nikes, Macintosh computers, and Red Hot Chili Peppers music tapes and CDs.[15] And Gucci, a luxury goods enterprise that targets affluent customers throughout the world, believes that similar demographics and income levels promote similar attitudes and behavioral patterns worldwide. Thus, in 1990, when it relaunched the Gucci name with print campaign, its "from the hand of Gucci" message was the same in the United States, the United Kingdom, Japan, France, and Italy. [16]

Subhash C. Jain, a professor of international marketing at the University of Connecticut, reviewed published sources to develop a framework for determining the extent of standardization feasible in a particular case. The determining factors in Professor Jain's framework are depicted in Figure 5-1.[17]

Service Strategy

As indicated above, a dilemma in global strategy for manufacturing businesses is the need to balance standardization with local customization. In contrast, in service delivery, in many cases, standardization and customization is equally feasible. There are three broad service categories: people-processing, possession-processing, and information-based services.[18]

People-Processing Services. In these services, customers become part of the production process. Such services include passenger transportation, health care, food services, and lodging services. The customer is present during the service. For example, Disney provides entertainment services in theme parks in Paris, France, and in Tokyo, Japan. (Of course, Disney also provides these services for foreign customers in California and Florida.) London hospitals maintain a lucrative business caring for wealthy Middle Eastern patients, as do Miami, Florida, hospitals caring for patients from Latin America.

Possession-Processing Services. Services of this nature involve tangible actions to tangible objects to enhance their value to customers. The customer need not be present. These services include transporting freight, installing equipment, and maintenance. For example, an American living near the Canadian border could go into Canada to have his or her car serviced because of lower costs resulting from favorable exchanges rates. For instance, if it costs $300 in both countries to have a car tuned-up, and the exchange rate is U.S. $1 equals Canadian $1.50, the American who goes into Canada for the service would save U.S. $100, less the expense of driving across the border. An international corporation might provide such services as bridge repair services or elevator repair services throughout the world.

FIGURE 5-1	Factors That Help Determine Standardization or Customization

➤ In general, standardization is more practical in markets that are economically alike.

➤ Standardization strategy is more effective if worldwide customers, not countries, are the basis of identifying the segment(s) to serve.

➤ The greater the similarity in the markets in terms of customer behavior and lifestyle, the higher the degree of standardization.

➤ The higher the cultural compatibility of the product across the host countries, the greater the degree of standardization.

➤ The greater the degree of similarity in a firm's competitive position in different markets, the higher the degree of standardization.

➤ Competing against the same adversaries, with similar share positions, in different countries leads to greater standardization than competing against purely local companies.

➤ Industrial and high-technology products are more suitable for standardization than consumer products.

➤ Standardization is more appropriate when the home market positioning strategy is meaningful in the host market.

➤ The greater the difference in physical, political, and legal environments between home and host countries, the lower the degree of standardization.

➤ The more similar the marketing infrastructure in the home and host countries, the higher the degree of standardization.

➤ Companies in which key managers share a world view, as well as a common view of the critical tasks flowing from the strategy, are more effective in implementing a standardization strategy.

➤ The greater the strategic consensus among parent-subsidiary managers on key standardization issues, the more effective the implementation of standardization strategy.

➤ The greater the centralization of authority for setting policies and allocating resources, the more effective the implementation of standardization strategy.

Source: Adapted from Subhash C. Jain, "Standardization of International Marketing Strategy: Some Research Hypotheses," *Journal of Marketing 53* (January 1989): 70–79. Used with permission from publisher. Copyright © 1989 American Marketing Association, Chicago, IL. All rights reserved.

Information-Based Services. The provision of these services involves collecting, manipulating, interpreting, and transmitting data to create value. Examples include such services as accounting, banking, consulting, education, insurance, legal services, and news. For instance, CNN provides news service in most countries. Prudential provides insurance services in many countries. Citicorp provides banking services in many parts of the world. Many American colleges and universities service a multitude of students from foreign countries around the globe in the U.S., and a number of them (American University in Cairo, Egypt, for example) have established satellites in foreign countries to service students abroad. Many American students are now pursuing college degrees in Canadian universities because the cost of tuition there is much lower than at home.[19]

Information Technology and Service Strategy

For all three types of services described above, use of current information technology, such as the Internet, may enable businesses to benefit from favorable labor costs or exchange rates by consolidating operations of supplementary services (such as reservations) or certain office functions (such as accounting) in just one or a few countries. Practical Perspective 5-5 describes a company in India that provides software services from home to businesses in other countries. Note that the costs of the software is about two-thirds cheaper in India than in the United States.

Diffusing Innovations

Not all products and services introduced in a foreign market will be immediately accepted by the prospective customers. Many products and services that are new to a market must go through the **diffusion process**. Basically, diffusion is "the process by which innovation is communicated through certain channels over time among members of a social system."[20] This means that the product or service is adopted by more and more members of the society gradually, over time. For example, in September 1998, Starbucks Coffee signed an agreement to open franchise outlets in Beijing, China. The

---

PRACTICAL PERSPECTIVE 5-5

Programmers From Abroad

The nation has a shortage of techies, as last week's government plan to help train more programmers made clear. But corporate America has already hit on a response. It's global telecommuting, through which this nation's technology companies have created a whole new realm of international trade by exporting their work and hiring programmers overseas to do it.

Having already scooped up any American programmers they could by offering them the chance to ride the Internet to work from their homes in Jackson Hole, Wyoming, or Boulder, Colorado, the corporations are now reaching out to places like South Africa and the Philippines.

So increasingly, the world's commerce involves not just tankers filled with Brent crude or container ships laden with VCRs but cables buzzing with computer programming code, product designs, and engineering, diagrams and formulas, not to mention overhauls of American software gone too soft. If computer systems squeak into the year 2000 without acting like they're back in 1900, foreign programmers will deserve much of the thanks.

Some companies bring the workers to work, searching the world for computer specialists willing to come to the United States. But virtual immigration, where the workers stay put, has become far more common, and remains much cheaper. The Software unit of a single company, Tata Sons Ltd. Of India, has 5,000 developers, a maquiladora of the mind that can immediately deploy 100 techies on a U.S. corporation's mission. India's software exports have grown from $225 million in 1992 to $1.15 billion in 1996, with a year 2000 goal of $3.6 billion.

On the Cheap

Technical advances have made this kind of rapid growth possible. Although banks, among other global institutions, have been electronically advantaged for years, the expense has fallen dramatically. Instead of high-capacity leased lines that can cost hundreds or thousands of dollars a month, a plain old phone connection and an Internet service provider will often do.

"It's no longer an international phone call. Now, it's an Internet file exchange," said Ester Dyson, author of "Release 2.0: A Design for Living in the Digital Age." A cyberdiplomat known for striving to make Eastern Europe at least as wired as its Western neighbors, Dyson also served on the board of the PRT Group in Barbados, a software and computer systems design firm, and Softstep, a company doing Year 2000 fixes from Kyrgyzstan in Central Asia.

While some global telecommunicaters, like many Americans, work at home, most are clustered in the foreign quarters of U.S. companies or in the offices of foreign contractors

like Tata. Projects can receive round-the-clock attention as they are handed from continent to continent. IBM teams in Europe, India, and the West Coast have kept the development of Java software for the Internet going at all hours, with handoffs over the Internet itself.

Even as the giants like Tata prospers, the Internet is also allowing pipsqueaks to be heard and seen, offering electronic sales pitches and work samples. Corporations like IBM find themselves hiring tiny foreign firms that could never have found their way through these companies' front doors.

Those specialists who do migrate to the United States have an advantage in spotting talent back home. Under Sanjiv Sidhu, a native of Hyderabad, India, and Sandy Tungare, an executive from Bombay, 12 Technologies of Dallas runs software development centers in Bombay and Bangalore, where the neighbors include Motorola, Intel, and Hewlett-Packard. Software developers who would earn at least $50,000 in the United States can be had for about a third as much in India, Tungare says.

Source: Excerpted from Allen R. Myerson, "Need Programmers? Surf Abroad," *The New York Times,* January 18, 1998, p. WK4. Copyright © 1998 by The New York Times Company. Reprinted by permission.

challenge Starbucks faces is to persuade a tea-drinking culture to switch to java.[21] (For another example, read Practical Perspective 5-6, which discusses how Budweiser diffused its brand name in China.) Many companies introducing a new product or service often incur losses in the beginning years because the company does not yet have the number of buyers required to cover the fixed costs of investment. In later years, however, after the product or service has been diffused, the enterprise should be able to earn enough money to recapture the early years' losses.

How Quickly Can a New Product/Service Be Diffused in a Culture?

The way people respond to a new product affects how quickly it is diffused. All new products and services can be categorized as to their varied degrees of newness, and the consumer reactions to each category affect the **quickness** or **slowness** of diffusion. Generally, the more disruptive the innovation

PRACTICAL PERSPECTIVE 5-6

Budweiser's China Challenge

When we arrived in 1995, virtually no one knew the name "Budweiser," says [Jack] Purnell [CEO, Anheuser-Busch International]. "So we focused immediately on simply building awareness. The first year we put most of our efforts into electronic media. We discovered the 'Ants' commercial created for use in the United States played very well in China, so we ran that, as well as specially created sequel showing the ants' party underground. We also developed another spot for China."

Although China is considered a developing country, the vast majority of Chinese households have access to TV sets, which means that the majority of people can be reached through mass electronic media.

The TV ads were supplemented with highly visible sponsorships, such as the World Cup. China National Basketball League, and the China Central TV World Sports Report, as well as with point-of-sale items and promotions at accounts.

The all-out effort worked. In Budweiser's first year on the market, awareness rose from zero to nearly 30 percent in the 22 key cities where the brand was sold.

Through all of theses challenges, product quality remained top of mind. After all, that is the single greatest competitive advantage that Anheuser-Busch offers. And it was never compromised.

After two years of operations in China, Budweiser's success speaks for itself. The brand will approach the million-barrel mark this year [1997], and the overall operations is on a strong path to begin to show a profit in the year 2000.

Purnell attributes this success to four things: "First, Budweiser has a appealing taste that is refreshingly different and consistent the world over. Second, the brand has a appealing image with American ties. As the best-selling beer in the world, it's an icon brand. That means a lot to Chinese consumers and elevates the brand's status. Third, we have an innovative and effective distribution system that allows us to gain effective placements in key accounts. And finally, we have a very enthusiastic and talented team of Chinese employees who have joined the Anheuser-Busch family. We are very proud of what they have accomplished in such a short period of time."

That winning formula has resulted in a 20 percent backlog on orders, which in turns has promised Anheuser-Busch to accelerate its brewery expansion schedule. The Wuhan brewery is currently being doubled in size. When completed in 1998, it will have a capacity of 2.1 million barrels, and Anheuser-Busch's investment in China will exceed $150 million.

"Our short-term goal is to double Budweiser sales to 2 million barrels in the next four years," says Purnell. "This will make Budweiser the fastest-growing premium beer and will result over the longer term in Budweiser becoming the No. 1 premium brand in China. We have a leadership position in 9 of the 27 markets we're in, and we're focusing on increasing that ratio. There are 70 more cities with a population of at least 1 million, so we'll expand our distribution area as we grow.

Source: Excerpted from "The China Challenge," *Anheuser-Busch Horizons* (Third Quarter 1997): 6. Reprinted with permission.

is, the longer the diffusion process will take. Innovations can be categorized as congruent, continuous, dynamically continuous, and discontinuous.[22]

Congruent Innovations. Congruent innovations do not disrupt established consumption patterns. Congruent innovation means introducing variety and quality or functional features, style, or perhaps a duplicate of an existing product. Introducing vegetable oil as a substitute for olive oil is an example of congruent innovation.

Continuous Innovations. Continuous innovation involves altering a product to enhance the satisfaction derived from its use. Menthol cigarettes, new model automobiles, and fluoride toothpaste are examples of continuous innovations. Continuous innovations have little disruptive influence on the culture's established consumption patterns.

Dynamically Continuous Innovations. Dynamically continuous innovation usually involves creating a new product or substantially altering an existing one to fulfill new needs created by changes in lifestyles or new expectations. Examples are frozen dinners, electric toothbrushes, and electric lawn mowers. These innovations are normally disruptive and therefore are resisted because the old patterns of consumption must be changed. Consumer behavior must be transformed if users are to recognize and accept the value of dynamically continuous innovations.

Discontinuous Innovations. Discontinuous innovation introduces an entirely new idea or behavior pattern. It means establishing fresh and untried consumption patterns. This would be the most disruptive innovation. An example is the introduction of a banking system into a traditional society where people tend to keep their money hidden at home or somewhere else.

Dualistic Technological Structures

Diffusion of new products or services is also affected by the technological structure of the country. A **dualistic technological structure** exists in the economies of most developing countries.[23] It refers to the simultaneous existence of a modern industrial sector and a traditional sector involved in agrarian and craft production. The modern sector involves large-scale, capital-intensive industries utilizing modern technologies and technically skilled labor to manufacture basic industrial goods such as energy, construction materials, and electrical and mechanical equipment. The traditional sector of many less developed economies is characterized by small-scale, labor-intensive industries using simple technologies with low capital investment and unskilled labor to produce agricultural and consumer products for domestic markets. For example, China is currently modernizing its industrial sector at a much faster rate than it is modernizing its agricultural sector. A reason for this might be that if modernization of the industrial sector is not substantially ahead of the modernization of the agricultural sector, the former may not be ready to employ those workers who became unemployed due to the modernization of the latter.

Managers should thus be aware that a developing nation may need advanced technologies in one sector and older technologies in another. They should also be aware that a developing nation may need both adaptive technological innovations and transformative technological innovations.[24] **Adaptive transformative innovations** are important to the modern industrial sector. They aim at modifying and adjusting modern technologies to the needs of domestic markets. An example of an adaptive technological innovation would be the introduction of a more modern tractor into an area where tractors are already in use. **Transformative technological innovations** are important to the traditional sector economically, socially, and culturally. An example of a transformative technological innovation would be the introduction of washing machines into a region where laundry is being done manually or the introduction of farming tractors into a region where horses and plows are being used.

PLACE/ENTRY STRATEGY

Managers of business enterprises must determine how their products or services will reach the consumer—the **place/entry strategy**. Distribution methods generally require variations from country to country as well as within each country. Generally, the methods are shaped by the size of the market, by the scope and quality of the competition, by the available distribution channels, and by the firm's resources. (For an illustration, read Practical Perspective 5-7, the case of Fusion Systems Corporation.) Distribution methods are also shaped by the laws of the country (the laws of some countries require foreign companies to use local distribution systems) and by the firm's entry strategy.

Basically, manufacturing enterprises can enter a foreign country by:

1. Manufacturing the product at home and exporting it to the foreign country for distribution in the local market.

2. Manufacturing parts at home and exporting them to the foreign country for assembly, for distribution in the local market, and/or for export to other markets (including back to the home market).

3. Manufacturing the product in the foreign country for distribution in the local market and/or for export to other markets (including back to the home market).

With respect to service enterprises,

1. Some, such as consulting companies, can provide the services from their home country or they can set up subsidiaries in the foreign country.

2. Others, such as insurance and banking companies, generally must establish subsidiaries in the foreign country.

The above suggests that firms enter a foreign market either by **exporting to it or setting up manufacturing facilities in it**. The ensuing sections describe various strategies enterprises use in exporting and manufacturing in foreign markets.

Exporting Strategy

When a firm decides to export, it must choose between indirect and direct exporting. **Indirect exporting** involves using experienced middlemen to handle export functions and **direct exporting** involves assigning the export functions to employees of the company. In general, when a firm lacks personnel with exporting expertise, it usually prefers to start out using the indirect method, and after the enterprise has developed personnel with exporting expertise, and if it is more efficient, it develops its own export division.

Indirect Exporting

There are two basic types of middlemen: **agent middlemen** and **merchant middlemen**. The agent represents the principal directly and the merchant takes title to the goods. Agent middlemen include the export management company (EMC), the manufacturer's export agent (MEA), the broker, and

---

PRACTICAL PERSPECTIVE 5-7

Fusion Systems Uses Local Distributor to Enter the Japanese Market

Fusion Systems Corporation, a Rockville, Maryland, company, makes sophisticated industrial equipment used to produce numerous goods, including optical fibers, automobile parts, graphic arts printing plates, and semiconductor chips.... Fusion has been in the Japanese market since 1975, four years after its founding by its president, Donald M. Shapiro, and four colleagues.... Because of its small size when it entered the Japanese market, Fusion lacked the resources to hire its own sales force there. It had to rely on a Japanese distributor.

"We knew we couldn't just hire a trade house that would buy and resell our product," said David Harbourne, a Fusion vice president and manager of its core business. "We can always teach a distributor how to sell our product, but if it doesn't have strong service, we can't do much about that. Our philosophy at Fusion is to look for strong service organizations that have a lot of after-sales support."

Source: Excerpted from Edward O. Welles, "Being There," *Inc.*, (September 1990): 143. Permission conveyed through Copyright Clearance Center, Inc.

buyers and selling groups. Merchant middlemen include export merchants and jobbers, export buyers and foreign importers, trading companies, and complementary marketers.

Middlemen may be located at home (**domestic middlemen**) or in the foreign country (**foreign middlemen**). Some firms prefer to deal with middlemen who are located in the foreign market. An advantage of using foreign middlemen is that they provide a channel that is closer to the customer than are domestic middlemen; that is, they provide personnel who are in constant contact with the foreign market. A disadvantage of using these middlemen is that the employing firm does not have the close contact it enjoys when dealing with a middleman located in the domestic market. Another disadvantage of using foreign middlemen is that language or communication barriers between the producer and the middlemen are more likely to develop than with the domestic middlemen. Elements that affect the indirect exporting strategy include the availability of middlemen, the cost of their services, the functions performed, and the extent of control the manufacturer can exert over the middlemen's activities.

Direct Exporting

To obtain greater control over their distribution systems and the volume of sales, firms often develop their own export organization. There are several approaches to establishing direct exporting means, among which are an international sales force, a sales branch, a sales subsidiary, setting up a company's own distribution system, and the Internet.

International Sales Force. An enterprise may establish an **international sales force** that travels abroad to sell the product. This may be the least expensive choice since the firm does not have to invest in any facilities abroad. This solution, however, would not give foreign customers immediate access to the firm's representatives, nor would the firm be able to effectively monitor foreign market changes.

Sales Branch. A firm may choose to establish a **sales branch** in the foreign country. This approach requires investment in foreign facilities. It enables the firm to be closer to the market, however.

Sales Subsidiaries. The manufacturer may also choose to establish a sales subsidiary abroad. A **sales subsidiary** differs from a sales branch in that it is an entirely separate entity, even though it is under the control of the company.

Setting Up Own Distribution System. If the foreign country's legal system permits it, a company can elect to set up a chain of wholly owned outlets, which may consist of retail shops.

The Internet/World Wide Web. Many firms now sell products and service on **the Internet or World Wide Web.** For example, many newly started businesses think globally from day one. Amazon.com, a bookstore on the Internet, relies on book lovers anywhere on the globe being able to tap into its site to place orders. During its fiscal year ending in 1997, the company sold $16 million worth of books to 180,000 customers in more than 100 countries.[25] Sony's president, Nobuyuki Idei, has indicated that Sony will soon revamp its distribution system. He doesn't see much future for traditional distribution of music CDs and movies from its Columbia TriStar studio. He is determined to transform the world's leading maker of consumer electronics into a fleet-footed player on the Web. He expects to provide interactive versions of music, movies, and games that can be downloaded onto Sony-made devices. And he expects Internet-related revenues eventually to surpass its $45 billion-a-year electronics sales.[26] Since many people around the globe still do not have access to PCs, businesses still must utilize a traditional distribution approach, thus increasing the costs. However, when using the Internet, a business cuts costs by cutting out the middleman. For example, Dell is able to lower the prices of computers sold in China because it sells them over the Internet. And to lower prices in China, Ford plans to sell its cars over the Internet.[27]

Firms should not adhere to any one approach; they should be flexible and conform to the situation. The choice of approach depends on a number of factors. Some of them include:

1. The philosophy and aims of the company.
2. The traditions of the target market.
3. The competition's behavior.
4. The existing and potential future size of the market.
5. Legal restrictions.
6. Usual patterns of distribution of the particular product(s).
7. Financial and staffing problems.[28]

Direct or Indirect Exporting?

There are advantages as well as disadvantages to both approaches. The advantages of the direct approach include:

1. The sales staff is more loyal than would be the sales staff of an intermediary.
2. The sales staff has greater knowledge of the product line of the firm than does an outside vendor.
3. The sales staff can be trained by the parent company according to its individual sales methods.
4. Salaries of the sales staff can be set in accordance with the long-term goals of the firm instead of on a commission basis.

5. The sales staff can keep personal contact with the end users and retailers.

6. The manufacturer has a channel to receive feedback information on new marketing opportunities and trends that might not be available to a firm using sales intermediaries.

7. The manufacturer has a means of getting information about competitors, evaluating product acceptance, and gathering a multitude of useful information.

8. The sales branch or subsidiary can spend promotional money to advertise a new product, concentrating on building product acceptance in a wide region, which might not be the goal of the sales intermediary.[29]

The disadvantages of using the direct approach include:

1. It is usually very expensive to start. (Refer again to Practical Perspective 5-7.)

2. A large inventory is usually needed.

3. The establishment of a complex organization, including a warehousing network, an administrative organization, and a trained staff, is often required.[30]

Manufacturing in Foreign Country Strategy

After they have acquired experience in the international arena, many enterprises find it profitable to produce in foreign countries. Six of the most common approaches to foreign production are licensing, franchising, management contracting, equity-based joint ventures, non-equity-based contractual alliances, and wholly owned subsidiaries. Many companies sometimes use a mix. For example, in 1989, Kentucky Fried Chicken had outlets in 58 countries, and these international outlets generated almost half of KFC's $5 billion per year in sales. But KFC's success was especially notable with its 1,324 outlets in the Pacific Rim. KFC's director of public affairs, Richard Detwiller, said, "We operate all our outlets on a joint-venture or franchise basis, and the licenses are mostly held by local nationals."[31]

Licensing/Franchising

Licensing involves granting a foreign enterprise the use of a production process, the use of a trade name, or permission for the distribution of imported goods for a fee. Licenses allow for expansion without a great deal of capital investment or personnel commitment. However, supervising licenses may sometimes be a problem and, because of the partnership, profits may be lower. Nevertheless, overall, licensing can be profitable for many companies, especially those that are no longer producing the product at home and could lose their patent protection for lack of use.

In **franchising**, the contractor provides a standard package of products, systems, and management services; grants permission to use a certain product, including a special name or trademark; and often incorporates a special set of procedures for making the product. Under franchising agreements, the parent firm maintains a reasonable degree of control. The Disneyland located in Tokyo, Japan, is a franchise arrangement. Under the agreement, Walt Disney Productions is to receive 10 percent of every admission fee from the Tokyo park and 5 percent of the revenues from restaurants and shops.[32]

Numerous other companies have been entering the complex Japanese market via franchising or licensing arrangements, including 7-Eleven Stores, Stained Glass Overlay, Tiffany & Company, and Barney's of New York.[33] Starbucks Coffee recently entered China via a franchising agreement.[34] Whirlpool Corporation entered China via joint ventures to make refrigerators and air conditioners, but is now withdrawing from the joint ventures and is expected to focus less on manufacturing its own products abroad and more on licensing.[35]

Management Contracts

Using the **management contract** method, a firm provides managerial know-how in all or some functions to another organization for a stated fee or a percentage share of the profits. For example, BBA Group of Britain possesses general airport-management skills. In the U.S., BBA operates the Indianapolis Airport under a ten-year management contract and provides retail management at the Air Mall in the Pittsburgh Airport.[36] The upside of this approach is that the firm is not investing its assets abroad, and when an enterprise licenses production abroad, it can maintain control. Furthermore, the enterprise can maintain control of an investment abroad in which it is a minority owner. The downside is that these contracts are often executed in hostile environments, thus exposing employees to danger. The approach is also used when a foreign nation's government nationalizes or takes over the industry, but needs the managerial know-how of the previous foreign owners to manage the enterprise. For a contracted fee, the previous owners manage the enterprise for the government.

Joint Ventures/Contractual Alliances

Many enterprises' entry strategy is via a joint venture or a contractual alliance. Many companies use a mix to attain the most efficient entry.

Joint Ventures. A **joint venture** is an arrangement whereby a company joins in a partnership or a merger between one or more other companies. Some governments require that their citizens have majority ownership of foreign-owned firms located in their country. Advantages of joint ventures include: (a) it enables a firm to utilize the foreign partner's skills; (b) it enables a firm to gain access to the foreign partner's distribution system; and (c) it requires less capital investment than if the investment were wholly owned, therefore reducing the size of the risk. For example, Toys "Я" Us Inc. planned to open 100 stores in Japan via joint ventures. Its strategy was to maintain 80 percent ownership. To compensate for its lack of understanding of Japan's real estate and cultural nuances, Toys "Я" Us teamed up with McDonald's Japan, whose management has experience in these matters.[37] Walt Disney Company likewise said it will build a theme park in Hong Kong—its third theme park outside the United States. The government and Disney will create the park through a joint venture, Hong Kong International Parks Ltd., held 57 percent by Hong Kong and 43 percent by Disney.[38] Practical Perspective 5-8 describes a joint venture between Suzuki and General Motors, and Practical Perspective 5-9 describes a joint venture between Telmex and Microsoft.

There are some disadvantages to this approach, however. First, profits must be shared with the partner, and second, because some nations require majority control by local people, the home company might lose managerial control. (A management contract, however, can mitigate this problem.) For example, in 1990, a U.S. household products company entered into joint venture in China with Shanghai Jahwa Corporation, China's largest cosmetics manufacturer. The U.S. side intended to capitalize on Jahwa's brand equity and distribution to push its own product line, and it hoped the Chinese partner would provide the connections required to do business in China. The Chinese partner hoped the U.S. side would upgrade its technology and increase its competitive capabilities both locally and abroad. The two companies, as it turned out, had different dreams; their dispute over direction and resources paralyzed operations for three years. In 1993, Jahwa withdrew its top brands from joint venture and sold its share, leaving the U.S. partner scrambling for another local partner to salvage its investment and save face.[39] As a result of experiences such as this one, currently many companies seek to enter the Chinese market via a wholly owned investment.[40] However, General Motors recently entered into a joint venture in China (becoming the largest U.S. venture in China). Many critics, including *Fortune*, have slammed General Motors for giving away too much technology and getting locked into making Buick sedans that are too expensive for the market. (General Motors acknowledges that the investment entails a lot of risk but defends the investment on the basis that it sees China as the world's last big growth market.)[41]

Contractual Alliances. Many joint ventures are in the form of a contractual alliance. **Contractual alliances** are formed to share costs, to share risks, to gain additional market knowledge, to combine technical and market knowledge, to serve an international market, and to develop industry standards together.[42] These organizations attain greater efficiency by focusing on their strengths. That is, they do what they can do best ("lead

PRACTICAL PERSPECTIVE 5-8

Frugal Head of Suzuki Drives Markets in Asia

In the U.S., Suzuki had some early success, introducing its small Jeep-like Samurai years before the Toyota RAV4 and Honda CR-V models. But Suzuki's fortunes sank after *Consumer Reports* magazine in 1988 branded the little truck prone to rolling over, a rating Suzuki still protests. U.S. sales peaked at 81,349 that year and dropped to 29,283 in 1997.

Suzuki has 60 plants in 27 countries from Hungary to Ecuador and Nigeria. Years ago, the company's products weren't good enough to get into the U.S. and Europe, Mr. Suzuki says. So he decided to enter the developing world.

His strategy is to start small. Mr. Suzuki describes the Vietnam factory as "just a hut" that produces 12,000 "two-wheelers" (motorcycles) and 500 "four-wheelers" a year. In India, Suzuki churns out 350,000 cars a year in a joint venture forged with the government. In China, it builds 260,000 cars and commercial vehicles a year at its five plants.

Suzuki pulled out of a joint venture in Spain about three years ago. Spanish regulations required paying workers until they were 65, even if they were laid off. So Suzuki sold out and now makes more money selling parts to its former plant than it did when it owned the facility.

Seeking to benefit from Suzuki's developing-world experience, GM has approached Suzuki about forging joint ventures in Asia and eastern Europe. Combining volumes in the smaller-car market could lead to purchasing economies of scale, says Lou Hughes, GM's executive vice president, but no agreement has been reached.

The two companies complement each other in a Canadian assembly joint-venture. Suzuki gets the benefit of GM's huge sales and purchasing network, while GM benefits from Suzuki's engineering skills.

But Suzuki holds the advantages in the developing world, and the two companies may not be as complementary there, Mr. Suzuki says. Mr. Suzuki makes most decisions himself, enabling his company to move more quickly than GM or other Japanese companies, which are ruled by consensus. A framed calligraphy of the Japanese characters for "being alone" hangs behind his desk.

Source: Excerpted from Valerie Reitman "Fresh Head of Suzuki Drives Markets in Asia," *The Wall Street Journal,* February 26, 1998, p. A12. Permission conveyed through Copyright Clearance Center, Inc.

from strength," as discussed in Chapter 4) and contract for other functions. For example, Nissan and Volkswagen have an arrangement whereby Nissan distributes Volkswagens in Japan and Volkswagen sells Nissan's four-wheel-drive cars in Europe.

In describing such an alliance, Professor Thomas G. Cummings of the University of Southern California used the label "transorganizational systems."[43] He described such systems as a group of two or more enterprises engaged in collective efforts to achieve goals they could not achieve by themselves. Riad Ajami, a professor at Ohio State University, proposed that such systems are characterized "by a shift from an equity-based investment...to

PRACTICAL PERSPECTIVE 5-9

Telmex and Microsoft Team Up on a Hispanic Portal

Over the years, Mexican mogul Carlos Slim spent billions assembling a sprawling communications empire. He started out with the acquisition of Teléfonos de México (Telmex), the former telecoms monopoly, in 1990. Investment in computers, media companies, and Internet service providers followed. But investors and analysts kept wondering when Slim would start up a truly multinational operation.

On October 18 they got their answer. Slim announced a $100 million joint venture with Microsoft Corporation to create a Spanish-language Internet portal for the Americas. For Microsoft, this is a chance to expand into foreign-language Internet services with a savvy Latin American partner. Telmex's pockets are nearly as deep as Microsoft's, to boot. For Slim, the venture will be key to his plans to go regional.

It's also part of his strategy to reduce Telmex's dependence on long-distance telephony, with its ever-smaller margins, and move into the fast-growing market for data transmission and Internet-related services. By the end of 2000, analysts expect that these services, along with cellular, will account for around 20 percent or $2 billion, of Telmex's annual revenues. "The Internet right now is in its diaper stage," says Slim. "We want to develop as many associated businesses as possible."

Telmex and Microsoft will be going head to head with big players throughout the region. U.S. heavyweights such as American Online Inc. and Yahoo! Inc. and homegrown Internet service providers such as Brazil's Universo Online are already battling for position. Early entrants such as New York-based StarMedia Network, Inc. will not give up market share easily. "We are far ahead not only in product development but audience creation," says Star-Media CEO Fernando J. Espuelas.

Source: Excepted form Geri Smith, "Mr. Slim, Meet Mr. Gates," *Business Week* (November 8, 1999): 5. Reprinted with permission.

that of a service-based organization providing technology know-how and other managerial services...ownership rests upon contractual arrangements rather than conventional ownership arrangements."[44] Ajami listed fifteen examples of such collaborative ventures, including Toyota–General Motors, General Electric–Salelni (Italian construction firm), and MW Kellogg Company of Houston–China Petrochemical International Corporation (SINOPEC).

Kenichi Ohmae, a management consultant for McKinsey, an international management consulting firm, described this type of arrangement as follows:

➤ There is no formal contract.

➤ There is no buying and selling of equity.

➤ There are few, if any, rigidly binding provisions.

➤ It is a loose, evolving kind of relationship.

➤ There are guidelines and expectations. But no one expects a precise, measured return on the initial commitment.

➤ Both partners bring to an alliance a faith that they will be stronger than either would be separately.

➤ Both believe that each has unique skills and functional abilities the other lacks.

➤ Both have to work diligently over time to make the union successful.[45]

Ohmae proposed that a non-equity-based alliance in many instances has advantages over the equity-based joint venture. He contended that when equity enters the picture, one becomes concerned with control and return on investment, and one cannot manage a global company through control—it demoralizes workers and managers. Furthermore, he contends that equity poisons the relationship, which can lead to the prevention of the development of intercompany management skills, which are crucial for success in today's global environment.[46]

There are certain problems in using this approach, however. Premature dissolution of the agreement by one partner can create problems for the other partner(s). There is always the risk that a partner may not really be in it for the long term—for example, a British whisky company used a Japanese distributor until it felt it had acquired sufficient experience to begin its own sales operations in Japan, and Japanese copier makers and automobile producers have done the same to their U.S. partners.[47] The effectiveness of the approach depends on a solid relationship between partners. It may be a very lengthy and expensive process to find the right partner(s) and develop the required relationship.

Wholly Owned Subsidiaries

Using the strategy of a **wholly owned subsidiary,** the firm establishes an entity in a foreign country, paying all of the costs incurred. To establish a wholly owned foreign subsidiary, an enterprise may acquire or merge with an existing company in the foreign country or build one from scratch. For example, to maintain its growth, Wal-Mart Stores, Inc. entered foreign markets. Moving to Europe for the first time, Wal-Mart acquired German retailer Wertkauf GmbH, giving it a foothold in a large market. The purchase was a key step for Wal-Mart in its continuing effort to expand internationally. The move parallels Wal-Mart's acquisition strategy in other countries, such as Canada, where in 1994 it acquired 120 stores from Woolworth Corporation. In December 1998, Wal-Mart bought another 74 German stores from Spar Handels Company.[48]

Recognizing that the U.S. market is close to the saturation point, Merrill Lynch made overseas acquisitions a central part of its strategy to capture more customers. The firm established objectives to make non-U.S. revenues account for 50 percent of its business within a five-year period. Within the first three years, Merrill acquired enterprises worldwide. In

1995, the company purchased the London-based broker Smith New Court PLC to improve its penetration into Asian markets. In 1997, Merrill acquired McIntosh Securities, one of Australia's leading brokerage houses. And Merrill's acquisition of Mercury Asset Management, Britain's second largest asset management company, cemented its position in Europe financial capital.[49]

In early 1998, it was announced that German carmaker Daimler-Benz and U.S. carmaker Chrysler Corporation, both international corporations, would merge to become the fourth largest car manufacturer in the world. The reason for the merger was that Daimler-Benz wanted a car company that was not dependent solely on luxury cars, and Chrysler wanted entry into the exclusive luxury car market that Daimler-Benz would provide.[50]

Advantages of the Wholly Owned Subsidiary:

1. The firm maintains total control and authority over the operation.
2. Profits need not be shared with anyone outside the company.
3. Since they do not need to consult a partner, firms have more flexibility to adapt faster to market demands and labor needs.
4. The enterprise is able to protect trade secrets.

Disadvantages of the Wholly Owned Subsidiary:

1. The breeding of **"badwill"** because profits are not shared with local people.
2. Government officials in many countries tend to view wholly owned foreign investments in their nation unfavorably.
3. The risk is greater since it is totally company borne.

Within the past two decades or so, government officials in many countries have become uncomfortable with the situation in which much of their nation's industrial sector is controlled by foreigners. As a result, many governments have established policies mandating that the majority of control of foreign investments in their country must be in the hands of local citizens—although this trend currently seems to be declining. China, for example, which in the past mandated entry via joint venture, now more readily allows entry via wholly owned investment.

Export or Manufacture Abroad?

Both approaches have advantages and disadvantages. The general advantages of investing in manufacturing facilities abroad, as opposed to exporting, include:

1. Capitalizing on low-cost labor.
2. Avoiding high import taxes.

3. Reducing transportation costs.

4. Gaining access to raw materials.

5. Developing **"goodwill"** in the foreign nation because direct investment may help in that nation's economic development.

The general disadvantages include:

1. Subsidiaries are far removed from the home country and are thus often difficult and expensive to control.

2. The risk of nationalization, confiscation, domestication, and expropriation exists to a greater degree than when using other methods.

Which strategy option, manufacture abroad or export, should a firm select? Naturally, the one that is the more efficient. And it is often most efficient for a company to manufacture in one country and export to another; that is, it is often most efficient to use a **mix.** Furthermore, firms sometimes shift back and forth from one strategy to another, as efficiency dictates.

For example, McIlhenny Company of Avery Island, Louisiana, the world's only maker of Tabasco pepper sauce, ships its product to Europe, where distributors get it onto grocery shelves. But McIlhenny did not always export its sauces abroad. The firm used to manufacture in England through a licensing agreement with a British company—a system that might be handy after 1992, according to Carlos E. Malespin, vice president in charge of the company's international operations. "Although it's more profitable for us to use distributorship arrangements," says Malespin, "we can fall back on our former strategy of licensing for manufacture in Europe if import tariffs are raised significantly after 1992."[51] (As of June 23, 1995, McIlhenny Company continued to export and had no plans to manufacture in Europe.) Another example is Guess? Inc.'s shift in strategy in Europe. In 1997, in Europe, a region targeted for particularly aggressive growth, Guess? took on a partner to share expenses. Earlier that year, Guess? sold part of its Italian unit and granted licensing rights to a joint venture. The move was taken, in part, to relieve Guess? of burden of financing the substantial capital expansion needed to build new Guess? stores in Europe.[52]

PRICE STRATEGY

Operating in foreign markets brings new price strategy challenges as there are new market variables to consider. For example, the attitudes of foreign governments are an important and serious problem that differs from one country to another. Sometimes foreign governments act as price arbiters. Therefore, effective price setting consists of much more than mechanically adding a standard markup to cost. International pricing strategy is much more complex than domestic pricing strategy.

International Pricing Strategy

International pricing strategy is made complex by monetary exchange factors as well as by firms often being required to countertrade; that is, to trade by barter or a similar system (which will be discussed more thoroughly later in the chapter). Pricing policy is also affected by the commercial practices of the country in which the firm is doing business, by the type of product being merchandised, and by existing competitive conditions. In establishing pricing policy, some firms are influenced by the view that pricing is an **active tool** by which to accomplish their marketing objectives, and some are influenced by the belief that price is a **static element** in business decisions. Furthermore, some firms emphasize control over final prices and some over the net price received by the enterprise.

Pricing as an Active Tool

Utilizing the view that pricing is an active tool, the firm uses pricing to accomplish its objective relative to a target return from its overseas operations or to accomplish a target volume of market share. (For an illustration of pricing as an active tool strategy, read Practical Perspective 5-10, the case of Dell Computer Corp. in Japan. Dell used pricing as an active tool in the early 1990s, and as indicated earlier, it is currently using the Internet to lower its prices.)

Pricing as a Static Element

If a firm follows the view that **pricing is a static element,** it will most likely be content to sell what it can overseas and consider it to be a bonus value.

Pricing as an active tool is more closely allied with firms that make direct investment in the foreign country, whereas pricing as a static element is more closely allied with firms that export.

Control over Final Prices

To achieve a desired level of foreign market penetration, a firm must have the ability to control the end price. Enterprises with the desire to attain a high level of market penetration therefore attempt to obtain all possible **control over the final price.** These firms are more likely to view pricing as an active tool than as a static element.

Net Price Received

Firms using this approach do not attempt to control the price at which the product is finally sold. The enterprise's main concern is with the **net price it receives.** This type of firm most likely shares the view of pricing as a static element more than as an active tool.

PRACTICAL PERSPECTIVE 5-10

Dell Computer Corporation Wages Price War in Japan

Dell Computer Corporation escalated a personal computer price war in Japan by unveiling plans to sell six types of high-end PCs in Japan at prices 25 to 60 percent lower than those of its rivals. At a news conference in Dell's Tokyo offices, Chief Executive Officer Michael Dell outlined the company's plans to target corporate customers through "direct sales," the company's preferred euphemism for mail order, its main avenue for PC sales in the U.S. According to Mr. Dell, the company's "more efficient mode" will allow Dell to undercut its competitors' prices because the company can avoid paying the added costs of distribution. Dell's kickoff of its full-scale Japanese operations, foreshadowed for weeks by press leaks and speculation about the company's sales strategy, marks the latest move in aggressive U.S. marketing tactics into the once-placid world of Japanese PC sales.

Dell joins Compaq Computer Corporation and International Business Machines Corporation, both of which announced low-priced PCs

for sale in Japan last fall [1992].... The U.S. companies have set their eyes on the world's second largest market for personal computers, once ruled by NEC Corporation. With an iron grip on its network of retail distributors and huge library of software, NEC has for years enjoyed a market share of more than 50 percent and the luxury of selling its computers at high prices.... Dell, the world's fifth largest PC maker, seems intent on pushing such competition even further. Officials at the news conference presented a price comparison of three Dell computers and machines from Compaq, IBM, and NEC with identical speed and memory and comparable hard-disk storage capacities. NEC's prices were as much as 60 percent higher than Dell's. Compaq's prices were generally closest to Dell's, at one point coming within 25 percent.

Source: Excerpted from David P. Hamilton, "Dell Computer Escalates Price War in Japan by Introducing Low-Cost PCs," *The Wall Street Journal*, January 22, 1993, p. 5. Permission conveyed through Copyright Clearance Center, Inc.

Foreign National Pricing and International Pricing

Pricing for foreign markets is further complicated by managers' having to be concerned with two types of pricing: foreign national pricing and international pricing. Basically, the former is pricing for selling in another country and the latter is pricing in another country for export.

Foreign National Pricing

A firm's **foreign national pricing** is influenced by its international pricing strategy, discussed above, as well as by foreign governments. A government can influence its nation's prices by taking various actions. It can institute **national price controls**. These controls may encompass all products sold within the nation's borders or impose them on only specific products. Some governments influence prices on foreign imports by levying higher import duties or subsidizing local industries. Governments can also affect prices by applying legislation relative to labor costs. For example, the government of Thailand, besides imposing steep taxes on cars, unofficially controls their prices. Of course, the steep taxes raise prices dramatically. For instance, in 1997, in Thailand, a Honda Accord, nearly identical to the one sold in the U.S., sold for $35,520, about a 50 percent premium.[53] Higher labor costs mean higher prices, and vice versa. A recent trend, however, among many nations is to open up their markets to price competition laws. Prices are likely to be lower in competitive environments. Because of globalization, competition is currently intensifying throughout the world. Therefore, many international corporations' strategies are now influenced by price. For example, European retailer Carrefour acquired Promodès Group, becoming Europe's No. 1 retailer. The merger aimed to create a much tougher playing filed for Wal-Mart Stores, Inc. in its drive to expand internationally. Carrefour is the No.1 retailer in Argentina, Brazil, and Taiwan, as well as in Belgium, France, Greece, Portugal, and Spain. To counter Wal-Mart, Carrefour seeks ways to slash prices—of course, Wal-Mart is doing the same.[54] Practical Perspective 5-11 describes IKEA's international pricing strategy. The product life cycle in a specific market also influences the price. If it is a new product and there is a demand for it, a higher price can often be charged. On the other hand, to achieve market penetration where the product is in a late life cycle stage, a firm may have to charge a lower price.

International Pricing

International pricing basically relates to the managerial decision of what to charge for goods produced in one nation and sold in another. A common practice of global corporations to establish a strong position in global markets is intracorporate sales. In applying this practice, a global corporation attempts to rationalize production by requiring subsidiaries to specialize in the manufacture of some items while importing others. The subsidiaries' imports may consist of components assembled into the end product, or they may be finished products imported to complement their product mix. This import-export practice among subsidiaries located in different countries enables the global corporation to control and transfer prices and to control the profits and losses of its subsidiaries. These corporations will realize no profits in a country where, for reasons discussed below, it is not beneficial to do so, and will realize them in a country where it is beneficial.

Avoiding a Country's High Tax Rate. Both foreign and domestic governments are interested in profits and the role of transfer prices in their attainment. This is because of the consequences profits have on the amount of taxes paid. Because of the differences in tax structures among nations, global corporations can often obtain significant profits by instructing a subsidiary in a country that has a **high corporate tax rate** to sell the product at cost to another subsidiary in a country where taxes are lower. The profit is thereby earned in the country where taxes are lower.

PRACTICAL PERSPECTIVE 5-11

IKEA: Furnishing A Big World

IKEA [a Swedish corporation] recognized that the value added in making furniture wasn't necessarily in manufacturing," explains Robert Atkins, a vice president of Mercer Management Consulting in Boston. "They designed kits that put the consumer in the middle of the value chain, giving them lots of things to do that were traditionally done by the manufacturer. This took incredible amounts of cost out of their system."

IKEA further reduced its costs by becoming production oriented. The company strives to carry out product development on the shop floor. It sends its 10 in-house designers into its suppliers' factories to learn the capabilities and limitations of their machinery so that product designs can be adapted to the machines, instead of the other way around. "Most designers look at the form and the function, but ours must

also look at the price," explains [Jan] Kjellman [president of IKEA North America]. "We don't want to make limited-edition products. We want to mass produce them."

Sometimes keeping costs down means that an IKEA design will be made of a lesser quality material. For example, the company does not hesitate to make a painted tabletop out of a lower grade of wood, or substitute a simpler material for a base that isn't seen. And furniture that would be too expensive to make in birch is made out of pine.

While the company aims to provide a good quality product, price is still the main reason people shop IKEA. "The easiest way to enter a market is with a low price," says Atkins.

Source: Excerpted form Sharen Kindely, "IKEA: Furnishing A Big World," *Hemispheres* (February 1997): 32. Reprinted with permission.

Avoiding a Country's Currency Restrictions. Transfer pricing may also be used to get around **currency restrictions.** For example, a nation suffering from a lack of foreign exchange may impose controls that limit the amount of profit that can be repatriated, that is, profits that can be transferred back to the corporation's home base. For instance, suppose nation X imposes controls on the amount of profits that can be repatriated and that there is trade with country Y, which does not have such controls. The corporation at home could instruct the subsidiary in country X to sell its product to a subsidiary in country Y at cost. This would transfer X's profit to Y, from where the global corporation can repatriate profits.

Avoiding Currency Devaluations, Having to Reduce Prices, and Having to Increase Wages. The international pricing approach could also be employed by global corporations when a foreign nation's **currency is devaluated,** when there is government pressure in the foreign country to **reduce prices** because of excessive profits, and when labor in the foreign country demands **higher wages** because of high profits earned.

Arms-Length Pricing. Because of these manipulative practices, many governments insist on **arms-length pricing;** that is, the price charged to company affiliates must be the same as that paid by unrelated customers. For example, under section 482 of the U.S. Internal Revenue Code, U.S. tax authorities have the authority to reconstruct an intracorporate transfer price. When they suspect that low prices were set to avoid taxes, the tax authorities may recalculate the tax. It should be noted that many U.S. executives prefer the arms-length approach because it enables them to properly monitor and evaluate foreign managements.[55] They also tend to prefer it because the transfers can demoralize the management of the foreign subsidiaries that do not show positive results—they were transferred to another subsidiary.

Fluctuating Exchange Rates and Costs

Fluctuating exchange rates force periodic adjustments in price. For example, Zenith Electronics Corporation incorrectly estimated the fluctuating direction of the U.S. dollar when it hedged in forward exchange contracts, resulting in a $13 million loss in its 1989 second quarter, even though its sales grew.[56] In 1996, Whirlpool lost $13 million in Europe, blaming it on the raising Italian lira.[57] To deal with the problems fluctuating currency exchange rates create for international businesses, the European Union has introduced a single currency—the Euro dollar. There is currently a move to introduce a single currency in Asia as well.[58] The same principle applies to fluctuating costs, including costs of raw materials and supplies, inflation, and interest rates. When a firm enters into a long-term contract at a fixed rate, shifts can prove disastrous if the firm cannot adjust its prices in some way. The lesson is that in international pricing, a firm must develop strong international money management skills. (Refer again to the case of Laker Airways, the British firm discussed in Chapter 3, which went into bankruptcy because it did not manage well in this respect.)

Countertrade

The swapping of goods is a practice that has been around for thousands of years. A well-known swap occurred in 1626 when European settlers in America traded with America's aborigines $24 worth of cloth and trinkets for Manhattan Island [New York].[59]

Pricing strategies are further complicated by the fact that not all foreign transactions can be in cash. For example, sales to communist countries and to Third World countries with "soft currency," currency that is not readily accepted in international transactions, often take place in the form countertrade, which fundamentally means the buyer of a product pays the seller with another product that has the equivalent monetary value. The pricing problem derives from the difficulty of assessing the value of the product received in exchange. A miscalculation could lead to financial disaster. There are four basic types of countertrade transactions: barter, compensation, switch, and counterpurchase.[60]

Barter

Barter is an arrangement in which the exporter sells goods to a foreign importer without the exchange of cash. That is, specified goods are sold to the importer for other specified goods.

Compensation

Using the **compensation** procedure, the exporter sells technology and equipment to an importer in the foreign market. The importer pays the exporter with goods produced with the imported technology or equipment.

Switch

In the **switch** procedure, the exporter transfers the commitment to a third party who may be an end user of the product received by the exporter or to a trading house employed to dispose of the product. An advantage here is that the third party can be highly effective in selling the product. A disadvantage is that the third party often seeks to obtain the product at a bargain price, therefore lessening profit and complicating negotiations.

Counterpurchase

Under a **counterpurchase** agreement, two parties agree to sell each other products or services with some balancing of values. The exporter sells goods, technology, or services to the foreign importer for cash, but agrees to purchase goods with the cash equivalent from the importer within a specified period—the goods are selected from a list that usually excludes those items produced by the technology being imported. An advantage of this approach is that the exporter has use of the cash for the specified period.

Exporters entering into countertrade agreements must often use a trading firm to market the goods they purchase. However, the goods purchased can often be distributed or used by a subsidiary of the exporter. For example, as mentioned in Chapter 4, PepsiCo has been selling to Russia the concentrate for a drink to be bottled and sold in Russia. In return, PepsiCo has been paid with vodka, which it has distributed through a subsidiary. Often, exporters receive raw materials or parts that can be used in their production process.

In general, the major problem in countertrade is determining the value and the potential demand of the goods offered by the other firm, and it is time consuming. Firms, however, are motivated to participate in countertrade for various reasons, including to make sales in nonmarket nations and in many less-developed countries and to adjust their accounting records to enable them to pay lower taxes and tariffs. This occurs when both parties underestimate the value of the goods.

PROMOTION STRATEGY

In general, problems related to international promotion strategy include the legal aspects of the country, tax considerations, language complexities, cultural diversity, media limitations, credibility of advertising, and degree of illiteracy. Some governments regulate advertising more closely than others. Laws in some nations restrict the amount of money that may be spent on advertising, the media utilized, the type of product advertised, the methods used in advertising, and the way in which the price is advertised. Some nations have special taxes on advertisements. Language translation, which will be discussed in Chapter 9, presents many barriers. For example, translation of semantic and idiomatic meanings across cultures are difficult to make, which presents huge impediments to communication.

Why International Promotional Strategies Fail

There are numerous reasons international promotional strategies fail. The reasons include insufficient research, poor follow-up, narrow vision, over-standardization, and rigid implementation.[61]

Insufficient Research

Insufficient research prior to making international strategic decisions generally leads to failure. For example, Lego A/S, the Danish toy company, had improved its penetration in the American market by offering "bonus" packs and gift promotion. Encouraged by its success in the U.S., Lego decided to apply the same approaches, unaltered, to other markets, including Japan, where penetration had been lagging. The Japanese customers were not attracted to those tactics. A later investigation revealed that Japanese consumers viewed the promotions as wasteful, expensive, and not too appealing. The results were similar in other countries as well.

Overstandardization

Some commodities, such as Coca-Cola, have a global appeal. In this situation, the message to be communicated can be much the same throughout the world. Many products, however, do not have universal appeal.[62] The message to be communicated must therefore be tied to individual motivation; the promotional campaign, instead of being **overstandardized**, must reflect local tastes. The foreign environment thus has a significant effect on promotional strategy. Failure to adapt promotional strategy to the foreign environment inevitably creates difficulties. Managers therefore need to determine whether or not a promotional message is appropriate for the foreign culture, and if not, what adoptions must be made.

For example, the Marlboro cigarette advertisements, which contain a man projecting a strong Western masculine image, were unsuccessful in Hong Kong. Philip Morris subsequently changed its ad to reflect a Hong Kong–style man, still a virile cowboy, but younger, better dressed, and owning the truck and the land he is on.[63] Another example is a laundry detergent company's promotional campaign in the Middle East. The advertisement pictured soiled clothes on the left, a box of soap in the middle, and clean clothes on the right. Since many people in that part of the world read from right to left, many individuals interpreted the message to mean that the soap soiled the clothes.[64] And in the 1970s, Polaroid began selling its pathbreaking SX-70 camera in Europe. It used the same advertising strategy, such as TV commercials and print ads, that was successful to launch the product in the American market. Although the product itself had global appeal, the TV commercials featuring personalities well known in the U.S. did not. Testimonials by well-known personalities did not stimulate European consumers' interest. Polaroid subsequently researched and adhered to European promotional practices that were known to work. (For further illustration, refer to Practical Perspective 5-12.)

Poor Follow-Up

Failure to monitor the promotional campaign for problems and solve them as they arise will contribute to failure. For instance, a U.S.-based computer company implemented a software house cooperation program in Europe to help penetrate the small- and medium-sized accounts market segment, where it was weak. The program needed a large change in sales force operation. The sales force, no longer in control of the hardware and software package, had to determine its content together with a software house that had access to the smaller accounts. The success of the new program depended on how effectively the sales force carried out its new assignments as well as on central coordination and attention, which it never got. Lacking central coordination and **follow-up,** there was no communication channel for sharing and building on the experiences of subsidiaries.

Narrow Vision

An enterprise may centralize promotional strategic decision making or it may decentralize it to its local managers. Both approaches have pros and cons. The centralized approach can be effective by providing an overall global perspective, but it can be ineffective because decision making is not close to the market. The decentralized approach may be effective since decision making is close to the market; however, it may be ineffective because it

PRACTICAL PERSPECTIVE 5-12

Advertising in Saudi Arabia Must Adhere to Local Customs

Saudi Arabia plays a key role in the Gulf Co-operation Council (GCC).... An understanding of advertising regulation in this gateway country thus becomes essential for marketers interested in the region.... As do many other developing countries, Saudi Arabia strongly adheres to local customs. Age-old traditions continue to be observed in dress, salutations, hospitality, and so forth. Although no laws specifically regulate the culture contents of ads, insensitivity may destroy credibility. A major tea company alienated Saudi customers after it aired a commercial that showed a Saudi host serving tea with his left hand to one of his guests. Moreover, the guest was shown wearing shoes while seated, which is considered disrespectful by traditional Saudis.

Source: Excerpted from M. Luqmani, Z. Quraeshi, and U. Yavas, "Advertising in Saudi Arabia: Content and Regulation," *The International Executive* (November–December 1989): 35–38. Reprinted with permission.

does not provide a global perspective. (For an illustration, refer to Practical Perspective 5-13.) Firms that apply just one of the two approaches possess **narrow vision.**

For example, in the 1970s, the Anglo-Dutch company Unilever targeted its household cleaner, Domestos, for international expansion. Management assigned development of a global "reference mix" to Britain, where the brand had been established. Several years and numerous market entries later, Unilever's top management was still waiting to repeat the success it had attained in the British market. Failure was attributed to the lead market's insistence that their strategy be followed in other markets (centralization), but success to deviation from the lead market's strategy (decentralization). However, in the markets where there was deviation, the global theme also deviated. For instance, the theme for Domestos in West Germany was as an "all-purpose sanitary cleaner," and in Australia it was as a "bathroom plaque remover." To attain a balance between centralization and decentralization, Unilever's detergent unit subsequently established a multisubsidiary structure, the European Brand Group, to coordinate brands in Europe. The group consisted of executives from the central headquarters and from numerous large subsidiaries.

Rigid Implementation

High-level managers sometimes ignore local managers' reservations about **rigidly implementing** a standardized promotional program and force compliance, which usually leads to failure. This is so because local managers' reservations are often based on a solid understanding of local conditions.

PRACTICAL PERSPECTIVE 5-13

Nestlé's Decentralization of Promotion Proves Less Than Satisfactory

Nestlé's experiences with *laissez-faire* in sales promotion are typical of the problems faced by many multinationals. In the early 1980s, management delegated to the local organizations many decisions that had traditionally been made or strongly influenced by the headquarters. Of all the marketing decisions, only branding and packaging were kept at the center. The rest, including consumer and trade promotions, became the domain of the company's country operations around the world. Although decentralization has helped enhance Nestlé's performance internationally, it has been less than satisfactory in sales promotion.

The problem has to do with two developments over time: a worldwide shift in emphasis and budget allocation in favor of sales promotion and away from media advertising and increasing reliance on price promotion to boost short-term local sales results, particularly in countries with a powerful trade and/or limited electronic media advertising. The outcome: reduced brand profitability, contradictory brand communication, and a serious potential for dilution of brand franchises with consumers. Today [1990] Nestlé is trying to put some central direction back into its worldwide communication practices, including sales promotion. Management is painfully aware of the damage "brand management by calculators" and "commodity promotion" can do to its international brands and their long-term profitability. *Laissez-faire* in sales promotion is no longer considered a virtue at Nestlé.

Source: Excerpted from K. Kashani and J.A. Quelch, "Can Sales Promotions Go Global?" *Business Horizons*, (May–June 1990): 37–43. Reprinted with permission.

For example, Nestlé launched an innovative cake-like chocolate bar in Europe. The British unit, however, refused to accept the product because of its knowledge that a soft bar would not appeal to British tastes. Forced adoption would therefore have resulted in failure.

Top management may also become inflexible to changing market conditions. For instance, Lego pioneered standardized marketing in its field and became a genuine global corporation by marketing its educational toys in the same way in more than 100 countries. However, Lego eventually encountered competition from look-alike and lower-priced rival products from Japan, the U.S., and other countries. Tyco, a leading competitor in the U.S., began placing its toys in plastic buckets that could be utilized for storage after play. Lego, however, used elegant see-through cartons standardized worldwide. American parents preferred the functional toys-in-a-bucket idea over cartons. Lego's U.S. managers sought permission from the central managers in Denmark to package Lego's toys in buckets. The central managers refused because they believed that the bucket could cheapen Lego's reputation for high quality, that it could change their reputation from innovator to follower, and that it deviated from the company's policy of standardization. Massive losses eventually led Lego to change and develop its own innovative buckets.

Developing an Effective International Promotional Strategy

To develop an effective international promotional strategy, strategists must determine (a) the promotional mix—the blend of advertising, personal selling, and sales promotions—needed for each market; (b) the extent of worldwide promotional standardization; (c) the most effective message; (d) the most effective medium; and (e) the necessary controls to aid in assessing whether or not the potential objectives are being met.[65] Practical Perspective 5-14 reports how Procter & Gamble penetrated the Japanese market with its Joy dishwashing soap. For another illustration, refer back to Practical Perspective 5-6, which describes Budweiser's development campaign in China.

WANT TO GO INTERNATIONAL? FACTORS TO CONSIDER

Chapters 3, 4, and 5 have discussed the international planning process. This section presents some questions that the strategist should answer, or factors that should be considered, to be successful doing business abroad.

➤ Does your firm have a mission statement? That is, do you know why the company exists and what it plans to do? If you don't, you won't have a sense of direction.

➤ Why do you want to go international? Is it for opportunity or threat reasons or both? Or is it because it is currently fashionable to internationalize? If it is the latter, you might not apply the intensity needed to be successful abroad.

➤ Are you ready to go abroad? Will going abroad really solve your problems? How long has the company been in business? Is it stable enough (financially and psychologically) to endure the initial hardship of internationalization? Does it have a national reputation? Being successful at home will help mitigate the internationalization hardship?

➤ Have you done your homework? That is, have you ascertained where there may be a demand for your product/service? Are you totally familiar with domestic and international environments? Have you

PRACTICAL PERSPECTIVE 5-14

P&G's Joy Makes an Unlikely Splash in Japan

Just two years ago, two powerful consumer-products concerns, Kao and Lion Corporation, each controlled nearly 40 percent of the kitchen-soap market with several brands and had essentially declared a truce. The rest of the market was cornered by private brands at chain stores.

Meanwhile, the Japanese were cooking less at home and thus buying less dish soap every year.

P&G actually washed out of the Japanese kitchen-detergent market during an earlier attempt. It withdrew in the late 1970s after failing to make a dent with Orange Joy, a product that it transplanted from the U.S. But by 1992, it had succeeded in marketing other products, such as Pampers, in Japan. The home office told its Japanese unit to find new markets for products in which P&G was strong elsewhere in the world.

So that year P&G sent out researchers to study Japanese dishwashing rituals. They discovered one odd habit: Japanese homemakers, one after another, squirted out more detergent than needed. It was "a clear sign of frustration" with existing Japanese products, says Robert A. McDonald, head of P&G's Japanese operations. He saw the research as a sign that

an "unarticulated consumer need" was more powerful soap. "We knew we had something to go after," he says.

Some P&G executives were concerned about entering such a mature market, says McDonald. But P&G's lab in Kobe went to work to create a highly concentrated soap formula, based on a new technology developed by the company scientists in Europe, specifically for Japan.

The first hint that Joy was a hit came in March 1995 in the region around Hiroshima, 400 miles west of Tokyo, where P&G started test-marketing it. Four weeks into the test, Joy had become the most popular dish soap in the region with a 30 percent market share.

P&G marketing pitch was deceptively simple: A little bit of Joy cleans better, yet is easier on the hands. The message hit a chord, says Ayumi Osaki, a 31-year-old homemaker who rushed off to buy Joy after seeing pilot commercials. "Grease on Tupperware, that's the toughest thing to wash off," says Osaki. A mother of three in Hiroshima. "I had to try it."

Source: Excerpted from Norihiko Shirouzu, "P&G's Joy Makes an Unlikely Splash in Japan," *The Wall Street Journal,* December 10, 1997, p. B1. Permission conveyed through Copyright Clearance Center, Inc.

thoroughly familiarized yourself with the potential market's cultural, economic, legal, political, competitive, trade and monetary barriers, and labor relations factors? That is, are your thoroughly familiar with the challenge you will be facing in internationalizing?

➤ Are you thoroughly familiar with your strengths and weaknesses? That is, do you have a thorough understanding of your international management capabilities? Do you have a clear understanding of the nature of your product/service? Do you know how to capitalize on your product's/service's strengths, how to minimize its weaknesses, how to correct its shortcomings, and how to customize it to fit the needs of the foreign market? How strong or weak is your firm with respect to e-commerce?

➤ Have you developed viable product/service, place/entry, pricing, and promotion strategies that are based on the answers to the questions posed above as well as to the ideas to be presented in Chapters 6–14?

In essence, the above means that, to be successful in internationalizing a business, the strategist must do his or her homework. As the many practical anecdotal cases presented throughout this book illustrate, those who do their homework have a far greater chance of succeeding abroad than those who do not.

SUMMARY

This chapter has proposed that when managers develop international product/service strategy, they must consider the SRC, which often leads one to assume that what sells at home will sell abroad in the same form—which usually is not true. Some products and services can be sold globally in standardized form, but most products and services must be customized to fit the varying needs of different societies. Managers must also consider that many products/services introduced into a society will not sell well right away; they must be diffused into the society over time.

The method of getting the product or service to foreign customers will vary from nation to nation. The fundamental approaches are exporting to it or manufacturing in it. Six approaches to manufacturing abroad have been discussed: licensing, franchising, management contracts, joint ventures, contractual alliances, and wholly owned subsidiaries. The chapter also described how various factors influence international pricing strategy, such as the foreign government, monetary exchange, and the requirement for barter trade. Some international firms use pricing strategy to develop foreign markets; others are content to simply get some revenue from the foreign market. Some international firms use a transfer pricing approach to get around a country's high tax rate, currency restrictions, currency devaluations, and mandate to reduce prices and increase wages. Four types of barter trade were discussed: barter, compensation, switch, and counterpurchase.

Relative to promotion strategy, it was proposed that various factors influence international promotions, including the legal aspects of the country, language differences, and cultural diversity. Several reasons international promotional strategies fail were discussed: insufficient research, overstandardization, poor follow-up, narrow vision, and rigid implementation.

Key Terms and Concepts

1. Product/service, place/entry, pricing, and promotion strategies
2. Self-reference criterion
3. Standardization versus customization
4. Cultural barriers
5. People-processing, possession-processing, and information-based services
6. The diffusion process
7. Quickness or slowness of diffusion
8. Dualistic technological structure
9. Adaptive transformative and transformative technological innovations
10. Exporting to or manufacturing abroad
11. Indirect and direct exporting
12. Agent and merchant middlemen
13. Domestic and foreign middlemen
14. International sales force
15. Foreign sales branch, foreign sales subsidary, and company's own foreign distribution system
16. Internet/World Wide Web sales
17. Firms should not adhere to any one approach
18. Licensing, franchising, management, contractual alliances, and wholly owned subsidiaries
19. "Badwill" and "goodwill"
20. A mix of strategies
21 International pricing strategy
22. Pricing as an active tool and as a static element
23 Control over final prices and net price received
24 Foreign national and international pricing
25. National price controls
26 Getting around a country's high tax, currency restrictions, currency devaluations, and requirements to reduce prices and increase wages
27 Arms-length pricing
28. Barter, compensation, switch, and counterpurchase
29. Insufficient research, overstandardization of promotion, poor follow-up on promotion program, narrow vision, and rigid implementation of promotion program

Discussion Questions and Exercises

1. Why is it important that managers of international firms remain informed about their enterprises' external environment and internal situation?
2. You are the strategic planner for a domestic firm that produces soft drinks. Your firm's sales at home are stagnant. As a solution, you have decided to sell your product in Europe and Asia. What should your next step be?
3. Briefly discuss the five different product strategies.
4. Some writers on international strategy contend that the effectiveness of international businesses is relying more and more on the offering of standardized products (a global strategy). Do you agree or disagree? Why?
5. Discuss the ways information technology enhances the provision of information-based services and products.
6. You are an international management consultant hired by a domestic company, which invented a unique product for its home market. The firm's management is now considering expansion into foreign markets and is currently considering the financial aspects of the transfer. With respect to revenues, what would you advise your client?

7. Discuss the dualistic technological structure.

8. A domestic firm, whose managerial personnel lack international business experience, is considering entering a foreign market. What would be its logical entry strategy? Why?

9. A domestic firm, whose managerial personnel have had considerable prior experience in international business in a similar industry, is considering entering a foreign market. What would be its logical entry strategy? Why?

10. Differentiate between an international sales force, sales branch, sales subsidiary, and own distribution system. Discuss some of the factors that affect the various approaches taken.

11. Discuss some advantages and disadvantages of direct exporting over indirect exporting.

12. Discuss the six strategic options to manufacturing abroad.

13. An international business has been exporting to a foreign market. The firm's product is well diffused in the market. Because of high local labor costs, rises in transportation costs, and increases in tariff costs, the firm has been incurring financial losses. The firm's management has decided that it is time to manufacture abroad. The management of the cash-short firm likes to be in control of total operations. Which of the six options to manufacture abroad do you believe is best suited for this firm? Why?

14. Discuss advantages and disadvantages of the wholly owned strategy.

15. Discuss advantages and disadvantages of manufacturing abroad over exporting.

16. Operating in foreign markets brings new pricing challenges. Discuss some of them.

17. Discuss the "pricing as an active tool," "pricing as a static element," "control over final prices," and "net price received" pricing strategies.

18. Differentiate between foreign national pricing and international pricing.

19. Why do international managers currently prefer arms-length pricing?

20. How do fluctuating exchange rates and costs affect pricing strategy?

21. Discuss the four approaches to countertrade. What is the major problem with countertrade?

22. Discuss the general problems related to international promotion strategy.

23. Discuss the factors with which a strategist should be familiar in developing an internationalization strategy.

24. You are an international promotion consultant hired by a firm getting ready to develop a massive international promotion program. What advice would you give your client?

Assignment

Interview an international executive of an international business firm. Ask him or her to describe the enterprise's general international strategies. How did the firm enter the foreign arena? What were some of the factors that affected the strategy? Has the firm changed strategies? If not, does it plan to do so? Prepare a short report for class discussion.

CASE 5-1

Keep on Trekking

Surrounded by Wisconsin's gently rolling hills, the town of Waterloo (population 2,888) is the last place you would associate with high-flying international business. License plates on the pickup trucks that dominate the roads here read *America's Dairyland*, football fans at Green Bay Packers games wear giant foam cheese wedges on their heads, and the conversations on Main Street are conducted in slow, flat Midwestern cadence, not the impatient shorthand of international trade—NAFTA, ASEAN, Mercosur, WTO. But here, in the heartland of America, a remarkable tale of globalization is unfolding. In the past ten years, international exports from Wisconsin have nearly quadrupled, reaching $10.6 billion in 1996, projections of $13 billion by 2000. Much of this growth has been generated by small and midsize firms that found themselves doing business around the world before they even thought much about it—companies like Trek Bicycle.

Trek made its first road bicycle in 1976 in a tiny workshop in a rented barn outside Waterloo, less than an hour from Milwaukee, the state's commercial center, and Madison, the state capital. The company still builds its high-tech, Y-suspension bicycle frames in that red barn, but in the intervening two decades, it has become the world's biggest specialty bicycle maker, ringing up nearly $400 million in sales in 1996, of which 38 percent comes from its international business. Mountain biking may have originated in the United States, but today it's a global obsession, and Treks are exported to more that seventy countries through seven wholly owned subsidiaries in Europe and Japan and 65 independent distributors on six continents. Last year, Wisconsin governor Tommy G. Thompson named Trek one of the state's top exporters. How a

tiny company that had just $18 million in sales in 1986, smack in the middle of Wisconsin farm country, managed to pull off this feat is a lesson in serendipity propelled by tenacity.

Joyce Keehn, Trek's worldwide sales director, still smiles in amazement when she recounts the events that catapulted international sales from zero in 1985 to well over $100 million in little more than a decade. It all began when a handful of letters came across her desk requesting information about exporting Trek bicycles to Canada. She was the telemarketing sales manager at the time, and Trek had no international sales division, so she took the letters to the national sales manager, John Burke. Those were the tight years of Reaganomics, of astronomical interest rates, bankruptcies, and the Third World debt crisis. Wisconsin was at the heart of the Midwest's rust belt, the depressed swath of the states where factories closed their doors when they were unable to ride out years of recession. Residents by the tens of thousands were moving south to try their luck in the booming Sun Belt. Exporting was the last thing on anyone's mind. When she proposed that Trek find out how to export to Canada. Keehn recalls, "Burke just looked at me for a while. Then he said, 'Okay. Do it.' I said, 'Me?' 'Yeah you.'" Keehn had absolutely no experience with the laws or the practice of international trade, but she rolled up her sleeves and set about learning how to export with the same diligence that had gotten her out of bed before dawn to milk the cows on her family's dairy farm.

It is not uncommon for small and medium-size companies to be introduced to international trade in just this way. Initially, most are content simply to fill overseas orders that arrive unsolicited. When results aren't immediately impressive or problems with tariffs and customs and distributors begin to crop up, many would-be exporters give up. But that didn't happen at Trek. Because Burke gave the telemarketing sales manager the leeway to develop the business and Keehn was determined to learn what it takes to be an exporter, the company was able to come up with the staff and budget to actually develop a global market rather than just fill orders for bikes. Following through made the difference.

Of course, it didn't hurt that Wisconsin had at that moment hit on the idea of international trade as a way out of its economic doldrums. Governor Thompson was setting up programs to teach local businesses about foreign markets, pushing through tax cuts for Wisconsin exporters, and leading trade missions all over the world. Because of the tone he set, when Keehn turned to the state export authority (a commercial office most states maintain), she found a staff that was enthusiastic and well-informed. They gave her advice on legal and logistical challenges and suggested she attend a state-sponsored trade seminar that brought together potential local exporters and international buyers. Keehn decided that Trek should sell directly to bicycle shops in Canada. The alternative, going through a distributor, would push the retail price too high. With that strategy in mind, Keehn flew to Canada, flipped through phone directories to find likely bicycle shops, then set out to visit each one. "You can tell which shops are at the high end, which ones are discounters, which you think you can work with," she says. "it's a lot of gut work." Back in Waterloo, with orders to fill, she handled all that paperwork needed to get each bicycle shipment through customs. And she made a trip to the warehouse before each shipment to make sure the papers were in order; even the tiniest slip could cause costly delays.

A year later, a Swiss dealer called, asking for bicycles to sell, and the whole process started again. By now, Keehn was an old hand. Within months, the Swiss orders multiplied from fifty bikes at a time to a hundred to a container of more than three hundred. Suddenly Keehn's boss realized he had good reason to pay attention to exporting. "It really didn't take a genius to figure out there were opportunities for us in Europe," says Burke, who is now Trek's president. The numbers told the story: Europeans buy fifteen million bikes a year, while Americans and Canadians together buy ten million. Because of the size of the European markets, Trek ponies up the money in the late '80s to establish its own wholly owned subsidiaries in six countries, including the U.K., Germany, and Austria, to distribute bicycles directly to retail outlets. The offices handle sales, inventory, warranties, and customer service. Although owning these operations was more expensive than using local distributors, it gave the company more control over how it sold its products, not to mention higher profits. That was the heart of the lesson Keehn was learning: Strive for as much control as possible, run your own operations on the ground, and build solid relationships worldwide.

As Trek set up European subsidiaries, Keehn began building a complementary network of independent distributors in countries where it made sense to do so. With greater distance and cultural and language barriers, Keehn had to rely on the expertise of local distributors rather than approach retailers on her own. To find partners, she attended trade shows and enlisted the help of private and state groups and the U.S. Department of Commerce. When she found likely prospects, she solicited proposals, then visited their offices and warehouses and asked questions. How would they advertise? How big was the market potential? Were there English speakers on staff? What were their marketing plans? How would they price the bikes? Did they sell competitors' bicycles? If so, the deal was usually off; Trek generally makes exclusive distributor agreements, renewable annually.

Often prospective partners came to the company. "Mountain biking was hot, and Trek was a hot brand. There was a lot of interest," Keehn says. At one trade conference, she offered a cough drop to a man sitting next to her with a terrible cold. When he thanked her, she noticed a Brazilian flag in his lapel pin and handed him a card; she was looking for a distributor in Brazil. His face lit up when he found out she was from Trek. He was looking for new products to add to his sports equipment business.

There were times, of course when her luck wasn't so good. In Brazil, Argentina, China, and Australia, Trek had to fight to protect its trademark. In South America and Indonesia, customs inspection delays sometimes held up shipments for so long that the letters of credit needed to ensure payment for the bicycles nearly expired. In Mexico, cargo was often pilfered while waiting to clear customs, making insurance hard to get. France and Denmark imposed all sorts of special requirements for the bikes, such as lights, bells, or engraved serial numbers, that made business difficult and costly.

And there was the constant risk of inadvertently offending customers through some cultural misunderstanding. Like the time Trek sent out catalogs decorated with pictures if Betty Boop, only to get a frantic fax the German subsidiary explaining that the character had adorned Allied bombers during World War II. A buyer from Singapore shied away from green helmets: in his country, he explained, if a man wears green on his head, it means his wife is having an affair. Often, however, international demands made the product better. Germany's strict environmental requirements led Trek to redesign its packaging, helping to bolster the company's environmentally conscious image.

The Internet, by making it much easier companies to advertise around the world,

posed another problem. About a third of the visits to Trek's Web site (www.trekbikes.com) come from abroad. But international sellers must charge more than their U.S. counterparts to make up for costs like shipping, customs duties, and currency exchange. If customers around the world could buy bicycles from the Web site, foreign distributors would be forced to compete with U.S. dealers. And price is no small matter: Trek's products are top of the line. Its famous Y-frame model, constructed of extremely light, strong carbon fiber, looks like something Batman might ride. The U.S. Secret Service uses it to patrol the White House grounds. Most of the mountain bikes the company exports are in the $300 to $1,500 range, with top models fetching more than $4,000. To protect its international sellers. Trek does not post prices on its Web site. It also forbids U.S. dealers to sell to international customers. Both policies demonstrate to Trek's overseas affiliates that it will stand behind them.

That is especially important for foreign partners, who have to grapple with red tape, wild swings in the value of their national currencies, and arbitrary import regulations. Last summer, for example, Brazil barred importers from borrowing for periods of less than 360 days, an extraordinarily long and expensive proposition for U.S. exporters, which normally don't extend credit for more than 90 days. And in 1996, the South African rand tumbled 30 percent on rumors (later proved false) that President Nelson Mandela had suffered a heart attack. American bicycles, therefore, were 30 percent more expensive for South Africans.

The last thing foreign distributors need is to sell against the more stable prices of the U.S. dealers. "Our local importer can absorb only so much of the price increase before it has to be passed on to the consumer," says Steve Bowman, a bike-racing champion whose Cape Town bike shop, Hopkins Cycle Inn, is Trek's top South African dealer. "From one month to the next, bike prices could go up

200 or 300 rand [about $40 to $60]." Trek brings dealers like Bowman to Wisconsin for regular visits to its factory and Madison store, where they've given sales and product training on Trek brands, including Fisher, LeMond, Klein, and Bontrager. In exchange, the company has high expectations of profits from Trek's team abroad. In five years, Trek projects exports to grow to 50 percent of its total sales.

What's next? Trek is considering building an assembly plant in Europe, a move that could cut delivery time by thirty days and eliminate 15.8 percent import duty it currently pays European Union member countries. Meanwhile, the company is active in seminars, mentoring programs, and state-level policy initiatives to help other firms get their global business going. Not that these efforts are completely altruistic: building a wider base of small-to-medium-size companies interested in export policies is good for business. A bunch of small companies can exert a lot of influence when it comes to trade policy. John Burke no longer greets international topics with blank stares but rather with impassioned arguments in favor of breaking down trade barriers. He's particularly incensed about China, which levies a hefty import tax on bicycles of at least 50 percent and pays only 11 percent on the three million bikes it ships to the United States every year. "They pay their workers a dollar a day and no benefits, they are subject to no environmental standards, and still they charge those kinds of tariffs," he says. "It's totally unbelievable to me that the U.S. government won't say to the Chinese. 'As of this date, we will permit no bikes to enter the United States until you open up your markets.'"

It's the kind of debate heard more often these days in small towns like Waterloo and in once-small companies like Trek Bicycle. But it shouldn't be surprising. The American economy is being fueled by two forces: small business and exports. The National Association of Manufacturers and the Institute for International Economics have found that exporters create 20 percent more jobs—and are 9 percent less likely to go under—than purely domestic firms. Exporters like Trek helped the Wisconsin job market grow 13 percent in the last five years, outrunning the 9 percent rate in the rest of the economy.

The latest bright idea to come out of Wisconsin is a kind of statewide export-import bank to finance new exporters. On a crisp fall day in Madison, in a brand new building covered with *Wet Paint* signs, Governor Thompson and three dozen of Wisconsin's international business pioneers mulled the matter over at a regular quarterly strategy session. "Every time you sell one billion dollars. "Every time you sell one billion dollars of goods and services, you create 22,000 good jobs here in the state of Wisconsin," the governor said in an interview after the meeting. Today that translates into 220,000 jobs in Wisconsin that are all directly related to exports, he said, "and we're not even scratching the surface."

Questions

1. Discuss Trek's internationalization strategies within the context of the 4 Ps. How effective was Trek?

2. How might the Internet enhance its international operations?

Source: First appeared in *Working Woman*, December–January 1998. Written by Michele Wucker. Reprinted with permission of MacDonald Communications Corporation. Copyright 1999 by MacDonald Communications Corporation. www.workingwoman.com. For subscriptions call 1-800-234-9675.

Notes

1. J. Friedland and L. Lee, "The Wal-Mart Way Sometimes Gets Lost in Translation Overseas," *The Wall Street Journal*, October 8, 1997, pp. A1, A12.
2. James E. Lee, "Cultural Analysis in Overseas Operations," *Harvard Business Review* (March–April 1966): 106–114.
3. Len Lewis, "Growing Global," *Progressive Grocer* 78, no. 9 (Septemeber 1999): 22–28.
4. Clifford Krauss, "Despite Uncertain World Markets, a Big U.S. Retailer Bulls into Latin America," *The New York Times*, September 6, 1998.
5. J. Flynn and L. Bongiorno, "IKEA's New Game Plan," *Business Week* (October 6, 1997).
6. Martha T. Moore, "Meeting the Cupholder Challenge," *USA Today*, May 2, 1994, p. 1B.
7. Whitaker Penteado, "Fast-Food Franschises Fight for Brazilian Aficionados." Used with permission of publisher from *Brandweek* (June 7, 1993): 20.
8. H. Riesenbeck and A. Freeling, "How Global are Global Brands?," *The McKinsey Quarterly* (November 4, 1991): 353.
9. Adapted from Allison Lucas, "Market Researchers Study Abroad," *Sales and Marketing Management* (February 1996): 13.
10. Warren J. Keegan, "Multinational Product Planning: Strategic Alternatives," *Journal of Marketing* (January 1969): 58–62.
11. Laurie M. Grossman, "PepsiCo Plans Big Overseas Expansion in Diet Cola Wars with Its Pepsi Max," *The Wall Street Journal*, April 4, 1994, p. B6.
12. Theodore Levitt, "The Globalization of Markets," *Harvard Business Review* 61 (May–June 1983): 92–102.
13. K. Naughton, E. Thorton, K. Kerwin, and H. Dawley, "Can Honda Build a World Car?," *Business Week* (September 8, 1997): 101–102.
14. Global Strategies, "The Colonel Comes to Japan," *The International Executive* (July–August 1989): 28–29.
15. Shawn Tully, "Teens: The Most Global Market of All," *Fortune* (May 16, 1994): 90.
16. H. Riesenbeck and A. Freeling, "How Global are Global Brands?," p. 349.
17. Subhash C. Jain, "Standardization of International Marketing Strategy: Some Research Hypotheses," *Journal of Marketing* 53 (January 1989): 70–79.
18. This discussion draws from C.H. Lovelock and G.S. Yip, "Developing Global Strategies for Service Businesses," *California Management Review* 38, no. 2 (Winter 1996): 64–86.
19. William M. Bulkeley, "Having High-Tuition Blues? Look North," *The Wall Street Journal*, November 26, 1997, pp. C1, C19.
20. Everett M. Rogers, *Diffusion of Innovations*, 3rd ed. (New York: The Free Press, 1983), p. 10.
21. Joanne Lee-Young, "Starbucks' Expansion in China is Slated," *The Wall Street Journal*, October 5, 1998, p. A27.
22. The discussion of these categories draws from P.R. Cateora and J.M. Hess, *International Marketing* (Homewood, IL: Richard D. Irwin, 1979), p. 377.
23. This discussion draws from Paul Shrivastava, "Technological Innovation in Developing Countries," *The Columbia Journal of World Business XIX*, no. 4 (Winter 1984): 23–39.
24. Ibid, p. 26.
25. Kevin Maney, "Technology is 'Demolishing' Time, Distance," *USA Today Tech Report*, September 2, 1997.
26. Irene M. Kunii, "Here Come the Sony Netman," *Buisness Week* (November 1, 1999): EB47.
27. Brian Palmer, "The View from China," *Fortune* (November 8, 1999): 214.
28. *Distribution in Asia/Pacific's Developing Markets* (Hong Kong: Business International Asia/Pacific Ltd., March 1978), pp. 1–3.
29. Ibid.
30. Ibid., pp. 3–4.
31. Global Strategies, "The Colonel Comes to Japan."
32. John Marcom, Jr., "Japan to Host World's 3rd Disneyland but Park May Run Short of Funds, Fans," *The Wall Street Journal*, November 17, 1982, p. 36.
33. Ted Holden, "Who Says You Can't Break into Japan?" *Business Week* (October 16, 1989): 49.
34. Lee-Young, p. A27.
35. Carl Quintanilla, "Despite Setbacks, Whirlpool Pursues Overseas Markets," *The Wall Street Journal*, December 9, 1997, p. B4.
36. "BBA Takes Majority Stake in Naples," *Airports International* (March 1997): 3.
37. Holden, "Who Says You Can't Break into Japan?".
38. Dirk Beveridge, "Disney to Build in Hong Kong," November 1, 1999, (http://dailynews.yahoo.com/h/ap/19991101/bs/hong_kong_disney_13. html)
39. Wilfried Vanhonacker, "Entering China: An Unconventional Approach," *Harvard Business Review* (March–April 1997): 131.
40. Ibid.
41. Hu Mao Yuan, "China's Car Guy," *Fortune* (October 11, 1999): 240.

42.J.G. Wissema and L. Euser, "Successful Innovation Through Inter-Company Networks," *Long Range Planning 24* (December 1991), p. 35.

43.Thomas G. Cummings, "Transorganizational Development," in B. Staw and L.L. Cummings, eds., *Research in Organizational Behavior, Vol. 6* (Greenwich, CT: JAI Press, 1984).

44.R. Ajami, "Designing Multinational Networks," in R.H. Kilmann and I. Kilmann, eds., *Making Organizations Competitive* (San Francisco: Jossey-Bass, 1991).

45.Kenichi Ohmae, "The Global Logic of Strategic Alliances," *Harvard Business Review* (March–April 1989): 151.

46.Ibid., pp. 147–149.

47.Ibid., p. 152.

48.L. Lee and C. Rohwedder, "Wal-Mart to Acquire German Retailer, Moving to Europe for the First Time," *The Wall Street Journal*, December 199, 1997, p. A2; "Wal-Mart Goes Shopping in Europe," *Fortune* (June 7, 1999): 105.

49.M. Bernstein and M. Weinstein, "Globalshakeout: The Changing Landscape of Financial Services," *Prudential Leader 3*, no. 2 (February 1998): 9, 17.

50.Frank Gibney Jr., "Worldwide Fender Blender," *Time* (May 24, 1999): 58–62.

51.Seth J. Margolis, "Middle Market Companies Prepare for '92," *The International Executive*, (January–February 1990): 41.

52.John R. Emshwiller and F. Rose, "Guess?'s Ambitious Design for Global Expansion Falters," *The Wall Street Journal*, November 26, 1997, p. B4.

53.Alex Taylor III, "Rough Road Ahead," *Fortune* (March 17, 1999): 116.

54.C. Matlack, I. Resch, and W. Zellner, "En Garde, Wal-Mart," *Business Week* (September 13, 1999): 55.

55.J. Greene and M. Duerr, *International Transactions in the Multinational Firm* (New York: The Conference Board, 1970), p. 8.

56.Stephen Kreider Yoder, "U.S. Technology Firms Go Global to Offset Weak Domestic Market," *The Wall Street Journal*, November 14, 1989, p. A1.

57.G. Steinmetz and C. Quintanilla, "Whirlpool Expected Easy Going in Europe, and It got a Big Shock," *The Wall Street Journal*, April 10, 1998, p. A6.

58.Barry Eichengreen, "Is There a Monetary Union in Asia's Future?" *The Brookings Review* (Spring 1997): 33–35.

59.Arley A. Howard and John A. Yeakel, "Who Wins in International Countertrade," *Financial Executive* (January–February 1990): 49.

60.This discussion draws from P. Maher, "The Countertrade Boom," *Business Marketing* (January 1984): 50–52; and "Countertrade Without Cash?" *Finance and Development* (December 1983): 14.

61.The following discussion is adopted from Kamran Kashiani, "Beware the Pitfalls of Global Marketing," *Harvard Business Review* (September–October 1989): 91–98.

62."Global Messages for the Global Village Are Here," *Business World* (Autumn 1983): 51.

63.David A. Ricks, *Big Business Blunders: Mistakes in Multinational Marketing* (Homewood, Il: Dow Jones/Irwin, 1983), p. 52.

64.Ibid., p. 55.

65.Adapted from Cateora and Hess, *International Marketing,* p. 417.

III

Organizing International Enterprises

Two key questions managers must answer when they decide to market their firms' products or services in the international arena are how they will handle their foreign business and how they will structure their organization to conduct that business in the most efficient and effective manner. The success of an international enterprise depends on many crucial factors. One is its organizational structure. The structure is the organization's "skeleton"; it provides support and ties together disparate functions. Therefore, it is imperative that managers totally understand the structuring factors to be considered and the structuring problems to be overcome when attempting to expand into foreign markets. Chapter 6 discusses various international organizational structures.

6

International Organizational Structures

To support Gillette's increasingly global focus, the company went through a restructuring in 1988, creating three principal divisions. The North Atlantic Group manufactures and markets the company's traditional shaving and personal care products in North America and Western Europe. The Diversified Group comprises the Stationery division's North Atlantic arm as well as the Braun, Oral-B, and Jafra companies, each organized on a worldwide product line basis. The International Group produces and sells the company's shaving, personal care, and stationery products in all markets except North America and Western Europe. The International Group is divided into three regions: Latin America; Africa, Middle East, and Eastern Europe (AMEE); and Asia-Pacific.[1]

Learning Objectives of the Chapter

Organizational structures generally establish internal authority relationships, responsibility for work performance, and paths of communication and control required for a company to achieve its objectives. These structures are typically set up to blend the specialized expertise needed to facilitate decision making on a variety of short- and long-range problems. The development of structures should generally be planned and managed. The type of structure managers select should take into consideration the social and psychological aspects of the environment and personnel and should be designed to achieve operational efficiency and control without inhibiting individual creativity and initiative. This task becomes much more complex when a domestic enterprise desires to internationalize its operations. This is because organizations' managers need to establish lines of authority and responsibility from top headquarters management to managers in a variety of foreign environments and at the same time keep open the necessary lines of communication required to manage effectively and efficiently in all the diverse environments.[2] After studying this chapter, you should be able to:

1. Describe the basic traditional international organizational structures.
2. Present the advantages and disadvantages of each structure.
3. Discuss contemporary thinking on the structuring of international organizations.

TRADITIONAL AND CONTEMPORARY INTERNATIONAL STRUCTURES

The three basic dimensions of an international business enterprise are technical or product needs, functional needs, and regional or environmental needs. *Technical or product needs* are specialized factors such as construction, operation, manufacturing, research and development, special knowledge, and experience. *Functional needs* are special knowledge of such functions as personnel, planning, purchasing, and finance. *Regional or environmental needs* are special knowledge of areas such as the foreign government, politics, trends, and economy. To attain maximum overall benefit and to ensure effective communication and develop the means to make effective decisions, the *international organizational structure* managers must effectively integrate these three basic dimensions throughout the organization.[3]

An organization's **international structure** is usually based on one of seven traditional or contemporary models. The traditional models include the functional structure, international division, foreign subsidiary, product division, and regional structure. The contemporary models include the matrix organization, the non-equity-based contractual/strategic alliance, and the mixed (hybrid) structure. These are discussed in the ensuing sections.

The Functional Structure

Under the **functional structure**, major functions are the focus. Product knowledge is centered in manufacturing, engineering, and marketing, and management of each of these departments is responsible for both domestic and international activities. Large international companies rarely use this structure at the corporate level; it is sometimes used in regions, divisions, and/or subsidiaries. The functional structure is traditionally European. It is typically used by smaller firms, or by larger firms with one major product and stable demand. Domestic firms whose internationalization strategy (discussed in Chapter 5) entails indirect exporting often use this structure.

A firm's low dependence on foreign sales and its staff's lack of international business experience often leads it to adopt this structure, as opposed to the international division structure (discussed next). A typical functional structure is illustrated in Figure 6-1. Note that the organizational chart in Figure 6-1 shows a manager of domestic operations and a manager of foreign operations for each function. However, these two roles are often carried out by one individual. Two people might be used when there is a large volume of international sales, but even then, the domestic manager may appoint an assistant manager to oversee international sales for him or her.

Advantages of the Functional Structure[4]

1. *Emphasis on functional expertise.* The key business tasks define work, and functional expertise is brought to bear on all aspects of the operation.

2. *Tight control.* This centralized functional approach permits a small staff to control the firm's operations. Top management has authority and operational responsibility.

3. *Prevents "We" versus "Them" conflicts.* The absence of secondary profit centers (there is no international division) prevents internal conflicts—the "we" versus the international division problem (discussed in the next section) is prevented.

Disadvantages of the Functional Structure

1. *Weak regional coordination.* Disputes between functional managers must often be resolved at the corporate level. The CEO is often asked to solve problems in areas in which he or she lacks expertise, such as international business.

2. *In firms with multiple product lines, functional structure can lead to top-heaviness.* In multiproduct firms, functional managers need expertise in each product, or a functional manager is needed for each product. The latter, which is often the case, would lead to an expensive, top-heavy structure. For example, if the volume of international business is high, a domestic functional manager and a foreign functional manager may be needed (as shown in Figure 6-1).

3. *Much greater emphasis is often placed on domestic sales than on foreign sales.* For example, in a study of 185 medium and large successful Australian exporters, it was found that those firms that make a commitment to support exports through the formation of a separate export unit within their organizations outperform firms that treat exports as just a part of their domestic business.[5]

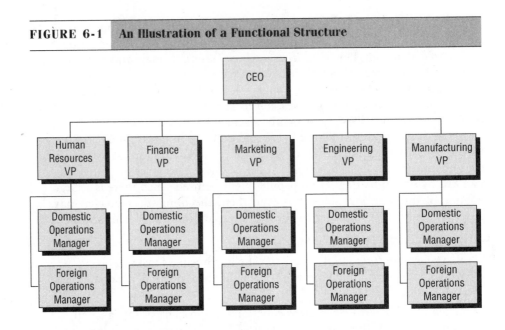

FIGURE 6-1   **An Illustration of a Functional Structure**

The International Division

After they have acquired some international business experience through indirect exporting and their reliance on international business has increased somewhat, many companies internationalize their operations further by creating an export department. Typically, the aim of the export department is simply to handle shipment of existing domestic products to foreign markets. But when firms' foreign transactions subsequently increase, the export department is generally developed into an international division. The *international division* usually supervises exports, distribution agreements, foreign sales forces, foreign sales branches, and foreign sales subsidiaries. Staff members in the international division are selected on the basis of their general familiarity with corporate products, technology, and culture, combined with their ability to be "hands-on" managers who are culturally sensitive and adaptable to the constraints imposed by the foreign environmental factors (as discussed in Chapters 1 and 3).

In the **international division structure**, functional staffs such as marketing, finance, and research and development are typically established, and an executive responsible for international operations is appointed. International businesses adopt this structure when they desire to have an expert responsible for managing each specialized function. Managing these functions across countries requires skills beyond those required for managing them in the home country. One of the earliest users of this type of structure was International Harvester.[6] Canon Corporation, before it became a multiproduct enterprise, also used this structure. Currently, to expand into markets abroad, Wal-Mart is using this structure, as is Bally's Total Fitness.

The international division is generally given total authority and responsibility for the enterprise's foreign operations and activities. Historically, some smaller enterprises for whom an international division was not really necessary (an export department would have sufficed) have nevertheless adopted such a structure because they saw it being used by larger, successful enterprises.[7] A typical international division structure is illustrated in Figure 6-2.

Advantages of the International Division[8]

1. *Focused international responsibility and authority.* Foreign operations are generally more complex than domestic operations and distant from the home base. An experienced executive whose sole responsibility and authority is the international division is therefore more free to react to the needs of such areas than would be an executive whose responsibility and authority is for both domestic and international operations.

2. *International executive development.* Managers and employees in such a division are forced to develop expertise in international busi-

FIGURE 6-2   An Illustration of an International Division Structure

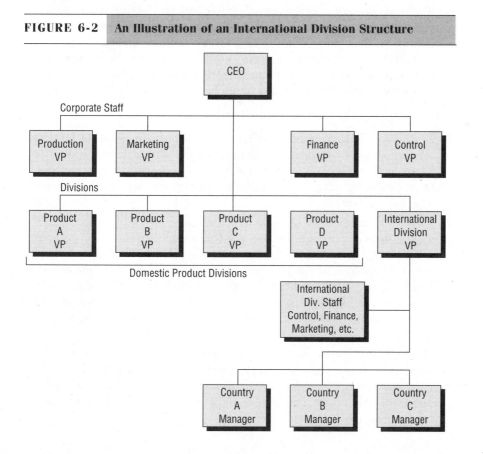

ness and will subsequently be able to participate in, or direct, operations in foreign sites.

3. *The international operation has a single, strong voice in the company's strategy/policy-setting process.* Since heads of international divisions are usually totally responsible for profits and losses of the foreign operations, they will be forceful in acquiring the share of resources necessary to accomplish the firm's international goals. On the other hand, an executive in charge of both domestic and foreign operations may focus more on obtaining resources for domestic activities than for foreign operations.

4. *Company-wide view of international operations.* Managers in the international division are usually concerned with the success of all of the firm's products in foreign markets. These managers are therefore impartial in determining the best overall corporate strategy for international profits. On the other hand, managers of individual product lines made responsible for both domestic and foreign operations may be partial to their own international operations as opposed to the firm's overall international strategy.

5. *Top management is cognizant of consequences.* Because of the complexity of international business, many domestic executives focus mainly on their home-country operations and lose themselves in domestic issues, therefore ignoring global operations. By having an international division, top management is made cognizant of the consequences of focused decisions on global operations.

Disadvantages of the International Division

1. *Bottleneck.* Managers of international divisions sometimes lack adequate product or technical expertise, and the physical separation between domestic and foreign operations often precludes enterprises from providing adequate technical support to international divisions. This causes bottlenecks.

2. *Exports slowdown.* Production divisions may not always adequately supply what the foreign division needs because they favor the domestic operations. Consequently, foreign orders may go unfilled even if the profit potential is higher than that for domestic orders. On the other hand, the heads of product divisions who are responsible for both domestic and foreign business may pay more attention to foreign operations when they see a higher profit potential than in the domestic market.

3. *Conflict between employees in the domestic division and the employees in the international division.* Organizational struggles between domestic and foreign operations often occur. Because the international division cuts across all product areas, a "we-they" situation can occur.

4. *International versus other divisions.* In the ideal corporate organization, operating divisions should be equal in size and profit. In reality, however, the international division often becomes more profitable than the product divisions. When this occurs, the product divisions sometimes "gang up" to reduce the international division's powers.

5. *International managers spread too thin.* Managers of international divisions are often made responsible for several disparate markets, such as South America, Europe, and Asia. This makes developing expertise difficult.

The Foreign Subsidiary Structure

Environmental changes, such as increased demand in foreign markets, or a foreign government's mandate, or changing conditions in the home market, often force international corporations to cease exporting and begin establishing manufacturing facilities in the foreign markets—they establish subsidiaries in foreign countries. These firms thus restructure their organization; they change from an international division structure to a **foreign subsidiary structure.** Each foreign subsidiary is treated as an entity. Each reports directly to top management at headquarters. Coordination between product and service departments is carried out at the headquarters office. These firms therefore apply the multidomestic strategy (discussed in Chapter 4). Applying a multidomestic strategy, the headquarters' managers generally allow the subsidiaries to function as a loose federation with **local managers** possessing substantial autonomy, allowing them to respond quickly to local situations.[9] (Refer to Practical Perspective 6-1). A typical foreign subsidiary structure is illustrated in Figure 6-3.

PRACTICAL PERSPECTIVE 6-1

Wal-Mart Spoken Here

Wal-Mart has had to cope with political and economic instability. In Mexico, for example, it first bought 80 percent of its goods locally to get the best prices. But customers, many of whom had shopped at Wal-Mart in the U.S., were disappointed at the lack of American products, so the retailer changed course. Then came the peso devaluation in December 1994, and Wal-Mart flip-flopped again. Now, only 10 percent of the goods sold in the Mexican stores are imported. What emerged from those early lessons is an overseas blueprint calling for a slightly different kind of Wal-Mart in each country. Though U.S. managers have been a big presence so far, the company hopes to create nearly autonomous units run by native managers who will handle their own buying, training, accounting, and other functions in two

(continued)

to three years. Managers will tweak the Wal-Mart formula to serve their local markets better. "We're building companies out there," says Martin. "That's like starting Wal-Mart all over again in South America or Indonesia or China."

But not everything will be decentralized. In the longer term, stores in different markets will coordinate purchasing to gain leverage with suppliers. Developing new technology—a key

Wal-Mart strength—and plotting overall strategy will be done from Bentonville. And in Mexico, Wal-Mart plans to merge its stores with CIFRA's successful chains, once it completes the takeover of its Mexican partner. That will let the chains streamline costs.

Source: W. Zellner, I. Katz, and D. Lindorff, "Wal-Mart Spoken Here," *Business Week* (June 23, 1997): 141. Reprinted with permission.

Advantages of the Foreign Subsidiary Structure[10]

1. *Autonomy of affiliates.* The affiliate subsidiaries operate free of layers of management between them and top management. These independent affiliate companies are generally allowed to operate with little control from above and can thus develop their own local identity.

2. *Direct top management involvement.* Problems beyond the affiliate's talents go to top management for response and resolution. This enables top management to reflect long-range corporate goals rather than parochial interests. Also, it forces top management to develop a stake in international business and acquire knowledge in that area.

FIGURE 6-3   **An Illustration of a Foreign Subsidiary Structure**

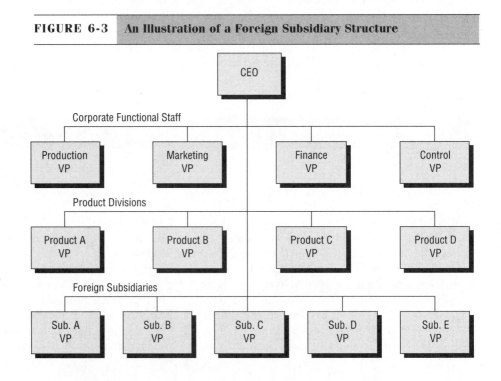

Disadvantages of the Foreign Subsidiary Structure

1. *Diffuseness of international responsibility.* There is no center for international operations responsibility. With so many groups reporting directly to the board, clarity and focus can be lost—although the board can delegate the responsibility to certain expert members.

2. *Potential unwieldiness.* Many items that could be resolved without board action, such as by experts, are often pushed to the board level—again, the board could delegate many responsibilities to expert members.

The Product Division Structure

Many corporations are diversified (multiproduct) and use the product division structure. Under the **product division structure,** each of the enterprises's product divisions has responsibility for the sale and profits of its product. Therefore, each division has its own functional, environmental, sales, and manufacturing responsibilities. When a product division decides to internationalize its operations, as in the case of one-product companies, it may first begin by indirect exporting, subsequently establishing its own export division, and then establishing foreign subsidiaries. This means that if sales in foreign markets by firms with numerous product divisions become substantial, these enterprises could end up operating numerous subsidiary companies in a single foreign territory. Ford Motors began restructuring itself along the product line in the early 1990s.[11] Canon Corporation used the product division structure when it became a multiproduct enterprise in 1962. (Practical Perspective 6-2 presents P&G's plan to restructure from a regional to a product structure by 2005.). A typical product division structure is shown in Figure 6-4.

Advantages of the Product Division Structure[12]

1. *Product and technology emphasis.* Since both the domestic and international units report to the product division and compared with the whole, product divisions tend to be small, closer ties could result. Therefore, because of the common product benefit and the closer ties, products and technology can be easily transferred between the domestic and international units.

2. *Worldwide product planning.* Foreign and domestic plans can be more easily integrated in a product division than in an international division. A worldwide division perspective could therefore evolve.

3. *Conflict minimized.* The problem of substantiating the difference between international and domestic needs may be less difficult than when the international function is in the international division. Having both functions in the same division may lead to similar loyalties and the "we-they" conflict often caused by placing the international function in an international division may be mitigated.

PRACTICAL PERSPECTIVE 6-2

From Country to Product

Procter & Gamble's Chief Executive John E. Pepper will step down about two years early to make way for President and Chief Operating Officer Durk I. Jager, who will drive the changes. It's a shift away from internal themes of recent years in which Procter focused heavily on such tasks as cost-cutting and shedding underperforming brands. But even as the giant revs its engines to push for faster sales growth, critics wonder if it can overcome both economic turmoil around the world and what will surely be cultural turmoil within its own ranks. "This is a very big deal, for Procter and for all the companies that watch Procter's moves," says Watts Wacker, chairman of consulting firm FirstMatter in Westport, Connecticut. "But great plans often come with great obstacles."

Simplify, Simplify

In preparation for the task, Pepper and other top execs have been traversing the country, visiting the CEOs of a dozen major companies, including Kellogg Company and 3M, in search of advice. Pepper went to Jack Welch at General Electric Company to learn how the company streamlined global marketing. He persuaded Hewlett-Packard Company CEO Lewis E. Platt to share enough secrets about new-product development to make a 30-minute instructional video for P&G staffers. The message from all was clear, says Pepper: "What thousands of people have been telling us is that we need to be simpler and move faster."

The result of this unprecedented road trip is Organization 2005, a shuffling of the P&G hierarchy and a new product-development process designed to speed innovative offerings to the global market. The old bureaucracy, based on geography, will be reshaped into seven global business units organized by category, such as baby care, beauty care, and fabric-and-home care. The global business units will develop and sell products on a worldwide basis, erasing the old system that let Procter's country managers rule as colonial governors, setting prices and handling products as they saw fit.

Source: Excerpted from P. Galuszka, E. Neuborne, and W. Zellner, "P&G's Hottest New Product: P&G," *Business Week* (October 5, 1998): 92, 96. Reprinted with permission.

Disadvantages of the Product Division Structure

1. *Weakness in worldwide know-how.* Managers of individual product divisions may become knowledgeable in operating in certain markets, but worldwide knowledge is often impossible. For example, in the past, many managers of U.S. domestic enterprises that internationalized their operations have developed strong skills in the Canadian and European markets but weaker skills in other parts of the world. This may result in weak performance in certain markets.

2. *Inherent weakness of multiproduct systems.* Managers of the overall corporate system may encounter conflicting international demands from the different product divisions. Since managers are part of the

FIGURE 6-4   An Illustration of a Product Division Structure

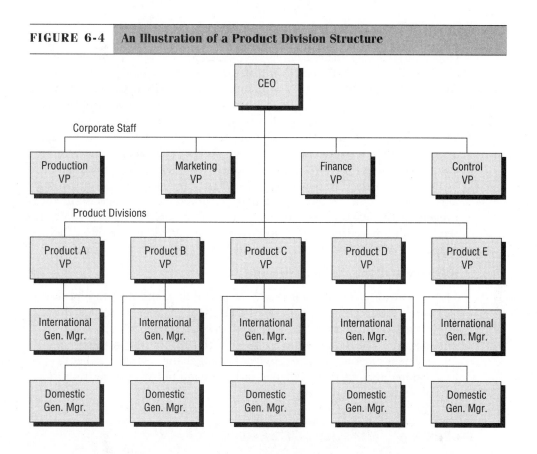

overall corporate system, they may not possess adequate abilities to handle such conflicting demands.

3. *Division managers often lack international skills.* International product managers are often selected on the basis of domestic performance and may therefore lack the required international skills. (This problem is addressed in Chapter 8.)

4. *Foreign coordination problems.* Managers of different product divisions operating in the same foreign country may not coordinate efforts to attain overall corporate efficiency because they are too busy looking out for each other's interests. For example, to cut costs, perhaps some support functions typically carried out in all product divisions, such as personnel and payroll, could be carried out by a single unit.

Canon Corporation has dealt with these disadvantages by developing a divisional structure at the corporate level as well. It has established a system consisting of eight product groups at the corporate level and 21 product divisions.

The Regional Structure

Under the **regional structure**, regional heads are made responsible for specific territories, usually consisting of areas such as Europe, Asia, South America, North America, etc., and report directly to their CEO or his or her designated executives at the headquarters. In general, firms with low technology and a high marketing orientation tend to use this structure. Firms whose foreign subsidiary or foreign product structure has become too large and too complex to manage from a single headquarters often restructure themselves using this form. This type of structure enables regional heads to keep abreast of, and provide for, the needs of their respective regional markets. Managers at regional headquarters are typically responsible for a range of activities, such as production for and marketing in their respective regions. Pharmaceutical, food, and oil companies tend to use this structure. A typical regional structure is illustrated in Figure 6-5.

Advantages of the Regional Structure[13]

1. *Decentralization.* Authority and responsibility, and therefore performance accountability, is delegated directly to the regional office. The management tasks of planning and strategy are less complex than if the central headquarters were to hold this responsibility. Also, management response time to environmental changes is shorter because a regional manager's knowledge of local conditions is greater than that of headquarters manager.

FIGURE 6-5   An Illustration of a Regional Structure

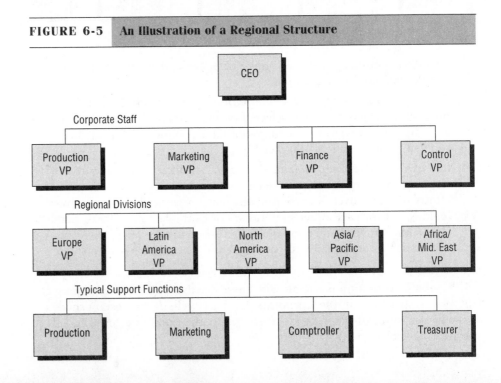

2. *Adaptation*. Regional managers are better able to adapt to local needs than headquarters managers because they are in closer touch with local changes and requirements.

3. *Single management units possess regional knowledge*. Regional managers develop local expertise because they are responsible for regional strategies and daily operations. Regional differences exist throughout the world. Inputs from knowledgeable regional managers can enable central headquarters managers to use these differences effectively in developing and attaining overall corporate objectives.

Disadvantages of the Regional Structure

1. *Weak worldwide product emphasis and technical knowledge*. Because technical knowledge is spread out, a global perspective on products is sometimes difficult to attain. And because the emphasis is usually on regional concerns, the formulation of worldwide strategy formulation can be difficult.

2. *Technology transfer barriers*. Employee loyalty is often focused on the region rather than on the overall organization, and each regional manager tends to claim that things are different in his or her region. Therefore, when headquarters managers attempt to implement new technology on an overall corporate basis, it may not be readily accepted by the regionals.

3. *Policy barriers*. Inconsistent overall corporate management practices may evolve. This is especially so when central management tries to, or is persuaded to, satisfy specific regional needs.

4. *Costly application*. The typical support functions shown in Figure 6-5 exist in each regional division. Costly duplication of effort results. Efficiency could result if these support functions were combines, but in this structure, the number of functional product staff specialists tend to increase through the years.

5. *Weak communications*. Necessary information may not reach top management because of the regional managers' focus on regional performance. Overall corporate performance may therefore be weakened.

The Matrix Structure

The ideal global corporation, as defined by Carl Lindholm, former executive vice president of international operations at Motorola, is strongly decentralized. It allows local subsidiaries to develop products that fit into local markets. Yet at its core it is very centralized; it allows companies to coordinate activities across the globe and capitalize on synergies and economies of scale.[14] To accomplish this, many international businesses have adopted **matrix structures**.[15] Companies such as Nestlé have adopted matrix organizations that allow for highly decentralized decision making and development while simultaneously maintaining a centralized corporate strategy and vision.

Nestlé, with many employees spread throughout a mutitude of sites in 60 countries, "develops as much as can be decided locally," said Peter Brabeck, executive vice president. "But the interest of the corporation as a whole has priority."[16] Many firms that apply a global strategy (firms that rely heavily on foreign revenues and view themselves as global corporations) tend to use this structure.[17] Practical Perspective 6-3 describes Gillette's matrix-like approach. Practical Perspective 6-4 describes H.J. Heinz Company's intent to scrap a system of managing a global company by country or region in favor of a matrix-like structure.

A typical matrix structure is shown in Figure 6-6. In general, managers from the functional side (e.g., Marketing, Africa) assign a staff to the product side (e.g., Product B). The staff leader is then responsible to both bosses. If conflicts arise, they are to be resolved between staff leaders if possible; then between general managers then between vice presidents; and finally by the CEO, sometimes called the fulcrum.

Advantages of the Matrix Structure[18]

1. Coordination and cooperation across subunits enable the firm to use its overall resources efficiently and therefore to respond well to global competition in any market.
2. Overall corporate global performance is highlighted.
3. Many internal conflicts are resolved at the lowest possible level, and those that cannot be resolved are pushed up.

PRACTICAL PERSPECTIVE 6-3

Gillette's International Organization

Gillette's global strategy includes a clear understanding of local differences—that each market presents unique challenges, requirements, and opportunities. In the rapid-growth Asia-Pacific region for example, Gillette has used merger integration as a vehicle for developing a wholly integrated approach to individual markets. In Singapore, the acquisition of Parker Pen in 1993 triggered the establishment of a new organizational structure that has allowed Gillette to show one face to the customer and act as a single, integrated entity to suppliers in the region. While the integration reflects a global strategy, the ability to pull it off required a local sensitivity and orientation. Indeed, the story of Gillette Singapore's merger with Parker Pen illuminates the link between global strategy and local mastery. It demonstrates how managing local integration is key to unleashing the power of global brands.

Source: Excerpted from R.M. Kanter and T.D. Dretler, "'Global Strategy' and Its Impact on Local Operations: Lessons from Gillette Singapore," *Academy of Management Executive 12*, no. 4 (1998): 62.

PRACTICAL PERSPECTIVE 6-4

Heinz's Johnson to Divest Operations, Scrap Management of Firm by Regions

SAN FRANCISCO—H.J. Heinz Company's newly appointed chief executive said he plans to centralize management, divest unrelated operations, and add another strategic business to the big food company.

William R. Johnson, unveiling his plans in an interview and a speech at a meeting of food brokers here Saturday, makes it clear that, in his opinion, Heinz could perform better. "We haven't been adept at internationalizing our business," he said.

The appearance came only days after Heinz, owner of Star-Kist Tuna and Weight Watchers in addition to the Heinz brand, announced that Johnson, its president and chief operating officer, would succeed Anthony O'Reilly as chief executive in April.

The 48-year-old Johnson said he will scrap a system of managing the global company by country or region. Instead, he will run the business by categories so that tuna managers in Europe will work with tuna managers in Asia, Latin America, and other regions, allowing the best brand manager to advise all the countries.

Johnson will also accelerate the expansion of successful products in one country or region into others. At the moment, he said, the company is test marketing in the U.S. products that have worked in Europe, such as frozen tuna filets and flavored tuna.

At the same time, Johnson said he intends to increase the role of Heinz's headquarters in monitoring sales performance and serving as a think tank for international growth.

Source: Excerpted from Rekha Balu, "Heinz's Johnson to Divest Operations, Scrap Management of Firm by Regions," *The Wall Street Journal*, December 8, 1997, p. B12. Permission conveyed through Copyright Clearance Center, Inc.

Disadvantages of the Matrix Structure

1. Worldwide responsibility may be given to product managers with weak international experience. (This problem is addressed in Chapter 8.)
2. The organization tends to create a mountain of paperwork.
3. The dual-boss, cross-communication system is expensive and complex.
4. Decisions sometimes must be made quickly. Quick decisions can be made by one person. In the matrix group decision-making process, decisions are usually made slowly.

Some international business enterprises have had an unhappy experience with the matrix structure. For example, in 1994, Digital Equipment announced that it was getting rid of its matrix system in a global restructuring that would cost $1 billion and 20,000 jobs. Dow Chemical has gone back to its conventional structure with clear lines of responsibility given to geographic managers.[19]

FIGURE 6-6   An Illustration of a Matrix Structure

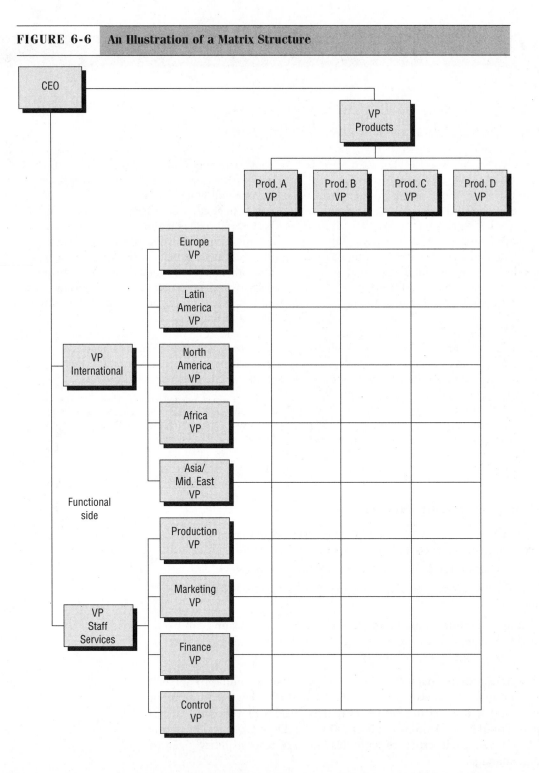

In 1999, the giant corporation General Electric established plans to restructure—to replace its matrix structure with a functional organization, marketing, sales, manufacturing, and so on[20] (although perhaps not in the same way as the functional structure described earlier).

Contractual Alliance Structures

As discussed in Chapter 5, many enterprises enter foreign markets via non-equity-based joint ventures, often referred to as contractual alliances and strategic alliances.[21] For example, one firm's strength may be production and another firm's distribution. Instead of these two firms forming an equity-based joint venture to capitalize on each other's strengths, they form a non-equity-based **contractual alliance**. Thus, when the two firms no longer need each other, in theory, they simply break up the partnership. The advantage of this partnership arrangement is that when there is a breakup, there is no long, drawn-out fight for the division of assets, as often is the case when equity-based partnerships break up.

There are disadvantages to this approach, however. For instance, when one partner acquires the other partner's skills, and the reverse is not the case, the learned partner may leave the unlearned partner in a dubious situation or the learned partner may easily take over the unlearned partner. Of course, this type of arrangement can work only when neither partner possesses an ulterior motive, for example, "I'm really going into this arrangement to acquire the partner's skills, and once I have done so, I will break up the partnership." Furthermore, these arrangements are extremely difficult to manage on a global scale. At one time, AT&T formed an alliance with Philips in Europe to swap technology for access to local markets. The alliance did not meet expectations, mostly because the companies failed to understand each other's strategic objectives.[22]

Networking

Somewhat similar to the contractual alliance arrangement is **networking**. Applying this approach, a corporation subcontracts its manufacturing function to other companies. For example, Nike, the American shoe maker, subcontracts the manufacture of its athletic shoes and clothing to forty separate locations, mostly in Asia.[23]

When an organization enters into such contractual alliances or network agreements, it must create a unit whose responsibility is to monitor the arrangement. For instance, IBM has created an alliance council of key executives who meet monthly to keep track of more than forty partnerships throughout the globe.[24]

But contemporary thinking is that these independent organizations must in some way be interconnected—read, for example, Practical Perspective 6-5. The well-known Harvard Business School professor,

PRACTICAL PERSPECTIVE 6-5

Asia's New Competitive Game

As the millennium approaches, business based on family ties is giving birth to a new type of organization. Instead of building either a centralized bureaucracy or a set of independent, far-flung subsidiaries to manage increasing complexity and geographic spread, Asia's new competitors are building extended networked organizations that rely on continual sharing of information among all their business units. In such organizations, information flows in many directions between nodes, each of which may act as an information supplier at one moment and as a receiver at the next. The process of information sharing is similar to the process by which data flow in a network of computers as opposed to in a centralized mainframe computer system. This style of sharing is especially important for Asian companies, for which key technologies and market intelligence are relatively hard to come by.

One of the companies that typify this new style of organization is Acer, which is driven by the vision of its chairman and CEO, Stan Shih. The structure of Acer's client-server organization is familiar: strategic business units (SBUs), each responsible for a group of products, and regional business units (RBUs), each responsible for a geographic area.

At Acer, each SBU and RBU has indepen-dent capabilities. RBUs, for example, are not simply distributors. They have the capability to assemble a product that has been locally customized to meet local needs, augmenting standard technologies and components in what Acer calls the fast-food model of the computer supply chain. Shih believes that as they develop, RBUs should move from being wholly owned subsidiaries of Acer to becoming minority-owned affiliates of the network, thereby ensuring that they develop as truly local competitors. In addition to acting as clients for the SBUs' products, the RBUs act as servers, providing local market intelligence and informing the SBUs and RBUs of local best practices.

Maintaining excellent multilateral communication among different groups within a company becomes more difficult when the groups are linked to the parent company only by minority shareholdings. But according to Shih, the advantage in such situations is that each group must continually prove the worth of its role in the network, an effort that reduces the risk of complacency. If the benefits of the linkages do not justify the costs, the subsidiary organization will be spun off.

Source: Excerpted from Peter J. Williamson, "Asia's New Competitive Game," *Harvard Business Review* (September–October 1997): 61–62.

Michael E. Porter, describes a similar arrangement as a "**cluster.**" According to him, clusters are "geographic concentrations of interconnected companies and institutions in a particular field." They encompass "an array of linked industries and other entities important to competition." And they include, according to Porter, "suppliers of specialized inputs such as components, machinery, and services, and providers of specialized infrastructure."[25] Practical Perspective 6-6 describes FedEx's and DHL's networking operations.

PRACTICAL PERSPECTIVE 6-6

Warehouses That Fly

DHL has assembled an extensive network of express logistic and strategic-parts center across Europe. For instance, in its Brussels logistics center, DHL does upgrading, repair, and final configuration of Stratus and Fujitsu computers, InFocus projectors, and Johnson & Johnson medical equipment. Adam Ludwig, operations manager at the center, says DHL is currently negotiating similar logistics contracts, each worth $15 million and more, with about 60 companies. The supply of spare parts and products replacements within Europe is another fast-expanding business. For instance, DHL stores and supplies parts for EMC and Hewlett-Packard and replaces Nokia and Philip mobile phones. "if something breaks down on a Tuesday at four o'clock, that warehouse knows at five past four, and the part is on DHL plane at seven or eight that evening," trumpets [Robert] Kuijpers [CEO, DHL International]....

Dell Computer's build-to-order, time-compression model hinges on fast and reliable air express service. FedEx consolidates parts for Dell at Subic, flies them to Dell's big plant in Penang, Malaysia, then, the next day, whisks the machines to Japan, where FedEx handles final configuration for the Japanese market.

DHL's arrangement with Lucent shows how a manufacturer's life can be simplified. DHL moves integrated circuits from Lucent plants directly to customers anywhere in the world within 48 hours. Cranfield's Peter says that the contract with DHL replaced contracts with 51 freight-forwarders and transporters. Likewise, before Toshiba Medical turned over its warehouses in Miami, Brussels, and Singapore, the Japanese firm stockpiled its medical systems and parts in 50 locations around the world.

Source: Excerpted from Andrew Tanzer, "Warehouses That Fly," *Forbes* (October 18,1999): 125. Reprinted by permission of *Forbes* Magazine © 1999. Forbes 1999.

The Mixed (Hybrid) Structure

The traditional and contemporary alternative structures described above are not independent entities that cannot co-exist within the same company. By **mixing** the structural types, the weaknesses of each type can be minimized. For example, companies with a worldwide product division structure can appoint regional coordinators who attempt to supply the concentrated environmental expertise that is usually absent in the product division structure. Similarly, companies with regional structures (either worldwide or within an international division) can set up positions for product coordinators. While such coordinator positions are not particularly new, giving them some real influence short of classical line authority is a relatively recent development.[26] Furthermore, international organizations can centralize some functions, such as an accounting division that provides services for all worldwide subsidiaries, while other functions, such as marketing, remain decentralized.

A General Framework for Decision Making

The preceding discussion described several traditional and contemporary international organizational structures and presented the general advantages and disadvantages for each. The word "general" was used because what is advantageous and disadvantageous does not apply to all situations. For example, one of the disadvantages of the international division structure is conflict; the structure often creates organizational struggles between employees in the domestic divisions ("we") and employees in the international division ("they"). In most cases it may be true that conflict causes harmful organizational disruptions, especially in organizations that rely on "team spirit" for effectiveness. But in some organizational situations, conflict can actually be advantageous, especially when it leads the groups to try to outperform each other. Thus, if the international division outperforms the domestic divisions, the latter may be stimulated to try to outperform the former, and so on. Therefore, the stated advantages and disadvantages are intended to serve as a general framework for decision making, not as a prescription. All situations must be examined separately because different situations sometimes require different prescriptions.

FLAT STRUCTURES

Regardless of which structure is used, it should be as **flat** as possible. That is, it should have fewer managerial layers than traditional hierarchical organizations. A flat structure is needed because a twelve-layer company cannot compete with a three-layer company. For example, a decade or so ago, General Motors, the U.S.-based car manufacturer, had an organizational structure consisting of more than fifteen managerial levels. General Motors had a problem competing with Toyota, the Japanese car manufacturer at least partially because Toyota's organizational structure contained only four managerial levels. (This is in part because Japanese employees are not as motivated by the opportunity to climb up the hierarchy as are American employees.) One reason companies with tall structures are less competitive than firms with flat structures is that they have to pay more managers at more levels, thus increasing their costs.

Another reason is that an organization can create an atmosphere of maximum creativity only if it reduces hierarchical elements to a minimum and creates a corporate culture in which its vision, company philosophy, and strategies can be implemented by employees who think independently and take initiative.[27] Furthermore, as Henry Mintzberg, a well-known professor at McGill University in Canada, proposed in his explanation of *adhocracy*, having many levels of administration restricts the organization's ability to adapt.[28]

The flatter structure means that managers have to communicate with more employees than do managers in tall structures. The ability to communicate with more subordinates has been made possible by the enormous advancements in communications technologies, which, as American management authority Peter F. Drucker noted, enables managers to communicate with a far wider span of individuals than was possible in the past.[29] Spans of control thus give way to spans of communication. For example, at Cypress Semiconductor, CEO T.J. Rodgers has a computer system that enables him to keep abreast of every employee (1,500) and team in his rapidly moving, decentralized, constantly changing organization.[30] The Asea Brown Boveri Group's structure is relatively flat. DuPont, the U.S.-based manufacturing and processing company that operates in 70 countries, has a goal to develop a flat organization that operates by network rather than by hierarchy. DuPont seeks to establish an organization with the flexibility to be able to quickly form and dissolve the local, regional, and global networks needed to solve business problems and meet customers needs.[31]

ORGANIC VERSUS MECHANISTIC STRUCTURES

Another problem confronting international managers is determining how organic or how mechanistic the organizational structure should be. Basically, managers in **organic** structures allow employees considerable discretion in defining their roles and the organization's objectives,[32] In **mechanistic** organizations roles and objectives are clearly and rigidly outlined for employees—managers and subordinates are allowed little or no discretion.[33] Historically, large organizations have tended to adopt the mechanistic form and small organizations the organic form; mass-producing organizations have tended to adopt the mechanistic form and firms producing specialized products have tended to adopt the organic form. Thus, the form an organization adopts is determined by varying situational factors.

In making a determination as to which approach is appropriate for an organization functioning across nations, managers also need to consider national cultural factors. For example, organizational structures tend to be more mechanistic in *strong uncertainty avoidance* cultures (discussed in Chapter 1), such as France and Germany, than in *weak uncertainty avoidance* cultures, such as Great Britain, and organic structures tend to be more prevalent in the latter cultures than in the former. See, for example, Jane Pickard's article "German Way Holds Sway in Britain."[34] This concept of national cultural factors, as well as the situational approach discussed in the paragraph above, will be discussed thoroughly in Chapters 11 and 13. As will be shown, national cultural factors provide international managers a starting point for decision analysis; but ultimately they must consider specific situations carefully. If one adheres to the national cultural factors model, subsidiaries in some nations will be more structured than subsidiaries in other nations; but if one adheres to the situational factors model, the same structure is applied in the same situation in all nations. As will be demonstrated in Chapters 11 and 13, reconciling the national cultural factors model and situational factors model as determinants of the appropriate structure is a monumental task confronting all managers of international organizations.

ADAPTABLE MANAGEMENT

The international organizational structure adopted by a firm's management is influenced by many factors, including the firm's economic situation, the type of product or technology, managerial preference (organizational culture), the foreign country's cultural, economic, technological, and political conditions, the wide separation of operations, and the different foreign market characteristics, including the nature of competition. Therefore, organizational structures that work well for domestic operations are often not suitable for multinational operations. For example, matrix organizations are very scarce in Latin America. This is in part because Latin America's patron system does not lend itself to the power sharing that characterizes matrices.[35] The structure is also influenced by the firm's level of experience in international business and its dependence on revenues from foreign markets. Table 6-1 presents the international organizational structures that might be appropriate for various levels of a firm's dependence on revenues generated from foreign sales.

Historically, when firms first ventured into foreign markets, and when both foreign sales and the diversity of products sold in the foreign country were limited, global companies generally managed their international operations through indirect exporting and subsequently through an international division. Companies that subsequently expanded their sales in foreign markets without significantly increasing foreign product diversity generally adopted the regional structure. Those enterprises that subsequently increased foreign product diversity tended to adopt the product division structure. Firms that increased both foreign sales and foreign product diversity tended to adopt the matrix structure.[36]

International business executives must be thoroughly familiar with the strengths and weaknesses of each organizational structure and be ready to switch from one form to another as a means of **adapting to changing environments** (including moving an important business unit's headquarters to foreign soil). (For an illustration, read Practical Perspective 6-7 and refer to Table 6-2.) The right structure must be matched to the right environment as both internal and external situations change. And the fit must attain a

TABLE 6-1	Dependence on Foreign Revenues and Organizational Structures		
Organization's Level of Dependence on Foreign Sales	**Unit Responsible for Foreign Business**	**Potential International Organizational Structure**	
Very little	Middle person (indirect exporting)	The functional structure; contractual alliance/network	
Somewhat	Export department	The functional structure; the international division; contractual alliance/network	
Substantial	International division	The international structure; contractual alliance/network	
Considerable	Foreign subsidiary	The subsidiary structure; the product structure	
Very much	Foreign subsidiary/ regional headquarters	The regional structure; contractual alliance/network	
Extensive	Foreign subsidiary/ central headquarters	The mixed (hybrid) structure; matrix	

PRACTICAL PERSPECTIVE 6-7

Moving Headquarters of Business Units Abroad

Increasingly, going global means "move 'em out"—by transferring world headquarters of important business units abroad. [Table 6-2 lists some of the MNCs that have made such a move.] In the process, many companies put a non-American in charge of the unit. And U.S. operations that once reported to Wilmington, Delaware, or Parsippany, New Jersey, now report to Tokyo—or the French Riviera. Multinational corporations are making these shifts, risking a loss of control, because they want to operate near key customers and tough rivals in fast-changing markets far from home. More big businesses "recognize that they can't rule the world from one single location" any longer, says Ingo Theuerkauf, an international man-agement specialist for consultants McKinsey & Company. In ten years, Theuerkauf predicts, "we will see maybe 50 percent of Fortune 500 companies making [such] moves."

This fall [1992], American Telephone & Telegraph Company moved the headquarters of its traditional corded-telephone business to France from Parsippany, N.J. It marked the first overseas move by a unit of AT&T, whose ranks of non-U.S. workers have jumped to 50,000 from 50 in 1984. The corded-telephone business had scant international sales until two years ago. Its approximately 2,000 employees around the globe now report to a Frenchman in Sophia Antipolis, a high-technology center near Nice on the Riviera. Other examples

(continued)

abound. In August, E.I. DuPont de Nemours and Company announced the shift of its worldwide electronics operation from the U.S. to Tokyo, nearer its big base of Asian customers. DuPont already manages its global agricultural-products operation and parts of two other large businesses from Geneva.

Going the other direction, Hyundai Electronics Industries Company in April moved its personal computer division to San Jose, California, from Seoul, South Korea, so it could better compete in that industry's biggest market. International Business Machines Corporation, Hewlett-Packard Company, and Germany's Siemens AG have taken similar steps since 1989 by moving units' global headquarters out of their home countries. "The name of the game is to get close to the customer and to understand the customer," says Jack Malloy, a DuPont senior vice president. With the

chemical giant growing fastest in non-U.S. markets, he says, "it wouldn't be surprising to see a couple more" units move their headquarters overseas.

Robert Bontempo, an assistant professor of international business at Columbia University, sees "a strategic competitive advantage" in uprooting operations from a parent's home country and basing them abroad. Relocated units often gain marketing power by acquiring the image of "a global firm with a global reach," he suggests. The strategy also helps to break down parochialism and to groom global managers, management experts say.

Source: Excerpted from Joann S. Lublin, "Firms Ship Unit Headquarters Abroad," *The Wall Street Journal*, December 9, 1992, p. B1. Permission conveyed through Copyright Clearance Center, Inc.

balance between organizational complexity and simplicity. Adopting an organizational structure too complex for its environmental demands can be as ineffective as adopting a structure too simplistic to operate in a turbulent environment.[37] Not adopting the right structure can be very costly—not only in the sense that it will be ineffective, but in the sense that reorganizing is very expensive. For example, AT&T indicated that global reorganization accounted for most of the $347 million it paid in fees to consultants in 1993.[38]

Information Technology and Organizational Structure[39]

The advent of new information technologies such as the Internet, World Wide Web, teleconferencing, and portable telephones now allows organizations to implement inter-and intra-organizational structures that were impossible or economically unfeasible not for too long ago. These technologies enable small, medium, and large organizations to access information from most parts of the world. This suggest that companies, usually smaller ones, organized under the functional structure, can now have access to the same information as large companies. Therefore, smaller companies, by selling their products/services through electronic commerce, can more effectively compete with larger corporations.

TABLE 6-2	**Firms Ship Unit Headquarters Abroad**			

Company	Home Country	New Location	Operation Shifted	Year Moved
AT&T	U.S.	France	Corded telephones	1992
DuPont	U.S.	Japan	Electronics	1992
Hyundai Electronics Industries	South Korea	U.S.	Personal computers	1992
IBM	U.S.	U.K.	Networking systems	1991
Siemens	Germany	U.K.	Air traffic management	1991
Siemens	Germany	U.S.	Ultrasound equipment	1991
DuPont	U.S.	Switzerland	Agricultural products and parts of fibers and polymers businesses	1991
Hewlett-Packard	U.S.	France	Desktop personal computers	1990
Siemens	Germany	U.S.	Nuclear medicine	1989
Cadbury Schweppes	U.K.	U.S.	Beverages	1987*
DuPont	U.S.	Switzerland	Lycra business	1987

*Moved back to London in 1991.
Note: Every relocated operation had its headquarters in the same country as its parent company.

Source: Joann S. Lublin, "Firms Ship Unit Headquarters Abroad," *The Wall Street Journal*, December 9, 1992, p. B1. Permission conveyed through Copyright Clearance Center, Inc.

Companies such as Wal-Mart that are organized under the international division structure with subsidiaries located in many parts of the world can now manage more effectively from single location and may often avoid the cost of establishing physical regional offices when they have grown. And many companies with regional offices throughout the globe can now revert to a single location or at least reduce the number of locations. For example, Eastman Kodak Company consolidated 17 data centers (on four continents) into seven.[40]

Perhaps some of the larger companies can even restructure themselves using the functional structure. As was mentioned earlier, General Electric, one of the largest corporations in the world, has plans it restructure itself from matrix to functional structure. Many of the functions carried out at several points in the matrix structure can now be performed more easily than in the past, when they were centralized. Therefore, the mixed structure is easier to manage, and the information technology makes global strategic alliances and networks easier to manage.

ORGANIZATION COMMUNICATION FLOW

Identifying the ideal international organizational structure is a huge challenge for the managers of any organization; there may not even be an ideal structure. Nevertheless, regardless of which organizational structure a firm adopts, a neat chart with neat boxes is useless unless **information and communications flow freely** to develop proper business decisions. The relationship of domestic, international, and senior corporate organization can be described by three general guidelines.[41]

1. The organization must be formulated in such a way that planning and decision making on every aspect of the firm's operations can be done by people with the breadth of functional, geographic, and/or product knowledge and responsibility necessary to develop the potential for a unified strategy.
2. The channels for the flow of important or recurring decisions and information should be as direct and as short as possible.
3. Individuals with expert international knowledge and competence in overcoming the obstacles to international communication should be readily available within the organization and be used wherever their capacities are needed.

This means that top management in all organizations must incorporate the following dimensions into their systems:[42]

1. The structure must allow for the development and communication of a clear corporate vision.
2. It must allow for the effective management of human resource tools to broaden individuals' perspectives and develop identification with corporate goals.
3. It must allow for the integration of individual thinking and activities into a broad corporate agenda.

Information Technology and Organizational Communication

The advent of the new information technology previously discussed also allows organizations to implement inter- and intra-organizational communication flows that were impossible or economically unfeasible not very long ago. These new **technologies enable companies to vastly increase information flows** across world operations. Companies can create globally integrated information infrastructure that electronically link their entire supply chains (refer again Practical Perspective 6-6)—their sales, production, and delivery processes—into one seamless flow of information across national borders and time zones with both real-time and store-and-forward access to information from any location. Some example are:[43]

➤ Nike, Inc. is implementing a global electronic supply chain to share information with its partners around the world and facilitate better decision making.

➤ The Body Shop is creating an intranet to link the head offices in each of the 47 countries in which it operates. Its headquarters is in United Kingdom.

➤ Tricon Global Restaurants, Inc., which operates 30,000 fast food restaurants worldwide (Pizza Hut, Taco Bell, and KFC) is standardizing its back office operations at all stores. Tricon's new proprietary global information system will allow all stores to order supplies through one global clearinghouse.

Of course, cross-country language and cultural barriers present a challenge for the implementers of such systems. (These problems are discussed in Chapter 9 and 10.) However, the problem is mitigated because English is rapidly becoming the international language for conducting commerce. For example, Cap Gemini Sogeti, a French company with operating units in the U.S. and Europe, recently made a $40 million investment to become more transnational. The firm chose English as common language for all correspondence and business documentation.[44]

SUMMARY

This chapter has discussed numerous international organizational structures, such as the international division and the matrix structure, adopted by international corporations, by multinational corporations, and by global corporations, and the advantages and disadvantages of each structure. Managers must be flexible regarding which structure to adopt for their organizations because different structures fit different environments, and environments change often. Regardless of which structure is adopted, it must allow information and communications to flow freely.

Key Terms and Concepts

1. International organizational structures
2. Functional structure
3. International division structure
4. Foreign subsidiary structure
5. Local managers
6. Product division structure
7. Regional structure
8. Matrix structure
9. Contractual alliances
10. Networks, clusters
11. Mixed (hybrid) structure
12. Flat structures
13. Organic vs. mechanistic organizations
14. Adaptable management
15. Information Technology and structure
16. Information and communications must flow freely
17. Information technology and communication flow

Discussion Questions and Exercises

1. In the functional structure, who is usually responsible for the firm's international business activities?

2. When an international corporation establishes a single subunit to manage all of its international business activities, the firm is using which international organizational structure?

3. Briefly discuss some advantages and disadvantages of the structure you gave as an answer to Question 2.

4. "Autonomy of affiliates" and "direct top management involvement" are advantages of which international organizational structure?

5. Which international structure is prone to "foreign coordination problems"?

6. A global corporation establishes a headquarters to manage its business activities in Africa and a headquarters to manage its activities in Asia. The firm is using which international organizational structure?

7. Which international organizational structure allows local subsidiaries to use discre-

tion in developing products or services to fit local markets and at the same time allows headquarters to coordinate activities around the globe to capitalize on synergies and economies of scale?

8. Discuss strategic alliances, networks, and clusters.

9. Which structure enables organizations to minimize the weaknesses of the other structures?

10. Managers must be flexible to the extent that they can adopt different structures to different environments. Discuss the environments that influence use of the international division, the regional structure, product division, and matrix structures.

11. Read Practical Perspective 6-7. Discuss some of the pitfalls of such a reorganization.

12. Discuss the impact of modern technology on structuring organizations.

13. Discuss the impact of modern technology on organizations' communication flow.

Assignment

Obtain the most current annual report of a multinational corporation. Prepare a short report describing the corporation's structure for class presentation.

CASE 6-1

Toys "Я" Us

Charles Lazarus founded Toys "Я" Us on the premise that "when Mama went back to work, department stores were dead." He argued that "working women wanted a store where they could shop for their children quickly, easily, and cheaply." Toys "Я" Us

offers a warehouse full of play items. Says Lazarus, "We don't want to decide which toys you should buy. We have everything." When focusing on domestic markets, Toys "Я" Us selects store locations where the rent is low, mainly along major highways as opposed to expensive shopping malls. The company's strategy of warehouse-size stores built away from shopping malls and slashing prices on merchandise is as effective today as it was four decades ago. Toys "Я" Us, in essence, invented the toy supermarket. By being big, Toys "Я" Us can buy merchandise at large volume discounts. Toys "Я" Us stocks about 8,000 items and it expects to raise that level to 15,000 over time.

Toys "Я" Us went international in 1984. The company began operating first in Canada, then it subsequently opened stores in Europe, Hong Kong, and Singapore. Japan was always tempting, but the country's Large-Store Law aimed at protecting Japan's small shopkeepers was too great a barrier to overcome...until December of 1991. Japan has the second largest toy market in the world. The Japanese spent $4.7 billion on toys in 1991. It was for this reason that Toys "Я" Us launched its Japanese effort. The first Japanese store was opened on December 20, 1991, in Ami, north of Tokyo.

Toys "Я" Us' international growth is as follows: During 1984, five stores were opened. By 1985, 13 had been opened. By 1986, 24 had been opened and by 1987, 37 had been opened. By 1988, 52 international stores were in operation, 74 by 1989, and in 1990, 97 international stores were open for business. As of January 1992, Toys "Я" Us was operating 497 stores in the United States, and 126 outlets overseas (including the two already opened in Japan), plus 189 Kids "Я" Us stores. Combined, these stores generated approximately $6 billion in sales in 1991.

Everyday low pricing has been a success in Europe, since it is virtually non-existent there. Toys "Я" Us plans to continue its aggressive pricing policy to obtain a greater market share. Toys "Я" Us has planned to open 10 foreign stores per year from 1993 through the end of the decade. According to Lazarus, at least 100 stores might be opened in Japan alone within the next 10 years, depending on

red tape and the ability to find real estate there. The goal of Toys "Я" Us for the future is to open 3001 European stores. The following is a list of Toys "Я" Us stores in the U.S. and abroad in 1999:

Store Locations

Stores Across the United States

	Toys	Kids	Babies
Alabama	8	I	2
Alaska	1	-	-
Arizona	11	-	2
Arkansas	4	-	-
California	87	23	8
Colorado	11	-	2
Connecticut	11	6	-
Delaware	2	1	1
Florida	47	10	10
Georgia	18	4	6
Hawaii	1	-	-
Idaho	2	-	-
Illinois	34	19	5
Indiana	13	7	2
Iowa	8	1	-
Kansas	5	1	1
Kentucky	8	-	1
Louisiana	11	-	1
Maine	2	1	1
Maryland	19	9	3
Massachusetts	19	6	1
Michigan	25	13	5
Minnesota	12	2	1
Mississippi	5	-	-
Missouri	13	5	3
Montana	1	-	-
Nebraska	3	1	-
Nevada	4	-	2
New Hampshire	5	2	-
New Jersey	26	18	7
New Mexico	4	-	-
New York	46	23	3
North Carolina	16	1	5
North Dakota	1	-	-
Ohio	33	18	6
Oklahoma	5	-	1
Oregon	8	-	1
Pennsylvania	33	15	3

	Toys	Kids	Babies
Puerto Rico	4	-	-
Rhode Island	1	1	1
South Carolina	9	-	3
South Dakota	2	-	-
Tennessee	14	2	4
Texas	54	9	13
Utah	6	3	1
Vermont	1	-	-
Virginia	22	7	7
Washington	14	-	1
West Virginia	5	-	-
Wisconsin	10	3	-
	704	212	113

TOYS "Я" US International—452

Australia	24	Netherlands	9
Austria	8	Portugal	6
Belgium	3	Saudi Arabia	3
Canada	64	Singapore	4
Denmark	10	South Africa	8
France	44	Spain	29
Germany	59	Sweden	5
Hong Kong	5	Switzerland	5
Indonesia	3	Taiwan	6
Israel	5	Turkey	5
Japan	76	United Arab	
Luxembourg	1	Emirates	4
Malaysia	5	United Kingdom	61

Source: 1998 Annual Report, http://www.toysrus.com (October 16, 1999). Reprinted with permission.

Questions

1. Design the appropriate international organization structure for Toys "Я" Us.

2. Why did you select that structure?

3. Will the structure be different in 10 years? Why or why not?

Source: Adapted from Stuart Gannes, "America's Sastest Growing Companies," *Fortune* (May 23, 1988); Holt Hackney, "How Do You Say Toys "Я" Us in Germany?" *Financial World* (September 5, 1989); Anthony Ramirez, "Can Anyone Compete with Toys "Я" Us?" *Fortune* (October 28, 1985); Robert Neff, "Guess Who's Selling Barbies in Japan Now?" *Business Week* (December 9, 1991); "Toys "Я" Us Seeks Bigger World Market," *Discount Merchandiser* (July 1989); Isadore Barmash, "Toys R Us: 1990 Outlook," *Stores* (December 1989); Patrick Oster, "Toys "Я" Us: Making Europe Its Playpen," *Business Week* (January 20, 1992).

Notes

1. Excerpted from R.M. Kanter and T.D. Dretler, "'Global Strategy' and Its Impact on Local Operations: Lessons from Gillette Singapore," *Academy of Management Executive* 12, no. 4 (1998): 62.
2. William A. Dymsza, *Multinational Business Strategy* (New York: McGraw-Hill, 1972), p. 17.
3. *Designing the International Corporate Organization* (New York: Business International Corporation, 1976), p. 17. For additional information about organizational structures refer to Michael Z. Brooke, *International Management: A Review of Strategies and Operations* (London: Hutchinson, 1986); W.H. Davidson and P. Haspeslagh, "Shaping a Global Product Organization," *Harvard Business Review* 59 (March–April 1981); C.A. Bartlett and S. Ghoshal, "Tap Your Subsidiaries For Global Reach," *Harvard Business Review* 64 (November–December 1986); Daniel Robey, *Designing Organizations: A Macro Perspective* (Homewood, IL: Richard D. Irwin, 1982); Thomas H. Naylor, "International Strategy Matrix," *Columbia Journal of World Business* 20 (Summer 1985).
4. Adopted from *Designing the International Organization,* pp. 32–33.
5. P.W. Beamish, L.G. Karavis, and C.A. Lane, "The Relationship Between Organizational Structure and Export Performance," *Management International Review* 39, no. 1: 37–54.
6. Dymsza, *Multinational Business Strategy,* p. 23.
7. John M. Livingstone, *The International Enterprise* (New York: John Wiley, 1975): 95.
8. Adopted from *Designing the International Corporate Organization,* pp. 19–25.

9. C.A. Bartlett and S. Ghoshal, *Managing Across Borders: The Transnational Solution* (Boston: Harvard Business School Press, 1989).

10. Adopted from *Designing the International Organization*, pp. 33–36.

11. "The Discreet Charm of the Multicultural Multinational," *The Economist* (July 30, 1994): 58.

12. Adopted from *Designing the International Organization*, pp. 25–29.

13. Ibid., pp. 29–31.

14. Joshua Greenbaum, "View from the Top: Survival Tactics for the Global Business," *Management Review* (October 1992): 50–51.

15. "The Discreet Charm of the Multicultural Multinational," p. 58.

16. Ibid.

17. Bartlett and Ghoshal, *Managing Across Borders*.

18. Stefan H. Robock and Kenneth Simmonds, *International Business and Multinational Enterprises* (Homewood, IL: Dow Jones-Irwin, 1983), pp. 387–388.

19. "The Discreet Charm of the Multicultural Multinational," p. 58.

20. Thomas A. Stewart, "See Jack, See Jack Run Europe," *Fortune* (September 27, 1999): 124–127.

21. See K. Ohmae, "The Global Logic of Strategic Alliances," *Harvard Business Review* 67 (March–April 1989): 143–154.

22. "The Discreet Charm of the Multicultural Multinational," p. 57.

23. Ibid.

24. Jeremy Main, "Making Global Alliances Work," *Fortune*, (December 17, 1990): 121.

25. Michael E. Porter, "Clusters and the New Economics of Competition," *Harvard Business Review* (November–December 1998): 77.

26. *Designing the International Corporation*, p. 36.

27. H.H. Hinterhuber and W. Popp, "Are You a Strategist or Just a Manager?" *Harvard Business Review* 70 (January–February 1992): 105–113.

28. Henry Mintzberg, *Structures in Fives: Designing Effective Organizations* (Englewood Cliffs, NJ: Prentice-Hall, 1983).

29. Jeremy Main, "The Winning Organization," *Fortune* (September 26, 1988): 60.

30. B. Dumaine, "The Bureaucracy Busters," *Fortune* (June 17, 1991): 46.

31. Sunny Baker, "Global E-Commerce, Local Problems," *Journal of Business Strategy* 20, no. 4 (July–August 1999): 32–38.

32. See John Miner, *The Management Process: Theory, Research and Practice* (New York: Macmillan, 1973), p. 270.

33. See Max Weber, *The Theory of Social and Economic Organization*, trans. A.M. Henderson and T. Parsons (New York: Oxford University Press, 1947).

34. Jane Pickard, "German Way Holds Sway in Britain," *People Management* 5, no. 17 (September 2, 1999): 15.

35. J.S. Osland, S. DeFranco, and A. Osland, "Organizational Implications of Latin American Culture: Lessons for the Expatriate Manager," *Journal of Management Inquiry* 8, no. 2 (June 1999): 219–234.

36. J. Stopford and L.T. Wells, Jr., *Managing the Multinational Enterprise* (New York: Basic Books, 1972).

37. S. Ghoshal and N. Nohria, "Horses for Courses: Organizational Forms for Multinational Corporations," *Sloan Management Review* (Winter 1993): 24.

38. "The Discreet Charm of the Multicultural Multinational," p. 57.

39. David O. Stephens, "The Globalization of Information Technology in Multinational Companies," *Information Management Journal* 33, no. 3 (July 1999): 67–71.

40. Ibid.

41. Adopted from John Fayerweather, *International Business Management—A Conceptual Framework* (New York: McGraw-Hill, 1969): 185.

42. Adopted from C.A. Bartlett and S. Ghoshal, "Matrix Management: Not a Structure, a Frame of Mind," *Harvard Business Review* 68 (July–August 1990): 138–145.

43. Stephens, "The Globalization of Information Technology."

44. Ibid.

IV

International Human Resource Management

The human resource management (HRM) function can contribute immensely to a firm's attainment of its goals and objectives. If properly administered, an HRM department helps the enterprise's management recruit, train and develop, and place the right people in the right places. It also helps identify the right motivational programs to keep employees working at their maximum pace. Administering the HRM function is indeed a challenging task in any organization. When the HRM function cuts across national borders, administering it becomes a monumental challenge because HRM managers face a complex set of problems that differ dramatically from those in the home country. One of the problems is selecting managers to staff the firm's foreign operations. This aspect is addressed in Chapter 7. Another problem is developing and implementing effective international programs. This aspect is addressed in Chapter 8.

7

International Managerial Staffing

Dear Mom...

For Americans sent to work in China, the word "adjustment" takes on new meaning, as is evident by these excerpts taken from a letter sent home by an American Anheuser-Busch employee shortly after his arrival in Wuhan:

"I have relocated to sunny (and hot!) Wuhan. Spring lasted about four days and now it is summer.

"We have recently started bringing restaurant menus to work to have them translated. The last one has such delicacies as 'fish stomach over rice' and 'beef tail.' You have to hand it to the people over here: they know how to get their money's worth out of an animal. Absolutely no waste....

"Well, I am in my new house. Everything has its own set of challenges. I taught myself how to use the alarm system. This may not seem like much, but you have to understand that while the instruction booklet is in English, the control panel is written in French....

"I did get my driver's license. Driving is certainly an adventure. This week I am learning how to ignore the stripes on the road, and next week I will work on ignoring red lights. Everything in its own time."[1]

Learning Objectives of the Chapter

Regardless of whether the nature of their business is in commerce, science and technology, education, entertainment, tourism, transportation, religion, or communications, domestic enterprises that want to remain competitive, as indicated in the previous chapters, must develop strategies in response to the intense global competition they face. When a domestic corporation develops a strategy to conduct business in a foreign country, its **human resource management (HRM) function** faces a complex set of managerial problems that differ substantially from those it faces at home. One of the complex problems is selecting the most effective managers to staff the firm's international operations. After studying this chapter you should be able to:

1. Describe the international HRM function.
2. Discuss the three types of managerial personnel commonly used by international corporations to staff their foreign subsidiaries.
3. Present the pros and cons of each type.
4. Describe the factors that influence the type selected.

THE INTERNATIONAL HRM FUNCTION

International human resource management (HRM) consists of an interplay among three dimensions:[2]

1. The broad function: procurement, allocation, and utilization.
2. Country categories: the home country, or where the headquarters is located; the host country, or where the subsidiary is located; and third countries, or other countries that may be a source of labor.
3. Types of employees: home-country employees, host-country employees, and third-country employees.

The factors that differentiate international from domestic HRM are additional functions and activities, a broader perspective, more involvement in employees' personal lives, changes in emphasis as the workforce mix varies, risk exposure, and more external influences.[3]

Additional Functions and Activities

Operating in an international environment, a multinational corporation's (MNC's) HRM department performs numerous activities that would not be required in the domestic environment. The department must deal with developing a global mindset, international taxation, international relocation and orientation, administrative services for expatriates (employees sent from the home country to manage firms' foreign subsidiaries), host government relations, and language training.

Developing a Global Mindset
Throughout the Organization
A key issue HRM is confronted with is how to transform the organization internally to become **globally oriented**. In today's environment, even for

employees who may not go abroad, it is necessary to constantly sensitize everyone to the notion that the company is in a global business.[4]

International Taxation

Expatriates normally have both home- and host-country tax liabilities. HRM must ensure that there is neither a tax incentive nor a tax disincentive attached to any particular assignment.[5]

International Relocation and Orientation

International relocation and orientation entails making arrangements for predeparture training; providing immigration and travel details; providing housing, shopping, medical care, recreation, and schooling information; and finalizing compensation details such as the issuance of salary in the foreign country, determination of various overseas allowances, and taxation treatment.

Providing International Administrative Services

Providing administrative services is a time-consuming and complicated activity, in part because policies and procedures are not always clear-cut and sometimes conflict with local conditions. For example, the practice of testing employees for alcohol and drugs may be legally required in a foreign country, but illegal in the home country, or vice versa. As another example, Chinese expatriates must take an AIDS test upon return to China after being away for a certain length of time. How does a Chinese company reconcile this with the prospective expatriate who may refuse the assignment because of such conditions?

Foreign Government Relations

It is usually much less difficult for HRM managers to obtain work permits and other important documents required by the expatriate if the international business enterprise maintains a good relationship with the host-country's government.

Providing Foreign Language Training

Providing verbal and nonverbal language training is another important activity of the international HRM. Expatriates require at least some basic knowledge of the language of the country in which they will be conducting business; otherwise, how will they communicate?

Broader Perspective

International HRM managers are confronted with the problem of designing and administering programs for more than one national group of employees.

As a result, they need to take a more global view; for example, they must make sure that employees are treated fairly, regardless of nationality.

More Involvement in Employees' Lives

Because the international HRM department must be involved in the selection and training of expatriates, and because it must ensure that expatriates understand housing arrangements, health care, cost-of-living allowances, taxes, and so on, it becomes much more involved in their personal lives than it does with those of domestic employees.

For example, Jeanne Dennison, director of HR of International Telecommunications Group at Bell Atlantic, has said that expatriate employees will often look to HR to learn all about things that affect their families, and you can get involved with them at a level unheard of with domestic employees.[6]

Changes in HRM Emphasis as the Workforce Mix Varies

As the corporation's foreign operations mature, the HRM department may have to change its international functions. If the enterprise employs mostly host-country nationals, the department would no longer place as much emphasis on expatriate training, relocation, and tax programs. The emphasis would probably shift to other programs such as bringing host-country nationals to the home office for development.

Risk Exposure

Possible terrorism in the foreign country, especially in countries where some groups hold hostile feelings toward "capitalists" or where there is a strong possibility of the expatriate being kidnapped for ransom, is of great concern to international business corporations and their expatriates. Mexico, for example, is a very high risk nation in this respect. In 1996, a Japanese Sanyo executive was taken hostage and only released after a $2 million ransom was paid. According to American International Group, an insurer, U.S. companies pay fat premiums for kidnapping insurance for their executives in Mexico. And many top American businessmen live as virtual prisoners of their own security.[7] Of course, kidnapping for ransom is not the only problem expatriates face—they are often sought out for robbery as well (see Practical Perspective 7-1). The training programs administered by the HRM department must therefore include briefing the expatriate about such **risk exposure**.[8] Figure 7-1 describes four steps for helping the expatriates abroad. Furthermore, preparing an employee to work abroad is very costly. This preparation investment is a high risk in the sense that many employees want to return home soon after they get to the foreign country.

PRACTICAL PERSPECTIVE 7-1

Very Risky Business

The last phone call Peter Zarate, an ex-Navy SEAL from California, made was to his wife. A commercial real-estate broker working in Mexico City, Zarate stayed late at the office one night in mid-December to close several big deals. Around 8 o'clock, he picked up his cell phone, called his wife and told her that he would be home soon. Ten minutes later, carrying a briefcase and dressed in a dark blue pin-stripe suit, he walked out of the three-story building on Galileo Street where his employer, the American company Cushman & Wakefield, has its offices.

Apparently Zarate had trouble getting a cab, because around 8:20 he called his wife again and said that he was going to walk to a taxi stand down the street. These would be "sitio" cabs—meaning they had license plates and were registered with the government—and so would be more or less safe. Unlicensed gypsy cabs have become infamous in Mexico City for elaborate mugging and kidnapping schemes, and in fact, a few days earlier an American had been savagely beaten in the back of one. The United States Embassy has issued strong warnings against taking them.

According to the account of a friend who was later involved in the police investigation, Zarate never made it to the taxi stand. He may have been shoved into a gypsy cab or he may have just gotten into one. At any rate, he found himself held at gunpoint by at least two men and tailed by several more in another gypsy cab. First they beat him—beat him so badly that the friend, who identified the body, thought Zarate had been shot in the head. And then they did what robbers in most gypsy cab holdups do: they drove him around from one automatic teller to another, taking out cash. The problem was that Zarate's bank account limited the amount of cash he could withdraw to around $200, and he wasn't even wearing any expensive jewelry. But the robbers looked in his briefcase and there they struck gold. They found papers that told them where he lived.

Source: Excerpted from Sebastian Junger, "Very Risky Business," *The New York Times Magazine* (March 8, 1998): 52. Used with permission of the author.

The international HRM department must make great efforts to lower the incidence of expatriates returning early from foreign assignments.

More External Influences

The type of government, the state of the country's economy, and the generally accepted business practices in the host countries are factors that affect international HRM. These factors vary from one host country to another. The cost of labor and the extent to which labor is organized also varies from country to country.

To find the right managers for foreign operations, managers of international HRM must study the complex situations that exist in each country.

FIGURE 7-1	Protecting Businesspeople Abroad

[Chris] Marquet [senior managing director of Kroll International, a New York–based security firm] describes four steps for helping protect businesspeople abroad.

Step 1: **Information and intelligence.** Companies should assess the risks in the countries where they send employees. Such information is available through the U.S. State Department, the British Foreign Office, and private firms. The information should include travel advisories, such as what parts of certain cities to avoid, and there should be a mechanism for getting that information to anyone who needs it via the Internet, company intranet, or fax.

Step 2: **Planning and preparation.** Have a crisis plan and test it frequently. The plan should describe specific solutions for hypothetical crises, such as kidnapping or extortion.

Step 3: **Prevention.** A preventive program involves special training on how to ward off incidents. For example, awareness training can teach people how to avoid being followed. Prevention also involves policies and procedures such as making sure all travelers are met at the foreign airport, sometimes with an escort or armored vehicle. It's also necessary to protect an expatriate's home as well as his or her office.

Step 4: **Response mechanism.** Companies should have plans in place to respond quickly and effectively to crises. In some countries, an evacuation plan may be necessary.

Source: Helen Frank Bensimon, "Is It Safe to Work Abroad?" *Training & Development 52*, no. 8 (August 1998): 20. Reprinted with permission.

In other words, to be effective in their role, international HRM managers must do their homework.

THREE APPROACHES TO STAFFING FOREIGN SUBSIDIARIES

A key problem confronting HRM managers is deciding whether to employ an expatriate, a host-country national, or a third-country citizen. An **expatriate** is a **home-country national,** usually an employee of the firm, who is assigned abroad to manage the enterprise's foreign subsidiary(s); a **host-country national** is a resident of the country where the firm's subsidiary is located, or is to be located, employed to manage the operations; and a **third-country national** is a resident of a country other than the home country and the host country employed to manage the operations. International HRMs must determine which approach is best suited to the needs of each situation.

Advantages and Disadvantages of Using Expatriates

When managers of international businesses are deciding whether to use an expatriate to manage a foreign subsidiary, they must consider both the advantages and disadvantages of the approach.[9]

Advantages

Knowledge of the Corporation's Culture. Using expatriates is a relatively easy way to obtain personnel with detailed knowledge of company policies, procedures, and corporate culture.[10]

Knowledge of the Company's Management Techniques. Expatriates, because they have worked for the company in the home country, are familiar with the company's management techniques and methods, as well as with the related technology and product development.

Loyalty. The expatriate approach enables international business corporations to select people with proven loyalty to the company. This helps provide credibility at headquarters when the expatriate conveys information, especially information concerning the adaptations the company must make to succeed in the foreign market.[11]

Influence at Headquarters. Using expatriates places individuals who are influential at the home headquarters in the foreign subsidiary.

Easier To Assess. Because the expatriate has been employed with the firm for some time, it is not difficult to assess his or her qualifications for the foreign assignment.

Foreign Image. Using expatriates enables companies to maintain a "foreign image" in the host country, which can be an important marketing strategy (many people, for example, the Chinese, like to purchase goods with foreign labels).[12]

Disadvantages

Expensive Orientation Programs Needed. Expensive programs (which are often unsuccessful) to orient the expatriate to the foreign country's culture and systems are required. This is not as much of a problem for large international business enterprises as it is for small and medium-size companies that compete in the global arena. Smaller companies often do not have the financial means to establish such programs. Smaller companies can send their expatriate candidates to a private training institution, but this is also costly. Yet, without such training, small firms' expatriates are likely to make costly blunders in conducting business abroad, thus putting them at a disadvantage. Small businesses can sometimes overcome this difficulty by entering into a partnership with a capable firm in the foreign market.

Unfamiliar With Foreign Environment. Initially, even after going through the orientation program, the expatriate is not familiar with the local culture, laws, political process, legal process, and other subtleties.

People can be taught the formal systems, but the informal ones have to be learned through field experience. Lack of information often impairs performance. (Read, for example, Practical Perspective 7-2.)

Communication Problems. The expatriate may encounter communication problems in the foreign country, especially if he or she does not have a good command of the local verbal and nonverbal language. This lack also impairs performance.

May Not Adapt to Foreign Culture. The expatriate and/or his or her **family may not adapt to the local culture** and have to be **repatriated** (brought back to the home country) early. This is an expensive proposi-

PRACTICAL PERSPECTIVE 7-2

Getting the Job Done

Although most expatriates will have prepared for working with Arab, Italian, Japanese, or other colleagues, there will be cultural and language obstacles for expats to overcome in the workplace. You can master the language, take cross-cultural diversity courses, and read the native literature and never be entirely prepared for all that idiosyncrasies of life in a foreign country.

Just ask Erin Crossland.

The last thing Crossland had to worry about while selling consulting services for Arthur D. Little in Belarus was cordiality. She quickly learned that many Belarussians live up to their reputations for enjoying a vodka or two. Her challenge: not to let their good nature get in the way of doing important business.

Crossland and her colleagues from the Arthur D. Little consulting group spent almost two years in Belarus working on a strategy with the local government to clean up an environmental-hazard site. It was cagey work that required both high-level planning and muscle-wielding manpower. Unfortunately, Crossland says, the work ethic of the Belarussians did not

always jibe with that of her American counterparts. She recalls being offered vodka at 10 A.M. breakfast meetings and having to fire a couple of Belarussians for being drunk on the job. But the most wrenching experience took place one night at a banquet Crossland oversaw for several international officials, including some from the U.S. Defense Department and the Environmental Protection Agency. The owner of the restaurant where the dinner was held offered to provide, at no expense, a cultural program as a thank-you for bringing him business. Crossland said sure, and gave it little thought. The oversight has since haunted her. That night, after dinner was served, several scantily clad women appeared in the banquet room to perform a racy dance for the guests. It left Crossland—and the executives—a bit red-faced. "I should have gotten a better explanation of what was meant by a cultural program," she now admits.

Source: Excerpted from Charles Butler, "A World of Trouble," *Sales & Marketing Management 151*, no. 9 (September 1999): 2. Reprinted with permission. Permission conveyed through Copyright Clearance Center, Inc.

tion—not only because is it expensive both to send the expatriate abroad and to prepare someone else for the assignment, but also because the expatriate may not have been very effective in the assignment. (In 1990, moving an expatriate and family members from the U.S. to Europe cost about $50,000, and twice that figure to send them to Japan.[13] In 1999, is was estimated to cost as much as $300,000.[14]) It was recently found that between 10 and 20 percent of all U.S. managers sent abroad returned early because of job dissatisfaction or difficulties in adjusting to a foreign country. Of those who stayed for the duration, nearly one-third did not perform up to expectations of their superiors, and one-fourth of those who completed the assignment left their company within one year after repatriation.[15]

The Best Qualified People Sometimes Do Not Want the Assignment. It may be difficult to find highly qualified people who want to work at the foreign subsidiary.[16] Many employees are motivated to elevate themselves in the corporate hierarchy, and they fear that by working in the foreign country, they may not rise as quickly as they would if they remained in the mainstream at home. For example, Ted Patlovich, vice chairman of Loctite Corp., has indicated that "generally, people are not champing at the bit to go [on a foreign assignment]." "It is a major plus to have international experience these days, but you may get lost there," says Chuck Campbell, senior vice president of Federal Signal Corporation. "You aren't as visible as the guy who is working away in front of the CEO's eyes."[17] And in a survey of personnel managers at 56 MNCs, 56 percent of the respondents believed a foreign assignment to be immaterial or detrimental to their careers.[18]

However, it is generally acknowledged that executives cannot elevate themselves in the organization without substantial foreign experience. According to Michael Angus, chairman of Unilever PLC, "Most people who rise toward the top of our business will have worked in at least two countries, probably three."[19] It may now be less difficult to find highly qualified people for foreign assignments than in the past.

Highly qualified executives may also refuse a foreign assignment because of a dual-career family situation, an increasing phenomenon in the United States. This means that to get highly qualified executives in such a partnership, international business enterprises may have to take on the costly burden of having to find a job in the foreign country for the spouse or pay for some other arrangement, such as commuter marriage support. The strategies that some companies are applying to this problem include intercompany networking, job-hunting/fact-finding trips, and intracompany employment.[20]

Very Expensive Incentives Required. To get these highly qualified people to accept a foreign assignment, very expensive incentives, such as much higher salaries and benefits, are often required. The average cost of an international assignment in 1998 was estimated at $1 million.[21] In 1999, a fully loaded expatriate package, including benefits and cost-of-living adjustments, cost anywhere from $300,000 to $1 million annually.[22] Because of such high costs, some companies in Asia terminated expatriate assignment during the recent economic downturn. (See Practical Perspective 7-3.)

Low Productivity in Early Part of Assignment. The expatriate may not be very productive in the earlier part of the assignment because he or she needs time to adapt to the new environment.

"Badwill." Employing foreigners could generate "badwill" among the local people, who may prefer to see citizens of their country managing the foreign subsidiary.

Expensive Repatriation Programs Needed. Expensive programs to reorient the expatriate when he or she returns (repatriation) are required. (This is discussed more throughly in Chapter 8.)

Expatriate May Have an Ulterior Motive for Accepting the Assignment. If an expatriate is resentful of his or her country's political

PRACTICAL PERSPECTIVE 7-3

Down and Out

Twenty-seven-year-old Ravi Menon arrived in Indonesia from India four years ago. Then, Indonesia was "expatriate heaven," a land of high salaries, big houses, company cars, great holidays, and full medical insurance. But this January, his employer, the giant Bakrie group, told Menon and its other expatriate staff that their U.S. dollar salaries would in the future be paid entirely in rupiah. What's more, the conversion would be at 3,500 rupiah to the dollar, less than half the market rate. "It was a good trip while it lasted," Menon says wryly.

Menon isn't the only one lamenting the end of the good times. Expatriates have been among the first to feel the heat of Southeast Asia's meltdown—dramatically so in Indonesia

but also in Thailand, Malaysia, and Singapore.

Before the crisis, replacing expensive foreigners with cheaper locals was a long-term goal for most employers of expatriates. Suddenly it has become a matter of immediate necessity.

Pummeled by currency devaluations, local companies can no longer afford U.S. dollar salaries. They and, to a lesser extent, multinationals are now trying to make their expatriates cheaper and more effective or getting rid of them altogether.

Source: Excerpted from Joanna Slater, with S. Jayasankaran, "Down and Out," *Far Eastern Economic Review* (April 2, 1998): 1. (http://www.feer.com/restricted/98apr_2/manage.html).

system and/or governmental policies, his or her motivation for wanting the foreign assignment may be "escaping" from the country. At the foreign site, the expatriate's energies may be used to attain his or her objectives instead of the company's. In the past, some expatriates from communist countries on assignment in democratic countries have spent much of their time finding ways to obtain political asylum.

Japanese Expatriates in the U.S. as an Illustration of the Disadvantages

An influential Japanese organization employed Matthew D. Levy, principal of WSY Consulting Group, and Soji Teramura, president of the consulting firm Teramura International, to analyze the experiences of 50 foreign-owned enterprises in the United States. The following are some of their findings:[23]

➤ A large majority of Japanese executives and about half of American executives find miscommunication (language barriers) to be a significant obstacle to successful operations.

➤ More than half of American executives, and nearly as many Japanese executives, find cultural differences in the U.S. workplace to be a problem.

➤ Smaller Japanese companies, which tend to be less experienced in international management, have the most difficulty managing cultural differences.

➤ Family adjustment and lack of preparation for life in the United States were cited as problems by about half of the Japanese executives.

➤ Japanese families have problems readjusting when they return to Japan.

➤ Some Japanese executives have problems dealing with American-style unions.

➤ Some Japanese executives, coming from a homogeneous society, encounter difficulties in dealing with America's culturally diverse workforce.

➤ Some Japanese executives have difficulty dealing with the negative feelings some American workers have toward Japanese management.

➤ Many Japanese executives have problems dealing with U.S. federal, state, and local government regulations.

➤ Some Japanese executives cannot effectively handle community relations.

Advantages and Disadvantages of Using Host-Country Locals

As indicated above, when managers of international enterprises are determining whether to use an expatriate to manage a foreign subsidiary, they must consider both the advantages and disadvantages. If the disadvantages of using an expatriate outweigh the advantages, they may have to consider the option of using a host-country national. This approach, too, has advantages and disadvantages.

Advantages

Familiar with Local Environment. Host-country nationals are already familiar with the local language, culture, and customs. They do not require expensive training in language proficiency or acculturation. Ted Patlovich, vice chairman of Loctite Corporation, sees great advantages in having a local manager running things overseas. "We would rather have nationals be country managers than foreigners," Patlovich says. "The national knows his [or her] way around. He [or she] knows the lawyers, the financial people, the bankers. He [or she] knows everybody."[24]

Can Sometimes Be Productive Right Away. Unlike expatriates, nationals do not need time to adapt to the local environment and can sometimes be productive from the beginning of the assignment.

Knows Local Business Subtleties. Nationals grasp the subtleties of the local business situation, information which may be vital to the establishment of a good relationship with customers, clients, government agencies, employees, and the general public.

"Goodwill." Having local nationals in management positions, especially at higher levels, may enhance the company's image (it develops "goodwill"), especially in very nationalistic countries. It may also enhance host-country employees' morale because these employees may appreciate working for a boss of the same nationality rather than for a foreigner, and/or they may appreciate the opportunity for growth in the organization.

Usually Less Expensive to Employ. Employing host-country nationals is often less expensive than employing home-country or third-country nationals, especially in lower-wage nations. Salaries and other benefit packages are often lower than the expatriate's and the third-country national's, and no expensive repatriation programs are needed.

Disadvantages

Loyalty May Be to Country, Not to the Company. In a conflict between national policy and the company's interests, host-country managers may favor national policy over the company's interests.[25]

Often Difficult to Find Qualified People. It is often difficult, especially in the less-developed countries, to find people at the local level with the right skills for the assignment.

More Difficult to Assess Abilities. It is usually more difficult to assess nationals' skills and abilities than to assess someone who is working for the corporation.

Does Not Understand the Corporation's Culture. The national probably does not have sufficient knowledge of the firm's policies and culture, including the informal decision-making network in the home office.

Problems in Communicating with Home Office. The national may have difficulty communicating with the home-office manager and other employees.

May Not Be Mobile. Host-country managers, once appointed, may be difficult to move; they may want to remain on the job until retirement. For example, the Japanese tend to prefer lifetime employment in the same company.

May Have Ulterior Motives. Local managers may become bored with the job itself and concentrate on building a name and reputation in the community for themselves, thus ignoring the managerial function.

May Be Weak in Dealing with Local Government Officials. A host country manager may be weak in dealing with local authorities.[26]

Expensive Training and Development Programs Needed. To deal with the problems outlined above, expensive programs, such as assigning the national to the corporate headquarters for a lengthy period of time to acquaint him or her with the corporation's formal and informal methods of operation, may be required. This would eliminate the advantage of the local manager's being productive right away. And the host-country local becomes an expatriate, thus inheriting the problems for the expatriate previously discussed. Nevertheless, as Morislav Lansky, human resource and corporate programs manager at IBM Czech Republic, has indicated, "It's better to train locals in corporate culture than to train expatriates in local culture."[27]

Advantages and Disadvantages of Using Third-Country Personnel

If the disadvantages of using an expatriate or a host-country national outweigh the advantages, managers can consider another option: using a third-country national to manage the foreign subsidiary. This approach, too, has advantages and disadvantages.

Advantages

Additional Source of Personnel. Third-country nationals are a source of personnel when there is a shortage of qualified host-country and home-country nationals who are able or willing to take foreign assignments.

Usually Costs Less Than the Expatriate. The costs of maintaining third-country nationals are often less than the costs of maintaining expatriates, especially if the expatriates are from high-income nations such as the U.S. and Japan.

Greater Adaptability Than the Expatriate. Third-country nationals from a country in the same region as the foreign assignment are likely to possess greater cultural adaptability and greater flexibility and ease of adjustment in the host country than home-country personnel. For instance, a Brazilian probably would adapt more readily in Chile than a Scandinavian. There will be even greater adaptability if the third country and the host country share a common language and a similar cultural background. A Portuguese citizen may be able to work in Brazil more easily than a British citizen because Portuguese is spoken in both Brazil and Portugal. And it would be easier for a Taiwanese to work in the People's Republic of China than it would for a French individual because Taiwan and the People's Republic of China, to a great extent, share a common culture and language (Mandarin). Over the years American companies have hired English or Scottish executives for top management positions in their subsidiaries located in countries that were former British colonies, such as Jamaica, India, and Kenya.

Advantageous When the Home Country Does Not Maintain a Good Relationship with the Host Country. Hiring a third-country national is especially advantageous when the home-country government does not maintain a positive relationship with the government of the nation in which the subsidiary is located. For instance, an Iranian enterprise with a subsidiary in the U.S. may be better off employing a Canadian citizen to manage the subsidiary because the Iranian government's relationship with Canada is better than its relationship with the U.S.

Disadvantages

The Employee's Country Does Not Maintain a Good Relationship with the Host Country. Problems arise with this staffing strategy if the qualified employee is from a country that does not maintain a good relationship with the country where the assignment is to take place. In certain parts of the world, animosities of national character exist between neighboring countries: India and Pakistan, Greece and Turkey, Ireland, and Northern Ireland, to name a few. Transfers of third-country nationals must take such factors into account very seriously, keeping in mind that local workers may dislike working for the third-country manager simply because he or she is from that third country.

Locals May Prefer Their Own Citizens in Managerial Positions. Another problem, similar to the use of the expatriate option, is the desire of the host-country's government to elevate its own people to responsible managerial positions. Even if the third-country national is better qualified, the government may prefer that a local citizen be appointed.

Appointee May Have an Ulterior Motive. Yet another problem, also similar to the expatriate approach, may occur if the candidate is dissatisfied with his or her country's political system and/or governmental policies. His or her motive for wanting the assignment may be to "escape," and he or she may work toward this end while ignoring the company's objectives.

FACTORS INFLUENCING THE CHOICE

Many factors influence the choice of whether to use an expatriate, a host-country national, or a third-country national. The factors include top management's staffing outlook, perceived needs, the corporation's characteristics, the characteristics of the personnel available at home, and the host country's characteristics.

Top Management's Staffing Outlook

The varying staffing views of international business corporations influence the decision. A company's view can be ethnocentric, polycentric, regiocentric, or geocentric.[28]

Ethnocentric

The **ethnocentric** view holds that key positions in the foreign subsidiary should be staffed by citizens from the parent company's home country. An enterprise develops such an outlook because its top management perceives a deficiency in the qualifications, experience, and competence of host-country nationals to fill management positions in the foreign subsidiary. These firms use expatriates to manage their foreign operations. Japanese international businesses are reputed to adhere strongly to this view. For example, Japanese international business corporations have been found to employ considerably more parent-country nationals at the senior and middle management levels in their foreign operations than do American and European international business enterprises, and they do not use third-country nationals at any level of management in their foreign operations, except in Africa.[29] Procter & Gamble endured a series of painful product failures because of its policy (now abandoned) of imposing managers from headquarters on overseas subsidiaries.[30]

Polycentric

The **polycentric** view holds that key positions in the foreign subsidiary should be staffed by locals (host-country nationals). A corporation's top management holding this view will employ host-country locals to ensure that the foreign subsidiary's operation follows overall company policy. However, polycentric enterprises do usually send expatriates to start the foreign subsidiary and to train and develop locals to assume the managerial responsibility. For example, in its international expansion efforts, Wal-Mart tries to have two American managers in each store for the first year or two, but in Mexico it employed more than two.[31] In addition, although Japanese international businesses have tended to apply the ethnocentric approach, some of them are starting to think polycentrically—for example, Sony now aims to give the top job in each of its subsidiaries to a manager from the host country.[32] Isao Tsuruta, senior vice president for JUSCO, a retail giant based in Tokyo with operations in many parts of the globe, including the U.S. and the U.K., has indicated that in their international expansion, as local people matured in the company, they gradually assumed key managerial positions. In Talbot's, their U.S. affiliate, according to Tsuruta, there is not a single JUSCO employee among its managers, and of the eight members of Talbots' board of directors, only four are JUSCO people.[33]

A company may behave polycentrically toward one country and at the same time behave ethnocentrically toward another. Polycentric firms send expatriates to the foreign subsidiary not only to train and develop the locals, but also to develop or enhance their managerial skills and to develop an informal communication network in the foreign market.[34] For example, Becton Dickinson promotes cross-posting of managers. The firm accomplishes this by sending managers to different foreign subsidiaries for a period of time and having them take on general management responsibilities. This gives members of the strategy teams a broad international profile, enabling them to be more effective when making organizational decisions.[35] Historically, hierarchical opportunities for host-country locals in these enterprises have generally been limited to top management of the local subsidiary.[36]

Regiocentric

The **regiocentric** view holds that key positions at the regional headquarters should be staffed by individuals from one of the region's countries. The firms will use expatriates to develop a regional organization and, as in the case of the polycentric approach, to enhance their skills and develop an informal communication network.[37] Hierarchical opportunity for host-country locals presented by these businesses (especially U.S. and European international business corporations) tends to be top management at the regional headquarters.[38] This opportunity evolved in part because polycentric companies realized that a way to keep effective local managers was to open regional top-level positions to them. Arthur Pappas, an American who (in 1991) headed Glaxo's regional operations in Asia, "had sent home ten Western managers since 1989, replacing them with locals or one of the growing number of Asians who work in the region but outside their home country. Among his current tasks: to train or recruit an Asian to take his place."[39]

International business enterprises typically do not provide locals the opportunity for top-level positions in the central, home-office headquarters. The lack of this opportunity demoralizes some local and regional managers.

Geocentric

The **geocentric** view holds that nationality should not influence the assignment of key positions anywhere (local subsidiary, regional headquarters, or central headquarters) and that competence should be the prime criterion for selecting managerial staff. Even though this view (referred to as that of the global corporation in Chapter 1), at least in theory, seems to be catching on, few international business enterprises practice it fully. David dePury, co-chairman of Asea Brown Boveri, the Swedish-Swiss electrical engineering giant, informed a recent international management symposium at St. Gallen in Switzerland that few multinationals produce more than 20 percent of their goods and services outside their immediate or wider home market, that most boards come predominantly from one culture, and that few multinationals are ready to let their shareholder base become as global as their business.[40]

Coca-Cola Company, however, appears to accept the geocentric view. It owns and operates businesses of all sizes in more than 195 nations. Two-thirds of its 31,000 employees work outside the United States. Third-country nationals make up the majority of the international service employees, and individuals of other nationalities are in charge of more of Coca-Cola's division offices than are North Americans.[41] In 1998, two of Gillette's four executive vice presidents, the traditional stepping-stone to the top, are Europeans. In some countries, Gillette management is beginning to resemble the U.N. Its business in the former Soviet Union, for instance, is headed by a Frenchman, backed up by an Egyptian controller, an English sales director, and officers from Pakistan and Ireland.[42] These corporations, too, use expatriates for development purposes. Ford Motor Company has recently embarked on a colossal plan to turn itself into a borderless firm.[43]

Top Management's Perceived Needs

Some top managers may perceive that an expatriate would work better for them than a local, and vice versa. Louis Jouanny, manager of international marketing for Grid Systems Corporation, a portable computer maker in

California, has stated that "The experience we had is that you need Europeans to sell in Europe and Asians to sell in Asia. You need local people to sell locally."[44] On the other hand, Jerry Johanneson, chief oper ating officer for Haworth Inc., an office furniture maker from Michigan, says, "because the pricing and design of furniture systems can get compli cated, and because we wanted to be certain Haworth's service would be excellent from the outset, we elected to station a U.S. national in the London office."[45]

Company's Characteristics

Companies' characteristics that influence the choice of staffing strategy include the following:[46]

Ownership of Foreign Subsidiaries

The type of staffing strategy an international business company adopts depends on whether the investment is for a short or a long term. If it is for a short term, the firm may utilize the expatriate approach because there is no time to develop locals; if it is for a long term, it may use a development-of-locals approach.

Industry Group

Staffing strategy is likely to vary between the manufacturing and service industries. Service industries such as banking, insurance, and law often hire locals because these people know the practices required to operate the for eign subsidiary effectively. On the other hand, manufacturing enterprises often hire expatriates because they have the technical knowledge required to develop and operate the foreign subsidiary effectively.

Technology

The level of technological sophistication and the amount of research needed to sustain it affects staffing strategy. If the level is high, an expatriate may be required. Furthermore, if the enterprise is protective of its tech nology, it is likely to use expatriates to avoid sharing private information.

Market Influences

Staffing strategies vary according to whether the market for the product is local or international. If the foreign subsidiary is producing for local dis tribution, employing managers with a local perspective may suffice. If, however, the production is for global distribution, managers with a broader perspective, which expatriates or third-country nationals are more likely to possess than locals, would be required.

Stage of Foreign Subsidiary Development

Traditionally, international business corporations have staffed foreign subsidiaries with expatriates in the early stages of establishing operations in a foreign country. To some extent, this is also true in the developed stages when higher-level positions are involved.[47] In the later **stages of subsidiary development,** at least at the lower levels, host-country nationals are employed. Research has revealed that in their first stage of internationalization, companies in the U.S. and Europe export their products to foreign markets. However, as the local market becomes large enough to support local manufacture of the product, home-country managers are sent to the host country to start the operations and manage them during the first few years. Subsequently, the companies replace the expatriates with host-country nationals.[48] The case of Motorola, which has been doing business internationally for many years, is an example:

> *Motorola has...U.S. managers serving on assignments in Europe, the Mid-East, Asia, Canada, Mexico, and Latin America. In virtually all our operations we use an American manager in the start-up process. We do this because it's very difficult for someone in a foreign country to acculturate to the company's management style and objectives while starting up a facility. It's an awful lot to learn. There are exceptions to that, mainly when we have a longer-than-normal lead time to get the facility going. But a lot of our expansion has happened fairly rapidly with only 9 to 12 months to get a plant up and running.*[49]

The cases of Wal-Mart and JUSCO discussed earlier serve as other examples. U.S. international businesses have a tendency to use host-country nationals at all levels of foreign subsidiary management to a much greater extent in the more advanced regions of the world than in the less advanced regions.[50] This suggests that U.S. international business corporations use the ethnocentric approach in less-developed countries and the polycentric approach in developed countries.

Organizational Structure

A company's **organizational structure** also affects its choice of staff. International business enterprises with multidomestic strategies (discussed in Chapter 4) may use locals more than enterprises with global strategies, which require an expatriate's or a third-country national's global perspective. (Of course, locals can also possess a global perspective.)

Dependence on International Business

Top management at firms with high dependence on international business may feel more secure with an expatriate managing foreign operations. Firms with low dependence may use locals because they cost less than expatriates.

Cost-Benefit Factors

The staffing approach with the most favorable cost-benefit ratio is chosen. There is, however, no standard formula for accurately determining the ratio. Decision makers must therefore rely on their intuition.

Style of Management

International business companies apply a staffing strategy that suits their organizational character (or corporate culture) and their **style of management.** For example, Japanese international businesses tend to staff their foreign subsidiaries' important decision-making positions with Japanese expatriates.

Characteristics of Personnel Available at Home

The choice of staffing strategy is also influenced by the **characteristics of the personnel available at home.** Are there individuals with

➤ Adequate qualifications and experience?

➤ A proven record of previous success?

➤ A commitment to international business, including aspirations for international assignments?

➤ The ability to adapt to cultural environments different from their own and the sensitivity to adapt to new situations?

➤ Family commitments that would not hinder the foreign assignment?

If the answer to most of the above questions is no, the firm may have to (1) look for staff in third countries and/or in the host country, (2) implement extensive training and development programs (to be discussed in Chapter 8), or (3) do both (1) and (2).

Host-Country Characteristics

The choice of staffing strategy is also influenced by factors associated with the **host country.** These factors include the following:

Level of Economic and Technological Development

If the country's level of economic and technological development is low, it may sometimes be difficult for the company's top management to find qualified personnel locally. Table 7-1 presents the profiles of country managers for 14 multinationals in Vietnam, an emerging market. None are Vietnamese.

Political Stability

If political stability in the country is low and nationalist sentiments are high, and there is great potential for the government to nationalize or

TABLE 7-1	Profiles of Vietnam Country Managers for 14 Multinational Corporations				
	Age	Nationality	Number Employed	Responsibility: Reporting Line	Vietnamese Connections and Experience
Consumer Products					
Company A	37	American	450	Reports to Singapore	Involved since 1987 in planning Vietnam operation
Company B	40	Swiss	300	Reports to Switzerland	French Vietnamese spouse: 5 years Asian experience
Company C	39	American	30	Also oversees Cambodia & Laos, report to Singapore	10 years Asian experience
Company D	37	British	160	Reports to Australia	Prior experience as manager in Vietnam operation
Company E	48	Japanese	90	Reports to Tokyo	Visited Vietnam often since 1978 to plan operations
Company F	38	French	10	Oversees all Indochina	Previous CM experience in other Asian markets
Industrial Products					
Company G	55	American	130	Reports to Singapore	10 years Asian experience
Company H	54	American	60	Reports to Singapore	3 years Asian experience
Company I	62	American	2	Reports to Thailand	Vietnam veteran
Company J	61	American	21	Reports to Singapore	24 years Asian experience
Company K	63	American	8	Reports to USA	Viet Kieu worked for same firm in Vietnam before 1975
Company L	49	Australian	24	Reports to Singapore	Had traveled in Asia in 1960s
Financial Services					
Company M	44	American	30	Reports to Singapore	Prior emerging markets (but no Asian) experience
Company N	40	American	5	Oversees all Indochina	Vietnamese spouse, in Vietnam since 1992

Source: J.A. Quelch and C.M. Dinh-Tan, "Country Managers in Transition Economies: The Case of Vietnam," *Business Horizons* (July–August 1998): 35. Reprinted with permission.

expropriate foreign-owned companies, an enterprise's top management may feel more secure sending an expatriate. (Of course, as suggested in Chapter 3, many companies will not establish operations in such a high-risk country.)

Control of Foreign Investments and Immigration Policies
Nations may have a policy mandating that foreign-owned subsidiaries place locals in managerial positions. As pointed out in Chapter 3, when Russia

started to attract foreign investment in the late 1980s, its policy was that top management in foreign-owned subsidiaries had to be Russians. Since the policy failed, Russia eliminated it, allowing foreigners to assume top management positions in foreign-owned subsidiaries.[51]

Availability of Capable Managerial Personnel

If managers with the appropriate abilities and experience are not available in the host country, the corporation may have to look for them in third countries or at home, and then implement programs aimed at training and developing locals for managerial positions.

Sociocultural Setting

Will it be too difficult for an expatriate to adjust to the country's cultural, racial, language, religious, and political boundaries? If so, the firm may have to look for locals or for third-country nationals. "The country you plan to expand into makes a big difference," says Steven Graubart, manager with the accounting and consulting firm Ernst & Young. "In Malaysia, Indonesia, Thailand, and the Middle East, for example, hiring a local executive to run the operation might be more necessary than it would be in Canada, the United Kingdom, or Hong Kong because differences in language, social customs, and government regulations are far more pronounced."[52]

Geographical Location

If the location is very isolated, adaptation may be very difficult for the expatriate. For example, it may be difficult to find an employee of a company in Hong Kong to accept an assignment in an isolated area of an African or a South American country. The corporation would then have to consider locals or third-country nationals.

The three sets of factors—company, home-country individuals, and host-country characteristics—may interact to affect the choice of one particular staffing strategy rather than another. These factors suggest that there may be situations in which international businesses will have to adapt their selection criteria to specific situations; in fact, they may sometimes have to lower their standards. For instance, a position at home may require an employee with a college degree, but in a foreign nation where college graduates are scarce and other factors dictate employing a local, the MNC may have to settle for a high school graduate.

TECHNOLOGY AND EXPATRIATION

Technology can play a role in easing some of the staffing problems discussed in this chapter. The Internet, e-mail, and computer networks now enable many companies in some situations to work globally in ways they could not before. For example, a group of computer programmers at Tsinghua University in Beijing, China, is writing software using Java technology. They work for IBM. At the conclusion of each workday, they send their work over the Internet to an IBM facility in Seattle, Washington. In Seattle, programmers build on it and use the Internet to send it to the Institute of Computer Science in Belarus and Software House Group in Latavia. From there, the advanced work is sent to India's Tata Group, which passes the software back to Tsinghua by morning, back to Seattle, and so on until the project is completed. Caterpillar is working on ways to let engineers in different countries collaborate on tractor designs by simultaneously working on a 3-D model over a computer network. And ParaGraph International, a software company started by Russian Stepan Pacikov, develops products in Moscow and Campbell, California, linking the two via Internet and e-mail.[53]

Furthermore, technologies such as videoconferencing, e-mail, cell phones, and frequent-flier miles now enable some expatriates to manage abroad but live at home (see Practical Perspective 7-4). Of course, even though global teams do not have to come together face-to-face and international managers can often carry out many of their managerial duties from the home office, they still must learn the other's cultures (to be discussed in Chapter 8).

PRACTICAL PERSPECTIVE 7-4

"Virtual" Expatriates Work Abroad but Live at Home

LONDON—Michael D. Bekins spent three years on a "virtual" assignment.

As head of Asia-Pacific operations for executive-recruiting firm Korn/Ferry International, of Los Angeles, Bekins was officially based in Singapore. But he didn't rent an apartment there because he wasn't spending enough time in the country to justify the expense. Instead, with his firm's approval, he lived in a hotel when he was in Singapore or elsewhere in Asia and kept his Los Angeles house as his home base.

With more employees refusing to uproot themselves and their families for foreign postings, "virtual" expatriates like Bekins are on

the rise, according to survey by PricewaterhouseCoopers.

Virtual expatriation arises when someone takes an assignment to manage an operation or area abroad without being located permanently in that country. By accumulating frequent-flier miles and using videoconferencing and communications technology to stay in touch with far-flung troops, the virtual expat is a new breed of manager that is multiplying.

For one thing, they are often less expensive than the traditional expatriate, whose allowances and other perks can end up costing employers three times as much as local hire.

More importantly, more executives are

(continued)

balking at an offer to pick up and move overseas for three or four years, particularly when working spouses and school-age children are involved. It is these reluctant employees who are forcing employers to come up with short-term and virtual international postings instead.

Virtual Postings Increase

According to the PricewaterhouseCoopers survey of 270 organizations in 24 European countries employing 65,000 expatriates, there has been an increase in shorter-term, commuter, and virtual assignment during the past two years. Since the last survey in 1997, 44 percent more employers report increases in virtual assignments, and 54 percent report a boost in short-term postings. Overall, about two-thirds of the companies surveyed employ virtual expats, up from 43 percent two years ago.

"Virtual assignments are a sign of how companies are being forced to become more flexible," says PricewaterhouseCoopers's Mari Simpson, who edited the study. "They have to, if they don't, more and more employees will refuse to go on assignment." The survey included responses from such companies as Italy's Flat SpA, Hoechst AG, of Germany, and Norsk Hydro ASA of Norway.

More than 80 percent of companies surveyed reported employees had turned down assignments because of dual-career problems or family issues. Other reasons for balking at overseas postings were the career risk of being far away from headquarters and less attractive overseas packages being offered by companies scrutinizing their expat costs.

Staying Close to Headquarters

Ian Hunter, for one, thinks it makes more business sense for him to be close to where budgeting decisions are made. Although he is in charge of the Middle East and Pakistan for SmithKline Beecham PLC, the Scottish-born Hunter isn't based in Istanbul, Turkey, or Dubai, United Arab Emirates, but rather at the drug maker's London headquarters. "My role is to get resources for my team, and being based at headquarters helps me lobby for them," he says.

Hunter, who is 57 years old, notes that being a "virtual" expat is less expensive for the company, even counting the cost of 16 to 17 weeks a year he travels. Yet he still sees a role for traditional expats, particularly as a way of quickly broadening the experience of promising young managers. Indeed, in the office next to his sits a young Arab assigned to London as an expatriate manager, and on the other side is a young Pakistani expatriate, who is his unit's newly appointed finance director.

To be sure, the survey found the traditional expat, with more than 50 percent of companies reporting growth in the number of assignments overall, is still out there. About 70 percent of companies also said they had focused on cutting expatriate costs during the past two years, with the main focus on reducing pay packages rather than cutting benefits such as housing and cost-of-living allowances.

It also found some companies were rejiggering compensation packages to reward expats who stuck it out through their entire foreign stint. One method: paying bonuses, allowances, or other forms of compensation near the back end of an employee's assignment, rather than spreading it out on a monthly basis, which is commonly done now.

Korn/Ferry's Bekins asked his employer for location flexibility. "My job required me to be out of the office most of the time, so it really didn't matter where I was based," says Bekins, who accepted a new assignment [in early 1999] as head of the executive-search firm's European operations based in London. In his new role, Bekins says he sees more employers offering virtual postings to help lure top executives to their companies.

Theoretically, the virtual posting allows an executive to take an assignment without subjecting his or her family to the culture shock of an overseas move. These arrangements also expose the employee to global management issues, while permitting closer touch with the home office.

Improved Technology Is Key

Technology has made that much easier. Gerald Lukomski, 63, a Detroit native now based in Slough, England, as Motorola Inc.'s corporate vice president and director of Central Eastern Europe, the Middle East, and Africa, estimates he spends about 75 percent of his working time traveling. He never leaves home without a laptop and cell phone. And as an empty-nester, he sometimes travels with his wife. "Our kids refer to us as 'runaway parents' because we are seldom in one place for very long," Lukomski says.

Of course, there are drawbacks to virtual assignments. Parachuting into a country for a few weeks every quarter may not be the most effective way of leading or building a local team. "Nothing can replace face-to-face communication," says Christine Communal, a senior researcher at England's Cranfield University's Center for Research into the Management of Expatriation. "If you do hit problems, the risk is that you haven't had time to properly build up a relationship with your local employees to help you work them out."

Source: Julia Flynn, "E-mail, Cell Phones and Frequent-Flier Miles Let 'Virtual' Expats Work Abroad but Live at Home," *The Wall Street Journal*, October 25, 1999, p. A26. Permission conveyed through Copyright Clearance Center, Inc.

SUMMARY

This chapter has briefly described how the international HRM function differs from the domestic HRM function. It has described three options for international business enterprises to use in selecting management staff for their foreign operations: send someone from the home country, hire someone in the host country, or hire someone from a third country. It has also discussed the advantages and disadvantages of each option and presented the factors HRMs must consider when deciding whether to use a home-country national, a host-country national, or a third-country national.

Key Terms and Concepts

1. International human resource management function
2. Global mindset
3. International relocation and orientation
4. Risk exposure
5. Expatriate
6. Home-country, host-country, and third-country nationals
7. Familiarity with internal aspects of the firm
8. Not familiar with local culture, laws,

    political process, legal process, and other subtleties
9. Family may not adapt to local environment
10. Repatriate
11. Adaptation
12. "Goodwill"
13. The ethnocentric, polycentric, regiocentric, and geocentric staffing views
14. Characteristics that influence the choice of strategy
15. Stage of subsidiary development

16. Organizational structure
17. Style of management
18. Characteristics of personnel available at home

19. Host-country characteristics
20. Technology and expatriation

Discussion Questions and Exercises

1. Fundamentally, the international human resource management (HRM) functions consist of an interplay among three dimensions. What are the three dimensions?
2. How does the international HRM function differ from the domestic HRM function?
3. Briefly describe the three approaches to international managerial staffing.
4. Discuss some of the advantages and disadvantages of each approach.
5. You are the manager of the international HRM function for a firm that needs to assign an executive to manage a subsidiary in a foreign country. You have approached a top-notch executive who refused the assignment because he or she wishes to remain in the home office because of upward movement aspirations. How would you convince the executive to accept the assignment? What would you say to him or her?
6. What are some of the problems Japanese expatriates encounter in the U.S. environment?
7. You are the manager of the international HRM function for a firm located in the U.S. that needs to assign an executive to Iran to establish operations there. The top management of the firm is inclined to send one of its own executives. What advice would you give to the top management?

8. You are the manager of the international HRM function for a firm whose staffing view is ethnocentric. You noticed that the firm has been spending far too much money assigning expatriates to manage its foreign operations, and that the host-country nationals working for foreign subsidiaries are disgruntled because their managers are foreigners. What would you advise the firm's management to do?
9. What is the appropriate staffing strategy for the following company characteristics?
   a. Has established foreign operations for a short period of time.
   b. Has established a banking subsidiary in foreign country.
   c. Is transferring advanced, sophisticated technology to the foreign country.
   d. Has an established foreign subsidiary in the foreign country to produce for local consumption.
   e. Is to establish a new subsidiary in the foreign country.
   f. Has developed a multidomestic strategy.
   g. Has total revenues that rely only slightly on foreign sales.
10. Discuss the host-country characteristics that influence the staffing method.
11. Discuss the way current technology aids HR managers in dealing with the international staffing problems discussed in the chapter.

Assignment

Contact the manager of an international business corporation's international HRM function. Ask him or her to describe the company's international managerial staffing approaches. Prepare a short report for class presentation.

CASE 7-1

Deep in the Republic of Chevron

The Delta region of Southern Nigeria, where the mighty Niger River drains into the Atlantic Ocean, includes some of the most inhospitable territory on earth. It's the world's largest mangrove swamp, 14,000 square miles of thickets, channels, and lagoons all but impenetrable to any but the most practiced eye. It's also oil country, dotted with wells and flow stations, where about two million barrels of crude are collected each day and piped to central stations for transport abroad.

Helicopter is the preferred mode of transport, for the lucky few who can afford it. One of those is Leonard Hutto, the superintendent of Chevron operations in the eastern Niger Delta, and on this day it was his chopper that hovered tentatively above one of Chevron's 30-odd oil stations in the area. The landing pad, a few hundred feet below, was thronged with hundreds of angry young Nigerians peering up at the midmorning sky, clearly shouting and shaking their fists. Seeing that they did not have guns, Hutto finally told the pilot to land.

At the same moment, down on the flow station, standing atop a table inside a tiny office, surrounded by dozen of young men brandishing machetes, Hutto's Nigerian assistant, Tony Okoaye. was relieved to hear the helicopter's engine drown out the shouts of his captors. To hear Okoaye tell it, a predawn phone call had jerked him out of bed: 400 villagers had invaded the site, carrying them a long list of demands. By 7 A.M. Okoaye had driven to the station, only to be taken hostage. Okoaye, an American-educated engineer normally prone to fits of delirious laughter, was not laughing. The young men, many drunk or high on marijuana, made him stand on the table for hours, slapping his pudgy frame and jabbing forefingers into the soft belly above his

Tommy Hilfiger jeans. "Ah, hah!" they taunted. "You're a big man!"

They ordered him to shut down the oil wells. Okoaye did so, reluctantly. "You don't want to lose one barrel." Then they demanded to see his boss, Hutto. "We want to see the white man," they told him. "The American."

And so after a half-hour helicopter ride from Chevron's eastern headquarters in the city of Port Harcourt, the American oilman from south Texas had arrived. "What a pain," Hutto remembers thinking, as his chopper descended from the sky and the Nigerians scattered.

What came next on this particular morning would nonplus the most seasoned executive at a Fortune 500 company, but to the Chevron oilman it was Kabuki. After the youths agreed to let him call a police escort, Hutto got into a Toyota pickup and drove a few miles to the village.

There, in the shade of a huge tree, he sat on a folding chair through the afternoon, listening to the community's grievances and demands: more scholarships for its youngsters and more regular meeting with Chevron, which the locals would get, and other demands, which they would not, including 25 jobs on the spot, about $27,000 in cash and an unspecified amount for wages they had lost while busy invading the oil station. Hutto instead slipped $50 to the town chiefs for drinks, $20 to the youths and another $20 to a group of young men who had let the air out of the tires of the Toyota—to reinflate them.

His assistant was released, the valves were opened at the oil wells and crude began coursing through the pipelines to the flow station. A few thousand barrels had been lost.

"Not a big deal," Hutto says.

Routine, in fact, in the Niger Delta, where

men usually focused on finding and extracting hydrocarbons are forced to act as politicians, diplomats, and mediators. These are roles that Western oilmen are increasingly playing as they seek crude in war-ravaged and lawless places like Angola and Congo, nations in name alone. Hutto spent 12 years in Congo, the former Zaire, where frequent crises forced him to sleep on an offshore oil platform, a fortress in the Atlantic Ocean several miles from a land of chaos....

After work, Hutto drives home in his white Toyota Landcruiser through Port Harcourt's "go slows," or traffic jams. Boys hawking everything from toilet paper to power tools dart to his side with cries of "Master!" But they turn away quickly: a Nigerian policeman, gripping a tear-gas rifle in his hands, rides shotgun.

More policemen guard Hutto's villa, a two-story white house. Never married, Hutto lives alone, not counting the houseboy in the backyard bungalow. In the kitchen, Hutto shows me a large refrigerator and freezer. He keeps inside the 50 New York sirloin and T-bone steaks that he brought back from his last visit to the United States and has been cooking, at the rate of one a week, on a grill that he keeps in his living room.

He drops off his briefcase and gets ready for a visit to an expat bar called Cheers. As Hutto pulls out of his driveway, a skinny African dog watches indifferently. When he moved in, Hutto explains, the houseboy told him that the previous tenant had left the dog behind.

"Now it's yours," Hutto told the houseboy.

Hutto, 43, grew up in the small town of Taft in south Texas, watching his father and grandfather supplement their farmers' incomes by working in oil fields. Hutto got a degree in petroleum engineering at Texas A & M, then joined Chevron and worked in west Texas and the company's headquarters in San Francisco. But it was the Congo that hardened him for battle. Like many expatriate oilmen in Africa, he worked nonstop for 28 days, then went home for 28 days, in his case to a ranch-style house in Las Vegas....

A year ago, Hutto accepted the assignment in Port Harcourt, a position Chevron considers difficult to fill because there is no rotation schedule, no other Americans, and constant interaction with Chevron's delta neighbors. In Lagos, the Americans live inside Chevron's headquarters, a sprawling campus surrounded by high walls, a surreal replica of America with wide streets and suburban houses straight out of Westchester County. Hutto is alone.

Questions

1. Discuss the appropriateness of Chevron's staffing approach, including Hutto and Okoaye in your discussion.

2. No doubt, this staffing approach is very expensive. Are there other viable staffing approaches available to Chevron? Why or why not?

3. Do you believe Chevron has a strong expatriate risk briefing program? Why or why not?

4. Is Chevron's staffing outlook in this case ethnocentric, polycentric, or geocentric? What in the case led you to that conclusion?

Source: Excerpted from Norimitsu Onishi, "Deep in the Republic of Chevron," *The New York Times Magazine* (July 4, 1999): 26–27. Copyright © 1999 by The New York Times Company. Reprinted by permission.

Notes

1.Excerpted from "The China Challenge," *Anheuser-Busch Horizons* (Third Quarter 1997): 3.

2.P.V. Morgan, "International Human Resource Management: Fact or Fiction," *Personnel Administrator 31*, no. 9 (1986): 43–47.

3.P.J. Dowling, R.S. Schuler, and D.E. Welsh, *International Dimensions of Human Resource Management* (Belmont, CA: Wadsworth Publishing, 1994), pp. 2–10.

4.K. Robert, E.E. Kossek, and C. Ozeki, "Managing the Global Workforce: Challenges and Strategies," *Academy of Management Executive 12*, no. 4 (1998): 95.

5.See D.L. Pinney, "Structuring an Expatriate Tax Reimbursement Program," *Personnel Administrator 27*, no. 7 (1982): 19–25.

6.Carla Joinson, "Why HR Managers Need to Think Globally," *HR Magazine* (April 1998): 2.

7.Sebastian Junger, "Very Risky Business," *The New York Times Magazine* (March 8, 1998): 53.

8.See J. Kapstein "How U.S. Executives Dodge Terrorism Abroad," *Business Week* (May 12, 1986): 41.

9.For a current account of the problems expatriates face, see R.L. Thornton and M.K. Thornton, "Personnel Problems in 'Carry the Flag' Missions in Foreign Assignments," *Business Horizons*, (January–February 1995): 59–65.

10.The source of this discussion is S.B. Prasad and Y.K. Shetty, *An Introduction to Multinational Management* (Englewood Cliffs, NJ: Prentice-Hall, 1976), p. 152.

11.C.K. Prahalad and K. Lieberthal, "The End of Corporate Imperialism," *Harvard Business Review* (July–August 1998): 75.

12.E.L. Miller and J.L. Cheng, "A Closer Look at the Decision to Accept an Overseas Position," *Management International Review 18*, no. 1 (1978): 25–27.

13.Charles Siler, "Recruiting Overseas Executives," *Overseas Business* (Winter 1990): 31.

14.Charles Butler, "A World of Trouble," *Sales Marketing Management 151*, no. 9 (September 1999): 45.

15.J.S. Black and H.B. Gregersen, "The Right Way to Manage Expatriates," *Harvard Business Review* (March–April 1999): 53.

16.Simcha Ronen, *Comparative and Multinational Management* (New York: John Wiley & Sons, 1986), pp. 505–554.

17.Charles Siler, "Recruiting Overseas Executives," p. 77.

18.Cecil G. Howard, "Profile of the 21st-Century Expatriate Manager," *HR Magazine* (June 1992): 93–100.

19.Ibid., p. 97.

20.C. Reynolds and R. Bennett, "The Career Couple Challenge," *Personnel Journal* (March 1991): 48.

21.Ken Coles, "Prudential Prepares People for Life Overseas," *Prudential Leader* (February 1998): 24.

22.J.S. Black and H.B. Gregersen, "The Right Way to Manage Expatriates," p. 53.

23.Matthew D. Levy and Soji Teramura, "Foreign Ownership: Japanese in U.S. Overcome Barriers," *Management Review* (December 1992): 10–15.

24.Siler, "Recruiting Overseas Executives," p. 77.

25.Prasad and Shetty, *Introduction to Multinational Management*, p. 153.

26.F. Adams, Jr., "Developing an International Workforce," *Columbia Journal of World Business 20* (20th Anniversary Issue) (1985): 23–25.

27.Byron Sebastian, "Integrating Local and Corporate Culture," *HR Magazine 41*, no. 9: 114.

28.H.V. Perlmutter and D.A. Heenan, "How Multinational Should Your Top Managers Be?" *Harvard Business Review 52* (November–December 1974): 121–132. See also S.H. Robock and K. Simmonds, *International Business and Multinational Enterprises* (Homewood, IL: Irwin, 1989); and J.L. Calof and P.W. Beamish, "The Right Attitude for International Success," *Business Quarterly* (Autumn 1994): 105–110.

29.Rosalie L. Tung, "Selection and Training Procedures of U.S., European, and Japanese Multinationals," *California Management Review 25*, no. 1 (1982): 61.

30."The Discreet Charm of the Multicultural Multinational," *The Economist* (July 30, 1994): 58.

31.W. Zellner, L. Shepard, and D. Lindorff, "Wal-Mart Spoken Here," *Business Week* (June 23, 1997): 141.

32."The Discreet Charm of the Multicultural Multinational," p. 8.

33.Deloitte and Touche Representatives, "One Company's Approach to Global Expansion," *Stores* (January 1998): S14.

34.A. Pazy and Y. Zeira, "Training Parent-Country Professionals in Host Organizations," *The Academy of Management Review 8*, no. 2 (1983): 262–272. See also Y. Zeira and A. Pazy, "Crossing National Borders to Get Trained," *Training and Development Journal 39* (October 1985): 53–57.

35. Denis McCauley, "How Becton Dickinson Uses Cross-Border Teams to Make 'Transnationalism' Work," *Business International* (February 26, 1990): 63–68.

36. Daniel Ondrack, "International Transfer of Managers in North American and European MNEs," *Journal of International Business Studies* (Fall 1985): 1–19.

37. Ibid.

38. Ibid.

39. Ford S. Worthy, "You Can't Grow If You Can't Manage," *Fortune* (June 3, 1991): 88.

40. "The Discreet Charm of the Multicultural Multinational," p. 57.

41. "Corporate Coaches Support Global Network," *Personnel Journal* (January 1994): 58.

42. William C. Symonds, "The Next CEO's Key Asset: A Worn Passport," *Business Week* (January 19, 1998): 76–77.

43. "The Discreet Charm of the Multicultural Multinational," p. 57.

44. Siler, "Recruiting Overseas Executives," p. 76.

45. Ibid.

46. Prasad and Shetty, *Introduction to Multinational Management*, p. 154.

47. M.Z. Brooke and H.L. Remmers, *International Management and Business Policy* (Boston: Houghton Mifflin, 1978).

48. Lawrence G. Franko, "Who Manages Multinational Enterprises," *Columbia Journal of World Business* 2, no. 8 (1973): 30–42.

49. David Pulatie, "How Do You Ensure Success of Managers Going Abroad?" *Training and Development Journal* (December 1985): 22.

50. Tung, "Selection and Training Procedures," p. 61.

51. R. Brady and R. Boyle, "Combustion Engineering's Dislocated Joint Venture," *Business Week* (October 22, 1990): 49–50.

52. Siler, "Recruiting Overseas Executives," p. 77.

53. This discussion draws from Kevin Maney, "Technology is 'Demolishing' Time, Distance," *USA Today*, September 2, 1997. (http://167.8.29.8/plweb-cgi/idoc.p...s+NEWS++international%26 management)

8

Effective International Human Resource Management

Michael Bonsignore, chairman and CEO of $7 billion instrument-controls maker Honeywell, may be the quintessential global executive. Having traveled extensively as the son of an Army doctor, during his own stint as an officer in the Navy and for Honeywell, Bonsignore has lived around the world—in Venezuela, Peru, Mexico, Germany, and Belgium. He speaks four languages: English, Spanish, French, and Italian. Since becoming head of the company in 1993, he has made sure that other executives at the Minneapolis-based company mirror his own broad exposure to various cultures. In several key instances, he's picked foreign-born managers for his most senior posts and ensured that other executives routinely are given short- and long-term assignment around the globe. Today, 40 percent of Honeywell's sales and one-third of its employees are outside the United States.[1]

Learning Objectives of the Chapter

As indicated in Chapter 7, international business enterprises use three types of executives to staff their foreign subsidiaries: home-country nationals (expatriates), host-country nationals (locals), and third-country nationals (by definition, also expatriates). Use of host-country nationals by companies to manage their foreign subsidiaries has become more and more popular in recent years. But there is no doubt that the home country and third countries will continue to be important sources of expatriate executives used by international businesses. This is especially true as more and more multinational corporations (MNCs) transform themselves into global corporations and establish a global strategy. These expatriate executives, referred to as global managers (discussed in Chapter 1), can move readily from country to country and perform effectively no matter where they are.

Using expatriates can be very costly, especially when the expatriate wants to return home prematurely from the foreign assignment or when the wrong person was selected for the foreign assignment—and these instances are numerous. A study of U.S. MNCs revealed that more than half (69 percent) of the firms surveyed had recall rates of between 10 and 20 percent; about 7 percent of the respondents had recall rates of between 20 and 30 percent; and 24 percent had recall rates of less than 10 percent.[2] This is consistent with another study's findings that nine of ten expatriates were significantly less successful in their assignments in Japan than they had been in their previous assignments in their home country, and four of five were considered to be failures by the home office.[3] This suggests that international business enterprises need to develop and implement effective international HRM programs. After studying this chapter you should be able to:

1. Discuss why many expatriates fail in their foreign assignments.
2. Propose how to reduce expatriate failures.
3. Point out how to select the right expatriate.
4. Discuss how to find and develop global expatriates.
5. Show how to administer expatriate programs.
6. Discuss expatriate compensation policy.

WHY EXPATRIATES FAIL

R easons for the failure of many **expatriates** in their foreign assignments include the foreign country's physical and social environments, varying technical sophistication, company-country conflicting objectives and policies, overcentralization, gender, inadequate repatriation programs, and pitfalls in the human resource planning function.

The Physical and Social Environments

When expatriates cross national boundaries, they often encounter **adaptation problems** caused by both the physical and the sociocultural environments. This is especially true when these environments are at odds with the expatriate's own value system and living habits. For example, geographical distance conflicts with an individual's need to feel secure in the community, and it may result in "separation anxiety" for expatriates and their family members.[4] Such reactions may impair the expatriate's on-the-job effectiveness and lower family morale. The problem is enlarged when the expatriate is not capable of communicating with the local people in their verbal and nonverbal language.[5] These problems will affect expatriates' ability to deal with individuals and business groups outside the subsidiary, including local partners, trade unions, bankers, and important customers.[6]

Varying Technical Sophistication

Expatriates often encounter **differences in technical sophistication** in the foreign country, a problem which conflicts with their expectations. The problem becomes critical when an expatriate views the technical differences as insurmountable.[7] Yet another problem for expatriates occurs when they attempt to apply successful home-country managerial and organizational principles in the foreign country. The expatriate may experience considerable frustration because differences in the local culture usually prevent effective implementation.[8]

MNC–Country Conflicting Objectives and Policies

Expatriates also encounter difficulties because they are links between corporate headquarters and the foreign subsidiary and because they are responsible for implementing the objectives and policies formulated by the home office. Problems often occur when the **objectives and policies conflict** with the managerial situation viewed by the expatriate manager and with the managerial mandates imposed on him or her by the local government.[9] That is, the expatriate manager must often conduct the subsidiary's operations within the constraints imposed by the immediate situation and the local government.

Overcentralization

Expatriates face another problem when the home office overcentralizes decision making. If the **expatriate manager's authority is visibly constrained,** his or her opportunity to establish and maintain an effective relationship with local associates is diminished. This is especially true in host environments where individuals place a high value on authority. If the expatriate manager lacks authority, he or she loses credibility in the eyes of locals.[10] (Refer to Practical Perspective 8-1.)

Gender

Still another problem is cultural resistance to expatriate women managers. **Cultural biases against women** in some host countries (especially in the Middle East, Japan, and Latin America) may deter the acceptance of women as managers. Subordinates in such host-country subsidiaries may interpret the assignment of a woman executive to mean that the central headquarters has low regard for its business with that subsidiary. They may

PRACTICAL PERSPECTIVE 8-1

Successful MNCs Have Flexible Practices, People, and HR Functions

If you want to be around 20 years from now, your people must be flexible and willing to make change—or the organization will be gone." This sentiment, expressed by André Rudé, an HR executive at the Hewlett Packard Corporation, summarizes well the opinions shared by the managers at the successful MNCs in our study. According to Rude, "Flexibility is IN" at Hewlett Packard. In the case of MNCs, flexibility is critical with respect to the policies and practices typically developed at headquarters and then implemented worldwide. Policies and practices are considered flexible if they allow for variation across nations, thereby taking national cultures into account. Yet, all too often, the goal is to maintain consistency across nations, and rigid and inflexible policies and practices are the result.

To illustrate this, some of the executives mentioned the conflict around diversity programs. This conflict arises between those advocating the need for consistency or centralization and those administering policy at the local level. In an extreme case of centralization, corporate headquarters may ask all the managers of the organization's foreign subsidiaries to implement the same very structured program. International managers are likely to become frustrated with the home office for being so culturally insensitive and naïve as to believe that people worldwide hold the same value concerning, for example, individualism and equal opportunity as a fundamental right....

Source: Excerpted from L.K. Stroh and P.M. Caligiuri, "Increasing Global Competitiveness Through Effective People Management," *Journal of World Business 33*, no. 1 (Spring 1998): 2–3. Reprinted with permission.

also worry that a woman will have less influence over decisions at headquarters; that is, they may think that she will have less autonomy in local negotiations, and will thus be less able to represent the subsidiary in local transactions.[11] However, using a female expatriate is becoming less and less of a problem—especially when she is viewed by locals as having the authority to make decisions.

Repatriation

Repatriation (reassigning the expatriate back home) is a special problem. A survey revealed that most of the responding companies had no formal **repatriation policy** to help returning employees readjust to the home country's environment.[12] Another survey revealed that employees found reentry into their home country and home company more difficult than the initial move to the foreign culture. This is in part because the **managerial skills that they had enhanced abroad generally were neither recognized nor utilized by the**

home-country organization. The returnees saw themselves as being most effective when they integrated their foreign with their home-country experiences and actively used these new skills. But their colleagues evaluated them most highly when they did not have characteristics of "foreigners" and did not use their cross-cultural learning in their domestic jobs.[13] In fact, the experience expatriates acquire in the foreign assignment often makes them more marketable outside the home corporation.[14]

The problem is magnified when the technological advances made at home make the expatriate's functional abilities obsolete.[15] It is also magnified when the returnee finds that he or she has **missed opportunities** in the organization. An investigation showed that returning managers encountered problems because important career and professional opportunities had passed them by.[16] Many expatriates have returned home only to find that their peers had been promoted ahead of them to higher-level positions.[17] Other problems include returnees' complaints that the length of their foreign assignment adversely affected their lifestyles, their ability to plan for their future professional careers, and their children's education.

Some returnees complained about losing social and professional prestige. For example, being in a country where the cost of living is relatively low, coupled with the higher salary expatriates normally draw, the executive may have had a very large house with servants, may have had children in an expensive private school, and may have been in top management at the subsidiary. Back at home, where the cost of living is relatively high, the employee may have to settle for a smaller house, no domestic help, and a less expensive, lower-quality school for the children. The returned is no longer in a focal position at work—even if the executive is promoted upon return, in many cases he or she may feel professionally "demoted," as the new position usually does not allow the same freedom and stimulation that the foreign position did.[18] Also, the repatriate and his or her family may experience **"reverse culture shock"** on return, as the environment is no longer as familiar as it was when they left.[19] Or the assignment may have been in a European cultural center and the returnee is assigned to a remote rural town. (Refer to Practical Perspective 8-2.)

These potential repatriation problems may hinder the expatriate's performance abroad, or, as pointed out in Chapter 7, the better-qualified executives may not even accept the foreign assignment, forcing companies to assign less-qualified people.

Pitfalls in the Human Resource Planning Function

The above reasons for expatriate failures stem in part from poor human resource planning. A study reveals that many pitfalls in the human resource planning function of U.S. multinationals help cause expatriate failures.[20] The human resource planning function in many U.S. international business enterprises tends to suffer because of several major limitations.

PRACTICAL PERSPECTIVE 8-2

Coming Home

In 1993 Thorpe McConville was sent to Shanghai to open Diebold, Inc.'s China subsidiary. As the general manager and CEO of the operation, McConville had considerable responsibilities. He would be preparing Diebold to tap a market with immense potential for his company's product, ATM machines. Over the course of the next five years, McConville accomplished a great deal: He had a manufacturing plant designed and built, recruited local sales and marketing executives, set up a distribution system, and negotiated tariff agreements with the government. Every day, he said, brought a challenge.

Today he is back at Diebold's headquarters in Canton, Ohio. His job? Head of internal auditing. Not exactly a sexy title befitting a cosmopolitan executive.

The entire time he was in China, McConville knew he would one day return to work in the Canton headquarters. He expected there would be a job—doing what, was in the back of his mind. "One of the things about foreign assignments is, it's very difficult to find a job back in the U.S. that fits you,"

McConville says. "After five years I knew I wanted to come home because companies tend to forget you by then. So about year four we came to an agreement that that was long enough. But I had mixed emotions about leaving." McConville is like many expats. After all the nagging issues of being sent abroad are overcome finding—housing, making new friends, developing a network within the organization—these workers finally get comfortable. It lasts for about a week. Then a creepy feeling envelops many. It's the fear that the home office will no longer need them when it's time to return. A merger might have eliminated jobs, or a mentor may have retired, or a host of other scenarios. The bottom line: The promise made earlier of a job, maybe even a promotion, has faded with the years. The reality is, there may be no position to promote an expat to once he or she returns. Even the most senior executives get anxious.

Source: Excerpted from Charles Butler, "A World of Trouble," *Sales & Marketing Management 151,* no. 9 (September 1999): 3. Reprinted with permission. Permission conveyed through Copyright Clearance Center, Inc.

Lesser Role Assigned to Human Resource Planning

Human resource managers generally play a less active role in companies' overall planning processes than do managers of other functions.[21] Based on a content analysis of interviews conducted to identify aspects of people management that were critical to MNCs' success in the global arena, it was concluded that the more successful companies have more effective initiatives to address the issue of including the human resource function as a strategic partner in global business than the less successful companies.[22] Evidence suggests that business failures in foreign countries are often linked to poor management of human resources.[23]

Inadequate Selection Criteria for Foreign Assignments

A study of international business enterprises' practices in selecting personnel for foreign assignments shows that international corporations with lower failure rates tend to use **criteria specifically appropriate for selecting expatriate personnel.** The study also reveals that most U.S. MNCs do not yet possess such criteria.[24] Another study shows that most U.S. international businesses use technical competence as the primary criterion for selecting expatriate personnel. This practice derives from two primary reasons: (1) the difficulty in identifying and measuring attitudes appropriate for cross-cultural interaction; and (2) the self-interest of the selectors: since technical competence usually prevents immediate failure on the job, particularly in high-pressure situations, the selectors play it safe by placing a heavy emphasis on technical qualifications.[25]

An abundance of research shows that while technical competence is the most important factor in the overall determination of success, relational abilities appear to increase the probability of successful performance considerably, and lack of relational skills is frequently the principal cause for expatriate failure. Research also indicates that U.S. MNCs seldom emphasize the relations skills criterion in the expatriate selection decision.[26]

Failure to Consider the Family Situation Factor

Another important reason for expatriate failure is the family factor.[27] This refers to the **inability of the expatriate's family to adapt to living and working in the foreign country.** This creates stress for the expatriate's family members, who then create stress for the expatriate, often resulting in on-the-job failure.[28] The majority of the respondents in a survey of personnel administrators indicated that they recognized the importance of this factor to successful performance in a foreign assignment, yet few U.S. MNCs actually take it into consideration in the selection decision.[29] Of 80 U.S. multinationals surveyed, 52 percent interviewed spouses as part of the selection procedure for managerial positions, and only 40 percent interviewed spouses for technically oriented positions.[30] The same study revealed that those U.S. multinationals that conducted interviews with the candidate and his or her spouse to determine his or her suitability for the foreign assignment experienced significantly lower incidents of expatriate failure than those that did not.

Lack of Adequate Training for Foreign Assignments

Among the 80 U.S. MNCs surveyed, only 32 percent of the responding firms had **formalized training programs to prepare candidates for foreign assignments.** Most of the firms that did sponsor training programs used environmental briefing programs only. When used alone, environmental briefings are inadequate for preparing expatriates for assignments requiring extensive contact with the local community in the foreign country. The use of more rigorous training programs could significantly improve the expatriate's performance in an overseas environment, thus minimizing the incidence of failure.[31]

However, changing the behavior of experienced managers could be an insurmountable task for a company's training system. First, prospective expatriates without a background in the behavioral sciences generally do not consider the training function to be an effective agent. Second, many prospective expatriates are inclined to believe that they are more familiar with the organizational environment and problems, both at the headquarters and at the foreign subsidiary, than the training department, and thus believe that they do not need its help. Third, a prospective expatriate whose past behavior has proven to be highly successful finds it hard to accept that similar behavior may be dysfunctional in the foreign assignment. Fourth, prospective expatriates may consider such training efforts as criticism of their past behavior; they may also interpret it to mean that top management has doubts about their ability to adapt their behavior on their own. Fifth, their workload in the midst of preparation for their transfer may not leave sufficient time for an intensive training program. Finally, top managers tend to underrate the need for such training.[32]

Duration of Assignment and Performance Evaluation[33]

Foreign assignments with a short duration are not conducive to effective performance because the expatriate is not allowed sufficient time to become acquainted with and **adapt to the new environment.** Many international businesses, especially U.S. companies whose management tends to be short-range-oriented, expect immediate results from their expatriates. These MNCs evaluate expatriates who do not produce positive results right away as low on performance. This evaluation is not reasonable because expatriates need time to adapt. To mitigate the acculturation problem and to avoid costly mistakes, expatriates should be exempted from active management activities during the first six months after arrival in the foreign market.[34] The amount of time expatriates require for adaptation has been estimated at six months, broken down into four phases: the **initial phase, disillusionment phase, culture shock phase, and positive adjustment phase.**[35] These are depicted in Table 8-1. The model presented in Table 8-1 is general, and some exceptions may occur.

Underutilization of Women as Sources of Expatriates

The option of using **women expatriates is underutilized** by international businesses. A 1983 study of 686 U.S. and Canadian firms revealed that only 3 percent of expatriate managers were women.[36] The October 21, 1994 edition of *The Wall Street Journal*, p. A1, reported this figure to be 5 percent. Today, the figure is likely to be only slightly higher. This underutilization of women for foreign assignments may derive from the presumption that, as pointed out earlier, for cultural reasons many male managers in foreign countries, do not accept women as business partners and equals. (See

TABLE 8-1	The Expatriate Adaptation Process
The Initial Phase	When the expatriate transfers to the foreign assignment, the newness of the culture creates a great deal of excitement for him or her.
The Disillusionment Phase	After about two months, the novelty of the new culture wears off, and day-to-day inconveniences caused, for example, by different practices in the local culture and by not being able to communicate effectively create disillusionment for the expatriate.
The Culture Shock Phase	After about two months of the day-to-day confusions, the expatriate faces cultural shock. By now the expatriate is ready to go back to his or her old, familiar environment.
The Positive Adjustment Phase	If the expatriate remains, at about month four of the assignment, he or she begins to adapt, and by month six he or she feels more positive about the foreign environment; he or she does not regain the "high" of the first two months, but does not repeat the "low" of the next two months.

Source: Based on data from K. Oberg, "Culture Shock: Adjustment to New Cultural Environments," *Practical Anthropology* (July–August 1960): 170–182.

PRACTICAL PERSPECTIVE 8-3

Work vs. Life vs. The World

Each country has different work/life issues to balance. It all depends on your perspective. In the U.S. the biggest work/life anxiety for an employee with flexible work arrangements might be arranging his or her schedule to finish a work assignment and still see his or her son's music recital and daughter's basketball game in the same day.

Elsewhere in the world, work/life concerns can be quite different—and much more basic. Indeed, the biggest work/life issue that Mhpo E. Letlape, human-resource director for IBM–South Africa, faces is simply the anxiety that sets in, she says, while "waiting for the gates to open at my home when I have to leave work after dark"—even though her home is only six kilometers from her office.

"Crime and violence are becoming a greater problem because the same work/life imbalances—workload problems, skills shortage, and business pressures—that exist around the world are surfacing in South Africa for the first time, creating [social] problems," says Letlape, one of the speakers at a recent seminar on international work/life issues cosponsored by the Conference Board and the Families & Work Institute. Indeed, she worries about her teenage children going to shopping malls where she says "drugs and rape are rampant."

By contrast, the most important work/life issues in Japan have been gender issues because there is little equity for women in the workplace. But even that equity issue has temporarily been pushed into the background by the economy. Now the key work/life issue in Japan—because of the unprecedented layoffs in firms that once boasted lifetime employment—is "simply survival as opposed to the perks and benefits" people in the U.S. often believe they are entitled to have, says Susan Seitel, president

(continued)

of Work & Family Connection, Inc. of Minneapolis, Minnesota.

Venezuela has similar gender issues. Women need a mentor—and their husbands' approval—to get a job, and it is taboo for women to be invited out for drinks, even for after-work business get-togethers, says Patricia Marquez Otero, associate professor of organizational behavior at the Institute of Higher Studies in Administration in Caracas, Venezuela. "How can we talk about work/life [issues], when we are not even willing to talk about gender differences?"

Unlike other countries, Venezuela has no difficulty balancing work and life issues because in that culture work is secondary to or part of social, personal, and family lives of people. "We work as part of our social life, not as a competitive thing," says Otero.

In Chile the quality-of-life issues are similar to those in Venezuela. "Women have conquered new places of work," says Aníbal Oyarzún-Lobo of Serviceo Médico Cámara, Chilena de la Construcción, Chile, "but there is still discrimination in [the kinds of jobs they can hold] and in compensation. And because government policies mandate 18 weeks of full pay for maternity leave, free medical care for newborns, and paid time off to take care of the sick children under age one, companies don't like to hire married women," he says.

Source: Excerpted from Michael A. Verespej, "Work vs. Life vs. The World," *Industry Week* (April 4, 1999). Reprinted with permission.

Practical Perspective 8-3.) While such barriers do exist, male managers in many countries do make a distinction between foreign women professionals and local women—many male managers may not accept local females in managerial roles but will accept foreign females. In a survey of female expatriates, many of the respondents indicated that they were viewed by locals as foreigners who happened to be women; they also said that the added visibility of being the first female manager in the region gave them greater access to clients because of the curiosity factor.[37] (For an illustration, refer to Practical Perspective 8-4.)

This suggests that MNCs need to explore the possibilities of utilizing female expatriates more than in the past. As noted earlier, many expatriates fail because of a shortage of relational skills. These skills are abilities generally ascribed to female managers. Women managers, compared with their male counterparts, experience significantly lower levels of boundary-spanning stress; that is, women cope better with the pressures and strains resulting from the foreign environment.[38] Practical Perspective 8-5 presents the story of a well-adjusted woman in Germany.

The writer's own experience in developing and managing an administrative division at a Native American reservation also provides support for the contention that women are more adaptable than men in a culture different from their own. Several years ago the writer was employed by a Native American tribe to aid in developing a division in the tribal organization. Non–Native American males and females were hired, but by the conclusion of the development period (three years later), the division

PRACTICAL PERSPECTIVE 8-4

An American Bussinesswoman's Guide to Japan

Japanese men aren't used to dealing with woman as equals in a business setting," says Diana Rowland, author of the book *Japanese Business Etiquette*, and owner of a San Diego–based cross-cultural consulting firm. "They are uncomfortable simply due to a lack of experience." That lack of experience can severely handicap an American woman executive working in Japan—but it can also be an asset. "I've been asked at meetings if I'm married and when I say no, then I've been asked why I don't want to be," Rowland says. "You just have to gracefully deal with these questions and move on."

As intrusive as they may appear, personal questions help a Japanese businessman determine how serious a woman might be about the project at hand. After all, lingering in his mind is the idea that a woman would rather be home, not on the job. Why an American woman would choose to work rather than raise a family is almost incomprehensible to the Japanese. It doesn't jibe with their cultural experience of what a woman ought to do.

In Japan, where gender roles are rigidly defined, most Japanese women choose to root their identities in motherhood and marriage.... Some Japanese businessmen—especially those accustomed to dealing with Americans—side-step the "female issue" altogether, preferring to somewhat desexualize their image of American women. "There are three kinds of people in Japan: men, women, and foreigners," says Nancy Noyes, who ran Salomon Brothers' hedge desk in Tokyo for six months in 1988. "In the Japanese male's mind, I was not a woman, but a foreigner."

Many American businesswomen say the sheer uniqueness of being a woman is an advantage in Japan. "Once I asked my Japanese associates how they felt about working with me," says a 32-year-old stockbroker for a large U.S. brokerage firm. "They said it was so easy to remember me because they'd always get Bob confused with Jim, Jim confused with John and John mixed up with Bob."... More and more Japanese men are discovering that they actually like working with American women. "As a group, we're probably more diplomatic and less threatening than American men," Rowland says. "Japanese men don't perceive us as trying to dominate them, nor do they feel the need to be overly competitive with us."

Source: Excerpted from Deidre Sullivan, "An American Businesswoman's Guide to Japan," *Overseas Business* (Winter 1990): 50–55. Reprinted with permission.

employed the writer (a male) and 15 females. The males had quickly become frustrated with the cultural differences and left, but many of the females who replaced the males were much more tolerant and stayed.

JAPANESE MNCs' EXPATRIATION PRACTICES

A comparative study of the expatriate selection and training procedures of U.S. and Japanese MNCs found that Japanese MNCs experienced a signif-

PRACTICAL PERSPECTIVE 8-5

Rooted in Germany

When Holly Methfessel left the United States for Europe five years ago, all she took with her were two suitcases and her dog. She left behind family, friends, and an established book of business.

An experienced insurance agent, Holly went to Germany to work for another American insurance company. Four years ago, she joined Prudential in Europe.

"It was difficult to move from a place where I was established to a new country," explains Holly. "I was afraid. But I knew that I couldn't let that fear hold me back. I had to work through it. And I'm glad I did because this move has turned out to be the greatest experience of my life. I don't know if I'll ever go back to the States."

If Holly does leave Germany at some time in the future, she won't be alone. About a year and a half ago she met her fiancé, Bill, also an American.

Establishing personal relationships hasn't been easy for Holly, though. "Because I do most of my business here with the military, that's also who I socialize with. But it's too transient of a population to establish lasting relationships," she notes.

Life in Germany does have its quirks. For example, expatriates purchase most of their electrical appliances from military PX, but they come with American pugs. "We have all kinds of adapters and converters so we can use these things at home," Holly notes.

Fluctuating exchange rates can be a bit of a hassle as well. Holly works with and earns U.S. dollars, yet makes purchases with the German mark. However, since she arrived in Germany, there has been a 10 percent increase in the value of the U.S. dollar against the mark.

Holly believes that a look at how retail operations are run reveals some of the most basic cultural differences between the United States and Germany. "Outside of the metropolitan areas of Germany, there aren't many malls," she explains, "mostly quaint outdoor shopping villages. It's wonderful way to shop. And the stores don't keep hours like they do in the states. They shut their doors for two hours at lunch time and don't open on Sundays. The Germans take their day of rest very seriously."

One of the cultural nuances that Holly has eagerly embraced is the Germans' love for the outdoors. "Walking and hiking are practically national pastimes here," she says. "And with the spectacular scenery you can understand why."

So what does she miss about the United States? Not much, she says. "You have to learn to accept the new culture as it is. You can't keep trying to make it into what you came from." But she will admit to an occasional craving for one culinary treat from the States. "I really do miss being able to get TCBY frozen yogurt. I used to get it at the airport on my return trips, but the shop's not there anymore."

Source: Excerpted from S.D. Adams and L. Esposito, "Culture Shock," *Prudential Leader* (February 1998): 22. Used with permission.

icantly **lower incidence of expatriate failure** than U.S. MNCs. Eighty-six percent of the Japanese companies reported a recall rate of less than 5 percent (in the U.S., 24 percent reported a recall rate of less than 10 percent), 10 percent reported a recall rate between 6 and 10 percent, and 14 percent reported a recall rate of between 11 and 19 percent.[39] The study's results provide numerous insights into the strengths of Japanese MNCs relative to their strategies in the human resource management function.

Importance of the Human Resource Function

The human resource function is centralized, and the head of the personnel division reports directly to the CEO.[40] The human resource division wields considerable authority in the overall aspects of the corporation's operation, such as recruitment, career development, evaluation, promotion, and the compensation of all employees.

Long Duration of Foreign Assignments

The average duration of foreign assignments in Japanese corporations is 4.67 years.[41] (Foreign assignments in U.S. companies are usually for three years or less.) During the first year of his or her foreign assignment, the Japanese expatriate focuses mainly on adaptation activities. In the second year, the expatriate becomes more active in managerial activities, but this year is still considered a period of adjustment. In the third year, the expatriate begins to function at full capacity.

Support System at Corporate Headquarters

Japanese firms provide a comprehensive support network established for the purpose of setting the expatriate's mind at ease once he or she arrives at the foreign market. The support network includes a division whose sole purpose is to look after expatriates' needs, including the provision of mental and financial support; a mentor system, which implies certain obligations and responsibilities on the part of the corporation toward the expatriate; the showing of greater concern for the total person, including the company's trying to find reasons for expatriates who went to the foreign country alone to periodically visit the headquarters or some other operation in Japan, enabling them to visit their families at the same time; and a practice of having expatriates who have been around for a long time provide assistance to the new expatriate.[42]

Criteria for Selecting Expatriates

Because the prospective expatriate has usually been with the enterprise for many years, managers of Japanese international firms normally have access to the information required to assess the candidate's suitability for the for-

eign assignment. The strong group orientation and the after-hours socializing practices of Japanese corporations enable managers to become
familiar with employees' family background. And most Japanese companies
keep a detailed personnel inventory on all their career staff.[43]

Training for Foreign Assignments

The system of lifetime employment and the long-range perspective of many
Japanese firms results in their investing large sums of money to train and
develop employees for future foreign assignments. The results of one study
indicate that 57 percent of the Japanese MNCs surveyed sponsored formal
training programs for their expatriates. The programs, in general, consist of
the following components: language training, general training, field
training, graduate programs in a foreign country, in-house training programs, and use of external agents.[44] The study also revealed that American
MNCs tend to be reluctant to invest as much as Japanese firms do in such
programs because employment in them tends to be short-term—if they
invest in an employee's development and he or she leaves, the company will
not recapture the costs.[45]

The above suggests that Japanese firms place much greater emphasis on
preparing expatriates than do American firms. This may be because Japan's
large population, in a small country with relatively few natural resources,
forces Japan to rely on international business much more than does the
U.S., which is a large country with an abundance of resources. Japanese
firms must therefore invest more in preparing expatriates than American
firms—although the changes that have taken place around the globe during
the past couple of decades are making American firms more and more
dependent on international business. In effective preparation of expatriates,
Japanese firms have an advantage over American firms, in part because of
the programs the Japanese have implemented and in part because they hold
a wider global business perspective.

However Japanese expatriation practices are not devoid of problems.
Lengthy foreign assignments often create problems in the children's education, and if the family adopts new cultural traits in the foreign country, they
may be ostracized by the community for "foreign" behavior when they
return to Japan. Furthermore, reluctance among the younger generation in
Japan to undertake a foreign assignment is increasing.[46]

EUROPEAN MNCs' EXPATRIATION PRACTICES

Like Japanese MNCs, European MNCs have a much lower expatriate recall
rate than U.S. MNCs. Evidence indicates that 59 percent of the European
MNCs have a recall rate of less than 5 percent (76 percent of the Japanese
MNCs reported a recall rate of less than 5 percent, and 24 percent of the
U.S. MNCs reported a recall rate of less than 10 percent), 38 percent have

a recall rate of between 6 and 10 percent, and 3 percent have a recall rate of between 11 and 19 percent.[47] The executives interviewed believed that the strong global orientation of the organization is a primary reason for the low expatriate failure rate. This orientation derives in part from the **"spirit of internationalism"** among European people. This spirit is attributed to several factors.[48]

Smallness of European Markets

Domestic markets in European nations tend to be small, and firms have had to export in order to expand market size. On the other hand, the vastness of the U.S. has been able to sustain most firms' growth objectives. Historically U.S. firms have not needed to transact business in foreign markets. As a result of these conditions, European firms have developed a much greater global perspective than have American firms.

Europeans Like to Travel Abroad

Europeans tend to travel extensively. Because of the size and proximity of neighboring nations, Europeans are naturally exposed to numerous foreign people and cultures, and they learn multiple languages, unlike Americans, who tend to learn only their own culture and language. Europeans therefore develop an international perspective to a much greater extent than do Americans.

A Tradition of Interaction in Foreign Lands

European traditions and economic conditions have for many centuries encouraged interaction in foreign markets, and even emigration to foreign lands. America has not developed such a tradition to the extent that Europe has.

A History of Colonization

In Europe, there is a legacy of "the empire," the colonization of nations around the globe. Portugal, Spain, England, and France once colonized much of the world. Therefore, European commercial enterprises have a long history of establishing operations in foreign nations and have accumulated much experience in dealing with people in other nations. Many European expatriates are therefore assigned to well-established foreign markets.

This "spirit of internationalism" provides European international businesses a large pool of individuals who can easily be developed for cross-national assignments. This spirit also makes European spouses more adaptable to foreign cultures than American spouses. In addition, as in the case of Japanese MNCs, European MNCs have a long-range orientation and a low rate of turnover among managerial personnel. As a result, they are also willing to invest heavily in training and development programs, and they have designed comprehensive expatriate support programs.[49] Therefore, European corporations, like their Japanese counterparts, have a greater pool of adaptable employees to transfer to foreign nations than do American businesses. Nevertheless, European companies now face new expatriation problems, such as the need to assign expatriates from dual-career families.

IMPLICATIONS OF U.S., JAPANESE, AND EUROPEAN MNCs' EXPATRIATE PRACTICES

Based on the analysis of the problems in human resource planning in many U.S. international business enterprises and of the comparative strengths of their Japanese and European counterparts, the following expatriate staffing implications may be drawn:[50]

1. Top management in international firms must pay a great deal more attention to the international HRM function. This function should have adequate representation in the overall corporate strategic planning.

2. Since inadequate relational skills contribute heavily to expatriate failures, managers selecting expatriates need to pay more attention to this criterion.

3. Top management in international businesses must sponsor rigorous training programs aimed to prepare expatriates for foreign assignments. This means choosing the right program for the right person and for the right nation. Since the expatriate's lack of sensitivity to the foreign country's culture is a primary reason for his or her failure, the programs must include cross-cultural sensitivity development. The programs should also address potential repatriation problems.

4. Top management may have to be flexible regarding the length of the foreign assignment. In some situations, a short-term assignment may be appropriate, for example, when an expatriate is sent abroad to repair some aspect of the manufacturing facilities. In other situations, however, such as sending an expatriate to develop a new foreign market, a longer-term assignment may be appropriate.

5. International business enterprises must also develop programs to attend to the needs and aspirations of expatriates, and eliminate the information gap so that expatriates do not feel too alienated from their old atmosphere. In this respect, the following ideas have been proposed:[51]

> ➤ A mentor program should be established to keep abreast of the expatriate's career progression throughout his or her international and domestic experience.

➤ The international business enterprise should establish a unit in its HRM function for career planning, meeting regularly with expatriates and repatriates.

➤ The firm's home office should maintain contact with expatriates by sending them newspapers, company newsletters, and mail.

And these days, the advent of view **new information technology**, such as the Internet, the Web, e-mail, voice mail, videoconferencing, on-line newsletters, and shared data bases, provides ways for global employees to remain linked to their home country and colleagues.[52]

6. Since the family is a prime reason for expatriate failures, managers making the selection must assess the expatriate's spouse and children to ascertain their adaptability to the foreign country.

7. International enterprises need to use women in their foreign operations to a much greater extent then they do now.

Incorporating the above framework into the international business enterprise's overall human resource management strategies will have positive consequences. It is likely to reduce the incidences of ineffective or poor expatriate performance. MNCs can no longer rely solely on technology to gain a competitive edge in international markets; they must also rely on international human resource management planning because the organization and technology are managed and operated by people.

REDUCING EXPATRIATE FAILURES

In essence, **expatriate failures can be reduced** by selecting the right person and implementing programs for assessing a prospective expatriate's effectiveness potential, finding and developing global executives, preparing expatriates, and providing effective compensation.

Selecting the Right Expatriate

As suggested above, expatriate failures can be reduced by selecting the right person for the assignment. "When an expatriate manager fails in a foreign assignment, it is usually not due to technical incompetence; it is due to improper selection."[53] To select the right expatriate for the assignment, David Pulatie, former vice president and director of employee relations at Motorola, Inc., recommends the following steps:[54]

1. Do an extremely sophisticated job of selecting the people you send to the foreign country—not only the expatriate, but his or her family as well. This requires private, extensive interviews to evaluate each candidate's family situation, lifestyle, and financial picture. For example, if the expatriate has family problems or schooling, medical, or financial

responsibilities, adjustment overseas will be difficult. The expatriate will not be able to devote his or her full attention to the assignment.

2. Find out why the candidate wants the foreign assignment, what he or she expects to get out of it, and if the expectations are realistic (see the accompanying cartoon), what his or her attitude is about living in a foreign country, and what his or her tolerance is.

3. Select only top-notch, proven people. This will help in both the expatriation and repatriation processes (to be discussed later).

4. Familiarize the expatriate and the accompanying family members with the country they are going to (to be discussed later).

5. Set up an administrative branch whose sole function is supporting your international staff (as previously discussed).

Rosalie L. Tung, a professor of international business at Simon Fraser University in Canada, has developed a flowchart of the expatriate selection process (see Figure 8-1).[55] Her model contains several notable features.[56] First, by requiring information about whether the position could be filled by a host-country national, it brings up the issue of employee nationality. Second, the model follows a low-risk strategy in selecting expatriates. Third, the model takes a contingency approach to selecting and training expatriates in that it recognizes that varying assignments require different degrees of interaction.

Assessing Expatriates' Effectiveness Potential

It is apparent from the preceding sections that individuals being considered for foreign assignments require certain characteristics that would not be required for local assignments. As executive search consultants agree, to be effective, expatriate managers must listen well, be patient, and have respect—perhaps even enthusiasm—for other cultures.[57] "You are looking for an open-minded person who is quite flexible and tolerant of other ways of doing things," says Kai Lindholst, managing partner for Egon Zehnder International Inc., a leading executive search firm. "If the person can only eat at McDonald's every day of the week, why go abroad? If the expatriate manager has a family also making the move, they must share in the enthusiasm in order for the relocation to work. Uprooting a family can be traumatic.... Most overseas managers seem to know of at least one divorce resulting from an overseas assignment."[58]

Based on existing published research, Professors Mark Mendenhall and Gary Oddou developed a framework outlining the special characteristics required by expatriates.[59] Their framework, which can be used to **assess expatriates' effectiveness potential,** consists of four dimensions as components of the expatriate adjustment process. The four dimensions and subfactors are outlined in Table 8-2. If a prospective expatriate demonstrates weakness on those dimensions, he or she may not be adaptable in a foreign

An Expatriate's Dream

Roger Roth

FIGURE 8-1 | The Expatriate Selection Process

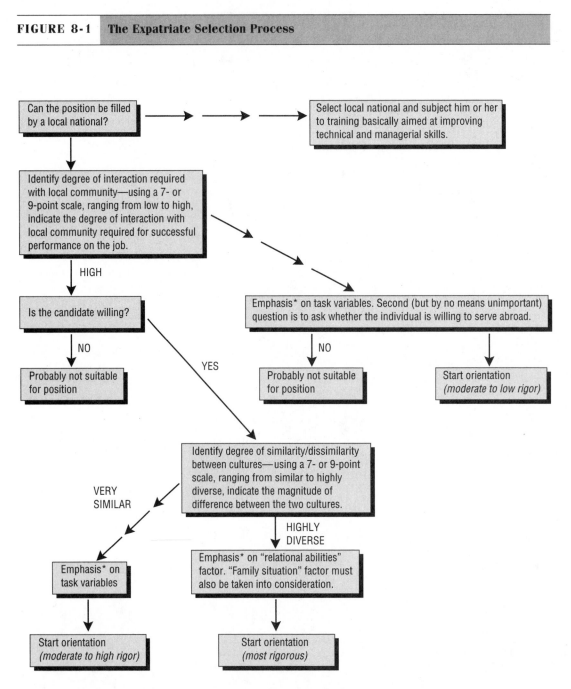

Can the position be filled by a local national? → Select local national and subject him or her to training basically aimed at improving technical and managerial skills.

Identify degree of interaction required with local community—using a 7- or 9-point scale, ranging from low to high, indicate the degree of interaction with local community required for successful performance on the job.

HIGH

Is the candidate willing?

NO

Probably not suitable for position

YES

Emphasis* on task variables. Second (but by no means unimportant) question is to ask whether the individual is willing to serve abroad.

NO

Probably not suitable for position

Start orientation *(moderate to low rigor)*

Identify degree of similarity/dissimilarity between cultures—using a 7- or 9-point scale, ranging from similar to highly diverse, indicate the magnitude of difference between the two cultures.

VERY SIMILAR

HIGHLY DIVERSE

Emphasis* on task variables

Emphasis* on "relational abilities" factor. "Family situation" factor must also be taken into consideration.

Start orientation *(moderate to high rigor)*

Start orientation *(most rigorous)*

*"Emphasis" does not mean ignoring the other factors. It only means that it should be the dominant factor.

Source: Rosalie L. Tung, "Selection and Training of Personnel for Overseas Assignments," *Columbia Journal of World Business* 16, no. 1 (Spring 1981): 73. Copyright © 1983, JAI Press Inc. Used with permission from JAI Press Inc. All rights reserved.

TABLE 8-2	Dimensions of the Effective Expatriate

The Self-Oriented Dimension

➤ Has the ability to replace pleasurable activities at home with similar, yet different, activities in the foreign culture. For example, can replace baseball in the United States with soccer in Brazil.

➤ Is able to deal with the stress that the foreign culture generally produces for expatriates. He or she has "stability zones," for example, meditation, writing in diaries, engaging in favorite pastimes, and religious worship, to which he or she can retreat when conditions in the host culture become overly stressful.

➤ Possesses the necessary technical competence.

The Others-Oriented Dimension

➤ Is able to develop long-lasting friendships with locals. The close relationship aids local mentors in guiding the expatriate through the intricacies and complexity of the new culture, for example, the local mentor provides feedback that helps the expatriate understand local worker expectations and attitudes, and helps the expatriate in his or her efforts to train and develop local replacements.

➤ Is able to communicate with locals (he or she has a good command of the local language). This enables the expatriate to become more familiar and intimate with locals and to create and foster interpersonal relationships.

The Perceptual Dimension

➤ Has the ability to understand why locals behave the way they do and to make correct attributions about the causes of locals' behavior. This helps the expatriate predict how the locals will behave toward him or her in the future.

➤ Is nonjudgmental and nonevaluative when interpreting the behavior of locals. Seeks to update his or her perceptions and beliefs as new information arises.

The Cultural-Toughness Dimension

➤ Is able to adapt to the toughness of the specific culture (for example, it may be more difficult for a Canadian expatriate to adapt in Nigeria than in England).

Source: Adapted from M. Mendenhall and G. Oddou, "The Dimensions of Expatriate Acculturation: A Review," *The Academy of Management Review 10*, no. 1 (1985): 39–47. Used by permission of the Academy of Management.

culture. Mendenhall and Oddou also identified some techniques currently available to test the strengths and weaknesses in the dimensions and subfactors outlined in Table 8-2.[60]

Relative to the self-oriented dimension, assessors already possess the means of evaluating technical expertise. They have access to various psychological tests and evaluation techniques, as well as to numerous instruments to measure stress levels and stress-reducing programs. To assess the others-oriented dimension, assessors can solicit in-depth evaluations from a prospective expatriate's superiors, subordinates, friends, and acquaintances. Regarding the perceptual dimension, there are numerous psychological tests available to measure the rigidity and flexibility of an individual's perceptual and evaluative tendencies. These tests include the

Cognitive Rigidity Test, the F-test, the Guilford-Zimmerman Temperament Survey, and the Alport-Vernon Study of Values. The prospective expatriate's **cultural-toughness dimension** can be assessed on the basis of the toughness of the specific country in concert with the above needs. That is, the assessor should feel confident that the applicant's scores on the battery of evaluation scores are high enough to handle the specific country.[61]

Professor S. Ronen also identified a group of attributes for expatriate success. The group includes the following: tolerance for ambiguity, behavioral flexibility, nonjudgmentalism, cultural empathy and low ethnocentrism, interpersonal skills, belief in the mission, interest in foreign experience, willingness to acquire new patterns of behavior and attitudes, adaptive and supportive spouse, stable marriage, and nonverbal communication skills.[62] A supportive spouse and a stable marriage are important because in the foreign country, work may be filled with frustrations, and the spouse may be the only one available with whom the expatriate can talk about them. The above framework also applies to the evaluation and selection of third-country nationals, who, because they are being assigned to a foreign country, are also expatriates, and even to the evaluation of host-country locals who are being expatriated to the home office for development.

However, psychological testing is not without its critics. Considerable debate goes on among scholars and practitioners about the reliability and accuracy of tests in predicting cross-cultural adjustments.[63] Furthermore, since these tests were developed in the U.S., they may be "culture-bound" and may be even less reliabile and accurate when applied to non-Americans.[64] Also, in some countries (Australia, for example) use of psychological tests is controversial.[65] Use of tests is limited by law in some countries, Italy, for example. And somewhat different conclusions regarding test use have been found, with a greater use of personality measures by the French compared to British organizations.[66]

Determining the effectiveness potential of expatriates is further inhibited by a nation's legal system. In some countries a candidate may not be asked about his or her religion, smoking habits, drug and alcohol consumption, and other such behaviors about which an assessor needs to know in order to make a determination about the candidate' adaptability. For instance, an individual who smokes and consumes alcohol may not adapt well to Saudi Arabia.

Finding and Developing Global Expatriates

Many international business enterprises, especially global corporations, require a group of executives who are ready to perform effectively in foreign assignments when and where needed (in Chapter 1, this kind of expatriate was referred to as a **global manager**). Many successful organizations, including Coca-Cola, have recently created a position labeled chief learning officer (CLO). Somewhat like a chief financial officer, who is dedicated to building the organization's financial strength, the CLO is responsible for developing—on a worldwide scale—the organization's human talent and for utilizing the human knowledge present in the organization.[67] Where do global corporations get such expatriate managers? Professor Cecil G. Howard identified a general recruitment and developmental process consisting of four sources: domestic operations; managers currently on a foreign assignment; external sources, including worldwide competitors; and educational institutions.[68]

Domestic Operations

A source available to international firms for recruiting and developing global expatriates is their home operations. The following are the steps an MNC can use when developing expatriate managers from its domestic operations:

1. Identify potential expatriate managers within the parent company at early stages of their careers. In other words, find out which young managers might do well in international assignments.

2. Prepare an individual development plan for each prospective expatriate manager. This entails conducting a training and developmental needs analysis, including discussions with the potential expatriate's supervisor and peers. (Development should include the characteristics identified in Figure 8-2.)

3. Give those selected as prospective expatriate managers training and skills development related to potential foreign assignments. The training and development should include practical on-the-job experience in a foreign site. (Practical Perspective 8-6 describes the development programs implemented by some international business enterprises.)

The domestic operations approach has at least three advantages: the MNC has a captive pool to tap, those selected are expected to be in tune with the corporate culture and its managerial philosophy, and the process of assigning those selected to foreign projects helps to eliminate those not really qualified for global managerial assignments. There are disadvantages, however. The process is quite costly and time-consuming, and there is a strong possibility that some of the trained executives will sell their newly acquired skills to another international business firm.

Managers Currently on Foreign Assignment

Another source for recruiting and developing global expatriates is the people working in a corporation's foreign subsidiaries. Using this approach involves the following steps:

1. Survey eligible expatriate managers worldwide. It should be noted that the managers in the foreign subsidiaries do not necessarily have to be

PRACTICAL PERSPECTIVE 8-6

Younger Managers Learn Global Skills

A growing number of global-minded U.S. companies are giving fast-track managers a global orientation much sooner in their careers. "It's a pretty significant trend," says David Weeks, a researcher who is completing a Conference Board study of 130 large multinational companies in the U.S., Europe, and Japan. The study found "a certain sense of urgency" among American companies about "trying to build an internationally experienced cadre of executives," Weeks says.

A number of European and Japanese corporate giants have already installed elaborate training and career-tracking mechanisms to develop such executives. Unless U.S. companies equip their best managers with global skills at younger ages, "they are going to come up short" in global competition, warns Michael Longua, Johnson & Johnson's director of international recruiting.

American Express Company's Travel Related Services unit gives American business-school students summer jobs in which they work outside the U.S. for up to ten weeks. [It] also transfers junior managers with at least two years experience to other countries. Colgate-

Palmolive Company trains about 15 recent college graduates each year for 15 to 24 months prior to multiple overseas job stints. General Electric Company's aircraft-engine unit will expose selected midlevel engineers and managers to foreign language and cross-cultural training even though not all will live abroad.

American Honda Motor Company, Inc. has sent more than 40 U.S. supervisors and managers to the parent company in Tokyo for up to three years, after preparing them with six months of Japanese language lessons, cultural training, and lifestyle orientation during work hours. PepsiCo, Inc.'s international beverage division brings about 25 young foreign managers a year to the U.S. for one-year assignments in bottling plants. Raychem Corporation assigns relatively inexperienced Asian employees (from clerks through middle managers) to the U.S. for six months to two years.

Source: Excerpted from Joann S. Lublin, "Younger Managers Learn Global Skills," *The Wall Street Journal*, March 31, 1992, p. A1. Permission conveyed through Copyright Clearance Center, Inc.

expatriates; they can be locals who have been developed or are being developed for local managerial assignments. Many international business enterprises, especially those with a multidomestic and global strategies, have training and development programs aimed at developing local managers. For example, Procter & Gamble asked the Chinese University of Hong Kong to develop a training program for young managers in its plant in Guangzhou, China. Japan's Matsushita's Human Development Center in Singapore trained more than 500 employees in 1990–1991.[69] And current general thinking is that the development of global leadership skills should not stop with home-country employees; it should involve host-country national as well. Prudential, for example, uses both.[70]

2. Identify the needs for further training and development for those who wish to fit a new and more demanding managerial role in the future.

3. Prepare independent development plans for those willing to fit the new managerial role.

4. Provide the skills and knowledge identified on the independent development plans.

5. Place expatriate managers in worldwide subsidiaries.

This approach, because the candidates are already working abroad, can be somewhat less expensive and less time-consuming than developing domestic talent, and they (other than the host-country nationals) have proven adaptability in a foreign culture. However, finding these individuals and administering and coordinating the development process can be a problem if the corporation's subsidiaries are geographically dispersed.

External Sources

Using this approach involves recruiting and developing people with foreign experience from outside sources. The steps in this recruitment and development process are as follows:

1. Recruit qualified individuals from competing and noncompeting companies, both at home and in foreign countries. Executive-search firms may be helpful in this respect.

2. Identify the training and development selectees need to fit into the new corporate culture.

3. Prepare an individual development program.

4. Provide the required skills and knowledge.

5. Place them in strategic foreign management positions.

The advantages of this approach include the fact that the new employee brings seasoned foreign management experience and personal maturity, reducing training and development costs and time. However, the search can be very expensive—the executive search companies, also known as "headhunters," charge a high finder's fee. Also, recruiting can take a long time, especially when local talent is scarce (refer to Practical Perspective 8-7). And the new hiree may take a long time to fit in the new corporate culture—or he or she may not fit at all. These factors add to the cost of this approach.

Educational Institutions

College and universities are another source for recruiting and developing global expatriates. Many of these institutions, especially in the United States, have recently implemented or are currently implementing programs aimed at internationalizing their students, including offering degrees in

PRACTICAL PERSPECTIVE 8-7

Consider the Quality and Availability of the Local Labor Force

The greatest challenge in entering a new market is often the work force, specifically senior management. "After you determine that you have a marketplace that's going to utilize what you're producing, you need to see if there is the capability and talent in the local workforce to support the endeavor," says Richard Bahner, human resources head at New York City–based Citicorp. "You really need to do a total, balanced evaluation. Some of these places offer less expensive labor, but if they don't have the capabilities you're looking for, it may not be a savings because you'll have to supplement it with a large amount of computer support, training, or expatriates."

The extent of the staffing challenges depends on your industry. "If you're distributing Pepsi™, you can manufacture it locally and teach people how to sell it easily enough, but if you're in global banking, you've got a lot more restrictions," Bahner explains.

Citibank has experienced this in the Asia-Pacific region. With relationships in China and Hong Kong for almost a century, it had an advantage when it looked to expand into Indonesia and Thailand. But it was hampered by the need for an educated workforce. Citibank developed the market in Indonesia and taught the people about electronic banking— eventually generating millions of Citibank Visa cardholders. But the HR issues were daunting.

"The biggest problem is the dearth of qualified locals," says Bill Fontana, formerly of Citibank in Indonesia and now vice president of international HR for the National Foreign Trade Council. It's a big, big problem. There are so few qualified people who can take senior positions (among 200 million Indonesians), that other U.S. companies will bid for this unique individual. "It jacks up the cost of your senior local person, and then you begin to pirate people away from other companies because they speak English, they've worked at another multinational organization, and therefore, you would pay almost anything to get them onto your payroll. It leads to spiraling inflation in the workforce."

As an example, Fontana was recruiting for a treasury head at Citibank in Indonesia. The position was staffed with an expat, and he wanted to fill it with a local. It took more than one year to identify a qualified person. Citibank offered the man $150,000 and a guaranteed base of $100,000. "He turned me down," says Fontana. "He told me that the Bank of Bali was offering him more money! And the expatriate was only making about $115,000."

Source: Excerpted form Charlene Marmer Solomon, "Don't Get Burned by Hot New Markets," *Global Workforce* (January 1998): 12–13. Reprinted with permission.

international business and programs encouraging study abroad. Gillette International has implemented a program to groom executives to fill global management positions. Initially, Gillette worked with New York City–based AIESEC (an international student exchange program) in identifying students for the program. Today, the personnel director and general manager for each of the company's worldwide operations are responsible for identifying the top business students in prestigious universities internationally.[71] Emerson Electric's biggest hurdle in entering China was finding the right managers. To jump that hurdle, Emerson woos graduates of top local universities with generous pay and brings them to the U.S. for intensive training.[72]

The college recruiter is encouraged to become familiar with the college's international program because an effective program will equip its students with professional skills, including cross-cultural sensitivity and linguistic capability. However, the programs in some colleges develop only a narrow functional specialization and a parochial perspective to managing in a foreign culture.

EXPATRIATE PREPARATION PROGRAMS

A selectee being sent to the foreign site needs extensive preparation. This means that international businesses require an **expatriate preparation program** and a program administrator who can effectively administer such a program. The preparation program should consist of four phases: understanding the corporate international environment, pre-expatriation, expatriation, and repatriation.[73]

The Corporation's International Environment

Before he or she can properly administer an expatriation program, the **program administrator** must become totally familiar with:

1. The enterprise's foreign involvements, including operations, investments, business goals, and strategies.

2. The staffing needs of overseas operations, including qualifications, duties, the expected duration of the assignment, and the goals and objectives of the position. For example, is the expatriate needed only to run the day-to-day operations, or to develop new operations, or to train locals for managerial positions, or to simultaneously run the operations and develop locals? Each job may require different skills. (This will be discussed more thoroughly in Chapter 12.)

3. The environmental aspects of the nation where the assignment is to take place, such as geographic isolation, level of urbanization, economic development, culture, and political and legal systems.

The above knowledge enables the program administrator to (a) better understand the organization's international commitments, (b) determine the skills, objectives, and relative hardships of foreign assignments, (c) make better selections for foreign positions, and (d) better judge the level of adjustment and readjustment necessary in each case.[74]

Pre-Expatriation

In the **pre-expatriation** phase, the selectee becomes involved in the preparation process. The objective of this phase is to make sure that:[75]

1. The individual has a complete understanding of the foreign assignment, including its purpose, goals, objectives, duties, and its relationship to his or her career objectives.

2. He or she is aware of the realities of expatriation, including the professional and personal problems foreign assignments often cause. This should include making the expatriate and his or her family aware (but not "scared to death") of the potential psychological and emotional strains created by being separated from friends and other family members. In other words, the expatriate and family should be made aware of all the advantages and disadvantages of the foreign assignment.

3. The expatriate and his or her family are educated and oriented about their temporary foreign home before leaving. The orientation should include the elements discussed in the following paragraphs.

Cultural Briefing

This should include the country's cultural traditions, history, government, economy, living conditions (including foods, education, medical facilities, and entertainment), climate, and clothing requirements. Books, maps, brochures, films, and slides would help in this respect. (Practical Perspective 8-8 describes the Prudential Intercultural Program.)

Assignment Briefing

This briefing includes details about the length of the assignment, vacation policy, holidays, allowances, tax consequences, and repatriation policy, as well as the expatriate's tentative workplan, the basis of his or her evaluation, and his or her authority and degree of autonomy in the foreign operations.

Relocation Requirements

Shipping, packaging, storage, and home disposal and acquisition should be addressed.

Language Training

Introducing the selectee to the country's language is essential. Not only does it help the communication process, but it also helps him or her better understand the country's culture. The language training methods commonly used include instruction at a language school and do-it-yourself kits such as records, cassette recordings, and books.

PRACTICAL PERSPECTIVE 8-8

An Olympic Moment for Prudential Intercultural

Prudential Intercultural brought new meaning to the phrase "training for the Olympics," when it provided cross-cultural training to 45 *USA Today* employees assigned to cover the 1998 Winter Olympics in Nagano, Japan.

Dr. Noel Miner, vice president of consulting for Prudential Intercultural and an authority on virtually every country in Asia, set up shop in the newspaper's Arlington, Virginia, headquarters to conduct the training seminars. He advised the journalists and executives on everything from Japanese history and cultural values to dining protocol and the correct way to exchange business cards, which, by the way, is to bow and lend an air of dignity and importance to the event.

One segment of the program included taking *USA Today*'s management committee to a Japanese banquet so they could get first-hand experience on how to conduct themselves during a formal dinner. They were briefed on topics like how to dress, where to sit, proper dining and drinking etiquette, and appropriate dinner conversation. A Japanese host gave explanations of various Asian dishes and the correct way to eat each.

"Using proper protocol is very important in Japanese culture, so knowing correct form is crucial to the *USA Today* employees' success," explains Miner, who has been living and working in Asia since 1966. "But we went beyond that; we tried to get them to understand the attitudes, beliefs, and values behind the protocol so they'll have every cultural advantage possible. They'll be under tight deadlines while there, and getting things done quickly is much easier if you understand the inner workings of Japanese society."

Judging from the turnout, the four-day program was a big success. "On our last day of training, ten addition *USA Today* employees showed up because they heard how helpful the program was," Miner says.

Source: Ken Coles, "An Olympic Moment for Prudential Intercultural," *Prudential Leader* (February 1998): 26. Used with permission.

Expatriation

The **expatriation** phase takes place while the expatriate is working in the foreign operations. It involves communication and information delivery. It is imperative that the home office

1. Keep the expatriate well-informed about domestic operations and plans—different time zones and the location of the assignment being out of the organizational mainstream make it easy for the home office to ignore the expatriate and make him or her feel professionally and personally isolated, thus increasing anxiety. As mentioned earlier, new technologies available, such as E-mail, help in this respect. Periodically bringing the expatriate to the home office for a meeting would help in this respect. (Refer to Practical Perspective 8-9.)

PRACTICAL PERSPECTIVE 8-9

Out of Sight, Out of Mind

Paris-based Stephen Gates, a senior research associate at the Conference Board, recently asked 152 HR managers with international work experience to identify the pitfalls of an overseas assignment. The survey's results appear in a recent report titled "Managing Expatriates' Return." Here are the key findings:

What's the single biggest problem for people who are working overseas?

Coming home. Almost 80 percent of repatriated executives say their international experience was not valued by their companies. The basic problem with a global assignment is the "out of sight, out of mind" mentality back at corporate headquarters.

How can expatriates keep in sight?

Get a mentor—someone who can keep you connected with the home office. If you're an expat at 3M, you must make an annual return trip to discuss your future with a designated mentor, who helps you keep track of company developments and job openings. Royal Duton/Shell has "technical mentors"—people who review technical developments and recommend the types of skills training you'll need when you return. If you don't have the technical expertise to keep up with people at the home office, you're in trouble.

How should people prepare for their return to the home office?

We found that operating managers typically haven't budgeted for an expat to return. And once budgets are set, it's difficult to squeeze someone back in. You really need to identify the key people who can help bring you back, make sure these people know you're actively seeking a position when you return, and mobilize the process yourself.

Source: Excerpted from Eric Matson, "How to Globalize Yourself." Reprinted from the April–May 1997 issue of *Fast Company* magazine. All rights reserved. To subscribe, please call 800-688-1545.

2. Review and discuss the expatriate's performance and career path, emphasizing the assignment's purpose and what the expatriate can expect to gain upon returning home. In other words, provide feedback and motivation.

Repatriation

After a lengthy assignment in a foreign country, the **repatriate** and the repatriate's family will encounter a high level of pressure and anxiety. The longer the assignment, the greater the pressure and anxiety. Upon the expatriate's arrival home, the following must be done:[76]

1. Provide intensive organizational retraining for the repatriate. The retraining should provide information on policy and procedures

changes, shifts in corporate strategy, new and promoted personnel, and a detailed description of his or her new position. (If the expatriate phase has been carried out effectively, this should not be too difficult.) He or she should not be pushed into a new position and be expected to produce immediately, but should be given ample time to adjust. Andy Knox of Korn/Ferry says it generally takes a returning expatriate up to 18 months to readjust to working in the States.[77] Also, the new position should, as much as possible, be challenging and should use the skills acquired in the foreign assignment.

2. Provide some form of financial counseling for the family, especially when there is a reduction of income.

3. Provide housing assistance. If the repatriate did not sell his or her house and instead rented it, help him arrange to have the house vacated and prepared for the family to move into it. If he or she has sold the house, help him or her obtain a new one, including a low-interest loan, a lump-sum bonus, or compensation for increased housing prices.

4. Assist the repatriate financially so that his or her children can continue receiving the quality education that the foreign country provided.

5. Help pay for psychological consultation if some repatriates and repatriate families experience personal and psychological problems readjusting.

EXPATRIATE COMPENSATION

Ineffective **expatriate compensation** can also lead to expatriate failures. Thus, international firms need to establish policies for effective management of expatriate compensation. To do so requires knowledge of the foreign country's laws, customs, environment, and employment practices, as well as understanding of the effects of currency exchange fluctuations and inflation on compensation. And, within the context of changing political, economic, and social conditions, establishing policy also requires an understanding of why certain allowances are necessary. Ron Ashkenas describes relocation problems that merit additional compensation:

> As more territories open up to global business, some will be remote, inconvenient, and disturbingly different. Organizations must develop programs to maintain fairness when hardship or disruption of families is an issue. While the manager may personally accept and even want the foreign assignment, he or she may have legitimate concerns about the schooling for the children, employment opportunities for the spouse, or the effects of cultural differences and language barriers.

TABLE 8-3	Top 10 Hardship Locations According to ECA Windham's Location Ranking System

Based on such criteria as security, sociopolitical tension, housing, and climate, here are the 10 countries or regions that ranked highest in hardship:

1. Kinshasa, Zaire
2. Almaty, Kazakhstan
3. Moscow, Russia
4. Beijing and Shanghai, China
5. New Delhi and Mumbai, India
6. Taipei, Taiwan
7. Lima, Peru
8. Sofia, Bulgaria
9. Warsaw, Poland
10. Jakarta, Indonesia

Source: Helen Frank Bensimon, "Is it Safe to Work Abroad?" *Training & Development* 52, no. 8 (August 1998): 24. Reprinted with permission.

New incentives and supports must be offered to help compensate for the feelings of loss that these situations trigger.[78]

An assignment in a hostile or undesirable environment would require greater compensation than an assignment to a friendly, desirable environment. For instance Frans Ryckebosch, who was overseas assignment general manager for Xerox in Shanghai, China, negotiated with Xerox for a 25 percent hardship allowance on top of the standard Xerox package before taking the assignment.[79] Table 8-3 presents the top 10 hardship locations.

Expatriate compensation policies seek to satisfy numerous objectives:[80]

➤ The policy should be consistent and fair in its treatment of all categories of expatriate employees.

➤ The policy must work to attract and retain expatriates in the areas where the corporation has the greatest need.

➤ The policy should facilitate the transfer of expatriates in the most cost-effective manner.

➤ The policy should be consistent with the overall strategy and structure of the organization.

➤ The compensation should serve to motivate employees.

A decision must be made about whether to establish an overall policy for all employees or to distinguish between home-country nationals (expatriates) and host-country and third-country nationals. It is common for international businesses to distinguish between them; they even distinguish between the types of expatriates. For example, different policies may be set on the basis of length of assignment or on the type of function to be carried out.[81] In all cases, the policy should be based on the idea that the expatriate must not suffer a loss because of his or her transfer. Furthermore, the approach selected should not demoralize the foreign subsidiary's staff; for example, **visible pay inequity** between the expatriate and their local peers can create bad feelings, thus undermining morale.[82] Table 8-4 presents the home-based balance sheet calculation of expatriate pay.

Expatriate Base Salary

MNCs tend to use the expatriate's home-country base salary as the primary component for determining his or her package of compensation for undertaking the foreign assignment. They tend to use third- and home-country nationals' home salary base to determine their compensation when they are selected for the assignment.

The conditions that force compensation policies to differ from those used for home-country expatriates include inflation and cost of living, housing, security, school costs, and taxation.[83] Furthermore, home-country expatriates often require a salary premium as an inducement to accept the foreign assignment or to endure the hardships of the foreign transfer. In the United States, when an international business enterprise has determined the type of hardship, it can refer to the U.S. Department of State's *Hardship*

TABLE 8-4	Calculation of Expatriate Pay

A pure home-based balance sheet calculation of expatriate pay works something like this:

1. Start with home-based gross income, including bonuses.

2. Deduct home tax, social security, and pension contributions (either a hypothetical tax or a real tax).

3. Add or subtract a cost-of-living allowance. Usually, companies don't subtract. Instead, they allow the expatriate to benefit from the negative differential.

4. Add a housing allowance, with or without a housing norm deduction.

5. Add incentive premiums, including general mobility premiums and possibly hardship premiums.

6. Add or subtract to equalize taxes. In other words, gross the net salary to protect against the double tax obligations in the home and host countries.

Of course, that can't be all there is to it. There are also many modified versions of the balance sheet approach and other unrelated compensation systems, including the host-based system. The balance sheet and host-based systems are at opposite ends of a continuum, with many hybrids in between.

Source: Valerie Frazee, "Is the Balance Sheet Right For Your Expats?" *Workforce* 77, no. 9 (September 1998): 19. (http://207.82.250.251/cgi-bin/getm...07076027.4). Reprinted with permission.

Post Differentials Guidelines to ascertain the appropriate level of premium compensation.

The practice of international businesses paying a higher salary to expatriate managers than to host- or third-country managers can demotivate the latter two categories, especially when they have an equal level of authority and responsibility. A problem currently confronting MNCs is how to deal effectively with such inequities. Some managers think that MNCs should have a global standard policy relating to compensation; that is, regardless of the varying costs of living existing in countries, all of the corporation's managers in all countries should be compensated on the basis of a standard global salary range based on the level of authority and responsibility. This policy, of course, is arguable and difficult to implement.

Taxation

For the expatriate, a foreign assignment can mean being **double-taxed**—by the home country and the foreign country governments. This problem, however, is mitigated in the United States by Section 911 of the Internal Revenue Service Code, which has an exclusion provision permitting a $70,000 deduction. It is also mitigated by the United States having a obligation agreement with some countries whereby an expatriate would pay taxes only in the United States and not in the host country—but in most cases double taxation applies.[84] International firms are subject to varying tax rates around the globe. The rates are different from country to country, and they change within countries from time to time. For example, the maximum marginal rate in Belgium was 72 percent in 1985 and 70.8 percent in 1988; in the United States it was 50 percent in 1985 and 33 percent in 1988.[85] (Current rates may be different.) A corporation's compensation packages must consider how specific practices can be adjusted in each nation to provide, within the context of the corporation's overall policy, the most tax-effective, appropriate rewards for expatriate, host-country, and third-country managers.

Benefits

Benefits such as pension and medical plans and social security are difficult to transfer across national borders. When considering expatriate benefits, international enterprises need to consider numerous issues, including[86]

➤ Whether or not to maintain expatriates in home-country programs, particularly if the company does not receive a tax deduction for it.

➤ Whether companies have the option of enrolling expatriates in host-country benefit programs and/or making up the difference in coverage.

➤ Whether host-country legislation regarding termination affects benefit entitlements.

➤ Whether expatriates should receive home-country or host-country social security benefits. (Refer to Practical Perspective 8-10.)

➤ Whether benefits should be maintained on a home-country or host-country basis, who is responsible for the cost, whether other benefits should be used to offset any shortfall in coverage, and whether home-country benefit programs should be exported to local nationals in foreign countries.

U.S. firms' home-country expatriates generally remain under their **home-company's benefit program.**[87] An agreement between the U.S., Canada, and several European countries which eliminates dual social security coverage of citizens from one country working in another on a temporary basis. In some nations, however, expatriates must participate in local social security programs. In these cases, the international companies normally incur the additional costs.[88]

Allowances

International businesses generally pay expatriates certain allowances. These include cost-of-living, housing, education, and relocation allowances. **Cost-of-living allowances** pay the expatriate for differences in expenses between the home and the foreign country. Housing allowances help the expatriate maintain his or her home-country living standards. Education allowances ensure the expatriate that his or her children will receive at least as good an education as they would receive in the home country. Relocation allowances usually pay for the expatriate's moving, shipping, and storage expenses, temporary living expenses, and other related expenses.[89]

The preceding discussions suggest that international business enterprises tend to apply an ethnocentric compensation policy—the home-country expatriate, as previously indicated, receives compensation and benefits that are different from those received by third-country and host-country managers. However, as companies become more globally oriented, they will rely more on third-country managers to manage global operations. These firms will apply a geocentric compensation policy, that is, a more globally uniform compensation and benefits package.

TECHNOLOGY AND CROSS-NATIONAL HRM

The advent of the new technologies described earlier, such as e-mail and videoconferencing, enable international organizations to develop a system to keep track of people and people's skills worldwide. For example, Cypress Semiconductor, a San Jose, California, maker of specialty computer chips,

PRACTICAL PERSPECTIVE 8-10

International Social Security

Around the globe, social security isn't just a tax to be avoided, it is a social policy that provides benefits including medical care, retirement, and disability pensions. Policies vary widely across countries.

For the expatriate, social taxation can become a complex issue that requires become a complex issue that requires careful planning to make sure that accumulated entitlements are protected in the home country, that benefits continue to accrue while on foreign assignment, and that the employee isn't taxed by both the home and host countries.

Within the European Union, and between the EU and the European Economic Area of Iceland and Norway, legislation specifies that normally an expatriate will enroll in the host-country program for the duration of the assignment and continue to accrue benefits. Similar agreements exist between the United States and most industrialized nations.

Reciprocal agreements between countries usually mean the employee can remain in the home-country system for a few years before being required to switch to the host-country scheme.

If expatriates eventually enroll in the host-country program, they will earn some benefits there. This situation can prove financially difficult if:

➤ The pension earned in the host assignment country is significantly less than home social security benefits;

➤ Pensions earned abroad are payable in the host country currency and exchange rates are expected to worsen prior to retirement; and

➤ Payment from the host country may be

difficult to claim and collect, especially if many years pass between the expat assignment and retirement.

Because of these concerns, many expats choose to remain in their home social security plan, even if this requires paying into both home and host country programs.

Assignments to countries without reciprocal agreements require protecting both existing and future social security benefits. "If the expatriate can be retained in his home country scheme, probably through voluntary contributions by employee and/or home employer, the problem is to a great extent solved," says Gunter Becher, director of international consulting in Europe for Watson Wyatt. "Certainly this is so in regard to continuing entitlement to long-term benefits. In these cases, short-term benefits such as medical care must often be arranged through private insurance.

"International social security matters require considerable knowledge and research," emphasizes Becher, "more particularly because systems are changing all the time."

To be safe, expats should remain in their home-country social security system whenever possible and for as long as possible. "In fact, this can frequently be achieved," says Becher, "and is the one solution that is readily acceptable to—and understood by—almost every expatriate."

Source: Excerpted from Leigh and Collinns Allard, "Managing Globe-Trotting Expats," *Management Review* (May 1996): 39. © 1996 American Management Association International. Reprinted by permission of American Management Association International, New York, NY. All rights reserved. http://www.amanet.org.

has developed a computer system that keeps track of its 1,500 employees as they criss-cross between different functions, teams, and projects. Apple has that developed a computer network called Spider—a system that combines a network of personal computers with a videoconferencing system and a database of employee records. A manager assembling a team can, using this system, call up profiles of employees who are stationed anywhere in the world. A color photo of the person can be seen on the screen, where he or she works, who reports to him or her, to whom he or she reports, and his or her skills. If the manager wants to interview a candidate in, for instance, Frankfurt, he or she can call him or her over the Spider network and talk with him or her in living color on the computer screen.[90]

Furthermore, **the Internet and intranets,** including e-mail, are the most democratic form of overseas deployment, enabling communication among employees regardless of organizational level. Videoconferencing has a similar advantage; however, such facilities are scarce compared with e-mail in most organizations. In the future, as costs of such systems are lowered, more organizations will be able to use videoconferencing. Dow and Merk have videoconferencing systems, and their managers said their videoconferencing rooms are in constant use.[91]

SUMMARY

This chapter has discussed several reasons expatriates fail, including the foreign country's physical and social environment, varying technical sophistication, gender, inadequate repatriation programs, and the pitfalls in the HR planning function. Based on Japanese, European, and U.S. MNCs' expatriation practices, a framework for reducing expatriate failure was presented. Other ways to reduce expatriate failure were also introduced, including a framework for selecting the right person for the foreign assignment. Also presented were frameworks for finding and developing effective expatriates, for administrating expatriate programs, and for administrating expatriate compensation.

Key Terms and Concepts

1. Expatriates
2. Adaptation problems
3. Differences in technical sophistication
4. Company-country conflicting objectives and policies
5. Visibly constrained authority of expatriate managers
6. Cultural bias against women
7. Repatriation
8. Repatriation programs
9. Skills acquired in foreign country not used at home
10. Missed opportunities
11. Reverse culture shock
12. Human resource managers play a less active role in companies' overall planning process
13. Inadequate selection criteria for foreign assignments
14. Inability of expatriate's family to adapt to foreign environment
15. Lack of adequate training for foreign assignments
16. Expatriates need time to adapt
17. The initial, disillusionment, culture shock, and positive adjustment phrases
18. Underutilization of women as expatriates
19. Lower incidence of expatriate failure experienced by Japanese MNCs than by U.S. MNCs
20. The "spirit of internationalism"
21. New information technology
22. Reducing expatriate failure
23. Selecting the right expatriate
24. Assessing expatriates' effectiveness potential
25. Cultural-toughness dimension
26. Finding and developing global managers
27. Chief learning officer
28. Expatriation programs and program administrators
29. Pre-expatriation, expatriation, and repatriation phases
30. Expatriate compensation policy
31. Visible pay inequity
32. Double taxation
33. Home-country's benefit package
34. Cost-of-living allowances
35. Internet and intranets

Discussion Questions and Exercises

1. Discuss the fundamental reasons expatriates fail.
2. You are the manager of the international HRM function for a firm whose top management is assigning an executive from the home office to head one of the firm's foreign subsidiaries. Relative to the cultural adaptation phases, what would you advise the top management?
3. What are the international staffing implications drawn from the Japanese, European, and U.S. MNCs' expatriate practices?
4. Refer back to exercise 2. What question would you ask the top management to be sure that the right expatriate has been selected?
5. To be effective, consultants agree, expatriates require certain characteristics. What are those characteristics?
6. Discuss the significance of the self-oriented, others-oriented, perceptual, and cultural-toughness dimensions in the selection of expatriates.
7. Discuss the four sources for recruiting and developing a pool of global expatriates.
8. Discuss the pre-expatriation, expatriation, and repatriation administration programs.
9. What type of knowledge is required for the effective administration of expatriate compensation?
10. What is meant by "a global standard policy" relating to compensation?
11. How do information technologies assist in managing global human resources?

Assignment

Contact the manager of the HRM function for an MNC. Ask him or her to describe the company's policy relating to expatriate development. Prepare a short report for your class.

CASE 8 - 1

Trouble Abroad

The line went dead. Steve Prestwick slowly hung up the telephone, wondering what he could possibly say to the executive committee monitoring the Singapore R&D center project. Shortly after being assigned to help staff the facility, he had attended a committee meeting that left him excited about tapping into the potential of the company's large global work force. "Get the best people from everywhere," said one executive. "Don't just rely on information from headquarters. Try to find out what the people in Europe or Japan might know," chimed in another. And from the CEO, "Let's use this as an opportunity to develop a global mindset in some of our more promising people." The vision sounded great, and Steve's role seemed simple: put together a team with all the experts needed to get the new facility up and running smoothly in its first two years.

Right away Steve began having trouble finding out who had the right skills, and even where the choices seemed obvious, he wasn't getting anywhere. The engineer who refused the assignment over the telephone was the best the company had in her field. She told him that spending two years in Singapore wouldn't really help her career. Plus, it would be hard on her children and impossible for her husband, a veterinarian with a growing practice.

Not only did he need a top engineering manager, but Steve also had to find a highly competent corps of technical researchers who knew about the company and its approach to R&D. He also needed technicians who could set up the facility. He thought he would bring in people from the U.S. to select and set up equipment, then lead a research team of local engineers that the U.S. engineers would train in company practices and technologies. To his chagrin, most of the U.S. technical people he had talked to weren't interested in such an assignment. A European perspective might be useful, but he didn't even have records on possible candidates from the other overseas offices. Steve was on his own, and he had less than a week to come up with a plan.

Questions

1. How could this problem have been avoided?
2. What can Steve do?

Source: Excerpted from K. Roberts, E.E. Kossek, and C. Ozeki, "Managing the Global Workforce: Challenges and Strategies," *Academy of Management Executive 12*, no. 4 (November 1998): 92. Copyright by Oxford University Press. Reprinted with permission.

Notes

1. Excerpted from "Today's Issue: What It Means to be a Global Corporation," *USA Today*, December 8. 1997, p. 15B.
2. Rosalie L. Tung, "Selection and Training of Personnel for Overseas Assignments," *Columbia Journal of World Business 16*, no. 1 (Spring 1981): 69–78.
3. E. Harari and Y. Zeira, "Training Expatriates for Assignments in Japan," *California Management Review 20*, no. 4 (1977): 56–61.
4. D.A. Heenan, "The Corporate Expatriate: Assignment to Ambiguity," *Columbia Journal of World Business* (May–June 1970): 49–54.
5. A.J. Almaney, "Intercultural Communication and the MNC Executive," *Columbia Journal of World Business 9*, no. 4 (1974): 23–28.
6. A. Rahim, "A Model for Developing Key Expatriate Executives," *Personnel Journal* (April 1983): 312–317.
7. Heenan, "The Corporate Expatriate."
8. F. E. Cotton, "Some Interdisciplinary Problems in Transferring Technology and Management," *Management International Review 13*, no. 1 (1973): 71–77.
9. Rahim, "A Model for Developing Key Expatriate Executives."
10. Heenan, "The Corporate Expatriate."
11. D.N. Israeli, M. Banai, and Y. Zeira, "Women Executives in MNC Subsidiaries," *California Management Review 23*, no. 1 (1980): 53–63.
12. J. Alex Murray, "International Personnel Repatriation: Culture Shock in Reverse," *MSU Business Topics 2*, no. 3 (1973): 59–66.
13. Nancy J. Adler, "Re-entry: Managing Cross-Cultural Transitions." Paper presented at the annual meeting of the Academy of International Business, October 1980.
14. L. Clague and N.B. Krupp, "International Personnel: The Repatriation Problem," *The Personnel Administrator* (April 1978): 32.
15. See Rosalie L. Tung, "Career Issues in International Assignments," *The Academy of Management Executive 2*, no. 3 (1988): 241–244.
16. Cecil G. Howard, "The Expatriate Manager and the Role of the MNC," *Personnel Journal 10*, no. 10 (October 1980): 830–844.
17. Michael G. Harvey, "The Other Side of Foreign Assignments: Dealing with the Repatriation Dilemma," *Columbia Journal of World Business 17*, no. 1 (Spring 1982): 53.
18. D.W. Kendall, "Repatriation: An Ending and a Beginning," *Business Horizons* (November-December 1981): 23.
19. Harvey, "The Other Side of Foreign Assignments."
20. Rosalie L. Tung, *Strategic Management of Human Resources in the Multinational Enterprise* (New York: John Wiley & Sons, 1984).
21. P. Lorange and D.C. Murphy, "Strategy and Human Resources: Concepts and Practices," *Human Resource Management 22*, no. 1–2 (1983): 111–113.
22. L.K. Stroh and P.M. Caligiuri, "Increasing Global Competitiveness Through Effective People Management," *Journal of World Business 1*, no. 1 (Spring 1998): 2.
23. R.L. Desatnick and M.L. Bennett, *Human Resource Management in the Multinational Company* (New York: Nichols, 1978).
24. Tung, "Selection and Training of Personnel."
25. Edwin L. Miller, "The Selection Decision for an International Assignment: A Study of Decision-Makers' Behavior," *Journal of International Business Studies 3*, no. 2 (1972): 49–65.
26. Tung, "Selection and Training of Personnel."
27. Charles Butler, "A World of Trouble," *Sales and Marketing Management 151*, no. 9 (September 1999): 5.
28. G.M. Harvey, "The Executive Family: An Overlooked Variable in International Assignments," *Columbia Journal of World Business* (Spring 1985): 84–91.
29. Rosalie L. Tung, "Selection and Training Procedures of U.S., *European, and Japanese Multinationals*," *California Management Review 25*, no. 1 (1982): 57–71.
30. Tung, "Selection and Training of Personnel."
31. Tung, "Selection and Training Procedures."
32. Harari and Zeira, "Training Expatriates."
33. For extensive coverage of this topic, refer to Charlene Marmer Solomon, "How Does Your Global Talent Measure Up? (International Personnel Performance Measures)," *Personnel Journal 73*, no. 10 (October 1994): 96–108.
34. Harari and Zeira, "Training Expatriates."
35. J.T. Gullahorn and J.E. Gullahorn, "An Extension of the U-Curve Hypothesis," *Journal of Social Sciences 19*, no. 3 (1963): 33–47.
36. Nancy J. Adler, "Cross-Cultural Management Research: The Ostrich and the Trend," *The Academy of Management Review 8*, no. 3 (1983): 226–232.
37. Ibid.
38. Tung, "Selection and Training of Personnel."
39. Tung, "Selection and Training Procedures."
40. J.C. Baker, K. Ryans, and G. Howard, *International Business Classics* (Lexington, MA: D.C. Heath and Co., 1988), pp. 283–295.
41. Ibid.

42. Ibid.

43. Ibid.

44. Tung, "Selection and Training Procedures."

45. Ibid.

46. Tung, *Strategic Management of Human Resources.*

47. Rosalie L. Tung, *The New Expatriate* (Cambridge, MA: Ballinger, 1988), pp. 161–172.

48. Ibid.

49. Ibid.

50. Adapted from Rosalie L. Tung, "Human Resource Planning in Japanese Multinationals: A Model for U.S. Firms," *Journal of International Business Studies 15*, no. 2 (Fall 1984): 139–150.

51. Tung, *The New Expatriate.*

52. Brian Croft, "Use Technology to Manage Your Expatriates," *Personnel Journal* (December 1995): 115.

53. Paul E. Illman, *Developing Overseas Managers and Managers Overseas* (New York: Ama Com, 1980), p.15.

54. David Pulatie, "How Do You Ensure Success of Managers Going Abroad?" *Training and Development Journal* (December 1985): 22–23.

55. Tung, "Selection and Training of Personnel."

56. P.J. Dowling and R.S. Schuler, *International Dimensions of Human Resource Management* (Boston: PWS-Kent Publishing, 1990), p. 53.

57. Charles Siler, "Recruiting Overseas Executives," *Overseas Business* (Winter 1990): 31.

58. Ibid.

59. M. Mendenhall and G. Oddou, "The Dimensions of Expatriate Acculturation: A Review," *The Academy of Management Review 10*, no. 1 (1985): 39–47.

60. For another framework on assessing expatriate candidates refer to Charlene Marmer Solomon, "Staff Selection Impacts Global Success," *Personnel Journal* (January 1994): 88–101.

61. Mendenhall and Oddou, "The Dimensions of Expatriate Acculturation."

62. S. Ronen, "Training the International Assignee," in *Training and Career Development*, ed. I. Goldstein (San Francisco: Jossey-Bass, 1989), p. 438.

63. I. Torbioro, *Living Abroad: Personnel Adjustment and Personnel Policy in the Overseas Setting* (New York: John Wiley, 1982).

64. H.L. Willis, "Selection for Employment in Developing Countries," *Personnel Administrator 29*, no. 7 (1984): 55.

65. P.J. Dowling, "Psychological Testing in Australia: An Overview and an Assessment," in *Australia Personnel Management: A Reader*, ed. G. Palmer (Sidney: Macmillan, 1988): 123–135.

66. A.M Ryan, L. McFarland, H. Baron, and R. Page, "An International Look at Selection Practices: Nation and Culture as Explanations for Variability in Practice," *Personnel Psychology 52*, no. 2 (Summer 1999): 359.

67. L.K.Stroh and P.M. Caligiuri, "Increasing Global Competitiveness Through Effective People Management," p. 11.

68. Cecil G. Howard, "Profile of the 21st Century Manager," *HR Magazine* (June 1992): 97–100.

69. Ford S. Worthy, "You Can't Grow If You Can't Manage," *Fortune* (June 3, 1991): 86.

70. L.K.Stroh and P.M. Caligiuri, "Increasing Global Competitiveness Through Effective People Management," p. 10.

71. Jennifer J. Laabs, "How Gillette Grooms Global Talent," *Personnel Journal* (August 3, 1993): 64–76.

72. Ronald Henkoff, "Growing Your Company: Five Ways to Do It Right," *Fortune Advisor 1998* (New York: Fortune Books, 1998), p. 84.

73. N. Sleveking, K. Anchor, and R.C. Marston, "Selecting and Preparing Expatriate Employees," *Personnel Journal* (March 1981): 197–200. See also Solomon, "Staff Selection Impacts Global Success"; and J.L. Calof and Paul W. Beamish, "The Right Attitude For International Success," *Business Quarterly* (Autumn 1994): 105–110.

74. Harvey, "The Other Side of Foreign Assignments," p. 54.

75. R.L. Thornton and M.K. Thornton, "Personnel Problems in 'Carry the Flag' Missions in Foreign Assignments," *Business Horizons* (January–February 1995): 59–65; Harvey, "The Other Side of Foreign Assignments," p. 56; Cecil G. Howard, "How Relocation Abroad Affects Expatriates' Family Life," *Personnel Administrator* (November 1980): 71; Michael A. Conway, "Reducing Expatriate Failure Rates," *Personnel Administrator* (July 1984): 31–34; David M. Noer, *Multinational People Management* (Bureau of National Affairs, Inc., 1975).

76. Sources: Harvey, "The Other Side of Foreign Assignments," p. 58; Clague and Krupp, "International Personnel: The Repatriation Problem," p. 32.

77. Charles Butler, "A World of Trouble," op. cit, p. 3.

78. Excerpted from Ron Ashkenas, "Breaking Through the Global Boundaries," *Executive Excellence 16*, no. 7 (July 1999): 8.

79. Eric Matson, "How to Globalize Yourself," *Fast Company* (April–May 1997): 134.

80. Dowling and Schuler, *The International Dimensions of Human Resource Management*, p. 117.

81. Ibid.

82. Valarie Frazee, "Is the Balance Sheet Right for Your Expats?" *Workforce* 77, no. 9 (September 1998): 19.

83. Dowling and Schuler, *International Dimensions of Human Resource Management*, pp. 120–121.

84. Carolina Esquenazi-Shaio, "Just Rewards: Compensating Managers Abroad is Tough," *International Business* (April 1996): 33.

85. Dowling and Schuler, *International Dimensions of Human Resource Management*, p. 124.

86. Ibid., p. 125.

87. Ibid.

88. Ibid., p. 126.

89. Ibid., p. 129.

90. B. Dumaine, "The Bureaucracy Busters," *Fortune* (June 17, 1991): 41.

91. K. Roberts, E.E. Kossek, and C. Ozeki, "Managing the Global Workforce: Challenges and Strategies," *Academy of Management Executive* 12, no. 47 (November 1998): 99.

V

Cross-Cultural Communication and Negotiations

Communication is the process of transmitting information, ideas, and attitudes (a message) from one person (the sender) to another (the receiver). In practice, this is an extremely difficult process to apply effectively because receivers often do not interpret messages as intended by the sender; messages are often not understood or are misinterpreted. This occurs when senders encode messages using words, symbols, and concepts/ideas that are unfamiliar to the receiver or receivers. Unfamiliarity results especially when senders' and receivers' frames of reference and means of communication have been developed in different cultures. Cultures typically develop unique ways of communicating; they develop formal languages, idioms, slang, jargon, and non-verbal means of communication (body language) as well as norms and values, which are unique to their own society. And they develop unique ways of conducting and negotiating business. This uniqueness makes communicating, and conducting and negotiating business, across nations/cultures challenging tasks for international managers. International managers who possess strong skills in this area are likely to be far more successful in international management than those who possess weak skills. Chapter 9 discusses cross-cultural communication, and Chapter 10, cross-cultural business practices and negotiations.

9

Cross-Cultural Communication

Stiff and ill at ease at first [at a training program], the Japanese said little, and some of what they said was hard to understand. The Americans talked too much and wondered when the Japanese would make a contribution.... [Professor Hirotaka Takeuchi from Hitotsubashi University, Japan] explained to the others why the Japanese spoke so little.... Unlike Americans, who like to jump in and grab control of a meeting, said Takeuchi, the Japanese prefer to wait and listen; the higher their rank, the more they listen. This group of Japanese was the elite, he explained, and therefore listened a lot. He added that the Japanese have a not-so-subtle saying: "He who speaks first at a meeting is a dumb ass." [1]

Learning Objectives of the Chapter

Effective communication across nations/cultures can take place only when the sender encodes the message using language, idioms, norms and values, and so on that are familiar to the receiver or when the receiver (or receivers) is familiar with the language, idioms, and so on used by the sender. Attaining familiarity with language, slang, norms and values, and so on across nations/cultures is by no means an easy task because words and concepts are often not easily translatable (and sometimes not translatable at all) from one culture to another. For example, the concept of "self-fulfillment" is well understood in the American culture, but such a concept is not translatable to many cultures throughout the world, who understand better the concept of "group-fulfillment." Furthermore, words often have different meanings when translated into another language. For instance, U.S. manufacturer

General Motors Corporation advertised on many of the automobiles it produced that the body was made by Fisher ("Body by Fisher"). The Flemish interpreted it to mean "Corpse by Fisher." The above suggests that communication is bound to create many problems for people conducting international/cross-cultural business. And international managers cannot generally be effective if they do not possess strong cross-cultural communication skills. After studying this chapter, you should be able to:

1. Discuss the communication process (ideation, encoding, transmission, and decoding) in an international/cross-cultural context.

2. Discuss the cultural and language barriers and the ways of dealing with them, including use of translators.

3. Discuss the ways to develop the ability to communicate effectively across cultures.

THE CROSS-CULTURAL COMMUNICATION PROCESS

Figure 9-1 presents the communication process. Communication is the process of conveying a message (a concept or idea) from one party to another or others. The message can be transmitted orally (spoken words), visually (written words), or nonverbally (body/facial expressions). Concepts have different meanings and different levels of importance in different cultures throughout the globe, and many societies have adopted a **unique language** or multiple unique languages (for example, China has more than 50 distinct spoken languages, such as Beijingnese, Cantonese, Shanghainese). Since meanings and languages vary so much from one culture to another, people conducting business across cultures and languages will often encounter communication difficulties that they would not encounter in their own culture and language. Therefore, to communicate effectively across cultures and languages, international businesspeople must develop the ability to adapt to the differences. Lacking this ability, they will often find themselves in embarrassing situations.[2]

Relative to differing verbal languages, **English appears to be emerging as the language of choice in conducting business** across countries. Nevertheless, cross-cultural, cross-national communication problems remain because different cultures have developed **different social values**. Thus, a concept perceived in a certain way in one culture is perceived differently in another. Also, different cultures have developed different nonverbal languages. Therefore, differing gestures and facial expressions still present cross-cultural communication problems. Furthermore, "it is blind provincialism to believe that English will continue to be used everywhere for all occasions."[3]

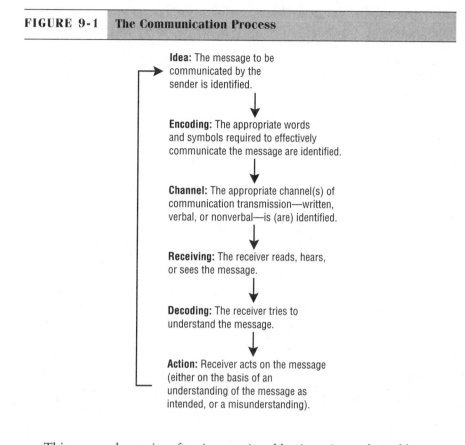

FIGURE 9-1   The Communication Process

Idea: The message to be communicated by the sender is identified.

Encoding: The appropriate words and symbols required to effectively communicate the message are identified.

Channel: The appropriate channel(s) of communication transmission—written, verbal, or nonverbal—is (are) identified.

Receiving: The receiver reads, hears, or sees the message.

Decoding: The receiver tries to understand the message.

Action: Receiver acts on the message (either on the basis of an understanding of the message as intended, or a misunderstanding).

This means that quite often international business is conducted between parties who speak different languages (either verbal or nonverbal or both). When senders of messages and the receivers speak different languages, communication barriers arise. To help eliminate the verbal and nonverbal barriers, the parties involved in the communication process must often employ a **language translator.** The ensuing sections describe the ideation, encoding, transmission, and decoding stages of the communication process in an international/cross-cultural context; discuss effective translation skills; propose a framework for communicating across countries using the English language; and propose ways to develop cross-cultural communication skills.

The Ideation Stage

At the ideation stage, senders (communicators) must identify clearly and specifically what it is that they want the receivers (the listeners) to do as a result of the communication—that is, they must determine what their objective is.[4] Is it to get the receiver(s) to buy a product or service? To perform a certain task? To sign a contract? To find a solution to a problem? To approve a solution to a problem? To provide certain information? To approve a certain recommendation?

When individuals are communicating in cultures different from their own (and realistically, differences do not occur only across nations; they can often be found within nations, as well as within nations' regions, cities/towns, and in cities such as New York, within blocks and even apartments in the same building), they should ask themselves two basic questions: In light of the culture, is the objective realistic? In light of the culture, is the time frame realistic?

Realistic Objective

A society's culture determines to what extent an **objective is realistic.** For example, an objective requiring that the receiver carry out the sender's directives may not be realistic in small power distance cultures such as Sweden, Norway, and Israel, where individuals culturally expect to participate in decision making. It may, however, be realistic in large power distance cultures such as France, where individuals culturally expect to be directed. (See Practical Perspective 9-1.) Objectives to sell beef in India or pork in Israel would not be realistic. An objective to sell toothpaste that

PRACTICAL PERSPECTIVE 9-1

An Illustration of Cross-Cultural Communication Ineffectiveness

Behavior	Attribution
American: "How long will it take you to finish this report?"	American: I have asked him to participate. Greek: His behavior makes no sense. He is the boss. Why doesn't he tell me?
Greek: "I don't know. How long should it take?"	American: He refuses to take responsibility. Greek: I asked him for an order.
American: "You are in the best position to analyze time requirements."	American: I press him to take responsibility for his actions. Greek: What nonsense! I'd better give him an answer.
Greek: "Ten days."	American: He lacks the ability to estimate time; this time estimate is totally inadequate.
American: "Take fifteen days. Is it agreed? You will do it in fifteen days?"	American: I offer a contract. Greek: These are my orders: fifteen days.

In fact, the report needed 30 days of regular work. So the Greek worked day and night, but, at the end of the fifteenth day, he still needed to do one more day's work.

Behavior	Attribution
American: "Where is the report?"	**American:** I am making sure he fulfills his contract.
	Greek: He is asking for the report.
	Both attribute that it is not ready.
Greek: "It will be ready tomorrow."	
American: "But we had agreed it would be ready today."	**American:** I must teach him to fulfill a contract.
	Greek: The stupid, incompetent boss! Not only does he give me the wrong orders, but he doesn't even appreciate that I did a 30-day job in sixteen days.
The Greek hands in his resignation.	The American is surprised.
	Greek: I won't work for such a man.

Source: From *Interpersonal Behavior*, 1st edition, by H. Triandis. Copyright © 1977. Reprinted with permission of Wadsworth, a division of Thomson Learning. Fax: 800-730-2215.

makes teeth sparkling white may not be realistic in many parts of Southeast Asia where betel nut chewing is an elite pastime and stained teeth are a symbol of high esteem. An objective to mass-sell Western-style, sitting-height toilet bowls in China, where ground-level bowls are widely used (to use, one squats over them), would not be realistic at this stage of China's economic transformation. An objective to obtain a signature on a lengthy contract may be realistic in America, where it is an accepted practice, but not in Japan, where verbal contracts ("a gentleman's agreement"/"a handshake") or written contracts consisting of only a few pages are the accepted practice.

An objective to obtain a firm employee commitment to a project in Islamic cultures—which exist anywhere from North Africa to the Middle East to Indonesia—may not be as realistic as it is in Western cultures. Islamic cultures tend to be guided by a fatalistic view that events are controlled by external forces ("God wills it") and they therefore have no power to make things happen, whereas the latter cultures tend to be guided by a master-of-destiny view that events are controlled by people themselves. An objective to discuss business during a lunch or dinner meeting in many parts of Asia, Europe, and South America, where such meetings are used mainly for the development of social relations, may not be a realistic objective, but it may be realistic in North America, where such meetings are typically held for the purpose of discussing business.

Realistic Time Frame

Culture also determines the definition of a **realistic time frame**. Different cultures hold different concepts of time. In some cultures, for example, Germany and Switzerland, timetables are exact and precise, and people tend to meet deadlines. In some cultures, including some Latin American and African cultures, individuals possess a relatively more relaxed attitude toward time; unlike in the United States, time is not a commodity and the completion of tasks moves relatively slowly. Deadlines given to employees in these cultures often will not be met and often will demotivate them. The objective to build a bridge in, for instance, a 24-month span of time is therefore more realistic in the former cultures than in the latter.

The Encoding Stage

After the message to be communicated has been ascertained, the next step is to determine and organize the words, expressions, and nonverbal signals needed to communicate the message effectively. Language and cultural differences exist among nations. Vast language differences occur even within a single nation, for example, Canada has two official languages, Switzerland has four, and China, as previously indicated, has more than 50 different languages. These differences create difficulties in identifying the words, expressions, and nonverbal signals required to communicate effectively across nations and cultures. Therefore, the encoding process for cross-cultural communication must take into consideration many language and cultural differences existing around the globe. Some of the differences are discussed below.

Language

Unique idioms, slang, similes, metaphors, and jargon are components of languages that people use without being aware that they are doing so, and many are not easily translatable from one language to another. For example, the promotional term "come alive with Pepsi" in the U.S. means to become invigorated or energetic, whereas when translated into German, it communicates the thought of "coming alive from the grave with Pepsi." Even though the Latin word *nova* actually means "new," the label on Chevrolet's Nova automobile was interpreted by many Spanish-speaking individuals to mean "doesn't go" (*no va*). Who would buy a car that does not go? America's Colgate-Palmolive Company introduced its Cue brand of toothpaste in French-speaking countries. The word *cue* in French translates into a pornographic word that offends many French-speaking people. How does a non-English-speaking person using a language translation dictionary readily translate the English phrase "as easy as duck soup" or "a ballpark figure" or "a monkey on my back" or "a pain in the neck" into his or her language? How does an English-to-Russian translator interpret such terms as "consumer market" or "market-driven economy" to a Russian?

Even within a language many **words have different meanings** to different people. For example, Parker, the well-known maker of ballpoint pens, had to change its advertising in Latin America after learning that *bola*, the Spanish translation of ball, does not mean ball in all Spanish-speaking countries; in some it actually means "revolution" or "lie." In the United States, "tabling" something means postponing it; in England it means discussing it now. In Canada, a "pothole" is where one goes swimming; in New York City it is where one smashes an automobile's wheels and shock absorbers. Imagine the embarrassment of an American named Randy, who when visiting in England approached a lady at a social gathering and introduced himself: "Hi, I'm Randy." In England, to be "randy" means to be sexually aroused. In the U.S., to be "pissed" means to be mad while in England it means to be drunk. And when United Airlines entered the Pacific market, one of United's in-flight magazine covers showed Australian actor Paul Hogan wandering through the Outback. The caption read, "Paul Hogan Camps It Up." Hogan's lawyer called United Airlines to let them know that "camps it up" is Australian slang for "flaunts his homosexuality."[5]

Letters and Characters

Letters and characters also differ across cultures. Chinese characters and English letters, for example, are very different. The Japanese language uses a combination of two syllabaries, *kana* and *kanji*. *Kana* is the phonetic sounds of the 113 possible syllables and *kanji* are Chinese characters that stand for sound plus meanings. To read a Japanese newspaper, the reader must know 2000 *kanji* characters, and the reader who knows 4000 characters is considered well educated. The Japanese language consists of about 40,000 picture characters. To overcome the problem created by having so many characters, many newspapers are published using *kana* interpretations, which are easier to understand.[6] (This may help explain why the Japanese culturally prefer oral over written communication and short as opposed to long written communication.) Such differences also make language interpretations difficult.

For example, when America's Coca-Cola Company initially introduced its beverage in China, only its Coca-Cola label appeared on the can. Since *Coca-Cola* is not translatable into Mandarin (the official language of China), to write the label, local vendors used Mandarin characters to phonetically spell the sound of *Coca-Cola*. The characters the vendors selected actually meant "bite the wax tadpole." To deal with this problem, Coca-Cola's translators eventually selected a group of characters that are interpreted by the Chinese to mean "may the mouth rejoice" and now place those characters on the cans along with the English letters.[7]

Effective translation of languages is therefore vital in cross-national business negotiations, in promotion and labeling as well as in writing of contracts and reports, in written and/or oral communications between domestic and foreign employees, and in the general management of foreign subsidiaries.

Expressions and Nonverbal Communication

Expressions and nonverbal communication play an important role in cross-cultural encoding. For example, U.S. movie-making firms export movies and television programs made for American audiences. Usually, these must be modified by dubbing in the local language. Accurate language translation is therefore essential. But what is also important is the nonverbal communication contained in the films. For example, the ways of depicting affection in American-made movies and television programs are viewed by some cultures as being offensive. Gestures are widely used as a means of communication in films and television programs, and the same sign has different meanings across different cultures. Some gestures may offend many foreign viewers and must therefore be edited out or somehow isolated before the film is distributed in the foreign culture. For example, Americans form a circle with their index finger and thumb to communicate that something is "OK." Imagine the embarrassment of a former U.S. president who visited Brazil, stepped out of the airplane, and made that gesture to a waiting crowd of Brazilians. The same sign in Brazil means that one is interested in having sex. The same OK sign means zero in France and is a symbol for money in Japan. In many cultures, including those of the United States and China, pointing one's thumb up is a gesture meaning "good" or "great," but in Australia it is a crude gesture.

The Role of Formality and Informality in Communication

Cultures vary in their **requirements for formality and informality,** and these variations also affect cross-cultural communication encoding. Some cultures, especially American and Australian, value informality in communication, but most cultures throughout the world value formality.[8] Individuals in cultures that value informality place low importance on the use of rank, status, and position in communication and often use first names when communicating with each other, even in business settings. On the other hand, individuals in cultures that value formality place high importance on the use of last names, titles, and other indications of rank and status in communication.

For example, in Italy many people are addressed as *Dottore* or *Dottoressa*, whether or not they hold the Ph.D. degree, and an individual can hold such a title by simply holding a college degree. In many Latin American cultures, the title is more important than the name. Therefore, the title *Inginero* (Engineer) is used before the person's last name (Inginero Vargas, for example). The French demonstrate status, rank, and privilege by the type of language used in correspondence. They often use flowery, effusive, complex syntax when communicating with higher ranking individuals. The French do not use the term "Dear" to begin a formal letter; the letter would simply start with the person's name, for instance, "P. Rousseau." In France individuals can work together in the same place for many years and still greet each other with a formal handshake and by the formal name—for example, "Bonjour, M. Rousseau." In Germany, a doctor is addressed as "Herr Doctor," not "Doctor Schilling," and one does not use first names until invited to do so.

In many cultures rank and status are shown by seating arrangements, by the way individuals enter a room, and by who speaks first. In Japan, for instance, the oldest male is normally the most senior, and he must not be the first to enter a room; he is preceded by his assistants, and followed by other assistants, and he sits in the middle. Correspondence to people of higher status must be written individually, and mass mailings are often disliked because they emphasize efficiency over the honoring of individuals' rank and position. People in cultures that value informality, such as Americans, often become frustrated when forced to pay deference to someone simply because of his or her status (family ties, schooling, age, and so on), and not because of the person's accomplishments.

How Much Information Is Needed?

Individuals in some cultures, such as Japan, France, and Germany, can be generally categorized as conservative or risk-avoidant. These individuals make decisions slowly, avoid risks, and dislike ambiguity. (Conditions of uncertainty and ambiguity make them feel uncomfortable.) They therefore have a strong need for much detail and information. On the other hand, people in some cultures, such as Singapore, the United States, and Australia, feel relatively more comfortable with risk and ambiguity, make decisions more quickly, and require less detail and information.[9]

Language Translation

The above suggests that cross-cultural, cross-national communicators, to communicate effectively, must make certain that the language used, including the words, symbols, slang, formal and informal behaviors, as well as nonverbal behaviors, is the one that will be understood by the receiver(s). In conducting global business, businesspeople often do not the possess the command of the language necessary to communicate effectively with foreign associates. These senders therefore have to find a way to convert the language they understand into the language understood by the foreign associates (the receivers).

Translating one language into another is a huge problem confronting cross-cultural, cross-national communicators. To overcome translation problems of written communications, international businesspeople often use the **dual-translation** approach. This involves having a translator in the home country interpret and convert the message into the foreign language, and before the message is communicated, having another translator in the foreign country interpret and convert the message back into the home country's language. For example, a communicator transmitting a message from the United States to Angola, where Portuguese is spoken, first has a translator of English to Portuguese in the United States interpret the message from English to Portuguese. The translated message is then sent to a translator of Portuguese to English in Angola to be interpreted back to English. The sender will transmit the message after he or she has been assured that the translated message will be understood by the receiver(s) as intended.

The Translator's Role

A translator acts as an interpreter for two or more people who wish to communicate with each other but speak different languages. The interpretation may involve written messages, oral messages, nonverbal messages, or a combination of the three types. The translator's job is complex, as he or she must effectively decode the sender's message and encode it into the receiver's language, and then decode the receiver's (now the sender's) reply and encode it into the sender's (now the receiver's) language. (See Figure 9-2.)

Oral Translators. There are two types of oral translators: those who are engaged in simultaneous interpretations and those involved in sequential interpretations.[10]

Simultaneous oral interpreters are usually used by speakers in formal presentation situations, such as conferences, where the audience (the receivers) and the speaker (the sender) communicate using a different lan-

---

FIGURE 9-2   Cross-Language Interpretation

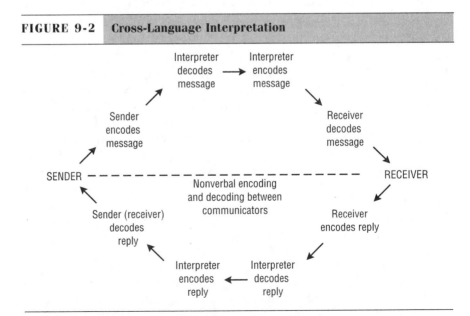

Source: Adapted from Lyle Sussman and Denise M. Johnson, "The Interpreted Executive: Theory, Models, and Implications," *Journal of Business Communications 30*, no. 4 (1993): 421. Reprinted with permission.

guage. In this situation, the translator interprets the sender's formal presentation and passes it on to the audience. (This type is used in United Nations' meetings.) Usually, the speaker communicates a small group of words, pauses to allow the interpreter to translate them and pass them on to the audience, and so on. For example, a few years ago, the writer spent three weeks lecturing in English at a university in Shanghai, China. The lecture topic was current Western management theory and research. The audience consisted of the university's management professors, some high-level executives from Chinese business enterprises, and several of the university's management graduate students. Most of the participants did not understand English or their understanding was weak. The presentations therefore required use of a translator. Two Mandarin-speaking graduate students at the university who also spoke English fairly fluently were assigned to the writer to act as translators. Both students were management majors who had studied Western management theory. They acted as translators in shifts—the lectures were daily from 9 A.M. to 4:30 P.M. with an hour and a half for lunch. It is virtually impossible for one person to be effective in a translator's role for such a long period of time. The writer made formal presentations with many pauses to allow the translator to interpret the message and pass it on to the audience.

Sequential oral interpreters are typically used by clients involved in cross-language business negotiations and social functions. Unlike the simultaneous interpreter, the sequential interpreter normally requires negotiation and diplomatic skills, the ability to transmit personality and style as well as knowledge of the language and culture.

The Effective Translator

It is obvious that the lack of an effective translator will lead to problems. Several factors help define the **effective translator**.[11]

Characteristics of the Message Itself. The translator is aware of the underlying substantive content of the message—both implicit and explicit—that the sender wishes to convey to the receiver(s). This suggests that a translator with a business background is likely to be more effective in business transactions than a translator with a liberal arts background. The former is likely to be more familiar with business jargon, idioms, etc., than the latter. For instance, the former is more likely to know what the business term *bull market* means than the latter. On the other hand, the translator with the liberal arts background may be more effective at social gatherings where a broad range of topics are typically discussed than the translator with the business background.

Characteristics of the Language Involved. The translator is familiar with the sociolinguistic properties of the languages, including formality (discussed above), the role of gender, status, verb tense, and standard syntax in the language. For example, the effective translator knows that it is not inappropriate to use first names in small power distance societies, but it is in large power distance societies, where use of titles is customary. As previously indicated, in the United States bosses and subordinates often communicate with each other on a first-name basis, but not so in France, where titles are used.

Interpreter's Relationship with the Client. The translator has personal involvement and familiarity with the client and the topic to be communicated. For example, when the writer was lecturing in China using two translators, both were familiar with the topic. A problem that arose, however, was that the writer did not meet with the interpreters before beginning the lectures to orient them specifically on the matters to be covered. Interpreters not given advance notice of the specific contents of the message can make translation errors and interrupt the flow of communication.

Context. The time, place, and purpose of the meeting affect a translator's ability. High-stakes negotiations that take place in a hostile environment and that must be accomplished in a short period of time create stress for the translator and for the communicator, reducing their effectiveness. Negotiations should therefore be arranged to cause minimum stress for the translator and the communicator.

Interpreter's Skills. The effective translator has command of the languages being interpreted, active listening skills, sensitivity to explicit and implicit meanings, and the ability to bridge cultural gaps. These skills must be optimum. Many language specialists believe that to master a language, especially idiomatic meanings and slang it is necessary to live in the foreign country for a few years. As a matter of fact, many expatriate professional translators periodically return to their native countries so that they can **update their translation skills.** They believe that prolonged absences reduce translation ability because idioms, slang, jargon, and cultural behaviors change rapidly.

For instance, in the United States, the meaning of the word *gay* not too long ago was generally taken to mean "happy"; today many people use the word to describe a homosexual male. The word *bad* has historically meant just that; today, in describing an individual's behavior, in some situations, such as in sports, the word is actually used to describe "good." For example, a basketball player is "bad" if he or she possesses "good" playing skills. His or her being so good makes it "bad" for the opposing team—therefore, he or she "is bad." And within the past few decades, the slang word used to describe unconventional individuals in the United States changed from *bohemian* to *beatnik* to *hippie.*

At a recent social gathering in New York, the writer met an expatriate from Portugal whose profession is translating English to Portuguese and Portuguese to English for businesses. She writes business contracts, is involved in oral translations, and so on. She said that, to maintain her translating skills, she goes back to Portugal every year and a half or so, and lives there for about six months, spending that time updating her Portuguese language skills. She believes that if a professional translator is away from the foreign language for much longer than a year and a half, his or her effective translation skills will diminish.

Characteristics of the Parties. The translator is familiar with the personal styles, idiosyncrasies, and communication strengths, including encoding and decoding abilities, of the parties for whom he or she is interpreting.

Cultural Norms and Values. The effective translator is familiar with the cultural norms and values of both cultures. For example, some cultures are high context and some are low context. When conducting business, people in **high-context cultures,** including the Chinese, Korean, Japanese, Vietnamese, Arab, Greek, and Spanish cultures, (1) establish social trust first, (2) value personal relations and goodwill, (3) make agreements on the basis of general trust, and (4) like to conduct slow and ritualistic negotiations.[12] People in these cultures prefer that messages not be structured directly, that they do not get right to the point and state conclusions or bottom lines first. Instead, they prefer that a message be indirect, building up to the point and stating conclusions or bottom lines last.[13] On the other hand, individuals in **low-context cultures,** including the Italian, English, North American, Scandinavian, Swiss, and German cultures, (1) get down to business first, (2) value expertise and performance, (3) like agreement by specific, legalistic contract, and (4) like to conduct negotiations as efficiently as possible.[14] Individuals in these cultures prefer that messages be structured directly, that they get immediately to the point and state conclusions or bottom lines first.[15]

The translator can guide the communication flow accordingly, and when the parties for whom he or she is acting as intermediary are opposites (one is high context and the other low context), the translator educates his or her clients accordingly and applies the most viable communication customs. For instance, if a Japanese businessperson is competing with other companies to obtain a contract from a German company, the German customs are likely to be the most applicable. If, however, a German businessperson is competing with other companies to obtain a contract from a Japanese company, the Japanese customs are likely to be the most applicable. (Practical Perspective 9-2 describes an American expatriate in Japan who became a cultural translator.)

Identify the Right Audience

To encode their messages effectively, senders must ascertain the correct receivers and see that the message appeals to them.[16] In many cultures, those persons involved in the decision or action phase are not readily obvious. Tailoring a message to the obvious receivers and appealing to them can often create communication problems. A culture's views on authority, rank,

PRACTICAL PERSPECTIVE 9-2

The Tale of a Cultural Translator

Joint ventures in Japan between Western and Japanese companies usually run into a series of small conflicts that escalate over the years. They easily become big emotional battles, mainly due to cultural differences. Both parties exclaim: "Here they go again. Can't they understand that..."

A company I [Gunnar Beeth] worked for as director of international operations avoided this entire problem thanks to an employee, George Schreiber. I will describe him because he became what I call a "cultural translator" between the American headquarters and its Japanese joint venture.

Schreiber was an installation engineer, in charge of starting up our equipment. The company needed to send a person to train the new Japanese employees in the unique technology. Schreiber accepted a two-year contract for temporary transfer to Japan. He was first sent to an intensive course in Japanese.

Schreiber did not belong to the management group in the American company but had a solid understanding of the technical products, their installation, and use. So he was highly qualified for training the Japanese engineers.

Schreiber became well accepted by all of the Japanese employees. The Japanese managers felt that the nonassertive Schreiber was no threat to their management careers, despite representing the U.S. owner. So they did not hesitate to ask his advice on a great many matters, some outside his expertise but within his good common sense. The engineers throughout the company appreciated Schreiber's frequent help with a multitude of problems they ran into in the beginning. It became their habit to ask him when they had a problem, any problem. The secretaries in the office were eager to help this nice *gaijin* bachelor with his wretched Japanese.

Before expected, the joint venture was profitable, thriving, and growing. Schreiber's first two-year contract came to an end. By then, he had learned Japanese habits. His spoken Japanese became good. He drank green tea at all hours, ate rice at all meals, and liked to sleep on Japanese tatami mats instead of a bed. He had become "tatamized."

Schreiber was offered a second two-year Japanese contract, which he accepted at once. Other contracts followed. The joint venture soon had more than 100 Japanese employees, and the Japanese engineers soon surpassed Schreiber in the intricacies of the new equipment, which changed rapidly, so he had nothing left to teach them in technical matters.

What could he do in that mature joint venture? Schreiber became a "cultural translator."

When a message arrived from the American headquarters and the capable Japanese joint-venture president felt offended, he stormed into Schreiber's small office and threw the message in front of him, fuming. George read it and explained in his calm manner that the Americans had not really meant it in the way such a message would be understood in Japan.

For communication from Japan to the United States, the written English of one of the Japanese secretaries was quite adequate. But at times something far more important than good English was needed, such as when the Japanese accountant explained to the American auditor why they had spent $46,534 on 847 December holiday presents or when the Japanese personnel manager explained why they continued to keep a chemist on the payroll whose specialty had become obsolete a year earlier.

In these instances, they all went to Schreiber with their drafted messages. Somehow or other, he made them sound at least halfway sane in the American environment. It wasn't easy.

At times, when not even Schreiber could get it to sound sane in the American culture, he would write over his own signature, "This will sound crazy in the United States, but you should go along with it anyway for the following reasons..."

When the western managers came traveling to Japan (myself included), Schreiber accompanied us to ensure that we didn't do or say anything too stupid, from the Japanese viewpoint. Whenever we did that anyway, he corrected us at once: "What you really mean is..." And he did the same thing in the opposite direction. He prevented many conflicts form arising, and he smoothed over small conflicts before they became big, emotional, and costly.

For international operations, especially countries such as Japan, China, India and Saudi Arabia, Western companies need a cultural translator even more than a language translator.

Source: Excerpted from Gunnar Beeth, "Multicultural Managers Wanted," *Management Review* (May 1997): 18–19. © 1997 American Management Association International. Reprinted by permission of American Management Association International, New York, NY. All rights reserved. http://www.amanet.org.

and group definition often force a sender to include additional or different **primary audience** members—those who will be receiving the message directly. They may also force a sender to include a **secondary audience**—those who will hear about the message, participate in decision making, or be affected by the message.

The sender must also identify the key decision makers in the audience. These could include superiors and subordinates, influential officials, opinion leaders, power brokers, contacts, tribe or sect members, or family members. How are the power brokers identified? In Western cultures, an individual's power is demonstrated by how much "proactivity" he or she brings to a situation. In Asia, the powerful do not reveal their inner feelings and thoughts, and they display their authority by the silence and stillness they maintain in response to situations. In Latin America, those in power are often also poets and musicians, and they are trusted because they are able to reveal their inner feelings and thoughts eloquently. The message must be tailored to these audiences and appeal to their motivations.

Appeal to Receivers' Motivations

Motivations are affected by the economic and political conditions confronting the audience. Obviously, an American sending a message to a group of locals in Rwanda about his or her mansion in California or his or her recent vacation in Hong Kong probably will not be heard; the Rwandans probably would hear a message about how to solve their hunger and other problems. That message also probably would not be heard by a group of individuals who are politically repressed; a message explaining how to attain more freedom would probably be heard by these people.

Individuals' motivations are also influenced by culture. For example, people in high masculinity cultures, such as the United States, Austria, and

Switzerland, may be motivated by material wealth and accumulation, while people in low masculinity cultures, such as Denmark and Norway, may value a clean environment and altruism more than material wealth. Thus, a message promising material wealth may be heard more by listeners from a high masculine culture than listeners from a low masculine culture. People in weak uncertainty avoidance cultures, such as Israel, the United States, and Denmark, may be motivated by task enhancement, career advancement, achievement, and challenge, while people in strong uncertainty avoidance cultures, such as France, Portugal, and Greece, may be motivated by job security and a safe work environment. Therefore, listeners from weak uncertainty avoidance cultures may be more interested in a message promising challenging tasks than listeners from strong uncertainty avoidance cultures. People in low-individualism cultures, such as Japan, may be more motivated by group relationships than by career advancement, while people in high-individualism cultures, such as Australia and the United States, may be motivated more by challenging work than by group relationships. A message promising individual rewards would probably be more appealing to listeners from high-individualism cultures than to listeners from low-individualism cultures.

Furthermore, individuals from some cultures, have a negative attitude toward work activities and a positive attitude toward leisure, community, religious, and family activities. The message must therefore appeal to these attitudes; otherwise, it may be difficult to get such people to listen. (Practical Perspective 9-3 presents an insight on making presentations across cultures.)

English as the Language of Communication in Global Business

As indicated above, English appears to be emerging as the universal language for conducting international business. English now has special status in more than 100 countries, far more than any other language. In addition, English is the most widely taught as a foreign language—in more than 100 countries worldwide. Nearly a quarter of the world's population, from 1.2 to 1.5 billion people, is already fluent or competent in English and the number is growing rapidly. No other language, Mandarin included, even comes close to this level of growth.[17] To deal with this evolution, many countries' governments now require that English be taught in their education systems, and in countries whose governments do not mandate the study of English, many students study English for competitive advantages in the job market, as many foreign businesses now require command of the English language as a basis for employment.[18] As a result, **English is often the second or third language** for many businesspeople around the globe. This, however, does not mean that these people are proficient in the use of the English language. Many of these individuals have learned English by reading and listening, and therefore possess a weak ability to communicate

PRACTICAL PERSPECTIVE 9-3

A Time to Talk, a Time to Dance

Picking up a little local color in advance, and using it appropriately, can endear you to an audience, says Richard Marker, a veteran of presentations in more than 20 countries, from Italy to Argentina.

"In Buenos Aires, I was invited to speak to a group of students at 10 P.M. on Saturday evening." He recalls. "We were convinced that we would arrive to an empty room, but found it was standing room only. In Buenos Aires, on the weekends, most people don't eat dinner until midnight, so this was the pre-dinner-and-dancing entertainment. The group was alive! And when I mentioned the local hot disco, El Cielo, I became a hero."

That, he adds, was a nice happenstance, considering that the conference organizer had inspired local derision by scheduling dinner for 6 P.M. and the evening sessions for an 8 P.M. start. "In Buenos Aires, even on weekdays, dinner isn't served until 9 or 10 P.M.," Marker points out, "The organizer had violated one of the basic principles of international business: Learn a little about the local scene."

Yogi Berra once noted that you can observe a lot just by watching. In planning your itinerary, reserve a little time after arrival to gain some familiarity with local conditions and culture.

"When you arrive you need to observe what the local people are doing," Bosrock says. "Ask whenever communication or expected behavior seems unclear. Listen actively and assertively to what people say."

Remember that the more you can acclimate to local customs and habits, the better your chance of presentation success. You need to be willing to try to greet people properly, taste the local food, and learn others' behaviors," Bosrock says. "People can tell when you're trying, and they appreciate it."

But in your quest to be culturally sensitive, don't obsess on tiny nuances of meaning. "We don't communicate perfectly even within our own culture, so we certainly shouldn't expect to do so in someone else's." notes Bosrock. "But when you try, people all over the world understand that you are taking a risk and making an effort to reach out to them."

Adjust to the Situation

Some cautions are so basic as to seem almost condescending—but as many veteran presenters can attest: The Basics are basic for a reason. "Speak more slowly and with less slang than to a U.S. audience," Marker says, repeating perhaps the most common caveat. Even articulate audiences will miss references to American cultural icons and misunderstand popular expressions.

Working with translators can present some unaccustomed challenges. In situations that require a translator, Marker advises modifying your pacing to speak in one or two-sentence bursts. The goal is not to slow down so much that the audience becomes restless, but to give the translator time to keep up with you—and to keep the audience involved. When hearing a lengthy paragraph in someone else's language, "people tune in and out," he points out.

For women presenters, there remain some special concerns. "In many countries, a woman may still need a male spokesperson with her, at least in the beginning," says Dana May Casperson, president of the Professional Resource Institute in Santa Rosa, California. "She needs to dress conservatively—dark neutrals are best—and in the highest-quality clothing and jewelry."

(continued)

The extra scrutiny women often receive in other countries extends to both what they say and how they say it. Here again, advance preparation is crucial. Before you go, you need to identify issues or presentation styles that might effect your credibility, offstage as well as on. That might include, in some cultures, being less open about family and personal matters, Casperson says.

Those, however, are the kind of subtleties that have to be dealt with on a country-by-country basis; broad rules simply don't apply. The support of credible local contacts can be invaluable in such instances not only for the advance heads-up they can provide but also for the role they can play as host, facilitators and sponsors.

Source: Excerpted from Dick Schaaf, "How to Prepare When You Are Presenting There," *Presentations 13*, no. 6 (June 1999): A1–A3. Permission conveyed through Copyright Clearance Center, Inc.

in English. In addition, many learn primarily just the English that relates to their specific industry, for example, large hotels often employ teachers to teach their staff English so that they can accommodate English-speaking customers. These hotels will invest just enough money to train employees in the language commonly used in the business, for example, "The restaurant is on the second floor" or "May I help you with you luggage?". Many understand only **dictionary (literal) translation** meanings. Therefore, quite often a correspondence in English from foreign business associates is the consequence of considerable time and effort on their part. Given a choice, most receivers with English as a second or third language would probably prefer to communicate in their native language and appreciate your acknowledgment of their first-language skills.

This suggests that senders from English-speaking countries should, when possible, attempt to communicate using the foreign receivers' language. They should learn the foreign language or at least have the communication translated. At the very least, senders should communicate some phrases using the foreign language. This shows respect for the culture, acknowledges that there are differences, and informs the receivers that they are not viewed as a branch of the English-speaking nation.[19] Furthermore, perhaps the most compelling reason for learning the language of one's international affiliate is that it provides considerable insights into that culture. It provides the means of entering into the "world view" of another culture—it reveals the important values found the culture, it gives insights into how directly or indirectly people in the culture communicate with one another, and it reflects social realities such as status differences within the culture.[20]

Although it is important that senders from English-speaking countries make some use of other languages, they should also be sensitive to the struggle that receivers with English as their second or third language encounter with the English language, and should attempt to maximize their use of English (practice makes perfect). Figure 9-3 provides some ground rules for communicating in English with receivers whose knowledge of English is secondary to their native language.

Identifying the Right Transmission Channel Stage

A message is typically transmitted in writing, orally, and nonverbally (body/facial expressions). Ongoing advancements in communications technologies present new means of transmitting messages. Written messages can now be transmitted via mail, computer, fax, and e-mail. Oral messages can be transmitted via meetings, telephone, and videoconferencing. Nonverbal messages can be sent via videoconferencing. Some of these communication channels are not available in many countries, especially in the less-developed countries.

Written or Spoken Message?

Regardless of the channels available, the sender must decide whether to transmit the message orally or in writing. Cultural norms affect the

FIGURE 9-3	A Framework for Dealing with Language Differences

➤ Keep your communications simple, short, and to the point. Do not use complicated English words. Monosyllables are fine, if they say what you mean.

➤ Try to eliminate all words that have more than one meaning (for example, does "right" mean "correct," "the opposite of left," or to "re-do"?).

➤ Don't make nouns into verbs.

➤ Don't use industry-specific jargon, acronyms, or abbreviations. Avoid all "professional-ese." There simply are no equal translations.

➤ Use action words and verbs to describe exactly what you mean (for example, don't say "take the bus"; instead, say "ride the bus"), and avoid word pictures unless they are exactly what you mean (for example, don't say, "walk me through this again," or "run that by me again").

➤ Always start out and stay formal unless and until your correspondent informs you to do otherwise; use titles, last names, and so forth.

➤ Avoid humor: It doesn't translate well. What is hysterically funny in one culture can be meaningless in another.

➤ Eliminate all slang, idioms, and sports-related terms from your English. Business English is loaded with them, and terms like "give me a ballpark figure," "hit a home run," "pinch hit for me in the morning," "that idea is out of left field," "he really threw me a curve ball," and "I'll touch base with you tomorrow" all have absolutely *no meaning* in cultures where they don't play baseball.

➤ On the telephone and in person, speak slowly, simply, and deliberately. Show respect and empathy. Never shout to be understood.

➤ On long-distance communications, the rule should be only one communication per item or question. A comprehensive fax of 15 major points and sub-points requiring a response, in English, to a group-oriented culture will either engender no response at all (they will be overwhelmed at the task), or can cause a delay of anywhere between several months to a decade or two.

➤ Be realistic: They don't speak English, they have to translate the document, they have to consider it as a group, and then find someone available who speaks English to retranslate their final answer back to you.

Source: Dean Foster, "Business Across Borders: International Etiquette for the Effective Global Secretary," *The Secretary* (October 1992): 24. Copyright © 1992 Stratton Publishing and Marketing Inc. All rights reserved. Used with permission.

decision. Some cultures prefer written messages and others prefer spoken messages. Individuals in high-context cultures, which value trust, tend to prefer spoken communication and agreements; confirming an idea in writing may be taken as an indication that you think their word is no good. On the other hand, people in low-context cultures, which value efficiency, tend to prefer written communication and agreements.[21] Also, as indicated earlier, many people who understand English as a second or third language learned it by reading and listening, and have not developed a strong command of the language. These receivers may therefore feel more comfortable with written communication than with oral communication, because written communication gives them more time to understand the message. The literacy level of the audience also affects the decision. If the illiteracy rate is high, oral messages would be more effective than written messages.

Format of Messages

There is no universal written message format. For example, standard paper sizes differ among many countries. The standard letter-size paper in the United States is 8.5" X 11"; in Europe, the page is longer, but in many countries it is narrower and shorter. This can create filing, printing, duplicating, and other problems. The physical format of the message must be adapted to different cultures. Similarly, presentation formats, including presentation length, timing, number of visual aids, flamboyance, and the nature of interaction with the audience, also vary among cultures.[22]

Body Language

Body language, including eye contact, physical distance and touching, hand movements, pointing, and facial expressions, which vary across cultures,[23] also affects the transmission of a message.

Eye Contact. Eye contact between superiors and subordinates is avoided in many Southeast Asian cultures because it is a sign of disrespect. On the other hand, in Western cultures avoiding eye contact is a sign of disrespect. Therefore, an American and a Malaysian subordinate may very well view each other as being disrespectful when the American attempts to make eye contact and the Malaysian avoids it.

Physical Distance and Touching. In Asia, once a relationship is established between individuals, physical distance is placed between them, and touching or display of emotions are substantially reduced. On the other hand, in Latin America, once a relationship is established between individuals, physical distance between them is reduced, and touching and display of emotions are increased.

Hand Movements. Some cultures make greater use of hand movements when communicating than others. For example, Italians tend to use their hands extensively, while Americans make limited use of hand movements—they believe that too much hand movement while communicating orally distracts the receiver(s).

Pointing. **Pointing** with the index finger is rude in some cultures, including those of Sudan, Venezuela, and Sri Lanka. Pointing your index finger toward yourself is insulting in Germany, the Netherlands, and Switzerland.

Facial Expressions. Russians do not use **facial expressions** very much and Scandinavians do not use many gestures. This does not mean that they are not enthusiastic.[24]

Transmission of Messages Through Mediators

Messages (written, spoken, and nonverbal) are typically sent directly to the receiver(s). In some situations in some cultures, it is not wise to send messages directly to the receiver(s); it is wise to use a **mediator**—the encoder sends the message to a mediator (a third party), who in turn conveys it to the receiver(s). For example, sincere Americans are often factually blunt and frank, even if it upsets the listeners.[25] The Japanese, however, culturally neither practice nor accept overt criticism and bluntness well. In Japan, to be sincere means having concern for the emotional, not the factual. In fact, to avoid being offensive (a concern for the emotional), a Japanese receiver may not even say "no" to a request from a sender with which he or she does not want to comply; instead, he or she would respond "maybe" (which really means "no" in Japan). Therefore, when a message being transmitted to a Japanese receiver must contain critical and blunt facts, it is better to submit it through a mediator. The bluntness is mitigated because the message was only indirectly passed from the sender to the receiver.

In Japan, when use of a mediator or message is too impractical, the Japanese use **informal get-togethers** to discuss formal matters. At the informal meeting's setting (often after work hours in bars, nightclubs, and restaurants), serious matters can be obscured as entertainment. Discussions in such settings can be semi-serious and hint of disagreements (the message can be blunt, but not too blunt) that would be unwelcome in formal settings.

Communication Principles

There is no doubt that the ability to communicate across cultures and languages is one of the most important skills required in global managers and businesspeople. Professors Ronald E. Dulek, John S. Fielden, and John S. Hill, all with the University of Alabama, devised a three-set series of cross-cultural communication *do*'s and *don't*s.[26] These are outlined in Figure 9-4. The three sets of principles are **conversational principles**, those that senders must remember in all aspects of cross-cultural communication; **presentation**

principles, those applicable when making oral presentations to a foreign audience; and **written principles,** those which must be remembered when transmitting written messages across cultures.[27]

The Receiving-Decoding Stage

In cross-cultural communication, decoding by the receiver of signals is subject to social values and cultural variables not necessarily present in the

FIGURE 9-4	Do's and Don'ts of Cross-Cultural Communication

Conversational Principles

1. *High-context* cultures need to know as much as possible about the sender, such as what makes him or her "tick" and the company he or she represents. Conversations about the sender's family, company, and current events are used to "warm up" relationships. And these people like to know about senders even before they meet them.

2. Foreigners often learn only formal English. Thus, the sender should speak slowly, clearly, and simply, and he or she should avoid use of jargon, slang, cliches, and idioms.

3. It is polite and diplomatic to learn and speak a few phrases using your host's language.

4. Pay close attention to your body language and tone of voice. Communicating disinterest or impatience will embarrass or insult many people. Loud oral communication is socially unacceptable in many parts of Asia and the Middle East, but it is acceptable in many parts of Europe and Central America.

Presentation Principles

1. Americans tend to like spontaneous, unrehearsed presentations. In most other nations, however, such presentations convey the impression that the speaker has not bothered to prepare sufficiently, thus demonstrating disrespect for the audience. Disrespect is further shown when a speaker writes on the blackboard or on transparencies during the presentation. Customized presentations are therefore appreciated in most cultures.

2. Be sensitive to the fact that different audiences in different cultures behave differently during presentations. In Japan, for example, during presentations, businesspeople generally sit quietly and nod their heads to indicate that they understand—not that they agree. When they talk frenziedly amongst themselves, it is an indication that the speaker has said something offensive. Also, be sensitive that in many cultures the audience's not looking at you while you speak does not mean that they are disinterested—in the United States, the audience's not looking at the speaker is a sign of disinterest.

3. Design your presentation's length, completeness, and interruptability to the culture and language capabilities. For example, Americans, Swiss, and Germans like fast-paced, efficient presentations. Most cultures, however, prefer slower, more deliberate presentations. Slower speaking paces are definitely mandatory when a translator is needed or when the audience does not have good command of the language that the speaker is using. Also, never show any sign of impatience when a member of the audience who does not have command of your language is struggling or is clumsy in encoding a question. In high-context cultures, presentations should be short, separate segments, with questions and answers in between. In low-context cultures, such as the United States, questions are usually reserved for the end of the presentation.

4. Match age and rank of presenter to the audience's cultural expectations. For example, in *high-context* cultures age and seniority is a major indicator of status and wisdom, so a young speaker in these cultures may not be appreciated. For instance, if an American firm sends a young executive to negotiate a business deal the other culture may interpret this as a lack of real interest in negotiations.

FIGURE 9-4	The Stages of Economic Development of Nations, *continued*

Writing Principles

1. In *low-context* cultures, where efficiency is highly valued, written communication should be organized so that the central point is immediately and directly stated. In *high-context* cultures, where efficiency is valued less, the communication should be less focused on getting the job done and more personally revealing. For example, people in *high-context* cultures will not read a detailed contract; they think that no one will be so ill-bred as to camouflage anything in fine print.

2. The style should be adapted to cultural preferences. Individuals in *high-context* cultures place great emphasis on respect and politeness, and writing etiquette requires that subordinates are asked to "consider" performing a task or "if at all possible" to complete a task. Arab and Latin American cultures tend to be poetic in their writing styles, and communications are filled with exaggerations, colorful adjectives, and metaphors. People in many cultures think that Americans tend to demonstrate egocentrism by overusing *I* and *my*.

3. If the message is important, enclose a translation in the receiver's native language whenever possible. Translations are both helpful and diplomatic.

Source: Adapted from Ronald E. Dulek, John S. Fielden, and John S. Hill, "International Communication: An Executive Primer," *Business Horizons* (January–February 1991): 21–24. Copyright © 1991 JAI Press Inc. Used with permission from JAI Press Inc. All rights reserved.

sender. Therefore, the most effective way to understand cross-cultural communication is to focus on the decoding process and the role of perception in communication. Communication itself is best understood from the perspective of the receiver, not the sender, the channel, or the encoded message itself.[28] This means that transmission of a message is by itself not communication; a conscious perception of signals at the receiver's end is necessary for communication to have occurred.

This suggests that an effective sender of a message understands the receiver's perceptions, which in essence means that he or she is both an encoder and a decoder. For effective communication to take place when the sender does not understand the receiver's perceptions, the receiver must understand the sender's perceptions; he or she is both an encoder and a decoder. Either the sender or the receiver (or both) must have knowledge of the other's **environmental, cultural, sociocultural, and psychocultural contexts.** Thus, when the amount of such knowledge is small on both sides, communication ineffectiveness results.

For example, in American culture it is quite acceptable to pass food at a dinner table using one's left hand, but in some Middle East cultures it is quite unacceptable. If an American transacting business in the Middle East is aware of this custom, when out to dinner or lunch with local clients, he or she will pass food only with his or her right hand. Doing so will permit communication between the American and the locals to proceed smoothly. If, however, the American is not aware of the custom and passes food with his or her left hand, it will offend the locals and the communication flow is impaired. On the other hand, if the local is aware that Americans instinctively pass food with either hand, depending on which is more convenient (efficient), and the local is "understanding," the communication flow may proceed smoothly.

In reality, it may be difficult to find "understanding" locals, as most will expect you to come to their territory prepared. If you are an American conducting business in China and go out to dinner with local business clients, it may be difficult to find one whose respect you will not lose if you ask for a fork, as opposed to eating with chopsticks. Also, it may be amusing if at first you are clumsy using chopsticks; however, in a long-term relationship, the clumsiness will cease to be amusing, and it may actually become a handicap. Of course, in the United States, the Chinese clients would have to be understanding, and they might have to use forks as well. But even in this situation, much may depend on who needs whom the most. It might be wise for the American to show courtesy by occasionally taking the Chinese visitors to a local Chinese restaurant where they can use chopsticks and the Chinese hosts might occasionally take visiting Western clients to a local Western restaurant where they can use forks. This would symbolize a show of mutual understanding and respect for both cultures. And it certainly would be intellectually self-enhancing if one learned to do it either way. The late CEO of Sony, Akio Morita, as shown in Practical Perspective 9-4, seemed to possess strong encoding-decoding ability.

The Nature of Received Signals

Receivers take **signals** transmitted by senders, decode them, and try to understand them. The receiver-decoded signal is a "sign" constructed of two parts: the signifier and the signified.[29] A sign is a signal that is recognized, structured into a category, and assigned meaning. The **signifier** is the sound or shape of the signal, which is sensorially perceived without meaning attached to it; the **signified** is the meaning attached to the signifier. "The linkage of new, unattributed signifiers to already-existing signifieds is a large part of the process of decoding communication messages."[30] Cross-cultural communication is ineffective "when signs are not recognized because they differ from the signs in the culture-driven repository."[31] (See Figure 9-5.)

Receivers of cross-cultural messages continually adjust and adapt incoming signifiers to the existing repository of signs, and adapt and adjust the repository of signifieds to create new signs. Thus, a competent cross-cultural receiver constantly challenges his or her repository of existing signs and expands it in order to participate in the matching of signs with the sender.[32] (Learning to use both a fork and chopsticks enhances cross-cultural competence.)

To communicate effectively across cultures, the transmission of signs to a receiver must take into account the cultural factors—values, attitudes, beliefs, and behaviors—that shape the structuring categories of the receiver's

PRACTICAL PERSPECTIVE 9-4

Mr. Sony's Struggle

In the 1970s and 1980s [Akio] Morita [the late CEO of Sony] built his presence in the global business establishment to a level not previously attained by any Japanese businessman. The phenomenon was so remarkable that it gave rise to perhaps the most important question above him; how did he do it?

What accounted for Akio Morita's unique ability as a businessman to establish and sustain beneficial relationships with the most important Western business and political leaders? There is striking agreement among those who knew him over time that he was special because he was someone who seemed to understand them and, as important, whom they could understand. Longtime acquaintance Peter Peterson, an investment banker and Sony board member, puts it as well as anyone: "When it came time for Akio to do business in the U.S., whether it was joint ventures or licensing or whatever, he could pick up the phone and talk to almost any businessman in America. And instead of its being 'Who is this again?' and interpreters and all that sort of thing, Akio knew these people at the human level, at the personal level. And let's be honest: To many American businessmen, the Japanese business culture is foreign: they don't feel comfortable with Japanese businessmen, and they don't know them to a large extent as human beings. But they did know Akio in that way, and therefore when he called, people listened."

Henry Kissinger was more theoretical: "First of all, the Japanese in my experience are not great communicators. They tend to operate within their consensus, and when they get dropped out of the consensus and get into dialogue with other cultures, it's tough because they don't feel they have the authority to make independent decisions. So even for many of us

who have Japanese friends whom we value, the problem of communication is very difficult. Morita could conduct a dialogue, and while he was a very patriotic Japanese and a firm defender of the Japanese point of view, he could communicate it in a way that was meaningful to non-Japanese... He was probably the single most effective Japanese spokesman I ever met."...

Morita was raised in a traditional Japanese family in which all things were understood implicitly, where communication, when it occurred, was oblique and equivocal. With this background, how can the aggressive outspokenness and confrontation at the heart of American business behavior have come naturally to him? How, indeed, can he have been naturally at ease with American social style in general? Was Akio Morita, the strict Japanese traditionalist, as effortlessly at home in the West as he appeared to be, or was he simulating Western behavior?

The following excerpt is from a televised dialogue with a well known Japanese commentator, Saburo Shiroyama, about the differences in Japanese and American management style:

Morita: Grammar and pronunciation aren't as important as expressing yourself in a way that matches the way Westerners think, which is very different from our thought process. You have to switch off your Japanese way of seeing things, or they will never understand what you are saying. First of all, they want to hear the conclusion right away; in English sentence structure, the conclusion comes first.

Shiroyama: I've heard that one of our Prime Ministers was in his way to the U.S. for the first time and asked you for advice, and you suggested the critical thing was to start right out with a "yes" or "no" followed by a brief explanation.

(continued)

Morita: When they ask questions or express an opinion, they want to know right away whether the other party agrees or opposes them So the English, "yes" or "no" comes first. We Japanese prefer to save the "yes" or "no" for last. Particularly when the answer is "no," we put off saying that as long as possible, and they find that exasperating.

Shiroyama: But in Japan, as you explained, we don't come out with "yes" or "no" but prefer expressions like, "I'll take this under consideration." Our feeling is that vagueness in these cases in less offensive. So when you're in America, you must be clear, and when you return to Japan you must be vague. Is it hard to switch back and forth?

Morita: It's more difficult than you can imagine.

Despite Westerners' impression that he was one of them, this small critique reveals Morita's appraisal from the opposite side of a cultural divide, as he worked hard to decipher the puzzle that stood between him and successful communication.

Source: Excerpted from "Mr. Sony's Struggle," *Fortune* (November 22, 1999): 237–248. A published excerpt from *Sony: The Private Life*, by John Nathan, published by Houghton Mifflin. Copyright by Houghton Mifflin. Reprinted by permission, all rights reserved.

repository. Cognitively learned knowledge of the cultures involved may be the basis for developing effective cross-cultural competence. Barriers to cross-cultural communication can be reduced by knowledge and understanding of varying cultural factors, along with a genuine desire to communicate effectively. All of this means that "intercultural communication competence is the encoding and decoding of attributed signifieds to signifiers in matches that correspond to signs held in the other communicator's repository."[33]

To communicate effectively across cultures also requires good listening skills. One must be able to listen to spoken as well as to nonverbal (such as facial expressions) messages. An impatient American who constantly looks at his or her watch is not likely to communicate effectively across cultures.

DEVELOPING CROSS-CULTURAL COMMUNICATION COMPETENCE

Professor Linda Beamer of California State University, Los Angeles, has developed a model for the purpose of describing the process of **developing cross-cultural communication competence.**[34] The model proposes five levels of learning: acknowledgment of diversity, organizing information according to stereotypes, posing questions to challenge the stereotypes, analyzing communication episodes, and generating "other culture" messages. The intent of the learning process, according to Beamer, "is to develop the ability to decode effectively signs that come from members of other cul-

FIGURE 9-5 | **Attaching Meaning to Signals**

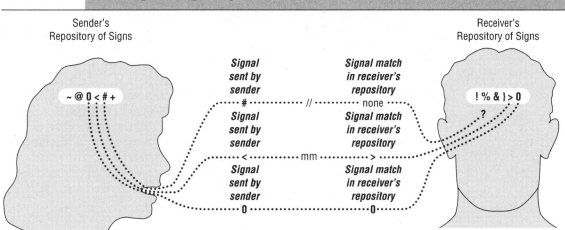

The # signal sent does not match a corresponding sign in the receiver's repository (?), so communication has taken place (//). The sign # may signify large in the sender's respository, but large is signified by & in the receiver's repository. Therefore, for effective communication to take place, either the sender must add & to his or her repository or the receiver must add # to his or her repository.

The < signal sent is matched by the receiver with the seemingly corresponding sign > in his or her repository. Both believe that the signs are the same and communication has taken place. But ineffective communication (*mm*) has actually taken place because while the signs appear the same, they actually point in different directions. The signs < and > may signify *He's old.* To the sender *He's old,* in a certain context, may mean *He's not qualified for the job;* but to the receiver, in the same context, it may mean that *He has wisdom and experience and is qualified for the job.* For effective communication to take place, either the sender or the receiver must understand the contextual differences and encode or decode the meaning accordingly.

The O signal matches the signal in the receiver's repository precisely. Effective communication has taken place.

tures, within a business context, and to encode messages using signs that carry the encoder's intended meaning to members of other cultures."[35] The five levels do not cease to exist once attained; they are continually revisited in the process of learning. This means that newer differences in a culture are constantly being discovered. The ensuing sections describe Beamer's model.

Acknowledging Diversity

At this level of learning, the learner becomes aware of cultural differences. He or she addresses the initial issue of perception—the recognition that formerly unknown and unrecognized signs are being sent. Individuals in homogeneous, high-context cultures, who possess limited experience of cultural diversity, need to start by acknowledging the diversity of signifiers for signifieds already understood. At this level, definitions of basic concepts for discussing diversity are important, such as *bias, ethnocentricity, stereotype, value,* and *culture.* Especially when discussing signifiers, language is the most apparent cultural difference—but becoming proficient in the target language does not always generate **cultural fluency.**

Organizing Information According to Stereotypes

At this level, **stereotypes** that distinguish a particular culture and its members are identified. Stereotypes are normally simple or brief: "Americans are efficiency-oriented"; "Latin Americans place the well-being of family members and friends ahead of organizational efficiency"; "the French are rude to non-French-speaking visitors." Stereotypes provide some familiarity with a culture, and they may be helpful and even accurate to some extent, but they are myopic insights that reveal only *part* of the entire culture. Therefore, knowledge of a culture's stereotypes does not constitute understanding of a culture, and it may actually be an obstacle to the development of cross-cultural communication competence. Stereotypes fail to challenge the signs within their own repository of meanings—they fail to ask if some other signified can be associated with the signifier. One must progress beyond this level of cross-cultural communication.

Posing Questions to Challenge the Stereotypes

At this level, **stereotypes are challenged.** The learner asks questions about how members of a business enterprise describe that organization, their relationships to one another and to their material environment, and their position in relation to the universe. Asking questions is apt to disclose attitudes that are crucial for understanding business activities, such as individuals' attitudes toward time, status and role, obligations in relationships, responsibility and the decision-making processes, the role of law, and the role of technology. Questions challenge stereotypes, and can be patterned to probe what members of a culture "value, how they behave in certain circumstances because of their values, [and] what their attitudes are toward institutions in their society and toward events beyond their control."[36] Primary and/or secondary research will help provide answers to the questions.

Beamer developed a framework outlining several questions that must be answered. The questions relate to the cultural differences in behavior and attitude that affect business communication. The framework develops five areas of value orientations: thinking and knowing, doing and achieving, the self, social organization, and the universe.[37]

Thinking and Knowing

This value orientation relates to how people in a culture obtain, organize, and communicate information about the culture. A group of questions about the culture must be answered:

1. *Ways to know.* In some cultures, an individual only knows something when it is conceptualized and abstracted; in others, what a person knows is contingent on firsthand experience.

2. *Activity that results in knowledge.* In some cultures, knowing is attained by probing, questioning, and atomizing; in others it is

attained by mastering a received body of knowledge to the point where it may be reproduced.

3. *Extent of knowledge.* In some cultures, everything is knowable; in others, the indescribable nature of some things precludes their being known totally.

4. *Patterns of thinking in the culture.* Some cultures use mainly cause-and-effect patterns; they value planning, and their conceptualizations, language, and institutions divulge linear thinking patterns. Other cultures stress "context in patterns of thinking: the interconnections and relationships between things are important and a lattice or net pattern emerges."[38]

Doing and Achieving

This orientation relates to activity and achievement. Some cultures identify goals, work to achieve them, and are results-oriented; other cultures emphasize the present, commemorate simply being, and are relationship-oriented. Furthermore, some cultures apply a sequential approach to the completion of tasks (for example, they can serve only one customer at a time), while others apply a simultaneous approach (they can serve several customers at a time). Some cultures have more tolerance for uncertainty and ambiguity than others. And some cultures view luck as a significant influence on outcomes; other cultures assign little or no importance to luck.

The Self

The self value refers to the relative importance of individualism versus interdependence. In cultures where individual efforts are rewarded, personal competitiveness is high; in interdependent cultures where people are not interested in individual achievement and groups are rewarded, competitiveness may be detestable. In some cultures age is more important than training and experience, but not in other cultures. In hiring practices some cultures prefer one sex over the other.

The Organization of Society

Cultures' value orientations relate to social structure contrast. The contrasts include (a) a tendency toward temporary versus permanent group membership; (b) a preference for private ownership of material goods versus community ownership; (c) a tendency to distrust form versus a preference for form; (d) an egalitarian versus a hierarchical structure; and (e) a general practice of approaching authority directly versus using a mediated link to authority. These orientations affect the format, organization, and tone of business communication documents as well as interpersonal communication.

The Universe

Cultural contrasts in this respect include humans dominating nature versus nature dominating humans; time being linear versus time being cyclical; human activity at the center of the universe versus divine beings at the center of all activities; change as good versus change as bad; and death as the end of life versus death as merely a part of life.[39]

Analyzing Communication Episodes

The understanding obtained by challenging cultural stereotypes can be used to analyze events in actual situations. Situations may reveal effective communication, ineffective communication, or both. As the situation is analyzed, new meanings for communication behavior can be ascribed. At this point of developing cross-cultural communication abilities, "learning focuses on depth of understanding, and application of the abstractions in level three [posing questions to challenge the stereotypes] during the plotting of a culture's value orientations."[40] The pool of questions about a culture's values is cultivated and enlarged with the addition of new insights from particular communication cases. This increases competence in both encoding and decoding cross-cultural messages.

Generating "Other-Culture" Messages

At this level, the communicator becomes cross-culturally competent "when messages may be encoded and directed as if from within the new culture and when messages from the new culture may be decoded and responded to successfully."[41] He or she has developed the ability to "become the other." At this level of cross-cultural competence, communicators continually evaluate "**other-culture**" **messages** against the **repository of signs** they have stored in their mental databases. They can modify the database or match incoming signs and messages to those already known. They are "able to manipulate information received as well as information stored and to make linkages between levels of understanding."[42]

INFORMATION TECHNOLOGY AND GLOBAL E-COMMUNICATION

On-line information technology, such as the Internet, e-mail, the Web, and videoconferencing, now enables organizations to more readily communicate with networks located around the globe. It also enables an organization's employees to more readily communicate with each other from sites located around the globe. This type of globalization, however, mandates the management of multilingual and multicultural implementation of applications and data, thus generating a new challenge for organizations. For example, consider the challenge of obtaining a consistent definition of data elements within only one business group. Anyone who has gone through the data definition process knows that it requires skill and patience to bring a group to consensus. Now consider the complexity of the problem when those same definitions must be shared worldwide among groups with different linguistic and cultural practices.[43]

Many of the problems and solutions discussed in this chapter have application in electronic communication; for example, simplifying the language and omitting idioms, slang, and so on, as outlined in Figure 9-3, helps mitigate the problem in **global e-communication.** Information technology itself is helping in this respect as well. It is interconnecting the world, which in turn helps advance learning about other cultures, thus facilitating effective cross-language and cultural communication.[44]

A few examples illustrate the point. Brazilian TV soap operas are very popular in Portugal. As a result, the Portuguese are thus learning about Brazilian culture as well as the Brazilian Portuguese verbal and nonverbal language. Also American TV programs are quite popular in other countries, as are American movies. This helps advance an understanding of American culture. To enhance their learning, many students of English watch TV programs and movies in which the local language has not been dubbed so students simultaneously learn the language and culture of the English-speaking characters. Many people now have access to the Internet, and therefore to information from all parts of the world (previously, governments could more easily control the information available to their citizens than they can today). This also helps develop cross-cultural awareness and understanding, which helps improve cross cultural and language communication effectiveness.

Furthermore, because of new technology, such as the Web, more and more domestic enterprises are able to internationalize their business activities. But companies that want to take on the global marketplace successfully via the Web will have to deal with four major issues.[45]

First, and most obvious, is the wide array of languages and localized settings that must be supported. For example, in international e-commerce, Web customers are three times more likely to purchase at sites that are presented in their native language. Again, the problems and solutions discussed in this chapter help in this respect. Second, some languages are not well suited to non-PC device rendering. For instance, Japanese characters and Thai accent marks do not display well in devices such as cellular phones. Global organizations will need to address such issues and implement technology solutions. The third and fourth issues concern multiple locales and content management. Many Web applications will require content that is created at different locations to support the local culture and customs of multiple countries simultaneously.

To help in this respect, there is Global Sight's Ambassador (www.globalsight.com), a product that provides Web-based workflow and tools that support distributed team creation of multilingual Web sites. The Ambassador is adept at that language translation. It can translate any source or target language as long as Web browsers support it—currently [1999], Web browsers support more than 50 languages. It also integrates easily with existing management products and Web servers that may be running. Once a translation is completed, it is available for subsequent reuse. For example, one can perform translation task on an entire Web site initially and then reuse the memory capabilities to shorten subsequent translation activities during site maintenance.

The new information technology is revolutionizing the ways organizations around the globe interact and communicate with each other. E-mail enables employee to communicate effectively with each other across 24 time zones, and it helps break down the communication hierarchy. (An employee at a lower level can readily communicate with an employee at a higher level.) But it also presents new challenges in the need to re-engineer organizations' communications systems and corporate cultures (including traditional nations' governmental culture).

SUMMARY

This chapter has presented the communication process in an international/ cross-cultural context. How cross-cultural communicators (senders) construct ideas to be communicated is influenced by the receivers' culture. The same concepts will be perceived differently across cultures. Thus, what works in one culture will not necessarily work in another, and adaptations must be made. The words, gestures, symbols, idioms, jargon, and slang a sender uses to communicate an idea are also affected by the particular receivers' culture. Different societies use different languages and social behaviors to communicate. Therefore, for effective communication to take place, the appropriate adaptations must be made.

The means—written, oral, or nonverbal—of transmitting the message is also affected by the receivers' culture. Culturally, some people prefer oral communication and others prefer written communication. Some cultures prefer flamboyant, flashy presentations; other cultures are offended by such presentations. The cross-cultural communicator must use the means most fitted to the receivers' culture. In essence, the sender of the message must know and use the words, concepts, and behaviors that the receivers will understand, which means that, to be effective, a cross-cultural communicator must learn to be both a sender and a receiver.

Key Terms and Concepts

1. Cross-cultural communication
2. Unique written, oral, and nonverbal languages
3. English as the language of communication in global business
4. Unique social customs and behaviors
5. Language translator
6. Realistic objectives
7. Realistic time frame
8. Same word, different meanings
9. Requirements for formality and informality
10. Dual-translation
11. Simultaneous and sequential oral translators
12. Effective translator
13. Updating translator skills
14. High-context and low-context cultures
15. Primary and secondary audiences
16. The audience's motivations
17. English as a second or third language
18. Dictionary translation
19. Body language
20. Eye contact, physical distance, and touching
21. Hand movements, pointing, and facial expressions
22. Mediators
23. Informal get-togethers
24. Conversational, presentation, and written principles
25. Environmental, cultural, sociocultural, and psychocultural contexts
26. Signal, sign, signifier, and signified
27. Cross-cultural message adjustment
28. Developing cross-cultural communication competence
29. Cultural fluency
30. Stereotyping
31. Challenging cultural stereotypes
32. "Other-culture" messages
33. Repository of signs
34. Global e-communication

Discussion Questions and Exercises

1. What are the major causes of cross-cultural communication ineffectiveness?
2. Discuss some of the factors that affect the development of an idea to be communicated across cultures.
3. Discuss some of the major factors that must be considered when encoding a message to be sent across cultures.
4. An American executive's firm has just completed negotiating a business deal with a company in Japan. You have been employed to help him or her write the contract. What would you advise your client to do?
5. Discuss some of the ways expressions and nonverbal communication affect the cross-cultural encoding process.
6. How do "formality" and "informality" affect the cross-cultural encoding process?
7. An American executive who is preparing to communicate with a French audience enlists your services to help him or her write the substance of the message. With respect to the amount of information a culture requires, what would you advise your client to do?
8. Discuss the dual-translation process.
9. Discuss the two types of translators.
10. Discuss the factors that describe an effective translator.
11. You are an executive from a low-context culture preparing a message to be delivered orally to an audience from a high-context culture. How would you structure the message?
12. Discuss the role audience motivation plays in encoding messages.
13. English appears to be emerging as the

language of global business. You are from England and you are going to speak to an audience whose English is a second or third language. Discuss the *do*'s and *don't*s of delivering the message.

14. Discuss the ways culture affects the selection of the right transmission channel.

15. How are mediators useful in cross-cultural transmission of messages?

16. What are the fundamentals of the three communication principles?

17. "The most effective way to understand cross-cultural communication is to focus on the decoding process and the role of perception in communication." Explain this statement.

18. Differentiate between "a sign," "the signifier," and "the signified."

19. Discuss how cross-cultural communication competence is developed.

20. You are a cross-cultural communication consultant employed by a domestic company that wants to internationalize its operations because of the current e-commerce revolution. What would be your advice to the firm's management?

Assignment

Select a short story written in English and write a dictionary translation of the story into a foreign language that you do not understand. Then have someone who speaks both English and the foreign language fluently interpret it back to English. How does the new translation compare with yours? Share the experience with your classmates.

C A S E   9 - 1

The Efficient Cross-Cultural Communicator

I [Dean Foster] was speaking recently with an American manager quite down in the dumps and befuddled over the fact that cooperation from the Mexicans, with whom his office did a great deal of work, was becoming increasingly difficult. He just could not figure out why. I asked him to outline all major changes he could think of that occurred around the time that cooperation began to change and he admitted that he had replaced his assistant around the same time. "Was this assistant responsible for communications between your office and the Mexicans?" I inquired, and got a positive response. "Is your new assistant similarly responsible?" Yes, he said.

By the look of things, the new assistant was certainly doing her job. There was no doubt about the efficiency of the letters, e-mails, faxes, and the like that went out like clockwork to the Mexico office. In fact, the new assistant had streamlined the communications system within the office significantly. Now there was a specific form to be used for different types of letters, more precise, straight to the point, and usable for mailing lists. Different criteria were now used for sending out different types of correspondence, time periods had been established that would automatically signal certain types of correspondence to be released to certain individuals, and so forth. Then I looked at the previous assistant's correspondence. It certainly was more cumbersome: Each letter was individually written, following no predetermined form, and was quite customized, depending upon to whom it was written and the circumstances. In fact, each correspondence usually acknowledged the individual to whom it was being written in quite personal ways. All correspondence seemed to be about 30 percent greetings, with much inquiry into the health and happiness of the reader's business and family. The significant issues—the reason for the letter in the first place—usually were embedded somewhere in the middle of all this, and constituted only about half of the total letter. A final 20 percent was spent at the end, once again, on all sorts of non-business-related issues, from hoping to see you next month in Guadalajara, to the recounting of a memorable meal that was shared the last time they were together.

Comparing these two very different styles of correspondence, my American manager friend agreed that he regretted replacing his former assistant, but that the company simply couldn't grow spending so much time and resources on old-fashioned, inefficient patterns and systems of communication. I asked him if Mexico constituted an important market for him. He answered that more than 80 percent of his business was with Mexico.

Questions

1. Discuss how the concept of low-context and high-context cultures led to this problem.
2. Assume that you are a consultant hired by this manager to solve the problem. What would you advise the manager to do?

Source: Excerpted from Dean Foster, "Business Across Borders: International Etiquette for the Global Secretary,:" *The Secretary* (October 1992): 20. Copyright © 1992 Stratton Publishing and Marketing Inc. All rights reserved. Used with permission.

CASE 9-2

The Elusive System

GBAH, the General Bureau of Animal Husbandry, is a division of the huge Chinese Ministry of Agriculture. It received its first grant from the UNDP—the United Nations Development Program—shortly after China joined the UN. It was a grant to study the feasibility of irrigation in the Mongolian grasslands, but one condition of the grant required the GBAH to demonstrate that it had adequate systems for safeguarding and accounting for the funds. So the GBAH reluctantly allocated some of the precious funds to employ a Western consulting firm to show them the systems they should have. That's what I [Roderick MacLeod] was in China for,

in part—to snag opportunities like that for my firm—so I was delighted. Since we looked upon it as an entry to the "China market," which we believed to be potentially huge and profitable, we scoured our worldwide resources for a UNDP expert and for Chinese-speaking staff.

Even though the fee would adequately compensate only for one, we sent a team of four people, a UNDP and cattle-farming expert, two Chinese-speaking consultants, and me, for the purpose of doing a bang-up job that we could use as a future reference.

We arrived as scheduled and went to the Beijing Hotel as directed. We weren't expected.

It took a couple of hours to get somebody from the GBAH, accompanied by a person from the ministry's Foreign Affairs Department, down to the hotel to work on the problem, and it took another twelve hours to get the four of us into rooms in the Yanjing Hotel, a couple of miles away and several steps down on Beijing's prestige scale. Sitting for fourteen hours in the barroom of the Beijing Hotel, anxious and helpless, unwashed and unloved, is not the best way to start coping with combined jet lag and culture shock.

The next day the GBAH officials came to the hotel, and the day was spent going over the contract, discussing arrangements, and having a congratulatory banquet. The day after that, twenty Mongolian accountants arrived to be trained in the UNDP accounting requirements. They looked like country people and farm people: weather-beaten faces, callused hands, worn Mao jackets, and the bemused expressions country people have all over the world on their first visit to the city. Each was the accountant for his "Banner" (Mongolian communes are called Banners, evoking images of troops of wild horsemen, although they are really political and economic units of up to several hundred thousand people) and thus was a responsible and experienced official.

We got to work, proud of the charts and tables we had laboriously drawn by hand and labeled in Chinese, and of the overhead projector we had brought along for displaying them. The two Chinese-speaking consultants had been told what to say by the expert, they had spent a week or more at the difficult task of translating it from English to Chinese, and they were ready to give all-day lectures in Chinese. The expert and I sat in ready to answer questions or help out as we could. The Mongolians listened quietly, diligently taking notes, for two days.

The third day the GBAH officials were back and a long discussion with the two Chinese-speaking consultants delayed the opening of the session. It appeared that what the Chinese were being told wasn't what they had contracted to find out. The Mongolians sat idly in the meeting room for another several hours while we tried to find out what the GBAH wanted and tried to convince them that they knew all there was to know and should be satisfied. The GBAH wasn't satisfied.

We stayed up all night, literally. The expert and I redid the lectures and charts, and the other two did their best to put them into Chinese. Ordinarily, it takes at least three times as long to put a lecture into Chinese as it does for the expert to write it in English. They didn't have that much time; they did it between eleven at night and seven in the morning.

The next day was a tiring one, and at the end of it the expert, who didn't like Chinese food, went off to call on his country's ambassador. (He happened to be Irish, but that's incidental; it seemed to me that all citizens of small countries treated their embassies in Beijing as homes-away-from-home.) The rest of us worked away at the charts and transparencies and lectures, and fell into bed exhausted.

Next day the GBAH officials were back. It still wasn't right. Since it was Saturday (the Chinese work a six-day week) we gave the Mongolians a long weekend and spent Saturday and Sunday trying to get it right. Except for the expert: He worked Saturday and then went to the embassy for Saturday night and Sunday.

Monday morning there was a conference to see if we were getting it. The expert said there were only so many ways you could slice up one piece of cake, and he thought they'd tried them all. The GBAH still wasn't satisfied. The Mongolian accountants had typically impassive faces, but not so much so that their irritation and frustration weren't showing through.

It went on and on like that. The GBAH had spent their money and wanted what they had paid for. The Mongolians wanted to be sure that they could measure up in the frightening new world of international agencies. We had our professional pride in our work, and also visions of future assignments driving us, and we were determined to get it right. Except for the expert, who spent more and more time at the embassy.

Finally, everybody was exhausted and the allotted time was up. The GBAH officials put a good face on it, saying the Chinese equivalent of "it had been a learning experience." Everybody went home, hurt and sad.

Questions

1. Based on what you learned in this chapter, what do you believe went wrong in this case? In answering the question, you should relate to the communication process.

2. How could the problem have been avoided?

Source: Roderick MacLeod, *China, Inc.: How to Do Business with the Chinese* (Toronto: Bantam Books, 1988), pp. 33–35. Copyright © 1988 by Roderick MacLeod. Used by permission of Bantam Books, a division of Bantam Doubleday Dell Publishing Group, Inc.

CASE 9·3

Training in Transition Economies

Here's a story of one training experience in a post-Soviet setting, with lessons for teaching new global concepts.

Thirteen eager Russian managers sat in the drab surroundings of an old plant facility in Tashkent, Uzbekistan. They had just finished an intense three-week training workshop on Western marketing principles. The table at the front of the room was covered with food and drink, typical of Uzbek celebrations. With great intensity, the managers filled out the evaluation form—a task taken very seriously as it was a new experience for them to be asked for their opinion.

The emotional graduation was videotaped by Tashselmash, the company where the training took place. It was to become part of

Tashselmash's history as the first such training provided by an American businessperson. Each participant came forward enthusiastically to receive his or her certificate of completion, which had been translated into Russian. Even though most of the participants understood only a few words of English, all wanted my [Schrage's] signature in English, not in Russian as I had planned.

Transition economies are truly different environments—uniquely naïve of what developed countries accept as commonplace. This knowledge gap can play a role in the day-to-day training experience, which makes the effort both challenging and exciting. In the scenario just described, the company, Tashselmash, is a 70-year-old farm equipment manufacturer that supplied the former Soviet Union with cotton harvesters. Before the independence of the Republic of Uzbekistan in September 1991, the company was considered a premier industrial facility. However, by Western standards, the facilities are primitive. The classroom is located on the third floor of a drab concrete high-rise office building characteristic of typical Soviet "realist" construction. Like most firms in Uzbekistan, Tashselmash was in a state of transition from total state control to private ownership.

The corporate culture within the post-Soviet transition economy in particular is difficult to describe. Still tainted with a Soviet style of bureaucracy, executives are struggling to cope with the transition to a market environment. In the past, production levels had been by government dictate, and a company had no responsibility for distributing or marketing its products. These post-Soviet companies realized that they had to become self-reliant, and staff were eager to learn Western marketing and business practices. Therefore, the need for training was imperative.

I was working on research in marketing and cross-cultural issues at the time and was contacted to serve as the instructor, and I agreed to work with Tashselmash executives. In January 1997, two Uzbek company representatives laid out their needs and desires for training in marketing. Managers from several departments would be the target audience, with the intent that the training would help them transform the company from a state-controlled entity into a self-marketed firm ready to deal in a competitive global market. My objective for developing and conducting the workshop was to gain an understanding of Uzbek culture and serve as a bridge in the company's transition toward privatization. Allen Jedlicka, who has worked in more than 30 developing economies in Latin America and Africa, would serve as an advisor to the project.

The New Capitalism

As executives in former centrally planned economies enter the brave new world of global competition, it's necessary to learn basic Western marketing principles, even if they choose later to modify or replace them with other approaches.

Consequently, the course focused on understanding basics of the marketing four Ps: product, promotion, place, and price. A government organization for 70 years, Tashselmash was told what to produce, how much to produce, and when to produce it. If the company was lucky, the government paid it an "acceptable price" for the product, which more or less covered the costs. The company didn't have to set up a distribution network to move products to customers, price products to make sure they were profitable, or determine what products to produce to maximize profits or satisfy a critical client base. Most of all, it definitely didn't have to promote the products. Even the basic economic law of supply and demand was totally new. The law Tashselmash understood was that the government demanded, the company supplied.

Questions

1. Discuss the basic cross-cultural communication problems Schrage will encounter in this training endeavor.

2. Based on what is described in this case and in the chapter, is Schrage qualified for the job?

3. What are some of the major obstacles she faces in teaching the four Ps to the Russian managers? Give examples.

Source: Excerpted form C.R. Schrage and A. Jedlicka, "Training in Transition Economies," *Training & Development 53*, no. 6 (June 1999): 38.

Notes

1. Excerpted from Jeremy Main, "How 21 Men Got Global in 35 Days," *Fortune* (November 6, 1989): 71.

2. See, for example, David Ricks, *Big Business Blunders: Mistakes in Multinational Marketing* (Homewood, IL: Dow Jones-Irwin, 1983).

3. R.E. Dulek, J.S. Fielden, and J.S. Hill, "International Communication: An Executive Primer," *Business Horizons 34*, no. 1 (1991): 20.

4. This discussion draws from Mary Munter, "Cross-Cultural Communication for Managers," *Business Horizons* (May–June 1993): 69.

5. J.R. Zeeman, "Service—The Cutting Edge of Global Competition: What United Airlines is Learning in the Pacific." Remarks before the Academy of International Business Annual Meeting, Chicago, IL, November 14, 1987.

6. L.S. Dillon, "Japanese Rules for Communication," *Personnel Administrator 19* (January 1984): 92.

7. "Going International, Part 1, Bridging the Culture Gap," video by Copeland Griggs Productions, San Francisco, California.

8. This discussion draws from Dean Foster, "Business Across Borders: International Etiquette for the Effective Global Secretary," *The Secretary* (October 1992): 20–24.

9. Ibid., p. 24.

10. This discussion draws from Lyle Sussman and Denise M. Johnson, "The Interpreted Executive: Theory, Models, and Implications," *The Journal of Business Communication 30*, no. 4 (1993): 415–434.

11. Ibid., pp. 419–420.

12. Edward T. Hall, "How Cultures Collide," *Psychology Today* (July 1976): 67–74.

13. Munter, "Cross-Cultural Communication for Managers," p. 74.

14. Hall, "How Cultures Collide," pp. 67–74.

15. Ibid., p. 74.

16. This discussion draws on Munter, "Cross-Cultural Communication for Managers," p. 73.

17. Cynthia L. Kemper, "Sacre Blue! English as a Global Lingua Franca?" *Communication World 16*, (June–July 1999): 42.

18. Alan Weiss, "Global Doesn't Mean Foreign Anymore," *Training* (July 1998): 51.

19. This discussion draws from Foster, "Business Across Borders," p. 24.

20. Gary P. Ferraro, "The Need for Linguistic Proficiency in Global Business," *Business Horizons* (May–June 1996): 40.

21. Munter, "Cross-Cultural Communication for Managers," p. 74.

22. Ibid., p. 75.

23. Ibid.

24. Ibid., p. 76.

25. This discussion draws from Jon P. Alston, "Wa, Guanxi, and Inhwa: Managerial Principles in Japan, China, and Korea," *Business Horizons 32*, no. 2 (March–April 1989): 27–28.

26. Dulek, Fielden, and Hill, "International Communication," pp. 21–24.

27. Ibid., p. 21.

28. This discussion draws from Linda Beamer, "Learning Intercultural Communication Competence," *The Journal of Business Communication 29*, no. 3 (1992): 285–303.

29. L.A. Saussure, *Course in General Linguistics*, trans. R. Harris, cited in Beamer, ibid., p. 247.

30. Beamer, p. 387.

31. Ibid.

32. Ibid., p. 289.

33. Ibid.

34. Ibid., pp. 291–301.

35. Ibid., p. 291.

36. Ibid., p. 294.

37. Ibid, pp. 296–300.

38. Ibid., p. 296.

39. Ibid., p. 300.

40. Ibid.

41. Ibid., p. 301.

42. Ibid.

43. This discussion is adapted from Sunny Baker, "Global E-Commerce, Local Problems," *Journal of Business Strategy 20*, no. 4 (July–August 1999): 32–38.

44. Dick Schaaf, "Speaking Abroad," *Presentations 13*, no. 6 (June 1999): A1–A15.

45. This discussion draws from Maggie Biggs, "Globalization Issues Forced to the Front Lines by Changing Online Demographics," *InfoWorld 21*, no. 36 (September 6, 1999): 52.

10

Cross-Cultural Business Practices and Negotiations

Companies that have a strong track record with expats put a candidate's open-ness to new cultures on an equal footing with the person's technical know-how. After all, successfully navigating within your own business environment and culture does not guarantee that you can maneuver successfully in another one. We know, for instance, of a senior manager at a U.S. carmaker who was an expert at negotiating contracts with his company's steel suppliers. When trans-ferred to Korea to conduct similar deals, the man's confrontational style did nothing but offend the consensus-minded Koreans—to the point where sup-pliers would not even speak to him directly. What was worse, the man was unwilling to change his way of doing business. He was soon called back to the company's home office, and his replacement spent a year undoing the damage he left in his wake.[1]

Learning Objectives of the Chapter

In this era of globalization of business activities, managers from one country will often be conducting business and/or sitting at negotiating tables with managers from other nations and cultures. Conducting business and negoti-ating in one's own culture are complex tasks; they are, however, far more complex when they are conducted across cultures. Each side tends to have perceivable differences in ways of conducting business, language, dress, pref-erences, and legal and ethical considerations. Understanding and minding the cultural variables of the country where business transactions are taking place is one of the most important aspects of being successful in any international business endeavor. A lack of understanding and/or a disregard for the variables will most likely lead to failure. Practical Perspective 10-1 presents an illustration of how an internationalizing firm's not heeding local culture led to problems. (Disney's managers insisted on doing things the way they did them at home.) After studying this chapter, you should be able to:

1. Discuss the ways business practices vary across cultures.
2. Discuss the ways negotiating tactics vary across cultures.
3. Discuss the ways negotiating styles vary across cultures.
4. Discuss the negotiating styles in numerous countries.

PRACTICAL PERSPECTIVE 10-1

Blundering Mouse

Europe got its first taste of the management style of Walt Disney Company when Joe Shapiro started kicking in a door at the luxury Hotel Bristol here [Paris]. It was 1986, and Disney was negotiating with the French government on plans to build a big resort and theme park on the outskirts of Paris. To the exasperation of the Disney team headed by Shapiro, then the company's general counsel, the talks were taking far longer than expected. Jean-René Bernard, the chief French negotiator, says he was astonished when Shapiro, his patience ebbing, ran to the door of the room and began kicking it repeatedly, shouting, "Get something cheap to break!" Shapiro doesn't remember the incident, though he adds with a laugh, "there were a lot of histrionics at the time." But Disney's kick-down-the-door attitude in the planning, building, and financing of Euro Disney accounts for many of the huge problems that plague the resort.

The irony is that even though some early French critics called the park an American cultural abomination, public acceptance hasn't been the problem. European visitors seem to love the place... Euro Disney's troubles, instead, derive from a different type of culture clash. Europe may have embraced Mickey Mouse, but it hasn't taken to the brash, frequently insensitive, and often overbearing style of Mickey's American corporate parent.... Disney's contentious attitude exacerbated the difficulties it encountered by alienating people it needed to work with, say many people familiar with the situation. Its answer to doubts or suggestions invariably was: Do as we say, because we know best. "They were always sure it would work because they were Disney," says Beatrice Descoffre, a French construction industry official who dealt with the U.S. company. "Disney," adds a colleague, "came here like the Marines going to Kuwait."

Source: Peter Gumbel and Richard Turner, "Fans Like Euro Disney But Its Parent's Goofs Weigh the Park Down," *The Wall Street Journal*, March 10, 1994, pp. A1, A12. Permission conveyed through Copyright Clearance Center, Inc.

CROSS-CULTURAL BUSINESS PRACTICES

As corporations become increasingly international and competition for global markets increases, business managers who are not attentive to cultural differences will not be able to function in foreign markets effectively—they will make their companies less competitive. Effective international managers have learned how varying cultural practices across societies affect business and management practices and how to adapt to the differences. Learning something about the culture of a country before transacting business there shows respect, and those who understand the culture are more likely to develop successful, long-term business relationships than those who do not.[2] Table 10-1 tests your current knowledge about customs around the world. The answers are provided at the end of the chapter (following the Summary). The ensuing section discusses business practices in a cross-cultural context.

The Impact of Culture on Business Practices

Approaches to conducting business vary from culture to culture, making the practice of business at the international level much more complex than in the home market. Some factors that affect **cross-cultural business** include time, thought patterns, personal space, material possessions, family roles and relationships, competitiveness and individuality, and social behavior[3] as well as whether a culture is high-context or low-context (discussed in Chapter 9).[4]

Time

"Time Equals Money" versus Relationships. Some cultures, the United States, for example, perceive time as a commodity and an asset, and a very high importance is placed on it—**"time equals money."** The conservation of time is therefore an efficient process in these cultures. Punctuality is expected behavior; tardiness is unacceptable behavior. People in other cultures, however, do not place as much of a premium on time and punctuality; to them, time does not equal money, and tardiness is quite acceptable; and in some cultures punctuality is viewed as unreasonable behavior. Individuals in these cultures place a much greater premium on relationships and a more relaxed lifestyle than they do on time and punctuality. (Table 10-2 presents the pace of life ranking for 31 countries.)

Businesspeople in these cultures generally would be offended by individuals applying time-oriented behavior in business transactions; they prefer that an amicable relationship be established before business is conducted. Charles Ford, commercial attaché in Guatemala, has said that:

The inexperienced American visitor in Guatemala often tries to force a business relationship. The abrupt "always watching the clock" style is often ineffective in Guatemala. A more informed businessperson

TABLE 10-1	How Much Do You Know About Customs Around the World?

You're sitting down to a dinner in a Bedouin home and when you look at the plate in front of you, the eye of a cooked lamb is staring back at you. What should you do? If you don't want to offend your hosts, you had better dig in because the eye is considered a delicacy and the highest honor given a guest. It makes the U.S. tradition of honoring a guest with a seat at the head of the table seem mundane, doesn't it?

Think you're knowledgeable about other global customs? The following quiz, courtesy of YAR Communications Inc., will help you find out. Check out their Web site at www.yar.com for more quiz questions.

1. In Taiwan, receiving a pineapple for a gift is a good omen for a businessperson.
   A. True
   B. False

2. What number in Chinese-speaking countries and also in Japan is as ominous as the number 13 in Western culture?
   A. 4
   B. 7
   C. 3
   D. 5

3. The executive of Chinese company is celebrating his/her 65th birthday. Which of the following is NOT appropriate?
   A. A silk tie
   B. A silver Mont Blanc pen
   C. A gold clock
   D. A crystal paperweight
   E. Gold and jade cufflinks

4. During a TV commercial, the announcer gives the OK sign on camera. In which country does this mean something entirely different?
   A. Australia
   B. Brazil
   C. Finland
   D. France
   E. Ireland

5. In England, it is inappropriate to discuss business after work over drinks.
   A. True
   B. False

6. You're creating a sales training manual for employees doing business in Japan. When would you tell them NOT to discuss business?
   A. At dinner
   B. Over lunch
   C. On the golf course
   D. At the start of a business meeting
   E. In your superior's office

7. OL is a widely used term in Japan that stands for:
   A. Obscene literature
   B. Office lady
   C. Old lady
   D. Outdoor life

8. Your company would like to send its top sales representatives abroad to meet with its distributors in August. In which countries is this most likely to become a problem?
   A. Italy and France
   B. Ireland and Sweden
   C. Japan and China
   D. Australia and New Zealand
   E. Hungary and Romania

9. At a business dinner in Korea, your counterpart's wine glass is half-empty. What should you do?
   A. Refill his glass immediately
   B. Sit back and let him refill his own glass
   C. Wait until his glass is empty and then refill it
   D. Fill your own glass and replace it with his

10. When writing names in Korea, what color is not appropriate to use?
   A. Blue
   B. Red
   C. Black
   D. None of the above

11. In the Philippines, people indicate directions with their
   A. Forefingers
   B. Mouths (accompanied by head movement)
   C. Feet
   D. None of the above

12. When you meet an Indonesian businessperson for the first time, you should:
   A. Bow deeply from the waist.
   B. Nod your head slightly with your hands in a praying position in front of your chest.
   C. Shake hands loosely and state your name.
   D. Shake hands vigorously and say, "How are you?"
   E. Kiss him/her on both cheeks.

Source: Printed in *Prudential Leader* (February 1998): 15. Used with permission of YAR Communications. All rights reserved.

would engage in small talk about Guatemala, show an interest in the families of his or her associates, join them for lunch or dinner, and generally allow time for a personal relationship to develop. This holds true for Latin America in general.[5]

TABLE 10-2	The Pace of Life

The chart below ranks 31 countries for overall pace of life; minutes downtown pedestrians take to walk 60 feet; minutes it takes a postal clerk to complete a stamp-purchase transaction; and number of minutes public clocks deviate from the actual time. Based on these measures, the Swiss are among the fastest-paced people in the world, with public clocks accurate to within one minute. Would you expect anything less from Swiss movement?

Country	Overall pace	Walking 60 feet	Postal service	Public clock
Switzerland	1	3	2	1
Ireland	2	1	3	11
Germany	3	5	1	8
Japan	4	7	4	6
Italy	5	10	12	2
England	6	4	9	13
Sweden	7	13	5	7
Austria	8	23	8	9
Netherlands	9	2	14	25
Hong Kong	10	14	6	14
France	11	8	18	10
Poland	12	12	15	8
Costa Rica	13	16	10	15
Taiwan	14	18	7	21
Singapore	15	25	11	4
United States	16	6	23	28
Canada	17	11	21	22
South Korea	18	20	20	16
Hungary	19	19	19	18
Czech Republic	20	21	17	23
Greece	21	14	13	29
Kenya	22	9	30	24
China	23	24	25	12
Bulgaria	24	27	22	17
Romania	25	30	29	5
Jordan	26	28	27	19
Syria	27	29	28	27
El Salvador	28	22	16	31
Brazil	29	31	24	28
Indonesia	30	26	26	30
Mexico	31	17	31	26

Source: Printed in *Prudential Leader* (February 1998): 13. Used with permission of *American Demographics*. All rights reserved.

Schedules. Schedules are important to individuals in some cultures, but relatively unimportant to people in other cultures. In other words, individuals in some cultures possess an "it must be done by tomorrow" mentality, but people in other cultures possess a "when it gets done is when it is done" mentality. Furthermore, in some cultures which task gets done first depends on task importance factors, but in other cultures it depends on factors such as relationship. For instance,

> *In the Arab East, time does not generally include schedules as Americans know and use them. The time required to get something accomplished depends on the relationship. More important people get fast service from less important people, and close relatives take absolute priority; nonrelatives are kept waiting.*[6]

Therefore, telling someone in the Middle East that something must be done now or by the end of the day or by tomorrow may prove to be a mistake. The recipient of the direction may stop work because he or she is placed under pressure and/or because he or she may view the person issuing the directive as being rude or "too pushy."

Time and Decision Making. Some cultures take a long time to make important decisions; other cultures make important decisions quickly. Consequently, low-level managers in cultures that take a long time to make important decisions often try to heighten their work status by lingering over routine decisions. And foreign managers who try to make important decisions quickly in these cultures are likely to downgrade their importance in local people's eyes. For example,

> *In Ethiopia, the time required for a decision is directly proportional to its importance. This is so much the case that low-level bureaucrats there have a way of trying to elevate the prestige of their work by taking a long time to make up their minds. (Americans in that part of the world are innocently prone to downgrading their work in the local people's eyes by trying to speed things up.)*[7]

Thought Patterns

Some cultures' thought patterns are circular. **Circular cultures** believe that since individuals can see what has happened in the past, their past is ahead of them, and since they cannot see into the future, their future is behind them. Many people in these cultures view change as being bad, so they do not see business opportunities that lie ahead. In contrast, some cultures' thought patterns are linear. **Linear cultures** like the United States view the past as being behind them and the future in front of them. Individuals in these cultures tend to view change as being good and attempt to take advantage of the business opportunities they foresee. Circular-oriented people are likely to view a future-oriented person's behavior as forward and aggressive. People in linear cultures are far more open to new ideas and the setting of objectives than are people in circular cultures.

Personal Space

Cultures generally develop informal rules on the distance individuals remain from one another in face-to-face interactions. People in the United States, for example, prefer a wide distance from those with whom they are involved in face-to-face communication, and they usually feel uncomfortable when the distance is narrow. In contrast, people in Arab cultures, for instance, prefer a very short distance between themselves and those with whom they are communicating, and they feel offended or rejected by those individuals who maintain a wide distance or keep backing away.

Americans tend to feel comfortable in the following zones of space: zero to 18 inches for comforting or greeting; 18 inches to four feet for conversing with friends; four to 12 feet for conversing with strangers; and more than 12 feet for public space (lobbies or reception areas). Venezuelans generally prefer much closer space and may view it as rude if someone backs away. On the other hand, the British tend to prefer more space and may view it as rude if one moves too close.[8]

Material Possessions

How individuals value material wealth varies from culture to culture. Individuals in high masculinity cultures tend to value **material possessions** more than do people in low masculinity cultures, who tend to place greater value on such things as a clean environment and a sense of equity/fairness. Individuals in some cultures, the United States, for example, equate success with material wealth—expensive clothes, automobiles, houses, large offices, expensive furnishings, and so forth. Individuals in many cultures, however, place relatively little importance on material possessions and view the flaunting of wealth as disrespectful.

> *Middle East businessmen look for something else—family, connections, friendship. They do not use the furnishings of their office as part of their status system, nor do they expect to impress a client by these means or to fool a banker into lending more money than he [or she] should. They like good things, too, but feel that they, as persons, should be known and not judged solely by what the public sees.[9]*

The American notion that "money talks" is far from true in many cultures. Furthermore, some cultures use material possessions differently from the way they are used in the United States. For example, the Japanese take pride in relatively "inexpensive but tasteful arrangements that are used to produce the proper emotional setting."[10] Europeans are embarrassed when guests compliment them on their personal possessions; they are not likely to value an object because of its monetary worth—they appreciate an object for its age, beauty, and form, for example, items that have been in the family for a long time.[11] Therefore, in most cultures, when one comments about the value of someone's material possessions, the comment should reflect the aesthetic value, as opposed to the monetary value, of the possession.

Family and Friendship Roles

In many cultures, family roles are highly traditional and personal. Members of the family have predictable, designated roles and a responsibility for maintaining the status quo. In these cultures, family responsibilities have greater influence on members' behavior than do work situations and business interactions; family-related matters are more important than work-related matters. On the other hand, in some cultures, especially in the United States, work matters often take precedence over family matters. Americans tend to make friends quickly and become disassociated from them just as fast. In other countries, however, friendships form more slowly and once made, they are deeper, last longer, and involve real obligations. Friends, as well as family, tend to provide some sort of social insurance.

> It is important to stress that in the Middle East and Latin America, your "friends" will not let you down. The fact that they personally are feeling the pinch is never an excuse for failing their friends. They are supposed to look out for your interests.[12]

Competitiveness and Individuality

Competitiveness and individuality are valued by Americans. A statement made by the late Vince Lombardi, a famous, highly successful American football coach, characterizes the typically American view of competition: "Winning isn't everything, it's the only thing." Many cultures, including European cultures, reject this attitude. Instead, they emphasize team and consensus values; they value modesty, team spirit, and patience. Individuals in these cultures are likely to be offended by those who apply **haste and aggressive behavior** in the pursuit of business transactions; they prefer business relationships that have a more relaxed atmosphere.

Social Behaviors

Many social habits, such as eating, types of foods eaten, gift giving, and greetings vary from culture to culture.

Eating. Behaviors such as noisy eating and belching are quite acceptable in some cultures and totally unacceptable in others. Eating noisily and belching mean that the meal is being enjoyed, and failure to do either may actually be offensive to the hosts because their absence indicates that the meal is not good. In some cultures, spitting residuals on the table, such as chicken bones and shrimp shells, is appropriate behavior at home or at a restaurant. Removing the residuals with your fingers and placing them on the table is actually crude behavior to people in these cultures. (The French, who think Americans are repulsive because they switch forks from one hand to the other while eating, may find these types of behaviors quite gross.)

Foods. Types of food vary from culture to culture, and what foreigners are expected to eat when dining with local hosts can be a traumatic cultural shock to many. For example, in China ceremonial lunches and dinners often consist of as many as 15 courses, and sometimes more. Chinese hosts typically expect guests to try at least a bit of each course—not doing so would be offensive. China, with a land-base smaller than Canada's, has a population of about 1.2 billion people (about 25% of the world's population). How, one might wonder, is such a population fed? One way is by being efficient, by not wasting foods and maximizing use of the foods "Mother Nature" provides. People in China generally eat a greater variety of foods than do people in most Western cultures. Therefore, a foreign guest should not be too surprised when he or she finds fish heads, chicken heads, chicken feet, and "night duck" soup (bat soup) included in the 15 or so courses.

An American in France might not enjoy snails, a popular local dish, and might not enjoy blood pudding sausages, which are popular in Portugal; he or she may not understand the appeal of "fragrant meat" (dog meat) eaten in Taiwan or horse meat once eaten in some parts of Italy. Global travelers who have participated in such lunches or dinners may suggest that in such situations it is best to just eat and not ask what it is. This writer's own experience, however, has been that it is polite and diplomatic to ask what food is being served is, but asking must be in a polite, curious, inquisitive way (the hosts appreciate that you have taken an interest in their culture). Never ask in a "What *is* that?" tone of voice, which may sound as if you find it strange that they would eat such a thing.

Gift Giving. In some cultures, gifts are expected, and failure to present them is considered an insult, whereas in other cultures, offering a gift is considered offensive. For example, gifts are rarely exchanged in Germany and are usually inappropriate—although small gifts may be appropriate. In some cultures, the present is given during the initial visit, while in others it is given afterwards. In some cultures, the gift is given in private, whereas in other cultures it can be given in public. In Japan, where gift-giving is an important part of doing business (it helps symbolize the depth and strength of a business relationship), the exchanging of gifts usually takes place at the first meeting. The gift given to a Japanese associate should consist of multiple contents that can be shared with the group. And gifts to the Japanese should not be too elaborate nor too expensive. Such gifts may create awkwardness.[13]

The type of gift given also varies from one culture to another. For example, white flowers are typically not given in Asia, where white is symbolic of death. In China, giving a clock shakes the superstitious. The phrase "to give a clock" sounds like a Chinese expression that means "to care for a dying patient."[14] In Belgium, gift-giving is not a normal custom—flowers may be given as a gift when invited to someone's home, but do not bring chrysanthemums, as they are used mainly for funerals.

Greetings. Knowledge of a culture's greeting behavior is important because first impressions are important to the development of relationships. Many cultures use a handshake as a major form of greeting, some use a hug, some a combination of a handshake and a hug, but some cultures do not greet by touching. For example, Australians and Americans use a strong handshake, but the French use a light, gentle, single shake. Many Latin European cultures greet with an abrazo—a combination of handshake, hug, and shoulder pats. The Japanese greeting is a bow, and the Laotian greeting involves bringing palms together in prayer-like form and bowing.[15]

High-Context versus Low-Context Cultures

Some cultures are high-context and some are low-context. The degree affects the business tempo in the society. As discussed in Chapter 9, in the transaction of business, people in high-context cultures, including the Chinese, Korean, Japanese, Vietnamese, Arab, Greek, and Hispanic cultures, establish social trust first, value personal relations and goodwill, make agreements on the basis of general trust, and like to conduct slow and ritualistic negotiations.[16] On the other hand, individuals in low-context cultures, including the Italian, English, North American, Scandinavian, Swiss, and German cultures, get down to business first, value expertise and performance, reach agreement by specific, legalistic contract, and like to conduct negotiations as efficiently as possible.[17] The following is the advice an American Embassy attaché gave to an executive from the United States (a low-context culture) seeking to do business in a high-context, South American Spanish-speaking country:[18]

1. "You don't do business here the way you do in the States; it is necessary to spend much more time. You have to get to know your man and vice versa."

2. "You must meet with him several times before you talk business...."

3. "Take your price list and put it in your pocket.... Down here price is only one of the many things taken into account before closing the deal. In the United States, your past experience will prompt you to act according to a certain set of principles, but many of these principles will not work here. Every time you feel the urge to act...suppress the urge...."

4. "Down here people like to do business with men who are somebody. In order to be somebody, it is well to have written a book, to have lec-

tured at a university, or to have developed your intellect in some way. The man you are going to see is a poet. He has published several volumes of poetry. Like many Latin Americans, he praises poetry highly. You will find that he will spend a good deal of business time quoting his poetry to you, and he will take great pleasure in this."

5. "You will also note that the people here are very proud of their past and of their Spanish blood, but they are also exceedingly proud of their liberation from Spain and their independence. The fact that they are a democracy, that they are free, and also that they are no longer a colony is very, very important to them. They are warm and friendly and enthusiastic if they like you. If they don't, they are cold and withdrawn."

6. "And another thing, time down here means something different. It works in a different way. You know how it is back in the States when a certain type blurts out whatever is on his mind without waiting to see if the situation is right. He is considered an impatient bore and somewhat egocentric. Well, down here, you have to wait much, much longer, and I really mean much, much longer, before you can begin to talk about the reason for your visit."

7. "There is another point I want to caution you about. At home, the man who sells takes the initiative. Here, they tell you when they are ready to do business. But, most of all, don't discuss price until you are asked and don't rush things."

Business Customs in China, Japan, and South Korea

People transacting business across cultures must be sensitive to the above dynamics, as well as to varying business customs. Culture affects business behavior and customs. This section describes how *guanxi* affects business culture and customs in China, how *wa* affects business culture and customs in Japan, and how *inhwa* affects business culture and customs in South Korea. Some other interesting business customs from around the world that differ from country to country are presented in Table 10-3. Note that the descriptions in Table 10-3 are generalizations. Not all residents of a country necessarily adhere to those customs—especially the immigrants in a country. For example, many people in Australia are from other countries, such as China and Italy. These people may adhere to the customs of their country of birth.

Guanxi

The Chinese are excessively polite, but are tough bargainers; they like to entertain and expect reciprocal dinner parties; and they avoid all unnecessary physical contact. In China, contracts are binding only if the conditions present at time the contract is signed are also present when the contract is executed.[19]

TABLE 10-3	Business Customs Around the World
Australia	Business is almost always conducted over drinks, and it is considered rude to buy out of turn. Australians like to be addressed by their titles.
Austria	Austrians prefer to be addressed by their titles and consider it rude if a business associate tries to pick up the tab for a lunch or dinner they have initiated. They enjoy discussing art and music as well as skiing.
Belgium	Belgians like to get down to business immediately and are very conservative and efficient in their approach to business meetings. One must address French-speaking Belgians as "monsieur" or "madame," while Dutch-speaking Belgians must be addressed as "Mr." or "Mrs."
Egypt	Egypt is dominated by the Moslem faith, and their business customs reflect this. Business is slow-paced and the red tape is limitless. Egyptians take offense at refusals and at the use of direct negatives.
France	Conducting business in France in August is difficult because most people are on vacation. The French use titles until use of first names is proposed. In negotiations, they like to debate issues; they like to show their intellect and to challenge your intellect. To successfully sell the French requires convincing them of the merits of the product/service through intellectual debate, not through flashy, high-powered presentations. They use sophisticated table manners.
Germany	One should expect much handshaking, but in order of the person's importance in the enterprise. Germans insist on using titles, seldom use first names, use surname preceded by title, dislike small talk, and are very punctual. Germans are competitive negotiatiors who get straight to the point and leave little room for debate. German executives tend to have an engineering and science background, and one must therefore appeal to their technical tastes—glitzy presentations are likely to fail. They do not strongly emphasize the development of personal relationships with business associates—they value their privacy and keep business and private matters separate.
Greece	The Greeks are famous for their extensive bargaining and for never discussing business without a cup of coffee. Building a personal rapport with Greeks is important. Business entertaining normally takes place in the evening at a local tavern, and spouses are often included. It is important that a business relationship be built on trust. Government plays an important role in business, which means that one must work through bureaucracy. Business is highly personalized—family connections, political connections, and business connections. How one connects is often more important than the quality of the product/service. In Greece, negotiations are not finished even after the contract has been awarded—a contract is viewed as an evolving document of agreement.
Guatemala	A luncheon set for a specific time means that some guests may arrive 10 minutes early, while others may be 45 minutes late.
India	Business is conducted at an extremely leisurely pace; therefore, Indians are very patient, unlike their American counterparts. When invited to dinner, one should accept and pass the food with the right hand only and expect to be asked many personal questions—which Indians see as a sign of politeness. Indians avoid discussing political issues with their business contacts.
Ireland, Republic of	Do not confuse it with Northern Ireland or the United Kingdom—it is politically and culturally distinct from both.
Italy	Italians use a handshake for greetings and goodbyes. Unlike in the United States, men do not stand when a woman enters or leaves a room, and they do not kiss a woman's hand—this is reserved for royalty. Appearance and style are very important to Italian businesspeople. The appeal and polish of a presentation reflect the quality of the product/service or the firm itself.

TABLE 10-3	**Business Customs Around the World,** *continued*
	Italian businesspeople are confident, shrewd, and competent negotiators, and they tend to rely mainly on their instincts and not as much on the advice of specialists.
Malaysia	Most Malaysians are Muslims, so they do not eat pork, drink alcohol, or party on Friday night, the eve of the Muslim sabbath. They are very status- and role-conscious, and therefore do not readily mingle at social gatherings, particularly if men and women are together at the same gathering.
Mexico	Local contacts (connections) are required prior to arrival in Mexico. It is impolite to make extended eye contact with Mexicans. Timeliness is not important—it is OK for your host to keep you waiting. Don't say "America" to mean the U.S.A. because Mexicans are Americans too, and don't say "the United States" to mean the U.S.A. because Mexico is a United States too—the United States of Mexico. Don't get down to business right away. First get to know your prospective Mexican clients and their families by socializing.
Netherlands	The Dutch are competitive negotiators who get straight to the point and normally have little conflict or debate.
Nigeria	Business is slow-paced and never conducted over the telephone.
Pakistan	The Islamic faith is a dominant factor in Pakistani life and in business as well. It is a male-dominated country where women are largely confined to the domestic sphere; hence Pakistani men are uncomfortable or may even refuse to transact business with a woman. They refuse alcohol, cigarettes, and pork. One should never try to take a picture of a Pakistani without his or her permission.
Portugal	One must take the time to establish a rapport with Portuguese business associates.
Saudi Arabia	Business is informal, slow paced, and male-dominated. The Saudies are insulted if forced to deal with a representative rather than with the main person. When invited to a Saudi home, never bring flowers or gifts to the lady of the house, never eat or drink with the left hand, and never praise the house furnishings unless you would like to receive them as a gift the following day.
South Africa	Businesspeople like to discuss politics with their peers, and they are generally ultra-conservative.
Spain	The Spanish work long days and break appointments often. The business lunch is an important part of conducting business in Spain, and great ceremony is applied in lunch meetings. Lunches stretch from 2:30 P.M. to 5:00 P.M.; then work goes on until 8:30 P.M. or 9:00 P.M. These lunches are used to develop the relationship required before business can be conducted.
Thailand	Thailand's traditional greeting is the *wai*, which is made by the placement of both hands together in a prayer-like position at the chin and bowing slightly. The gesture means "thank you" and "I am sorry" as well as "hello." The higher the hands, the more respect is symbolized. The fingertips, however, should never be raised above the eye level. Failure to return a *wai* is equivalent to refusing to shake hands in the West. In Thailand it is considered offensive to place one's arm over the back of the chair in which another person is sitting, and men and women should not show affection in public. First names are used, and last names are reserved for very formal occasions or in writing.
United Kingdom	In the U.K., never sit with the ankle resting on the knee; one should instead cross his or her legs with one knee on top of the other. Avoid backslapping and putting an arm around a new acquaintance. Use titles until use of first names is suggested. Gift-giving is not a normal custom in the U.K. The British are very civil and reserved, they do not admire overt ambition and aggressiveness, and are offended by hard-sell tactics. They do not brag about their finances or positions. And they are good negotiators, but do not have a high regard for bargaining in general.

(continued)

TABLE 10-3	**Business Customs Around the World,** *continued*
United States	Americans often feel that the European practice of meticulously cultivating personal relationships with business associates slows the expedient conduct of business; they agree that time is money, and the Europeans waste time. Business comes first, and friendship or pleasure comes later, if at all.

Source: Excerpted from David Altany, "It Takes Cultural Savvy," *Industry Week* (October 2, 1989); M. Katherine Glover, "Do's and Taboos: Cultural Aspects of International Business," *Business America* (August 13, 1990): 3; Dean Foster, "Business Across Borders: International Etiquette for the Effective Secretary," *The Secretary* (October 1992): 23; and excerpted from Valeria Frazee, "Getting Started in Mexico," *Workforce* 2, no. 1 (January 1997): 16, 17.

A major dynamic of Chinese society is *guanxi,* which refers to the special relationships two people have with each other.[20] The two individuals who share this relationship assume that each is fully committed to the other; that they have agreed to exchange favors, even when official commands mandate that they act neutrally. The *guanxi* relationship, even though it is preferred, does not have to be between friends. In the relationship, an individual who refuses to return a favor loses face and becomes known as untrustworthy. Foreigners wishing to do business in China who have not established a *guanxi* relationship may very well have to deal with uninterested officials. When the relationship is between two people of unequal rank, the relationship favors the weaker person. The weaker person can claim inadequacy and ask for special favors that he or she does not have to reciprocate equally. The unequal exchange gives respect and honor to the stronger party who voluntarily gives more than he or she receives. Thus, to do business in China effectively, good personal connections must be established first. Note that the decision-making process in China is slow even when bureaucracy is circumvented by *guanxi.* This is because decisions in China are made hierarchically, and superiors in each *guanxi* link must agree.[21] This Asian value contributed to Asia's recent financial crisis. Many Asian banks made loans, not on the basis of merit (as defined in the Western financial systems), but on the basis of these types of connections.[22]

Wa

The Japanese entertain exhaustively, but in a very businesslike manner. To them, business is family, and therefore they are usually selfless—unlike the cutthroat business styles of many Americans. The Japanese, like the Chinese, avoid physical contact as much as possible, and they require even more space than Americans. No matter how poorly negotiations may be going, the Japanese see direct negative statements as rude and offensive. They consider it rude to be late for a business meeting, but it is quite acceptable to be late for a social occasion. The Japanese bow is a well-known form of greeting; it symbolizes respect and humility. When receiving a business card, take it with both hands, observe it carefully, acknowledge it with a nod that you have taken in the information, and make a relevant comment or ask a polite question about it. In other words, treat the card as you would treat its owner—with respect. When presenting the card, use both hands and position the card so that the recipient can read it. The information should be printed in Japanese on the reverse side of the card.

The Japanese concept of *wa* necessitates that members of a group, be it a work team, a company, or a nation, cooperate with and trust each other. Consequently, the Japanese usually prefer, or even demand, that business dealings occur among friends, and they do not like to deal with strangers. Therefore, proper introductions are crucial when business relationships are launched. Before business transactions can begin, the Japanese must first place the foreigner within some group context (a *wa* relationship must be established).[23] Furthermore, in Japan telling the truth, or, as it is called in the United States, "laying one's cards on the table," does not work well because it may upset someone and threaten the group's *wa*. The Japanese thus prefer ensuring harmony and goodwill over the truth, as well as long-term over short-term relations.[24]

Inhwa

South Korean business behavior is heavily influenced by *inhwa,* which stresses harmony; linking of people who are unequal in rank, prestige, and power; loyalty to hierarchical rankings; and superiors being concerned for the well-being of subordinates.[25] Corporations are viewed as a "family" or a "clan." As a consequence, Korean businesspeople prefer to establish personal ties with strangers before they transact business deals with them. Unlike the Japanese, but like the Chinese, the binding of Koreans' relationships is between individuals, and there is no strong loyalty to the organization—they will readily change companies when it is beneficial to them. *Inhwa* relationships are long-term and require a long time and much patience to cultivate. Once relationships have been established, they must be continually maintained and strengthened. Business contracts are interpreted through the personal relationships of those who agree. Therefore, an agreement is only as good as the personal relations that made it possible; lawyers should not take over from the originators.

Furthermore, in Korea contracts are not simply documents indicating mutual obligations and rights; they are declarations of intentions supported by the integrity of the signers. As a result, renegotiation of contracts is expected behavior in Korea. Koreans do not consider a contract binding if conditions change. Since the emotional aspects are more valuable than the contents of a contract, foreigners must cultivate a strong relationship with their Korean associates before signing a contract. The original signers should be prepared to continually maintain that relationship and interest in the project after the contract has been signed because a change of those in power could lead to problems.

Government officials direct much of Korea's economy; therefore, most major ventures require the support of one or more governmental offices. Foreign businesspeople must establish relationships in government circles as well. Senior Korean officials deal only with other senior officials, not junior officials. If the Korean company is using its president as the negotiator, the foreign corporation should use its president as well. Also, Koreans do not like bad news, and when it must be delivered, it should be done toward the end of the workday and unexpectedly.[26]

Cross-Cultural Generalizations: A Caveat

The international businessperson should be aware that while the culture influences the mode of doing business in a country, the introduction of new technology changes culture. Historically, cultural borrowing between countries has been common. Strategists should thus be cautious about older information on a nation's culture, since it may be outdated. They should also be aware that generalized information about nations serves mainly as a stereotype, and stereotypes are useful mainly as starting points for analysis.[27] Ultimately, specific situations must be analyzed and considered to make the final decision. For example, it may be true that some Americans tend to regard time as money, but not all of them do.

Cross-Cultural Adaptation: A Caveat

Those who offer advice on international negotiations advocate adaptation—an attempt to obtain approval from members of a foreign culture by becoming behaviorally similar to them. (**"When in Rome, do as the Romans do."**) This advice is based on research findings that when individuals were perceived as similar in areas of beliefs, attitudes, dialect style, and socioeconomic class, they were viewed more favorably. These advocates do not specify a degree of adaptation, however. Other research findings suggest that the positive correlations between similarity and attraction may be true only at moderate levels of similarity and that substantial levels of adaptation actually result in negative relationships.[28] In other words, if one does not adapt to local culture, a negative relationship will occur, as it will if one attempts to adapt too much. It is therefore moderate adaptation that leads to a positive relationship. A possible explanation for this is that substantial adaptation efforts may be perceived as presumptuous, while moderate adaptation efforts may reflect respect and sensitivity to the local culture.[29]

For example, a male Japanese executive conducting business in Texas may actually be offensive if at a business meeting with his traditionally dressed Texan associates he dresses in traditional Texas clothes (big hat, big boots, and so forth). In the same context, an American conducting business in Malaysia may offend some Malaysians if he or she dresses in traditional

Malaysian clothes. Simply acknowledging and respecting that traditional dress style differs in many countries would suffice. Not violating local rituals, such as hurrying the conducting of business in a culture where business activities typically are not hurried, will result in a better relationship. Furthermore, a male Texan conducting business in India may actually command respect if he dresses in traditional Texas clothes—it would be interesting to the locals.

CROSS-CULTURAL NEGOTIATIONS

Negotiating across cultures is far more complex than negotiating within a culture because foreign negotiators have to deal with differing negotiating styles and cultural variables simultaneously. In other words, the negotiating styles that work at home generally do not work in other cultures. As a result, cross-cultural business negotiators have one of the most complicated business roles to play in organizations. They are often thrust into a foreign society consisting of what appears to be "hostile" strangers. They are put in the position of negotiating profitable business relationships with these people or suffering the negative consequences of failure. And quite often they find themselves at a loss as to why their best efforts and intentions have failed them. (Practical Perspective 10-2 presents an insight in this respect.)

PRACTICAL PERSPECTIVE 10-2

Be Aware of Cultural Differences When Selling Abroad

When Shannon Small began her marketing presentation, she had no idea it was about to backfire on her.

A vice president for Bethesda, Maryland–based IconixGroup and a seasoned pro at corporate image-building and technology branding, Small started her pitch to a French firm recently with a tactic that had proven effective for Iconix when presenting to domestic companies. She showed the firm a side-by-side comparison of its Web site and those of its competitors. She evaluated the strengths and weakness of each, including where the prospective client's Web site fell short. The reaction was swift.

"They said, 'If you send us anything like this again, we will never work with you,'" Small recalls of the response. Far from viewing the comparison as constructive and insightful criticism, the clients perceived it as "confrontational, rude, typical ugly American," Small says.

(continued)

For a young technology company doing business overseas, the episode was a telling lesson in negotiating Old World cultural subtleties.

"Basically what they told us was, 'You can tell us those things, but we don't want to know anyone is doing it better,'" Small says. With a little finesse, she ultimately salvaged the account. What Small took away from that unexpected encounter was that the American penchant for the cards-on-the-table, straight talk approach in business meetings must give way to coaxing egos and using polite gestures in France.

This type of scenario may be ancient history for large American corporations that have been working in overseas markets for decades now. But as technology companies run by headstrong entrepreneurs are going international at earlier and earlier stages in their life cycles, they are facing such subtleties for the first time.

No longer the exclusive province of Fortune 500 companies, international markets are opening up to small firms riding the Internet's conquest of the globe. As digital connectivity eliminates the cost of doing business over long distances and as language barriers become a thing of the past, young tech executives are rushing into foreign markets hungry for American Internet and software expertise. But the roadblock time and time again for this aggressive generation is its lack of Miss Manners properness in dealing with other cultures. For all the talk of the Internet breaking down barriers and making the world a cozy global village, the reality is that age-old cultural differences still persist.

These cultural differences in the tech world include misunderstandings of behavior and speech, and societal differences in the proper ways of relationship building and deal signing. And gender issues, though not included in this list, still affect many international business ventures—after all, professional American women still encounter sexism and unequal treatment when doing business in certain countries of South America, the Middle East, and the East Asia.

Large tech companies, like IBM, Hewlett Packard, and General Electric, learned their overseas cultural lessons 30 or more years ago. But the next generation is up against the same curve.

"The smaller companies have so much learning to do," says Neil Goodman, who heads Global Dynamics, an international business protocol consulting firm in Randolph, New Jersey. "They stumble a lot more in international settings, and it's very hard to recoup from that bad first impression."

Source: Excerpted from Dan Egbert, "The New Generation Learns an Age-Old Lesson Overseas," *Tech Capital 3*, no. 4 (July 1999): 78. Reprinted with permission.

How to Avoid Failure in International Negotiations

Negotiators in a foreign country often fail because the local counterparts have taken more time to learn how to overcome the obstacles normally associated with international/cross-cultural negotiations. Failure may occur because of time and/or cost constraints. For example, a negotiator may be given too a short period of time to obtain better contract terms than were originally agreed to in a country where negotiations typically take a long time. A negotiator may think that "what works in the home country is good enough for the rest of the world," which is far from the truth. In fact, strategies that fail to take into account cultural factors are usually naive or misconceived. Typically, the obstacles to overcome include

➤ **Learning the local language,** or at least being able to select and use an effective language translator.

➤ **Learning the local culture,** including how the culture handles conflict, its business practices, and its business ethics, or at least being able to select and use an effective cultural translator.

➤ **Becoming well-prepared for the negotiations,** that is, along with the above, the negotiator must have a thorough knowledge of the subject matter being negotiated.

Effective cross-cultural negotiators understand the cultural differences existing between all parties involved; and they know that failure to understand the differences serves only to destroy potential business success.[30]

How Much Must One Know About the Foreign Culture?

Realistically, it is nearly impossible to learn everything about another culture, although it may be possible if one lives in the culture for several years. The reason for this is that each culture has developed, over time, multifaceted structures that are much too complex for any foreigner to understand totally. Therefore, foreign negotiators need not have total awareness of the foreign culture; they do not need to know as much about the foreign culture as the locals, whose frames of reference were shaped by that culture. However, they will need to know enough about the culture and about the locals' negotiating styles to avoid being uncomfortable during (and after) negotiations.[31] Besides knowing enough to not fail, they also need to know enough to win. For example, in negotiations between Japanese and American businesspeople, Japanese negotiators have sometimes used their knowledge that Americans have a low tolerance for silence to their advantage.

In other words, for negotiation to take place, the foreigner must at least recognize those ideas and behaviors that the locals intentionally put forward as part of the negotiation process—and the locals must do the same for the foreigners. Both sides must be capable of interpreting these behaviors sufficiently to distinguish common from conflicting positions, to spot movement from positions, and to respond in ways that sustain communication.[32] Practical Perspective 10-3 describes negotiating in Mexico. Tables 10-4 and 10-5 present the recommended behavior for negotiating with the Japanese, Table 10-6 for negotiating with the French, and Table 10-7 for negotiating in China. Appendix 10-1 presents the negotiating styles of various European nations, and Appendix 10-2 presents the negotiating style in Asia. (Both appendices are presented at the end of the chapter.) It cannot, however, be overemphasized that these are stereotypes or generalizations, which, while they are often accurate, should serve only as starting points in understanding a culture. Not all individuals in a culture adhere to these

PRACTICAL PERSPECTIVE 10-3

Negotiating Successfully In Mexico

Negotiating in Mexico is non-confrontational; it may seem more like a polite conversation than the give-and-take process many Americans are accustomed to. Agreements are developed in a more casual environment, but the deal is expected to be honored. Mexicans keep their word and expect us to do the same.

Although our counterparts will likely speak English, bring someone who speaks Spanish, preferably someone from Mexico. This encourages familiarity, which will be conductive to negotiations.

Warming Up

Mexicans have a warm-up period that greatly influences how negotiations will proceed and their outcome. U.S. political and military interventions in Mexico are still alive in Mexican education, so Mexicans are wary of being taken advantage of by "gringos." Wariness needs to be overcome, and trust must be built. Demonstrate that you are willing to negotiate on a level playing field.

Mexicans need to feel their counterparts are *simpático* (being warm and likable) to feel comfortable negotiating and enjoy doing business with them. This comes from a cultural emphasis on the importance of relationship. U.S. businesspeople are sometimes perceived as *antipático* (impersonal or aloof). Mexicans use the warm-up period to determine whether their counterparts are *simpático* or *antipático*. Decisions are based not only on the decision maker's assessment of the negotiations but also on feelings about the U.S. company and the individuals representing it.

In the United States, decisions tend to be reached by committee or group consensus. This is not the case in Mexico. The decision maker is one person, which comes from a historical and cultural emphasis on *personalisimo* (personalism). This value has developed strong political leaders and predominates in Mexican businesses. Americans should use the warm-up period to determine who the decision maker is.

Mexicans are very hierarchical, and by interacting with your counterparts socially, you may discover that the person you are dealing with defers to someone else. Also, many Mexican companies are family businesses. By doing research, you will know what family names are associated with the owners of the company. If you are not dealing with the decision maker, you are going through an extra step in the negotiations.

It's How You Say It

Mexican society is high-context, meaning much of the information transferred between people, especially in negotiations, is in the context rather than the content. A great deal of information is transmitted nonverbally. Less emphasis is placed on words, numbers, and written documents, and much more on inflection, tone of voice, setting, past history of your relationship, how they feel about you, trust, and so on.

Because it is a high-context culture, Mexicans use body language. Less eye contact would indicate reluctance to commit. Less distance, more touching, and warm *abrazos* (hugs) are signs of acceptance.

Lengthy proposals written in legalese will intimidate your Mexican counterparts and can scare them away from the deal.

Negotiations may not proceed in an orderly fashion by U.S. standards. Discussions are not necessarily sequential or logical. Mexicans are quite comfortable with this as it allows them to be creative and demonstrate their personal flair. If you present a checklist-style negotiation schedule and stick to it rigidly, the Mexicans may feel confined and pressured.

The Mexican culture is far more concerned with status than ours is. Therefore, it is important that your negotiators' status matches theirs. If the U.S. company sends mid-level managers, the Mexicans may be offended. If the opposite is true, you will be wasting your time because the decision will come from higher ranks. The larger company and the buyer will have more status.

Dealing With Difficulties

Your Mexican counterparts have less control over things than we might have in this country. Rather than pretend difficulties will not arise (for example, delivery dates might not be met), it is much more useful for both companies to recognize these potential problems and build into the contract a way to deal with them. This foresight will also show your counterparts that you understand their business environment.

If negotiations are not working out, it is important not to end abruptly. If you have an attitude that indicates, "This is our bottom line. We cannot go any farther, and the negotiations are over," you may hinder future business opportunities. They need to feel they can come back to you later and still have a *simpático* relationship.

Reaching An Agreement

We like to end negotiations on a clear, definitive note. Mexicans need a more flexible ending. This "open-endedness" allows Mexicans to deal with unforeseen eventualities—changes in price, political climate, etc. Mexican businesspeople deal with much more change and uncertainty than we do and would be uncomfortable with an iron-clad document at the end if negotiations. This does not mean they are trying to find an escape clause. The real substance of the agreement is in the quality of the relationship that has been established.

Source: International Business (February 1997): 15. Reprinted with permission.

practices. Ultimately, cross-cultural negotiators must determine their counterparts' personal motivations and agendas and adapt the negotiation style to them.

The purpose of the ensuing sections is to develop a cross-cultural negotiations process. The process includes both strategy and tactics. **Strategy** refers to a long-term plan, and **tactics** refers to the actual means used to implement the strategy.[33]

STRATEGIC PLANNING FOR INTERNATIONAL NEGOTIATIONS

Strategic planning for international negotiations involves several stages: preparation for face-to-face negotiations, determining settlement range, selecting the form of negotiations, determining where the negotiations should take place, deciding whether to use an individual or a group of individuals in the negotiations, and learning about the country's views on agreements/contracts.

TABLE 10-4	Recommended Behavior for Negotiating with the Japanese

Employ

➤ Use "introducer" for initial contacts (e.g., general trading company).
➤ Employ an agent the counterpart knows and respects.
➤ Ensure that the agent/advisor speaks fluent Japanese.

Induce

➤ Be open to social interaction and communicate directly.
➤ Make an extreme initial proposal, expecting to make concessions later.
➤ Work efficiently to get the job done.

Adapt

➤ Follow some Japanese protocol (reserved behavior, name cards, gifts).
➤ Provide a lot of information (by American standards) up front to influence the counterpart's decision making early.
➤ Slow down your usual timetable.
➤ Make informed interpretations (e.g., "it is difficult" means no).
➤ Present positions later in the process more firmly and more consistently.

Embrace

➤ Proceed according to information-gathering, *nemawashi* (not exchange) model.
➤ "Know your stuff" cold.
➤ Assemble a team (group) for formal negotiations.
➤ Speak in Japanese.
➤ Develop personal relationships, respond to obligations within them.

Improvise

➤ Do your homework on the individual counterpart(s) and circumstances.
➤ Be attentive and nimble (improvising entails different behaviors for different Japanese).
➤ Invite the counterpart to participate in mutually enjoyed activities or interests (for example, golf).

These are examples, not a complete listing, of attitudes and behaviors implied by a negotiator's use of each strategy.

Source: Stephen E. Weiss, "Negotiating With 'Romans'—Part 1," *Sloan Management Review* (Winter 1994): 58. Copyright © 1994, Sloan Management Review Association, Massachusetts Institute of Technology, Sloan School of Management. Used with permission. All rights reserved.

Preparation for Face-to-Face Negotiations

Generally, at the preparation stage, the issues to be identified are common interests, desired outcomes, possible conflicts (and tactics for handling them), participants' abilities and limitations, business markets, financial status, participants' reputation, and similar products/services.[34] Typically, the negotiating strategy that is effective in the home market will have to be

TABLE 10-5	How to Behave During Negotiating Sessions in Japan

➤ Don't get too involved with details of the contract too early in the session. The Japanese may feel that the details can be worked out as the relationship continues to grow.

➤ Try not to use an aggressive approach to selling your idea. Japanese believe that your idea or product should speak for itself. A low-key approach is better.

➤ Don't interrupt when someone is speaking. This is considered rude by most Japanese.

➤ Try to be formal. Do not ask if it would be OK to call them by their first names or if everyone can take off their suit coats to relax. This type of atmosphere or approach tends to give the Japnese a feeling of a lack of sincerity.

➤ Always bring as much information as possible about your plans and your firm. Published articles are of great advantage.

➤ It is better to not approach the Japanese alone. Send a group (two or three) to conduct negotiations. This is a sign of earnestness to the Japanese. Make certain you send the appropriate individuals who can make the decisions.

➤ Do not demand an immediate decision on points covered in the meetings. As most decisions are made in groups, the Japanese team needs time to compare notes and discuss matters.

➤ Do not be offended if the Japanese inquire about your religious or political beliefs. These are common questions used in Japan because they are interested in knowing as much about you and your company as possible. It is a confidence builder.

➤ If you get stuck on a point, don't continue to beat away on it. Move on to other points and come back when the other team has had time to think about it.

➤ Keep reviewing those points that were agreed upon during the meeting, trying to move forward in a constructive manner.

➤ Maintain good communication with your interpreter. The interpreter may be able to inform you on the progress of the contact or perhaps of possible conflicts that may be avoided.

➤ Speak slowly and with patience. Do not rattle off numbers to indicate your knowledge of the project. Numbers can be studied in detail by the Japanese at a later date.

➤ Be prepared for misunderstandings and clarify the points with sincerity and willingness to assist.

➤ Don't cover difficult points first on the agenda. Work toward a common ground, but be flexible enough to realize that ground may totally change before the contract is signed.

Source: Robert T. Moran, *Getting Your Yen's Worth: How to Negotiate with Japan, Inc.* (Houston, TX: Gulf Publishing, 1985), pp.123–124. Copyright © Gulf Publishing Company, Houston, Texas, 800-231-6275. All rights reserved.

modified for negotiating with foreign businesses; as indicated above, cultural factors, business customs, and ethical standards of the foreign country must be considered.[35] For instance, in negotiating with the Chinese, Americans want to agree on specific terms first while the Chinese want to determine general principles (the "spirit of the contract") and then discuss specifics. In other words, Americans tend to be concerned with short-term goals, such as profits, while the Chinese are more concerned with long-term interests, such as the procurement of American technology and business techniques.[36]

TABLE 10-6	Recommended Behavior for Negotiating with the French

Employ

➤ Employ an agent well-connected in business and government circles.
➤ Ensure that the agent/advisor speaks fluent French.

Induce

➤ Be open to social interaction and communicate directly.
➤ Make an extreme initial proposal, expecting to make concessions later.
➤ Work efficiently to get the job done.

Adapt

➤ Follow the French protocol (greetings and leave-takings, formal speech).
➤ Demonstrate an awareness of French culture and business environment.
➤ Be consistent between actual and stated goals and between attitudes and behavior.
➤ Defend views vigorously.

Embrace

➤ Approach negotiation as a debate involving reasoned argument.
➤ Know the subject of negotiation *and* broad environmental issues (economic, political, social).
➤ Make intellectually elegant, persuasive, yet creative presentations (logically sound, verbally precise).
➤ Speak in French.
➤ Show interest in the counterpart as an individual but remain aware of the strictures of social and organizational hierarchies.

Improvise

➤ Do your homework on the individual counterpart(s) and circumstances.
➤ Be attentive and nimble (improvising entails different behaviors for different French).
➤ Invite the counterpart to participate in mutually enjoyed activities or interests (for example, dining out, tennis).

These are examples, not a complete listing, of attitudes and behaviors implied by a negotiator's use of each strategy.

Source: Stephen E. Weiss, "Negotiating With 'Romans'—Part 1," *Sloan Management Review* (Winter 1994): 58. Copyright © 1994 Sloan Management Review Association, Massachusetts Institute of Technology, Sloan School of Management. Used with permission. All rights reserved.

Determining a Settlement Range

At this phase, a negotiation or **settlement range** (all possible settlements a negotiator would be willing to make) must be established. The "least acceptable result" (LAR) and a "maximum supportable position" (MSP) must be identified. In this respect, the Japanese have a saying, "*Banana no tataki uri,*" which means "ask outrageous prices and lower them when

TABLE 10-7	**Culturally-Based Guidelines for Negotiating Business Conflict Resolutions in China**

---

1. Expand Your Cultural Comfort Zone.

Underlying Chinese Value: "Learn something from 5,000 years of Chinese history," –Jiang Zemin

Implications for American Managers Who Are Negotiating Conflict Resolutions in China:
   a. Embrace the unusual as normal.
   b. Get rid of any misplaced sense of (American) cultural arrogance.
   c. Seek all forms of knowledge about China's history and culture.
   d. As a result of this cultural immersion, seek to absorb strategic thinking unconsciously. Then strive to accept the mental "thrust-and-parry" associated with strategic thinking as a natural part of human interaction in China.

---

2. Last Things First.

Underlying Chinese Value: "*Reng Qing,* the belief that the human element should never be removed from business affairs." –Confucius

Implications for American Managers Who Are Negotiating Conflict Resolutions in China:
   a. Learn that in the face of Chinese conflict not having goals may be worse than not being able to achieve them.
   b. Welcome conflicts as an opportunity for creative expression within the context of the business relationship.
   c. Learn how to create obligations (in one's Chinese counterparts) through gestures or actions that cost little. Also, learn when and how to subtly call the debt due. In short, learn the essence of *Reng Qing.*

---

3. Anticipate Conflict.

Underlying Chinese Value: "He who excels at resolving difficulties does so before they arise. He who excels in conquering his enemies triumphs before threats materialize." –Sun Tzu

Implications for American Managers Who Are Negotiating Conflict Resolutions in China:
   a. Learn that active measures should be taken in anticipation of conflict rather than dispassionately waiting for disagreements to arise.
   b. Learn that the opportunity to act in China turns on the ability to make small adjustments or corrections in advance of significant disagreements.
   c. Learn to separate essential (hard-boundary) issues or concepts from nonessential ones and do not allow hard-boundary issues to be violated by Chinese partners.
   d. Learn to specify hard-boundary issues or concerns to Chinese counterparts very early in the relationship; otherwise, doubts may arise.

(continued)

TABLE 10-7	**Culturally-Based Guidelines for Negotiating Business Conflict Resolutions in China,** *continued*

4. Do Not Resist Resistance.

Underlying Chinese Values: "Travel where there is no enemy." –*Bing Fa*	Implication for American Managers Who Are Negotiating Conflict Resolutions in China:
"Understand your adversary thoroughly and lead him to where he is without fault." –*Chuang Tzu*	a. Accept Chinese resistance to Western business practices.
"Become your opponent." –*Bing Fa*	b. Learn to maintain organizational flexibility (except with respect to hard-boundary issues) in the face of conflict; then strive to blend with and redirect attacks.
	c. Put yourself in your opponent's place, consider his goals, and develop empathy toward him.
	d. Work toward a solution that allows each party to achieve what it desires.

5. Retreat Gracefully.

Underlying Chinese Values: "Retreat is another form of advance. Good men do not fight losing battles." –*Bing Fa*	Implications for American Mangers Who Are Negotiating Conflict Resolutions in China:
"If I can fight and win, I fight. If I cannot fight, I will escape." –Ancient Chinese schoolchild adage	a. Develop alternatives for every negotiating response expected from the Chinese and create exit strategies for each business negotiation.
	b. When original positions are knocked down, compensate as gracefully as possible and retreat slowly toward hard-boundary issues.
	c. Accept that U.S. firms in China will sometimes find it necessary to accept temporary defeat and attempt to preserve strength for other days (and future conflicts).

6. Understand The Role Of Deception.

Underlying Chinese Values: "Offer the enemy a bait to lure him; then feign disorder and strike him."	Implications for American Managers Who Are Negotiating Conflict Resolution in China:
"Pretend inferiority and encourage his arrogance."	a. Do not idealize Western traditions of openness and fair play while in China.
"Do not gobble proffered baits." –*Bing Fa*	b. Be aware of the likelihood that deception will be used in China. These illusions are likely to assume the form of "hiding the truth," "showing false strength," or "bait and switch" tactics.
	c. Reserve a place for illusion in one's own business practices in China, but use the tactic sparingly, selectively, and properly.

faced with buyer objections."[37] Establishing a range provides negotiators the ability to make concessions and therefore more flexibility in the negotiations. Some cultures, Russia, for example, view concessions as a sign of weakness, not gestures of goodwill or flexibility. To be able to establish a reasonable negotiating range, an accurate analysis of the nature of all relevant markets must be conducted.[38] If there are other options, that is, if

TABLE 10-7	**Culturally-Based Guidelines for Negotiating Business Conflict Resolutions in China,** *continued*

7. Give Your Opponent Face.

Underlying Chinese Value: "Gentleman call attention to the good points in others; they do not call attention to their defects." –Confucius

Implications for American Managers Who Are Negotiating Conflict Resolutions in China:

a. Acknowledge opponents' potential for future excellence.
b. Remember that taking away an opponents' face is perhaps the worst tactical error that can be made in China.
c. Always acknowledge the value, dignity, and position of one's adversaries. Whenever possible, feed their self-worth.
d. Remember that if your firm is the selling partner in a Chinese business alliance, it operates under a culturally induced obligation to defer to the buying partner.

8. In Death Ground, Fight.

Underlying Chinese Value: "In death ground, fight" –Sun Tzu

Implications for American Mangers Who Are Negotiating Conflict Resolution in China:

a. When encountering a worst-case scenario, recognize the danger.
b. Quickly and accurately analyze the direct threat to your firm's survival in China.
c. Integrate all available resources and energies into a single, focused ("zero-doubt") strike at the heart of your adversary.
d. Use this sort of "zero-doubt" negotiating style only when absolutely necessary.

Source: David Strutton and Lou Pelton, "Scaling the Great Wall: The Yin and Yang of Resolving Business Conflicts in China," *Business Horizons* (September–October 1997): 26–27. Reprinted with permission.

either the seller or the buyer has other forms of leverage or enticement, he or she may not need to make as many concessions or may not need to make any concessions at all.

Technological Forms of Negotiation

International negotiations can take place via telephone, telex, e-mail, or fax; face-to-face videoconferencing; face-to-face in-person negotiations; and use of third parties.[39] Using a telephone, telex, e-mail, or fax is relatively inexpensive, but because it lacks personal presence, it is usually not a viable approach in important negotiations.

Global videoconferencing can be an effective negotiating form. There is face-to-face communication; yet, unlike face-to-face in-person negotiations, negotiators do not have to travel to strange physical environments and the costs of airfare and lodging are saved. However, the development of global videoconferencing technologies is still at an early stage. It is not yet widely used by negotiators, but as technological advancements are made, its use is more likely. Note that videoconferencing will not be a viable form for all face-to-face negotiations. In many cultures, China, for example, carrying out certain rituals and ceremonies are an important part of negotiations, and in many negotiating situations an in-person presence is needed. (Refer to Table 10-7 for guidelines for negotiating business in China.) In important negotiations, the **face-to-face in-person form** is the most widely used, and this is likely to continue. Using a **third party** in face-to-face in-person negotiations sometimes works best, especially when one or both of the parties involved are not knowledgeable about cross-cultural negotiations and when there is much political and/or social hostility between the two countries involved in the negotiations.

Where Should Negotiations Take Place?

Negotiations can take place in the home country, in the counterpart's home country, or at a neutral site. Most negotiators would prefer that negotiations take place on their home turf. Familiar surroundings and easy access to information provide more leverage; fatigue and stress associated with foreign travel are not experienced; and, of course, lower travel costs are incurred.[40] On the other hand, negotiating in the foreign country does have its advantages, such as sometimes receiving certain concessions because you have endured the burdens of traveling. And quite often it is a good idea to base decisions on site observations—for example, it is a good idea to see the plant where your product is going to be manufactured. A neutral site that is equally advantageous to both parties is often ideal. For example, an American executive from Park Avenue in New York City may not adapt well in a Brazilian village in the Amazon, and an executive from this village may not adapt well in New York City. A negotiating site that falls between the two extremes may be the most viable.

Individual or Team Negotiations?

An organization can assign one individual or a group of individuals to conduct the negotiations. The obvious advantages of using **one person** are that it is cheaper and a decision can be made quickly. An obvious disadvantage is that one person may not have sufficient ability to deal with the other side, which typically consists of a group of experts and negotiating specialists—an advantage of the group approach. Furthermore, in Japan, for instance, not using a group may be interpreted to mean that you are not very serious about the negotiation or the business deal. Also, the individual negotiator often finds himself or herself pressed to make a decision when it is not the right time to do so. In a group, the members can always take a break to confer, therefore "buying time" to assess the situation and develop new strategies and tactics. (The Japanese typically use this method because their decisions usually require group consensus.) Thus, in negotiating situations where the cost and speed of a decision are more important than the other factors, use one negotiator; otherwise, use a group of experts and negotiating specialists.

To speed up decision making a bit and still have access to expert input, a **team of negotiators** can be used, but one member is given full negotiating authority (Americans generally use this approach). Of course, the other side may know this. And in the negotiations game, for tactical reasons, both parties try to learn who the decision maker is. In this respect, American decision makers usually reveal themselves quickly because they tend to be very active in the negotiations. On the other hand, Japanese decision makers are usually not very active in the negotiations—they simply remain silent and listen. It should also be noted that the Japanese tend to include several young executives in the negotiations team simply for exposure and on-site development purposes.[41]

What Are the Country's Views on Agreements/Contracts?

Countries existing on a high commercial level have generally developed a working base on which agreements can rest. The base may be on one or a combination of three types:[42]

1. Rules that are spelled out technically as laws or regulations.
2. Moral practices mutually agreed upon and taught to the young as a set of principles.
3. Informal customs to which everyone conforms without being able to state the exact rules.

Some cultures favor one type, and some another. Americans, for example, rely heavily on written contracts, and they tend to consider the negotiations ended when the contract is signed. Many societies, however, do not place much importance on written contracts; they rely more on the development of a social relationship. And in many countries, Greece, for instance, a signed contract is simply a starting point for negotiations, which end only when the project is completed—the clauses in the contract are subject to renegotiation. Thus, the international negotiator must understand the nature of the other country's **views and practices relating to agreements and contracts.**

TACTICAL PLANNING FOR
INTERNATIONAL NEGOTIATIONS

Tactical planning for international negotiations involves determining how to obtain leverage, use delay, and deal with emotions.

Leverage

In negotiations, it is generally accepted that the more options you have, the more leverage you have, and the more concessions your opponents may be willing to make. For example, if you are negotiating with the Argentinean government to establish a manufacturing subsidiary in Argentina, and the Argentinean negotiators know that their site is the only viable one you have, they will not make any concessions, and are likely to ask you for some concessions. But if the Argentinean negotiators believe that you can just as easily set up the subsidiary in Peru or Brazil, and they need the technology—as most less-developed nations do—they are likely to be willing to make concessions.

Less-developed countries appear to have leverage over multinational corporations because they control access to their own territory, including markets, local labor supplies, investment opportunities, sources of raw materials, and other resources that multinational corporations need or desire. China, for instance, is developing economically rather quickly these days. Its more than one billion prospective customers, along with its relatively inexpensive cost of labor, make China an attractive place for many foreign companies to establish operations. This, it seems, would give Chinese negotiators considerable leverage, and concessions would often have to be made by foreign negotiators. This may be true in some cases, but in many instances, multinational corporations have negotiating advantages because they possess the capital, technology, managerial skills, access to global markets, and other resources that governments in less-developed countries need for economic development.[43]

Delay

Applying **delay tactics** is another form of leverage. If you walk away from the negotiations and your opponents become overly anxious, they may be willing to make some concessions. On the other hand, if you become anxious before your opponent does, you may have to make some concessions. Furthermore, the pause in the negotiations enables you to rest and recuperate, assess progress, obtain other information, and reformulate strategy.[44] In this context, patience is generally recognized as being a key personal attribute in negotiators. Americans tend to be low on patience, while the Japanese tend to be high. For an illustration, refer to Practical Perspective 10-4.

PRACTICAL PERSPECTIVE 10-4

Don't Just Sit There—Do Something!

A close friend and executive in a large Japanese company spoke very frankly to me one day. He said, "You Americans are fond of the expression 'Don't just sit there—do something.' Once in a while, you should reverse that advice. We Japanese would prefer to say 'Don't just do something—sit there.' Contemplation may be more productive than action."

It is true that U.S. businesspeople have always been action-oriented. Only when rushing to an endless series of appointments and conferences do they really feel productive. For many, perpetual motion seems to be their ultimate goal. It was Santayana who once observed that Americans are possessed by an obscure compulsion that will not let them rest, that drives them on faster and faster—not unlike a fanatic who redoubles his effort when he has lost sight of his goal. The greatest compliment that can be paid a U.S. executive is to call him dynamic....

Furthermore, foreign visitors are startled by Americans' typically low tolerance of silence. Most Asians, in contrast, can endure long periods during which nobody says anything. They feel that these opportunities for organizing and evaluating one's thoughts may be the most productive in any conference or negotiation.

Their relative inability to tolerate long periods of silence has gotten many American negotiators into serious trouble when the other side feels no comparable frustration and tension. As one foreign consultant cautions, "This is a bad trait indeed when the negotiation game is being played in a boardroom in Rio or in a Ginza nightclub, and when the other side is playing by Brazilian or Japanese rules."

The international vice president of a large U.S. corporation confessed to his own experience with the consequences of failing to understand foreign negotiating patterns. He said, "In one of my company's deals overseas, our buyer was sitting across the table from the Japanese manufacturer's representative for the purpose of bidding on an item in which we were interested. Following the usual niceties, our man offered $150,000 per batch. On hearing the bid, the Japanese sat back and relaxed in his chair to meditate. Our buyer, interpreting this silence to be disapproval, instantly pushed his offer higher. It was only after the session was over that he realized he had paid too much."

It is true that Americans are considered an outspoken lot. Masaaki Imai contrasts this with the behavior of his own compatriots in saying, "Sitting mute is clearly a minus at the Western conference, while silence is still silver, if not golden, in the Japanese mind-set. Many Japanese sit silently throughout the conference. Nobody thinks the worse of them for that. They are like oxygen; their views may not be visible, but they are making a positive contribution nonetheless."

Unless and until American business leaders can learn to live more comfortably with silence and to value thinking and listening as highly as mere physical activity, foreign executives will enjoy an easy advantage. It has been suggested that top U.S. executives keep a tiny replica of the giant Buddha of Kamakura, Japan, on their desks at all times. Its typical posture of quiet and peaceful meditation should serve as a constant reminder that great leaders are remembered for their thoughts as well as their deeds.

Emotions

Even though behavior in negotiations is mainly intuitive, it should never be judgmental. To be able to listen to other negotiators, one should exclude his or her subjective opinions, preconceptions, and emotional filters. By becoming aware of your **emotions,** you can learn to change your reactions and avoid being manipulated by others or by the emotions themselves—you prevent emotion from controlling a negotiation. On the other hand, if you negotiate solely on the basis of logic, you will miss emotional signals sent out by the other negotiator. Thus, the key to negotiations is to be perceptive of feelings (yours and theirs) without being reactive.[45] For an illustration, refer again to Practical Perspective 10-4.

ETHICAL CONSTRAINTS

Business ethics and corporate social responsibility, which were discussed in Chapter 2, place constraints on negotiators. For example, a negotiator's ethical concerns for honesty and fair dealings, regardless of the power status of negotiating parties, will affect the outcome. As was pointed out in Chapter 2, there is no global standard or view of what is ethical or unethical behavior in business transactions—what is viewed as unethical behavior in one culture may be viewed as ethical in another culture, and vice versa. For instance, if a negotiator on one side "pays off" an influential decision maker on the other side to obtain a favorable decision, it would be an unethical business practice in some cultures (and illegal in the U.S.), but it would be quite acceptable in other cultures.

SUMMARY

This chapter has discussed how differing cultural views on time, material possessions, family roles, relationships, and so forth affect the ways one transacts business across societies. For example, in the United States, "time is money," but in many parts of the world, people value relationships more than time. Thus, the "hurry up" business approach used by Americans would not be effective in, for instance, Spain, where establishing a relationship is more important than "time equals money." The practices in a number of countries have been briefly discussed. How negotiating styles vary from culture to culture has also been discussed. If a cross-cultural negotiator does not become familiar with, and adapt to, the style of the society where he or she is negotiating for business contracts, the consequence is likely to be failure. Issues related to strategic and tactical planning for international negotiations were addressed. The negotiation styles of numerous nations were examined.

Answers to Multicultural IQ Quiz from Table 10-1

1. A. In Taiwan, receiving a pineapple as a gift means the recipient will start a successful new business.

2. A. In the Chinese (and Japanese) language, the pronunciation of "four" is exactly the same as "death" and is considered bad luck.

3. C. A gold clock is an inappropriate gift for a Chinese executive because the Chinese pronunciation of the word "clock" is a homonym for "being at the deathbed of a loved one" and symbolizes severing of ties.

4. B. A TV announcer would not want to give the OK sign in Brazil, where it is considered a derogatory gesture.

5. A. The English don't like talking about work when the business day is over.

6. D. Business in Japan is discussed around the clock—except at the start of a business meeting. It is a brief but important time where greeting are exchanged and impressions are made.

7. B. In Japan, an OL is a female office worker.

8. A. During August, scheduling a business meeting can be a problem in Italy and France, where most firms close for vacation.

9. C. Korean men fill each other's glasses only when they are empty. However, do not wait too long because your companion may fill it himself. This would be regarded as impolite. And in mixed company, never let a woman fill anyone's glass, not even her own.

10. B. Korean are not likely to write names in red ink as they believe that someone who is close to them will die if they do.

11. B. Filipino folklore says that you can lose your finger if you point at things. So it became a Filipino habit to point out directions with their mouth.

12. C. Although bowing is the custom in other Asian countries, Indonesians shake hands. A person who shakes hands vigorously, uses physical gestures, or asks questions such as "How are you?" is likely to appear boorish.

Source: Prudential Leader (February 1998): 3.

Key Terms and Concepts

1. Cross-cultural business practices
2. "Time is money"
3. Circular- and linear-oriented cultures
4. Material possessions
5. Haste and aggressive behavior
6. *Guanxi, wa,* and *inhwa* relationships
7. "When in Rome, do as the Romans do"
8. Cross-cultural negotiations
9. Learning the local language and culture
10. Strategic and tactical planning for international negotiations
11. Settlement range
12. Face-to-face in-person negotiations
13. Use of a third party in negotiations
14. Individual versus team negotiations
15. Countries' views on agreements/contracts
16. Leverage
17. Delay tactics
18. Emotions
19. Ethical considerations

Discussion Questions and Exercises

1. Discuss how a culture's views on "time is money," relationships, and material possessions affect cross-cultural business transactions.

2. Discuss the effect of a culture's thought patterns—linear or circular—on cross-cultural business activities.

3. "Winning isn't everything, it's the only

thing." Discuss this statement in a cross-cultural context.

4. Discuss some of the ways social customs differ across cultures.

5. Describe the business tempo for the following cultures: Greece, Spain, Italy, England, and Germany.

6. Discuss the major business dynamics of China, Japan, and South Korea.

7. How does one avoid failing in cross-cultural negotiations?

8. You are the vice president of marketing for Y Company. You need to send an executive to Brazil to negotiate a contract. Your firm's personnel files indicate that one of your marketing executives has a college degree with a major in Brazilian culture. Would you feel comfortable sending this executive to Brazil to negotiate the contract? Why?

9. You are the negotiator for a firm that wishes to negotiate a contract in a foreign country. What must you do before you depart?

10. What are the forms of international negotiations?

11. You are a cross-cultural consultant specializing in negotiating in Japan and China. Two clients come to you for guidance—one on Japan and the other on China. In broad terms, what would you tell your clients to do?

12. As a classroom exercise, your professor will appoint two groups of at least five students each. One group will act the part of a team of negotiators sent to China by a U.S. automaker to negotiate a contract with Chinese government officials and businesspeople. The company has decided to establish a subsidiary in the People's Government of Yue Cheng District Shaoxing (about 200 miles southwest of Shanghai) to manufacture automobile parts to be sold back to the parent company in the U.S. The group has decision-making authority. *If available, these actors should be students who are U.S. citizens.*

The second group is to represent the Chinese side. This group is represented by the district head and vice-head, who are concerned with the long-range economic development of their district, and by three top-level local factory executives who are seeking to import the manufacturing technology they need to update their current unproductive operations. This group also has decision-making authority. *If available, these actors should be students who are from an Asian nation or some nation other than the U.S.*

The demands are as follows:

➤ The Chinese side wants Chinese managers in charge of the subsidiary; the American side believes that the Chinese do not yet have managers capable of managing this type of advanced technology and wants Americans in charge.

➤ The Chinese side does not want the parent company to repatriate any profits for ten years. (They want profits to be reinvested in China.) The Americans, who have short-range pressures to increase employee salaries and issue dividends to stockholders, want to be able to repatriate profits after two years.

➤ The Chinese want the American side to pay for all the expenses of building a new plant or refurbishing an old one; the Americans believe that since they are contributing the technology, which is very important to China's economic development, the Chinese side should pay for the entire investment.

In 45 minutes or less, the two groups should negotiate an agreement in class. The groups should draw on this chapter, including Appendix 10-2 and Table 10-7, as well as on previous chapters, especially those on international human resource management. After the agreement is negotiated, hold a class discussion about the negotiating difficulties and possible compromises.

Assignment

Select a country that was not extensively discussed in the chapter. Research the country and prepare a short report on how to transact business there—the *do*'s and *don't*s. Present your findings (in three to five minutes) to your class.

CASE 10-1

The Impatient American Sales Manager

A Latin American republic had decided to modernize one of its communication networks to the tune of several million dollars. Because of its reputation for quality and price, the inside track was quickly taken by American company "Y." The company, having been sounded out informally, considered the size of the order and decided to bypass its regular Latin American representative and instead send its sales manager. The following describes what took place. The sales manager arrived and checked in at the leading hotel. He immediately had some difficulty pinning down just whom he had to see about his business. After several days without results, he called at the American Embassy where he found that the commercial attaché had the up-to-the-minute information he needed. The commercial attaché listened to his story. Realizing that the sales manager had already made a number of mistakes, but figuring the Latins were used to American blundering, the attaché reasoned that all was not lost. He informed the sales manager that the Minister of Communications was the key man and that whoever got the nod from him would get the contract. He also briefed the sales manager on methods of conducting business in Latin America and offered some pointers about dealing with the minister.

The next day the commercial attaché introduced the sales manager to the Minister of Communications. First, there was a long wait in the outer office while people kept coming in and out. The sales manager looked at his watch, fidgeted, and finally asked whether the minister was really expecting him. The reply he received was scarcely reassuring, "Oh yes, he is expecting you but several things have come up that require his attention. Besides, one gets used to waiting down here." The sales manager irritably replied, "But doesn't he know I flew all the way down here from the United States to see him, and I have spent over a week already of my valuable time trying to find him?" "Yes, I know," was the answer, "but things just move much more slowly here."

At the end of about 30 minutes, the minister emerged from the office, greeted the commercial attaché with a *doble abrazo*, throwing his arms around him and patting him on the back as though they were long-lost brothers. Now, turning and smiling, the minister extended his hand to the sales manager, who, by this time, was feeling rather miffed because he had been kept in the outer office so long. After what seemed to be an all-too-short chat, the minister rose, suggesting a well-known café where they might meet for dinner the next evening. The sales manager expected, of course, that, considering the nature of their business and the size of the order, he might be taken to the minister's home, not realizing that the Latin home is reserved for family and very close friends.

Until now, nothing at all had been said about the reason for the sales manager's visit, a fact that bothered him somewhat. The whole setup seemed wrong; neither did he like the idea of wasting another day in town. He told the home office before he left that he would be gone for a week or 10 days at most and made a mental note that he would clean this order up in three days and enjoy a few days in Acapulco or Mexico City. Now the week had already gone and he would be lucky if he made it home in ten days. Voicing his misgivings to the commercial attaché, he wanted to know if the minister really meant business, and, if he did, why could they not get together and talk about it?

The commercial attaché by now was beginning to show the strain of constantly having to reassure the sales manager. Nevertheless, he tried again: "What you don't realize is that part of the time we were waiting, the minister was rearranging a very tight schedule so that he could spend tomorrow night with you. You see, down here they don't delegate responsibility the way we do in the States. They exercise much tighter control than we do. As a consequence, this man spends up to 15 hours a day at this desk. It may not look like it to you, but I assure you he really means business. He wants to give your company the order; if you play your cards right, you will get it."

The next evening provided more of the same. Much conversation about food and music, about many people the sales manager had never heard of. They went to a night club, where the sales manager brightened up and began to think that perhaps he and the minister might have something in common after all. It bothered him, however, that the principal reason for his visit was not even alluded to tangentially. But every time he started to talk about electronics, the commercial attaché would nudge him and proceed to change the subject.

The next meeting was for morning coffee at a café. By now the sales manager was having difficulty hiding his impatience. To make matters worse, the minister had a mannerism he did not like. When they talked, he was likely to put his hand on him; he would take hold of his arm and get so close that he almost "spat" in his face. As a consequence, the sales manager was kept busy trying to dodge and back up.

Following coffee, there was a walk in a nearby park. The minister expounded on the shrubs, the birds, and the beauties of nature, and at one spot he stopped to point at a statue and said: "There is a statue of the world's greatest hero, the liberator of mankind!" At this point the worst happened, for the sales manager asked who the statue represented and, being given the name of a famous Latin American patriot, said, "I never heard of him," and walked on.... The sales manager did not get the order.

Questions

1. It appears that the sales manager did not follow the commercial attaché's instructions. What do you believe were the attaché's instructions?
2. The sales manager was sent to a foreign country to negotiate a business contract. Discuss what should have been done before he or she was sent to the foreign country.

Source: Edward T. Hall, "The Silent Language in Overseas Business," *Harvard Business Review 3*, no. 3 (May–June 1960): 93–96. Copyright © 1960 by the President and Fellows of Harvard College. All rights reserved.

CASE 10-2

A Failed Cross-Cultural Negotiations Attempt

An Italian director of a construction company went to Germany to negotiate for a project. He began the discussion with a presentation of his company that vaunted its long history and its achievements. The German managers first looked startled, then bored, then they excused themselves and walked out the door, without even listening to the Italian manager's offer.

Questions

1. Discuss what you believe went wrong.

Source: Alex Blackwell, "Negotiating in Europe," *Hemispheres*, United Airlines (July 1994): 43.

CASE 10-3

The Long Printed Contract

There is a popular story making the rounds of Japanese business circles. So legalistic was the representative of an American candy company that he ruined his chances to establish a potentially profitable joint venture with a Japanese corporation. The product was a top-quality, prestige chocolate with a fine reputation already established in the United States. The goal was to establish a plush retail outlet on Tokyo's glittering Ginza. Many days were spent by the U.S. company's legal department in drawing up a lengthy, complete contract *before* their representative packed his bags for a trip to Tokyo. He was proud of the leather-bound, printed contract with almost 50 pages of fine print. No detail had been omitted. All that was lacking were the two signatures needed to launch the new enterprise.

With no knowledge of the Japanese language or culture, the U.S. representative faced a half dozen Japanese negotiators. He had a copy of the contract for each member of the Japanese team. But he was crushed when not one of them even opened the impressive legal document before them. Instead, a pleasant and inconclusive discussion of general business conditions in the two countries took up the whole afternoon. No decision on the proposed joint venture was made then—nor was the possibility ever discussed again.

Questions

1. Discuss what you believe went wrong.

Source: Arthur M. Whitehill, "American Executives Through Foreign Eyes," *Business Horizons* (May–June 1989): 46. Reprinted with permission.

CASE 10-4

Profitable Genuineness

Years ago, when I [Gunnar Beeth] was starting the European operations of an American company, I was considering appointing a popular general distributor for France. This family-held company was a leader in the industry and was located in the small town of Amboise in the Loire valley. My repeated letters and calls to them, though, did not produce a sufficiently large initial order.

So I went to see them. A long, heavy day's work in their offices with all their specialists, discussing packaging, branding, designs, advantages, prices, delivery, and competitors, did not produce the order. Despite my efforts, all I got was an invitation to dinner with the owner, *le patron*.

Even during dinner, my attempts to turn the conversation from wine, food, theater, liter-ature, and our families to business were waived away by *le patron*. I admit that with each bottle of wine my attempts grew feebler, while the conversation grew livelier and more inter-esting.

Questions

1. What must Beeth do to secure the order?

Source: Excerpted form Gunnar Beeth, "Multicultural Managers Wanted," *Management Review* (May 1997): 21. Copyright © 1997 American Management Association International. Reprinted by permission of American Management Association International, New York, NY. All rights reserved. http://www.amanet.org.

Notes

1. Excerpted form J.S.Black and H.B. Gregersen, "The Right Way to Manage Expats," *Harvard Business Review* (March–April 1999): 58.
2. M. Katherine Glover, "Do's and Taboos: Cultural Aspects of International Business," *Business America* (August 13, 1990): 3.
3. Adapted from R. Knotts, "Cross-Cultural Management: Transformations and Adaptations," *Business Horizons* (January–February 1989): 29–33.
4. This idea draws from Edward T. Hall, "How Cultures Collide," *Psychology Today* (July 1976): 67–74.
5. Glover, "Do's and Taboos," p. 3.
6. Edward T. Hall, "The Silent Language in Overseas Business," *Harvard Business Review* (May–June 1960): 87.
7. Ibid.
8. Mary Munter, "Cross-Cultural Communication for Managers," *Business Horizons* (May–June 1993): 77.
9. Hall, "The Silent Language," p. 90.
10. Ibid.
11. John Hill and Ronald Dulek, "A Miss Manners Guide to Doing Business in Europe," *Business Horizons* (July–August 1993): 50.
12. Hall, "The Silent Language," p. 90.
13. Amanda Mayer Stinchecum, "Everyone Gives at the Office," *World Traveler* (June 1997): 20.
14. Frederick H. Katayama, "How to Act Once You Get There," *Fortune* (Pacific Rim, 1989): 88.
15. Munter, "Cross-Cultural Communication for Managers," p. 77.
16. Hall, *Beyond Culture* (Garden City, NY: Doubleday, 1976).
17. Ibid.
18. Hall, "The Silent Language," p. 96.
19. Cindy P. Lindsay and Bobby L. Dempsey, "Ten Painfully Learned Lessons About Working in China: The Insights of Two American Behavioral Scientists," *Journal of Applied Behavioral Science* 19, no. 3 (1983): 265–276.
20. This discussion draws from Jon P. Alston, "Wa, Guanxi, and Inhwa: Managerial Principles in Japan, China, and Korea," *Business Horizons* 32, no. 2 (March–April 1989): 28–29.

21.Ibid., p. 29.

22.Paul Krugman, "Saving Asia: It's Time to Get Radical," *Fortune* (September 7, 1998).

23.Alston, "*Wa, Guanxi*, and *Inhwa*," p. 27.

24.Ibid.

25.Ibid., pp. 29–30.

26.Ibid.

27.See A. Bird, J.S. Ogland, M. Mendenhall, and S.C. Schneider, "Adapting and Adjusting to other Cultures: What We Know But Don't Always Tell," *Journal of Management Inquiry* 8, no. 2, (June 1999): 152–165.

28.Cited in June N. P. Francis, "When in Rome? The Effect of Cultural Adaptation on Intercultural Business Negotiations," *Journal of International Business Studies* (Third Quarter, 1991): 403–428.

29.Ibid.

30.Dean Allan Foster, *Bargaining Across Borders* (New York: McGraw-Hill, 1992), p. 5.

31.Ibid.

32.Stephen E. Weiss, "Negotiating With 'Romans'— Part 1," *Sloan Management Review* (Winter 1994): 52.

33.Hokey Min and William Galle, "International Negotiation Strategies of U.S. Purchasing Profes-

sionals," *International Journal of Purchasing and Materials Management* (Summer 1993): 43.

34.Trenholme J. Griffin and W. Russell Daggatt, *The Global Negotiator* (New York: Harper Business Publishers, 1990, p. 74.

35.Min and Galle, "International Negotiation Strategies," p. 42.

36.Robert O. Joy, "Cultural and Procedural Differences That Influence Business Strategies and Operations in the People's Republic of China," *SAM Advanced Management Journal* (Summer 1989): 31.

37.Griffin and Daggatt, *The Global Negotiator*, p. 77.

38.Min and Galle, "International Negotiation Strategies," p. 43.

39.Ibid., pp. 43–44.

40.Ibid.

41.Ibid., p. 44.

42.Hall, "The Silent Language," p. 93.

43.Shah M. Tarzi, "Third World Governments and Multinational Corporations: Dynamics of Host's Bargaining Power" (n.d., n.p.), p. 237.

44.Griffin and Daggatt, *The Global Negotiator*, p. 120.

45.Ibid., p. 106.

APPENDIX 10-1

Negotiating in Europe

The following are generalizations, based on expert opinion, about the negotiating style found in Europe's major markets:

Germany

In the preliminary stages of negotiations, German managers are often tough, cold, and impassive. They grill their prospective partners on all the technical aspects of their businesses, and it's bad luck for them if they don't have all the answers. "A mistake at this stage means that you're lost," comments cross-cultural negotiating consultant Prabhu Guptara, chairman of ADVANCE: Management Training Ltd. in London. Once the Germans are satisfied about technical matters, they begin to think they can trust the other negotiators. The difficulty at this point is to make German managers change their position. "At times they can stick to one point

and refuse to budge," says [Ann] Bengtsson [a management consultant based in Stockholm]. Still, consultants agree that German managers are, in general, quite practical at this stage. Finalizing a negotiation is not difficult with German mangers. However, it is important to know if the person you are dealing with has the authority to close the deal. Germans believe in "consensus management," comments [Vincent] Guy [a consultant specializing in international business communication with Canning International Management Development in London]. Patience may be required to get the final word.

Italy

Human relationships are most important here. Italian managers need to believe that they can get along as well with their foreign partners as they would with managers from Italian companies.

Initial negotiations with Italians can include a lot of idle talk and some chess playing. These preliminaries will last until they feel secure and comfortable. When they do, the negotiation process actually starts. But here the foreign businessperson may be baffled by circumlocutions: Italian managers may take ages to get to the point, Guptara points out. But be sure not to interrupt. As far as Italians are concerned, they are simply giving you the benefit of a complete understanding of their position. Concluding a negotiation with Italian managers can go quite quickly. But a surprise may be in store for the foreign manager because of the fluid nature of Italian corporate hierarchy. Titles mean relatively little in Italian companies, and very often the person who would normally have decision-making authority turns out to need approval. "Watch for someone sitting on the sidelines who's said nothing so far," warns Bengtsson. That person may leap into the fray at the end, make some changes, and then conclude the negotiation.

France

The French have their own way of doing most things, and negotiation is no exception. As a result, the French do not quite fit into the North-South dichotomy. The art of diplomatic negotiations was invented in France in the 14th century, and the French embrace that long tradition. Yet because French education stresses mathematics and logic, doing business is a highly intellectual process for French managers. "They see the negotiating process as a means to solve a logical problem," points out Robert Moran, professor of cross-cultural communication and international studies at the American Graduate School of International Management in Glendale, Arizona.

French managers will have carefully prepared for the negotiations, but they will generally begin with some light, logical sparring. "The French love discussion and often handle negotiating as though it were a debate," Moran adds. In general, French managers don't like to work on one point at a time. "They like to outline the entire structure of a potential agreement abstractly," explains Guptara. "Then they look at the details briefly, moving quickly from one to another." Throughout the preliminary and middle stages of negotiating, the French manager will judge the partners carefully on their intellectual skills, their ability to reply quickly and with authority. As one French businessman puts it, "sometimes I am more impressed by a brilliant sally than by a well-reasoned argument." But generally one has to be able to do both. Because the details come last in French negotiations, the finalizing stage can be very tricky. "French managers tend to slip in little extras when finalizing, like executive bonuses," comments Bengtsson. It's important to insist on what one wants at this stage and be prepared to refuse, even if days have been spent getting to this point.

Scandinavia

While it is always difficult to generalize about four separate nations like Norway, Sweden, Finland, and Denmark, consultants agree that the business culture is quite similar in these countries. Scandinavian managers tend to be frank, open, and relatively sincere. They like to get right down to work, and expect their partners to do the same. This makes the preliminary stages relatively brief, but the foreign manager should not confuse Scandinavian frankness with the easy establishment of a relationship of trust. "If the foreign manager becomes too friendly too quickly, the Scandinavian partner will construe this as weakness," comments Bengtsson. In fact, time must be taken to develop a real relationship. In the middle stages of negotiations, foreigners may be surprised to find a Scandinavian manager become inflexible, sticking to a technical point. "These are often not negotiable in Scandinavia," Guptara says. "It is best to research technical questions carefully beforehand to be prepared for the Scandinavian's reaction." After this stage, finalizing is usually relatively quick and simple.

Spain

Preliminaries to negotiations in Spain may take several days. The foreign businessperson may be asked to spend a day touring the city, having long meals, with business barely being mentioned. Here the establishment of a good, friendly relationship with a partner precedes all else. "It is very important not to appear impatient, not to seem in a hurry to get it over with," says Thorne. The foreigner should show interest in Spain and its culture without being unctuous. When finally the Spanish managers get down to business, the negotiation process can be elaborate and theatrical. "Sometimes a Spanish manager will just storm out of the room, right in the middle of negotiations," Bengtsson says.

One has to be prepared for long and complex discussions in the middle stages. It is important at this time to earn the respect of the Spanish manager with intelligence and straightforward replies. Finalizing can be difficult in Spain because of the strict hierarchy in Spanish companies. Approval may take a long time.

Britian

British managers tend to be curious negotiators. They are usually open in preliminary stages of negotiations, and they like to get down to work fairly quickly. They are very practical and well prepared. Yet in the middle stages of negotiations, British managers may become "a bit vague," Bengtsson points out. Sometimes they can become cagey about details, refusing to provide information. Here the foreign manager must be patient. Finalizing can be complex in Britain because it may take time and more negotiating to

get approval from the right people. Patience and tact are required in order to reach a conclusion.

The Netherlands

Dutch managers are generally among the most cosmopolitan of Europe's businesspeople, consultants agree. With a long history of trade, the Dutch are experienced at adapting to foreign cultures. They are likely to be familiar with customs in a foreigner's country and to change their negotiating style accordingly. It is possible to offend your Dutch partners, though. Beating around the bush and too much dallying will eventually make the Dutch manager annoyed and ultimately distrustful. The Dutch appreciate efficiency above all.

Eastern Europe

The countries of Eastern Europe are rapidly learning modern negotiation techniques, but it is too early to analyze cultural differences, Moran points out. These countries need to attract business from all the industrialized nations, and that makes the negotiating process somewhat special. The same general rules apply in Eastern Europe as they do in all international negotiations. Be polite, earn the trust and respect of the partner, and you will succeed. All the consultants agree that this approach applies everywhere in the world.

Source: Alex Blackwell, "Negotiating in Europe," *Hemispheres*, United Airlines (July 1994): 43–48. Reprinted with permission from *Hemispheres*, the inflight magazine of United Airlines, Pace Communications Inc., Greensboro, N.C. and the author.

███ **A P P E N D I X   1 0 - 2** ███

Asian Bargining Tactics

Westerners can enhance their negotiating power in Asia be recognizing a set of *strategic archetypes* used by Asian negotiators. Most Asian negotiators imitate military tactics developed in China thousands of years ago and passed down through mentor-apprentice relationships. Eight strategic archetypes are commonly encountered in Asia.

Strategy 1. Playing the Orphan

Use humility to make them haughty.–Sun Tzu Throughout Asia, one encounters business situations in which the Asian company claims to be weaker and more vulnerable than it really is. The Asian side claims it is a small or backward company in order to elicit sympathy in the form of concessions. This seems odd to North American executives who typically try to convince a negotiating partner that their company is large and powerful. Sun Tzu taught: "Even though you are competent, appear to be incompetent." Sun Tzu's commentator, Mei Yaochen, elaborated: "Give the appearance of inferiority and weakness, to make [your enemy] proud."

Asians may open a negotiation by dwelling on their company's vulnerabilities, small size, and other feigned weaknesses to swell Westerners' confidence and induce them to ask for less in return for the concessions that the Westerners are prepared to request. Some Westerners might think the orphan strategy is an expression of Asian humility. Instead, it often conceals a hidden agenda. For example, a claim of weakness is soon followed by a request that the foreign side ease its credit terms to lighten the financial burden on the Asian side. Or, the Asians demand conciliatory "favors" outside the contract.

Strategy 2. Team-Driven Intelligence Gathering

Comparisons give rise to victories. –Sun Tzu By the comparisons of measurements, you know

where victory and defeat lie," Cao advises in *The Art of War.* What Asian counterparts can find out about a Western company will be used against the company during negotiations—how large or small the company is, what sort of technological know-how it possesses, and the tone of its financial muscle. A concerted effort may be underway to transfer to the Asian side as much of the company's know-how as possible, free of charge.

Westerners who have negotiated in Asia report that Asians value detail in formulating their business decisions; they consider information gathering to be the heart of a negotiation. However, what they call a "know-how exchange" often becomes "information rape," with the Asian side planning to reverse-engineer a Western product from the outset of collaboration with the firm. The effort will be a concerted team objective. If Western negotiators are not on guard against it, their firm is likely to find itself the victim of information rape.

The Asians' objective of sharing in a company's know-how without paying for it may be partially cultural in origin. In Asia, no notion of proprietary know-how took root; new technology was shared by all. Knowledge was kept public, and to imitate or adopt someone else's methodology was considered virtuous, and a great compliment to the person who created it. Borrowing another person's expertise was considered neither thievery nor unethical. The Japanese have long conducted a policy of "selective borrowing" from foreigners. Industrial Japan borrowed extensively from the West and adapted Western production and quality control techniques to its own needs.

All of this is *not* to suggest that Asia hasn't developed technologies on its own; its well-known inventions through the centuries have had dramatic effects on all of civilization. Today, technological innovations travel back and forth across the Pacific with amazing frequency. The flow of innovation, however, is moving faster toward the East than toward the West. Japanese companies, for example, purchased over half of American high-technology firms that were sold during a 30-month period from 1989 to 1991, according to a study by the Economic Strategy Institute, a Washington think tank. Increasingly, North American corporations have found it necessary to forge "strategic alliances" with Asian companies (mostly Japanese) in order to acquire know-how from Asia, rather than vice versa. Facilitating the flow of technical information and human know-how has proven easier said than done.

Strategy 3. The Haughty Buyer

The customer is God. Sellers of products and services in the West defer to their buyers to some degree, but sellers and buyers ultimately deal with one another as social equals. Not so in Asia: buyers and sellers differ fundamentally in social status.

In North America, buyers and sellers maintain a somewhat adversarial relationship; in order to get a lower price, buyers ask vendors to bid against each other, and sellers seek out those buyers who will pay a premium price. When monetary advantage can be found elsewhere, buyers have few qualms about terminating their relationship with a seller. Business is business.

In much of Asia, however, buyers and sellers forge long-term bonds of trust and partnership. Sellers tend to respond to every wish and whim of their buyers. In Japan, and increasingly in Korea, as well as in other parts of Asia, the customer is not only king, but God. Asian buyers look after their suppliers in ways their North American counterparts do not.

Asian sellers tend to *overserve* their buyers because they can trust them to stay loyal if times get tough. A buyer might pay an above-market price, find a seller new customers, and even help [protect] the seller's business from foreign competitors. In Japan, the relationship between buyer and seller is based on *amae* (a paternalistic, dependent relationship). Paternalistic buyer-seller bonds are hard to break, especially for a newcomer in the market.

Westerners' typical unwillingness to accept the lower-status position of suppliers in Asia and to enter into paternalistic relationships with buyers is a primary reason, though not the sole one, that American executives often hear their potential Asian customers say, "We'll contact you when we are prepared to buy," which means, "Thanks anyway." Asian buyers are not exactly "haughty" as part of a strategy; they are demanding, and possibly condescending, because of conditioning.

To sell, Westerners may have to enter *amae* relationships and accept the lower status. They have to satisfy what they may consider unreasonable demands such as fast delivery, costly product modifications, and strictly enforced quality specifications. Some companies have not survived the rigorous requirements of being sellers in Asia. Still, there are ways to reach arrangements that will satify both sides.

Strategy 4. Outlasting the Enemy

It is easy to take over from those who have not thought ahead. –Li Quan in *The Art of War* Asian negotiations can, as the Chinese saying goes, be like "grinding a rod down to a needle." When the Taoist concept of *wu wei* (nonassertion) is applied to business negotiation, the strategy is to seek long-term success through minimal short-term effort: state a position and wait, hoping that opponents will yield on concessions in order to close the deal. Time is *not* money for Asian negotiators; it's a weapon.

Asian negotiators often open a negotiation, extend an invitation to visit their country, supply some technical information, and dedicate time and resources to forging an agreement. Unfortunately, the final contract remains elusive. Some Japanese investors, according to a number of American real estate developers I know, will sit down with them and sign on for a mutually beneficial deal, but problems set in at the last minute, when they balk and push for concessions. Then they initiate delay tactics, all the while pushing for more and more concessions in the gray areas of the contract. The foreign side often gives in because a costly delay may jeopardize firm financial commitments.

When Asian negotiators use delay tactics that push foreigners to the brink of anger, they may be seeking more than concessions. They may be testing the Westerners' commitment to a deal or their accountability. They may want to clarify the unequal status between buyer and seller. By delaying, they send a message that their interest may be waning; the Westerners may weaken in their resolve to hold out for a stated price.

I've seen this strategy used on youthful foreigners (myself included) as a way of testing their will and trying to intimidate them—to put them in their youthful place. Another possible reason for delay is that an Asian wants to kill a deal without losing face and hopes that the Westerner will take a hint and walk away as a friend, not a frustrated foe.

Strategy 5. Hidden Identities

The inscrutable win, the obvious lose. –Du Mu in *The Art of War* In the city of Hefei, in China's Anhui Province, I came across two Canadian representatives of a water purification equipment company. They were to have an important meeting with local import officials the following morning in the conference room at our hotel.

I met them the next day as they emerged confidently from their meeting. I also recognized a past acquaintance, the leading official from the Ministry of Foreign Economic Relations and Trade. After he left the hotel, I complimented the Canadians on obtaining a meeting with such a prominent official and suggested that this official's presence indicated significant interest in the water purification system on the part of the Chinese.

"Who, him?" one of the Canadians blurted. "He said he was just our interpreter for the meeting!"

This high official had concealed his true identity in order to eavesdrop on the Canadians in the guise of an interpreter. They had been burned by the hidden identity strategy.

Although a meeting in Asia usually begins with an exchange of business cards and handshakes, the true identities of the real decision makers on the Asian negotiating team may

remain unknown—sometimes indefinitely. Ascertaining precisely who the key players are and how much influence they wield is difficult because some persons may vanish and later reappear at a banquet or sightseeing excursion.

The hidden identity strategy may also involve sudden changes among the Asian side's negotiating personnel. The number of Asian negotiators may swell over time, while the foreign side generally depends on the same team throughout. Being forced to defend a proposal before a new team can be maddening or can lead to making extra concessions or giving up some that have already been won. More innocently, the Asian negotiator whom the company hosted in the West for a factory visit and a side trip to Disneyland may have suddenly moved to another division of the Asian company. All the concessions won with him are now gone, and the process must start all over again with a new negotiator. In China, this problem has been exacerbated by the massive reorganization that has taken place since the Tiananmen Square massacre.

It would be unfair to Asians, however, not to mention that the same problem occurs in North America for different reasons. With the constant merging of North American companies and the high turnover of their executives, whether through departure, relocation, or promotion, the appearance of new negotiators can be difficult and disconcerting for Asians who desire to forge long-term, ongoing relationships with Western companies.

Strategy 6. The Trust Game

Honey in mouth but dagger in heart. –Chinese saying A well-known American cable television company recently signed a deal with a comparable cable network in Taiwan. The agreement was based on a royalty to be paid by the Taiwanese company to the U.S. company for each television show aired. To guarantee its 10 percent share, the American company requested that the contract enable it to periodically view the Taiwanese company's accounting books.

The president of the Taiwanese company took the request as a grave insult. He was livid and nixed the entire deal, which had taken months to put together. "The American company is implying that we are liars," he railed. "If the Americans can't trust us, then we won't trust them!"

The irony is that *most* Taiwanese companies (this one included) keep two, or even three, sets of books, and a demand to have the accounting records made public in a deal of this size would be reasonable anywhere else in the world.

As part of what I call the trust game, the Asian doesn't want to trust the Westerner but reacts negatively to any suggestion that the mistrust is mutual. Asians may even purposefully personalize negotiations in order to give Westerners a feeling that trust has been generated, and thus lure them into a deal; Westerners may find they are being called "old friend" at the second meeting. The Asian side's personalization of the negotiation may be a good thing for the long-term relationship between the two companies. However, it may be merely a tactic to obtain proprietary information about the firm—its size and past endeavors, the price and marketability of its products, its experience in Asia, and so on. Trust has to work both ways.

The trust game in Asia can be especially brutal on "middlemen" and firms that share their technology. "When the hares have been killed, the hounds are cooked," as the Chinese say. That is, the middlemen are discarded once they have fulfilled their purpose. I recommend that middlemen sign a bomb-proof contract with the manufacturer they represent, guaranteeing them total exclusivity to represent the product in Asia. They should conclude the contract before they disseminate information or quote prices of equipment among potential Asian customers.

Often Asian customers will contact the manufacturer directly and attempt to cut the middlemen out. The motive may not be to avoid paying an added commission, but simply to forge a relationship directly with the manufacturer and get closer to its technology.

In another trust game, the Asian side signs a "symbolic agreement." The Asians win over the Western firm by signing a well-drafted contract but then fail to *implement* what they have agreed

to do. Some Asians may sign a "symbolic contract" knowing full well that governing bodies with oversight of the venture will not accept the conditions of the deal. Requests for major revisions in the contract arrive soon after.

A recent case in Korea involved the purchase of agricultural goods from the United States. The goods were refused by Korean Customs. The Korean customer had guaranteed that the government would enact a regulation allowing the import of the goods long before the contract was signed. Unfortunately, the Korean government was unwilling to enact the law. The deal died, along with a shipment of perishable product.

Strategy 7. Sacrifice Something Small for Something Big

Cast a brick to attract a piece of jade. –Chinese saying In this strategy, Asian counterparts attempt to trick Westerners into trading something significant for something insignificant. An Indonesian or Chinese joint venture partner might assure a Western company of access to a large untapped market or offer unlimited numbers of inexpensive workers in exchange for cash, technology, and worker training.

Many gullible Westerners have fallen victim to this strategy, believing the numbers that appear in feasibility studies presented by the Asians. The market may be both smaller than the numbers claim *and* quite inaccessible despite promises of access. The building space and land offered may appear to be a real break but could cost a fortune to upgrade.

Some Asian managers wish to connect with a foreign firm to gain the benefits that accrue to an Asian factory that forges a joint venture with a foreign company. In China, for example, these benefits can include the right to hire and fire workers, the unilateral right to buy imports without government approval, and the right to pay more to workers than regular Chinese enterprises can, thus allowing the manager to attract more workers with higher skills.

Some foreign companies have been asked by Chinese enterprises to form a joint venture but to station only one foreign manager in China—an easy way for the Chinese enterprise to enjoy the benefits of being a "foreign-invested enterprise." They sign a contract to manufacture and sell a foreign product, but the interests of the foreign partner become secondary to their own the moment the contract is signed.

A weak Asian company can obtain a new lease on life by merging with an unsuspecting, richer foreign partner. Even a near-bankrupt Asian company gains leverage over its Asian competitors by becoming a partner of a large foreign company. "If you forge alliances with strong partners, your enemies won't dare plot against you," Cheng Shi comments in *The Art of War*. For the foreign company, having an Asian partner with this objective usually leads to disaster.

Strategy 8. The Shotgun Approach

Foreign business negotiators most often experience the "shotgun approach offer" when dealing with individual overseas Chinese entrepreneurs (briefcase companies); their locale is just about all of Asia except Japan and Korea. The Westerners begin by presenting a product for sale to the Asian side, and within minutes they find themselves talking about transferring technology, transferring a management model, and setting up a manufacturing joint venture in Asia. They have been lured off course by the "shotgun strategy."

We don't need to dwell long on this tactic; most of us have dealt with it in some form on our home turf. Chinese Malay business people might negotiate like the proverbial used car salesmen of the West; they want a deal, any deal, *now*. Owners of Asian "trading companies" tend to work alone and to negotiate as individual (one-person) companies.

They start by saying, "I can get you anything in Asia that you want. Bamboo furniture, tropical fish, orchids, anything. My brother has an orchid farm near Kuala Lumpur, you know." "Okay, okay," you say, "let's concentrate on orchids. Can you get 8,000 stems by February?"

"Well, I don't know, 8,000 is a lot of orchids. Let me call my brother. Maybe we start slow with about 200 per week."

Your expected sigh only triggers another onslaught.

"We should grow orchids here! Set up a greenhouse. Start small. Big profit. You make a mint. Why didn't you guys think of it? It'll be like having the right to print money!"

You sigh again and balk at the whole idea of collaborating at all.

These dealmakers try to make Westerners feel guilty about not trusting them. In fact, the obstacle in the negotiation is that they can't perform what they originally claimed they could do. Wise Westerners stay polite and collected, and they keep communication lines open. Getting irate is the only sin that Westerners can commit in dealing with these "pushy" overseas Chinese: it robs Westerners of face and gets their name around as a company to avoid.

Source: Excerpted from Christopher Engholm, "Asian Bargaining Tactics: Counter Strategies for Survival," *East Asian Executive Reports* (July 1992): 9, 22–25 and (August 1992): 10–13. Copyright © 1992, International Executive Reports, Ltd. and Christopher Engholm. Reprinted with permisssion. All rights reserved.

VI

Cross-Cultural Coordination

Some managers make decisions participatively; they involve those subordinates who will be affected by the decision in the decision-making process. Others make decisions authoritatively; instead of involving subordinates who will be affected by the decision, they make the decision by themselves. One theory posits that a manager's approach is influenced by national culture. Another theory is that the approach is influenced by specific situations in all cultures. These theories are discussed in Chapter 11. American-based theories posit that participative leadership behavior produces better results than authoritative behavior. However, in many cultures, authoritative behavior produces better results. Culture also has an effect on employee motivation. In some cultures, employees are motivated by the opportunity to obtain challenging work, but in other cultures, they are motivated by the opportunity to socialize. Cross-cultural leadership and motivation are discussed in Chapter 12.

11

Cross-Cultural Decision Making

Bosses in France tend to be Napoleonic. They are, as a rule, graduates of one of the elite Grands Ecoles and are expected to be brilliant technical planners, equally adept at industry, finance, and government. They can be vulnerable to surprise when the troops below fail to respond to orders from on high. Stiff hierarchies in big firms discourage informal relations and reinforce a sense of "them" and "us." Managers in Italy tend to be more flexible. Firms' rules and regulations (where they exist) are often ignored. Informal networks of friends and family contacts matter instead. Decision making tends to be more secretive than elsewhere, and what goes on in a meeting is often less important than what happens before and after.[1]

Learning Objectives of the Chapter

In essence, every aspect of management (planning, organizing, staffing, coordinating, and controlling), in one form or another, involves decision making. Decision making is thus the manager's most difficult task, and when managers cross national borders and cultures, the task becomes even more difficult. This is because people in different cultures view problems differently and apply unique decision-making processes. (For illustrations, read Practical Perspectives 11-1 and 11-2.) **A decision or a decision-making process that works in one culture is often ineffective in another culture.** Furthermore, different situations also require different decision-making styles. After studying this chapter, you should be able to discuss:

1. The decision-making process in a cross-cultural context.

PRACTICAL PERSPECTIVE 11-1

Choosing a Local Manager in Russia

In choosing a general manager [in Russia], Western companies are often misled by the false conventional wisdom that insists there never was such a thing as effective Soviet management. Considering the enormous handicaps imposed on them by perennial shortages and centralized command and control, the general managers of many Soviet enterprises accomplished wonders. These managers still have no training in Western management theory and practice, of course, but their own Russian management style, deeply rooted in the resilient culture of the Russian *mir*, or collective, has its own considerable strengths. For example, Russian executives are often strong personal leaders who practice hands-on, walk-around, face-to-face management. They develop direct bonds of loyalty with employees at all levels. They also practice a unique form of decision making that combines consultation and command by alternating periods of open, widespread discussion of options with moments of strong, top-down authority in making final decisions.

Source: P. Lawrence and C. Vlachoutsicos, "Joint Ventures in Russia: Put Locals in Charge," *Harvard Business Review* (January–February 1993): 45.

2. The differing cultural factors that affect managers' decision-making style, authoritative/consultative or participative.

3. The varying environmental factors/situations that affect the decision-making style.

THE DECISION-MAKING PROCESS: A CROSS-CULTURAL PERSPECTIVE

When making decisions, managers in organizations apply either a programmed or a nonprogrammed decision-making process. Both processes are affected by the culture of the society in which the decision is being made. For example, managers in countries with relatively low tolerance for ambiguity, such as Japan and Germany, avoid nonprogrammed decisions as much as possible by using standard operating procedures (programmed decision making). Operating manuals in organizations in these cultures tend to be relatively thick. In contrast, managers in countries with relatively high tolerance for ambiguity, such as the United States and Norway, seek responsibility for nonprogrammed decision making.[2]

The Programmed Decision-Making Process

The programmed decision-making process, which is by far the most commonly used in organizations, entails making decisions based on precedent,

PRACTICAL PERSPECTIVE 11-2

The Quiet Indonesian

Machmud had recently been promoted to a position of authority and was asked to represent his company and Indonesia's needs at the head office in Butte, Montana. Relationships with fellow workers seemed cordial but rather formal from his perspective. He was invited to attend many policy and planning sessions with other company officials where he often sat, rather quietly, as others generated ideas and engaged in conversation. The time finally came when the direction the company was to take in Indonesia was to be discussed. A meeting was called to which Machmud was invited to attend. As the meeting was drawing to a close after almost two hours of discussion, Machmud, almost apologetically, offered a suggestion—his first contribution to any meeting. Almost immediately, John Stewart, a local vice president, said, "Why did you wait so long to contribute? We needed your comments all along." Machmud felt that Stewart's reply was harsh. In Indonesia, the group often comes before any action of the individual. Machmud was acting as one would in a meeting in his home country. Rather than standing out as an idea-person seeking attention, suggestions are often quickly presented toward the close of a meeting, with hope that little attention will be paid to the originator of the idea.

Source: Excerpted from R.W. Brislin et al., *Intercultural Interactions: A Practical Guide*, vol. 9 (Newbury Park, CA: Sage Publications, 1986), pp. 169, 185. Copyright © 1986, Sage Publications, Inc. Reprinted with permission. All rights reserved.

custom, policies and procedures, and training and development. An advantage of this approach is that the basis for a decision can be pretested for efficiency, which reduces risk and stress for decision makers ("I followed the procedures manual," "I did it the way it is supposed to be done," or "I did it the way it has always been done"). A disadvantage of this approach is that when the organization's environment changes, the programmed bases for decision making often become obsolete and ineffective, which can lead to decision-making ineffectiveness. Of course, some of the advantages and disadvantages are culturally determined. For example, people in some cultures do not like too much challenge; they prefer a structured environment that provides certainty and become frustrated in ambiguous, challenging situations. People in other cultures prefer challenge and become bored in an environment that provides too much structure. (This will be discussed in more detail later in this chapter.)

The Nonprogrammed Decision-Making Process

The **nonprogrammed decision-making process** entails analyzing current data and information, obtained through a systematic investigation of the current environment, for the purpose of identifying and solving a problem.

Two approaches to this process are rational decision making and "satisficing."

The Rational Decision-Making Process

In Western culture, the steps in the rational decision-making process are as follows: (1) through investigation, define the problem; (2) identify a set of minimum criteria on which to base the decision; (3) identify multiple viable choices; (4) quantitatively, evaluate each viable choice on the basis of each criterion; (5) select the optimum choice, the one with the highest quantitative value, and (6) implement the choice. In Western cultures, the "ideal" decision model thus presumes an optimum choice among viable alternatives.

The Satisficing Decision-Making Process

The satisficing approach assumes that there is an incompleteness of information; that is, decision makers do not possess the information necessary to optimize.[3] Therefore, they *satisfice*; they select the first choice that meets some minimum criteria, that is, the first choice that is "good enough." They do not identify multiple viable choices. An advantage of satisficing over the rational approach is that it is quicker and thus less expensive. A disadvantage is that you may be foregoing a better solution.

The Impact of Culture on Nonprogrammed Decision Making

The validity of the nonprogrammed decision-making process as a prescription for decision-making behavior is affected by culture. Culture has been defined as "the interactive aggregate of common characteristics that influence a group's response to its environment."[4] Since the characteristics vary from group to group, people in different cultures are likely to have different preferences for a certain state of affairs, for specific social processes, and for "general rules for selective attention, interpretation of environmental cues, and responses."[5] As such, people in different cultures view and react to problems differently. What is rational in one culture may be irrational in another, and vice versa. In a broad context, we do not know whose views are right.[6] Presented below are some examples of how contrasting views affect the decision-making process.

Problem Recognition

The master-of-destiny and fatalistic cultural concepts described in Chapter 1 affect problem definitions. Managers in **master-of-destiny cultures** tend to perceive most situations as problems to be solved, and they seek improvement through change. On the other hand, managers in **fatalistic societies** tend to accept situations as they are, and they do not seek improvement or change; they believe that fate or God's will intervene in decision making.

The United States society is an example of the master-of-destiny culture, and Indonesia an example of a fatalistic society.[7] American decision makers would thus act more quickly on a problem than would Indonesian decision makers.

Criteria

Some cultures possess a "collective" orientation (discussed in Chapter 1 and to be discussed later on in this chapter as "low individualism") and some, an "individualistic" orientation (also discussed in Chapter 1 and to be discussed later on in this chapter as "high individualism"). The collectivist orientation implies that individuals in the culture possess a group orientation; they emphasize group objectives in arriving at decisions, the rights of both current and future generations, and group harmony and discipline. In contrast, the individualistic orientation implies emphasizing the functional definition of relationships, utilitarianism in problem solving, a shorter time perspective, and the freedom to choose and compete.[8] Decision makers in the two cultures are thus likely to use different criteria to make a decision. For example, collectivist decision makers may use maintaining group harmony as the major criterion on which to base the decision; in contrast, individualistic decision makers may use cost-benefit as the major criterion (evident in the United States, an individualistic society).

Information Gathering

As pointed out in Chapter 1, decision makers in some cultures rely on "hard facts" and data as bases for a decision. The nonprogrammed approach to decision making would therefore be applied in these cultures. In many cultures, however, decision makers do not place a high premium on factual information and data; instead, they rely more on their instincts as a basis for decision making. Since decision makers in these cultures rely on their intuition, they would not be highly receptive to the application of the nonprogrammed decision-making process.

Choice and Implementation

In some cultures, such as the United Kingdom and Canada, the choice and implementation tactics are determined either by the highest-ranking member of the decision-making team or by a majority vote. But in collectivist cultures, such as Japan and Africa, to maintain **harmony** and unity, decisions are made by **consensus**. When group consensus is required, decisions normally take a long time to make. The process of obtaining consensus is often more important than the choice itself. In contrast, choice and implementation decisions in individualistic societies are normally made quickly because decision makers tend to be autocratic and make decisions by themselves. (The ensuing sections will discuss this more thoroughly.) Furthermore, decision makers in individualistic cultures are likely to select the most economically efficient choice. On the other hand, decision makers in collectivist societies are likely to select a choice that does not offend members of the group. Thus, in troubles times, an American corporation might lay-off employees as a way of dealing with the problem, whereas a Japanese corporation would not—it would seek to maintain group harmony and therefore seek other solutions.

In some cultures, decision makers are very methodical, and they carefully evaluate numerous alternative choices before making a selection; in other cultures, decision makers use an incremental approach—they discuss alternatives in a preplanned sequence, making decisions as they go along. Furthermore, as will also be discussed in the ensuing sections, individuals in some cultures take greater risks than individuals in other cultures. For instance, in deciding on a foreign market entry strategy, decision makers in the lower-risk-taking cultures may select the safer exporting approach; decision makers in the higher-risk-taking cultures may select a riskier approach, such as producing abroad.

DECISION-MAKING BEHAVIOR: AUTHORITATIVE OR PARTICIPATIVE?

Decision makers use two basic types of decision-making behavior: authoritative and participative. Decision makers using **authoritative behavior** decide alone what is to be done and/or how it is to be done and tell subordinates; however, they may consult their subordinates about decisions before they finalize them. Using **participative behavior**, decision makers ask their subordinates what should be done and/or how it should be done, and together they reach an agreement and/or a consensus. Both approaches have advantages and disadvantages.

An advantage of the authoritative approach is that decisions can be made quickly. A disadvantage, however, is that not involving the subordinates in the decision-making process can lead to their demoralization, which often leads to decision sabotage and slow implementation. An advantage of the participative approach is that it can lead to greater subordinate satisfaction and performance, especially when participation makes work more challenging for them, and the multiple input obtained from the subordinates can result in higher quality decisions than those made authoritatively by one person. A disadvantage is that the decision process can take too long, although this disadvantage can be offset by the decision-making not being sabotaged and therefore being implemented more quickly.

Management theorist Rensis Likert has hypothesized that authoritative decision making leads to "mediocre" organizational performance, consultative to "good" organizational performance, and participative to "high levels of productivity."[9] It should be noted, however, that the concept of authoritative or participative decision-making behavior is explained from a Western cultural perspective. Some cultures may not even possess such a perspective. In other words, many concepts are not readily transferrable across cultures. For example, many people in Western cultures perceive the authoritarian decision maker in a negative way: "Who made him/her king/queen?" But in some cultures, the same decision-making behavior is perceived favorably: "By dictating to me, he or she is communicating God's will to me, so I feel good."

Furthermore, many Westerners perceive participative decision-making behavior positively. In many cultures, however, it is **perceived negatively**: "He or she is asking me what I think…. Doesn't he or she know how to do his or her job? It's not my responsibility to make decisions." In these cultures, the participative decision maker loses credibility in the eyes of subordinates and may even frustrate and demoralize them. For example, in their study of Mexican workers in a Mexican plant and of American workers in a U.S. plant, cross-cultural management researchers T. Morris and C.M. Pavett concluded that U.S. management systems do not have to be applied in the Mexican plant to extract the same level of production as in the U.S. plant. They found that the management systems used in the two plants

> *reflect some of the salient cultural differences between the U.S. and Mexico. Americans have been characterized as less accepting of authority, autocratic decision making, and unequal power distributions [to be discussed in the ensuing sections] than are people of Mexico…. Mexican workers are characterized as expecting an authority figure to make decisions and assume responsibility.*[10]

It should be noted that in applying participative decision making, some managers apply the management by objectives (MBO) approach, while others apply the *ringi* approach. The use of these approaches is also dictated by culture. The major features of a typical MBO program are as follows:[11]

1. Manager and subordinate meet and together set objectives for subordinate.

2. Manager and subordinate attempt to establish realistic, challenging, clear, and comprehensive objectives related to organizational and personal needs.

3. Criteria for measuring and evaluating the objectives are agreed upon by both the manager and the subordinate.

4. The manager and the subordinate establish review dates when objectives will be reexamined.

5. The manager plays less the role of a judge and jury and more of a coach, counselor, and supporter.

6. The overall process depends on results accomplished and counseling subordinates, and not on activities, errors, and organizational requirements.

7. After establishing goals and objectives and identifying the activities necessary to accomplish them, subordinates are allowed to pursue

their goals and objectives essentially in their own manner. However, as indicated above, there are periodic reviews by the manager. The subordinate also reviews his or her own progress.

Many decision makers, especially in Japanese organizations, use a group-oriented consensus building process known as *ringi* to establish objectives. The *ringi* participative approach is as follows:[12]

1. All subordinates who are to be involved in the execution of the decision must have the opportunity to voice their views.

2. The manager meets with the group responsible for carrying out the decision.

3. During the meetings, all issues are considered and all members of the group contribute to the discussion of options, facts, and philosophy underlying the decision. Therefore, when a decision is reached, everyone involved knows what he or she must do. And because everyone has agreed to the decision, its execution can proceed quickly.

The MBO process is likely to work best in "individualistic" cultures such as the United States, where individuals tend to prefer to work on their own, and the *ringi* process is likely to work best in group-oriented, "collectivist" cultures such as Japan, where people tend to like to work in groups.

Subordinates' views on how they should be used in the decision-making process vary from culture to culture, as do managers' views. For example, French executives tend to assume that the authority to make decisions is a given right of office and a privilege of rank, and therefore they make decisions authoritatively. On the other hand, executives in the Netherlands, Scandinavia, and the United Kingdom expect their decisions to "be challenged, discussed or, more probably, made on a consultative, group basis in the first place."[13]

Which approach works best? It is, as suggested above, contingent on many factors. The aim of the ensuing sections is to explain the concept of **contingency decision-making behavior.** Different situations and cultures require dissimilar behavior, and decision makers therefore have to be flexible in their decision-making style when confronted with varying situations and when crossing national boundaries and cultures. Failure to apply the right decision-making behavior will result in ineffective decisions, which in turn will make the enterprise less competitive in the global economy.

DECISION-MAKING BEHAVIOR: TWO CONTINGENCY FRAMEWORKS

Decision makers who are not bound to just one approach or style are often confronted with the problem of determining which decision-making behavior (DMB)—authoritative/consultative or participative—is applicable in a given situation. Using several existing theories, concepts, and research findings, the ensuing sections develop two contingency DMB frameworks that can assist cross-cultural managers in determining the appropriate DMB for specific situations and cultures. The first framework, labeled the **country-related cultural factors framework**, identifies certain national cultural dimensions and their impact on DMB. This framework is **"culture-specific"**; it assumes that different societies possess distinct and relatively stable cultures that serve as determinants of the DMB.[14] The second contingency framework, labeled the universal factors model, identifies various situations and their impact on DMB. This model is **"culture-free"**; it assumes that certain situational factors have an impact on DMB in all cultures.[15]

The Country-Related Cultural Factors Framework

A key study used in developing *the country-related cultural factors framework* was conducted by Professor Geert Hofstede. Hofstede developed a typology consisting of four national cultural dimensions by which a society can be classified: power distance, uncertainty avoidance, individualism, and masculinity.[16] (These were discussed in Chapter 1.) As pointed out in Chapter 1, Hofstede and his colleague, Michael Bond, subsequently identified a fifth dimension, labeled the *Confucian dynamism* dimension.[17] The ensuing section describe these five cultural dimensions and discuss whether DMB tends to lean toward authoritative/consultative or participative (see Table 11-1). Table 11-2 lists the 50 countries included in Hofstede's study and their cultural classifications as well as the Confucian measure for 18 of the 50 countries.

TABLE 11-1	The Country-Related Cultural Factors Model	

Factors	DMB>
Large power distance	A
Small power distance	P
Low individualism	A
High individualism:	
Employees show low concern for organization's well-being	A
Employees show high concern for organization's well-being	P
Strong uncertainty avoidance	A
Weak uncertainty avoidance	P
Confucianism	A
High masculinity	A
Low masculinty	P

DMB> = Decision-making behavior leaning toward

A = Authoritative; P = Participative

TABLE 11-2	Cultural Profile of Fifty Countries				
Country	**PD**	**IN**	**MA**	**UA**	**CF**
Argentina	LG*	LO	ST	ST	—
Australia	SM	HI	ST	WK*	LO
Austria	SM	HI	ST	ST	—
Belgium	LG	HI	ST*	ST	—
Brazil	LG	LO	ST*	ST	HI
Canada	SM	HI	ST*	WK	LO
Chile	LG	LO	WK	ST	—
Colombia	LG	LO	ST	ST	—
Costa Rica	SM	LO	WK	ST	—
Denmark	SM	HI	WK	WK	—
Ecuador	LG	LO	ST	ST	—
Finland	SM	HI	WK	ST*	—
France	LG	HI	WK*	ST	—
Germany	SM	HI	ST	ST	LO
Great Britain	SM	HI	ST	WK	LO
Greece	LG	LO	ST	ST	—
Guatemala	LG	LO	WK*	ST	—
Hong Kong	LG	LO	ST	WK	HI
Indonesia	LG	LO	WK*	WK	—
India	LG	LO	ST	WK	HI
Iran	LG	LO	WK*	ST*	—
Ireland	SM	HI	ST	WK	—
Israel	SM	HI	ST*	ST	—
Italy	LG*	HI	WK*	ST	—
Jamaica	LG*	LO	ST	WK	—
Japan	LG	LO	ST	ST	HI
Korea (S.)	LG	LO	WK*	ST	HI
Malaysia	LG	LO	ST*	WK	—
Mexico	LG	LO	ST	ST	—
Netherlands	SM*	HI	WK	WK*	HI*
Norway	SM	HI	WK	WK	—
New Zealand	SM	HI	ST	WK	LO
Country	PD	IN	MA	UA	CF
Pakistan	LG	LO	ST*	ST	LO
Panama	LG	LO	WK*	ST	—
Peru	LG	LO	WK*	ST	—
Philippines	LG	LO	WK	WK	LO
Portugal	LG	LO	WK*	ST	—
So. Africa	LG*	HI	ST	WK	—
Salvador	LG	LO	WK*	ST	—

TABLE 11-2	Cultural Profile of Fifty Countries, *continued*				
Country	PD	IN	MA	UA	CF
Singapore	LG	LO	WK*	WK	HI
Spain	LG	HI	WK*	ST	—
Sweden	SM	HI	WK	WK	LO
Switzerland	SM	HI	ST	ST*	—
Taiwan	LG	LO	WK*	ST	HI
Thailand	LG	LO	WK	ST*	HI
Turkey	LG	LO	WK*	ST	—
Uruguay	LG	LO	WK*	ST	—
United States	SM*	HI	ST	WK	LO
Venezuela	LG	LO	ST	ST	—
Yugoslavia	LG	LO	WK	ST	—

PD = Power Distance; IN = Individualism; MA = Masculinity;

UA = Uncertainty Avoidance; CF = Confucianism

LG = Large; SM = Small; HI = High; LO = Low;

ST = Strong; WK = Weak

* But near the line that divides the two extremes.

Note: The PD, IN, MA, and UA dimensions are adopted from Geert Hofstede, "The Cultural Relativity of the Quality of Life Concept," *Academy of Management Review 9*, no. 3 (1984): 391–393. The CF dimension is adopted from G. Hofstede and M.H. Bond, "The Confucius Connection: From Cultural Roots To Economic Growth," *Organizational Dynamics* (Spring 1988): 12–13. This study categorized only 18 countries.

DMB as a Factor of the Country's Power Distance

As indicated in Chapter 1, Hofstede found that some of the countries included in his study are classified by a **moderate-to-large power distance** cultural dimension. Individuals dominated by this dimension, according to him, tend to accept centralized power and depend heavily on superiors for structure and direction. Hofstede also noted that different laws and rules for superiors and subordinates are accepted. Therefore, authoritative DMB probably would be preferred by subordinates dominated by this cultural dimension. On the other hand, Hofstede found that some nations are classified by a **moderate-to-small power distance** cultural dimension. Individuals dominated by this dimension do not tolerate highly centralized power and expect to be consulted in decision making. Furthermore, Hofstede remarked that status differences (large power distance) in these countries are suspect. Thus, subordinates in these cultures probably would favor participative, or at least consultative, DMB. For example, subordinates in the United States, a moderate power distance society, tend to favor consultative DMB.

Cross-cultural researcher O.J. Stevens conducted a research project including MBA students from Germany, Great Britain (both small power distance societies), and France (a large power distance society). This study provides some support for the above propositions about a country's power distance measure influencing DMB. He asked the students to write their diagnosis of and solution to a case problem. The majority of the French referred the problem to the next higher authority—they sought direction. The British handled the problem. The Germans attributed it to a lack of formal policy and proposed establishing one.[18] Studies by researchers S. Kakar and by L. Williams, W. Whyte, and C. Green also lend support for these conclusions.[19] Kakar reported that the paternal type of superior-subordinate relationships, especially in the form of assertive behavior, dominates the authority relations in organizations in India, a large power distance society. He attributed this pattern to sociocultural factors, as well as to the hierarchical development of modern work organizations in India.[20] Williams and his colleagues concluded that in societies where there are small power differences, such as Sweden, Austria, and Israel, subordinates and managers are highly interdependent in the completion of tasks, and status differences are downplayed. In cultures where there are large power differences, such as the Philippines, Mexico, and Venezuela, a more autocratic management style is not only more common but also expected by subordinates.[21]

DMB as a Factor of the Country's Individualism Measure

Hofstede found that many societies are classified by a **moderate-to-low individualism** (**collectivist**) cultural dimension. Low individualism societies are tightly integrated, and individuals belong to "in-groups" from which they cannot detach themselves. People think in "we," as opposed to "me," terms and obtain satisfaction from a job well done by the group. Since most of the societies that measured low individualism also measured large power distance (as shown in Figure 1-5, Chapter 1), the DMB applied by decision makers in organizations in these countries probably leans toward the authoritative.

On the other hand, Hofstede concluded that some nations are classified by a **moderate-to-high individualism** cultural dimension. Individuals in these societies look primarily after their own interests. Since employees in these cultures often consider their own objectives to be more important than the organization's, decision makers are likely to apply DMB leaning toward the authoritative, as evidenced by the authoritative/consultative DMB usually applied by decision makers in U.S. organizations, a country with a high individualism measure. And, as Practical Perspective 11-3 indicates, the management of Japanese MNCs tend to behave authoritatively with American executives working for their subsidiaries in the United States. In these societies the subordinates themselves probably would prefer that participative or at least consultative DMB be applied. This contention is based on Hofstede's conclusion that, for these individuals, a high quality of life means individual success and achievement, which is perhaps best

PRACTICAL PERSPECTIVE 11-3

The Authoritative Japanese Management

The Japanese need American executives' expertise to sell their products in the United States and are willing to pay top salaries to get them. But in company after company, the Americans complain about a system of subtle and debilitating discrimination in which they are treated as necessary but inferior outsiders—lacking both the authority to get things done and upward mobility.... This is hardly surprising, given the chasm that separates the American and Japanese corporate cultures. The qualities admired in American managers—ambition, risk taking, independence—are handicaps in Japanese companies, where group cooperation and a strict decision-making hierarchy prevail. Japanese managers generally choose a company for life, and they move up the corporate ladder very slowly and according to seniority rather than ability....

Japanese companies have been described as Machiavellian bureaucracies where absolute loyalty is demanded.... As a result, the Japanese have a hard time dealing with the mobility of

American executives, whose tendency to move from company to company to take advantage of better opportunities breeds distrust and makes their loyalty automatically suspect.... A study on the organization of Japanese subsidiaries in the United States by the Boston Consulting Group shows that while the formal corporate chain of command includes American executives at the second and third level, the actual decision-making system cuts out the Americans altogether. "You have a situation in which business is conducted at night on the telephone in Japanese between Japanese," says Kazuo Nomura, who is consul for the Boston Consulting Group and helped put the study together. "They come back in the morning and tell the Americans what has been decided, and sometimes they even make it seem like the Americans made the decision."

Source: Excerpted from Leah Nathans, "A Matter of Control," *Business Month* (September 1988): 46, 50. Reprinted with permission.

attained in organizations whose decision makers apply participative DMB. Therefore, in societies with a high individualism measure, decision makers in organizations whose employees are strongly concerned with the enterprise's well-being probably apply DMB leaning toward the participative.

The above contentions are partially supported by researchers E.F. Jackofsky and J.W. Slocum, Jr. They argue that in low individualism cultures, employees attach more importance to structure than to freedom in their jobs and are more emotionally and morally involved with their organizations than are employees in cultures that stress high individualism.[22]

DMB as a Factor of the Country's Uncertainty Avoidance Measure

Many societies, Hofstede found, are classified by a **moderate-to-strong uncertainty avoidance** cultural dimension. Individuals in these cultures feel uneasy in situations of uncertainty and ambiguity and prefer structure and direction. Therefore, authoritative DMB, because the uncertainty involved in decision-making is assumed by someone else, probably would be preferable to these subordinates. Hofstede has proposed that improving the quality of life for employees in these societies implies offering more security and perhaps more task structure on the job. On the other hand, Hofstede found that numerous countries are classified by a **moderate-to-weak uncertainty avoidance** cultural dimension. People in these cultures tend to be relatively tolerant of uncertainty and ambiguity and require considerable autonomy and low structure. Since it allows for some degree of autonomy, participative DMB probably would be preferred by subordinates dominated by this dimension.

This conclusion is supported by cross-cultural researchers R.N. Kannungo and R. Wright, who discovered that many managers in Britain, a weak uncertainty avoidance culture, placed much greater importance on individual achievement and autonomy than managers in France, a strong uncertainty avoidance society. The French valued competent supervision, sound company policies, fringe benefits, security, and comfortable working conditions.[23] This suggests that British subordinates prefer participative DMB and the French authoritative DMB.

DMB as a Factor of the Country's Masculinity Measure

Many countries, Hofstede found, are classified by a **moderate-to-strong masculine** cultural dimension. Societies classified by this dimension stress material success and assertiveness and assign different roles to males and females. Males are expected to carry out the assertive, ambitious, and competitive roles in the society; females are expected to care for the nonmaterial quality of life, for children, and for the weak—to perform the society's caring roles. In such societies a male might be the manager of finance, and a female might be his secretary; a role reversal would be an exception to the rule. In strong masculine countries, where such behavior is perceived as inequitable, mandating authoritative DMB emphasizing reduction of such social inequities would probably be applied in many organizations. One finds evidence of this in recent programs in the United States, a society with a moderate-to-strong masculine dimension, which enacted programs such as the Equal Pay Act of 1963, Title VII of the Civil Rights Act of 1964, and affirmative action and equal employment opportunity; in Japan, with its very strong masculine culture, which enacted the Employment Opportunity Law of 1986; and in Great Britain, another high masculinity culture, which enacted strong equal opportunity laws in 1976. Furthermore, the assertive behavior of male managers is likely to lead them to making decisions authoritatively. It has been proposed that in Latin American cultures, which tend to rank high on masculinity, women's leadership style may be more participative than autocratic (but this proposition may be difficult to test, since there are few female leaders in Latin American organizations).[24]

Hofstede also concluded that numerous nations are classified by a **moderate-to-weak masculine** cultural dimension. Societies classified by this dimension stress interpersonal relationships, a concern for others, and the overall quality of life, and they define relatively overlapping social roles for males and females. In these cultures, neither male nor female need be ambitious or competitive; both may aspire to a life that does not assign great value to material success and that respects others—both may perform the society's caring roles. Male secretaries, female truck drivers, and male nurses would be far more acceptable in such societies than they would in societies classified by a strong masculine cultural dimension. According to Hofstede, improved quality of work life for individuals in these societies means offering opportunities for developing social relationships on the job, which is perhaps best accomplished through participative/consultative DMB. Sweden, a weak masculine society, which generally exhibits participative DMB, is a good example. Findings by cross-cultural researchers B.M. Bass and L. Eldridge provide support for Hofstede's contention. They discovered that successful managers in Denmark (a low masculine society) emphasized societal concerns in decision making, whereas successful U.S., British, and German (all high-masculine societies) managers strongly valued a profit motive.[25]

DMB as a Factor of Confucianism

As pointed out earlier and in Chapter 1, research by Hofstede and Bond revealed a fifth cultural dimension labeled the **Confucian dynamism** dimension by which many societies can be classified. This dimension applies mainly to East Asian cultures based on Confucian philosophy (the People's Republic of China, South Korea, Japan, and Singapore)[26] As indicated in Chapter 1, Confucianism is not a religion but a system of practical ethics; it is based on a set of pragmatic rules for daily life derived from experience. The key tenet of Confucian teachings is that unequal relationships between people create stability in society.

In essence, individuals in Confucian-based organizations are forced to adhere to rigid, informal group norms and values, which include the subservient relationships aspects of Confucianism described in Chapter 1. Since individuals are so strictly bound to group norms, decision makers in organizations based on the Confucian cultural dimension, in reality, apply authoritative DMB. Support for this contention is provided by cross-cultural studies conducted by K.H. Chung and by W.S. Nam, who found that South Korean managers demonstrate the Confucian virtues of loyalty and obedience to authorities; and by G.W. England and R. Lee and by J. Harbron, whose studies revealed that South Korean managers tend not to adopt systems of shared management and power equalization within organizations. It is also supported by research conducted by L.W. Pye and by R.H. Solomon, who described Chinese subordinates as passive and as preferring that others make decisions for them.[27] And it is generally known that Japanese culture teaches its children submissiveness to elders and authority.[28]

As discussed earlier, Japanese managers use a participative approach called *ringi*. Many Japanese managers, however, prior to the group's meeting, "discuss" the issue or decision one-on-one with individual members. They use a technique called *nemawashi*—a term borrowed from gardening, which refers to the process of gradually snipping the roots of a tree or bush which is to be transplanted in order to reduce the shock to the plant. In business terms, **nemawashi** means many private or semiprivate meetings in which true opinions are shared before a major decision-making meeting takes place.[29] In essence, the *ringi* method appears to be subtle authoritative decision making—not only does the manager enforce rigid group norms and values, but so do the group's members. The real objective of participative decision making is to generate and allow the introduction of varying views and alternative choices. The group-oriented cultures, however, tend not to allow the introduction of views that differ from the group's norms and values—which, in a Westerner's view, translates into repressive, authoritative behavior. In fact, a trend currently catching on in Japan is Japanese executives' seeking employment in foreign companies where they can be more autonomous.[30]

Other Support for the Country-Related Cultural Framework

Numerous theorists accept the country-related cultural factors model.[31] They conclude that managerial attitudes, values, and beliefs are functions of a society's culture, and many studies support these theorists' contention. **Cross-cultural researchers** A. Sorge and M. Warner, for example, found substantial differences between West German and British factories with respect to shape of organizations, functional differentiation and integration mechanisms, basic features of industrial systems, and the process of education; they attributed these differences to distinct national technical cultures.[32] Researchers M. Maurice, A. Sorge, and M. Warner studied similar factories in France, West Germany, and Great Britain and proposed that organizational processes of differentiation and integration interact with the processes of educating, training, recruiting, and promoting manpower; that these processes develop within an institutional logic that is distinct to a society; and that nationally different shapes of organization result.[33]

Cross-cultural researcher D. Gallie studied the work attitudes of employees in four oil refineries owned by a multinational corporation. The refineries, two situated in Great Britain and two in France, were matched for technology and size. Gallie found considerable contrast in the attitudes of workers and their relations with management; he attributed the differences to national culture.[34] Professor A. Laurent researched employees in a multinational enterprise in different nations and found that the employees retained their culturally specific work behaviors despite the existence of common management policies and procedures.[35]

Researcher P. Blunt studied an organization employing about 160 people in Brunei to determine whether or not the employees' values compared with Brunei's national values of large power distance, strong uncertainty avoidance, and low individualism. Brunei was not included in Hofstede's study, but Blunt equated Brunei with similar countries in the region that Hofstede had categorized as such. Blunt found that commonalities did exist between the firm's employees and Brunei's national values. For example, employees showed a considerable unwillingness to make a decision without referring it to the most senior manager in the organization—an indication that the employees were exhibiting large power distance and strong uncertainty avoidance.[36]

Jackofsky and Slocum examined published sources to ascertain whether or not the behaviors of two French CEOs, three West German CEOs, two Swedish CEOs, one Taiwanese CEO, and three Japanese CEOs compared with their respective country's culture as identified in Hofstede's study. Although they detected a few deviations, for the most part they found commonalities in the CEOs' behavior and their country's value system.[37] The above cited cross-cultural studies thus provide strong support for the "cultural-specific" theory.

Questions About the Country Factors Framework

Despite support for the country-related cultural factors framework, many unanswered questions remain. For example, how does the framework apply to **multicultural centers,** such as the United States and Canada? For instance, British Americans can be individualistic and Japanese Americans collectivistic; German Americans can have strong uncertainty avoidance and Swedish Americans weak uncertainty avoidance. From a global perspective, can we even conceptually define the meaning of the labels used, such as uncertainty avoidance? Are not the more educated members of societies generally better equipped to deal with conditions of high uncertainty than the less-educated members? If so, does this framework apply only to the less-educated members of the society? In the same sense, does the framework apply more to the lower-level members of an organization than to the upper-level members?

Furthermore, how does this framework apply to the archetypes described by researchers W.D. Guth and R. Tagiuri, Economic Man, Theoretical Man, Political Man, Religious Man, Aesthetic Man, and Social Man, labels that reflect the personal values of decision makers existing in societies?[38] For instance, the Theoretical Man, who relies on tangible evidence in seeking the truth, would probably have low tolerance for power from above and high tolerance for uncertainty. The Religious Man, who relies on mysticism (faith) and the intangible, would probably have higher tolerance for power from above and lower tolerance for uncertainty. The Economic Man is practical and concerned with what is immediately useful, the Social Man is driven by benevolence, the Political Man is driven by challenge, and the Aesthetic Man is driven by savoring the moment's beauty—would not these individuals also have different tolerances for different decision-making styles, and would not they themselves apply different decision-making behaviors? For instance, would not the more liberal values of the Aesthetic Man generate more participative decision-making behavior than would the more power-oriented values of the Political Man? These questions thus lead us to the universal factors framework.

The Universal Factors Model

Many theorists argue that, irrespective of a society's culture, individuals are forced to adopt attitudes and behaviors that comply with the imperatives of industrialization.[39] (For an illustration, read Practical Perspective 11-4.) These theorists believe that other transnational factors affect DMB in all countries. For example, management theorists V. Vroom and P. Yetton contend that participation is not an ideological or cultural phenomenon but an "instrumental" phenomenon. They propose that U.S. managers use participation to enhance both quality and acceptance.[40] Therefore, many cross-cultural theorists adhere to a universal factors framework, which posits that DMB is influenced not as much by broad cultural factors as by varying situational factors, such as **subordinates' work environment, motivation, maturity level, and managerial level and functions.** These situations and the DMB behavior associated with each are discussed below. (See Table 11-3.) It should be noted that numerous management textbooks, especially those addressing leadership, list many other situations that affect DMB. These few were selected to illustrate the framework.

The Subordinates' Work Environment

Regardless of national culture, in crisis situations and in conditions where a group of individuals are under extreme pressure to perform a difficult task or survive in a hostile atmosphere, they generally prefer that the decision maker behave in a directive manner.[41] A decision maker who authoritatively makes and communicates decisions to correct the undesirable conditions is likely to be welcomed. Individuals confronted with ambiguous or unclear assignments also generally prefer a manager who provides much structure, clearly defining roles and expectations.[42] On the other hand, in situations where individuals feel competent, an effective decision maker is likely to be one who asks them to participate extensively in the decision-making process. This is because competent people, those with a higher degree of perceived ability relative to the task demands, usually have low tolerance for authoritative behavior.[43]

Individuals' Motivation

In many societies, some individuals are motivated by the need for affiliation, others by the need for achievement, and still others by the need for power.[44] Individuals whose primary motivator is the need for affiliation are interested in warm, friendly relationships, social interaction, communication and collaboration. Such people generally dislike making unpopular decisions, even when it is necessary for organizational effectiveness. These

PRACTICAL PERSPECTIVE 11-4

Participative Management Comes to the Far East

Taiwan and South Korea, the two heavy-weights among the newly industrialized economies, face not so much a quantitative shortage as a qualitative one: The skills its managers have are simply no longer appropriate for the changing competition they face. As wages have risen, the region's traditionally low-tech companies have had to move into higher-value-added products dependent upon expertise—overseas marketing sophistication, for instance—that their old-line managers often do not have. As authoritarian governments in both countries loosened up, workers began to challenge their bosses for the first time, creating a whole new set of managerial problems. Says Lee Hak-chong, a dean at Yosei University in Seoul: "Democratization has produced a tough and loud labor force." The search for more of the right kind of managers is challenging some of the region's most basic values....

A new wave of thinking is bringing forward a fresh generation of managers, men like Ng Pock Too and Nelson An-ping Chang. After getting an MBA degree from New York University, Nelson Chang went back to Taiwan. He heads an innovative computer services firm and a large cement manufacturing company that his father founded in 1954.... Chang, 38, could easily fill the part of the omnipotent dictatorial boss, the role favored by his father's generation. He has instead renounced that style because he thinks it stifles productive ideas. Says he, proudly: "I am a participative manager." The participation can get rough. To make certain that his senior executives take issue with him, Chang sometimes deliberately sets overambitious goals that they must argue against—or suffer penalties if the objectives are not met.

Belatedly, the region's universities are trying to respond.... Business schools are broadening curriculums in response to criticism that they have been turning out narrow specialists. In 1991, began requiring the National University of Singapore, business majors to take courses in such areas as psychology and Japanese culture. Chow Kit Boey, director of the school's Centre for Business Research and Development, says professors are now challenging students to become more "participative" and "free-thinking."

Source: Excerpted from Ford S. Worthy, "You Can't Grow If You Can't Manage," *Fortune* (June 3, 1991): 83–88. Copyright © Times, Inc., New York. Reprinted with permission. All rights reserved.

individuals may not like the responsibilities that come with participative decision-making behavior, and they may prefer authoritative DMB with consultation. People motivated by the need for achievement are interested in attaining specific objectives, will work hard to achieve them, and tend to be more interested in personal success. It is likely that these individuals will want to be very involved in making decisions. People motivated by the need for power are interested in controlling and influencing situations; they like to get things done through people, and they like to teach and inspire other individuals. Since such people want to have an impact on the organization, they probably would prefer to participate extensively in the decision-

TABLE 11-3	The Universal Factors Model	
Factors		**DMB>**
Subordinates' Work Environment:		
Crisis conditions		A
Ambiguous conditions		A
Competent individuals		Pe
Individuals' Motivation:		
Need for affiliation individuals		Ac
Need for achievement individuals		Pe
Need for power individuals		Pe
Individuals' Maturity Level:		
Low-maturity individuals		A
Low-to-moderate-maturity individuals		Ac
Moderate-to-high-maturity individuals		P
High-maturity individuals		Pe
Managerial Level and Functions:		
Upper-level managers		Pe
Lower-level managers		A
Structured functions		A
Unstructured functions		P

DMB> = Decision-making behavior leaning toward
A = Authoritative; Ac = Authoritative/Consultative;
P = Participative; Pe = Participative/Extensive

making process—although they themselves may prefer to apply authoritative DMB with their subordinates.

Individuals' Maturity Level

According to theorists Paul Hersey and Kenneth Blanchard, individuals function at four maturity levels: low maturity, low-to-moderate maturity, moderate-to-high maturity, and high maturity.[45] Individuals at a low maturity level have a negative attitude; they are unwilling and unable to assume responsibility. With such people, the effective manager applies directive (authoritative) DMB. Some individuals attain a low-to-moderate maturity level. These people are willing to assume responsibility, are confident, and have a positive attitude but lack the skills to make decisions. A combination of directive (authoritative) and supportive (consultative) DMB would work best with them. The manager, engaging in both kinds of DMB and using two-way communication, tries to improve the subordinates' decision-making abilities.

Other individuals develop to a moderate-to-high maturity level. Through coaching, training, and development, they have acquired the ability to make decisions but are unwilling to do so because of a lack of confidence. Participative DMB, which provides strong emotional support and encouragement and helps build confidence, would work well with these individuals. People with a high maturity level are able and willing and possess the confidence to make decisions. Because they are at a maturity level where they need little direction and little emotional support, these individuals are likely to prefer a participative approach that allows them a great deal of responsibility in the final decision. Hersey and Blanchard's theory thus suggests that DMB is not a factor of national culture but a factor of individuals' differing maturity level in their culture.

Decision-Making Level and Functions

Regardless of national culture, lower-level decision makers generally provide more direction than do upper-level decision makers; upper-level decision makers normally delegate more than those at a lower-level.[46] This means that upper-level decision makers apply participative DMB more so than lower-level decision makers, and lower-level decision makers apply authoritative DMB more so than upper-level decision makers. Decision makers for functions such as production, especially when the tasks are structured, tend to be directive and apply authoritative behavior. Decision makers for functions such as sales, where much of the employees' work is self-initiated, usually apply participative DMB.[47]

Other Support for This Model

Cross-cultural researchers P.C. Bottger, I.G. Hallein, and P.W. Yetton explored the effects of task structure and leader power on participative leadership across Australian, African, Papua-New Guinea, and Pacific Island managers. They reported that "differences in leadership style between developed and developing nation managers would appear to arise from instrumental considerations rather than cultural or ideological ones."[48] Researcher D.B. Stephens studied textile workers in three plants in Peru and in three plants in the United States. He concluded that

> *the cultural differences assumed to affect management processes in different countries may not transfer completely to the management context or may be attenuated by a somewhat universal management experience…. Based on this research, there is little reason to conclude that leadership styles are much different in Peru than in the U.S.*[49]

Some Problems with This Framework

The above discussion has presented some ideas that may aid decision makers in determining the appropriate DMB for certain situations in all national cultures. One problem in applying the above framework is reconciling the conflicting demands of a situation. For example, when a crisis confronts a group of achievers, which behavior would be most appropriate?

Another problem is how to identify individuals' motivation at all levels—not all upper-level managers are willing to delegate authority to the lower-levels, nor do all lower-level managers want to behave autocratically. Furthermore, some organizational behavioralists have questioned the utility of complicated situational theories as a means of improving managerial effectiveness.[50] They believe that these theories can only be applied when the manager has time to analyze the situation and select the style that works best. But managers, according to those behavioralists, are so busy making decisions and responding to crises in a hectic and fragmented fashion that they do not have adequate time to evaluate the situation. The complexity of managing in the international environment is likely to increase, which means that managers will have even less time to analyze and apply a situational approach in the international environment than they do in the domestic one.

WHICH FRAMEWORK IS CORRECT?

Since the two frameworks are well supported by existing literature, can they both be correct? An analysis of the study by Jackofsky and Slocum, cited earlier, can be used to lend support to both models. They found that in some instances the behavior of one of the French CEOs was influenced more by his own personal characteristics than by his country's cultural characteristics. This CEO acted boldly in acquiring two competing firms—behavior that stands in marked contrast to France's culture of strong uncertainty avoidance (conservative behavior). He also decentralized management in the acquisitions—conduct that also is opposed to France's large power distance culture. Jackofsky and Slocum surmised that this CEO's behavior of not conforming to national culture eventually led to his demise—which supports the country-related cultural factors framework. However, this CEO's behavior also violated the universal factors framework. This contention is based on the idea that often acquisitions are made when the firm being acquired is encountering difficulties (crisis) and that ambiguous conditions often arise in newly acquired firms. In such situations, the universal framework proposes application of directive DMB,[51] yet the CEO decentralized decision making. This CEO's unorthodox behavior, which led to his failure within the company, thus also can be interpreted to support the universal framework.

The other CEO, also eventually released from his position, generally conformed to France's national culture. He made conservative decisions (high uncertainty avoidance behavior), even when his firm was confronted with crisis conditions. However, his behavior contradicts the universal framework, which proposes that individuals confronted with a crisis generally prefer an authoritative manager who makes decisions that communicate potential for correcting the situation. This CEO did make a somewhat bold decision in trying to cut 9,000 jobs to save money. But this action seems to go against both models. It violates the universal framework in the sense that the solution does not develop hope for subordinates confronted with crisis conditions, and it violates the country-related framework in the sense that the French display strong uncertainty avoidance and search for security; eliminating 9,000 jobs certainly does not make one feel secure.

The cases of these French CEOs, therefore, lend validity to both frameworks—as does Professor Herbert Simon's famous, older work. He discusses the "zone of acceptance" concept, which is the extent to which a subordinate accepts another's decisions as governing his or her behavior. Individuals with a wide zone accept more; individuals with a narrow zone accept less. Simon proposes that the zone is socially determined and varies with the social situation, which in some ways equates with the country-related framework. On the other hand, he notes that "there are wide differences, too, among different types of employees in their expectation of authority relations in their positions. Professional men and skilled workmen are apt to have relatively narrow zones of acceptance."[52] This provides support for the universal framework.

Even though we know that both frameworks can be used to help predict DMB in organizations, we do not know yet which one is the best predictor. That is, we do not know when the determinants in one framework have a greater impact on DMB than the determinants in the other. Are there any situations (for example, crisis) that make the determinants in one framework more dominant than the determinants in the other? For example, would the two French CEOs discussed above have been more effective if their behavior emphasized the universal model's determinants when they seemed the most relevant and the country-related determinants when they seemed the most appropriate? How is such a determination made? It seems that, to make such a determination, managers require a great deal of managerial savvy, including global, cross-cultural savvy.

IMPLICATIONS OF THE TWO FRAMEWORKS FOR CROSS-CULTURAL DECISION MAKING

The two frameworks developed in this chapter are still being refined, but they do have some implications for cross-cultural decision making. The country-related cultural factors framework can serve as a general starting point for analysis. For example, it may be accurate to state that culturally the British tend to be highly individualistic and the Portuguese tend to be less individualistic. But it would be risky to make a blanket decision based on this belief, as not all British rank high on individualism, nor do all Portuguese rank low on individualism. Thus, ultimately, each specific situation must be studied. For instance, when the Japanese Honda Motor

Company penetrated the European market, it discovered that it was not sufficient to have abstract knowledge about a foreign country—a deeper understanding had to be developed. Honda learned the importance of adopting a locally oriented approach and building up a new way of doing work in the host country. As its success indicates, Honda learned how to blend its corporate culture with the cultural background of the host nation.[53]

The two frameworks also imply that cross-cultural decision makers need to determine to what extent individuals in different situations and cultures tolerate or expect different DMB. They also imply that effective cross-cultural decision makers are flexible in their approach to making decisions in different situations and across cultures; they understand that the behavior that works in one situation or culture will not necessarily work in another.[54] Historically, managers doing business across foreign borders have made many costly blunders, in part because they did not adopt managerial styles appropriate to specific situations and cultures.[55] For example, David Pulatie, vice president and director of employee relations at Motorola, Inc., stated that there has been a tendency on the part of American managers to simply go into nation X, Y, or Z and try to introduce the American mentality and decision-making process without considering the reactions of the host country's citizens.[56] For example, there was a situation in which an Asian employee working in an American firm was threatened with termination. The reason given was that he asked too many questions. The Asian was deeply bewildered by this criticism; he could not imagine how to act differently. The manager, being a good American, expected employees to act independently after receiving initial instructions. The manager was annoyed by the Asian's constant questions and decided he was too ignorant for the job. Actually, however, the Asian was asking questions as a way of strengthening his dependent relationship with his supervisor and to be sure he was proceeding properly.[57] In view of the huge costs managerial blunders can generate in the global economy, it is imperative that international decision makers learn and apply the appropriate managerial behavior to the situation and culture.

Before a corporation sends someone abroad, it must identify the effective management style for that place and, as indicated in Chapters 7 and 8, select and train the right person for the assignment. For example, Reynolds International's training director, Thomas Kruse, explained that in order to determine the right management style for a country, they rely on managers who have worked there before, and they talk to Peace Corps volunteers who have worked in the country. They also obtain information from the American Management Association in New York, which offers country profiles and arranges seminars in which natives of a specific nation provide information on management styles that work in their country.[58] In the long run, the investment of time and effort put into assessing the situation, culture, and appropriate managerial behavior will be recaptured by avoiding costly blunders.

GROUP DECISION MAKING AND INFORMATION TECHNOLOGY

More and more international organizations (and domestic ones as well) are now making important decisions by using input from groups consisting of employees and sometimes outsiders. In face-to-face group decision making, it is well known that, in both small and large power distance societies, a certain member or certain members of the group (often those with status) usually influence the other members' decisions. Questions one might ask include: Can the use of newer technologies, for example, using e-mail instead of face-to-face communication, in offering input for group decision making, reduce the powerful group member's influence on the group's decision-making process? Can the not-face-to-face **group decision-making means presented by the Internet** induce group members holding a large power distance cultural orientation to participate more in the organization's decision-making process? Some initial research in this respect involving computer-mediated communication (CMC) conducted using U.S. (small power distance) and Singapore (large power distance) decision-making groups suggests that the answer to the above questions might be yes—the groups supported by CMC were less influenced by member status than groups that were not supported by CMC.[59] This suggests that in the future the Internet might have a positive effect on the democratization of societies throughout the world.[60]

SUMMARY

This chapter has discussed the programmed and the nonprogrammed decision-making processes in a cross-cultural context, including a discussion on how a society's culture affects the rational decision-making process. The MBO and *ringi* participative decision-making approaches were also described in a cultural context. Two frameworks, each presenting several factors that influence decision-making behavior (DMB)—authoritative or participative—were discussed. The country-related cultural factors framework proposes that certain cultural dimensions affect DMB. The universal factors framework posits that certain specific situational factors affect DMB in all cultures. Questions about how to apply both frameworks were posed. The implications of both frameworks were put forth—mainly that cross-cultural decision makers, to apply the appropriate DMB, must understand each situation and culture thoroughly.

Key Terms and Concepts

1. An effective decision-making process in one culture may be ineffective in another
2. Programmed and nonprogrammed decision making
3. "Master of destiny" and "fatalistic" cultures
4. Consensus; group harmony
5. Authoritative and participative decision making
6. Participative DMB is perceived negatively in many cultures
7. MBO and *ringi*
8. Contingency decision making
9. The country-related cultural factors framework
10. The universal factors framework
11. The "culture-specific" and "culture-free" theories
12. Power distance
13. Individualism
14. Uncertainty avoidance
15. Masculinity
16. Confucianism
17. *Nemawashi*
18. Cross-cultural research
19. Multicultural centers
20. Subordinates' work environment
21. Individuals' motivation
22. Individuals' maturity level
23. Decision-making level and function
24. Group decision making and information technology

Discussion Questions and Exercises

1. Discuss the ways culture affects programmed and nonprogrammed decision making.
2. Discuss the fundamentals of the country-related cultural factors and the universal factors frameworks.
3. What type of DMB, authoritative or participative, would you apply in the following cultures:
   a. Large power distance
   b. Low individualism
   c. Strong uncertainty avoidance
   d. Low masculinity
   e. High Confucianism
4. What type of DMB, authoritative or participative, would you apply in the following situations:
   a. Crisis conditions
   b. Subordinates are motivated by the need for affiliation
   c. Subordinates function at a high level of maturity
   d. Subordinates carry out the sales function
5. Discuss the problems with the country-related cultural factors and the universal factors frameworks.
6. Fundamentally, what do the two frameworks tell the global manager?
7. Analyze Figure 10-2, and based on the country-related cultural factors framework, determine the appropriate DMB—authoritative or participative—for each of the 50 countries.
8. Discuss how technology affects cross-cultural group decision making.

Assignment

Interview an executive involved in international business. Ask the executive to describe his or her experiences in making decisions across cultures. Did he or she apply the country-related factors framework or the universal factors framework? Prepare a short report for class discussion.

Cultural Traditions

If you are involved in business with Third World countries, you need to understand three widespread traditions that affect business transactions: the inner circle, future favors, and gift exchange.

Inner Circle

Communal societies divide people into two groups: those with whom they have relationships, and those with whom they have none—the goal being group prosperity and protection. There are the "in" people and the "out" people. The "ins" are family; the "outs" are strangers. In East and West Africa, inner circles can be true relatives, comrades, or persons of similar age or region. In China, they may be those who share the same dialect; in India, members of the same caste. These are not unlike the "old boy networks" in the United States. The effect in many of these countries is to restrict social and business dealings to those with whom the business person has safe, trusting relationships.

Future Favors

The system of future favors operates within the inner circles. In Japan it is known as "inner duty," in Kenya, "inner relationship," and in the Philippines, "inner debt." In these traditions, the person is obligated to another to repay the favor sometime in the future. Some form of favor or service will repay the earlier debt; this repayment then places the grantor of the original favor under future obligation. Life-long shifting obligations create relationships of trust and are the basis for doing business.

Gift Exchange

In many non-Western circles, the gift exchange tradition has evolved into a business tool: Gifts begin a process of future favors. They are an immediate sign of gratitude or hospitality, but upon acceptance, they generate an obligation that the recipient must someday repay.

Questions

1. Discuss some of the ways the above cultural traditions affect the rational decision-making process described in this chapter.
2. Compare the Inner Circle to the "low-individualism" cultural dimension. What type of decision-making approach, participative or authoritative, is likely to be preferred in the Inner Circle cultures? Why?

Source: Ken Hodgson, "Adapting Ethical Decisions to a Global Marketplace," *Management Review* (May 1992): 55.

CASE 11-2

From Napa Valley, California, to Paris, France

John Terwilick, an executive for Shonteur, Inc., a wine wholesaler based in Massachusetts, was appointed to head Shonteur France, Inc., a subsidiary in Paris, France. The subsidiary had been established to procure wines in Europe for distribution in the U.S. market. The subsidiary employs 179 people. The employees are mostly locals (French), but numerous employees are from Germany, Spain, and Portugal—which are sources of European wines. The company selected Terwilick for the assignment because of his successful experience managing another wine sourcing subsidiary in Napa Valley, California.

Over the years Terwilick has attended many management development seminars, where he was taught that participative management, involving employees in the decision-making process, would produce wonders. It did work well for him at the Napa Valley subsidiary, and it helped establish his reputation at the Massachusetts headquarters as an effective manager. These days, however, to climb to the top of a corporation's headquarters, managers require extensive cross-cultural experience—that is, experience managing diverse cultures. In view of this current managerial trend, Terwilick, with the goal of a high-level appointment at corporate headquarters, happily accepted the appointment in France.

Terwilick was determined to be at least as successful in France as he had been in Napa Valley. Upon assuming his managerial post as the head of the French subsidiary, Terwilick began applying basically the same managerial style he had applied in Napa Valley. For example, he began delegating some of his decision-making duties to the French supervisors, and in making major decisions, he often solicited their input—he involved them in the decision-making process. Terwilick had been taught in management development programs and learned through experience at Napa Valley that this would improve employee morale, and thus productivity. To his surprise, however, he noted that the French supervisors nonverbally expressed anxiety, dissatisfaction, and low morale. Terwilick thought to himself: "What is wrong here? What is the problem?"

Questions

1. What did the company do wrong in sending Terwilick overseas?
2. Can you help Terwilick solve the problem with which he is confronted?

Source: This case was created by the author.

Notes

1. "The Business of Europe," *The Economist* (December 7, 1991): 64.
2. J.S. Black and L.W. Porter, *Management: Meeting the New Challenges* (Upper Saddle River, NJ: Prentice Hall: 2000), p. 54.
3. See Herbert A. Simon, *Administrative Behavior* (New York: The Free Press, 1976).
4. Geert Hofstede, *Culture's Consequences: International Differences in Work-Related Values* (Beverly Hills, CA: Sage Publications, 1980), p. 19.
5. D.K. Tse et al., "Does Culture Matter? A Cross-Cultural Study of Executives' Choice, Decisiveness, and Risk Adjustment in International Marketing," *Journal of Marketing* 52 (October 1988): 82.
6. See R. Theobald, "Management of Complex Systems: A Growing Societal Challenge," in F. Feather, ed., *Through the 1980s: Thinking Globally, Acting Locally* (Washington, D.C.: World Future Society, 1980), pp. 42–51.

7.Nancy J. Adler, *International Dimensions of Organizational Behavior*, 2d ed. (Boston: PWS-Kent Publishing, 1991), p. 162.

8.Tse et al., "Does Culture Matter?" p. 82.

9.Rensis Likert, *The Human Organization: Its Management and Values* (New York: McGraw-Hill, 1967).

10.T. Morris and C.M. Pavett, "Managing Style and Productivity," *Journal of International Business Studies* (First Quarter 1992): 177.

11.Anthony P. Raia, "A Second Look at Management Goals and Controls," *California Management Review* (Summer 1966): 49–58; and Peter F. Drucker, *The Practice of Management* (New York: Harper & Row, 1954).

12.J. Johnston, "Ringi: Decision Making Japanese Style," *Management Review 70* (May 1981): 15–21.

13.R. Neale and R. Mindel, "Rigging Up Multicultural Teamworking," *Personnel Management* (January 1992): 37.

14.See J. Child and A. Kieser, "Organizations and Managerial Roles in British and West German Companies: An Examination of the Culture-Free Thesis," in C. Lammers and D. Hickson, eds., *Organizations Alike and Unlike* (London: Routledge and Kegan Paul, Ltd., 1979), pp. 251–271.

15.See Child and Kieser, "Organizations and Managerial Roles in British and West German Companies;" W. Heydebrand, *Comparative Organization: The Results of Empirical Research* (Englewood Cliffs, NJ: Prentice-Hall, 1973); D.J. Hickson, C.J. Hinings, and J.P. Schwitter, "The Culture-Free Context of Organization Structure: A Tri-National Comparison," *Sociology 8* (1974): 59–80; M. Haire, E.E. Ghiselli, and L.W. Porter, *Managerial Thinking: An International Study* (New York: John Wiley, 1966).

16.Hofstede, Culture's Consequences; Geert Hofstede, "The Cultural Relativity of the Quality of Life Concept," *Academy of Management Review 9*, no. 3 (1984): 389–398.

17.G. Hofstede and M. Bond, "The Confucius Connection: From Cultural Roots to Economic Growth," *Organizational Dynamics* (Spring 1988): 5–21.

18.Cited in Geert Hofstede, "Motivation, Leadership, and Organization: Do American Theories Apply Abroad?" *Organizational Dynamics* (Summer 1980): 42–62.

19.S. Kakar, "Authority Patterns and Subordinate Behavior in Indian Organizations," *Administrative Science Quarterly 16* (1971): 93–101; L. Williams, W. Whyte, and C. Green, "Do Cultural Differences Affect Workers' Attitudes?" *Industrial Relations 5* (1966): 105–117.

20.See also Z. Aayan, R.B. Kanungo, and J.B.P. Sinha, "Organizational Culture and Human Resource Management Practices," *Journal of Cross-Cultural Psychology 30*, no. 4 (July 1999): 501–526.

21.J.K. Harrison and R. Hubbard, "Antecedents to Organizational Commitment Among Mexican Employees of a U.S. Firm in Mexico," *The Journal of Social Psychology 138*, no. 5 (1998): 609–623; J.S. Osland, S. Franco, and A. Osland, "Organizational Implications of Latin American Culture: Lessons for the Expatriate Manager," *Journal of Management Inquiry 8*, no. 2 (June 1999): 219–234.

22.E.F. Jackofsky and J.W. Slocum, Jr., "CEO Roles Across Cultures," in D.C. Hambrick, ed., *The Executive Effect: Concepts and Methods for Studying Top Managers* (Greenwich, CT: JAI Press, 1988).

23.R.N. Kannungo and R. Wright, "A Cross-Cultural Comparative Study of Managerial Job Attitudes," *Journal of International Business Studies 14*, no. 2 (1983): 115–129.

24.H.J. Mullen and M. Rowell, "Mexican Women Managers: An Emerging Profile," *Human Resource Management 36*, no. 4: 423–435; J.S. Osland, L. Hunter, and M.M. Snow, "A Comparative Study of Managerial Styles in Nicaraguan and Costa Rican Female Executives," *International Studies of Management and Organization 28*, no. 2 (1998): 54–73.

25.B.M. Bass and L. Eldridge, "Accelerated Managers' Objectives in Twelve Countries," *Industrial Relations 12* (1979): 158–171.

26.Hofstede and Bond, "The Confucius Connection."

27.K. H. Chung, "A Comparative Study of Managerial Characteristic of Domestic, International, and Governmental Institutions in Korea." Paper presented at the Midwest Conference of Asian Affairs, Minneapolis, Minn., 1978; W.S. Nam, "The Traditional Pattern of Korean Industrial Management," *ILCORK working paper no. 14*, Social Science Research Institute, University of Hawaii, 1971; G.W. England and R. Lee, "Organizational Goals and Expected Behavior Among American, Japanese, and Korean Managers: A Comparative Study," *Academy of Management Journal 14* (1971): 425–438; J. Harbron, "Korea's Executives Are Not Quite the New Japanese," *The Business Quarterly 44* (1979): 16–19; L.W. Pye, *The Spirit of Chinese Politics* (Cambridge, MA: MIT Press, 1968); R.H. Solomon, *Mao's Revolution and Chinese Political Culture* (Berkeley, CA: University of California Press, 1971).

28.Brock Strout, "Interviewing in Japan," *HR Magazine* (June 1998): 72

29.J.S. Black and L.W. Porter, *Management: Meeting the New Challenge*, p. 254

30. "Changing Jobs Catching On in Japan," *Focus Japan* (March 1993): 6.

31. See M. Crozier, The Bureaucratic Phenomenon (London: Tavistock Publications, 1964); S.M. Davis, Comparative Management: Cultural and Organizational Perspectives (Englewood Cliffs, NJ: Prentice-Hall, 1971); R. Nath, "A Methodological Review of Cross-Cultural Research," *International Social Science Journal 20*, no. 1 (1968): 35–62; W. Glasier, "Cross-National Comparisons of the Factory," *Journal of Comparative Administration* (May 1971): 67–83; Hofstede, "Culture's Consequences;" Haire, Ghiselli, and Porter, *Managerial Thinking*.

32. A. Sorge and M. Warner, "Culture, Management and Manufacturing Organizations: A Study of British and German Firms," *Management International Review 21* (1981): 35–48.

33. M. Maurice, A. Sorge, and M. Warner, "Societal Differences in Organizing Manufacturing Units: A Comparison of France, West Germany, and Great Britain," *Organization Studies 1* (1980): 59–86.

34. D. Gallie, *In Search of the Working Class* (London: Cambridge University Press, 1978).

35. A. Laurent, "The Cultural Diversity of Management Conceptions," *International Studies of Management and Organization* (Spring 1983): 75–96.

36. P. Blunt, "Cultural Consequences of Organization Change in a Southeast Asian State: Brunei," *The Academy of Management Executive 2*, no. 3 (1988): 235–240.

37. Jackofsky and Slocum, "CEO Roles Across Cultures."

38. See W.D. Guth and R. Tagiuri, "Personal Values and Corporate Strategy," *Harvard Business Review* (September–October 1965): 126.

39. See R.E. Caves, "Industrial Organization, Corporate Strategy and Structure," *Journal of Economic Literature 18* (1980): 317–334; Hickson, Hinings, and Schwitter, "The Culture-Free Context of Organization Structure"; W. Heydebrand, *Comparative Organization: The Results of Empirical Research*.

40. V. Vroom and P. Yetton, *Leadership and Decision-Making* (Pittsburgh: University of Pittsburgh Press, 1973); F. Heller and B. Wilpert, *Competence and Power in Managerial Decision-Making* (New York: John Wiley & Sons, 1981).

41. See A.W. Halpin, "The Leadership Behavior and Combat Performance of Airplane Commanders," *Journal of Abnormal and Social Psychology 49* (1954): 19–22; E.P. Torrence, "The Behavior of Small Groups Under Stress Conditions of Survival," *American Sociological Review 19* (1954): 751–755; M. Mulder and A. Stemering, "Threat, Attraction to Group, and Need for Strong Leadership," *Human Relations*, no. 16 (1963): 317–334.

42. E. Burack, *Organizational Analysis: Theory and Applications* (Hinsdale, IL: Dryden Press, 1975), pp. 315–318.

43. See A.S. Ashour and G. England, "Subordinates' Assigned Level of Discretion as a Function of Leader's Personality and Situational Variables," *Journal of Applied Psychology 56* (1972): 120–123; A.C. Filley, R. House, and S. Kerr, *Managerial Process and Organizational Behavior*, 2d ed. (Glenview, IL: Scott, Foresman and Co., 1976), p. 215; F. Heller, *Managerial Decision Making: A Study of Leadership Style and Power Sharing Among Senior Managers* (London: Tavistock Publications, 1971).

44. See D.C. McClelland, "Business Drive and National Achievement," *Harvard Business Review 40* (July–August 1962): 35–42; D.C. McClelland, *The Inner Experience* (New York: Irvington, 1975).

45. P. Hersey and K. Blanchard, *Management of Organizational Behavior*, 4th ed. (Englewood Cliffs, NJ: Prentice-Hall, 1982).

46. See F. Heller and G.A. Yukl, "Participation, Managerial Decision Making, and Situational Variables," *Organization Behavior and Human Performance 4* (1969): 227–241; W.W. Tornow and R.R. Pinto, "The Development of a Managerial Job Taxonomy: A System for Describing, Classifying, and Evaluating Executive Positions," *Journal of Applied Psychology 61* (1976): 410–418; R.A. Webber, *Time and Management* (New York: Van Nostrand-Reinhold, 1972).

47. See J.K. Hemphill, "Job Descriptions for Executives," *Harvard Business Review 37* (September–October 1959): 55–67; R. Stewart, *Contrast in Management* (Maidenhead, Berkshire, England: McGraw-Hill U.K., 1976); B.M. Bass, "A System Survey Research Feedback for Management and Organizational Behavior," *Journal of Applied Behavioral Science 12* (1976): 151–171; Heller and G.A. Yukl, "Participation, Managerial Decision Making, and Situational Variables"; Webber, *Time and Management*.

48. P.C. Bottger, I.G. Hallein, and P.W. Yetton, "A Cross-National Study of Leadership: Participation as a Function of Problem Structure and Leader Power," *Journal of Management Studies 22*, no. 4 (July 1985): 365.

49. D.B. Stephens, "Cultural Variation in Leadership Style: A Methodological Experiment in Comparing Managers in the U.S. and Peruvian Textile Industries," *Management International Review 21*, no. 3 (1981): 54.

50. See M.W. McCall, Jr., "Leaders and Leadership: Of Substance and Shadow," in J. Hackman, E.E. Lawler, Jr., and L.W. Porter, eds., *Perspectives on Behavior in Organizations* (New York: McGraw-Hill, 1979).

51. E.P. Torrence, "Behavior of Small Groups."

52. H.A. Simon, *Administrative Behavior.*

53. H. Sigiura, "How Honda Localizes its Global Strategy," *Sloan Management Review 31*, no. 1 (Fall 1990): 77–82.

54. "Cultural Differences Affect Decision-Making," *IIE Solutions 31*, no. 6: 8.

55. See D. Ricks, *Big Business Blunders: Mistakes in Multinational Marketing* (Homewood, IL: Dow Jones-Irwin, 1983).

56. D. Pulatie, a section of "How Do You Ensure Success of Managers Going Abroad?" *Training and Development Journal* (December 1985): 22–23.

57. Cornelius Grove, "Easing Overseas Workers into the U.S. Business Environment," *HR Focus 76,* no. 10 (October 1999): 9.

58. T. Kruse, a section of "How Do You Ensure Success of Managers Going Abroad?" *Training and Development Journal* (December 1985): 23.

59. N. Adam, B. Awaerbuch, J. Slonin, P. Wegner, and Y. Yesha, "Globalizing Business, Education, Culture Through the Internet," *Communications of the ACM 40*, no. 2 (February 1997): 115–121.

60. B.C.Y. Tan, K.K. Wei, R.T. Watson, and R.M. Walczuch, "Reducing Status Effects With Computer-Mediated Communication: Evidence From Two Distinct National Cultures," *Journal of Management Information Systems: JMIS 15*, no. 1 (Summer 1998): 119–141.

12

Cross-Cultural Leadership and Motivation

"Companies tend to take good advice on contractual and legal problems but don't tend to take account of the cultural problems," said [Stephen] Burke [Düsseldorf-based director of recruitment consultants Michael Page International]. Not clearly understanding the way people work and the attitudes they have towards work can cause real difficulties, as explained by [Michael] Howlin [a barrister with Dickson Minto in Edinburgh]: "For example, in a highly unionized country such as Italy, even when a company is acting fairly, the workforce may be suspicious because there is a tradition of conflict." However, "there are no real differences in work aspirations between nationalities, more differences in the way such aspirations are expressed," explained Rosemary Neale, managing consultant with Warwick Weston.... "For instance, British and American workers felt that to do well, they had to work longer hours and stay late to show commitment, whereas Scandinavians believed that working beyond your allotted hours just demonstrated that you were not doing your job right." "There are also differences in management style. A French executive, for example, will tend to make the assumption that the authority to make decisions comes as a right of office, whereas Dutch, British, or Scandinavian managers expect a more consultative, team approach to decision making."[1]

Learning Objectives of the Chapter

Leadership is the act of one person guiding another or others toward the attainment of an objective, and *motivation* is the act of the leader providing the incentives necessary to induce the follower or followers to attain the objective. Leadership and motivation are therefore interrelated and interdependent. However, the leadership style and the types of inducements to which individuals respond vary from one culture to another. Thus, the managerial behavior that works well in one culture will not necessarily work well in another. For example, culturally, the French and the Swedish tend not to respond to the same leadership style. Americans and Japanese tend to be driven by somewhat different motivations.

Therefore, managers of multinational corporations are likely to be ineffective if they attempt to rashly transfer the leadership style and inducements that work in their home country to the management of subsidiaries in other countries. This means that, along with having to adapt their business, negotiation, and communication approaches to different cultures, cross-cultural managers must adapt their leadership style and motivation inducements to different cultures as well. After studying this chapter, you should be able to:

1. Discuss how culture affects leadership style.
2. Point out that American-based leadership theories do not have global application.
3. Describe the traits, abilities, and behaviors leaders require in varying international strategic situations.
4. Discuss how culture affects motivation.
5. Point out that American-based motivation theories do not have global application.
6. Discuss how work goals vary across cultures.

CROSS-CULTURAL LEADERSHIP

There are some universal leadership similarities. For example, managers throughout the globe tend to want to be more proactive and to get work done by applying less authority, and those with greater rates of career advancement view themselves as possessing greater effective intelligence.[2] However, in most cases, national boundaries make a substantial difference in managers' goals, inclination for taking risks, pragmatism, interpersonal skills, and leadership style.[3] This is because, overall, the environments that affect leader-subordinate relations vary across countries and cultures.[4] What is valued in one society in terms of leadership behavior may not be valued as much in another society. For example, the ambitious behavior of American managers is valued less by the British than it is by the Americans.[5] And in the United States it is quite common for a leader/manager with good technical abilities to be younger than his or her subordinates. But in Africa this would not work well. There, a person younger than his or her subordinates would feel highly uncomfortable supervising them—even if he or she possessed superior technical abilities.[6]

Therefore, to be effective, **cross-cultural managers** are often required to assume different **leadership styles,** depending on the culture with which they are interacting. (For illustration purposes, read the case of Glaxo in Practical Perspective 12-1.) It should be noted, however, that, as pointed out in Chapter 11, cross-cultural managers may sometimes find themselves confronted with situations in which other factors are more important determinants of the appropriate leadership style than cultural factors. For example, a manager confronted with the need to make a decision very quickly may not have the time to involve employees who culturally want to be involved in the decision-making process.

American-Based Management Theories

Popular **American-based leadership theories** include Douglas McGregor's *Theory X versus Theory Y manager* and Rensis Likert's *System 4 management.*[7] Fundamentally, these theories advance the notion that participative leadership behavior is more effective than authoritarian leadership behavior. As pointed out in Chapter 11, this may be true more in small power distance cultures, such as the United States and Denmark, than in large power distance cultures, such as France, Mexico, Spain, and Turkey, where employees tend to expect authoritative leadership.

Relationship-Oriented and Task-Oriented Leadership

In leader-subordinate relationships, some leaders are by nature *relationship-oriented* and some *task-oriented*. *Relationship-oriented leaders* place much more emphasis on maintaining a good relationship with their subordinates

PRACTICAL PERSPECTIVE 12-1

Leaders Require Cultural Sensitivity

Global corporations are those that consider all nations as sources of managerial, leadership, and technical resources. Glaxo, a pharmaceutical corporation headquartered in London, has intentionally spread its operations throughout the globe in pursuit of cultural diversity and human resource talent. It has research centers in the United States, Italy, Japan, and France. Cross-country partnership means that open-minded leaders must coordinate activities in Glaxo plants. An authoritarian style or a "best way" technique is not suited to Glaxo's approach to cultural diversity. Glaxo's work force, managers, and orientation are built on the premise that cultural values must be respected and can be utilized to the advantage of the enterprise.

Source: Adapted from Paul Girolami, "Why Glaxo Seeks Cultural Diversity," *World Link* (September–October 1990): 108–109.

than they do on the performance of tasks. *Task-oriented leaders* place more importance on the performance of tasks than they do on maintaining a good relationship with their subordinates.[8] Robert R. Blake and Jane S. Mouton surveyed 2,500 managers from the United States, South Africa, Canada, Australia, the Middle East, and South America, who were participating in Managerial Grid seminars. Most agreed that the ideal leadership style was an integration of the relationship and task orientations, but when these managers described their actual behavior on the job, the practice was more task-oriented than relationship-oriented.[9]

However, culture has an impact in this respect as well.[10] For instance, Indian leaders have been found to emphasize the task orientation.[11] A strong task orientation is also generally found in leaders in North America and in most Western European countries, and strong relationship orientation is generally found in leaders in African, Arab, and Latin American countries.[12]   Using the Least Preferred Coworker (LPC) questionnaire, it was found that high-performing managers in the Philippines had a low score (task-oriented) while their counterparts in Hong Kong had a high score (relationship-oriented).[13] In a study of American, Indian, and Japanese managers, the Japanese managers indicated that they received more social support from their superiors than did the American and Indian managers, and for Americans and Indians, relatives were more important providers of social support.[14] The Chinese, as Practical Perspective 12-2 indicates, also prefer relationship-oriented leadership. And in Africa, employees prefer a manager who is highly visible, approachable, and genuinely concerned with their welfare.[15]

PRACTICAL PERSPECTIVE 12-2

Managers in the People's Republic of China

Ignoring me [James A. Wall, Jr., University of Missouri] as well as her customers, the young salesclerk slowly leafed through her paperback. This I had heard was the best-run clothing store in Nanjing, and I was waiting to talk with its manager. "He's not here," said the translator. "He's on a buying trip, so we'll have to come back later." As we left, I asked the salesclerk, "Would you be reading that book if your manager were here?" "Of course," she snapped. "He's not a cold machine. He's progressive and lets me enjoy my work. He has a reformed management style." I had just been given my first

lesson in contemporary Chinese management....

"Dictatorship of the proletariat" dovetails quite easily with ancient Chinese values. In the feudal system, the rulers, landowners, and businessmen treated their subordinates as a large family. The superiors expected obedience, loyalty, and labor from the subordinates. In return, the superiors provided food, care, and protection. Chinese society still views firms from this feudal perspective. The firm is expected to provide for the families of the workers, and managers are expected to attend to the workers' personal problems. Reared under these traditional values and 40 years of socialism, Chinese managers willingly accept their paternal roles....

Chinese managers, it seems, are squeezed into power positions and at the same time instructed by their government to utilize scientific management in which pay is tied to productivity. The problem, however, is that the discretionary pay (bonus) of about $5 a month is not large enough to serve as an incentive. As they recognize that they have no effective pay system, the Chinese managers, like their counterparts in the U.S., build and rely on other forms of power. And they do so quite pragmatically.

A seemingly preferred method for building power is to loosen the rules; in street jargon, managers "cut workers some slack." Specifically, managers allow cooperative workers to be tardy, take days off, sleep on the job, play cards, or earn extra income using plant tools.... In return for their laxness, managers expect to glean workers "on" (obligation), so that they will perform when production is necessary, and give moderate attention to quality. In Western terminology, we say the Chinese managers develop idiosyncracy credits with each worker and then call these in as they need loyalty, hard work, and high performance. Managers labor diligently to establish and maintain a strong, warm relationship (that is, referent power) with each worker. Since the leader traditionally is viewed as a patriarchal figure, this relationship is highly valued by the subordinates.... The importance of the leader-subordinate relationship cannot be overly emphasized. It enables leaders to gain worker conformity and it proves to be an important source of worker satisfaction....

Reform, even though it breaks sharply from tradition, is heartily embraced by managers. Every manager emphasizes that he or she practices a "reformed" leadership style. In practice, though, most pick and choose from the reform package.... Many managers, workers complain, lead as they wish and then label their approaches "reformed" management. My interviews with managers in the Nanjing and Shanghai areas strongly validated this assertion. Many were autocratic, expecting subordinates to work hard without complaining. Some held that workers should work for and appreciate their "elementary" pay because it provided them with rice (i.e., life). And others admitted eschewing risk—"No achievement but no failure"—and following the rules. In all these cases, the managers referred to their styles as "reformed."

Bonuses, while used and praised by most managers, are administered effectively by a small percentage. One set of managers pretends to reward productive employees with differential bonuses. Actually they spread the bonuses around arbitrarily and parrot the reform propaganda. Some only preach bonuses because they do not care to devote the time and resources to monitoring individual production levels. And others eschew bonuses because they do not want the reform system to work.

Source: Excerpted from James A. Wall, Jr., "Managers in the People's Republic of China," *Academy of Management Executive* 4, no. 2 (1990): 19–32. Used with permission from the Academy of Management. All rights reserved. Permission conveyed through Copyright Clearance Center, Inc.

Initiating Structure and Consideration

Leadership behavior, which is similar to the task and relationship orientations consists of *initiating structure*, which refers to the leader's efforts in organizing and getting things done, and *consideration*, which relates to the extent of trust, friendship, respect, and warmth that a leader extends to subordinates.[16] It was once believed in the United States that leaders applying consideration behavior were more effective than those applying structure. However, this leadership behavior, too, is affected by culture. For example, it has been found that consideration behavior applied by leaders in a mixed cultural setting in New Zealand did not contribute to managers' effectiveness.[17] A twelve-nation study revealed that leaders tend to view the need for more consideration at the lower levels than at the upper levels of management—except for the French and Latin Americans, who regarded being considerate as relatively unimportant at all levels of management. Germans and Austrians viewed consideration as important at all levels. Consideration was highlighted by fast-rising but not by slow-rising managers in Italy, Spain, Portugal, and the United States, and it was deemphasized by managers with accelerated careers in Belgium, Scandinavia, France, Latin America, and India.[18] And in line with consideration, *respect-oriented* leadership behavior, which is characterized by avoiding confrontation, displaying patience, listening to others, and avoiding losing face, is prevalent in China, Japan, Korea, Singapore, and Turkey.[19]

Japanese PM Theory of Leadership

American managers' authoritative leadership approach is poorly suited to Japan's group-controlled style. Building on the American task and relationship leadership ideas, during the past few decades, the Japanese have developed their own theory, labeled **the PM theory of leadership.** *P* stands for performance and *M* for maintenance. Fundamentally, in Japanese PM leadership, the *P* refers to leadership oriented toward forming and reaching group goals, and *M* refers to leadership oriented toward preserving group social stability.[20] Therefore, as in the case of the American task and relationship leadership style, *PM* is concerned with both output and people.

However, a fundamental difference between Japan's PM leadership theory and the American task and relationship leadership theory is that the Japanese emphasize groups and Americans emphasize individuals. Another fundamental difference is that in practice Americans tend to emphasize the task more than the relationship aspects of leadership, while the Japanese emphasize P and M equally. (Table 12-1 shows a comparison between some American and Japanese management styles.)

Cross-Cultural Leadership Traits, Abilities, and Behavior

Figure 1-11 in Chapter 1 and Table 8-2 in Chapter 8 present the characteristics of effective cross-cultural, cross-national managers. Along with those characteristics, cross-cultural leaders also require certain other traits, abilities, and behaviors, as well as the ability to apply different traits, abilities, and behaviors to different leadership situations.

Innovator, Implementor, and Pacifier Leadership

Different situations require a manager with particular leadership characteristics. Three types of leaders, **the innovator, the implementor, and the paci-**

TABLE 12-1	A Comparison of American and Japanese Managers	
The American Manager	**The Japanese Manager**	
Is a decision maker	Is a social facilitator	
Heads a group	Is a member of a group	
Is directive	Is paternalistic	
Often has conflicting values	Has harmonious values	
His or her individualism sometimes obstructs cooperation	Facilitates cooperation	
Is confrontational	Avoids confrontation	
Top-down communication	Top-down, bottom-up communication	
His or her authority and responsibility are limited and specified	His or her authority and responsibility limits are not specified	
Is held responsible for performance	Groups are held responsible for performance	
Is held responsible for subordinates' poor decisions	Accepts symbolic responsibility when things go wrong	
Top managers initiate problem statements and propose solutions	Top managers initiate problem statements, and those affected are involved in identifying solutions	
Makes final decision	Codifies final decision	
Needs to show immediate results because he or she is reviewed on a short-term basis	The longer term review period enables him or her to concentrate on long-term plans	

Source: Adapted from Sang M. Lee and George Schwendiman, *Japanese Management: Cultural and Environmental Considerations* (New York: Praeger Publishers, 1982); Sang M. Lee and George Schwendiman, *Management by Japanese System* (New York: Praeger Publishers, 1982).

fier, require different characteristics (the characteristics are described in Table 12-2). Each type works best in specific situations. Figure 12-1 depicts three problem phases (situations) organizations normally encounter and the appropriate type of leader for each.[21]

As Figure 12-1 indicates, an organization needing an infusion of new ideas (often an organization undergoing crisis) requires a leader with the characteristics of the innovator. This is because under crisis conditions, subordinates generally prefer a forceful leader who can solve the problem—leadership behavior characteristic of the innovator. The innovator identifies new ideas and visions and "sells" them to the institution. Some aspects of the leadership behavior of Jack Welch, General Electric's CEO, provide a good illustration of an innovator leader. He recognized the problems created by global competition and redirected GE into broadcasting, investment banking, high-tech manufacturing, and other high-risk ventures. Lee Iacocca's behavior at Chrysler is another example of innovator leadership. Hired by Chrysler when it was confronted with extreme financial crisis, he came up with the radical idea of getting the U.S. Congress and the United Auto Workers to aid him in saving the company. He persuaded the U.S.

TABLE 12-2	The Traits, Abilities, and Behavior of Three Types of Leaders
The Innovator	Likes to compete and win
	Keeps on trying to succeed
	Assumes responsibility for success and failures
	Takes moderate as opposed to high risk (is bold)
	Likes to commit unit to a major course of action
	Is actively searching for new ideas to improve unit
	Seeks organizational growth
	Is motivated by the need to achieve, to be creative
	Centralizes decision making (is in control)
	Wants to stand out from the rest of the group (dares to behave differently)
	Believes the environment can be controlled and manipulated (can "sell" his or her ideas)
	Is long-range oriented (foresees positive results in the distant future)
The Implementor	Desires to exercise power, to control and influence situations
	Is actively assertive
	Is able to get things done through others
	Has the ability to assume responsibility for decision making
	Is systematic in analysis and in problem solving
	Is able to integrate decisions and analysis
	Is both long-range and short-range oriented (attends to distant needs as well as to today's)
The Pacifier	Has a positive attitude toward authority figures
	Is willing to carry out administrative functions (willing to do the "paperwork")
	Is interested in friendly relationships
	Likes to communicate and collaborate with employees (is socially oriented)
	Likes to improve the social atmosphere in the unit
	Makes decisions that keep everyone moderately happy
	Makes decisions based on feedback from what others have decided
	Allows employees to make many of the unit's decisions (delegates decision making)
	Accepts that decisions in the unit are not in harmony (individuals make conflicting decisions)
	Seeks to satisfy influential individuals
	Believes the environment cannot be controlled and manipulated (cannot "sell" ideas)
	Makes short-range decisions (deals only with day-to-day problems)

Source: Carl A. Rodrigues, "Identifying the Right Leader for the Right Situation," *Personnel* (September 1988): 46.

government to guarantee bank loans, he put the president of the union on Chrysler's board, and he received major concessions from the union.

The new ideas introduced by the innovator often create an ambiguous atmosphere in the organization. When individuals cannot tolerate ambiguous or unclear assignments, they generally prefer to have a leader who provides systematic structure to create a stable working environment within the organization. Thus, after the new vision has been initiated, the insti-

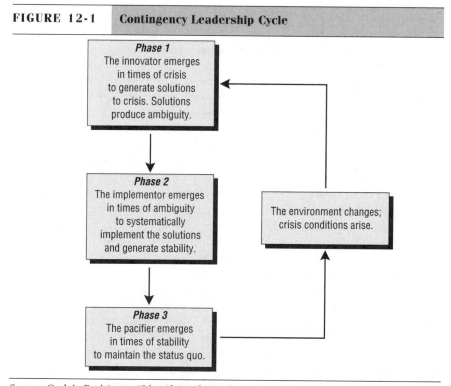

FIGURE 12-1   Contingency Leadership Cycle

Source: Carl A. Rodrigues, "Identifying the Right Leader for the Right Situation," *Personnel* (September 1988): 44.

tution needs a leader who can systematically put into operation the desired changes, someone whose personality is similar to the implementor's. Some aspects of the behavior of Alfred Sloan, Jr., serve as an example of implementor leadership. He generated structure in General Motors after William C. Durant conceived the company. Sloan was a talented operations executive who also possessed competency in financial and organizational matters. He studied the situation at GM and prepared the "Organizational Study," a program proposing a new organizational and business philosophy for GM.[22]

When the organization has attained a certain stability and daily operations are running smoothly, members usually feel more competent and believe that they can perform the task at hand. The higher the degree of perceived ability related to task demands, the less willing subordinates will be to accept strong direction and oversight. In this situation, an organization needs a pacifier-oriented leader. In some respects, the leadership of Reginald H. Jones, Jack Welch's predecessor at General Electric, illustrates pacifier behavior. Prior to the placement of Welch in the top position, Jones emphasized the role of corporate statesman.[23] Figure 12-1 shows that when a crisis arises again the leadership cycle is repeated.

Managerial Strategy and Application of the Three Leader Types

Table 12-3 depicts foreign subsidiary managerial strategy and application of the three types of leaders. As Table 12-3 shows, when a company needs to send an expatriate abroad to start a new subsidiary, an individual with the innovator's creative characteristics probably would work best. But once the innovator has conceived the idea for establishing the subsidiary, an individual with the implementor's capabilities to systematically operationalize the innovator's ideas and to train locals for managerial positions would probably work best. (Many innovators do not possess the implementor's characteristics.) Once the implementor has fully developed the subsidiary and trained local managers, a pacifier-oriented leader is needed to transfer managerial duties to the locals. Subsequently, a manager with the characteristics of the pacifier is needed at the firm's headquarters to monitor the foreign subsidiary's activities. This type of manager is needed because he or she will not interfere as much in local activities as would the innovator and the implementor, who are hands-on managers.

Some individuals possess the characteristics of both the innovator and the implementor. Thus, instead of sending two individuals, one who has been properly developed to act both ways would be the most cost-efficient. And some individuals actually possess the traits, abilities, and behaviors of all three types—as three-dimensional leaders, they know when it is time to create, when it is time to rally others to get the creation operationalized, and when to stay out of the way. Three-dimensional leaders would therefore be the ideal. They, however, are hard to find—but can be developed.

It should also be noted that national culture also has an impact on the appropriate leadership style. For example, small power distance individuals, because they want more control over their affairs, would be open to the relatively "hands-off" managerial approach of the pacifier type. On the

TABLE 12-3	Managerial Strategy and Application of the Three Leader Types		
		Type of Leader Needed	
Managerial Strategy	Innovator	Implementor	Pacifier
Expatriate to create a new subsidiary abroad	X		
Expatriate to operationalize the new subsidiary		X	
Expatriate to train locals for managerial positions		X	
Expatriate to transfer autonomy to local managers			X
Home-office manager to monitor subsidiary activities			X
Expatriate/local manager to solve crisis in subsidiary	X		
Expatriate/local manager to operationalize solution		X	
Local manager to carry out activities under conditions of stability			X

PRACTICAL PERSPECTIVE 12-3

Learning to go Against Japan's Corporate Grain

A Japanese executive was describing his company's efforts to spin off a smaller unit when he suddenly leaned forward and asked that his name not be used.

In a low voice, he said with a touch of embarrassment: "If this happens, we will have an image as an innovator."

Horrors!

This desire to innovate while not being openly seen as doing so may explain why the Japanese have not quite embraced a concept that has built the United States and contributed to its vitality: entrepreneurship.

They don't even have a good word for it. They have a few expressions, like *kigyo ka* ("one who starts a business"), but somehow the terms don't quite have the same ringing spirit in a nation not known for a go-it-alone attitude.

So the Japanese have just imported the word *an-torepurenah* whole, along with launching rounds of discussions about its spirit.

As the Asian economic crisis continues, it has become painfully obvious here that traditional Japanese values are interfering with the country's attempt to build the kind of entrepreneurial spirit that could lead it out of its seven-year slump.

Japan fears that it will fall behind the United States and Europe, and perhaps even Asian countries like South Korea, unless it can change the dynamic of its economy.

A Fear of Losing Ground

Although Japan may have the second biggest economy in the world, its companies are vast, bureaucratic conglomerates at a time when entrepreneurial, information-age companies are dominant.

In short, they are too much like Mitsui and not enough like Microsoft. Government officials and business executives fear the country is losing ground in an emerging global economy that will increasingly reward creativity, flexibility, and entrepreneurship, which is a rarity here. While entrepreneurship is not looked down on, it doesn't merit much prestige either.

"It's not receiving the appropriate attention or respect," said Yoshihiko Miyauchi, a creative iconoclast and the president of Orix Corporation, a leasing company. "People do not aim to become like Bill Gates."

Japan is now grappling with ways to inspire entrepreneurship and innovation in a society that looks askance at those who venture out alone. The new campaign to create individuals in the most communitarian of societies—and nurture risk takers in a nation exceedingly risk averse—faces huge obstacles....

Upstarts

Now, the need is for software engineers, and Japan lags.

Besides creativity, entrepreneurship also needs a system of venture capital to finance companies so that they can expand.

Japan has almost no true venture capital funds nor a system of venture capital. Banks are loath to lend to upstarts, high taxes discourage success, and stock market listings are extremely difficult to secure.

The government has made a start, particularly in setting up programs to encourage new business with special loans.

On a broader level, Japan is trying to re-educate its people, starting with kindergartners in hopes of cultivating greater creativity and independent thinking.

(continued)

Now entrepreneurship has become a buzz-word among board directors, salarymen, government officials and young students.

Lectures, seminars, and books abound, all of them offering step-by-step guidance on how to become an entrepreneur.

The stature of the handful of new entrepreneur, like Masayoshi Son, who began distributing software and then bought high technology companies here and in the United States, has been rising within the business community.

But, ultimately, some scholars say, a fundamental shift is needed since Japan's capitalism differs from that of the United States and tends to be less friendly to small start-ups.

"For entrepreneurship to work, you have to have a free market, one where the strong win and the weak lose," said Daizaburo Hashizume, a sociologist at Tokyo Institute of Technology.

"With this kind of market, old companies disappear and new companies rise. But there is no such free market in Japan."

Source: Sheryl WuDunn, "Learning To Go Against Japan's Corporate Grain," *The New York Times*, Sunday, March 8, 1998, p. wk 3. Copyright © 1998 by The New York Times Company. Reprinted by permission.

other hand, large power distance individuals are likely to appreciate the strong "hands-on" managerial approach of the implementor type. And in comparison with weak uncertainty avoidance people, strong uncertainty avoidance people, since they have relatively low tolerance for ambiguity, probably would prefer the structure the implementor provide and probably would be closed to the innovator's creative thinking.[24] In a broader sense, the United States appears to develop more managers with entrepreneurial skills than does Japan—which Japan, in light of its current financial crisis, views as problem. (Refer to Practical Perspective 12-3.) Practical Perspective 12-4 attempts to explain this phenomenon.

CROSS-CULTURAL MOTIVATION

In discussing the topic of *motivation*, some individuals may argue that there are no major differences in what motivates people across countries; that people everywhere, in general, are the same and respond to the same stimuli. This may be true in some respects but not in all. Certainly, just about all individuals are driven by such basic needs as food, water, air, and shelter. However, people are also driven by psychological needs, such as self-esteem and social status. Psychological drives tend to be *culture-specific*; the stimuli to which an individual responds differs across cultures. For example, people in individualistic-oriented cultures, such as the United States, may work toward **self-actualization** as an end, while people in collectivistic oriented cultures, such as China, may work toward self-actualization as a means to an end—**to better serve society/the group.**

Many of the popular motivation theories were developed by Western scholars using Western subjects and concepts. The ensuing sections discuss some of these theories in a cross-cultural context.

PRACTICAL PERSPECTIVE 12-4

In Japan, Nice Guys (and Girls) Finish Together

My intention, honest, was not to scar these Japanese kids for life. I just wanted to give them a fun game to play.

It was the fifth birthday party last year for my son Gregory, and he had invited all his Japanese friends over from the Tokyo kindergarten that he attended. My wife and I explained the rules of musical chairs, and we started the music.

It was not so awful for the Japanese boys. They managed to fight for seats, albeit a bit lamely. But the girls were at sea.

The first time I stopped the music, Gregory's five-year-old girlfriend, Chitose-chan, was next to him, right in front of a chair. But she stood politely and waited for him to be seated first.

So Gregory scrambled into her seat, and Chitose-chan beamed proudly at her own good manners. Then I walked over and told her that she had just lost the game and would have to sit out. She gazed up at me, like luminous eyes full of shocked disbelief, looking like Bambi might after a discussion of venison burgers.

"You mean I lose because I'm polite?' Chitose-chan's eyes asked. "You mean the point of the game is to be rude?"

Well, now that I think of it, I guess that is the point. American kids are taught to be winners, to seize their opportunities and maybe the next kid's as well. Japanese children are taught to be good citizens, to be team players, to obey rules, to be content to be a mosaic tile in some larger design.

One can have an intelligent debate about which approach is better. The Japanese emphasis on consideration and teamwork perhaps explains why Japan has few armed robbers but also so few entrepreneurs. The American emphasis on winning may help explain why the United States consistently racks up Olympic gold medals but also why its

hockey players trashed their rooms in Nagano.

The civility that still lingers in Japan is the most charming and delightful aspect of life here today. Taxi drivers wear white gloves, take pride in the cleanliness of their vehicles, and sometimes give a discount if they mistakenly take a long route. When they are sick, Japanese wear surgical face masks so they will not infect others. The Japanese language has almost no curses, and high school baseball teams bow to each other at the beginning of each game.

One can go years here without hearing a voice raised in anger, for when Japanese are furious they sometimes show it by becoming incredibly formal and polite. Compared with New York, it's rather quaint.

The conundrum is that Japan is perhaps too civilized for the 1990s. To revive its economy, mired in a seven-year slump, the country now needs an infusion of economic ruthlessness, a dose of the law of the jungle. Japan desperately needs to restructure itself, which is to say that it needs to create losers—companies need to lay off excess workers, Mom-and-Pop rice shops need to be replaced by more efficient supermarkets, and failing banks need to go bankrupt.

But Japan is deeply uncomfortable with the idea of failures or losers. The social and economic basis of modern Japan is egalitarianism, and that does not leave much room for either winners or losers. In Japan winning isn't everything, and it isn't the only thing; in elementary schools it isn't even a thing at all....

Of course, competition is inevitable in any society, and in Japan it is introduced in junior high schools, when children must compete intensely to pass high school and college entrance examinations. But the emphasis remains on "wa" or harmony on being one with the group.

(continued)

Ask a traditional Japanese housewife what she wants for her child, and you will sometimes hear an answer like: "I just want my kid to grow up so as not to be a nuisance to other people." Hmmm. Not a dream often heard in America....

The emphasis on *wa* perhaps arises because 125 million Japanese, almost half of the United States population. Are squeezed into an area the size of California. How else could they survive but with a passion for protocol and a web of picayune rules dictating consideration for others? If 125 million Americans were jammed into such a small space, we might have torn each other to shreds by now.

Building teamwork in Japan starts from birth. When our child, Caroline, was born in Tokyo last fall, the hospital explained that the mothers were to nurse their babies all together in the same room at particular meal times. So on her first day of life, Caroline was effectively told to discipline her appetites to adjust to a larger scheme with others....

So now, Japan is trying to become nastier. Workers are being pushed out of their jobs, occasionally even laid off. Employees are no longer being automatically promoted by seniority. Pay differentials are widening. Companies are becoming more concerned with efficiency and share prices, less concerned with employee welfare.

Source: Nicholas D. Kristof, "In Japan Nice Guys (and Girls) Finish Together," *The New York Times*, April 12, 1998, p. wk 7. Copyright © 1998 by The New York Times Company. Reprinted by permission.

A Comparison of Western and Southeast Asian Motivation Theories

More than three decades ago, Douglas McGregor proposed that managers adhere to one of two opposing theories about people: *Theory X* and *Theory Y*.[25]

Theory X

Theory X posits that the average human being has an inherent dislike of work and will avoid it if he or she can. Because of this human characteristic of dislike of work, people must be coerced, controlled, directed, or threatened with punishment to get them to put forth adequate effort toward the achievement of organizational objectives. The average human being prefers to be directed, wishes to avoid responsibility, has relatively little ambition, and wants security above all.

Theory Y

Theory Y puts forth that the expenditure of physical and mental effort in work is as natural as play or rest. External control and the threat of punishment are not the only means of bringing about effort toward organizational objectives. People will exercise self-direction and self-control in the service of objectives to which they are committed. Commitment to objectives is a function of the rewards associated with their achievement. The average human being learns, under proper conditions, not only to accept but to seek responsibility. The capacity to exercise a relatively high degree of imagination, ingenuity, and creativity in the solution of organizational problems is widely, not narrowly, distributed in the population; under the conditions of modern industrial life, however, the intellectual potential of average human beings is only partially utilized.

Several years ago Geert Hofstede, the European researcher, analyzed these two theories in the context of Southeast Asian culture. He believed that McGregor's assumptions, which are common to both theories, stem from the United States, an individualistic and masculine society. Hofstede outlined the assumptions upon which McGregor's theories rest as follows:[26]

➤ Work is good for people. It is God's will that people should work.

➤ People's potentialities should be maximally used. It is God's will that you and I should maximally use our potentialities.

➤ There are "organizational objectives" that exist separately from people.

➤ People in organizations behave as unattached individuals.

Theory T and Theory T+

Hofstede proposed that American assumptions do not apply in the collectivist (low individualism), large power distance Southeast Asian cultures. He replaced them with Southeast Asian assumptions.[27]

Southeast Asian assumptions:

➤ Work is a necessity but not a goal itself.

➤ People should find their rightful place, in peace and harmony with their environment.

➤ Absolute objectives exist only with God. In the world, persons in authority positions represent God, so their objectives should be followed.

➤ People behave as members of a family and/or group. Those who do not are rejected by society.

Hofstede proposed that since these assumptions are culturally determined, McGregor's Theory X and Theory Y distinction becomes irrelevant in Southeast Asia. He developed a **Southeast Asian distinction** (although he qualifies his distinction in that he is a European and may thus have made cultural mistakes). Theory X and Theory Y are mutually exclusive opposites. Unlike the American distinction, the Southeast Asia distinction that Hofstede proposed, which he labeled **Theory T and Theory T+** (T standing for traditional), is a complementary one—Theory T and Theory T+ fitting harmoniously together. According to Hofstede, Southeast Asian management could be as outlined in Table 12-4.[28] Theory X posits that people dislike work and will avoid it if they can, and Theory T contends that people dislike change and will avoid it if they can. This suggests that both Theory

TABLE 12-4	Southeast Asian Management
Theory T:	There is an order of inequality in this world in which everyone has his or her rightful place. High and low are protected by this order, which is willed by God.
	Children have to learn to fulfill their duties at the place where they belong by birth. They can improve their place by studying with a good teacher, working with a good patron, and/or marrying a good partner.
	Tradition is a source of wisdom. Therefore, the average human being has an inherent dislike of change and will rightly avoid it if he or she can.
Theory T+:	In spite of the wisdom in traditions, the experience of change in life is natural, as natural as work, play, or rest.
	Commitment to change is a function of the quality of the leaders who lead the change, the rewards associated with the change, and the negative consequences of not changing.
	The capacity to lead people to a new situation is widely, not narrowly, distributed among leaders in the population.
	The learning capacities of the average family are more than sufficient for modernization.

Source: Geert Hofstede, "The Application of McGregor's Theories in Southeast Asia," *Journal of Management Development 6*, no. 3 (1987): 16. Copyright © 1987 MCB University Press. Used with permission. All rights reserved.

X and Theory T propose that all people would attempt to avoid challenging work. A difference, however, is that Theory T espouses development of people, while Theory X advocates control. Theory T+ indicates that, in spite of the wisdom of tradition, the experience of change in life is natural, and, similar to Theory X, it is the function of the leader to coerce those who resist change.

People in cultures throughout the world thus behave in dissimilar ways because of the differences in how they view their environment. Their thinking is partly conditioned by national cultural factors, which are passed on from one generation to the next. It would therefore be a critical mistake for an international manager to attempt to **apply a set of motivational techniques on a worldwide basis**—to reiterate, what works in one culture does not necessarily work in another. Of course, people's thinking does not remain static from generation to generation. Cultural factors do change gradually over time as new technologies are introduced into the society. For example, the new economic systems introduced into the former communist nations are changing the ways managers lead and what motivates employees. (For illustration purposes, refer again to Practical Perspective 12-2 and review the case of China presented in Practical Perspective 12-5, as well as the case of Russia in Practical Perspective 12-6.)

PRACTICAL PERSPECTIVE 12-5

Money Works Wonders in China

Attracting workers [in China] can be a lot easier than holding on to them. Money is king in contemporary China. Workers will jump to other companies for a $5 raise. Stories abound of women from the inner provinces arriving to work long, backbreaking days for a few years and then returning home flush with cash to start businesses or to start up a local gentry. To provide some stability to their workforces, companies are moving to individual contracts. "We want total commitment from our workers," says Mr. Yen of Xian-Janssen [Pharmaceutical Ltd., a China-U.S. joint venture]. "They have to sign a pledge. Signing something is very significant here. So once they sign, they are committed."

"Have them sign it before training takes place, so you can protect your investment," advises Ralph McIntyre, area director for Asia of Mine Safety Appliances Company in Pittsburgh. Incentives also help restrain potential wanderers and boost performance. "Simple performance-related incentives work best," says [Andrew] Mok [vice president] of Philips [Inc., the Hong Kong subsidiary of a Dutch multinational]. "If a unit exceeds its target, the members get extra money. Some of our partners refuse to use incentives, and you can see a marked difference in output." The disinclina-

tion to take individual action or responsibility is another trait that can be tackled via incentives. "Anyone who takes a risk is immediately rewarded," says Xian-Janssen's Jerry Norkskog. "I don't care how wrong the risk is."

Of course, even money takes time to move attitudinal mountains. Rich Brecher of the U.S.–China Business Council cites an American company that recently took over a state-run enterprise. The plant now has one expatriate officer on the floor with hundreds of Chinese workers. The transformation from communism to capitalism is proving slow. "That guy can't do everything," observes Brecher. "The workers have to understand that all decisions don't have be made by the president. But that takes years to teach." All the time and effort will be worth it, however, if China continues shedding communism as an economic philosophy. Companies with well-trained management teams and workforces in place stand to enjoy a great advantage over those who are delaying [entering China] until they can see exactly how [now deceased] Premier Deng Xiaoping's long march to capitalism pans out.

Source: Excerpted from John R. Engen, "Getting Your Chinese Workforce Up to Speed," *International Business* (August 1994): 44. Reprinted with permission.

Chinese Social Motivation versus Western Individual Motivation

The *Hierarchy of Needs* theory developed by Abraham H. Maslow proposes that certain individual needs serve as motivators.[29] Maslow contended that people are first motivated by activities that aim to satisfy their *basic needs*. Once these needs are reasonably satisfied, they seek to satisfy the next level, their *safety needs*. Subsequently, they satisfy the next higher level, their *social needs*. Once the social needs are reasonably satisfied, the individuals satisfy their *esteem needs*. And once these are reasonably satisfied, they satisfy their *self-actualization needs*, which, according to Maslow, is the highest level of the needs hierarchy.

Maslow's theory has not been empirically verified, however. In fact, it has been widely criticized. Such terms as "belonging" and "esteem" are vague. The meaning of "satisfaction" is unclear. For example, after a big meal an individual would be full, and he or she, according to the theory, would not be motivated by food. However, this is not true in all cases—some individuals may still remain motivated by food because they have a memory and the ability to anticipate the future when hunger will occur again. Also, there is no evidence that satisfaction of one need activates the next higher need, and there is little support for the proposition that the level of satisfaction of a need diminishes its importance as a motivator.[30] In an international context, the hierarchy has been criticized as being based on Maslow's personal choice—American individualistic, middle-class values that put self-actualization and autonomy on top.[31] Furthermore, a study by cross-cultural management researchers Haire, Ghiselli, and Porter concluded that workers in different cultures tend to have a different hierarchy of needs. For example, managers in the United States and Italy ranked security as being relatively less important than other needs (basic needs were omitted from the study); in India, Spain, and Germany, security ranked as relatively more important.[32] Maslow's individual-based theory thus does not have universal application. The ensuing section demonstrates how the theory has a different application in the Chinese culture.

I-Ching: Beyond Self-Actualization

Professors David V. Gibson and Francis Woomin Wu of the University of Texas at Austin and Fordham University, respectively, have used the *I-Ching* to form what they label the ***social interaction paradigm of human cooperative behavior.*** The *I-Ching* ("The Book of Change") was written by ancient Chinese philosophers and social leaders between 3000 and 1000 B.C. and was interpreted by Confucius (551–479 B.C.). (*I-Ching* has also been translated to mean "The Bible of Practicality.") The social interaction paradigm, which is used to explain the inherent cooperative culture behind the economic success of the Pacific Rim economies, extends the hierarchy of needs beyond the self-actualization need.[33] Gibson and Wu state:

> *Maslow's theory of human needs is not comprehensive enough to address the complexity of business and social communication required by increased human interaction and the emerging global economy. It does not provide a paradigm for social interaction in relation to real-world problems of the coming decades. Although Maslow's theory describes "love" as an important motivation, it refers mostly to "self-centered" social needs, or love receiving. "Society-based" social needs for undertaking cooperative tasks for the survival and prosperity of collectives from the level of groups to nations are not mentioned.*

PRACTICAL PERSPECTIVE 12-6

Human Resource Management (HRM) in Russia

HRM in Russia in the Communist Era

In order to understand how to design efficient human resource management systems for Russia today, it is important to understand traditional human resource management practices in Russia prior to end of communism. Traditionally, Russian firms have viewed employees as a cost rather than as a resource. In addition, while Russia has had a well-developed and demanding educational system that Russians went through prior to beginning work, relatively little attention was paid to skill development once a Russian was employed in a firm.

The Russian labor market has also historically been inefficient. Artificial constraints (for example, poor labor mobility due to needing a permit to live in each town) have limited career progression and thereby decreased incentives for people to work hard. Furthermore, salary differentials were very small in Russia during communist times. Even if you could obtain extra money, it had limited value since there were few goods available to purchase. In Russia, it was products and contacts, not money, that had the greatest value. All adults were expected to have a job in Russia, and many jobs were created to ensure full employment. Since there was limited focus on the enterprise making money, less attention was given to finding ways to motivate employees to work hard than was case in the West.

It is also important to note that employment security has been a hallmark of Russian labor policy.

HRM in Russia Today

When the government was privatizing a firm, a key consideration was often finding a foreign firm that would agree to guarantee job security for at least some of the original employees. Many foreign firms in this situation encountered a problem with the acquired employees not understanding new market conditions. The change in mentality that must occur to facilitate the customer focus needed for success in today's Russia has been difficult to achieve for many firms. HRM is critical for assisting in phasing out the old culture and replacing it with a new one. For many Russians, the concept of HRM is new. One HR manager we interviewed commented that "people are surprised to find out that so much attention is given to personnel management in Western firms.

Many successful foreign companies in Russia today are growing at very rapid rates. This growth increases the HRM difficulties because there is little time to explore different HRM policies. As Dennis M. Krianin, human resource manager at Coca-Cola, explained, "Business in Russia right now is very intensive. Such companies as ours are covering in one year the history that our colleagues in Europe have covered over five years. We are developing incredibly fast."

The high rate of change in Russia is also problematic for firms. As Vera Panova, personnel manager at GPT, explained, "In Russia...daily work conditions could be compared to a jungle where you really don't know what is going to fall on your head in the next

(continued)

minute." In order for firms to survive in this jungle, competent employees are essential. As the HR development director at McDonalds said, "It is not possible to build a successful business without cultivating a base of people who will able to manage the business and take over the operations in the future. One has to think long term."

Being flexible and willing to adapt to the Russian environment has been found to be a key success factor for operating in Russia. Margaret Jones, HR manager at Cadbury, explained that her firm initially set up very strict recruiting policies, requiring two years' work experience in a foreign company and specific education. However, the firm quickly realized that this was too stringent and thus Cadbury became more flexible.

Coca-Cola follows a general country-specific policy and this is the case as it is in any other country in the world. Despite being an international company with an international image, Coca-Cola adjusts its operations to the conditions of the local environment. Coca-Cola has found that a good way to facilitate this local adaptation is to hire predominantly local personnel. Only 5 of Coca-Cola's 660 employees in Moscow are expatriates....

[A study of Russian HR practices today reveals that] having a good fixed salary is important to Russian workers and companies with non-competitive salaries will have difficulty attracting, motivating, and retaining workers. However, the study shows that the optimal compensation package combines bonuses and non-monetary benefits as well. The study also revealed that most Russians value training and badly need some. As a result, effort should be placed on competence development. The benefits of using training as a tool for motivation and retention were also demonstrated. The study also highlights that while a competitive salary is important in retaining workers, probably the most important factor in retaining key personnel is having them believe that the firm is committed to Russia.

Source: Excerpted form C. Fey, P. Engstrom, and I. Bjorkman, "Doing Business in Russia: Effective Human Resource Management Practices for Foreign Firms in Russia," Part 1 of 2 and Part 2 of 2, *Organizational Dynamics 28*, no. 2 (Autumn 1999): 69–80. Reprinted with permission of Elseviere Science.

Although these collectives are important in coordinating individual effort toward mutual benefit, the formation of social entities, such as organizations or communities, cannot be fully explained in terms of individual self-actualization or love and belongingness needs.... Instead, individual effort that is directed toward developing larger cooperative entities may result in the satisfaction of others' needs rather than just the needs of oneself. Collectives may actually restrain the individual from actualizing his or her own talent and power in order to facilitate intra- and interorganizational cooperation. When individuals act in ways that they perceive as rational in terms of pursuing their own goals, they may actually be disadvantaging themselves and others at the collective level.... Striving for high social needs without regard for immediate personal gain is symbiotic with the I-Ching philosophy, which emphasizes that as social beings, people must deal with social responsibilities throughout their lives. The greatest social welfare is achieved though the joint efforts of individuals creating better social and physical environments in which others can actualize their capacities. Greater value is placed on the ability to lead individuals and groups to cooperative output than on the actualization of one's own individual talent.[34]

To help illustrate the above quotation, assume that an American corporation's headquarters executive who monitors the activities of the firm's subsidiary in Japan notices that a young Japanese employee has strong capabilities and is highly productive. To reward the employee, the executive decides to promote him or her to a managerial position in charge of the group. This would be a mistake because it would demoralize both the capable employee and the group; it would disturb the group's *wa* (discussed in Chapter 10). The disruption of the group's harmony would result from the violation of the accepted Japanese practice of promoting elders and from the violation of the Japanese practice of rendering rewards to groups, not to an individual member of the group—even if his or her performance is outstanding. And individual members of the group do not want to be singled out for exceptional performance. In Japan, individuals adhere to the notion that "the nail that sticks out will be hammered down." (The corresponding Chinese saying is "the bigger trees catch the wind.") This means that a group member who receives individual recognition will be ostracized and emotionally punished by the group.

The Chinese symbol of the dragon, which depicts the Eastern thought that the ultimate aim of the individual is to contribute to the larger collective, derives from the *I-Ching*.[35] The **dragon** symbolizes both individual freedom (it can fly) and the creation of shared social benefits (its flying through the clouds causes rain, which benefits all). Thus, as symbolized by the dragon, "individual self-actualization is not an end in itself, but merely a preparation for the more noble goal of contributing to the betterment of society."[36] Therefore, the social interaction paradigm of human cooperative behavior suggests that personal freedom is a necessary step toward social cooperation.

Gibson and Wu's addition of the stages of the social interaction paradigm of human cooperative behavior to Maslow's theory of human needs is depicted in Figure 12-2. The following discussion describes the additional stages.[37]

Stage 6: Social Awareness

The stage of **social awareness**, understanding human/social needs outside one's own individual-based ends, furnishes a base for interorganization cooperative behavior and for molding effective strategies to merge human endeavors to solve difficult problems. Confucian philosophy posits that the most effective leaders often possess humble origins where they were exposed to basic human needs. Such origins equip leaders with the ability to recognize the needs of others.

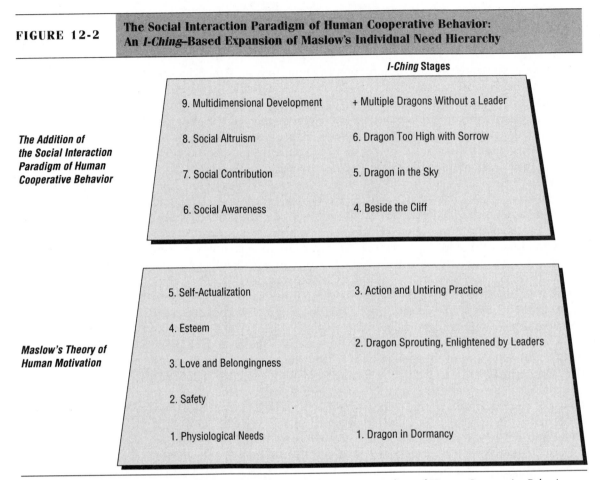

FIGURE 12-2   **The Social Interaction Paradigm of Human Cooperative Behavior: An *I-Ching*–Based Expansion of Maslow's Individual Need Hierarchy**

I-Ching Stages

The Addition of the Social Interaction Paradigm of Human Cooperative Behavior

9. Multidimensional Development   + Multiple Dragons Without a Leader

8. Social Altruism   6. Dragon Too High with Sorrow

7. Social Contribution   5. Dragon in the Sky

6. Social Awareness   4. Beside the Cliff

Maslow's Theory of Human Motivation

5. Self-Actualization   3. Action and Untiring Practice

4. Esteem

                                   2. Dragon Sprouting, Enlightened by Leaders

3. Love and Belongingness

2. Safety

1. Physiological Needs   1. Dragon in Dormancy

Source: David V. Gibson and Francis Woomin Wu, "The Social Interaction Paradigm of Human Cooperative Behavior: Societal Motivation Beyond Maslow's Need Hierarchy," *Proceedings of the Fourth International Conference on Comparative Management,* National Sun Yat-sen University, Taiwan, 1991. Reprinted with permission from Professor David V. Gibson. All rights reserved.

Stage 7: Social Contribution

Social contribution refers to the mixture of striving to fulfill other people's needs while simultaneously pursuing one's own personal growth and social power. At this stage, an individual searches for opportunities that benefit the collective. He or she looks for "win-win" situations.

Stage 8: Social Altruism

At this stage, an individual's major concern is the functioning of society. He or she acts to generate vital long-term benefits for others without wanting or needing to acquire rewards for himself or herself. Social altruism must be voluntary, and the individual must expect little overt appreciation because the beneficiaries are usually not aware of, or do not appreciate, the long-term benefits of his or her efforts. **Social altruism** requires the support of a wide range of people with influence. This support is generated in Stage 7, where the individual builds networks of organization and community ties, as well as a cooperative spirit.

Stage 9: Multidimensional Development

A key facet of **multidimensional development** is "stepping aside," that is, leaving an important position and distributing political and economic power across public and private sectors. One downplays one's social power by helping others develop their leadership abilities and networks, so that many individuals, besides the dominant few, will have strong intra- and interorganizational connections and social power. This philosophy magnifies the effectiveness of cooperative action through intensified participation, and it stimulates the sharing of rewards. Consequently, a society's benefits are enhanced because more people contribute to the common good, and greater stability is attained because power and rewards are diffused and individuals network across multiple leaders and groups.

As shown in Figure 12-2, *I-Ching* articulates the stages of leadership development by using the dragon as a metaphor:

1. *Dormant:* Dragon in dormancy.
2. *Growth:* Dragon sprouting, enlightened by leaders.
3. *Actualization:* Action and untiring practice.
4. *Take-off:* Beside the cliff.
5. *Service-delivering:* Dragon in the sky.
6. *Leading:* **Dragon too high with sorrow,** with a compensation strategy of multiple dragons capable of governing themselves.

The *I-Ching's* dormant stage compares with the physiological and stages of Maslow's theory; the growth stage compares with Maslow's love and esteem stages; and the actualization stage compares with Maslow's self-actualization stage. As indicated in Figure 12-2, the *I-Ching's* stages 4, 5, and 6 are not captured by Maslow's theory.[38]

Gibson and Wu also develop their theory from the perspective of Buddhism. They divide Buddhism into two sects: *Hinayana,* which stresses the importance of self-restraint, and *Mahayana,* which stresses selfless devotion to society. Basically, *Hinayana* compares with self-actualization in Maslow's theory in the sense that it underscores the energy it takes to contain one's mind and to exercise one's full physical and mental strength. *Mahayana* compares with the *I-Ching's* later stages in the sense that it requires great initiative and compassion for others.[39]

The leadership motivation of the *I-Ching* contrasts with Western leadership motivation. Western leaders tend to be motivated by the need for power, while Asian leaders tend to be motivated more by a need resembling the Western need for affiliation.[40] The Asian leaders' "sorrow" (stage 6) derives from their having to make decisions that affect others—Western leaders generally do not experience such "sorrow." In other words, leaders motivated by the philosophy of the *I-Ching* lack the arrogance typically demonstrated by Western leaders.

Cross-Cultural Behavior Modification

All organizations around the globe seek to attain organizational effectiveness. Effectiveness, however, may be defined differently across cultures. For example, in American organizations, effectiveness is often measured by profits, but in some cultures profits are less important than other measures, such as quality of life (for instance, a clean, safe environment). One thing that is common around the globe, however, is that the attainment of organizational effectiveness requires employees to practice behavior desired by the organization. For instance, the export division of an international company requires certain staff to be present at certain times to process certain documents in a certain way. If the staff members decide not to be present at those times or decide to process the documents in their own way, organizational ineffectiveness may result. The company therefore needs to be assured that the staff members will be present when needed and that they will process the documents in the specified way. For example, it has been found that Saudis are unwilling to observe strict rules and regulations, while, in contrast, Iraqi managers show a strong tendency to follow rules and regulations.[41] The organization must then have programs in place to **modify the behavior** of employees—to develop employee behavior that conforms to the organization's needs.

All organizations attain the desired member behavior through reward and punishment techniques. But the importance level attached to the rewards and punishments varies across cultures. For example, giving money as a reward for desired behavior or not giving money because of undesired behavior may be a highly effective behavior modifier in some cultures but not as effective in other cultures. In some cultures, the prospect of being rewarded with a big individual office may encourage an employee to work hard and to conform to the behavior desired by the organization. But in other cultures it may not—for instance, American managers may work hard for such a reward, but Japanese managers are quite satisfied with a small individual office or simply sharing an office with other employees. In the same context, employees in some cultures are motivated by the prospect of being rewarded with challenging work and more job responsibility, while employees in other cultures may prefer job security. For example, British workers may be motivated more by challenging work, and French workers may be motivated more by job security.

Total Quality Management and Empowerment

Relative to the awarding of challenging work as a reward, today's popular **Total Quality Management** (TQM) concept advances the notion of **empowering** employees (usually in groups) as a means of improving organizational effectiveness.[42] Fundamentally, TQM calls for giving employees more challenging work. It is believed that employees must be given the responsibility for deciding the most effective and efficient way to service the organization's customers (both internal and external customers). However, individuals in some cultures are more receptive (or less receptive) to TQM/empowerment programs than individuals in other cultures.[43] For example, people in collectivistic (low individualism) societies are likely to work much better in groups than people in high individualism societies, who tend be competitive and prefer to work on their own. (A TQM framework is described in Chapter 14.)

Furthermore, TQM and empowerment theories assume that individuals will take the initiative in getting things done. However, individuals in strong uncertainty avoidance cultures are likely to take less initiative than individuals in weak uncertainty avoidance cultures, and vice versa. This is because taking initiative normally means taking risk, and people in weak uncertainty avoidance cultures tend to take greater risk than people in strong uncertainty avoidance cultures.[44] For instance, "industrial democracy" in Sweden, a weak uncertainty avoidance culture, was initiated in the form of local experiments and was subsequently given a legislative framework. But in Germany, a strong uncertainty avoidance culture, industrial democracy was initiated by a legislative framework first and then localized in organizations.[45] Also, individuals in some cultures tend to perceive managers' efforts to apply TQM/empowerment programs as efforts to manipulate them. (Practical Perspective 12-7 describes Motorola's efforts to implement TQM/empowerment programs in its Malaysia and Florida plants.)

WORK GOALS AND VALUES
VARY ACROSS CULTURES

In the industrialized world, the role of work in an individual's life is extremely important. What sort of work goals do people seek? About three decades ago, Frederick Herzberg, an American researcher, identified numerous work goals, including salary, work conditions, security, supervision, achievement, and recognition, and the importance level individuals attach to them.[46] Herzberg's findings posit that factors such as an increase in pay, improvement in working conditions, more security, and improved supervision do not motivate employees to increase production, but they will demotivate employees and cause them to produce less when perceived as inadequate. What motivates employees, according to Herzberg's findings, is

PRACTICAL PERSPECTIVE 12-7

Importing Enthusiasm

Inside Motorola, Inc.'s glistening walkie-talkie plant in Penang [Malaysia], the atmosphere resembles a high school sports department. Group shots of exuberant Malaysian production workers, charts with performance statistics, and morale-boosting slogans line the walls. A trophy case is filled with awards hauled back from quality competitions across the U.S. and Asia by teams with names such as "Orient Express" and "Road Runners." The messages are hammered home: We are a family. This is your company. This is a grand global experiment in plant management by one of the best-run American companies. The methods used to promote worker excellence at the Penang plant are a big part of Motorola's blueprint for developing a well-trained, motivated, and highly productive workforce, especially in emerging markets such as China and Vietnam.

This is potentially frightening news for American and even Japanese workers, who think they still have a lock on more demanding jobs. But in Motorola's case, the company is trying to allay that fear by improving the productivity and motivation of workers in its U.S. plants as well. And Motorola is using lessons learned in Penang to boost the morale and involvement of workers back home.... The [Penang] plant's quality-control program... relies in part on the thousands of recommendations it receives from workers. Last year, employees submitted 41,000 suggestions for improving operations, which resulted in $2 million in savings. "Here," says Managing Director Ko Soek King, "everyone marches in the same direction."

The Motorola approach means a great deal in a developing country such as Malaysia, where workers are used to being treated by management as disposable robots. To the typical American worker, though, it may sound more like the usual corporate motivational pap. But the "I Recommend" program, so successful in Malaysia, is also part of Motorola's approach to boost quality in the U.S. That's especially so at the company's 2,300-worker factory in Plantation, Florida, which makes products similar to those in Penang. The goal, pursued by Motorola worldwide, is to get employees at all levels to forget narrow job titles and work together in teams to identify and act on problems that hinder quality and productivity. The Plantation plant now displays lists of star employees, and managers hand out everything from "golden attitude" pins to cash bonuses for good ideas. New applicants are screened on the basis of their attitude toward "teamwork."

But getting them to match the Malaysians' enthusiasm hasn't been easy. "The whole plant in Penang had this craving for learning," says Jerry Mysliwiec, director of manufacturing in Plantation, who spent three years in Penang in the late 1980s. "People in the U.S. are less trusting and believing." And at first, many of the recommendations that came in weren't very helpful. Recalls Craig Kenyon, another manager in Plantation: "They were things like 'Move the garbage can from point A to point B.'" After a slow start, "empowerment" is starting to take hold in Florida, too.... The U.S. and Malaysian workers share one reason to stay on their toes: fear of losing their jobs. Not long ago, a quality team was assembled in Florida to examine a component production line whose workers' morale was at rock bottom. Hourly output was one-third of the counterpart line in Penang. The Plantation team boosted output by nearly 150 percent by, among other things, reducing 18 work stations to 6. Now, a product change and a highly automated line are giving the team a new goal: to find new jobs for the workers no longer needed.

Malaysians also must stay alert. Just as the Penang plant had its origins as a source of cheap labor, the workers' fear is that Motorola someday could shift work to an even cheaper locale. So managers are trying to increase the plant's share of R&D and looking for ways to boost efficiency even further. Says Managing Director Ko: "I constantly tell them that we will lose out to other places if we aren't cost-competitive." Ko knows firsthand about the

coming competition. Her next post is Tianjin, China, where she will be in charge of a new factory. "In China, we are starting with people with a higher level of technical training," she says. "I give them five years before they catch up with us." If that's an accurate prediction, workers in both the U.S. and Malaysia will have even more reason to keep hustling. For both production workers and engineers, staying competitive is the only real job guarantee in the global economy.

Source: Excerpted from Peter Engardio and Gail DeGeorge, "Importing Enthusiasm," *Business Week, 21st Century Capitalism,* special edition (1994): 122–123. Copyright © 1994, McGraw-Hill, New York. Used with permission.

the presence of factors such as opportunity for personal growth, challenging work, and recognition—but the absence of these factors does not cause demotivation. It should be noted that his research subjects were professionally homogeneous Americans (accountants and engineers). Does the importance level employees attach to various **work goals vary across countries?**

Do Work Goals Vary Across Cultures?

To obtain an answer, Itzhak Harpaz, a researcher at the University of Haifa, Israel, surveyed employees from seven countries. The countries and the number of respondents from each country were as follows: Belgium (5450), Great Britain (773), Germany (1,278), Israel (973), Japan (3,226), the Netherlands (996), and the United States (1,000). The employees were asked to rank eleven work goals.[47]

The results are shown in Table 12-5. As Table 12-5 shows, employees in Belgium, Great Britain, Israel, and the United States ranked "interesting work" as the most important facet of their work lives, and employees in Japan, the Netherlands, and Germany ranked it second or third respectively. The Japanese employees ranked "match between person and job" as the most important facet of their work lives, employees in the Netherlands ranked "autonomy" as the most important, and German employees ranked "pay" as number one. "Pay" was ranked number two in Belgium, Great Britain, and the United States, number three in Israel, and number five in Japan and the Netherlands. Thus, as Table 12-5 depicts, while the "interesting work" value is fairly consistent across the seven nations, many of the other values are not. For example, while "autonomy" was ranked number one in the Netherlands, it was fourth in Belgium and Israel, eighth in the United States, and tenth in Britain.

TABLE 12-5 | **Mean Ranks and Intracountry Ranking of Work Goals**

Work Goals	Belgium	Britain	Germany	Israel	Japan	Netherlands	USA
Opportunity to learn	5.80[a] 7[b]	5.55 8	4.97 9	5.83 5	6.26 7	5.38 9	6.16 5
Interpersonal relations	6.34 5	6.33 4	6.43 4	6.67 2	6.39 6	7.19 3	6.08 7
Opportunity for promotion	4.49 10	4.27 11	4.48 10	5.29 8	3.33 11	3.31 11	5.08 10
Convenient work hours	4.71 9	6.11 5	5.71 6	5.53 7	5.46 8	5.59 8	5.25 9
Variety	5.96 6	5.62 7	5.71 6	4.89 11	5.05 9	6.86 4	6.10 6
Interesting work	8.25 1	8.02 1	7.26 3	6.75 1	7.38 2	7.59 2	7.41 1
Job security	6.80 3	7.12 3	7.57 2	5.22 10	6.71 4	5.68 7	6.30 3
Match between person and job	5.77 8	5.63 6	6.09 5	5.61 6	7.83 1	6.17 6	6.19 4
Pay	7.13 2	7.80 2	7.73 1	6.60 3	6.56 5	6.27 5	6.82 2
Working conditions	4.19 11	4.87 9	4.39 11	5.28 9	4.18 10	5.03 10	4.84 11
Autonomy	6.56 4	4.69 10	5.66 8	6.00 4	6.89 3	7.61 1	5.79 8

[a]Mean ranks are shown in the top line of each cell.

[b]The rank of each work goal within a given country is shown in the bottom line of each cell. Rank 1 is the *most* important work goal for a country, and rank 11 is the *least* important.

Source: Itzhak Harpaz, "The Importance of Work Goals: An International Perspective," *Journal of International Business Studies 21*, no. 1 (First Quarter 1990): 81. Copyright © 1990, *Journal of International Business Studies.* Reprinted with permission.

An interesting point in this study is that Japan was the only country Geert Hofstede classified as a collectivist (low individualism) society. People in these cultures value group harmony to a greater extent than do people in high individualism societies. This would help explain why "match between person and job" was ranked the number one work value by the Japanese employees—being in the right job helps maintain harmony. Israel and the Netherlands were the only countries classified by Hofstede as feminine societies—the others were classified as masculine societies. According to Hofstede, people in feminine cultures strongly value the maintenance of good interpersonal relations, and people in masculine cultures tend to need to perform and to assert themselves.[48] Israel and the Netherlands were the only two of the seven societies included in this study to rank the "good interpersonal relations" work value higher than the "pay" work value.

The results of the above study indicate that the importance people place on work goals tends to vary from culture to culture. It should be noted that the study included only advanced industrialized countries. Therefore, those work goals that match across cultures may be generalizable only to advanced countries. Thus, the same study conducted in industrially less-advanced countries is likely to produce different results—if people are not well fed or are relatively illiterate, they may not rank "interesting work" or "challenging work" very high and may rank money very highly. For example, cross-cultural researchers Philip Hughes and Brian Sheehan interviewed Eastman Kodak employees in Australia and Thailand work sites to determine what they valued most about their work. Australian employees valued interesting and challenging work, and Thai employees valued work primarily for the friends with whom they worked.[49] (Practical Perspective 12-5, presented earlier, and Practical Perspective 12-8 illustrate how money is very important to Chinese workers.)

The Full Appreciation of Work Done

The work values included in the above study are not all-inclusive—there are other work values. For example, Professor Colin P. Silverthorne of the University of San Francisco conducted a study to compare employee work motivation in the U.S., Russia, and Taiwan. Silverthorne's study contained some work values that were not contained in Harpaz's study, for instance, "full appreciation of work done." The results of Silverthorne's study are included in Table 12-6.

Silverthorne asked managers in the three countries to rank the ten work values based on how they believed their employees would rank them.[50] Their rankings are indicated by *M* in Table 12-6. The professor then asked the managers' employees to rank the same ten values. Their rankings are indicated by *E* in Table 12-6. Note that American employees ranked "Full appreciation of work done" as number one and "interesting work" (ranked number one in the Harpaz study) as number two. Note also that "Full appreciation of work done" was ranked number seven by the Russian employees and number four by the Taiwanese, and "interesting work" was ranked number five by the Taiwanese. As illustrated in Table 12-6, American managers' and employees' rankings are far more closely matched than are the Russians' and the Taiwanese's matchings. One explanation as to why U.S. managers' and employees' rankings are more closely matched may be that U.S. management theories and managerial development programs, which have been administered in Russia and Taiwan to a lesser extent, have in the past several decades sensitized American managers to the fact that organizational effectiveness depends on their being aware of motivating factors. Note also that the Russian employees rated "promotion and

PRACTICAL PERSPECTIVE 12-8

In China, Firms Find Some Employees Just Keep Going and Going and Going

Chantelle Qian is bright, personable and resourceful. Fluent in Mandarin, English, and Japanese, experienced in human-resources management and marketing, the 27-year-old Shanghai native has put her skills to work.

A bit too well, some would say. Qian has held four executive positions in 4 years.

In China, thousands of highly skilled people make it a practice to hop from job to job, often within a matter of months. "The average turnover in China for many midlevel to senior-level executive posts is 8 to 12 months," says Polly Yip, China division manager for KPMG Peat Marwick's human-resources consulting service in Hong Kong. "The talent pool is small, job opportunities are numerous, and people are constantly looking for better career prospects."

High Turnover

Roughly 17 percent of the local managers working for joint ventures in Guangzhou switched jobs during the year ended Feb. 1, according to a survey by compensation consultant Watson Wyatt Worldwide. Turnover rates are marginally lower in Shanghai and Beijing—about 12 percent, down from roughly 15 percent last year.

The people most in demand, and most likely to job hop, are in finance and accounting and sales and marketing and include those filling general-manger posts, according to Yip and Mona W. Chan, a director at Watson Wyatt in Hong Kong.

But times are changing. Recruitment and compensation consultants say local professionals in China are holding on to jobs longer as joint-venture companies launch retention programs that often provide training, regular salary reviews, more executive benefits and, most importantly, a clearly defined career path.

"When [markets in] China first opened" in the 1980s, "many people made job moves simply for money," recalls Chan. "For 20 percent more, they'd take a new job. Now, they're more concerned about career development than just monetary rewards," she says. Job candidates are asking about training, promotions, housing, savings programs, and recently, retirement benefits, she says.

Professionals Wanted

But this doesn't mean the days of frequent job-hopping are over. The pool of skilled professionals in China with overseas work experience or advanced degrees from abroad can't meet current demand, estimated by some experts as ten jobs for every qualified person.

And demand is growing quickly. The need for executive among large corporations will increase by at least 400 percent during the next decade, according to a 1996 study by human-resource consultants Korn/Ferry International. That estimate might even be conservative as the number and size of foreign-funded enterprises grows and state-operated enterprises try to reform to be competitive, says Ng Sek-hong, an associate professor at the University of Hong Kong who studies employment issues in China.

Part of the problem may be differing perceptions about what constitutes short-term and long-term employment, observes Nigel P.R. Isherwood, human-resources director at Nestlé (China) Investment Services in Beijing. "Many new hires can't see beyond six months to a year, while we see a minimum commitment of three to four years," Isherwood explains.

After a year at Nestlé, people are itching for a promotion or a new job, Isherwood says. But Nestlé, which employs 5,000 people in China and manufactures and sells instant coffee, tea, creamer, and milk products, finds most executives aren't up to speed until their second year, he notes. "We look to the long term—a career," Isherwood explains. "We want people who will stick with us, who have management aspirations and potential."

Focus on Retention

To keep staff, Nestlé and other companies are hustling to install retention programs that meet employee demands.

Qian, the Shanghai job-hopper, says money used to be a prime motivator. Now, she says,

her priorities have shifted. "Training and benefits are important," she says. "And, it's important that the company provide career development."

Some companies offer training as an incentive. Motorola, Inc. has a full-blown internal university, teaching language and computer courses to support staff, technical courses to engineers, and management to its managers. Coca-Cola China Ltd., a unit of Coca-Cola Company has a management school in China for its staff. And Ericsson China Ltd., a unit of Sweden's Telefon AB L.M. Ericsson, opened a Beijing training center in mid-1995 to hone employees' managerial and technical skills.

Source: Excerpted from Hal Lipper, "In China Firms Find Some Employees Just Keep Going and Going and Going," *The Wall Street Journal*, December 5, 1997, p. B13A. Permission conveyed through Copyright Clearance Center, Inc.

growth in the organization" as number one. This compares to the more recent findings discussed in Practical Perspective 12-6, wherein training programs were found to serve as a strong employee motivator in Russian organizations. This suggests that when international corporations hire locals to manage their foreign subsidiaries, their HR managers must make sure that the locals are put through the appropriate development programs.

Work Values: A Study of a Chinese Factory

Addressing the problem of cross-cultural human resource management, Professors John C. Beck and Martha Nibley Beck conducted a study of a factory in China whose top management was experimenting with cross-cultural management.[51] The factory, located in southern China in the town of Zhongshan, was operated by a Hong Kong subsidiary of a Japanese corporation. One part of the plant was managed by local Chinese managers, another part by Hong Kong managers, and a third part by Japanese expatriates. The factory was originally built by the communist government to produce cardboard boxes. In the late 1970s, it was purchased by the Hong Kong Japanese subsidiary to manufacture small electronic consumer goods for foreign markets, such as the United States, Japan, and Europe. Due to rising costs at home, the Japanese firm began to use this factory more and more in the mid-1980s.

In order to produce "Japanese-quality" products, the Hong Kong subsidiary's top management decided to mix the managerial style at the fac-

TABLE 12-6	Rankings of Work Values in the U.S.A., Russia, and Taiwan					
	U.S.A. 1990–1991		Russia 1991		Taiwan 1990–1991	
	M	E	M	E	M	E
Full appreciation of work done	2	1	8	7	1	4
Feeling "in" on things	8	7	9	2	3	8
Sympathetic help on personal problems	9	10	1	8	8	6
Job security	1	3	5	6	6	1
Good wages	4	5	7	10	4	2
Work that keeps you interested	3	2	10	3	2	5
Promotion and growth in organization	5	4	6	1	7	3
Personal loyalty to workers	6	8	2	4	9	9
Good working conditions	7	6	3	9	5	7
Tactful disciplining	10	9	4	5	10	10

M = The rankings of the work goals manager believed their employees valued

E = The rankings by the employees

Source: Adapted from Colin P. Silverthorne, "Work Motivation in the United States, Russia, and the Republic of China (Taiwan): A Comparison," *Journal of Applied Social Psychology* 22, no. 20 (1992): 1634. Copyright © V. H. Winston & Son, Inc., 1992. Used with permission. All rights reserved.

tory. Top management attempted to implement a mix of the Japanese, Hong Kong, American, and mainland Chinese styles. The factory was divided into three different sections. The first section, which consisted of the first and second floors of the plant's largest building, was managed by a supervisor from mainland China. The second section, which consisted of the third and fourth floors, was overseen by Hong Kong managers. And the third section, which consisted of the fifth floor, was overseen by two Japanese supervisors.

Before conducting their own study, Beck and Beck interviewed the Hong Kong subsidiary's top management. The researchers were informed that the section run by the mainland Chinese supervisors was sloppy and lazily managed. The section operated by the Hong Kong managers was highly productive but somewhat ramshackle and disorganized. And the section operated by the Japanese supervisors, "just like the Japanese," was clean, efficient, and highly coordinated. The professors thus concluded that Hong Kong top management believed that the managers with superior skills that had proven effective in one culture could be applied effectively in another cultural setting. Beck and Beck subsequently studied the situation at the factory. Their findings and conclusions are described below.

Differences Between the Three Sections

Chinese Managers. The first section was managed by a mainland Chinese supervisor left over from the factory's cardboard box–producing days. This section contained the facilities for producing the plastic casings the firm uses in its radios and stereo headsets. The production technology was simple and required little labor from the eight workers in the section. The mainland Chinese manager was thus assigned to a section with very low production technology. The section, according to the professors, appeared to live up to its reputation of being similar to Chinese-managed factories, which are usually unkempt and lackadaisically operated. The workers appeared to take little interest in their jobs.

Hong Kong Managers. The second section, operated by the Hong Kong managers, consisted of 180 floor workers. The majority of these employees spent their working hours arranged along two assembly lines, assembling small radios and portable cassette players. The Hong Kong managers were therefore assigned to a more advanced production technology. The professors observed that the emphasis in this section appeared to be on speed of production, and little attention was being paid to tidiness—there was debris of all types. There were shelves where workers were supposed to leave their shoes after replacing them with rubber slippers—which was mandatory. But most of the employees did not take off their shoes and did not put on the rubber slippers. The Hong Kong managers told the professors that it was **"mandatory," but not "required"** (organizations often have policies mandating certain behaviors that are not enforced by management, and employees practice a different behavior). The professors also observed that managers publically "scolded" employees when they made mistakes.

Japanese Managers. The third section, managed by the Japanese expatriates, contained 103 line workers. They were responsible for producing polyvaricon capacitors, tiny coil-like components utilized in small audio electronic devices. The Japanese managers were thus assigned to a very advanced production technology. According to Beck and Beck, this section demonstrated a glaring contrast to the first and second sections. The room was very clean and orderly. All employees were mandated, as well as required, to take off their shoes and put on their rubber slippers. There were no exceptions, and all the shoes were tidily arranged in the proper area. Unlike the Hong Kong managers, the Japanese managers did not apply rushed behavior nor public scolding.

Which Sections Were Most Successful?

Beck and Beck sought to determine which sections were the most effective. The professors omitted the first section from the analysis because it contained so few employees. Thus, only sections two and three (Hong Kong and Japanese managers) were analyzed. They centered their analysis around determining worker satisfaction and disaggregating levels of dissatisfaction determined by the nature of the task and factors specifically related to managerial tactics on the part of the supervisors. Their investigation used in-depth interviews and broad-scale questionnaires.

The Second Section (Hong Kong Managers). According to the professors, the workers in the second section were "old" employees who had been well trained in all aspects relating to the line. The section was doing very well, quality standards were being met, and most days the workers produced more than their quotas.

The Third Section (Japanese Managers). The third section had a high employee turnover, which was very costly to the company. Thus, employees in the second section were more satisfied (or less dissatisfied) than the employees in the third section.

Differences Attributed to Management Styles

Beck and Beck attribute the differences to the leadership styles applied by the Hong Kong and Japanese managers. The employees in the second section were more satisfied with their leaders than were the employees in the third section. The styles used by top managers in the second and third sections differed. The leadership approach used by the managers in the second section adhered to local culture; the approach applied by the managers in the third section did not. For example, the Chinese and Japanese societies share the traditional value of removing one's shoes before entering a home and walking on the floor. However, in China the value is loosely followed, while in Japan it is rigidly followed. Thus, the professors found, the Japanese managers' rigid insistence that the employees in the third section follow this practice irritated them and led to resentment (dissatisfaction). As noted earlier, the Hong Kong managers in the second section did not enforce this value, so there was no employee resentment (no dissatisfaction).

Beck and Beck also concluded that whether managers practiced **open criticism** also affected employees' satisfaction level. The Japanese managers practiced quiet, nonaccusatory behavior, while the Hong Kong managers practiced open criticism. Culturally, the practice of public scolding (*ma ren*) is quite acceptable in China, while in Japan such practice is highly unacceptable. The Chinese view such practice as open communication and view the practice of quiet, subtle criticism as "sneakiness" or lack of open communication. The Japanese managers' subtle approach thus contributed to employee dissatisfaction.

Somewhat related to the above practice, the management of a large department store in Xian, China, selects its forty worst sales clerks each year and has them write self-criticisms and analyze their shortcomings. The managers then hang a plaque with a picture over their workplace.[52] This observation, as well as Beck and Beck's observation, took place in the 1980s. This writer visited two model Chinese factories in Shanghai in June 1994. At each factory there were large glass cases with large color pictures of individual employees (such as mechanical engineers who work alone) and of groups of employees being recognized as outstanding employees and groups of the month. This may mean that employees' work values in China are changing or that Chinese values differ from region to region.

FLEXIBILITY IN CROSS-CULTURAL LEADERSHIP AND MOTIVATION

As suggested above, there are no leadership and motivation theories with clearly global application. The following section discusses how leadership styles and motivation approaches differ in Germany, France, the Netherlands, and Chinese societies.[53] (How the leadership style differs between the United States and Japan was discussed earlier.)

Leadership and Motivation Approaches

Germany

In Germany, highly skilled and responsible workers do not necessarily require a manager to "motivate" them American-style. These workers expect their superiors, who generally possess an engineering background, to assign their tasks and to be the expert in solving technical problems. German workers thus require little supervision. This means that German organizations would require relatively fewer supervisors than would organizations in many other cultures. For example, a comparison of similar organizations in Germany, Britain, and France showed that Germans have the highest rate of personnel in productive roles and the lowest in both leadership and staff roles.

France

Unlike Americans, the French do not think in terms of managers versus nonmanagers. Rather, they think in terms of cadres versus noncadres. One becomes a member of a cadre by attending the right schools and remains a member for the rest of his or her life. Furthermore, regardless of task, cadres possess the privileges of a higher social class, and it is very rare for noncadres to cross the ranks.

The Netherlands

Leadership in the Netherlands is different from what it is in the United States. Leadership in the United States presupposes assertiveness, as opposed to consensus and modesty in the Netherlands. However, in the Netherlands there are time-consuming ritual consultations to conserve the appearance of consensus and modesty.

Chinese Societies

Chinese businesspeople living/operating in other than mainland China countries, such as Taiwan, Singapore, and formerly Hong Kong, tend to prefer economic activities in which large gains can be attained with few human resources. They employ few professional managers. They do employ their sons and sometimes daughters who have graduated from prestigious business schools, but they continue running the family business the Chinese way. (For an illustration of an exception, refer to Practical Perspective 12-9.) They keep their enterprises small because of their perception that nonfamily employees will not be loyal and, if they are competent, they will start their own business. This type of view is found in the history of Chinese society,

PRACTICAL PERSPECTIVE 12-9

First Pacific's Pearls

For all their money-making abilities, the ethnic Chinese business clans have a major weakness. They jealously keep decision making within the family. Only by marriage into the patriarch's clan can a nonfamily employee acquire real power within the group.... This reluctance to share power or wealth limits the ability of many Chinese-owned businesses to grow and assures that many will suffer under inept heirs. Indonesian multibillionaire Liem Sinoe Liong is a glaring exception to the rule. The Indonesian surname of the Liem family's Chinese name is Salim. Based in Jakarta, Liem/Salim's main business, Salim Group, has holdings in everything from cement to noodles.

In the late 1970s Liem/Salim encouraged his son, Anthony Salim, to recruit nonfamily talent. Anthony Salim approached Manuel Pangilinan, a young investment banker then working for American Express Bank in Hong Kong. Pangilinan was a Filipino who was educated in Jesuit schools before receiving an M.B.A. from Wharton in 1968. Would Pangilinan set up a Hong Kong–based investment arm for the Liem family? He would. In 1981, at age 35, Pangilinan acquired for the Liem/Salims a tiny Hong Kong finance company for $1.5 million. From this seed has sprouted Hong Kong–based First Pacific Co. Ltd., an emerging trans-Asia conglomerate that probably earned over $120 million after taxes in 1994, on sales of about $3.5 billion....

"The Salims are unique," says Pangilinan. "They are one of the few Chinese groups that's recognized the distinction between ownership and management." And profitably so. Their 35 percent holding in First Pacific is currently worth $400 million, and Manny Pangilinan is considered a member-in-very-good-standing of the extended Liem/Salim family.

Source: Excerpted from Andrew Tanzer, "First Pacific's Pearls," *Forbes* (February 13, 1995): 48, 50. Reprinted by permission of *Forbes* magazine © 1999. *Forbes* 1995.

where there have been no formal laws, only formal networks of influential people steered by general principles of Confucian virtue. The authorities were often unreliable, thus no one could be trusted except one's family.[54]

The above suggests that international managers are confronted with an enormous challenge. They are faced with the complex task of having to determine the leadership style and the motivation preferred by different people in different cultures and adapt to them appropriately. This suggests that effective international managers must be highly versatile; they must know how to manage in multicultural settings. (The development of these global managers was discussed in Chapter 8.)

THE IMPACT OF INFORMATION TECHNOLOGY ON CHANGING VALUES ACROSS CULTURES

Much of the practical and academic media report that current information technology (IT), such as the Internet, e-mail, e-commerce, movies, and television, is linking the many cultures around the globe, which is leading toward the Westernization of the world, and thus toward globalization. As an illustration, Practical Perspective 12-10 describes the changes currently

PRACTICAL PERSPECTIVE 12-10

India's Youth

Every day at 8 A.M., her straight black hair tied neatly in a braid, 16-year-old Neelam Aggarwal rides three miles to school in a horse-drawn buggy. She would like to be a doctor someday. But for girls like Neelam, who lives in the dusty, impoverished village of Farah in India's northern state of Uttar Pradesh, such a vocation seems remote. For starters, her school—like most village schools in India—doesn't even offer science classes for girls.

But Neelam, one of eight daughters of a sweets maker, has no intention of becoming a housewife even if she doesn't get that medical degree. "I want to make something of myself," she says. So each day after school, Neelam operates what amounts to the village's only pubic telephone—a cellular phone owned by Indian cellular operator Koshika. By charging her fellow villagers to make calls, Neelam can make as much as $25 on a really good day. She's saving the money for computer classes, which she hopes will lead to a good job.

Ten years ago, few girls in India would have dared to be like Neelam. But today, she is the very embodiment of the Indian youth—ambitious, technology-oriented, and confident. Her generation is the product of the incredible sociological change wrought by eight years of economic liberalization in India, a period of

(continued)

How The Young Are Different

Older Generation

➤ Idealized Gandhi-style poverty, Socialist theory

➤ Grew up amidst famines

➤ Had only one state-run TV channel

➤ Mostly technophobic

➤ Tended to be avid savers

➤ Grew up with stable government led by one party; upper-caste domination

➤ Favored medicine, engineering, or civil service as careers

➤ Average literacy levels of 30 percent

➤ Tastes tended towards tradition: drinking tea, eating at home

New Generation

➤ Wants to get rich, admires Capitalism

➤ Grew up amidst food surpluses

➤ Can watch 50 TV channels via cable and satellite TV

➤ Mostly technology-savvy

➤ Tend to be guiltless consumers

➤ Grew up with constantly shaky coalitions; more voice for lower castes

➤ Favor computer-driven and other high-paying career choices

➤ Average literacy levels of 52 percent

➤ Tastes tend toward modern: Western food and sodas, eating out

painful transition from one-party, socialist rule to an economy where free markets play a much bigger role. Indian society also has been transformed by the Internet and cable television—forces young people are best equipped to exploit.

India's youth are already having an enormous impact: on the economy, on companies hoping to sell them products, on the media, and on the culture. Unlike previous generations, today's youth are not obsessed with the ins and outs of politics. Thus the current election, which pits the ruling Bharatiya Janata Party against the Congress Party, has failed to ignite the passions of the young. "Today, even if Parliament blew up, no one from this generation would notice," says Rama Bijapurkar, a marketing consultant, "It has little relevance for them." Liberalization's children also differ from their conservative, insular parents in that they proudly mix Indian values with Western packaging. They enjoy wearing saris and still admire Mahatma Gandhi. But they also like wearing blue jeans, drinking fizzy sodas, and watching MTV.

Source: Excerpted form Manjeet Kripalani, "India's Youth: Capitalist Generation," *Business Week* (October 11, 1999): 128E2, 128E4. Reprinted with permission.

taking place in India. But the changes that IT is inducing may merely be the modernization of societies, neither Westernization nor globalization.[55] As nations modernize, they will still maintain their own deeply rooted cultures, some of which, such as China, are thousands of years old. Thus, while the practical aspects (how technical things are done) of **a culture may change as a result of IT**, the value aspects of the culture will remain intact for at least several generations.

SUMMARY

This chapter has proposed that the appropriate leadership style and the motivational incentives a cross-cultural manager applies are for the most part determined by the culture in which he or she is managing. But in some situations, as discussed in Chapter 11, other factors may supersede the cultural factors in importance as the determinants of the appropriate style and incentives. The chapter has also suggested that United States–based theories do not have cross-cultural application. And it concluded that culture also influences the degree of importance people place on work values.

Key Terms and Concepts

1. Cross-cultural leadership
2. American-based leadership and motivation theories
3. Respect-oriented leadership
4. The PM theory of leadership
5. Innovator, implementor, and pacifier leadership
6. Self-actualization
7. To better serve society/the group
8. Southeast Asian management
9. Theory T and Theory T+
10. Application of one approach on a worldwide basis
11. Social interaction paradigm of human cooperative behavior
12. *I-Ching*
13. The dragon
14. Social awareness, social contribution, and social altruism
16. Multidimensional development ("stepping aside")
15. Collective
17. "Dragon too high with sorrow"
18. *Hinayana* and *Mahayana*
19. Cross-cultural behavior modification
20. Total quality management and empowerment
21. Work goals vary across cultures
22. "Mandatory" but not "required"
23. Open criticism
24. Information technology and changing values

Discussion Questions and Exercises

1. What is the notion of Theory X and Theory Y and System 4 management with respect to leadership style? Do you agree? Why?
2. What is the impact of culture on empowerment?
3. You are a cross-cultural training specialist. Your client is a global corporation that has employed you to train one of its home country employees who is being prepared to manage the corporation's foreign subsidiary in the Philippines. At home, the employee has been an effective manager by applying a "relationship-oriented" leadership style. What would you tell the employee?
4. You are the HR manager assigned to recruit three top-level managers for three of the company's foreign subsidiaries. One of the subsidiaries is in the strategic planning stages and has not yet been started. The second subsidiary has recently been started amid much chaos. The third subsidiary has been established and is now operating under conditions of stability. For each subsidiary, describe the leader-

ship characteristics each manager requires to be effective. Discuss why you chose those characteristics.

5. How do Theories X and Y differ from Theories T and T+?

6. The assumptions on which Theories X and Y are based do not apply in Southeast Asia. Why not?

7. Maslow's hierarchy of needs theory does not have global application. Discuss this statement.

8. How does Maslow's hierarchy of needs theory differ from the social interaction

paradigm of human cooperative behavior?

9. How are work goals affected by culture?

10. You are a cross-cultural training specialist. Your client is a global corporation that has employed you to train one of its home country employees who is being prepared to manage the corporation's foreign subsidiary in mainland China. With respect to motivation and work values, what would you tell the employee?

11. Discuss information technology and how it changes values across cultures.

Assignment

Contact a manager who has had experience managing an enterprise in a foreign country. Ask him or her to share his or her experience relative to leadership and motivation in the particular country. What were the differences he or she perceived? Prepare a brief report for presentation in class.

CASE 12-1

Putting on the Ritz

When Horst H. Schulze stood before the core staff of the Ritz-Carlton, Hong Kong, he gave his usual talk about team ownership and the need to correct "challenges" (a euphemism for problems) as soon as they occurred. After speaking animatedly for 50 minutes, the German-born Schulze asked a young man trained as a bellhop, "In what hotel did you work previously?" The young man smiled broadly and answered in perfect English, "My pleasure, Mr. Schulze." Reflects Schulze, 53, "In that culture, they want to say yes and are eager to please, but they didn't get what I was saying at all."

Shaking his head at the memory he adds, "I knew at that moment I had seriously underestimated what it would take to operate in the Far East. I was used to a quick start: Going in with a cross-trained team ten days before

opening and putting the finishing touches on the local staff and then leaving. I will never do that again." As president and COO of the Atlanta-based Ritz-Carlton Hotel Company, one of the world's most renowned hotel-management companies, Schulze has high standards, yet he doesn't expect any more from his employees than he does from himself. Before the grand opening of a new luxury hotel or resort, Schulze flies in to conduct orientations personally. He dons blue jeans to work alongside his employees, ensuring that every detail is letter-perfect.

That drive for excellence helped the Ritz-Carlton became the first and only company to capture the U.S. Commerce Department's Malcolm Baldrige National Quality Award in 1992.... Schulze attributes much of the victory to the Ritz-Carlton's infusing its 14,000-

employee organization with a team spirit and a sense of individual empowerment. For example, any employee is authorized to spend as much as $2,000 to satisfy a disgruntled guest. Although that award-winning management style brought the rapidly expanding company international kudos, Schulze only recently learned that doesn't necessarily translate into ready acceptance. "Our first efforts in the international market were opening two hotels in Australia," he says. "Because we spoke the same language, in my mind it wasn't going to be any different than managing a hotel in California. In hindsight, however, the Australians viewed teams and total quality management with a great deal of skepticism. They have been won over to the Ritz-Carlton way now, but it took about a year before they no longer thought of it as 'a bunch of American hype.'"

After his epiphany in Hong Kong, Schulze—a slim elegant man who is decidedly passionate about the hotel business—is still firmly committed to hiring locals to run the hotel. "They have an understanding of the local culture that outsiders cannot possibly attain quickly enough," he says. However, to ensure that Ritz-Carlton corporate culture isn't lost in the equation, the core staff of locals will now be hired a full year before the hotel is scheduled to open. "There is such a thing as a different culture," says Schulze, who began in the hotel business as a 17-year-old busboy in Germany and came to the U.S. in 1965 to work with Hilton.... "We knew that, yet we didn't fully appreciate the importance of it until Hong Kong. Now, we are being careful to teach the Ritz-Carlton culture while allowing the locals to combine it with their own so as to better relate it to their compatriots in their style."

Throughout most of the 1980s, Schulze had his hands more than full with expansion in the United States. Then, when the luxury hotel market took a major hit with the collapse of the real estate market, he began looking to export Ritz-Carlton's credo: "We are ladies and gentlemen serving ladies and gentlemen." Besides the foreign properties in Hong Kong and Australia, the 11-year-old [as of 1994] privately held company...operated a resort in Cancún, Mexico, and was scheduled to open the Hotel Arts Barcelona. The latter was the company's first property in Europe. (It didn't own the rights to the Ritz-Carlton name in France, England, Spain, or Canada.) And the Spaniards employed in Barcelona received a year-long training within the organization.

Schulze was primarily focusing on expanding Ritz-Carlton's franchise in the Pacific Rim. "That's where most of our opportunity is because that's where the business traveler is going," he said. "We go to the strategic locations because we want to build loyalty with our existing customers. The Pacific Rim and Asia are the most dynamic regions in the global economy and represent the cornerstone for our second decade of development." The Ritz-Carlton broke ground in Osaka, Japan, in December 1993] and had agreements to provide technical service and support for properties in Tokyo, Jakarta, Nagoya, Singapore, Bangok, Kuala Lumpur, Seoul, Auckland, and Bali. The company established a development office in Hong Kong and was negotiating to develop properties in Shanghai, Cheju Island, Guangzhou, Taipei, Melbourne, Pusan, Manila, a second site in Tokyo, Beijing, Shenzhen, and Gold Coast and Adelaide, Australia.

The Ritz-Carlton's reputation...was one of its most precious assets.... "Our guests expect a certain level of service and having demands met on time is one of the keys," says Schulze. "However, in Hong Kong that same rapidity is viewed as rude and intrusive. It was hard to convince them that Europeans and Americans who sat in a restaurant for two or three hours for lunch would not be coming back." Overcoming such skepticism and suspicion is paramount to the company's overseas success. In this case, Schulze discovered that the

Chinese have a great respect for written information. By showing Hong Kong employees the extensive surveys the company had done regarding guests' requirements, he was able to convince the staff that speed was paramount.

Among the most difficult hurdles he faced in Hong Kong was convincing the staff that management valued their input. Schulze always opens orientation by declaring imperiously, "My name is Horst Schulze. I am president of this company, and I am very important." After a dramatic pause, he adds, "And so are you. You are equally important." In the United States, that statement was met with approval and nods. In Hong Kong it was met with disbelief. "When I started setting silverware on the tables in the restaurant the day before orientation started, the Chinese supervisors said, 'Why are you doing that? The workers come tomorrow.'" Recalls Schulze, "They couldn't fathom the idea of leading by example—a management technique we take for granted in the United States. Understanding the idea of mutual respect was difficult, too. They were used to being the boss, period."

Companies that use management styles readily accepted in the United States must gird themselves for such battles. Schulze noticed that although the Hong Kong Chinese were clearly unconvinced that team management would work initially, they were loath to admit their disbelief. In Mexico, he knew immediately that the employees were dubious. "When I was working through the mission statement with the dishwashers, a practice I complete with each department, I asked if they had any questions," says Schulze. "The Mexicans were very open about their lack of faith in individual empowerment. They questioned everything, but they were also quicker to rally to our ways once they understood that we were sincere." In hindsight, Schulze believes it took the Australians almost three years to get with the Ritz-Carlton program. "That was completely our fault. Because English was the language there, I took it for granted that they understood us."

Questions

1. What type of leader—an innovator, an implementor, a pacifier, or a combination of two or three—do you believe Schulze is? Which facts in the article led to your conclusion?
2. Do you believe Schulze is an effective cross-cultural leader? Why?
3. Why did the Australians view teams and TQM with skepticism?

Source: Exerpted and adapted from Echo Montgomery Garrett, "Putting on the Ritz," *World Trade* (April 1994): 52–56. Copyright © 1994. *World Trade* magazine. Used with permisssion. All rights reserved.

CASE 12-2

The New Chief Auditor

Mr. Chartchai is a the new chief auditor of a large agro-business [in Thailand]. He is 29 and has an MBA from Thammasat University. He is recognized as a hard worker who accomplishes his tasks quickly and competently. He amazed his manager by studying for the MBA and finishing so quickly. This is one of the reasons he was selected to be the chief auditor. There are 10 other auditors in the department. Mr. Chartchai has been working in the department for seven years and has several close friends. He has thought of being the top manager in the department for a long time and has taken charge of the department very fast. Now that he is in charge, he wants things done his way. He takes a very strong interest in the smallest details of what the auditors do. He also keeps after the other staff. He feels that this is "his" department and that he is responsible for everything that goes right and everything that goes wrong.

Sometimes he has to complain to his friends. They keep doing things their own way, not his. He feels bad when he does it, but he has decided that running the auditing department the way it is supposed to be run is more important than friendship. From his business studies, he learned that management is not a popularity contest. Still, he would like to keep his friends and to enjoy the work and their activities after work. He misses the sense of closeness, but being a manager, he feels, is worth the sacrifice.

Questions

1. Thailand is high on power distance, low on individualism, and high on Confucianism. Is the chief auditor's leadership behavior the appropriate one for the culture? Why?
2. Does Chartchai's behavior contrast or support the *I-Ching* philosophy? How?
3. Do you believe Chartchai will be an effective manager? Why?

Source: Fredric William Swierczek, "Culture and Training: How Do They Play Away from Home?" *Training & Development Journal* 42, no. 11 (November 1988): 76. Copyright © November 1986, American Society for Training and Development. Reprinted with permission. All rights reserved.

CASE 12-3

The Rewarded Chinese Olympic Stars

For China's Olympic stars, the gold medals around their necks in Barcelona were just a forecast of what was to come. As symbolism of China's invincibility in the swimming pool and on the ping-pong table, the athletes returned home to be showered with gold and cash to an estimated value of $182,000 each, tax-free.

In a country where the average annual income [in 1992] was under $400, it was perhaps inevitable that the awards provoked feelings of envy and claims from other professionals. Rocket scientists pointed out that the launch of a Long March rocket carrying an Australian communications satellite was also considered a patriotic victory. As a result, 20 rocket scientists have each been awarded 5,000 yuan (about $900).

Questions

1. Discuss the case within the context of the hierarchy of needs framework described in this chapter. How does the rocket scientists' behavior relate to the *I-Ching* philosophy?
2. Discuss the scientists' work values.

Source: Exerpted from "China: New Rich," *The Economist* (October 10, 1992): 36. Reprinted with permission.

CASE 12 - 4

Volvo's Enriched Job Strategy

Volvo executives decided that one way to improve job conditions was through a job enrichment program. Volvo experimented with this idea by converting its Uddevalla, Sweden, plant to a job-enriched facility. Automobiles were built in small workshops by teams of approximately 12 autonomous workers. Each team member was trained to be capable of doing every job the team was responsible for in building the automobile. There were very few supervisors in the plant. Thus, members of the team learned and received feedback from the other members—not from supervisors. Volvo declared the experiment at Uddevalla a success and implemented it at its three other plants in Sweden. Volvo found the program motivational, efficient, and profitable.

Questions

1. Using a cultural perspective, why do you think the program worked so well at Volvo?
2. Do you believe the program would work as well with American employees at a U.S. car builder? Why?

Source: Adapted from William E. Nothdurft, "How to Produce Work-Ready Workers," *Across the Board* (September 1990): 47–52. Reprinted with permission.

CASE 12 - 5

F. Susanne Jenniches at Westinghouse

F. Susanne Jenniches, who previously was a high school biology teacher, joined Westinghouse in 1975 as an associate test engineer. As of 1992, she was general manager of Westinghouse's Civil Systems Division. On motivation, Jenniches stated, "I believe the best thing you can do for people in terms of recognizing and rewarding them is to give them a higher level of responsibility and authority. That doesn't necessarily mean a promotion to top management because many people don't want that kind of responsibility— many of them want more technical responsibility, more recognition of their technical expertise, or to be a team leader."

Questions

1. Based on what you have learned in this chapter, does Jenniches's belief about motivation have universal application? Why?
2. Discuss Jenniches's leadership style.

Source: Adapted from "F. Suzanne Jenniches," *Industry Week* (March 2, 1992): 32–36. Reprinted with permission.

Notes

1. "Foreign Bodies," *CA Magazine* (November 1993): 21.
2. B.M. Bass et al., *Assessment of Managers: An International Comparison* (New York: Free Press, 1979).
3. Ibid.
4. V. Terpstra, *The Cultural Environment of International Business* (Cincinnati, OH: South-Western Publishing, 1978).
5. P.T. Terry, "The English in Management," *Management Today 1*, no. 11 (1979): 90–97.
6. M.P. Mangaliso, N.A. Mangaliso, and J.H. Burton, "Management in Africa, or Africa in Management? The African Philosophical Thought on Organizational Discourse." Paper presented at the *International Management Division, Academy of Management Annual Meeting* (August 6, 1998): 21.
7. Douglas McGregor, *The Human Side of the Enterprise* (New York: McGraw-Hill, 1960); Rensis Likert, *The Human Organization: Its Management and Value* (New York: McGraw-Hill, 1961).
8. Robert R. Blake and Jane S. Mouton, *The Managerial Grid* (Houston, TX: Gulf Publishing, 1964).
9. Cited in Bernard M. Bass, *Bass & Stogdill's Handbook of Leadership: Theory, Research, & Managerial Applications*, 3d ed. (New York: The Free Press, 1990), p. 796.
10. See Robert Westwood, "Harmony and Patriarchy: The Cultural Basis for 'Paternalistic Headship' Among Overseas Chinese," *Organization Studies 18*, no. 3 (1997): 445–480.
11. Ibid. Bass, *Bass & Stogdill's Handbook*.
12. Claude Cellich, "When Cultures Collide: Managing Sussessfully Across Cultures," *International Journal of Conflict Management 8*, no. 2 (April 1997): 176.
13. M. Bennett, "Testing Management Theories Culturally," *Journal of Applied Psychology 62* (1977): 578–581.
14. J.M. Ivancevich, D.M. Schweiger, and J.W. Ragan, "Employee Stress, Health, and Attitudes: A Comparison of American, Indian, and Japanese Managers." Paper presented at the annual meeting of the Academy of Management, Chicago, 1986.
15. "Companies With Happy Staff Have More Success," *Business Times* (South Africa), Appointments Section, May 2, 1999, p. 1.
16. See V.V. Baba and M.E. Ace, "Serendipity in Leadership: Initiating Structure and Consideration in the Classroom," *Human Relations 42* (June 1989): 509–525.
17. L.R. Anderson, "Management of the Mixed-Cultural Work Group," *Organizational Behavior and Human Performance 31* (1983): 303–330.
18. Bass et al., *Assessment of Managers*.
19. Claude Cellich, "When Cultures Collide: Managing Successfully Across Cultures," p. 1.
20. Mark F. Peterson, "PM Theory in Japan and China: What's in It for the United States," *Organizational Dynamics* (Spring 1988): 22.
21. This discussion draws from C.A. Rodrigues, "Identifying the Right Leader for the Right Situation," *Personnel* (September 1988): 43–46; C.A. Rodrigues, "The Situation and National Culture as Contingencies for Leadership Behavior: Two conceptual models," in S.B. Prasad, ed., *Advances in International Comparative Management 5* (Greenwich, CT: JAI Press, 1990); and C.A. Rodrigues, "Developing Three-Dimensional Leaders," *Journal of Management Development 12*, no. 3 (1993): 4–11.
22. J.P. Wright, *On a Clear Day You Can See General Motors* (Grosse Pointe, MI: Wright Enterprises, 1979).
23. R. Mitchell, "Jack Welch: How Good a Manager?" *Business Week* (December 14, 1987): 92–95.
24. For a more complete discussion of this topic, see C.A. Rodrigues, "Application of High-Quality Leadership as an International Competitive Advantage," in A.J. Ali, ed., *How to Manage for International Competitiveness* (Binghampton, NY: The Haworth Press, 1992).
25. Cited in Geert Hofstede, "The Applicability of McGregor's Theories in Southeast Asia," *Journal of Management Development 6*, no. 3 (1987): 16.
26. Ibid., pp. 16–18.
27. Ibid., p. 17.
28. Ibid., pp. 17–18.
29. Abraham H. Maslow, "Theory of Human Motivation," *Psychological Review 50* (July 1943): 370–396.
30. J.C. Williams, *Human Behavior in Organizations* (Cincinnati, OH: South-Western Publishing, 1982), pp. 80–81.
31. Geert Hofstede, "The Cultural Relativity of the Quality of Life Concept," *Academy of Management Review 9*, no. 3 (1984): 396.
32. M. Haire, E.E. Ghiselli, and L.W. Porter, *Managerial Thinking: An International Study* (New York: John Wiley & Sons, 1966).

33. David V. Gibson and Francis Woomin Wu, "The Social Interaction Paradigm of Human Cooperative Behavior: Societal Motivation Beyond Maslow's Need Hierarchy," *Proceedings of the Fourth International Conference on Comparative Management* (1991), Taiwan, National Sun Yat-sen University. Used with permission from professor David V. Gibson. All rights reserved.

34. Ibid., p. 99.

35. Ibid.

36. Ibid.

37. Ibid., pp. 100–101.

38. Ibid., p. 101.

39. Ibid.

40. For a discussion on the three learned motivation needs, the need for achievement, the need for power, and the need for affiliation, refer to David C. McClelland, *The Achieving Society* (Princeton, NJ: Van Nostrand Reinhold, 1961).

41. M. Alaki, *Business Administration in Saudi Arabia* (Jeddah, Saudi Arabia: Dar AlShorouq, 1979); Z.B. Al-Musavi, "The Administrative Staff on the Scale," *The Economist* (Iraq) *35*, 6670 (1973); and A. Ali, "A Comparative Study Of Managerial Beliefs About Work in the Arab States," In R. Farmer (Ed.), *Advances in International Comparative Management* (Greenwich, CT: JAI Press, 1989).

42. See Carl A. Rodrigues, "A Framework for Defining Total Quality Management," *Competitiveness Review 5*, no. 2 (1995); and Richard S. Johnson, *TQM: Leadership for Quality Transformation* (Milwaukee, WI: ASQC Quality Press, 1993).

43. See Carl A. Rodrigues, "Employee Participation and Empowerment Programs: Problems of Definition and Implementation," *Empowerment in Organizations: An International Journal 2*, no. 1 (1994): 29–40.

44. See Bass et al., *Assessment of Managers; Geert Hofstede, Culture's Consequence: International Differences in Work-Related Values* (Beverly Hills, CA: Sage Publications, 1980).

45. Geert Hofstede, "Motivation, Leadership, and Organization: Do American Theories Apply Abroad?" *Organizational Dynamics* (Summer 1990): 57.

46. Frederick Herzberg, "One More Time: How Do You Motivate Employees?" *Harvard Business Review 46* (January–February 1968): 53–62.

47. Itzhak Harpaz, "The Importance of Work Goals: An International Perspective," *Journal of International Business Studies 21*, no. 1 (First Quarter 1990): 81.

48. Hofstede, *Culture's Consequence.*

49. Philip Hughes and Brian Sheehan, "Business Across Cultures: The Comparison of Some Business Practices in Thailand and Australia," *Asian Review*, Institute of Asian Studies, Chulalongkorn University (1993): 263.

50. Colin P. Silverthorne, "Work Motivation in the United States, Russia, and the Republic of China (Taiwan): A Comparison," *Journal of Applied Social Psychology 22*, no. 20 (1992): 1631–1639.

51. This discussion draws from John C. Beck and Martha Nibley Beck, "The Cultural Buffer: Managing Human Resources in a Chinese Factory," *Research in Personnel and Human Resources Management*, Suppl. 2 (Greenwich, CT: JAI Press, 1990), pp. 89–107.

52. Adi Ignatius, "Now if Ms. Wong Insults a Customer, She Gets an Award," *The Wall Street Journal*, January 24, 1989, p. 1.

53. This discussion draws from Geert Hofstede, "Cultural Constraints in Management Theories," *The Academy of Management Executive 7*, no. 1 (1993): 81–94.

54. See also Andrew Tanzer, "First Pacific's Pearl's," *Forbes* (February 13, 1995): 48, 50.

55. See Hellmut Schutte, "Asian Cultures and the Global Consumer," *Mastering Marketing* (September 21, 1998): 2–3.

VII

International Control

The intention of the control process is to enable managers to compare actual activities with planned activities. Planning (discussed in Chapter 4) and controlling are thus closely linked. When the organization establishes tactical objectives (discussed in Chapter 4), management must establish feedback mechanisms to verify that those objectives are being attained. The question, however, is how much control? The aim of Part Seven is to address the question of how much control is appropriate in a global context. When corporations establish subsidiaries in foreign countries, the managers at headquarters must decide how to best maintain control over foreign activities, that is, how to be assured that activities in foreign markets are being carried out as planned. These managers are therefore confronted with the task of deciding whether to give the subsidiaries autonomy (loose, decentralized control) or make decisions at home (rigid, centralized control), or, since either extreme is ineffective, how to attain a balance between the two. Chapter 13 discusses this aspect of control.

13

Headquarters–Foreign Subsidiary Control Relationships

Multinational companies, like Phillips, Unilever, and ITT, have relied on a decentralized structure and a diversified strategy to be responsive to local conditions. Global companies, like Matsushita and Kao, are organized around a strong central headquarters and treat the world market as an integrated whole, where universal consumer demand outweighs local preferences. International companies, like General Electric and Procter & Gamble, are structured to adapt and transfer the parent company's knowledge to foreign markets and to allow national units to adapt products and ideas from the parent company to local markets.[1]

Learning Objectives of the Chapter

When businesses establish operating subsidiaries in foreign countries, their headquarters managers must establish an effective **headquarters–foreign subsidiary control relationship**. Traditional management thinking is that a relationship may be one of **centralization**, in which headquarters managers do not give much autonomy to managers of the subsidiaries and make most of the important decisions about local operations. Or it may be one of **decentralization**, in which the subsidiaries managers are given a great deal of autonomy, and they make most of the important decisions relating to local operations. Both centralized and decentralized controls have pros and cons. Contemporary management thinking promulgates the control relationship in terms of three headquarters–foreign subsidiary governance mechanisms: centralization (a top-down hierarchical relationship), formalization (a bureaucratic, prescribed procedures relationship), and normative integration (a relationship that relies neither on centralization nor formalization, but on shared overall behavior). The appropriate control relationship is contingent on cultural and situational factors.

Regardless of the thinking they adopt, headquarters managers of effective international business enterprises must establish the headquarters–foreign subsidiary control relationship that best attains the overall goals and objectives of the corporation. After studying this chapter, you should be able to:

1. Discuss centralized and decentralized headquarters–foreign subsidiary relationships.
2. Describe the factors that affect the decision of whether to establish a centralized or a decentralized relationship.
3. Describe centralization, formalization, and normative integration relationships.
4. Discuss the cultural and situational factors that influence the use of the three relationships.
5. Discuss how a balanced relationship is accomplished.

GLOBAL CONTROLS: CENTRALIZATION AND DECENTRALIZATION

To maintain proper control systems, an appropriate organizational structure (discussed in Chapter 6) is essential. Along with identifying the appropriate structure, headquarters management must decide whether the headquarters–foreign subsidiaries relationship should be centralized or decentralized. In a centralized system, most of the important decisions relative to local matters are made by the headquarters management. In a decentralized system, managers at the subsidiary are given the autonomy to make most of the important decisions relative to local matters.

Both approaches have advantages and disadvantages. For example, it is difficult for the headquarters managers located in Paris, France, to know what type of benefits best meet the expectations of workers in a subsidiary located in Rio de Janeiro, Brazil. Local managers would know best. Joanne Webster, human resource director for Gupta Corporation, a 260-employee software company based in Menlo Park, California, stated that she has seen multiple kinds of organizational structures and now views her own ideal: "At my last company, Europe was operated like a separate company that mirrored the United States. When we were acquired, it all went into corporate in the United States, which had the responsibility for overseeing everything, even the salary surveys." Webster now finds herself leaning toward establishing human resource departments in geographic areas, with managers handling employee relations and training but reporting to her office. Webster does not believe that "we in the United States can develop the expertise in all the employment regulations. We would want to hire someone closer to the action. They would have that expertise and base their compensation and benefits on what works in Europe."[2] (Practical Perspective 13-1 presents a human resources director's view on decentralization.)

Also, foreign markets now change rapidly, and since local managers are closer to the market, they are able to keep abreast of local changes better than headquarters managers. Therefore, unduly centralized control can rob global aspirants of vital contacts with foreign customers.[3] The case of AT&T illustrates this point:

> AT&T employs about 54,000 workers in foreign markets, of which about half are in AT&T's traditional lines of equipment and communication services and the rest in its NCR computer unit. But local management is spotty, and equipment and long-distance businesses report up through separate units based in Basking Ridge, New Jersey. Virtually all major decisions are made in the United States, requiring

PRACTICAL PERSPECTIVE 13-1

Bridging Cultural Gaps

Deng Tao is Director of Human Resources for Greater China at Allied Signal and the winner of the China STAFF Beijing HR Manager of the Year Award 1998. His career path has moved from five years as a soldier of the People's Liberation Army (PLA) in Xinjiang province, northwest China, to five years in a state-owned enterprise (SOE), to a career as a Human Resources professional in multinational corporations. In 1984 he joined Hewlett-Packard, and then he moved to Mersk Shipping Company, before joining Allied Signal in 1997. Allied Signal, which produces automotive and aerospace equipment, has 12 legal entities in China, 6 of which are wholly–foreign owned enterprises (WFOEs) and 6 are joint-ventures. The firm employs over 1,000 people in China.

[In an interview by the editor of] China STAFF [Deng Tao was asked]: "If a company decides to localize, how should they go about it? What is the role of training, development, and assessment?"

[Deng Tao responded,] "With a multina-tional doing business in China, we [local managers] are the people who have experience; we know China; we know how to run a company. We can bridge the difference between the corporate headquarters far away in the United States and how we run the business in China. Whenever there is an initiative from the corporate headquarters, we ask how can it be implemented successfully in China and in different cities (because development stages vary from city to city—Xian is quite different from Shanghai). It is challenging because Allied Signal is a very decentralized culture and diversified business. The challenge for me is how to tell the U.S. counterpart how to implement things in China. We have to make some changes [to their initiatives] because some initiatives are very complex. We try to make them simple, easy to use, easy to implement."

Source: Excerpted from "The Long March from the PLA into HR Management," *China STAFF 5,* no. 6 (May 1999): 18–21. Reprinted with permission.

*foreign proposals to snake their way up through myriad departments
before getting approval. "That's much too far from our customers" to
achieve on-site, rapid decision making, said Victor Pelson, chief of
AT&T Global Operations. "The market is changing very rapidly."*[4]

Decentralizing such decisions would therefore be advantageous. On the
other hand, when decision making is decentralized, judgments made by
local managers may sometimes have negative consequences for other subsidiaries and/or may not be the best decision when the overall firm's objectives are considered. For instance, a decision made by managers at the Rio
de Janeiro subsidiary to pay generous benefits to their workers may demoralize workers in other subsidiaries if they perceive their benefits to be
comparatively unfair. Centralized decision making would thus enable headquarters managers to consider the consequences of a decision on all of the
firm's subsidiaries. Centralization, in this respect, would be advantageous.

As another example, managers of a subsidiary with decision-making
power may decide to expand their subsidiary's market. In their efforts, they
may unknowingly (or knowingly) be competing with another of the firm's
subsidiaries. For example, in the 1980s, top management at such firms as
Ford, IBM, Digital Equipment, and Texas Instruments saw their increasingly important international operations become slow-moving clones of
corporate headquarters. Little communication or coordination occurred
among regions. Even worse, country organizations sometimes spent more
energy competing with each other than they did fighting with the competition.[5] In its fiscal year ending March 1994, Japan's Matsushita realized
nearly 50 percent of its $64.3 billion in sales in overseas markets, and its
foreign factories supplied two-thirds of the goods sold abroad. Matsushita,
at the time, let its plants set their own rules, fine-tuning manufacturing.
Many of Matsushita's overseas plants began competing with the company's
factories back in Japan.[6]

Centralized control would have helped avert such a situation, and it
would have been advantageous in this respect. On the other hand, centralized controls requiring local managers to obtain permission to apply their
creativity may actually inhibit local initiatives that would benefit the
overall organization. The case of Japanese corporations' practices illustrates
how centralization can be disadvantageous:

*Unwillingness to give foreigners much clout could put Japanese com-
panies at a disadvantage. Even at Uniden, where 277 out of 10,000
employees work in Japan, Japanese executives run all the foreign subsidiaries, and most key decisions are made at headquarters.
Overcentralized management compounds the problem. Taku Ogata,
an advisor on China for Nomura Research Institute, Ltd. and author
of a Japanese bestseller,* The Secret of Success in China, *thinks the
unwillingness of Japanese companies to give authority to foreign executives is causing them to fall behind their Western competitors in
China. Westerners hire Chinese managers, turn them loose, and*

reward them lavishly if they do well. By contrast, Japanese companies hesitate to hire Chinese at high levels, and Chinese prefer to work for Western companies because the pay is better.[7]

Headquarters managers are therefore often confronted with the problem of deciding whether to maintain central control over decisions relating to the firm's foreign subsidiaries or allow local managers to use their own discretion in decision making. Of course, when an organization adopts an approach, it does not adhere to it rigidly; it changes approaches when needed. For example, when an enterprise operating on a decentralized basis is confronted with the need to transform itself due to environmental changes, headquarters management will centralize decision making. But after the transformation has been accomplished, central management may again decentralize decision making to the local subsidiaries to enable them to establish a strong **local presence.** The case of Berkel illustrates this point:

Maatschappij Van Berkel's Patent N.V., a Dutch-based MNC supplier of weighing and food processing equipment, took action to meet competitive cost pressures by transforming itself into a sales and service firm. To manage the complicated process of rationalizing its manufacturing and engineering activities and phasing in an outsourced product line, Berkel temporarily adopted a highly centralized decision-making structure. But once the transformation was accomplished, the headquarters loosened control over its national operating companies and resumed the more autonomous decision-making style that in the past had helped build a strong local presence.[8]

Some of the traditional factors used by top management to determine whether to centralize or decentralize are outlined in Table 13-1.[9] The ensuing sections present contemporary thinking relative to headquarters–foreign control relationships.

HEADQUARTERS–FOREIGN SUBSIDIARY GOVERNANCE MECHANISMS

A contemporary idea on headquarters–subsidiary governance (control) relationships (HSRs) has been discussed by business professors Sumantra Ghoshal and Nitin Nohria, from INSEAD, France, and Harvard Business School, respectively. They described the relationships in terms of three basic headquarters–subsidiary **governance mechanisms:** centralization, formalization, and normative integration.[10] According to them, **centralization** concerns the role of formal authority and hierarchical mechanisms in the company's decision-making processes; **formalization** represents decision making through bureaucratic mechanisms such as formal systems, established rules, and prescribed procedures; and **normative integration** relies

TABLE 13-1	Traditional Determinants of Centralization and Decentralization
Industry	Firms in an industry that requires product consistency across many foreign markets (such as firms with a global strategy) tend to centralize control. On the other hand, firms in an industry that must produce to suit the needs of specific foreign markets (such as firms with a multidomestic strategy) tend to decentralize decision making. This is because the former needs much more central coordination than the latter.
Type of Subsidiary	Foreign manufacturing subsidiaries are likely to be more controlled by headquarters managers than foreign marketing subsidiaries. This is because manufacturing technologies tend to be consistently applicable across foreign markets and can therefore be centrally coordinated. On the other hand, marketing technologies generally require a great deal of cross-cultural adaptation, which is generally best accomplished by local managers.
Function	International functions such as finance and accounting are likely to be more centrally controlled than functions such as hiring local workers. Top management generally likes to control "the purse" (money), and local managers would have a better grasp of the local labor market than would central headquarters managers.
Range of Subsidiary's Market	Those foreign subsidiaries that provide a wide range of products for diverse markets tend to be less centrally controlled than those that provide uniform products for uniform markets. The latter is not too complicated for headquarters managers to control, while the former would be too complex for central managers to control, and local managers are best able to make adaptations required by the diverse markets.
Number and Size of Subsidiaries in a Market	Companies with a few large subsidiaries in a foreign area tend to decentralize more so than firms with many small units. Many small units in a market would require more central coordination among the units than would a few large units, which can more easily coordinate in matters among themselves.
Ownership Structure	Partially owned foreign subsidiaries, for example, joint ventures, are more likely to be less centrally controlled than wholly owned foreign subsidiaries. The expertise, such as knowledge of the local culture, markets, and legal systems, often lies in the foreign partner, while in the wholly owned subsidiary the expertise often lies in the home office.
Date of Acquisition	Newly acquired foreign subsidiaries that continue manufacturing their old product lines under their same managers tend to be less centrally controlled because the old managers possess the expertise. However, when the subsidiary subsequently grows and begins to expand into other products and markets, central control increases because central expertise and coordination is now needed.
Headquarters' Interest and Expertise	The greater the headquarters management's personal interest in the subsidiary and the greater expertise in the subsidiary's business area, the greater central control over the foreign subsidiary it maintains. If management's personal interest is low and the expertise is little, central control will be lower. (For an illustration, refer to Practical Perspective 13-2.)
Distance	Distant foreign subsidiaries tend to be less centrally controlled—although, as indicated earlier, recent advances in global communications technologies have shortened the distance.
Environment	Subsidiaries located in countries with environments that are unfamiliar to headquarters management tend to be given greater autonomy than those that are located in familiar environments. Also, if the foreign subsidiary is located in a dynamic, changing local environment, the tendency is for headquarters management to decentralize. Local management is more familiar with the local environment and more in touch with the rapid changes that take place locally than headquarters management, and is therefore better able to cope.
Corporate Goals	If the goal of headquarters managers is to maintain maximum power, then more central control is applied. If it is to maximize local market share, however, control tends to be decentralized.

TABLE 13-1	Traditional Determinants of Centralization and Decentralization, *continued*
	Local managers are generally more familiar with the local market conditions and are therefore better equipped to carry the growth objective. (For an illustration, refer to Practical Perspective 13-3.)
Ownership	If the enterprise is owned and managed by a few individuals, these managers may maintain a closer watch over their foreign interests than would professional managers of an enterprise that is owned by a large number of stockholders. (Of course, the other factors must also be considered.)
Headquarters' Confidence in Subsidiary's Management	When the confidence in the foreign subsidiary's managerial abilities increases, decision making tends to become more shared and less dictated by headquarters' management. And vice versa: when it decreases, the tendency is to apply central controls.
Success of the Subsidiary	If the foreign subsidiary is perceived as being highly successful, headquarters control tends to lessen. But when things are not going well locally, headquarters management becomes more involved and centralist.
Intersubsidiary Transactions	A firm with a substantial volume of intersubsidiary transactions tends to be centralized because when organizational effectiveness depends on several subunits, central coordination is usually required.
Importance of Foreign Market	Headquarters management may want to monitor an important foreign market very closely. Therefore, control over a foreign subsidiary in that market would be more centralized than it would be for subsidiaries located in markets that are of less importance.
Foreign Laws	The government of the nation in which a foreign subsidiary is located may require that the subsidiary be managed by locals. Central control would thus be less.
Individuals	If managers of the foreign subsidiary require autonomy, the tendency is to apply less central control. Attempts to control these individuals from the headquarters would result in ineffectiveness. On the other hand, some individuals, culturally, prefer that decisions be centrally made.

PRACTICAL PERSPECTIVE 13-2

Managing Headquarters

Since the days the East India Company, the country manager (CM) has been the eyes and ears of the multinational corporation in foreign markets. Despite the globalization of markets and the pressures on many MNCs in favor of greater headquarters coordination, studies confirm the continued importance of CMs with profit and loss responsibility as drivers of business growth, especially in emerging markets.

Here we [J.A. Quelch and C.M. Dinhtan] present the first country-specific study of CMs

in an emerging market—in this case, Vietnam. From in-depth personal interviews with 14 CMs in Vietnam, representing MNCs across a diverse range of goods and services, our aim was to identify who the CMs were and why they had been selected, how they spent their time and how they expected to spend their time in the future, and what they regard as their principal challenges and how they dealt with them. Although we cannot claim that our findings are generalizable] Vietnam, we do believe they

(continued)

reflect the experiences of CMs in other transitional economies around the world....

Almost all the CMs in our study reported to a regional headquarters, typically located in Singapore. Six of the 14 CMs believed their required interactions with regional and world headquarters were more of a hindrance than a help. This was especially the case when no headquarters managers had Vietnamese experience or relevant experience from other emerging markets. Common complaints included the frequency and scope of financial reporting, often in formats that were inappropriate for emerging markets; numerous "parachute" visits from headquarters personnel, especially when the Vietnam operation had been accorded a high profile in the MNCs annual report; and a consequent impatience for quick results, including, for example, achieving break-even in the second year of operations.

The level and frequency of oversight from regional and world headquarters is a function not merely of the scope of operations but also of the MNC's experience in emerging markets (less experience implying more oversight) and

the perceived competence of the CM. In our study, a typical reporting pattern required four face-to-face meetings per year with the CM's regional manager. However, the relatively inexperienced CM of one of the smallest operations we examined was required to visit regional headquarters twice a month.

Managing the Vietnamese opportunity successfully calls for decentralization to a highly competent, culturally sensitive CM whom government officials and joint venture partners can respect. The market is highly competitive, with many MNCs jockeying for position, and customers are savvy, often unwilling to accept anything less than the latest product technology. Such circumstances call for CMs with the power to respond quickly to the local environment. It is essential to success that MNCs invest in their selection processes and appoint CMs to whom they feel comfortable delegating authority.

Source: Excerpted from John A. Quelch and Christine M. Dinh-Tan, "Country Managers in Transitional Economies: The Case of Vietnam," *Business Horizons* (July–August 1998): 34–39. Reprinted with permission.

neither on direct headquarters involvement nor on impersonal rules but on the socialization of managers into a set of shared goals, values, and beliefs that then shape their perspectives and behavior.[11] (Organizations that adopt the matrix organizational structure, discussed in Chapter 6, also tend to adopt the normative integration approach.) The ensuing sections present two schemes that identify factors to help determine the right headquarters–foreign subsidiary control relationship. The first scheme posits that national cultural dimensions affect the relationship. The second proposes that certain situational factors influence the relationship in all countries.

The National Culture Scheme

As discussed in Chapter 1, cross-cultural researcher Geert Hofstede[12] proposed a paradigm to study **the impact of national culture on individual behavior.** He developed a typology consisting of four national **cultural dimensions** by which a society can be classified: power distance, individualism, uncertainty avoidance, and masculinity. He later added a fifth dimension—Confucianism. The ensuing section indicates whether the headquarters–subsidiary relationship (HSR) with subsidiaries located in

PRACTICAL PERSPECTIVE 13-3

China's Car Guy

Nearly two years ago Hu Mao Yuan, 48, the first president of Shanghai General Motors, found himself enduring a sleepless night at the Renaissance Center Hotel in Detroit, far from his home in China. A veteran manager of state-owned corporations, Hu was kept awake by fears that the $1.5 billion enterprise with GM—the largest U.S. joint venture in the People's Republic—would wind up "as an auto company that just produces quarrels" between its partners. He spent that night fretting over a set of cooperative principles that would stress the independence of the joint venture. As it turns out, Hu could have rested peacefully: The project has been a hit: The Buicks now rolling out of a state-of-the-art plant in Shanghai are the highest-quality cars of that model being produced anywhere in the world—and they are also selling.

Hu has drawn much of the credit for this promising start. Top officials at General Motors are quick to attribute the early success of this ambitious and risky investment to his leadership and his ability to bridge the gap between Western and Chinese business practices. Says Rudolph A. Schlais, Jr., president of General Motors Asia Pacific: "He's a businessman and hard-charger who understands the Chinese system."…

His performance has pleased not only GM but his Chinese bosses as well. In July, Hu was appointed president and chief executive of Shanghai Automotive Industry Corporation. (SAIC), the largest and most successful automotive manufacturer in China—and GM's partner.…

Selected by Shanghai government as one of the 100 most promising managers in the city, Hu was dispatched to Georgia Tech in 1995 to study business administration. Before leaving for Atlanta, he finished a master's thesis at Fudan University in Shanghai on zero defects in quality control at Hui Zhong, a producer of trucks and components that he had headed. Shanghai authorities pulled him out of Georgia Tech after three months to lead the Chinese team forming the GM joint venture. Recalls Hu: "Both parties had to overcome a lot of obstacles—differences in social, political, and legal systems. I wasn't surprised that we had difficulties."…

Later Hu tells *Fortune* how he has made a fifty-fifty joint venture work, which he says "is difficult anywhere in the world." A joint board sets broad policies, but the top SGM executives in Shanghai—two from each of the owners—make the company's operating decisions. Says Hu: "If you hand a problem to your boss, he may not think you are capable. I like to solve things myself." In doing so, Hu has helped fit GM's strategic goal of capturing a significant share of the Chinese market while operating in an environment in which government support is crucial to business success.

From the start, the joint venture partners agreed that GM would inject technology and management skill to support a world-class car company, complete with exclusive Chinese dealers and vigorous marketing. Making that happen in the People's Republic proved to be tougher than either partner expected. The Chinese government, for instance, still dictates what products automakers can build, as well as how many and at what price. Moreover, GM is required to use locally made components, 40 percent in terms of value this year [1999] and 60 percent next year. And while sharing its latest technology, GM is restricted by Chinese law to owning just half of the joint venture.

Hu notes, "GM naturally wanted control." Bitter disputes long bedeviled SGM, even

(continued)

though the two partners spent 17 months negotiating contracts that stack about a foot high.
Remarks Hu: "They were just done to meet
legal requirements, and we never had time to
took at them afterward." Inside the joint venture, officially formed in March 1997, the
arguments raged so intensely that Hu told his
GM associates, "I think Ford and Volkswagen
would be very happy to see us quarrel." Says
Philip Murtaugh, 44, executive vice president
and the senior GM manager in the joint venture: "We had a lot of shooting matches but
finally established a level of trust." Murtaugh
credits Hu with moving American and Chinese
managers from confrontation, unavoidable in

negotiations, to cooperation, and says, "He
could run a company anywhere in the world."

Dealing with the egos of leaders of the
biggest corporation on earth proved to be an
enormous challenge for Hu, who says, "In
many other places GM won't listen to its local
partners. That made my job more creative. It's
not easy to change the attitudes of GM
people." Nonetheless, he broke through dead-
locks by establishing great rapport with Murtaugh, a bright young charger himself.

Source: Excerpted from Louis Kraar, "China's Car Guy,"
Fortune (October 11, 1999): 238–244. Copyright © 1999 Time
Inc. Reprinted by permission.

these cultures leans toward low or high centralization (C), low or high formalization (F), or low or high normative integration (NI). (See Table 13-2.)

Power Distance

Moderate-to-Large Power Distance. Individuals in societies dominated
by this dimension tend to accept centralized power and depend heavily on
superiors for direction. Therefore, an HSR leaning toward high C probably
would be preferred by subsidiary managers who are dominated by this cultural dimension.

Moderate-to-Small Power Distance. Individuals in societies dominated
by this cultural dimension do not tolerate highly centralized power and
expect to be consulted, at least, in decision making. Furthermore, Hofstede
remarked that status differences in these countries are suspect. Thus, subsidiary managers who are dominated by this cultural dimension probably
would favor an HSR leaning toward low C, high NI, or high F.

The research project previously discussed including MBA students
from Germany, Great Britain (both small power distance societies), and
France (a large power distance society)[13] provides some support for the conclusions about a country's power distance measure influencing HSR. The
students were asked to write their own diagnosis of and solution to a case
problem. The majority of the French referred the problem to the next
higher authority—they sought direction (high C). The British handled the
problem (low C or high NI-like behavior), and the Germans attributed it to
a lack of formal policy and proposed establishing one (high F). Decision
making in many of the Latin American cultures, which generally measure
high on the power distance dimension, tends to be centralized.[14]

TABLE 13-2	The National Culture Framework
Cultural Determinants	**Headquarters–Foreign Subsidiary Control Relationship**
Large power distance	HC
Small power distance	LC, HF, or HNI
High individualism	HC or HF
Low individualism	LF, HNI
Strong uncertainty avoidance	HF or HC
Weak uncertainty avoidance	LC or HNI
Confucianism	LF, HC, HNI
High masculinity	HF
Low masculinity	LC, HNI
C = centralization; F = formalization; NI = normative integration; H = high; L = low	

Source: Carl A. Rodrigues, "Headquarters–Foreign Subsidiary Control Relationships: Three Conceptual Frameworks," *Empowerment In Organizations: An International Journal 3*, no. 3 (1995).

Individualism

Moderate-to-High Individualism. Individuals in societies dominated by this dimension think in "me" terms and look after primarily their own interests. Since these individuals often consider their own objectives to be more important than the organization's, the HSR that evolves in subsidiaries managed by people influenced by this cultural dimension probably leans toward high C or high F.

Moderate-to-Low Individualism. Low individualism societies are tightly integrated and individuals belong to "in-groups" from which they cannot detach themselves. People think in "we" as opposed to "me" terms and obtain satisfaction from a job well done by the group. Individuals in these societies are controlled mainly by the group's norms and values. These people would therefore require less formal structure than individuals who think in "me" terms. An HSR leaning toward high NI would thus fit these societies.

Findings by some researchers lend support to the above contentions. These researchers concluded that control systems in the United States (a high individualism culture) are designed under the assumption that workers and management seek "primary control" over their work environments.[15] Primary control is manifested when employees with individualistic tendencies attempt to shape the existing social and behavioral factors surrounding them, including co-workers, specific events, or their environments, with the intention of increasing their rewards.[16] Thus many employees exhibit behaviors and establish goals that may diverge from those desired by the organization. For these reasons, control systems consisting of rules, standards, and norms of behavior are established to guide, motivate, and evaluate employees' behavioral performance (high F).[17] On the other hand, organizations in Japan (a low individualism culture) rely more on "secondary controls," controls that rely mostly on informal peer pressure (high NI).[18] And Japanese corporations with subsidiaries in the United States tend to give American managers working for them little or no authority.[19]

Uncertainty Avoidance

Moderate-to-Strong Uncertainty Avoidance. Individuals in these cultures feel uneasy in situations of uncertainty and ambiguity and prefer structure and direction. Therefore, because it tends to reduce uncertainty for individuals, managers of subsidiaries who are influenced by this cultural dimension probably would prefer an HSR leaning toward high F or high C. Hofstede has proposed that improving quality of life for employees in these societies implies offering more security and perhaps more task structure on the job (high F).

Moderate-to-Weak Uncertainty Avoidance. Hofstede found that in countries dominated by a moderate-to-weak uncertainty avoidance dimension, individuals tend to be relatively tolerant of uncertainty and ambiguity; they do not require as much high C or high F as do people in strong uncertainty avoidance cultures. Thus, an HSR leaning toward low C or high NI, since it provides more challenge than does high C and high F, probably would be preferred by managers of subsidiaries who are dominated by this cultural dimension.

For example, managers in Britain, a weak uncertainty avoidance culture, tend to value achievement and autonomy (low C or high NI behavior) and managers in France, a strong uncertainty avoidance society, value competent supervision, sound company policies, fringe benefits, security, and comfortable working conditions (high C and high F).[20] French managers do not believe matrix organizations (discussed in Chapter 6), which tend to apply high NI-like behavior, are feasible; they view them as violating the principle of unit of command.[21]

Confucianism

As pointed out in Chapter 1, individuals in East Asian cultures (the People's Republic of China, South Korea, Japan, Hong Kong, and Singapore) are also influenced by the Confucian cultural dimension. In essence, individuals in Confucian-based organizations are forced to adhere to rigid, informal group norms and values (high NI-like relationship). Since individuals are so strictly bound to group norms, organizations based on the Confucian cultural dimension probably apply less formalization (low F) than do organizations in the West. This contention is partially supported by research findings that organizations in China, where the Confucian influence is still strong, tend to be far less formalized than Western organizations.[22] There is evidence that Confucian-based organizations apply high C. For example, South Korean managers demonstrate the Confucian virtues of loyalty and obedience to authorities and they tend not to adopt systems of shared management and power equalization within organizations.[23] Chinese subordinates have been found to be passive, preferring that others make decisions for them (high C).[24]

Masculinity

Moderate-to-High Masculinity. Societies dominated by this dimension stress material success and assertiveness and assign different roles to males and females. To review, males are expected to carry out the competitive roles in the society; females are expected to care for the nonmaterial quality of life. In strong masculine countries where people perceive such behavior as being inequitable, an HSR leaning toward high F, emphasizing reduction of such social inequities would probably be preferred. One finds evidence of this in recent programs in the United States, a society with a moderate-to-high masculine cultural dimension—the Equal Pay Act of 1963, Title VII of the Civil Rights Act of 1964, affirmative action and equal employment opportunity programs; and in Japan with its very high masculine culture—the Employment Opportunity Law of 1986.

Moderate-to-Low Masculinity. Hofstede also concluded that those nations dominated by a low masculine cultural dimension stress interpersonal relationships, a concern for others, and the overall quality of life, and define relatively overlapping social roles for males and females. In these cultures, neither male nor female need be ambitious or competitive; both may aspire to a life that does not assign great values to material success and respects others. According to Hofstede,[25] improved quality of work life for individuals in these societies means offering opportunities for developing relationships on the job, which is perhaps best accomplished through low C or high NI-like HSR. For example, people in Sweden, a low masculine society, generally prefer organic (low C, NI-like) organizational structures, and they like to be involved in the decision-making process.

The Situational Scheme

The above presented a national culture scheme as a means of determining HSRs. However, as pointed out in Chapter 11, the scheme serves mainly as a generalization—as a starting point for analysis—and many organizational theorists[26] have argued that, irrespective of a society's culture, individuals are forced to adapt attitudes and behaviors that comply with the imperatives of industrialization. This means that HSRs are affected more by situational factors than cultural factors. Thus we arrive at the **situational scheme.** See Table 13-3.

TABLE 13-3	The Situational Framework	

Situational Determinants	Headquarters–Foreign Subsidiary Control Relationship
The Subsidiary's Local Context	
Low complexity; low level of resources	HC, LF, LNI
Low complexity; high level of resources	LC, HF, HNI
High complexity; low level of resources	MC, LF, HNI
High complexity; high level of resources	LC, MF, HNI
The Organization's Size	
Large-scale organization	HF
Large-scale organization with global strategy	LC, HC, HNI
Large-scale organization with multidomestic strategy	LC, HF
Small-scale organization	HNI or HC
Organizational Function	
R&D-like functions	HNI, LC, LF
Production-like functions:	
With multidomestic strategy	HF
With global strategy	HNI, MC
Cash management-like functions	HC, HF
Organization under Crisis Conditions:	
In an environment of scarcity	HC or HF
In an environment of abundance	LC, HNI
Management's Preference:	
Likes to maintain strong control	HC
Likes to maintain stability	HF
Likes to maintain adaptability, flexibility	HNI
Information Technology: Communication Costs:	
Costs are high	LC
Costs fall	HC
Costs continue falling	HNI

C = centralization	F = formalization	NI = normative integration
H = high	L = low	M = moderate

Source: Carl A. Rodrigues, "Headquarters-Foreign Subsidiary Control Relationships: Three Conceptual Frameworks."

The Subsidiary's Local Context

Ghoshal and Nohria believe that headquarters–subsidiary relationships are not identical for all subsidiaries throughout the company, that each headquarters–subsidiary relationship can be governed by a different combination of the three mechanisms (C, F, NI), and that companies adopt different governance modes to fit each **subsidiary's local context.** The local context, according to them, can vary in a number of ways, but two of the most important ways are **environmental complexity** (the level of technological dynamism and competitive intensity) and the **amount of local resources** available to the subsidiary.[27] Some subsidiaries may be managing advanced technologies (computers, for example) in a very competitive market (high environmental complexity), while others may be managing older technologies (steel production, for example) in a stable market (low environmental complexity). Some subsidiaries may have an abundance of resources, while others have scarce resources. Ghoshal and Nohria developed a scheme that matches headquarters–foreign subsidiary control relationships to subsidiary contexts. The scheme is as follows:[28]

1. Low environment complexity and low levels of local resources dictate a high level of centralization and low levels of formalization and normative integration.

2. Low environment complexity and high levels of resources dictate a low level of centralization and high levels of formalization and normative integration.

3. High environment complexity and low resource levels indicate a moderate level of centralization, a low level of formalization, and a high level of normative integration.

4. High environment complexity and high resource levels indicate a low level of centralization, a moderate level of formalization, and a high level of normative integration.

Size of the Organization

The **size of the organization** has been found to be a factor in determining HSRs. Large-scale organizations have tended to apply structural relationships leaning toward high F and small-scale organizations tend to apply a high NI or high C structural relationship.[29] However this factor is influenced by the organization's strategy. Some international businesses establish a global strategy. The global corporation uses all of its resources against its competition in a very integrated fashion. All of its foreign subsidiaries and divisions are highly interdependent in both operations and strategy. As an expert said,

> In a global business, management competes worldwide against a small number of other multinationals in the world market. Strategy is centralized, and various aspects of operations are decentralized or centralized as economics and effectiveness dictate. The company seeks to respond to particular local market needs, while avoiding a compromise of efficiency of the overall global system.[30]

Companies that apply the global strategy include IBM in computers; Caterpillar in large construction equipment; Timex, Seiko, and Citizen in watches; and General Electric, Siemens, and Mitsubishi in heavy electrical equipment. Many corporations that adopt the global strategy approach also adopt the matrix organizational structure. In the matrix structure there is extensive cooperation among all the operating subsidiaries. Therefore, the global corporation relies on an HSR with a combination of low C, high C, and high NI.

Many international firms establish a multidomestic strategy. The multidomestic firm has a different strategy for each of its foreign markets. In this type of strategy, "a company's management tries to operate effectively across a series of worldwide positions with diverse product requirements, growth rates, competitive environments, and political risks. The company prefers that local managers do what is necessary to succeed in R&D, production, marketing, and distribution but holds them responsible for results."[31] In essence, this type of corporation competes with local competitors on a market-by-market basis. A multitude of American corporations use this strategy, for example, Procter & Gamble in household products, Honeywell in controls, Alcoa in aluminum, and General Foods in consumer goods. Large organizations that adopt a multidomestic strategy tend to apply low C; but for accountability reasons, they also tend to rely on bureaucratic (high F) HSRs.

Type of Organizational Function

The **internal aspects of the organization** are also determinants of structural relationships.[32] Some subunits apply high organic, NI relationships, while other subunits in the same organization apply high C or F relationships. Thus, R&D subsidiaries, because their functional effectiveness often depends on an integration of numerous individuals' ideas, probably function more effectively with a relationship leaning toward low F, low C, and high NI. Subunits such as production, a function that usually requires high structure to ensure production efficiency, probably work best with a relationship leaning toward high F—this, however, may be more so for corporations with a multidomestic strategy than for companies with a global strategy. To ensure overall production efficiency, global corporations often integrate production across all subsidiaries by use of the matrix organization structure, thus applying a high NI with some degree of central coordination (moderate C). Functions such as cash management are usually centralized (high C) and formalized (high F). For example, Broken Hill Proprietary Company Ltd., a U.S.-based producer/distributer of minerals, petroleum, and steel, has centralized cash management in the corporation but has decentralized and localized the management of resource gathering, marketing, and distribution.[33] (Practical Perspective 13-4 illustrates how BICC Cables dealt with the problem of needing to decentralize certain functions while at the same time needing to centralize the information technology function.)

Organizations under Crisis Conditions

Numerous studies have revealed that organizations confronted with **crisis conditions**—environmental hostility, turbulence, and financial adversity—tend to increase the formalization and standardization of procedures, to place greater emphasis on previously established rules, and to centralize and involve fewer people in the decision-making process.[34] (The case of

PRACTICAL PERSPECTIVE 13-4

Getting the "Hardware" Right: The Case of BICC Cables

One of the primary challenges in an organisation is to set up an IT function. How well the function is set up is a major factor in its effectiveness. Yet setting the functions up well requires highly effective IT management in the first place. And what constitutes a well-structured IT function can change over time with the strategic needs of the organisation and with the characteristics of IT.

For many years BICC Cables had allowed its worldwide operations great local decision-making authority. Customers usually made local purchasing decisions. The company believed that managers of local operating units would make the best business decisions if they had responsibility for all factors affecting profitability—including IT.

Two issues caused the company to rethink its IT management strategy. First, managers anticipated a shift toward customers purchasing globally—a trend that would require greater interdependence among local operations. Second, they became aware of developments in IT that seemed to require a different management approach. The company's capital budgeting committee found itself simultaneously considering requests from two different operating units to replace aging legacy information systems with an enterprise software package. The two had done a thorough evaluation to determine the best package for their needs—and had chosen two different packages.

Members of the committee asked themselves several questions. Didn't the two units do basically the same things? If so, how could two different packages both be best? How much would it cost to adopt different IT solutions in different parts of the company? And how would different IT solutions in different parts of the company hinder it from responding to likely future business trends? Preliminary investiga-

tions revealed that a corporate approach to acquiring enterprise software would yield major saving over a decentralised approach.

Of course, the committee's questions raised a number of red flags. How would local units react to any recentralisation of IT management? Would this seriously undermine the autonomy that operational managers needed to control profitability? These were clearly serious concerns, requiring careful handling.

The committee put both requests on hold pending further study of the need for common systems, and Andrew Cox, the company's chief financial officer, hired its first chief information officer, Alan Harrison. To combat fears of "IT empire-building," Harrison operated for several years as a "department of one". He convened a company-wide task force to chart the major business processes of one of the local operations. Each site was then asked to review the charts, noting local differences. The results were quite compelling: the commonalties in business processes across local operations were far greater than the differences. Thus it looked possible to select a single enterprise package representing what was best for the company as whole.

The next step was to form a company-wide software selection task force to evaluate several options, including the two first championed by local units. The evaluation criteria were rigorously defined in advance to forestall any criticism from the "losers." When the committee completed its selection, Harrison negotiated a very favourable corporate contract with the software vendor.

The corporate purchase agreement was not the last of the new IT management decisions raised by enterprise software. Still to be decided were which units would adopt the software,

(continued)

how much local autonomy there would be in software configuration, and how implementation and support would be managed. To ensure local commitment to implementing software successfully, units were still required to apply to the capital budget committee for funding. All were expected to justify their applications but they were granted freedom to justify their applications in locally relevant terms. Some cited business benefits such as inventory reductions; others emphasized IT cost savings.

To enable a coordinated response to customers in the future, BICC Cables decided to develop a common enterprise model. Local operations could request changes but these would be treated as changes to the core model rather than as changes in local implementations. On the other hand, local operations were expected to implement the software themselves with consulting support from the vendor and from the still small (but no longer one-man) IT function. Because enterprise software involves a long-term commitment to a vendor's product

family (and therefore a series of future upgrades), the local units were thought to require the capacity to manage implementations locally.

The case of BICC Cables illustrates several points about improving the effectiveness of the IT function. First, decisions about the "hardware" of the IT function (its size; structure; mission; and tasks, including the activities to be outsourced) are critical. Second, these decisions must be revisited from time to time as changes occur in the nature of the business and in the opportunities and challenges posed by new information technologies. Third, these decisions will not be the same for all companies but will depend on such things as the industry in which a company operates; the company's specific business strategies; and its size, structure, and historical management culture.

Source: Excerpted from "Organising a Better IT Function," *Financial Times* (London), Survey Edition 1 (February 15, 1999): 5. Reprinted with permisssion.

Samsung in Practical Perspective 13-5 illustrates this point.) In other words, headquarters managers of organizations confronted with crisis conditions usually apply an HSR leaning toward high F or high C. It has been found, however, that this occurs more frequently when the organization exists in an environment of scarcity than when it exists in an environment of abundance.[35] Organizations confronted with crisis conditions in an environment of abundance tend to decentralize (low C, high NI behavior).

Management's Preference

Culturally, **management's preference** may be to maintain strong control over activities (high C); strong organizational stability, and thus a bureaucratic system (high F); or a flexible, adaptable organization, and therefore an interactive approach (high NI). U.S.-based giant Johnson & Johnson is an illustration of a company whose management has over the years developed a corporate culture that promotes decentralization but encourages managers to act in a global, concerted fashion when necessary.

Johnson & Johnson is performing an act that defies gravity. It runs no fewer than 33 major lines of business with an astounding 168 operating companies in 53 countries. And runs them well. Johnson & Johnson may have mastered the art of decentralized management

PRACTICAL PERSPECTIVE 13-5

The Man Who Shook Up Samsung

Even in a year of remarkable recovery for Asia, some of the region's leading companies were foundering because of old bad habits. That wasn't the case with Samsung Electronics, whose CEO, Yun Jong Yong, used Asia's current chaos to reinvent a company that seemed near death—a feat that has earned Yun *Fortune*'s title of Asia's Businessman of the Year.

When Yun took command of Samsung three years ago, earnings had largely evaporated because of a long decline in the prices of memory chips—then Samsung's main source of profit. And the company was losing money on its low-priced me-too models of TVs and microwave ovens. "There was a sense that this company could go down. It was that extreme," says Yun. So extreme, in fact that Samsung's chairman authorized Yun, an electrical engineer who has been with the company since its founding in 1969, to make changes shocking to most Koreans—chopping one-third of the payroll and replacing half of the senior managers; selling off $1.9 billions in assets, from an executive jet to an entire semiconductor division; refusing to tolerate long presentations or reports; and welcoming a foreigner to the corporate board. Then Yun launched a slew of leading edge products, including Internet music players, flat-panel displays, and a line of 5.5 oz cell phones with both voice-activated dialing and Internet access. The result: Analysts estimated that 1999 earnings would rise more than tenfold, to $2 billion...and the company's stocks, listed in Korea and widely held internationally, rose 233 percent, to $227 a share, last year [1999].

Source: Louis Kraar, "Asia's Businessman of the Year," *Fortune* (January 24, 2000): 28. Copyright © 2000 Time Inc. Reprinted by permission.

better than any other company in the world. Long before the rest of Corporate America made "empowerment" a management buzzword, J&J was practicing it. As early as the 1930s, longtime chairman Robert Wood Johnson pushed the idea of decentralization. Believing that smaller, self-governing units were more manageable, quicker to react to their markets, and more accountable, the son of a J&J co-founder encouraged such early mainstays as Ethicon, Inc., a sutures maker, and Personal Products Company, the feminine-hygiene business, to operate independently.[36]

Information Technology: Communication Costs

Current information technology, such as the Internet, the Web, and video-conferencing, is forcing many organizations to rethink and reengineer their organizational structures and their information systems. This chapter presents numerous factors that influence the type of organizational structures and controls managers adopt. Another factor that influences organizational structure and control is **communication costs.** As improvements in technology reduce communication and coordination costs, the preferred way to make decisions moves in three stages.[37]

In the first stage, when communication costs are high, the best way to make decisions is via independent decentralized decision makers (LC). As communication costs fall, it becomes more feasible in many decision-making situations to bring remote information to one point, where centralized decision makers (HC) can have a broad perspective of the whole organization and therefore can make better decisions than the isolated, local decision makers.

As communication costs continue to fall, many organizations will be more effective in many decision-making situations if connected, decentralized decision makers make the decision (HNI). For example, Swisscom, one of Europe's leading telecommunications and networking companies, has installed a new workflow system supplied by CSE Systems Corporation, an Austrian document technology company. The primary objective is to accelerate the flow of information throughout the company, which employs approximately 21,000 people. The system provides an intranet gateway for distribution of documents and data within the enterprise and to external parties.[38]

International Managers Must Consider Both Schemes

As pointed out in Chapter 11, both the cultural and the situational schemes are well supported by research. Therefore, when making a decision about the right headquarters–foreign subsidiary control relationship, international managers will have to consider both the situational and the cultural schemes. When international managers make a mistake and select the wrong HSR, it usually costs their company a great deal of money to correct, and there will be nonmonetary costs as well, such as low employee morale. Either extreme—too much centralization and too little decentralization or too little centralization and too much decentralization—eventually leads to managerial problems. Hence, international managers must seek a balance between centralized and decentralized headquarters–foreign subsidiary control.

A FRAMEWORK FOR ATTAINING A BALANCED HSR

As Kenichi Ohmae, head of McKinsey's office in Tokyo, proposes,

> *The conditions in each market are too varied, the nuances of competition too complex, and the changes in climate too subtle and too rapid for long-distance management. No matter how good they are, no matter how well supported analytically, the decision makers at the*

*center are just too far removed from the intricacies of individual mar-
kets and the needs of local customers.*[39]

But decentralizing key decisions creates its own problems, and no
company can operate effectively for a long period of time through a totally
centralized or a totally decentralized control relationship. In other words,
as classical U.S. management principles indicate, there must be a balance
between centralization and decentralization. (This means that Johnson &
Johnson, previously described, may not be as decentralized as the media
make it out to be.) A major problem confronting headquarters' managers is
how to attain an HSR with balanced centralization and decentralization:
how to obtain assurance that decisions made by subsidiary managers are in
tune with the enterprise's overall objectives and that decisions made by
headquarters management are not sabotaged by subsidiary management.
(Note that in Practical Perspective 13-3, General Motors attains a balance.)
The ensuing section describes a framework for attaining a balanced HSR.

Due Process as a Means of Attaining Balanced HSRs

Historically, when headquarters managers made decisions (such as establishing strategic plans) that had to be executed by subsidiary managers,
many managers relied on implementation control mechanisms such as
incentive compensation, monitoring systems, and rewards and punishments. W. Chen Kim, associate professor of strategy and international management, and Renee A. Mauborgne, research associate of management and
international business, both at INSEAD, France, conducted extensive
research to ascertain what it takes for multinationals to successfully execute
global strategies. The subsidiary top managers they interviewed indicated
that these implementation control mechanisms alone are not sufficient nor
effective, that they were not particularly motivating, and that they were
easy to dodge and cheat.[40]

The subsidiary managers indicated that effective implementation
requires that due process be exercised in global decision making. The due
process is depicted in Figure 13-1. Due process means (1) that the head
office is familiar with subsidiaries' local situations; (2) that two-way communication exists in the global strategy-making process; (3) that the head
office is relatively consistent in making decisions across subsidiary units; (4)
that subsidiary units can legitimately challenge the head office's strategic
views and decisions; and (5) that subsidiary units receive an explanation for
final decisions.[41] This model means that organizations can attain a balance
between centralization and decentralization if they apply extensive **vertical
and horizontal communication** throughout the overall system. Application
of the **matrix organization structure** (discussed in Chapter 6) can help attain
this type of communication. More is needed, however. Practical
Perspectives 13-6 and 13-7 suggest that the development of corporate
global core values, which cut across all foreign subsidiaries, would help
provide a balance.

FIGURE 13-1   **What Is Due Process in Global Strategic Decision Making?**

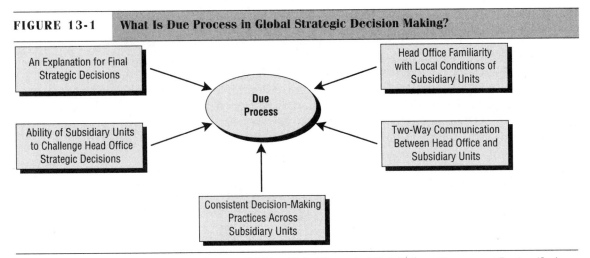

PRACTICAL PERSPECTIVE 13-6

Transplanting Corporate Cultures Globally

Asea Brown Boveri, Inc. (ABB), the electrical-engineering giant, is the quintessential global company. It has a clearly defined mission statement and a culture that supports the mission.... "We think about ABB as a company without any regard to national boundaries," says Richard P. Randazzo, who, as ABB's vice president of HR, works out of the company's Stamford, Connecticut, base and oversees the company's HR operations in the United States. "We just operate on a global basis. A lot of other companies see boundaries and barriers, but from a business standpoint, this company is intent on transcending those boundaries." Indeed, more than 50 percent of its sales are in Europe, 20 percent are in North America, 20 percent in Asia, and the rest are in South America and Africa. The official language is English; the official currency is the dollar....

It's a highly decentralized business (the United States alone has 50 companies, each with its own president). Divisions treat each other as vendors and customers, invoicing one another and maintaining accounts payable and receivable from other divisions. Characterized by *Forbes* as a company that has no discernible national identity, ABB's corporate culture is one of its strong defining features. The company embodies the phrase *think globally, act locally*. According to Randazzo, ABB's culture is focused tightly on making money. Its personality profile is a hands-on, action-oriented, travel-to-the-opportunity kind of business. Each division acts locally in response to customers and employees. But managers are required to think globally about sourcing. For example, if the dollar is strong relative to the Swedish krona, then the company sources more from Sweden because goods and services are cheaper there. When that changes, sourcing also changes.

Corporate culture mixes with the culture of the country in which ABB operates. "There's no attempt by the corporation to tell us in the United States how we should behave relative to our customers or to our employees," says Randazzo. (Other HR executives oversee ABB's HR operations in its different business segments and the different countries in which the company operates.) The senior management team is composed largely of Europeans, so at times they give Randazzo quizzical looks when he says that they can't ask a person's age or marital status when recruiting. "They don't understand some of the affirmative-action targets we have, but they don't attempt to influence any of that. The rationale is that we know more about the United States marketplace than the Germans, the Swedes, or the Swiss will ever know, and therefore, we're better able to deal with it."

But cultures aren't static. They influence each other. For one, HR management plays a much more significant role in the United States than it does in Europe. According to Randazzo, this is the arena in which Americans have had significant influence on ABB's Europeans, addressing such issues as employee involvement, empowerment, and total quality. In fact, the U.S. HR staff developed materials for conducting management training, some of which were translated into German.

Likewise, the Europeans have influenced the Americans. They've brought a sense of business urgency to the company. They helped with downsizing, lowering the break-even point and getting the organization focused. Understanding local attitudes helps corporate cultures take root. Not all corporate cultures transplant well overseas. Companies that try to graft the Stars and Stripes forever in a foreign location will likely encounter resistance. Those that are sensitive to local attitudes and customs are bound to be more successful.

Source: Excerpted from Charlene M. Solomon, "Transplanting Corporate Cultures Globally," *Personnel Journal* (October 1993): 80–81. Reprinted with the permission of *Personnel Journal*, ACC Communications, Inc., Cosa Mesa, California. All rights reserved.

Global Corporate Culture and Core Values as a Means of Attaining Balance

Some cross-cultural researchers have broken down the meaning of corporate culture into symbols, heroes, and rituals, which they defined as organizational **practice,** and into **values,** such as good/evil, beautiful/ugly, normal/abnormal, rational/irrational. These researchers contend that corporate cultures "reflect nationality, demographics of employees and managers, industry, and market; they are related to organization structure and control systems; but all of these leave room for unique and idiosyncratic elements."[42] Among national cultures, comparing "otherwise similar people," these researchers found "considerable differences in values." Among corporate cultures, the opposite was the case; they found "considerable differences in practices for people who held about the same values."[43]

Therefore, according to these researchers, the value aspects of corporate culture are attributed to nationality, but the practice aspects (symbols, heroes, and rituals) are attributed to the corporation, and the corporation

PRACTICAL PERSPECTIVE 13-7

Global Vision and Core Values

In April 1992, Chairman Riley P. Bechtel issued the company's [Bechtel Corporation] new strategic plan called *Toward 2001*. In it, he articulated his global vision and core values, making a commitment to analyze and change the corporate culture within a global context. To be most effective, it was essential to learn about employees' beliefs and attitudes. Gaufin's HR staff issued a 102-question survey to 22,000 employees. Questions asked employees about communication, training and advancement opportunities, the work environment, and the importance of international and domestic field experience to professional development. The staff followed up with more than 200 focus groups at the firm's domestic and international locations.

In response to the results, each large office developed specific action plans to address employee concerns, which included communication between management and employees and the availability of training programs for people at field locations....

"The survey is a way of listening to employees. It gives us ways to implement the corporate culture more effectively," says Gaufin. The 1992 survey is the baseline. Periodic surveys will provide means of measuring progress. There are a lot of challenges when it comes to implementing some of the changes, says Gaufin. For example, different cultures perceive performance reviews in different ways. "We have to be sure that we're not going against accepted practices in other parts of the world," she says. Furthermore, part of the new strategic plan focuses on empowered teams. Gaufin says that will be a challenge, too....

Of course, state-of-the-art telecommunications facilitate the cultural exchange. Many employees have considerable international phone contact with each other. Videoconferencing and in-person meetings with foreign

changes practices in response to environmental demands. Since the environment changes at different times for different organizations, the practice aspects will differ from corporation to corporation, even when the values remain relatively similar. This means that individuals in the same national culture may possess broad behavioral similarities, but different practices, depending on the corporation they work for.

The development of **global corporate core values**, that is, values that cut across all subsidiaries located around the globe, would help provide a **balance**. For example, Asea Brown Boveri, Inc. (ABB), the electrical engineering giant, is the quintessential global company. It has a clearly defined mission statement and a culture that supports the mission. "We think about ABB as a company without any regard to national boundaries," says Richard P. Randazzo, who, as ABB's vice president of HR, works out of the company's Stamford, Connecticut, base and oversees the company's HR operations in the United States. "We just operate on a global basis. A lot of other companies see boundaries and barriers, but from a business standpoint, this company is intent on transcending those boundaries."[44]

colleagues build social relationships. The company also televises major company meetings to Europe.

These are key ways to convey corporate culture. In Bechtel's case, this is particularly important. As the speedy mobilization to help fight the Kuwait fires attests, employees sometimes are called on to move to another location on a few days' notice. A highly decentralized, flexible structure makes this rapid response possible. Work often is done with project teams. They form to accomplish specific tasks. U.S. expatriates, other expatriates, and local nationals do the job and then demobilize. This type of work arrangement, the speed at which the company can respond, and the company's flexibility also make it imperative that employees fully comprehend the company's mission.

"Obviously, you have to communicate the company's purpose and its objectives," says Morgan. "The culture provides guidance for the employee on how the company wants to achieve those objectives."... In addition, the HR staff...uses pre-employment interviews to communicate some of the company's culture, particularly when hiring managers. The issue of *fit* not only involves technical skills and qualifications but also assurance that the employee will be comfortable with Bechtel's way of doing things....

Training and development are other areas in which Bechtel communicates its goals and values. Morgan, who is Australian and has lived in a variety of off-shore settings, says that international training is heightened when you teach mixed groups of U.S. expatriates and local nationals. The training goes both ways. U.S. expatriates communicate the company's ideals and personality to local nationals, and the nationals transmit the host culture to the Americans.

In April 1992, Chairman Riley P. Bechtel issued Bechtel Corporation's new strategic plan called *Toward 2001*. In it, he articulated his global vision and core values, making a commitment to analyze and change the corporate culture within a global context: "The culture provides guidance for the employee on how the company wants to achieve those objectives."[45] "It's vitally important that the [transnational] company have a strong company culture," says Calvin Reynolds, senior fellow at the Wharton School of the University of Pennsylvania and senior counselor for New York City–based Organization Resources Counselors. "If you don't have a strong set of cultural principles from which to function, when people get overseas, they're so lacking in clarity that no one knows where he or she is going."[46]

Nurturing Balance

The above suggests that a global corporation can develop a value system with global application, in which individual subsidiaries adapt practices to the local situation. David Whitwam, CEO of Whirlpool Corporation, also supports this contention, stating that:

When we acquired Philips [a floundering European appliance business in 1989]...Wall Street analysts expected us to ship 500 people over to

Europe, plug them into the plants and distribution systems, and give them six months or a year to turn the business around. They expected us to impose the "superior American way" of operating on the European organization.... If you try to gain control of an organization by simply subjugating it to your preconceptions, you can expect to pay for your short-term profits with long-term resistance and resentment. That's why we chose another course. During the first year, I think we had two people from the United States working in Europe, and neither was a senior manager. By the end of the second year, we had maybe a half a dozen U.S. managers there—again, none at the senior level. We listened and observed. We worked hard to communicate the company's vision, objectives, and philosophy to the European workforce. Building a shared understanding takes time, and we had to learn how to do that in a multilingual, multinational environment. Today we have 15,000 employees in Europe with only 10 from U.S. operations. They all report to European bosses, with the exception of Hank Bowman, executive vice president of Whirlpool Europe.[47]

Gurcharan Das, formerly chairman and managing director of Procter & Gamble India, said the same thing:

Globalization does not mean imposing homogeneous solutions in a pluralistic world. It means having a global vision and strategy, but it also means cultivating roots and individual identities. It means nourishing local insights, but it also means reemploying communicable ideas in new geographies around the world.[48]

Practical Perspective 13-7 describes Bechtel Corporation's approach to changing corporate culture within a global context. Figure 13-2 depicts the

---

FIGURE 13-2   **Attaining a Balanced Headquarters–Foreign Subsidiary Control Relationship (HSR)**

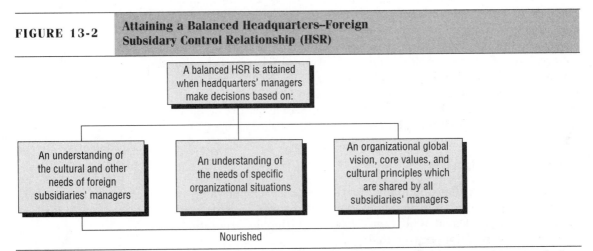

Source: Carl A. Rodrigues, "Headquarters-Foreign Subsidiary Control Relationships: Three Conceptual Frameworks."

framework for **attaining a balance** between centralization and decentralization and therefore a balanced headquarters–foreign subsidiary control relationship.

SUMMARY

This chapter has addressed the topic of headquarters–foreign subsidiaries control relationships. It has presented the traditional concepts of centralized and decentralized headquarters–foreign subsidiaries control relationships as well as several factors that help headquarters managers determine the appropriate relationship. It has also addressed the contemporary concepts of centralization, formalization, and normative integration headquarters–foreign subsidiary control relationships and presented cross-cultural and situational factors that help headquarters managers determine the appropriate relationship. It has proposed that effective global corporations need to establish a balanced headquarters–foreign subsidiary relationship and that balance can be attained through the implementation of a global corporate culture and core values.

Key Terms and Concepts

1. Subsidiary
2. Headquarters–foreign subsidiary control relationships (HSRs)
3. Centralization; decentralization
4. Headquarters management's confidence in the foreign subsidiaries' management abilities
5. Local presence
6. Governance mechanisms
7. Formalization; normative integration
8. The national culture scheme
9. Cultural dimensions affect relationships
10. The situational scheme
11. The subsidiary's local context
12. Environmental complexity and amount of local resources
13. Size of the organization; type of organizational function; crisis conditions; management's preference; and communication costs
14. A balanced headquarters–foreign subsidiaries control relationship
15. Vertical and horizontal communication
16. Matrix structure
17. Practices and values
18. Adapting practices to local situation
19. Corporate core value system has global application
20. Global corporate culture and core values as a balance
21. Nurturing balance

Discussion Questions and Exercises

1. Describe the centralized and decentralized headquarters–foreign subsidiaries control relationships and some of the pros and cons of each.

2. Foreign manufacturing and foreign marketing subsidiaries are likely to generate what types of headquarters–subsidiary relationships?

3. The function of recruiting and selecting personnel in foreign subsidiaries is likely to generate what kind of headquarters–foreign subsidiary control relationship?

4. Why are foreign subsidiaries that provide a wide range of products less centrally controlled than those that provide a narrow range of products?

5. Describe the centralization, formalization, and normative integration headquarters–foreign subsidiaries control relationships.

6. What type of headquarters–subsidiary relationship—centralization, formalization, or normative integration—fits low individualism cultures? Why?

7. Managers of foreign subsidiaries who are dominated by a small power distance cultural dimension are likely to favor a normative integration or a formalization headquarters–subsidiary relationship. Do you agree or disagree? Why?

8. You are from the headquarters of a U.S.-based company. You are assigned to create subsidiaries in France, Germany, Britain, and China. What type of headquarters-subsidiary–relationships—centralization, formalization, or normative integration— would you establish in each country? Why?

9. Describe the degrees of centralization, for-

malization, and normative integration in a headquarters–subsidiary relationship when the foreign subsidiary is confronted with a high environment of complexity and low level of local resources.

10. You are the headquarters executive responsible for the financial aspects of the overall corporation. What type of headquarters–foreign subsidiary control relationship—centralization, formalization, or normative integration—are you likely to establish? Why?

11. How does current information technology enable organizations to shift from a highly centralized control system to a high normative integration system?

12. How do global corporate cultures and core values help provide a balanced headquarters–foreign subsidiaries control relationship?

13. Top management of a global corporation that manufactures and distributes product Y has decided to divest its manufacturing operations and concentrate on its distribution operations. How is the transformation best approached? (Refer to Practical Perspective 13-6.) Which headquarters–foreign subsidiary control relationship is likely to emerge?

Assignment

Contact a senior international executive of a corporation. Ask him or her to describe his or her company's foreign subsidiary control rela-tionship. Write a short report for presentation in class.

CASE 13-1

Electrolux

Global business or product-division managers have one overriding responsibility: to further the company's global-scale efficiency and competitiveness. This task requires not only the perspective to recognize opportunities and risks across national and functional boundaries but also the skill to coordinate activities and link capabilities across those barriers. The global business manager's overall goal is to capture the full benefit of integrated worldwide operations.

To be effective, the three core roles a business manager must play are strategist for his or her organization, architect of its worldwide asset and resource configuration, and coordinator of transactions across national borders. Leif Johansson, now president of Electrolux, the Swedish-based company, played all three roles successfully in his earlier position as head of the household appliance division.

In 1983, when 32-year-old Johansson assumed responsibility for the division, he took over a business that had been built up through more than 100 acquisitions over the previous eight years. By the late 1980s, Electrolux's portfolio included more than 20 brands sold in some 40 countries, with acquisitions continuing throughout the decade. Zanussi, for example, the big Italian manufacturer acquired by Electrolux in 1984, had built a strong market presence based on its reputation for innovation in household and commercial appliances. In addition, Arthur Martin in France and Zoppas in Norway had strong local brand position but limited innovative capability. As a result of these acquisitions, Electrolux had accumulated a patchwork quilt of companies, each with a different product portfolio, market position, and competitive situation. Johansson soon recognized the need for an overall strategy to coordinate and integrate his dispersed operations.

Talks with national marketing managers quickly convinced him that dropping local brands and standardizing around a few high-volume regional and global products would be unwise. He agreed with the local managers that their national brands were vital to maintaining consumer loyalty, distribution leverage, and competitive flexibility in markets that they saw fragmenting into more and more segments. But Johansson also understood the views of his division staff members, who pointed to the many similarities in product characteristics and consumer needs in the various markets. The division staff was certain Electrolux could use this advantage to cut across markets and increase competitiveness.

Johansson led a strategy review with a task force of product-division staff and national marketing managers. While the task force confirmed the marketing managers' notion of growing segmentation, its broader perspective enabled Johansson to see a convergence of segments across national markets. Their closer analysis also refined management's understanding of local market needs, concluding that consumers perceived "localness" mainly in terms of how it was designed or what features it offered. From this analysis, Johansson fashioned a product-market strategy that identified two full-line regional brands to be promoted and supported in all European markets. He positioned the Electrolux brand to respond to the cross-market segment for high prestige (customers characterized as "conservatives"), while the Zanussi brand would fill the segment where innovative products were key (for "trendsetters").

The local brands were clustered in the other two market segments pinpointed in the analysis: "yuppies" ("young and aggressive" urban professionals) and "environmentalists" ("warm and friendly" people interested in basic-value products). The new strategy provided Electrolux with localized brands that responded to the needs of these consumer groups. At the same time, the company captured the efficiencies possible by standardizing the basic chassis and components of these local-brand products, turning them out in high volume in specialized regional plants. So, by tracking product and market trends across borders, Leif Johansson captured valuable global-scale efficiencies while reaping the benefits of a flexible response to national market fragmentation. What's more, though he took on the leadership role as a strategist, Johansson never assumed he alone had the understanding or the ability to form a global appliance strategy; he relied heavily on both corporate and local managers. Indeed, Johansson continued to solicit guidance on strategy through a council of country managers called the 1992 Group and through a set of product councils made up of functional managers.

Newly developed business strategies obviously need coordination. In practice, the specialization of assets and resources swells the flow of products and components among national units, requiring a firm hand to synchronize and control that flow. For organizations whose operations have become more dispersed and specialized at the same time that their strategies have become more connected and integrated, coordination across borders is a tough challenge. Business managers must fashion a repertoire of approaches and tools, from simple centralized control to management of exceptions identified through formal policies to indirect management via informal communication channels. Leif Johansson coordinated product flow—across his 35 national sales units and 29 regional sourcing facilities—by establishing broad sourcing policies and transfer-pricing ranges that set limits but left

negotiations to internal suppliers and customers. For instance, each sales unit could negotiate a transfer price with its internal source for a certain product in a set range that was usually valid for a year. If the negotiations moved outside that range, the companies had to check with headquarters. As a coordinator, Johansson led the deliberations that defined the logic and philosophy of the parameters, but he stepped back and let individual unit managers run their own organizations, except when a matter went beyond policy limits.

In contrast, coordination of business strategy in Johansson's division was managed through teams that cut across the formal hierarchy. Instead of centralizing, he relied on managers to share the responsibility for monitoring implementation and resolving problems through teams. To protect the image and positioning of his regional brands—Electrolux and Zanussi—he set up a brand-coordination group for each. Group members came from the sales companies in key countries, and the chairperson was a corporate marketing executive. Both groups were responsible for building a coherent, pan-European strategy for the brand they represented. To rationalize the various product strategies across Europe, Johansson created product-line boards to oversee these strategies and to exploit any synergies. Each product line had its own board made up of the corporate product-line manager, who was chair, and his or her product managers. The Quattro 500 refrigerator-freezer, which was designed in Italy, built in Finland, and marketed in Sweden, was one example of how these boards successfully integrated product strategy.

In addition, the 1992 Group periodically reviewed the division's overall results, kept an eye on its manufacturing and marketing infrastructure, and supervised major development programs and investment projects. Capturing the symbolic value of 1992 in its name, the group was chaired by Johansson himself and included business managers from Italy, the

United Kingdom, Spain, the United States, France, Switzerland, and Sweden.

The building blocks for most worldwide companies are their national subsidiaries. If the global business manager's main objective is to achieve global-scale efficiency and competitiveness, the national subsidiary manager's is to be sensitive and responsive to the local market. Country managers play the pivotal role not only in meeting local customer needs but also in satisfying the host government's requirements and defending their company's market positions against local and external competitors.

The need for local flexibility often puts the country manager in conflict with the global business manager. But in a successful transnational like Electrolux, negotiation can resolve these differences. In this era of intense competition around the world, companies cannot afford to permit a subsidiary manager to

defend parochial interests as "king of the country." Nor should headquarters allow national subsidiaries to become the battle-ground for corporate holy wars fought in the name of globalization.

Questions

1. What type of headquarters–subsidiary relationship did Johansson establish?
2. Did he nurture corporate culture across the firm's subsidiaries? If so, how?
3. Discuss the role information technology might play in Electrolux.

Source: Reprinted by permission of Harvard Business Review. An excerpt from C.A. Barlett and S. Ghoshal, "What Is a Global Manager?" *Harvard Business Review* (September–October 1992): 125–128. Copyright © 1992 by the President and Fellows of Harvard College. All rights reserved.

CASE 13-2

See Jack. See Jack Run Europe.

You don't become head of General Electric by being scaredy-cat, but one thing frightens Jack Welch, even after 18 years in the job; the sheer size of the company. "Don't talk to me about how big this place is," he says, nearly shouting. "I hate it." Size means sloth, systems, and smugness rather than speed, simplicity, and self-confidence. Over and over, Welch urges people to "tear this place apart."

At the same time, of course, he has grown GE so much it's, well, scary. GE is the ninth-biggest and second most profitable company in the world. Since Welch took over in 1981, GE's sales have risen 3.7 times (from $27.2 billion to $100.5 billion), and profits have grown 5.7 times (from $1.6 to $9.2 billion). Size is a burden if you try to lug it around, but

it's an advantage if you can make it work for you. "Jack always says, 'You can't manage a company the size of GE. You leverage it,'" says Claudio Santiago. Spanish-born Santiago, 42, works in Florence, Italy, as CEO of one of GE's bigger divisions, a $2.1 billion-in-sales compressor and turbine manufacturer, Nuovo Pignone.

Welcome to global GE. Businesses like Nuovo Pignone symbolize one of the biggest stories of Welch's storied career: how America's most admired company, and a very American one, has become a truly global corporation. It is the story of how GE leveraged its businesses to buy and build, in just over a decade, a European business nearly as large as all GE was when Welch became CEO, and now intends to do the same in Asia, only faster. It is the story of how GE leverages its intellectual capital—an incomparable management tool kit that has turned a bunch of state-run sinecures and niche businesses into a powerhouse whose net income, now a fifth of the company's, is compounding at 34 percent a year. And it's the story of the lever itself, the reason this Gargantua can be as agile as Nijinksy: a leadership-development system that won't let GE stop improving.

Since 1990, GE has paid nearly $30 billion for 133 European acquisitions; some 90,000 people are on GE's payroll there, about as many as Euro-giant Axa and BP Amoco employ worldwide. Europe accounted for $24.4 billion of 1998 revenue, of which only $2.7 billion, or 11 percent, came from exports from America. Inflation-adjusted, that's less than at the start of the decade.

When you do a lot of deals—GE made 108 acquisitions worldwide last year—you get good at it. One secret is an "integration model" developed chiefly at deal-hungry GE Capital Services. It rests on an obvious fact, but one many companies fudge: There are no "mergers of equal" here; there are acquisitions. "If you won't want to change, don't be acquired, "says Norris Woodruff, a general manager in Industrial Systems and an in-house expert on the subject. Sure, GE wants to inspire change rather than compel it, to learn as well as teach, but GE is boss.

A second key point: Integration begins before the deal, with a due-diligence team that's not just financial but includes human resources and general management. They draft a plan to take effect the instant the pens are capped. Says James Conheady, an unsentimental Irishman who runs HR for GE Power Controls, which makes circuit breakers and the like and is based in Barcelona, "You have to move very, very quickly. There's a window of opportunity—an expectation of change—so you must deliver it fast."

First to arrive is someone from finance who is expected, literally on day one, to take control of the books, with the general ledger set up in the format GE uses worldwide. An "integration manager" is a half-step behind—usually a high-potential youngster brevetted into the acquired company. The integration manager doesn't supplant the people running the business. He works full-time on integration; the general manager runs the shop and owns the P&L.

There's nothing special about these changes except the speed with which GE does them. But they're worth two to eight percentage points of operating margin, says Joaquim Agut, the Catalonian CEO of GE Power Controls, an $800 million operation composed of ten acquisitions in eight countries, including his family-owned company, sold in 1993.

After generic change comes GEneric change. Agut ticks off a list of GE tools—CAP, CMS, MGPD, bullet trains, QMI, Six Sigma, and more—and says they're worth another eight points of margin. That's an astonishing number, but you can make the case: Ten businesses that today represent about half of GE's European revenues had a combined operating margin of 5 percent in their first year of GE ownership, vs. an expected 13 percent margin for 1999.

Says Welch: "These companies have nothing in common except leadership and best practices," but that's not chopped liver. In the view of Merrill Lynch analyst Jeanne Terrile, GE is not so much a collection of businesses as it is "a repository of information and expertise that can be leveraged over a huge installed base." The ability to leverage expertise is why GE's globalization works.

Among GE management tools, several are particularly powerful aids to globalization. One of them, Work-Out, is so fundamental that GE trademarked the term and in its values statement says, "GE leaders...are committed to Work-Out." Work-Outs, begun in 1989, are meetings that can be called by anybody to address any problem, from niggling to humongous, with no boss in the room. When the participants have a plan—kill that stupid form, replace that balky pump—the boss must say yes or no on the spot, no haggling, no waffling. Work-Outs have become so common that there's probably one every day in each sizable GE facility, without management's knowing about it till someone pops in saying, "We had a Work-Out and need to talk to you."

Its simplicity is deceptive. Piazzolla says, "We saw 'committed to Work-Out' and asked, 'What's Work-Out? A meeting? Why should we spend time in meetings?'" But Work-Out's few rules totally subvert traditional executive power, and that's radical, especially in Europe.

Says Welch: "Getting a company to be informal is a huge deal, and no one ever talks about it." Informality is the key to GE's in-your-face, just-do-it culture. It allows the other tools to work QMI, for example, is "quick market intelligence," a tool adapted from Wal-Mart. A regularly scheduled, intense meeting where managers, salespeople, and others pore over data and share anecdotes to get a pulse of the market, QMI can't succeed if people are afraid to tell the boss he's all wet....

GE's European work force has taken to its style with surprising ease. Says Anneliese Monden, who runs GE's leadership development programs in Europe: "Respect for titles isn't what GE is about, and it's a little strange in the beginning. Once people understand it's safe to think, they love it." According to Kary Wright, an American who is site manager of the aircraft-engine repair facility in Wales. "Personal contact is the key. You need it to share best practices."

"GE is a language—it is a world—and at the beginning it is difficult," says Pier Luigi Ferrara, 62, Nuovo Pignone's chairman.

More and more, the language of GE is the language of Six Sigma, the quality initiative begun in late 1995. It has become central to GE's ability to operate as a global whole. "Six Sigma" refers to a standard of excellence defined as having no more than 3.4 defects per million—in anything, whether it's manufac-

turing, billing, or loan processing. GE says it will spend $500 million on Six Sigma projects this year and will get more than $2 billion in benefits.

A global company needs a common language. Six Sigma is it, more than English. The shared lexicon makes it easier to swap ideas around GE. Before, two plant managers, even making the same product, probably had different performance measures. Says Piet van Abeelen, vice president for Six Sigma: "without Six Sigma, if you run a plant and I run a plant, it's tough to understand your numbers. Then you can say, 'Your ideas won't work, because I'm different.' Well, cry me a river. The commonalties are what matter. If you make the metrics the same, we can talk."

And they talk: Never in business history have so many people talked so much to so many other people as they do at GE. In 1988, when GE started benchmarking other companies and sharing best practices internally, people embraced the notion, but with reluctance, as one might embrace a loved one who had come in from a hard run on a hot day.

It's obvious to anyone who spends time in GE that hesitation has turned to obsession. Says Welch: "This is all about moving intellectual capital—taking ideas and moving them around faster and faster and faster." There is no "GE Europe" per se—no Rome to which all roads lead; the businesses report in to Schenectady, Cincinnati, Milwaukee, Kansas City, etc. But there are dozens of councils: In Europe alone, a Corporate Executive Council for the pooh-bahs, a Marketing Council, Technical Council, Sourcing Council, Finance Council, Human Resources Council, Sales Council, Manufacturing Council, Quality Council, and more. Each business operates similar cross-business or cross-functional networks, which meet for a day or two every few months. Probably every professional in the company—tens of thousands of people—sits on at least one cross-business council. At meetings, everybody is excepted to bring something—an idea that made a few bucks, a process that's quicker than the old one. "Go to the European Corporate Executives Council," says Larry Johnston, just named to head it, "and you see 30 people writing all day long."

GE's culture is both deeply competitive and furiously collaborative. It's a company joke that within minutes of Welch's leaving a site, the phone starts ringing as other businesses ask. "What's this thing you told Jack about?" More and more best practices flow both ways across the Atlantic. A system for managing sales forces developed in Barcelona is spreading worldwide. In May 1998, in Florence, Welch heard how a Six Sigma team making turbine packages had cut the total cost by 30 percent. Show me, Welch demanded, and spent an hour grilling the team so he could, when he left, tell everybody else in GE to call Nuovo Pignone.

Ultimately people, not money or tools, make the global GE work. From the beginning, Welch has poured money and energy into creating a massive iceberg of leadership ability. The tip is Crotonville, the company's spiffy executive development campus in New York State; it was a "hovel" when Welch took over, according to one GE executive. What's beneath Crotonville is more important—a passion for leadership development everywhere in the company. The heads of GE's European businesses, asked how much of their time is spent on HR subjects, give answers ranging from 30 to 50 percent.

There's nothing egalitarian about GE's HR philosophy. It finds the best and culls the rest—period. It can be a cultural shock. Says Tone Rongstand, 32, who has been promoted twice in 1999 and now heads risk management for GE Consumer Finance in Norway: "When I was young I went to a ski competition, and the winner was the one who went in the average time. This is not like GE!"

Leadership development ranks with Work-Out, Six Sigma, and idea swapping as GE's best tools for globalization. It starts with new hires—or people at newly acquired companies. Engineers might get into TLP, a tough, two-year technical leadership program that involves three eight-month projects interwoven with classroom work in project management, process-improvement methods, and so on. Similar courses exist in every functional discipline from finance to information management, as well as Six Sigma training leading to "black belt" and "master black belt" status. Still more courses are offered at intermediate and advanced levels, always with lots of time in the field.

Questions

1. Discuss GE's headquarters–subsidiary control relationship.
2. Compare and contrast this case to Practical Perspectives 13-6 and 13-7.

Source: Excerpted from Thomas A. Stewart, "See Jack. See Jack Run Europe," *Fortune* (September 27, 1999): 124–136. Copyright © 1999 Time Inc. Reprinted by permission.

Notes

1. Ron Ashkensas, "Breaking Through the Global Boundaries," *Executive Excellence 16*, no. 7 (July 1999).
2. Cited by Stephanie Overman, "Going Global," *HR Magazine* (September 1993): 49–50.
3. Joann S Lublin, "Too Much, Too Fast," *The Wall Street Journal*, September 26, 1996, p. R8.
4. John J. Keller, "AT&T to Give Foreign Units More Autonomy," *The Wall Street Journal*, December 13, 1993, p. A4.
5. P. Dwyer et al., "Tearing up Today's Organization Chart," *Business Week: 21st Century Capitalism* (1994 Special Issue): 81.

6. Brendan R. Schlender, "Matsushita Shows How to Go Global," *Fortune* (July 11, 1994): 162.

7. Dwyer et al., "Tearing up Today's Organization Chart," p. 90.

8. John Dupuy, "Learning to Manage World-Class Strategy," *Management Review* (October 1991): 40.

9. The factors contained in Table 13-1 are adapted from Richard D. Robinson, *Internationalization of Business: An Introduction* (New York: The Dryden Press, 1984), pp. 268–269.

10. Sumantra Ghoshal and Nitin Nohria, "Horses for Courses: Organizational Forms for Multinational Corporations," *Sloan Management Review* (Winter 1993): 28.

11. Ibid.

12. Geert Hofstede, *Culture's Consequences: International Differences in Work-Related Values* (Beverly Hills, CA: Sage, 1980).

13. Cited by Geert Hofstede, "Motivation, Leadership, and Organization: Do American Theories Apply Abroad?" *Organizational Dynamics* (Summer 1980): 60.

14. J.S. Osland, S. DeFranco, and A. Osland, "Organizational Implications of Latin American Culture: Lessons from an Expatriate," *Journal of Management Inquiry 8*, no. 2 (June 1999): 219–234.

15. J.R. Weisz, F.M. Rothbaum, and T.C. Blackburn, "Standing out and Standing in—The Psychology of Control in America and Japan," *American Psychologist 39* (1984): 955–969.

16. R.N. Bellah et al., eds., *Individualism and Commitment in American Life* (New York: Harper & Row, 1987).

17. W.G. Ouchi, "The Relationship Between Organizational Structure and Control," *Administrative Science Quarterly 22* (1987): 95–113.

18. Weisz et al., "Standing out and Standing in."

19. Leah Nathans, "A Matter of Control," *Business Month* (September 1988): 46–52.

20. R.N. Kannungo and R.W. Wright, "A Cross-Cultural Comparative Study of Managerial Job Attitudes," *Journal of International Business Studies 14*, no. 2 (1983): 115–129.

21. Cited by Hofstede, "Motivation, Leadership, and Organization," p. 60.

22. S.G. Redding and D.S. Pugh, "The Formal and the Informal: Japanese and Chinese Organizational Studies," in S.R. Clegg, D.C. Dunphy, and S.G. Redding (eds.), *The Enterprise and Management in East Asia* (Hong Kong: Center for Asian Studies, 1986).

23. K.H. Chung, "A Comparative Study of Managerial Characteristics of Domestic, International, and Governmental Institutions in Korea." Paper presented at the *Midwest Conference of Asian Affairs*, Minneapolis, Minn., 1978; W.S. Nam, *The Traditional Pattern of Korean Industrial Management* (ILCORK working paper No. 14, Social Science Research Institute, University of Hawaii, 1971); G.W. England and R. Lee, "Organizational Goals and Expected Behavior Among American, Japanese, and Korean Managers: A Comparative Study," *Academy of Management Journal 4* (1971): 425–438; J. Harbron, "Korea's Executives Are Not Quite the New Japanese," *The Business Quarterly 44* (1979): 16–19.

24. R.H. Solomon, *Mao's Revolution and Chinese Political Culture* (Berkeley, CA: University of California Press, 1971).

25. Geert Hofstede, "The Cultural Relativity of the Quality of Life Concept," *Academy of Management Review 9*, no. 3 (1984): 389–398.

26. R.E. Caves, "Industrial Organization, Corporate Strategy and Structure," *Journal of Economic Literature 18* (1980): 64; M. Haire, E. Ghiselli, and L.W. Porter, *Managerial Thinking: An International Study* (New York: John Wiley, 1966); D.J. Hickson et al., "The Culture Free Context of Organization Sructure: A Tri-National Comparison," *Sociology 8* (1974): 59–80.

27. Ghoshal and Nohria, "Horses and Courses: Organizational Forms Multinational Corporations."

28. Ibid.

29. H. Aldrich, Organizations and Environments (Englewood Cliffs, NJ: Prentice-Hall, 1979); L. Greiner, "Evolution and Revolution as Organizations Grow," *Harvard Business Review* (July–August 1972): 41.

30. Thomas Hout, Michael E. Porter, and Eileen Rudden, "How Global Companies Win Out," *Harvard Business Review* (September–October 1982): 103.

31. Ibid.

32. .Lawrence and J.W. Lorsch, *Organization and Environment: Managing Differentiation and Integration* (Cambridge, MA: Division of Research, Graduate School of Business Administration, Harvard University, 1967).

33. "Decentralizing for Comptitive Advantage," *Across the Board 31* (January 1994): 26.

34. R.E. Miles, C.C. Snow, and J. Pfeffer, "Organization Environment: Concepts and Issues," *Industrial Relations 13* (1974): 244–264; K. Weick, *The Social Psychology of Organization* (Reading, MA: Addison-Wesley, 1969); R. F. Zammuto, "Growth, Stability, and Decline in American College and University Enrollments," *Educational Administration Quarterly 19*, no. 1 (1983): 83–89.

35. M. Yasai-Ardekani, "Effects of Environmental Scarcity and Munificence on the Relationship of Context to Organizational Structure," *Academy of Management Journal 32*, no. 1 (1989): 131–156.

36. Excerpted from Brian O'Reilly, "J&J Is on a Roll," *Fortune* (December 26, 1994): 178–192; and Joseph Weber, "A Big Company That Works," *Business Week* (May 4, 1992): 125.

37. This idea draws from Thomas W. Malone, "Is Empowerment Just a Fad? Control, Decision Making, and IT," *Sloan Managaement Review 38*, no. 2 (Winter 1997): 23–25.

38. David O. Stephens, "The Globalization of Information Technology in Multinational Corporations," *Information Management Journal 33*, no. 3 (July 1999): 66–71.

39. Kenichi Ohmae, "Planning for a Global Harvest," *Harvard Business Review* (July–August 1989): 136.

40. W.C. Kim and R.A. Mauborgne, "Making Global Strategies Work," *Sloan Management Review* (Spring 1993): 11.

41. Ibid.

42. G. Hofstede et al., "Measuring Organizational Cultures: A Qualitative and Quantitative Study Across Twenty Cases," *Administrative Science Quarterly 35* (1990): 286–316, 311.

43. Ibid., p. 312.

44. Charlene M. Solomon, "Transplanting Corporate Cultures Globally," *Personnel Journal* (October 1993): 80–81.

45. Ibid.

46. Ibid.

47. Regina Fazio Maruca, "The Right Way to Go Global: An Interview with Whirpool CEO David Whitwam," *Harvard Business Review* (March–April 1994): 139.

48. Gurcharan Das, "Local Memoirs of a Global Manager," *Harvard Business Review* (March–April 1993): 38.

VIII

International Management: A Future Perspective

It seems certain that the word *globalization* will continue to be used extensively, that companies will conduct their business activities in a highly interconnected world, and that in this "shrinking world" managers will need to reengineer organizations that can respond quickly to developments in foreign markets. Many organizations are attempting to implement total quality management (TQM) as a way of coping with these global changes. TQM, this chapter proposes, can be achieved only when the organization develops the ability to cater to customers' needs; monitor the internal and external environments on an ongoing basis to obtain and disseminate information needed by empowered group decision makers; establish and maintain an atmosphere where there is strong vertical and horizontal communication, collaboration, and cooperation among individuals in internal units as well as among individuals in external units; develop and maintain a bond and a "sense of ownership" among employees; and develop and maintain ongoing training programs. Implementing such a program is a challenge to managers of any organization in any country, and it is even more challenging when they attempt to implement it across nations. Future advancements in information technology, however, will help managers meet the challenge.

14

Total Quality Management and Implementation Challenges

New markets, rapid advances in communications, and new sources of brain-power and skilled labor are forcing businesses into their most fundamental reorganization since the multidivision corporation became standard in the 1950s. "We're talking about a new order, a sea of change, that will go on for the rest of my career," says [Richard J.] Callahan [CEO of U.S. West International]. "It's almost like Halley's comet arriving unannounced." Senior managers are struggling to adapt themselves and their organizations to the twenty-first-century business world that's rapidly taking shape. Boundaries will be even less important than they are today. The rate of technological progress will accelerate, with breakthroughs in biotechnology or digital electronics coming from such unexpected places as Israel, Malaysia, or China. At the same time, the huge demands of the new middle classes and their governments will revive such supposedly mature businesses as household appliances and power-plant construction. All this means that business opportunities will explode—but so will competition as technology and management know-how spread beyond brand-name companies to new players in Asia and Latin America. Thriving in this fast-paced environment requires a new kind of company and a new kind of CEO. Just as much of the world is embracing a liberalized economic model, so businesses of all stripes seem to be converging on a common management model to run their far-flung operations. Although that model is still a work in progress, the outlines of what is likely to be the early twenty-first century's world standard are beginning to take shape. This model will rely on Western-style accounting and financial controls yet stress Japanese-style teamwork. It will value ethnic diversity, though less from high-mindedness than from prag-matism. It will be centrally directed by multicultural, or at least cosmopolitan, executives who will set overall tone and strategy but give entrepreneurial local managers a long leash.[1]

Learning Objectives of the Chapter

Within the past few decades, as suggested in previous chapters, many coun-tries around the globe have made substantial progress toward achieving their industrialization objectives. As a result, intensive global competition has evolved, and it is expected to continue to intensify. Numerous organi-zations have implemented, or are attempting to implement, total quality management (TQM) to cope with these environmental changes. The term TQM has many meanings. In general, however, it refers to an organization having a long-term commitment to ongoing improvement of quality throughout its whole system, with all employees at all levels in all subunits and subsidiaries actively participating.[2] It also means an organization pro-ducing goods and/or services that meet or exceed consumers' expectations at the lowest possible cost[3] as well as doing things right the first time.[4] According to quality management writer J.M. Juran, quality consists of two basic dimensions: "product performance that results in customer satisfac-tion" and "freedom from product deficiencies, which avoids customer dis-satisfaction."[5]

The American Society of Quality Control supports the term "manage-ment of quality" to mean the activities that are generally associated with quality improvement in the organization.[6] Built into the TQM concept is the notion that all employees in the organization provide a service, not only to the external customer, but also to their colleagues. Therefore, the cus-tomer is anyone for whom a service is rendered—both inside and outside organizational boundaries.[7] The Baldrige Award also helps describe TQM. Building on the quality concept, the Baldrige Award was established in 1987 to provide a systematic national framework for assessing quality levels in U.S. companies. In Britain, the concept of quality is described by British Standard 5750 and in the European Union by ISO 9000 and by such labels as quality improvement program (QIP), total customer delight (TCD), and total customer satisfaction (TCS). In Japan it is described by such labels as total quality control (TQC) and quality circles (QC). However, the **International Organization for Standardization (ISO) 9000** is likely to have a greater impact on quality practices around the world than any other quality concept. Thus, when doing business globally, ISO 9000 certification is becoming increasingly important. Figure 14-1 describes the five standards that collectively make up ISO 9000. ISO 9000 standards do not specify how an organization should develop its quality processes; rather, it requires each enterprise to define and document its own quality processes and provide evidence of implementing them.

FIGURE 14-1	ISO 9000: International Standards for Quality Management
ISO 9000 Quality Management And Assurance Standards— Guidelines for Selection and Use	This is the road map for the series. Its purpose is to provide the user with guidelines for selection and use of ISO 9001, 9002, 9003, and 9004.
ISO 9001 Model for Quality Assurance in Design, Development, Production, Installation, And Servicing	This standard is for when conformance to specified requirements is to be assured by the supplier during several stages, including design, development, production, installation, and servicing.
ISO 9002 Model for Quality Assurance in Production and Installation	This standard is for use when conformance to specified requirements is to be assured by the supplier during production and installation.
ISO 9003 Model for Quality Assurance in Final Inspection and Testing	This standard is for use when conformance to specified requirements is to be assured by the supplier solely at final inspection and test.
ISO 9004 Quality Management and Quality System Elements—Guidelines	This standard describes a basic set of elements by which quality management systems can be developed and implemented. There is heavy emphasis on "meeting company and customer needs."

Source: ISO 9000: 1987 (E).

In spite of the many definitions of TQM, there does not seem to exist a general framework that defines the abilities (or characteristics) an organization must possess in order for TQM programs to be effective.[8] Many organizations fail in their attempts to implement TQM programs, and many of the successfully implemented TQM programs eventually failed because the companies were not able to maintain them. This suggests that "simply being aware of the new management paradigms or being willing to act on them will not produce a competitive advantage. International competition demands not only a knowledge of what is required to be a global player but also a superior ability to implement that knowledge."[9] After studying this chapter, you should be able to:

1. Describe a general TQM framework.

2. Describe the challenges/barriers managers face in implementing and maintaining such a framework.

3. Describe the ways information technology aids managers in meeting the challenges.

TOTAL QUALITY MANAGEMENT: A FRAMEWORK

As suggested above, **total quality management (TQM)** means an organization being more efficient and effective than its competitors. The ensuing sections propose that this can be achieved only if the organization attains and maintains the abilities described below (see Figure 14-2). These abilities are all interdependent, and neglecting any one is thus likely to lead to ineffective TQM programs. The good news is that the current information technology will aid organizations in attaining and maintaining these abilities (refer to Practical Perspective 14-1). It will unlock for businesses the ability to infuse customer-centered innovation into everything they do: creating new markets; creating new products and services; creating new business opportunities; creating new reward systems for employees, customers, and other stakeholders; creating new networks of suppliers, competitors, partners, distributors, sellers, and prospects; and creating new value for customers.[10]

Responsive to Customer Needs

The effective TQM organization is culturally highly responsive to the needs of markets; it does not produce first, then find markets for its goods. Its managers ask: "What does the world really need that our company can and should provide?"[11] For example, Honda Motor Company, a Japanese firm that since 1948 has grown into a huge international corporation, places

FIGURE 14-2	Characteristics of the TQM Organization

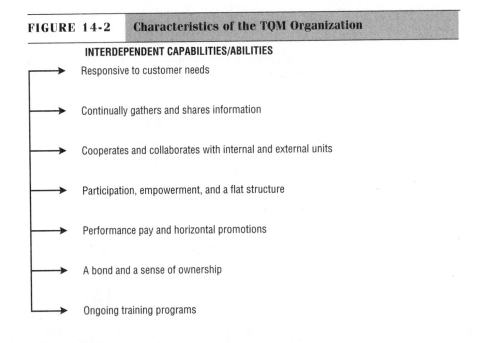

INTERDEPENDENT CAPABILITIES/ABILITIES

Responsive to customer needs

Continually gathers and shares information

Cooperates and collaborates with internal and external units

Participation, empowerment, and a flat structure

Performance pay and horizontal promotions

A bond and a sense of ownership

Ongoing training programs

PRACTICAL PERSPECTIVE 14-1

Now It's Electron Jack

This is clearly the biggest revolution in business in our lifetimes—and I've got all the tools to go after it." Jack Welch is talking about electronic commerce, the passion of his final year as CEO of General Electric.

Welch used GE's annual top executive meeting at Boca Raton, Florida, in January [1999]—the meeting where he is likely to name his successor next year—to order a major companywide e-commerce initiative. Welch had been skeptical about the power of the Internet, but there's no zealot like a convert; these days people at headquarters in Fairfield, Connecticut, call him e-Jack.

Welch himself is not skilled on the computer—his assistant Rosanne Badowski is used to his hollering for help when he accidentally closes an application on the Dell PC in his office. But if Welch is no power user, no one is quicker student of power. Welch sees the Web changing everything:

➤ "It will change relationships with employees. We will never again have discussions where knowledge is hidden in somebody's pocket. You will have to lead with ideas, not by controlling information."

➤ "It will change relationships with customers. Customers will see everything. Nothing will be hidden in paperwork. Where is the inventory? Where is that part? They will see it all. Execution is very important. Look what quality will do to the Internet, and vice versa. Every error you make is transparent on the Web, so without Six Sigma quality you can't win."

➤ "It will change relationships with suppliers. Within 18 months, all our suppliers will supply us on the Internet or they won't do business with us."

Welch won't give companywide targets for the e-commerce initiative. Instead, he says, "I've got to go crazy over the next months to make e-commerce happen." He can't imagine being better equipped. At Crotonville, GE's corporate university, every business management course—a four-week, action-learning program offered to 50 high-potential managers each quarter—will do an e-commerce project. Every GE business is appointing a maverick, an e-commerce fanatic, who reports to the business's CEO and is empowered to break every GE rule except the company's values.

His one worry: "Do we have the right gene pool—do people who join big companies want to break glass? We've got to break this company to do this—there's no discussion, we've just got to break it."

Characteristically, Welch wants in on the brick-throwing. To that end, he's sponsoring his own e-commerce blitz-krieg: 90-day, all-company Work-Out, which will run through December. The Work-Out will take place on the company intranet; its subject is how to use the Web to eliminate bureaucracy and move to electronic commerce.

"The attic's getting full again," Welch says. "This way we'll get an Internet focus and clear out some crap," handing his successor a wired company newly scoured of administrivia. E-Jack is ionized: "I just wish we were faster—I never move fast enough."

Source: "Now It's Electron Jack," *Fortune* (September 27, 1999). Copyright © 1999 Time Inc. Reprinted by permission.

utmost importance on localization. According to its retired chairman Hideo Sugiura, localization means "developing, manufacturing, and marketing products best suited to the actual and potential needs of the customers and to the social and economic conditions of the marketplace."[12] Some automakers have gone as far as paying foreign exchange students living with American families to study the families' habits as a means of determining what might serve their needs better—for instance, they have placed cup holders in cars because people were observed carrying cups of coffee while driving. To determine customers satisfaction, some organizations such as Ford Motor Company often involve key customers in making product decisions.[13] Professors R. Blackburn and B. Rosen interviewed executives at organizations that have won the Baldrige Award in order to codify these organizations' human resource policies and practices. In discussing the Baldrige Award–winning companies, Blackburn and Rosen cite **customer satisfaction** as a characteristic of the TQM culture.[14] And, as cited earlier, the responsibility for customer satisfaction in a TQM organization must lie with all employees at all levels. As illustrated in Practical Perspective 14-2, the current **information technology** revolution will aid organizations in developing and maintaining this ability. The Web has forever changed the way businesses and customers (whether they be consumers or other businesses) buy and sell with other, learn about each other, and communicate.[15] For example, Toshiba America's copier and fax machine business gives its dealers on-line access to machine-level profitability data they have never had before. United Airlines is bringing information technology to bear on virtually every aspect of its customer experience.[16]

PRACTICAL PERSPECTIVE 14-2

Mass Customization Will Change the Way Products Are Made—Forever

A silent revolution is stirring in the way things are made and services are delivered. Companies with millions of customers are starting to build products designed just for you. You can, of course, buy a Dell computer assembled to your exact specifications. And you can buy a pair of Levi's cut to fit your body. But you can also buy pills with the exact blend of vitamins, minerals, and herbs that you like, glasses molded to fit your face precisely, CDs with music tracks that you choose, cosmetics mixed to match your skin tone, textbooks whose chapter are picked out by your professor, a loan structured to meet your financial profile, or a night at a hotel where every employee knows your favorite wine. And if your daughter does not like any of Mattel's 125 different Barbie dolls, she will soon be able to design her own.

Welcome to the world of mass customization, where mass-market goods and services are uniquely tailored to the needs of the individuals who buy them. Companies as diverse as BMW, Dell Computer, Levi Strauss, Mattel, McGraw-Hill, Wells Fargo, and a slew of leading Web businesses are adopting mass customization to maintain or obtain a competitive edge. Many are just beginning to dabble, but the direction in which they are headed is clear. Mass customization is more than just a manufacturing process, logistics system, or marketing strategy. It could well be the organizing principle of business in this new century, just as mass production was the organizing principle in the last one.

The two philosophies couldn't clash more. Mass producers dictate a one-to-many relationship, while mass customers require continual dialogue with customers. Mass production is cost-efficient. But mass customization is a flexible manufacturing technique that can slash inventory. And mass customization has two huge advantages over mass production: It is at the service of the customer, and it makes full use of cutting-edge technology.

A whole list of technological advances that make customization possible is finally in place. Computer-controlled factory equipment and industrial robots make it easier to quickly read-just assembly lines. The proliferation of bar-code scanners makes it possible to track virtually every part and product. Databases now store trillions of bytes of information, including individuals customers' predilections for everything from cottage cheese to suede boots. Digital printers make it a cinch to change product packaging on the fly. Logistics and supply-chain management software tightly coordinate manufacturing and distribution.

And then there's the Internet, which ties these disparate pieces together. Says Joseph Pine, author of the pioneering book *Mass Customization*: "Anything you can digitize, you can customize." The Internet makes it easy for companies to move data from an on-line order form to the factory floor and makes it easy for manufacturing types to communicate with marketers. Most of all, the Internet makes it easy for a company to conduct an ongoing, one-to-one dialogue with each of its customers, to learn about and respond to their exact preferences. Conversely, the Internet is also often the best way for a customer to learn which company has the most to offer—if he or she is not happy with one company's wares, nearly perfect information about a competitor's is just a mouse click away. Combine that with mass customization, and the nature of a company's relationship with its customers is forever changed. Much of the leverage that once belonged to companies now belongs to customers.

Source: Excerpted from Erick Schonfeld, "The Customized, Digitized, Have-It-Your-Way Economy," *Fortune* (September 28, 1998). Copyright © 1999 Time Inc. Reprinted by permission.

It should be noted that the meaning of quality varies among countries, and even among people in countries. Many people are more concerned with **value** (the usefulness, desirability, or worth of a thing[17]) than with **quality**. As Jack Welch, General Electric's CEO, observed in 1993,

> *Everywhere you go, people are saying, "Don't tell me about your technology; tell me your price." To get a lower price, customers are willing to sacrifice the extras they used to demand. The fact is many governments are broke, and people are hurting, so there is an enormous drive to get value, value, value.[18]*

Furthermore, in some countries, such as the formerly communist European countries, the notion of customer satisfaction or customer responsiveness has not yet taken root—a challenge international managers will be facing.[19]

Continually Gathers Information

The above characteristic suggests that effective TQM organizations require the ability to gather vast amounts of information from many parts of the world. They must be able to obtain information about what customers or prospective customers want, where, and when. To react effectively, they require information about their capabilities as well as the ability to get the information to where it is needed. (Refer to Practical Perspective 14-3) This means that effective TQM organizations have developed **cybernetic**[20] and **scanning**[21] systems to obtain and disseminate the needed information.

Cybernetic System

The concept of cybernetics includes information transmission, processing, and storage.[22] Cybernetic behavior requires that a focal unit monitor internal occurrences on an ongoing basis, not as much for the purpose of

PRACTICAL PERSPECTIVE 14-3

Competing in a Nonlinear World

Because companies now operate in a non-linear world, the value of a business lies increasingly in its ability to capture information and generate new ideas, according to Sherman and Schultz [authors of *Open Boundaries: Innovation Through Complexity*]. Analysts have traditionally valued businesses by calculating the net cash flow generated by their assets. But if new entrants can suddenly make a company's assets obsolete, those assets are no longer useful even in describing how a business works, let alone in valuing a company. This is particularly true of material assets—good information about market demands, for example, can render most inventory unnecessary. But even such intangible assets as brands can lose their competitive strength.

This need to capture new information has far-reaching effects. Japan's banks, for example, are in trouble not just because they made too many bad real estate loans but, more importantly, because they know how to evaluate only hard assets like buildings and machinery. So they make loans only on the basis of those assets. They don't have experience with evaluating "soft" credits that have to be managed according to probabilities, as U.S. banks and venture capitalists do. Today's risk assessments are all about the flow of information.

Accordingly, Sherman and Schultz argue that a company should aim to maximize its information and minimize its infrastructure. Information, as they define it, is not just data but "the gathering of patterns and ways of informing and learning." Infrastructure is "everything from physical support systems and physical structures to philosophical constraints and preconceptions." That is, information is everything that helps create new ideas; infrastructure is everything that can get in the way.

Source: Excerpted from Thomas M. Hout, "Are Managers Obsolete," *Harvard Business Review* (March–April 1999): 163. A book review of H. Sherman and R. Schultz, *Open Boundaries: Innovation Through Complexity* (Reading, MA: Perseus Books, 1998).

control as for the purpose of coordinating effective and efficient problem-solving/decision-making activities. For example, computer monitoring has often been used by managers to control and punish employees. At Hughes Aircraft, however, computer monitoring is used to gather information about production and quality strategy that provides needed information to a diverse team of workers.[23]

Scanning System

Scanning behavior involves monitoring the external environment. The term "environment" has been defined as the relevant physical and social factors outside the boundary of an organization that are considered during organizational decision making.[24] Environmental scanning should be a continuous process.[25] Analysis of the social, economic, technological, political, and regulatory aspects of the global environment is ongoing. The analysis involves the examination of current and potential changes and the ways those changes affect the organization.[26] When a monitoring focal unit finds that the environment is dictating change, organizational transformation activities are initiated. Organizations that are unable to effectively scan and react to their environment are likely to decline when faced with more capable competition. It has been found that top-level managers in high-performance companies scan their environment more often and more broadly in response to strategic uncertainty than do their counterparts in low-performance firms.[27] The performance of many of today's organizations thus relies on how effectively they respond to their external environment.[28]

For example, to help monitor the internal occurrences and the external technological environment and to nourish the domestic and international transfer of technology, Japan formed the Japan Industrial Technology Association at the macro level. This organization helps facilitate the dissemination and exchange of technical information between the Agency of Industrial Science and Technology research laboratories and foreign countries. It attempts to keep abreast of technological developments at home and abroad, and it facilitates the transfer of technical information and technology between the source and the potential user.[29] In Japanese companies managers are trained to make competitive intelligence everyone's business.[30] In the United States, General Electric has been a pioneer in the application of the scanning system. In fact, in the past it has sold information obtained from the global marketplace through its scanning system to other enterprises.

Many organizations have not applied this type of organization in the past because the costs would have been huge. Today, however, the advent of enormous communications technologies that generate information at relatively low cost should enable more organizations to implement this type of system. Obviously, customer satisfaction cannot be attained unless, first, the organization knows what the customer wants, and second, it is able to get this information to the employees at all levels who are responsible for customer satisfaction. TQM thus requires such an information-gathering system—a system that enables the organization to create an organic network in which everyone is linked and interconnected and where there is a free exchange of ideas and data.[31]

Cooperates and Collaborates with Internal and External Units

Internal Cooperation and Collaboration

Systems-approach management, popularized in the 1960s,[32] posits that all subunits in an organization are interrelated and that positive decisions made in one unit often have a negative impact on other units, thus leading to an unhealthy internal atmosphere. It was proposed that managers could improve organizational efficiency if they considered the effect their decisions might have on other units and averted the foreseen negative consequences. This requires managers to get feedback from all of those whom the decision might affect. This type of decision-making approach therefore requires downward, upward, and horizontal communication within the organization as well as a focal point to coordinate the communication. In this respect, American scholar Rensis Likert developed the "linking-pin" concept of a strong vertical and horizontal organizational communication link.[33]

The effective TQM organization has thus developed a culture in which there is much cooperation, communication, and collaboration among individuals within the organization and quite often with individuals in other organizations. In such an environment, managers and employees do not work at cross-purposes. For example, in efforts to obtain acceptance of and mobilize support for their new visions, some U.S. corporations have applied a variation of the linking process. Bank of America established a program, labeled the Management Forum, to link all levels in order to obtain support for its new vision. The program's objective was to provide tools to the top 100 executives by which they would link others to generate support.[34] Southwestern Bell linked 55,000 employees and spouses in 57 locations via satellite.[35] Blackburn and Rosen found that the Baldrige Award–winning organizations practice this type of information-sharing behavior.[36]

External Cooperation and Collaboration

As noted above, the effective TQM organization often cooperates, collaborates, and communicates with individuals in other organizations, and it often forms **strategic alliances** with competitors.[37] For example, Phillips and DuPont collaborate to develop and manufacture compact discs.[38] AT&T has links with many of the world's biggest telephone and electronics companies; IBM has created an alliance council of key executives who meet monthly to keep track of more than 40 partnerships around the globe; and

Boeing took on three Japanese allies—the heavy industry divisions of Fuji, Mitsubishi, and Kawasaki—to make a new plane.[39] And, as indicated in Chapter 5, Toyota and General Motors, General Electric and Salelni (an Italian construction firm), and MW Kellogg Company of Houston and China Petrochemical International Corporation (SINOPEC) have formed such collaborative ventures.[40] Organizations enter such an arrangement to share costs and risks, to gain additional technical and market knowledge to complement each other, to serve an international market, to strengthen themselves against other competitors, and to develop industry standards together.[41] Practical Perspective 14-4 discusses the advantage of this type of alliance over the traditional alliance through merger or acquisition. Note that this type of alliance, often referred to as a **network,** which numbered 20,000 in 1998 in the United States, Europe, and Japan, also provides flexibility—it can quickly grow or shrink as needed.[42] This type of arrangment is especially beneficial for smaller companies that now must become global players. Alone, they would not have the resources required to effectively compete against the larger multinational corporations. For example, such an arrangement enables firms to service customers worldwide without having to invest very many resources in those markets—the lower overhead makes them more competitive.

Organizations attain greater efficiency by being aware of the available resources in their internal units (subsidiaries, divisions, departments, and so on), as well as in external units (other companies, governments, and so on), and forming mutually beneficial alliances that make wise use of those resources. For example, a subunit in the organization suddenly requires additional production capacity. Instead of investing resources to acquire it, the focal monitoring unit knows of available production capacity in another internal or external unit and arranges a mutually beneficial alliance between the two units to use the idle capacity.

The organization also attains greater efficiency by focusing on its strengths; it does what it can do best and contracts for other needed functions. For instance, a firm's strength may be engineering and design. Instead of doing manufacturing, it would be efficient for the firm to farm it out to a company whose strength is manufacturing. For example, as pointed out in Chapter 4, Apple vice president Al Eisenstat said, "If I can loop off one area of activity and say, 'Gee, I can join with such and such company,' then I can focus my resources on what I do best."[43] Firms such as Apple, Nike, and IBM have established themselves as design, engineering, and marketing companies, farming out much of their manufacturing to those who are able to do it cheaper and better. Maatschappij Van Berkel's Patent N.V., a Dutch-based multinational supplier of weighing and food processing equipment, met competitive cost pressures by outsourcing its manufacturing and engineering activities and transforming itself into a sales and service company.[44] As Jack Welch of GE put it, "tomorrow's organization will be boundaryless. It will work with outsiders as closely as if they were

PRACTICAL PERSPECTIVE 14-4

Is This Baby Built for Cyberspace?

America Online founder Steve Case has shown a keen ability for seizing on a world-changing vision and sticking with it. The boyish entrepreneur has defied the odds and the calamitous predictions to create the largest and most profitable company in cyberspace. And his audacious plan to take over Time Warner is the greatest manifestation of the vision yet—a behemoth that can place more digital content in front of more consumers than anyone on the horizon. In short, a General Motors for the New Economy.

Dated Strategy

Case's remarkably bold stroke is in fact reminiscent of the architecture designed by Alferd P. Sloan at GM in the 1920s. Through monumental acquisition and vertical integration, Sloan created a giant that outdistanced its rivals on every measure and dominated the world auto industry for nearly half a century. Sloan's strategy was simple but powerful. GM built a car "for every purpose and purse" and sewed up more of the market than anyone else.

Seven decades later, Case is pursuing a similar strategy of vertical integration and conglomeration to rule cyberspace. There is, however, an inherent problem in the analogy: Case is using Old Economy tools in a New Economy that he has helped to define.

Leaders in this economy have generally understood that, unlike in the world of iron foundries and stamping plants, the attributes of size—access to greater resources, economies of scale, and stability—are not nearly as crucial as flexibility, speed, and agility. They know that partnerships, without the fixed costs, inventories, and management headaches of pure ownership are the antithesis of vertical integration. An they've learned that melding a sleek, fast-growing organization with a big established enterprise is the quickest way to slow growth and smother creativity.

Source: Excerpted from John A. Byrne. "Is This Baby Built for Cyberspace?" *Business Week* (January 24, 2000): 40. Reprinted with permission.

insiders."[45] Organizations that cannot work with outsiders will not be as competitive and as capable of serving the customer as those that can. This TQM characteristic is thus dependent on the organization's ability to continually gather information about internal and external occurrences as well as on the ability to share information openly.

Participation, Empowerment, and a Flat Structure

Blackburn and Rosen found that Baldrige Award winners apply participative management, empower groups, and have a flat organizational structure.[46] (For an illustration, read Practical Perspective 14-5.)

PRACTICAL PERSPECTIVE 14-5

Ford's Ambitious Global and Product Plans for the '90s

Ford has ambitious plans to expand global activities in all three of its product areas—vehicles, components, and financial services—while maintaining a lean staff and production base. To get there, Ford's people must develop broader capabilities and learn to work together in teams. Flexibility is the key word.

Ford's specific goals for the remainder of the twentieth century included establishing production bases in China and other Asia/Pacific markets, growing worldwide component sales by 50 percent, increasing engineering productivity by 50 percent, maintaining a 70/30 split between automotive and financial profits, maintaining strong technical and design capabilities, and increasing cash reserves to prepare for the next downturn....

Ford's vision of the future involves the merging of customer satisfaction, employee satisfaction, and profitability. If these objectives are met, market share will take care of itself, says Edward E. Hagenlocker, executive vice president–Ford North American Automotive Operations (NAAO). "Part of the strategy we're working on within NAAO that will be implemented over the next year focuses heavily on empowering people," Hagenlocker says. To facilitate this environment, Ford is shifting from strong functional organizations such as marketing, accounting, engineering, and manufacturing, to empowered teams with authority to function as independent units.

Source: Excerpted from Stephen E. Plumb, "Trotman Team Eyes Ford's Future," *Ward's Auto World* (November 1993): 25–26. Reprinted with permission.

Participation

Participative management is an all-encompassing term meaning such activities as setting goals, solving problems, direct involvement in decision making, and including employees in consultation committees, representation on policy bodies, and selection of new co-workers.[47] It has been argued that participative management is an ethical imperative.[48]

The effective TQM organization uses a **participative** approach in decision making, either in the initial stages of the decision or at least in the implementation stages. It does so because participation offers a number of benefits.[49] One is that people will accept a decision more readily when they are involved in making it. Another is that diverse input often leads to a high-quality decision. Yet another is that it helps develop an environment of trust, which helps develop an achievement orientation among employees. For example, observation of a General Motors plant revealed that both the workers and their union were very enthusiastic about the new emphasis on quality—participating in determining high-quality standards provides workers with a feeling of self-worth and dignity.[50] It is also beneficial because it is the lower level employees who are close to the customer, and therefore they know better what the customer wants—as has been proposed, in the old days, the "tool maker" and the "tool user" were one and the same. The "tool maker" could thus easily judge what would best serve the "tool user."[51] According to Babbar and Rai, managers can facilitate institutional involvement by regularly discussing environmental issues and information gathered through scanning.[52]

Group and Team Empowerment

Effective organizations consist of smaller, more adaptable, interdependent, parallel problem-solving and information-sharing, relatively self-sufficient subunits.[53] For example, in recent years many U.S. enterprises have begun applying a managerial form labeled "team self-management."[54] Other labels include "self-managed work teams" and "quality circles."[55] Many employers use self-management teams, and by the end of the 1990s, experts predicted, 40 to 50 percent of all U.S. workers could be managing themselves through such mechanisms.[56] For example, at General Electric, teamwork, not authority, is the key. Almost every GE factory, in every business, uses manufacturing cells, where teams share work, rather than assembly lines, which isolate workers.[57]

The basic idea of team self-management is that members of the team possess a high degree of decisional autonomy and control of activities (**empowerment**), which were previously a prerogative of management.[58] Blackburn and Rosen[59] cite Pauline Brody, chairwoman of Xerox's Quality Forum, who stated that human resources practices in TQM organizations must be congruent with corporate culture, including a shift from working as individuals to working as teams. Performance measurement and evaluation are based on team goals. In Japan, this team orientation is referred to as total quality control or *jidka*.[60]

Ad Hoc Group Empowerment

Many of the organization's decisions are made in what has been labeled an "*ad hoc* center," which is defined by task-relevant, specialized knowledge; centers of control, authority, and communication are problem-specific and dependent on where the expertise to solve a problem rests.[61] Another label used is "problem-solving groups."[62] The Baldrige Award–winning companies studied by Blackburn and Rosen practice this behavior. Charles Sabel, a sociologist at Massachusetts Institute of Technology, describes this type of organization as a geometric form that has no identifiable top or bottom (the Mobius strip organization), "a body that constantly turns on itself, in an endless cycle of creation and destruction."[63] As contended by Kenan Sahin, president of Kenan Systems Corporation, a Cambridge, Massachusetts, software consulting firm, in this type of organization managers will have to change gears readily, following those who know most about the subject.[64] Therefore, a skilled scientist, marketer, or engineer who is a leader on one project may have to be a follower on the next. Raymond Miles, a professor of management at the University of California at Berkeley, describes this idea as a network where managers function like switchboard operators, coordinating the activities of employees, suppliers, customers, and joint-venture partners.[65]

When a problem arises, an *ad hoc* **group** consisting of members who possess the relevant knowledge is formed by a coordinator to serve temporarily as decision makers. The group, which may consist of shop-floor workers, managers, technical experts, suppliers, and customers, come together to do a job and then disband, with everyone going back to his or her regular job or to the next assignment. For example, large construction firms such as Bechtel Corporation pick groups of employees and outside contractors with the right skills for each new dam, refinery, or airport. Becton Dickinson, according to its former CEO [Raymond] Gilmartin, organizes its own cross-functional **teams** including not only its own people but also vendors, suppliers, and people from other divisions.[66]

The above means that the organization requires a system to keep track of people and their skills. For example, Cypress Semiconductor, a San Jose, California, maker of specialty computer chips, has developed a computer system that keeps track of its 1,500 employees as they criss-cross between different functions, teams, and projects. As previously described, Apple has developed a computer network called Spider, a system that combines a network of personal computers with a videoconferencing system and a database of employee records. A manager assembling a team can call up profiles of employees who are stationed anywhere in the world. A color photo of the person can be seen on the screen as well as information about where he or she works, who reports to him or her, to whom he or she reports, and his or her skills. If the manager wants to interview a candidate in, for instance, Frankfurt, the manager can call the person over the Spider network and talk with him or her in living color on the computer screen.[67]

Participative management and empowerment generate an organizational culture that challenges workers. Babbar and Rai proposed that the organization "must challenge employees and engage them intellectually so as to optimize the use and development of human resource."[68] Clearly, one of the stronger components of TQM is a commitment to the development of human resources. Babbar and Rai indicated that "Managers can make this possible by providing the necessary infrastructure required to bring out the best in their employees and building in mechanisms for them to use in order to draw from the environment. This in turn should facilitate continuous improvement in basic processes and raise the productivity of individuals."[69] This aspect of TQM is thus dependent on the organization's ability to gather and openly share information as well as to apply participative management and empowerment in a genuine way. The recent advancement made in information technology and the reduction of its costs should in the future enable managers to exploit the benefits derived from the application of participation and empowerment.[70] These advancements will enable organizations to develop a team culture, to establish virtual teams, and develop a system of multicultural teamwork.

Team Culture. Be it ongoing or *ad hoc,* to be effective, team members need to establish the behaviors outlined in Table 14-1.

Virtual Teams. The team culture outlined in Figure 14-3 can lead to an inflexible organization. But today's global environment dictates that organizations must develop strategically flexible organizations. Application of the virtual team approach will enable organizations to become more flexible. Virtual teams are groups of geographically and/or organizationally dispersed coworkers that are assembled using a combination of telecommunications and information technologies to accomplish an organizational task. (For an illustration, refer to Practical Perspective 14-6.) Virtual teams rarely, if ever, meet in a face-to-face setting. They may be *ad hoc* or ongoing, and membership is often fluid.[71]

Multicultural Teamwork. Today's organizations must be innovative. Innovation is often best generated through teams whose members have diverse views, that is, members who come from varied cultures. But people typically have difficulty accepting views that are different from their own and seek to eliminate diversity. Therefore, implementing multicultural

TABLE 14-1	Characteristics of the Effective Team

1. *Members trust and respect each other.*
    Trust is the antidote to a proliferation of rules and regulations. It simplifies life. Without trust, the team would not be able to effectively deal with external threats.

2. *Members protect and support each other.*
    Members of the team must share the conviction that they can rely on each other. As such, each member's self-esteem must be maintained.

3. *Members engage in open dialogue and communication.*
    obedience to authority figure is minimal and all members must participate—every member can expect it, every member can demand it, and every member is supposed to participate.

4. *Members share a strong common goal.*
    Certain mutually agreed upon qualitative and quantitative target need to be established by the team. This helps them determine the degree of their success in pursuing their tasks.

5. *Members have strong shared values and beliefs.*
    Shared values and beliefs define the team's attitudes and norms that guide their behavior—and they play the role of social control mechanism.

6. *Members subordinate their own objectives to those of the team.*
    Teams members operate within the boundaries of team rules, they understand personal and team roles, and they do not let their own needs take precedence over the team's needs.

7. *Members subscribe to "distributed" leadership.*
    Team members are not intimidated by rank, seniority, or status. All members of the team are empowered to make decisions. Team leadership is based on knowledge and expertise.

Source: Abstracted from Manfred F.R. Kets De Vries, "High-Performance Teams: Lessons from the Pygmies," *Organizational Dynamics* 27, no. 3 (Winter 1999): 66–77.

PRACTICAL PERSPECTIVE 14-6

Siemens: Building a 'B-School' in Its Own Backyard

For Siemens, it bordered on the embarrassing. The $65 billion German conglomerate makes 12 million mobile phones a year, but its own use of mobile-phone service was stuck in the wireless Stone Age. Managers in different units in Britain were acting like the Lone Ranger, buying phone service for their thousands of employees from a bevy of far-flung suppliers instead of huddling like a team to negotiate a cut-rate contract from one source. Co-workers were dialing each other up over costly wireless networks when they could have been patching calls through Siemens's own less expensive network. One of the mobile-phone use manuals was prehistoric—it hadn't been updated since 1991. No surprise then that all this was wasting $4 million a year.

In-House Talent

Usually when global companies find themselves in such straits, they hire a slew of high-priced consultants. But instead of tapping the brainpower outside of headquarters, Siemens executives started thumbing through their own worldwide employee directory. The problem, it turned out, was a perfect case study for "Siemens University." This is Siemens' in-house corporate training program, in which Siemens analysts and engineers act like MBA students and use Siemens's business problems as the case studies to be solved. For the Munich-based giant, whose wide array of product includes semiconductors, washing machines, high-speed trains, offshore oil-rig equipment, and telephone systems, its like having your kids pay back college tuition upon graduation—along with a generous tip. Indeed, Siemens may be one of the only companies in the world whose management education program not only pays for itself but also saves the company money—

about $11 million so far this year, according to Siemens. "Why should management learning be a cost center?" ask Matthias Bellmann, one of the program's architects, who also heads up human resources for Siemens's Information & Communication Products unit. "Why shouldn't it be a profit center?"

The company isn't the first to link theory and practice in executive education. But the success at Siemens, a lumbering bureaucracy for decades, shows that nearly any business can unlock entrepreneurial spirit by getting managers to work beyond their accustomed roles instead of hiring outside help. Siemens CEO Heinrich von Pierer says the program is an important part of getting executives to be just as networked with one other as are the company's phones. "The interest we get [in the program] from all over the place is a good indicator that we are on the right track," says von Pierer.

Part of the program's success has to do with the way it takes a wrecking ball to the walls between the company's divisions, which have long operated as their own inefficient fiefdoms. Managers are thrown into teams with the "students," peers from other business units, often from abroad. That can make for a lot of diversity in problem-solving, since Siemens has 444,000 employees scattered across 190 countries. "To compete globally, they have to be able to share resources and share ideas," says James H. Vander Weide, a professor at Duke University's Fuqua School of Business, who teaches finance in the Siemen management learning program. "that's one of the purposes of this."

Just how does it work? The students identify what's known in the program jargon as a Business Impact Project, an unexploited way to

(continued)

make or save money. Usually the project is outside the students' area of expertise. They don't get a penny to solve the problems, so the only resource they have to start with is their ingenuity in forging alliances in other departments. The point is to force managers beyond the well-worn grooves and make them work across corporate lines of authority.

Source: Excerpted from Jack Ewing, "Siemens: Building a B-School in Its Own Backyard," *Business Week* (November 15, 1999): 281–282. Reprinted with permission.

teamwork is a challenge organizations face. Organizations will need to implement programs that bring the members together for the purpose of:[72]

➤ Providing team members with an awareness of culture difference and its impact on organizational structure and systems, management style, decision making, and interpersonal behavior.

➤ Helping team members become aware of their different roles, preferences, and strengths and how these complement each other.

➤ Helping team members develop methods of communication swiftly and effectively with each other.

➤ Helping team members develop a set of shared ground rules for maintaining team effectiveness when working together and working apart.

➤ Begin the process developing a shared vision for the team and an implementation strategy.

Relatively Flat Organizational Structure

The effective TQM organizational structure is relatively **flat**. That is, there are fewer managerial layers than in traditional hierarchical organizations. This is because, as well-known management writer Tom Peters has said, "A twelve-layer company can't compete with a three-layer company."[73] In part this is because paying many managers at many levels and the slowness of hierarchal decision making in tall structures would make organizations existing in a dynamic environment less efficient and hence less competitive. Also, an organization can only create an atmosphere of maximum creativity if it reduces hierarchical elements to the minimum and creates a corporate culture in which its vision, company philosophy, and strategies can be implemented by employees who think independently and take the initiative.[74] Furthermore, as management scholar Henry Mintzberg proposed in his explanation of *adhocracy,* many levels of administration restrict the organization's ability to adapt.[75] This means that to flatten an organization, many managerial positions must be eliminated; it also means that those managers who remain must supervise more workers. For example, one area of a General Electric plant, which handles accessories such as hydraulic controls and fuel pumps from 70 different suppliers, has just one manager for 130 workers.[76]

A flatter structure is made possible by the enormous advancements in communications technologies, which, as the well-known management expert Peter F. Drucker noted, enables managers to communicate with a far wider span of individuals than was possible in the past.[77] Spans of control thus give way to spans of communication. For example, at Cypress Semiconductor, CEO T.J. Rodgers has a computer system that enables him to keep abreast of every employee and team in his rapidly moving, decentralized, constantly changing organization. Each of his 1,500 employees maintains a list of 10 to 15 goals such as "Meet with marketing for product launch" or "Make sure to check with customer X." Noted next to each goal is when it was agreed upon, when it is due to be completed, and whether it has been completed yet or not. Mr. Rodgers stated that he can review the goals of all the employees in about four hours, which he does each week. He searches only for those falling behind, and then contacts them not to scold but to ask if there is anything he can do to help them accomplish the goal.[78]

It should be noted that the *path-goal theory* suggests that wide spans of control are possible if the employees are well trained and experienced.[79] This aspect of TQM therefore depends on the developmental aspects of the participation and empowerment components, as well as on training and development programs (to be discussed later). The participative-empowerment aspects of TQM therefore depend on a flat structure.[80] One of the characteristics of the TQM culture identified by Blackburn and Rosen is "a wide span of control."[81]

While effective TQM organizations are relatively flat, they still maintain the three basic management levels: institutional, administrative, and operational.[82] The institutional level still monitors the organization's internal and external environments and establishes objectives and policies to align the two; the administrative level still interpolates structure or improvises; that is, it implements the policies and objectives in its respective subunit; and the operational level still uses the structure provided to keep the organization operating effectively. However, the fixed actors at these levels use participative management and empowerment, and decisions at these levels are often made by problem-specific, *ad hoc* groups and by relatively autonomous groups.

Performance Pay and Horizontal Promotions

In effective TQM organizations, the reward system is viewed by employees as being equitable. Employees' perceptions of equity affect their decisions to join, remain, and produce for a firm. Equity includes an external and individual process.[83] External equity refers to employees' perception of how they are rewarded in proportion to the external market, and individual equity relates to employees' perception of how they are rewarded in proportion to their individual performance.[84] If rewards are perceived to be inequitable, employees are likely to leave; if they stay, they are likely to be low producers.

Performance Pay

Individual equity suggests that "better workers should receive higher wages on the same job than poorer workers."[85] This wage differentiation supposedly helps motivate workers to produce closer to their maximum potential.[86] This suggests that the effective TQM organizational culture requires some form of a pay-based-on-performance system.

Performance pay became a major area of strategic management change in the 1980s.[87] In a survey of more than 1600 U.S. organizations, 75 percent indicated having some form of incentive scheme, with more plans having been introduced in the past five years than in the previous twenty years.[88] Performance pay is distinct from "merit pay" in that it is systematic and open; employees have at least some awareness of the criteria being applied to measure performance and the consequent rewards. Using the merit-pay approach, increases are often based on arbitrary management decision.[89]

R. Semler, CEO for the Brazilian firm Semco, S.A., reported that at his company, employees at the lower level can actually, through incentives, earn more money than middle-level employees.[90] According to Blackburn and Rosen, Baldrige Award winners offer a variety of formal and informal financial and nonfinancial rewards for individuals and teams. However, it has been found that intrinsic job motivation declined when extrinsic rewards, such as pay, were involved,[91] and workplace participation and job enrichment were far more closely associated with employee motivation than with pay.[92] This means that this TQM factor is dependent on the participation, group involvement, and empowerment factors. As Frederick Herzberg found, money does not motivate workers, but it does demotivate them when it is viewed as being inequitable or inadequate; what motivates them is challenging work.[93]

Horizontal Promotions

As people move from one team to another, they and the firm consider their careers and pay in new ways. Instead of slowly climbing up the organizational ladder (the TQM organizational structure is flat), workers and managers make more **lateral moves**, acquiring expertise in different functions such as marketing or manufacturing. Becton Dickinson, for example, is trying out lateral promotions for those who do well in teams, rotating, for example, a financial person into a marketing or manufacturing job. In 1990, in one division the company rotated 10 managers out of 50. They received a raise and change of title, just as they would with a regular promotion, but they were not necessarily put in charge of any more workers.[94]As previously indicated, at Semco, quite often lower-level employees make higher salaries than the middle-level employees, and they are able to increase their status and compensation without entering the management line. This aspect of TQM depends on the flat component because a tall organization's promotion opportunities would disrupt the system and would inhibit application of empowerment.

A Bond and a Sense of Ownership

The effective TQM organization requires high **employee commitment.** In high-commitment organizations, the relationship between labor and the organization is expanded "well beyond the traditional arrangement [high compliance]. The employee becomes committed to the organization and its goals and is matched by an additional commitment by the employer to the employee's welfare."[95] Similarly, it has been proposed that "provision must be made to ensure that each member (called an associate) is bonded to the organization as a whole and to the position held. Moreover, the position must be bonded to the organization."[96]

However, the bonds must not be unbreakable. If an employee is committed to a course of action, and he or she subsequently finds that course is no longer suitable, the employee is encouraged to develop a new suitable course and submit it through the approval process. For example, one U.S.-based firm depends on mechanical organizational behavior for attaining efficiency. The mechanics are agreed upon through a participative process. If, however, an employee later becomes bored or disenchanted with the mechanical job, he or she is encouraged by management to develop a new and more interesting way of accomplishing the task and to submit a proposal through the agreed upon process. Once the change is agreed upon, the new way becomes part of the routine. The firm's executive with whom the writer spoke claimed that this behavior may be temporarily inefficient (while the employee is redefining his or her job), but in the long run it is highly efficient. This suggests that the TQM organization is paradoxical—it resembles the organic form in that it is flexible and adaptable and at the same time it resembles the bureaucratic form in that it must adhere to many processes—not rigid rules and procedures, however.

To enhance commitment, effective TQM organizations develop a **"sense of ownership"** in their employees. The sense of ownership makes employees less afraid of losing their jobs. This in turn makes them object less to learning about new technology and proposing process improvements.[97] For example, to help develop such a sense, Semco issues profit sharing in each division twice a year, divided equally among employees, and every month, each employee gets a balance sheet, a profit-and-loss analysis, and a cash-flow statement for his or her division. Furthermore, the company provides additional job security for employees who have been with the company for more than three years or who are more than 50 years old. Wal-Mart gives everybody a piece of the action. Through profit sharing, incentive bonuses, and stock purchase plans, all the people who handle the goods and the customers have a direct stake in doing well.[98] In Japan, lay-offs are less common for those employed under Japanese-style tenured employment. Thus, because they generally are not afraid of losing their jobs, employees are not usually opposed to learning about new technology and suggesting process improvements.[99]

Ongoing Training Programs

TQM culture requires a change "from a focus on results to a focus on con-tinuous improvement of the processes that deliver the results."[100] TQM thus requires developing more flexible cultures and structures, new organiza-tional practices, and **socializing employees** to them. Continuous improve-ment in basic processes and raising the productivity of employees can be facilitated by challenging them and engaging them intellectually. Managers can make this possible "by providing the necessary infrastructure required to bring out the best in their employees and building in mechanisms for them to use in order to draw from the environment."[101]

Training programs are a primary mechanism through which organiza-tions socialize employees to new organizational values; they also signal an organization's desire for greater employee involvement and its reciprocal commitment to inproving employee welfare. TQM requires the empower-ment of workers and the reduction of managers' relative power.[102] (For an illustration, refer to Practical Perspectives 14-1, 14-6, and 14-7.) It has been suggested that such a power shift and cultural change can cause increased aggression for all parties and severe problems with authority relation-ships.[103] The training programs must address this problem. For example, in a discussion of the implementation of a Japanese-style just-in-time (JIT) system in American organizations, it was proposed that "The greater the number of high-quality training programs related to power shifting between management and workers, the faster its [JIT] rate of adoption and the better the firm's performance."[104] As Blackburn and Rosen reported, "the Baldrige companies focus their training efforts on quality. Their quality training programs are comprehensive, well funded, and fully supported by top management."[105] Of course, since the environment is constantly changing and TQM organizations respond to changes, training programs to change the organization's culture must be ongoing. With the current infor-mation technology such as the Web and e-mail, ongoing training and devel-opment programs can now be administered via long distance. It is not always necessary that the trainees in the program meet at a central point. The Web and e-mail enable participants to interact with the trainer and among themselves.[106]

The Call for Training

Business schools in Europe and the United States are beginning to understand the requirements for these new managerial marvels and modify their programs. The educational infrastructure is coming, but not soon enough. We need to retool an entire generation of managers and professionals over the next decade.

We should look to three familiar sources for this training, but each source will have to reorder its priorities, change its curriculum, and deliver in wholly new ways. The first source, business schools, are rushing to change their curriculum to include global management issues. But that's not enough. Every course should be designed from a global perspective, with cases on cross-border alliances, cross-cultural issues, and global markets and competition. Today's student in the United States must understand how Japanese and Indian managers think, not just to compete against them but also to partner with them.

Many companies also are already investing in internal development programs and sending managers to executive courses offered by graduate business schools to help develop the level of understanding needed in alliances. But most are not taking the necessary actions.

Motorola University has multiple course offerings on cultural awareness and alliances training. Bell South and Nortel have built training engines to ensure that their alliances run smoothly. Hewlett-Packard has an intense alliance development program. Internally, its best practices program in alliance management consist of training sessions, case histories, tool kits, and checklists. Externally, HP obtains assessments form its partners and benchmarks the best practices of other successful companies.

The third source is the individual. Anyone who wishes to be a business leader in the twenty-first century should read as much as possible about managing in an intercultural environment and participative management. Accept an assignment to live outside your home country, be part of a team managing a strategic alliance, put yourself in the line of fire.

Source: Excerpted from Cyrus, F. Faidheim, Jr., "The Battle of the Alliances," *Management Review 88*, no. 8 (September 1999): 46–51.

CHALLENGES IN IMPLEMENTING AND MAINTAINING TQM PROGRAMS

Effective implementation and maintenance of a TQM program requires a new organizational culture.[107] Organizational culture is not easily changed, however. **Organizational culture** has been defined as the "pattern of basic assumptions that a given group has invented, discovered, or developed in learning to cope with its problems of external adaptation and internal integration and that have worked well enough to be considered valid and therefore to be taught to new members as the correct way to perceive, think, and feel in relation to those problems."[108] Organizational culture is thus defined by the organization's members' frames of reference, which are articulated and codified by organizational statements of purposes, policies, myths, stories, and rituals.[109] As pointed out in Chapter 13, the meaning of organizational culture has been broken down into **practice**, such as symbols, heroes, and rituals, and into **values**, such as good/evil, beautiful/ugly, normal/abnormal, rational/irrational. The value aspects of organizational culture are determined by national culture, and the practice aspects are determined by the organization as a means of adapting to environmental demands for change.[110] The notion of culture thus presents numerous challenges to the implementation and maintenance of TQM programs across cultures.

How Are the Practice and Value Aspects of Culture Changed?

To implement TQM programs, do organizations need to change both the practice and value aspects of organizational culture? How are the practice aspects changed? For example, a firm's traditions "frequently have their origins in the ideology of an entrepreneurial founder who set out both a strategic perspective on the task of the organization and a philosophy on the form of the labor process to accomplish it."[111] Thus, when implementing change, past design choices are likely to influence the type of job design and coordination and control strategies chosen.[112] Bartlett and Ghoshal have shown how an organization's administrative heritage and ingrained management norms constrain its ability to reconfigure itself.[113] Similarly, Professor R.E. Quinn's competing values model provides one means of examining how **different value orientations** underlying organizational culture affect design choices. Some organizations possess flexibility-oriented values, which emphasize decentralization and differentiation, and some possess control-oriented values, which emphasize centralization and integration.[114] The former is likely to encounter much less difficulty in implementing TQM programs than the latter. How do the latter organizations deal with the implementation difficulties?

Quinn and fellow researcher J.R. Kimberly Jr., have indicated that no organization is likely to reflect only one value; instead, organizations reflect a combination of values, although one could be more dominant than the others.[115] This suggests that an organization may apply strong controls in a certain function, for example, finance, and at the same time apply looser controls in another, for instance, marketing or R&D. How do organizations attempting to implement such programs address the need for different approaches for different functions?

How are the value aspects changed? For example, the education system in the United States fosters individual efforts and in Germany and Japan it fosters group harmony and cooperation. Therefore, to implement TQM, which requires group cooperation, do the United States and similar cultures need to transform their education system? In light of the fact that Americans and people in similar cultures tend to adhere strongly to the individualistic approach, how is the transformation accomplished?

Organizations that have implemented TQM programs rely heavily on **informal group controls.** It has been suggested that in American-like cultures people join group activities voluntarily "on the basis of enlarged benefits that will accrue to them for participation, balanced against the loss of individual freedom that is surrendered to the group."[116] How do organizations address employees who do not want to participate in group activities because they do not want to lose their individual freedom? The Japanese are forced, in many instances, to become members of groups others feel are appropriate for them.[117] Can people in American-like cultures be mandated to join groups? Even if they could be, it may not be effective—as has been proposed, employee involvement "with **voluntary membership** status works best for the firm [boldface added]."[118] And research shows that the effectiveness of self-managed work teams is not uniformly positive.[119] How do managers of organizations attempting to implement and maintain effective TQM programs confront these challenges?

How Are Participation and Team Programs Implemented in Resistant Cultures?

As explained in Chapter 1, societies consist of multiple cultural dimensions: large or small power distance, strong or weak uncertainty avoidance, group-oriented or individualistic, and so on. Individuals dominated by a large power distance and/or a strong uncertainty avoidance cultural dimension (for example, the French) do not necessarily want the responsibilities that come with the participation and empowerment aspects of TQM programs. And people dominated by an **individualistic cultural dimension** (such as Americans) do not fit well into the team aspects of TQM programs.

Japan, for example, is a **group-oriented culture**. Implementation and maintenance of such programs would thus be possible there. However, Japan is also a large power distance culture (employees prefer direction), which suggests that it would not be possible there. But the popular press reports that such programs have been effectively implemented in Japan. How? Or is it that Japanese organizations do not really apply these programs in the way they are understood in the West? For instance, it has been observed that there is strong social pressure in Japan to make "voluntary" suggestions for improvement in the work place.[120] Some companies such as Nissan have a quota of suggestions for each employee that must be met each month.[121] In addition, Japanese managers use peer pressure to force employees to master their jobs in order to not call attention to themselves too often.[122] These kind of pressures cause stress for workers—Japanese or American.

Also, many people like to be consulted on decisions but do not necessarily want to participate in making them. Furthermore, it has been proposed that for participation to work, there has to be enough time, issues must be relevant to workers' interests, employees must have the ability to participate, and the organizational culture must support employee involvement.[123] In this dynamic environment there is not always enough time, and when quick decisions are needed, it is often best that one person make them. Also, a multitude of studies have looked at the participation-performance relationship. When the results of numerous studies are examined closely, it seems as if participation has only a moderate impact on variables such as motivation, productivity, and job satisfaction.[124] How do organizations address **barriers** to the implementation and maintenance of TQM programs?

What If Customers Do Not Want to Pay for TQM?

Major cultural changes and structural change efforts are very expensive and time-consuming due to the need to build **trust**, develop skills, and overcome resistance. For example, shifting from a mechanistic to an organic form is time-consuming and costly because of the requirement that lower level employees, supervisory personnel, and middle managers be retrained in the knowledge, skills, and abilities needed to carry out their new roles. These changes disrupt existing power and status networks, making resistance likely as well as costly and time-consuming to overcome.[125] Also, organizations incur substantial ongoing training costs after their initial investment because of the need to continually update employee knowledge and skills.[126]

In other words, quality is expensive, and ultimately the consumer must bear these expenses. What if customers do not want to pay for these costs? Or what if consumers can get the product for less from companies that do not incur as many costs in implementing such programs? What if customers no longer want to pay for TQM? For example, Baldrige Award winner Wallace Company's customers eventually rebelled at paying higher prices to fund the costs of the firm's quality program. The enterprise lost money, laid off employees, and was forced to operate in Chapter 11.[127] If the latter occurs, what happens to the "bond" aspects of TQM? How will these problems be dealt with?

Can Organizations Really Guarantee Quality?

Labels such as "A TQM Organization" or "A Baldrige Award Winner" or "An ISO 9000 Company" symbolize the organization's commitment to quality both at the employee level and the organizational level. The label therefore symbolizes organizational worth. But often it becomes a "rubber stamp."[128] Some of the firms included in Peters's and Waterman's famous list of "excellent" corporations soon after turned out not to be so excellent, and TQM organizations tend to fail very quickly.[129] Wallace Wilson, CEO of Wilson Industries, has said: "I think some companies use it [TQM] and promote it strictly for marketing advantages. They hype it and talk about it, but it really isn't valid. If you talk to their people, they really do not believe in it and they really are not doing that much."[130] Following her investigation of two firms in England that failed in their attempts to implement quality programs, researcher Carole Brooke questioned whether quality techniques can be taken seriously: "Could it be that heavy emphasis on quality symbols and ritual processes can mask what is really going on and that experience may contradict the quality objectives, resulting in organizational shambles?"[131] And, according to Jo Broux, senior vice president of human resources at Unilever Home and Personal Care Europe, such systems have proven their worth in many organizations, but they can also be counterproductive. Such a concept carries the risk of becoming an end in itself. When that happens, it runs into a religion, complete with high priest, rituals, and detailed procedures that take on the status of holy writ.[132] How can organizations address this problem?

Can TQM Be Implemented in New, Small Firms?

Another question has to do with entrepreneurship. According to Henry Mintzberg, the entrepreneur, who is functional in smaller, newer enterprises and does not work well in a structured organization, centralizes decision-making and has little interest in employee involvement.[133] Does this mean that TQM programs cannot be implemented in new, small organizations?

What If Those in Power Refuse to Relinquish Power?

Still another question has to do with individuals' need for power and empowerment. Many people are motivated by the need for power.[134] What if such individuals do not want to surrender their power? How do organizations deal with these individuals? Can they be taught the practice of empowerment? Furthermore, if these individuals refuse to relinquish power, how will organizations establish a flatter structure?

In Strategic Alliances, How Can Trust Be Built?

As indicated in the TQM framework, to be effective in the global marketplace, organizations must often enter into strategic alliances. However, strategic alliances are typically laden with tensions, most of them run into trouble at some point, and tensions tend to arise between each parent company.[135] The success rate of alliances is not documented, but Jordan D. Lewis, a consultant based in Washington, D.C., believes it is not high. "The biggest reasons for failure," he said, "are corporate cultures and misplaced control. Cultural differences can also be magnified by a strategic alliance."[136] How do managers address this problem?

How Is an International Telecommunications Network Established?

For firms seeking to compete in the global marketplace, managing information technology and systems presents monumental challenges.[137] One challenge is that global information technology managers must understand the overall global strategy of the parent company as well as the strategy of each of the business units. Another challenge involves establishing an **international telecommunications network.** This is a complex and frustrating undertaking. Telecommunications service offerings, pricing schedules, and policies differ from country to country. Furthermore, telecom services must be arranged separately with each regional PTT office (national public utility organizations, similar to AT&T in North America). Each PTT has different rules and regulations and often different languages.[138] And, as Drucker indicated, so far no one has figured out how to get meaningful outside data in any systematic form. When it comes to outside data, we are still very largely in the anecdotal stage. It can be predicted that the main challenge to information technology in the next 30 years will be to organize the systematic supply of meaningful outside information.[139] These are just a few of the challenges involved in establishing a global cybernetic and scanning system required for effective TQM. How will managers meet these challenges? As has been proposed, "few companies have really mastered the skills of gathering and exploiting information from around the world."[140]

IS TQM REALLY ATTAINABLE?

These questions suggest that while we may know that TQM programs are imperative for organizational effectiveness, there is still much to be learned about what such programs really are and what they are really for. Are they a **quick-fix** business solution? Are they a methodology? It has been inferred that TQM is neither; that it is an attitude, a set of values, and that there is very little discussion in the literature of what is required in order for TQM to work.[141] This chapter has attempted to show what is needed. Notwithstanding all the barriers, the concept of total quality management is still valuable. It provides, at least, a framework for thinking in terms of organizational and managerial improvement.

SUMMARY

This chapter has suggested that as global competition continues to intensify, organizations must look for ways to serve customers better than their competitors do. One way is by developing better managerial capabilities. One managerial tool that can aid organizations in this respect is total quality management (TQM). A TQM framework was described. Many questions need to be answered, however, before such a framework can be effectively implemented and maintained.

Key Terms and Concepts

1. ISO 9000
2. Total quality management (TQM)
3. Customer satisfaction
4. Information technology
5. Quality; value
6. Cybernetic; scanning
7. Internal cooperation and collaboration
8. External cooperation and collaboration
9. Alliances
10. Network
11. Participation; empowerment
12. *Jidka*
13. Teams; *ad hoc* groups
14. Team culture, virtual teams, multicultural teamwork
15. Flat structure
16. Performance-based pay
17. Horizontal promotions
18. Commitment
19. A sense of ownership
20. Socializing employees to new organizational values
21. Organizational culture
22. Practice; values
23. Different value orientations
24. Informal group controls
25. Voluntary membership
26. Individualistic cultures
27. Group-oriented cultures
28. Barriers
29. Trust
30. Labels
31. International telecommunications network
32. Quick fix

Discussion Questions and Exercises

1. Describe the general meaning of total quality management (TQM).
2. Describe the difference between *quality* and *value*.
3. You are an international management consultant hired by a domestic firm in Sweden. The firm's top-level management is aware of the opportunities and threats that are emerging throughout the global marketplace. In light of these changes, management has decided that the firm must internationalize its operations. As has been emphasized in this and other chapters, to remain competitive in this changing world, many businesses will have to develop superior international management skills. As the consultant, prepare for the firm's management:
   a. An outline of the capabilities/abilities the firm will need to develop to be effective in international management.
   b. An outline of the difficulties/barriers the management will face in implementing those capabilities/abilities and in maintaining them.
4. Discuss the way information technology aids managers in implementing and maintaining TQM.

Assignment

Contact an executive of an international organization who has extensive international management experience. Ask him or her to describe the future international management challenges he or she foresees. Prepare a short report to share with the class.

CASE 14-1

Implementing TQM in Poland

The globalization of organizations, partially brought on by rapid improvements in information flow capabilities, increased competition from emerging economies, and newly opened markets has transformed organizational life. Managers are now faced with a growing set of issues of how to manage and motivate individuals from diverse cultures who hold very different assumptions about work, time, and the world. The ways in which people from different cultures interact has become varied and complex. Multinational corporations, cross-cultural joint ventures, transnational teams, international consulting, and marketing have all provided vehicles for this interaction. While we may recognize the need to address management of individuals who view the world differently, we often fail to see how the implicit cultural assumption embedded in well-known managerial programs may be implemented in a way that is inconsistent with dominant cultural values. Total Quality Management (TQM) is one of these well-known programs and Valvex, a Polish company, illustrates the problem.

TQM is an integrated approach to management that represents a holistic management philosophy rather than a series of techniques. As such, TQM is embedded with cultural values and assumptions that are consistent with its culture of origin (predominantly Japanese). When TQM was implemented in a valve manufacturer in a farming village in southern Poland, the impact of cultural differences between the management approach and cultural context became clear.

For Valvex, as for most Polish companies, the ripple effect of the dramatic changes of 1989 have turned the company virtually upside-down. In an attempt to make massive change quickly, the management has introduced TQM. Valvex employs approximately 600 employees and has supplied valves to the construction industry in Poland, the former Soviet Union, other east European countries, and Cuba for 25 years. The company was privatized in early 1994 through a lease/buy plan. Valvex has remained a profit-making enterprise throughout the pre- and post-communist periods. Increasing competition from other European suppliers and difficulties generating new customers for the product have threatened their previously secure financial picture. The Polish-American owner's recent effort to introduce TQM to Valvex represent his attempt to address these challenges.

Questions

1. In Poland, power is assigned through ascription: "Who you are." In TQM philosophy, power is assigned through achievement: "What you do." Polish culture is "fatalistic": belief in a "powerful" other and lack of control over destiny. TQM philosophy is "deterministic": belief in personal power over destiny. Drawing on this chapter,
   a. Discuss the challenges Valvex's managers will face in implementing TQM
   b. Describe the implementation approach you would use. That is, how should Valvex's managers go about implementing the TQM program?

Source: Excerpted from Jennifer Roney, "Implementing TQM in Poland," *Journal of World Business* 32, no. 2, (1997): 152–153. Reprinted with permission.

What Makes a Company Great?

When J.P. Morgan grants its twice-annual options awards to top employees, it specifically evaluates leadership, teamwork, and people management skills. Those who do well on these counts get plumper rewards than those who don't. At Bristol-Myers Squibb, managers are subject to "360 degree" assessments, in which individual performance is reviewed not only by the immediate supervisor but also by subordinates, colleagues, and customers. Toyota, faced with falling sales in Asia, is sending people to extra training rather than laying them off. The decisions in all these instances were defined by a set of shared values, expectations, and behavior. This "corporate culture" can set the context of everything a company does.

In last year's *Fortune* survey of most admired companies, the single best predictor of overall excellence was a company's ability to attract, motivate, and retain talented people, notes Bruce Pfau, a vice president of the Hay Group, the Philadelphia-based management consultancy that produced the survey with *Fortune*. "CEOs said that corporate culture was their most important lever in enhancing this key capability." So in 1998, *Fortune* asked, What kind of corporate culture works?

To answer the question, the Hay Group asked teams of executives from ten companies that ranked at or near the top of their industries—Asea Brown Boveri, American Airlines, Bristol-Myers Squibb, Dow Chemical, Intel, J.P. Morgan, Southwest Airlines, 3M, Toyota, and United Parcel Service—to participate in a formal study. Using Hay's Targeted Culture Modeling technique, the teams described their company's current and desired cultures by ranking 56 behavioral attributes, such as attracting top talent and improving

operations. The profiles of this group were then compared with the norms from the Hay Group's 300-company database. The result?

The corporate cultures of high-performing companies," says Pfau, an expert in culture assessment, are dramatically different from those of average companies." In the most admired companies, the key priorities were teamwork, customer focus, fair treatment of employees, initiative, and innovation. In average companies the top priorities were minimizing risk, respecting the chain of command, supporting the boss, and making budget.

Perhaps, the most compelling insight of the study: The most admired companies all have consensus at the top regarding cultural priorities. Hay's assessment allowed for a precise gauging of the level of agreement or disagreement within each team. The most admired teams show more consensus than almost any company we've examined," says Mel Stark, another Hay consultant. "There is unanimity not only on culture goals but also on where the company stands relative to those goals."

Fortune's most admired companies also appear to be more successful at breathing life into their corporate culture, not just giving it a few lines in the company handbook. "In most companies, the actual culture bears little resemblance to the ideal culture," says Stark, "but in the benchmark group, the correlation is strong." Intel, for example, seeks to keep the egalitarian and cooperative ethic that it started with. In practice, that means there are no reserved parking spaces, no executive lunchrooms, no corner offices—and everyone can get stock options. By contrast, it is all too common for average companies to say they value teamwork but then to award bonuses only on the basis of individual achievement.

Although the most admired companies are more successful at translating their vision into reality, they are often hard on themselves and admit to falling short of their own standards. Their priorities: faster decision-making, better training, and swift action on new opportunities. Such improvements are more likely when the company has a strong corporate culture to start with. A fear of complacency is also useful.

Questions

1. Discuss the comparisons in this case to the framework described in the chapter.

Source: Excerpted from Jeremy Kahn, "Global Most Admired Companies: What Makes a Company Great?" *Fortune* (October 26, 1998): 218. Copyright © 1998 Time Inc. Reprinted by permission.

Notes

1. B. Dwyer, P. Engardio, Z. Schiller, and S. Reed, "Tearing Up Today's Organizational Chart," *Business Week: 21st Century Capitalism* (1994 Special Issue): 81.
2. R. Collard and G. Sivyer, "Total Quality," *Personnel Management* (May 1990): Factsheet 29.
3. W.E. Deming, *Out of the Crisis* (Cambridge, MA: Massachusetts Institute of Technology, Center for Advanced Engineering Study, 1986); and A. V. Feigenbaum, *Total Quality Control* (New York: McGraw-Hill, 1983).
4. H.J. Harrington, *The Improvement Process: How America's Leading Companies Improve Quality* (New York: McGraw-Hill, 1987).
5. J.M. Juran, *Planning for Quality* (New York: The Free Press, 1988), p. 332.
6. S. Cavalery and K. Obloj, *Management Systems: A Global Perspective* (Belmont, CA: Wadsworth Publishing, 1993), p. 176.
7. Collard and Sivyer, "Total Quality."
8. This framework builds on Carl A. Rodrigues, "A Framework for Defining Total Quality Management," *Competitiveness Review* 5, no. 2 (1995).
9. Spitzer and Tregoe, "Thinking and Managing Beyond the Boundaries," *Business Horizons* (January–February 1993): 36.
10. Bob Evans, "Imagine the Possibilities," *InformationWeek*, no. 752 (September 13, 1999): 10.
11. W.G. Bennis, "Managing the Dream: Leadership in the 21st Century," *Training: The Magazine of Human Resources Development* 27 (May 1990): 48.
12. H. Sugiura, "How Honda Localizes Its Global Strategy," *Sloan Management Review* 32, no. 1 (1990): 78.
13. John H. Byrne, "Strategic Planning," *Business Week* (August 26, 1996): 46-52.
14. R. Blackburn, and B. Rosen, "Total Quality and Human Resources Management: Lessons Learned from Baldrige Award–Winning Companies," *The Academy of Management Executive* 7, no. 3 (1993): 49–66.
15. Stewart Alsop, "e or Be Eaten," *Fortune* (November 8, 1999): 87.
16. Clinton Wilder, "E-transformation," *Information Week*, no. 752 (September 13, 1999): 44-62.
17. J.J. Kaufman, "Total Quality Management," *Ekistics* 56, no. 337 (July–August 1989): 182–187.
18. "Jack Welch's Lessons for Success," *Fortune* (January 26, 1993): 86.
19. C.R. Schrage and A. Jedlicka, "Training in Transition Economies," *Training & Development* 53, no. 6: 38-41.
20. For more information on this concept, see A. T. Schick, "Toward the Cybernetic State," *Public Administration in Time of Turbulence*, D. Waldo, ed. (New York: Chandler Publications, 1971).
21. For more information on this concept see R. Vernon, "The Product Cycle Hypothesis in a New International Environment," *Strategic Management of Multinational Corporations: The Essentials*, H.B. Wortzel and L.H. Wortzel, eds. (New York: John Wiley and Sons, 1985).
22. J. Klir, *Cybernetic Modelling* (Princeton, NJ: D. Van Nostrand, 1965).
23. T.L. Griffith, "Teaching Big Brother to Be a Team Player: Computer Monitering and Quality," *The Academy of Management Executive* 7, no. 1 (1993): 73–80.

24. R.B. Duncan, "Characteristics of Organizational Environments and Perceived Environmental Uncertainty," *Administrative Science Quarterly 17*, no. 3 (1972): 313–327.

25. S. Babbar and A. Rai, "Competitive Intelligence for International Business," *Long Range Planning 26*, no. 3 (1993): 103–113.

26. P.M. Fahey and V.K. Narayanan, *Macro-environmental Analysis for Strategic Management* (St. Paul, MN: West Publishing, 1986).

27. D.L. Daft, J. Sormunen, and D. Parks, "Chief Executives Scanning Environmental Characteristics, and Company Performance: An Empirical Study," *Strategic Management Journal 9*, no. 2 (1988): 123–139.

28. P.M. Ginter, and W.J. Duncan, "Macro-environmental Analysis for Strategic Management," *Long Range Planning 23*, no. 6 (1990): 91–100.

29. S. Gee, *Technology Transfer, Innovation, and International Competitiveness* (New York: John Wiley and Sons, 1981).

30. Babbar and Rai, "Competitive Intelligence for International Business," p. 110.

31. Ron Ashkenas, "breaking Through Global Boundaries," *Executive Excellence 16*, no. 7 (July 1999): 7–8.

32. See C.W. Churchman, *The Systems Approach* (New York: Dell Publishing, 1968).

33. R. Likert, *New Patterns of Management* (New York: McGraw-Hill, 1961).

34. R.N. Beck, "Visions, Values, and Strategies: Changing Attitude and Culture," *The Academy of Management Executive 1*, no. 1 (1987).

35. Z.E. Barnes, "Change in the Bell System," *The Academy of Management Executive 1*, no. 1 (1987).

36. Blackburn and Rosen, "Total Quality and Human Resources Management: Lessons Learned from Baldrige Award–Winning Companies."

37. See K. Ohmae, "The Global Logic of Strategic Alliances," *Harvard Business Review* (March–April 1989).

38. G. Hamel, L.Y. Doz, and C.K. Prahalad, "Collaborate with Your Competitor—and Win," *Harvard Business Review* (January–February 1989).

39. J. Main, "Making Global Alliances Work," *Fortune* (December 17, 1990): 121.

40. R. Ajami, "Designing Multinational Networks," *Making Organizations Competitive*, R.H. Kilmann and I. Kilmann, eds. (San Francisco: Jossey-Bass, 1991).

41. J.G. Wissema, and L. Euser, "Successful Innovation Through Inter-Company Networks," *Long Range Planning 24* (December 1991): 33–39.

42. Michael A. Verespej, "Work vs. Life vs. The World," *Industry Week* (April 19, 1999).

43. B. Dumaine, "The Bureaucracy Busters," *Fortune* (June 17, 1991): 46.

44. J. Dupuy, "Learning to Manage World-Class Strategy," *Management Review* (October 1991): 40.

45. Dumaine, "The Bureaucracy Busters," p. 46.

46. Blackburn and Rosen, "Total Quality and Human Resources Management: Lessons Learned from Baldrige Award–Winning Companies."

47. J.L. Cotton, D.A. Vollrath, K.L. Froggatt, M.L. Lengnick-Hall, and K.R. Jennings, "Employee Participation: Diverse Forms and Different Outcomes," *The Academy of Management Review 13*, no. 1 (1988): 8–22.

48. M. Shashkin, "Participative Management Is an Ethical Imperative," *Organizational Dynamics* (Spring 1984): 5–22.

49. See S.P. Robbins, *Organizational Behavior* (Englewood Cliffs, NJ: Prentice-Hall, 1993).

50. R.E. Cole, "Quality Improvement in the Auto Industry: Close But No Cigar," *California Management Review 33*, no. 5 (1990): 71–85.

51. J.M. Juran, and F.M. Gryna, Jr., *Quality Planning and Analysis* (New York: McGraw-Hill, 1970).

52. Babbar and Rai, "Competitive Intelligence for International Business," p. 109.

53. J.W. Dean, Jr., and G.I. Susman, "Strategic Responses to Global Competition: Advanced Technology, Organizational Design and Human Resources Practices," *Strategy, Organization Design, and Human Resource Management*, C.C. Snow, ed. (Greenwich, CT: JAI Press, 1989).

54. C.C. Manz and H.P. Sims, Jr., "Leading Workers to Lead Themselves: The External Leadership of Self-Managing Work Teams," *Administrative Science Quarterly 32* (1987): 106–128.

55. R.F. Magjuka, "Survey: Self-Managed Teams Achieve Continuous Improvement Best," *National Productivity Review* (Winter 1991–1992): 51–57.

56. J.S. Lublin, "Trying to Increase Worker Productivity, More Employers Alter Management Style," *The Wall Street Journal*, February 13, 1992, p. B1.

57. Thomas A. Stewart, "See Jack Run Europe," *Fortune* (September 27, 1999): 128.

58. P.K. Mills, "Self-Management: Its Control and Relationship to Other Organizational Properties," *The Academy of Management Review 8* (1983): 445–453.

59. Blackburn and Rosen, "Total Quality and Human Resources Management: Lessons Learned from Baldrige Award–Winning Companies," p. 50.

60. R. Chase and N. Aquilino, *Production and Operations Management* (Homewood, IL: Irwin, 1989).

61. K.E. Weick, "Theorizing About Organizational Communication," *Handbook of Organizational Communication*, L.L. Putnam, K.H. Roberts, and L.W. Porter, eds. (Newbery Park, CA: Sage Publications, 1987).

62. Magjuka, "Survey: Self-Managed Teams Achieve Continuous Improvement Best."

63. Dumaine, "The Bureaucracy Busters," p. 42.

64. Ibid., p. 50.

65. Ibid., p. 42.

66. Ibid.

67. Ibid., p. 41.

68. Babbar and Rai, "Competitive Intelligence for International Business," p. 109.

69. Ibid.

70. Thomas W. Malone, "Is Empowerment Just a Fad? Control, Decision Making, and IT," *Sloan Management Review 38*, no. 2 (Winter 1997): 23–35.

71. A.M. Townsend, S.M. DeMarie, and A.R. Hendrickson, "Virtual Teams: Technology and the Workplace of the Future," *Academy of Management Executive 12*, no. 3 (1998): 18.

72. This concept draws from R. Neale and R. Mindel, "Rigging Up Multicultural Teamwork," *Personnel Management* (January 1992): 37.

73. J. Braham, "Money Talks," *Industry Week* (April 17, 1989): 23.

74. H.H. Hinterhuber, and W. Popp, "Are You a Strategist or Just a Manager?" *Harvard Business Review* (January–February 1992): 105–113.

75. H. Mintzberg, *Structures in Fives: Designing Effective Organizations* (Englewood Cliffs, NJ: Prentice-Hall, 1983).

76. Thomas A. Stewart, "See Jack Run Europe."

77. J. Main, "The Winning Organization," *Fortune* (September 26, 1988): 60.

78. Dumaine, "The Bureaucracy Busters," p. 46.

79. R.T. Keller, "Test of the Path-Goal Theory of Leadership with Need for Clarity as a Moderator in Research and Development Organizations," *Journal of Applied Psychology* (April 1989): 208–212.

80. K. Shelton, "People Power," *Executive Excellence* (December 1991): 7–8.

81. Blackburn and Rosen, "Total Quality and Human Resources Management: Lessons Learned from Baldrige Award-Winning Companies," p. 51.

82. See D. Katz and R.L. Kahn, *The Social Psychology of Organizations* (New York: John Wiley and Sons, 1966).

83. M.J. Wallace and C.H. Fay, *Compensation Theory and Practice* (Boston: PWS-Kent, 1988).

84. Ibid.

85. Ibid., p. 18.

86. W.F. Cascio, "Do Good or Poor Performers Leave? A Meta-Analysis of the Relationship Between Performance and Turnover," *The Academy of Management Journal 30*, no. 4 (1987): 744–762.

87. See S. Kessler, and F. Bayliss, *Contemporary British Industrial Relations* (Basing-stroke: Macmillan, 1992).

88. J. McAdams, "Performance-Based Pay Reward Systems: Towards a Common Fate Environment," *Personnel Journal* (June 1988): 103–113.

89. Kessler and Bayliss, *Contemporary British Industrial Relations.*

90. R. Semler, "Managing Without Managers," *Harvard Business Review* (September–October 1989).

91. E.L. Deci, "The Effects of Contingent and Non-Contingent Rewards and Controls on Intricate Motivation," *Organizational Behavior and Human Performance 8* (1972): 217–219.

92. N.P. Lovrich, "Merit Pay and Motivation in the Public Workforce: Beyond Technical Concerns to More Basic Considerations," *Review of Public Personnel Administration 7*, no. 2 (1987): 54–71.

93. F. Herzberg, F. Mausner, and B.B. Snyderman, *The Motivation to Work* (New York: John Wiley and Sons, 1959).

94. Dumaine, "The Bureaucracy Busters," p. 42.

95. R.E. Walton, *Up and Running: Integrating Information Technology and the Organization* (Boston: Harvard Business Press, 1989), p. 81.

96. K.D. MacKenzie, "Holonomic Processes for Ensuring Competitiveness," *Making Organizations Competitive*, R.H. Kilmann and I. Kilmann, eds. (San Francisco: Jossey-Bass Publishers, 1991), p. 244.

97. C. Johnson, "Japanese Style Management in America," *California Management Review 31*, no. 4 (1988): 34–45.

98. "Wal-Mart," *Business World*, ABC-TV, April 21, 1991.

99. Johnson, "Japanese Style Management in America."

100. Blackburn and Rosen, "Total Quality and Human Resources Management: Lessons Learned from the Baldrige Award–Winning Companies," p. 50.
101. Babbar and Rai, "Competitive Intelligence for International Business," p. 109.
102. Walton, *Up and Running: Integrating Information Technology and the Organization.*
103. L. Hirschhorn, and T.N. Gilmore, "The Psychodynamics of Cultural Change: Learning from the Factory," *Human Resources Management* 28 (1989): 211–233.
104. S.M. Young, "A Framework for Successful Adoption and Performance of Japanese Manufacturing Practices in the United States," *The Academy of Management Review* 17, no. 4 (1992): 692.
105. Blackburn and Rosen, "Total Quality and Human Resources Management: Lessons Learned from Baldrige Award-Winning Companies," p. 55.
106. For further discussion, refer to Pat Hall, "Distance Education and Electronic Networking," *Information Technology for Development* 7, no. 2 (October 1996): 75-89.
107. Much of this discussion is excerpted from Carl A. Rodrigues, "Employee Participation and Empowerment Programs: Problems of Definition and Implementation," *Empowerment in Organizations: An International Journal* 2, no. 2 (1994): 29–40.
108. E. Schein, "Coming to a New Awareness of Organizational Culture," *Sloan Management Review* (Winter 1994): 3.
109. P. Shrivastava and S. Schneider, "Organizational Frames of Reference," *Human Relations* 37 (November 10, 1984): 795–805.
110. G. Hofstede, B. Neuijen, D. D. Ohavy, and G. Sanders, "Measuring Organizational Culture: A Qualitative and Quantitative Study Across Twenty Cases," *Administrative Science Quarterly* 35 (1990): 311–312.
111. J. Child, "Managerial Strategies, New Technology and the Labor Process," *New Technology as Organizational Innovation*, J.M. Pennings, and A. Buitendam, eds. (Cambridge, MA: Balinger, 1987), p. 171.
112. M.R. Kelley, "Programmable Automation and the Skill Question: A Reinterpretation of Cross-National Evidence," *Human Systems Management* 6 (1986): 141–147.
113. C.A. Bartlett and S. Ghoshal, *Managing Across Borders: The Transnational Solution* (Boston: Harvard Business School Press, 1989).
114. R.E. Quinn and J Rohrbaugh, "A Spatial Model of Effectiveness Criteria: Towards a Competing Values Approach to Organizational Analysis," *Management Science* 29 (1983): 363–367.

115. R.E. Quinn and J.R. Kimberly, Jr., "Paradox, Planning and Perseverence: Guidelines for Managerial Practice," *Managing Organizational Transitions*, J.R. Kimberly and R.E. Quinn, eds. (Homewood, IL: Dow Jones-Irwin, 1984): 295–313.
116. S.P. Sethi, N. Namiki, and C.L. Swanson, *The False Promise of the Japanese Miracle: Illusions and Realities of the Japanese Management System* (London: Pitman, 1984): 243.
117. Ibid.
118. R.F. Magjuka, "Should Membership in Employee Involvement Programs Be Voluntary?" *National Productivity Review* (Spring 1992): 208.
119. See, for example, J.L. Cordery, W.S. Mueller, and L.M. Smith, "Attitudinal and Behavioral Effects of Autonomous Group Working: A Longitudinal Field Study," *The Academy of Management Journal* 34, no. 2 (1991): 464–476.
120. J. Junkerman, "We Are Driven," *Mother Jones* (1982): 21–40.
121. "The Darker Side of Japanese Management," *Frontline*, PBS-TV New Documentary (1984).
122. K. Susaki, "Japanese Manufacturing Techniques: Their Importance to U.S. Manufacturers," *Journal of Business Strategy* 5 (1985): 10–19.
123. R. Tannenbaum, I.R. Weschler, and F. Massarik. *Leadership and Organization: A Behavioral Science Approach* (New York: McGraw-Hill, 1961).
124. For example, J.W. Graham and A. Verna, "Predictors and Moderators of Employee Responses to Employee Participation Programs," *Human Relations* (June 1991): 551–568; and K.L. Miller and P.R. Monge, "Participation, Satisfaction and Productivity: A Meta-Analytic Review," *The Academy of Management Journal* 29, no. 4 (1986): 727–753.
125. Child, "Managerial Strategies, New Technology and the Labor Process."
126. P.L. Nemetz and L.W. Fry, "Flexible Manufacturing Organizations: Implications for Strategy Formulation and Organization Design," *The Academy of Management Review* 13 (1988): 627–638.
127. Blackburn and Rosen, "Total Quality and Human Resource Management: Lessons Learned from Baldrige Award–Winning Companies," p. 61.
128. C. Brooke, "Symbols and Shambles: Quality and Organizational Change," Proceedings of *Organizations and Symbols of Transformation*, Standing Committee on Organizational Symbolism, Barcelona, Spain (June 27–30, 1993).

129. E.E. Lawler III, S. Mohrman, and G. E. Ledford, Jr., "The Fortune 1000 and Total Quality," *National Productivity Review* (Autumn 1992): 501–515.

130. R.C. Hill, "When the Going Gets Rough: A Baldrige Award Winner on the Line," *The Academy of Management Executive* 7, no. 3 (1993): 78–79.

131. Brooke, "Symbols and Shambles: Quality and Organizational Change," p. 4.

132. Anat Arkin, "Excellent Adventure," *People Management* 5, no. 17 (September 2, 1999): 40–43.

133. H. Mintzberg, "Strategy Making in Three Modes," *California Management Review* 16, no. 1 (1973): 44–53.

134. D.C. McClelland, *The Inner Experience* (New York: Irvington, 1975).

135. J. Bleeke and D. Ernst, "The Way to Win in Cross-Border Alliances," *Harvard Business Review* (November–December 1991): 135.

136. Martha H. Peak, "Developing an International Style of Management," *Management Review* (February 1991): 33.

137. S.L. Huff, "Managing Global Information Technology," *Business Quarterly* (Autumn 1991): 71.

138. Ibid., p. 73.

139. Peter F. Drucker, "Management's New Paradigms," *Forbes* (October 5, 1998): 176.

140. Dwyer et al., "Tearing Up Today's Organization Chart," pp. 83–84.

141. A. Wilkinson, "TQM and Employee Development," *Human Resource Management Journal* 2, no. 4 (1992): 1–20.

IX

Integrative Cases

This part contains nine cases: "Internationalization Process of the President Enterprise Corporation," "Providing Local Care on an International Scale," "Steering Around Culture Clashes," "U.S. Fiber Industry Players Look Overseas," "Euro Disneyland," "Sony in America," "Thai Chempest," "The Case of the Floundering Expatriate," and "McDonald's Conquers the World."

In each chapter, this textbook has presented practical perspectives, exercises, and cases which, along with the instructor's lectures, will help students understand the chapter's contents. The nine cases in this part will help students develop an integrated understanding of the textbook's contents. These cases should be read and analyzed after students have read all the chapters and practical perspectives and completed all the exercises and previous cases.

To help students develop an integrated view, the instructor will provide a set of questions for each case to guide the analysis. The instructor may also assign individual and group exercises, which aid in the integrative development process. The integration will be enhanced if the analyses are discussed in class.

Internationalization Process of the President Enterprise Corporation

In the late 1980s, Taiwan recognized the need to diversify its infrastructure for labor-intensive industries in order to become more competitive in the global market. Because local markets also became saturated, a number of Taiwanese companies undertook the challenge to become more globalized. One of these companies was the President Enterprise Corporation (PEC), the largest food company in Taiwan. By 1996, internationalization had brought numerous challenges to PEC. Specifically, PEC's executives were concerned with necessary changes regarding the company's strategy, structure, and human resources.

BACKGROUND

President Enterprise Corporation was founded on July 1, 1967 by Wu Shiu Chi and Kao Chin Yen in Tainan, Taiwan, in response to Taiwan's deregulation of the flour industry. Kao Chin Yen started his career as a teenage apprentice in a textile shop known as the Tainan Spinning Company. In the late 1960s, the Tainan Spinning Group was made up of approximately 20 firms, mainly in the fields of textiles and construction.

Kao, by his late 30s, now the sales manager for Tainan Spinning, discussed a business plan with the owner, Wu Shiu Chi, in the late 1960s. During that time, Taiwan experienced a sudden flour shortage accompanied by black-market price increases. This event prompted the Taiwan government to open up the sector of the state-monopolized flour mills to private investment. Kao persuaded Wu to launch President Enterprise Corporation in order to take advantage of the policy changes.

Soon after PEC was founded, the food company was quickly diversified by Wu and Kao. The flour was used for noodle production, while the by-products were sold as animal feed. The Animal Feed Division was later divided into separate divisions for fish food, livestock, and dairy products. A new division was created to manufacture edible oils. Soy milk and soy sauce were also added as new product lines. Largely because of the booming local economy, PEC soon bypassed the parent company, Tainan Spinning, to become a market leader in the food industry in Taiwan.

By 1996, PEC had grown to contain more than seventeen divisions and employ over 6000 employees. PEC's domination of consumer products later led to a new distribution system, which was managed under a new convenience-store division. The company ran a number of retail outlets, including the 7-Eleven convenience stores in Taiwan, and managed joint ventures with foreign partners such as Kentucky Fried Chicken, PepsiCo, Frito-Lay, Maxwell House, and Kikkoman Soy Sauce.

Local successes, however, could not propel further growth. Kao Chin Yen, PEC's president, described the company's vision of "becoming the world's largest food producer by the year 2017." This global vision, if successful, would transform PEC into a company with sales of 120 billion U.S. dollars, tripling the size of the world's largest food company, Nestlé of Switzerland. As explained by President Kao, PEC's two corporate strategies had been in "pursuit of high growth" based on a GNP strategy and on the "diversification of business." These strategies, however, were not sufficient to achieve PEC's vision. Facing a maturing Taiwanese market, Kao believed that successful internationalization efforts, especially in the People's Republic of China, would be key to the company's vision of becoming the world's largest food company.

While PEC intended to become the largest food corporation in the world, top management feared the company lacked the necessary brand name recognition that worldwide customers could associate with a particular product category; for example, Coke as colas, Nestlé as candy, and Campbell's as soup. The lack of international brand names has resulted in PEC's strategy to become the world's largest food group by actively tracking the GNP of host countries and by concentrating primarily on the Asian markets. As one senior executive commented on PEC's international goals,

> *Stage one is to capitalize on large project growth of consumer markets in China and southeast Asia. PEC's ten- to fifteen-year plan is to make inroads into Brazilian and Indian markets because of projected increases in disposable income and projected growth rate of population.*
> *PEC will use Nestlé as our benchmark to determine market successes. Nestlé is one of PEC's largest and most aggressive competitors.*

The strategy to analyze disposable incomes was developed when PEC captured the Taiwan market. It was done by producing products that fit the host country's GNP growth. For example, when Taiwan's GNP per capita was less that 700 U.S. dollars, PEC used a manufacturing-oriented strategy through the mass production of edible oils, flour, and animal feeds. When GNP per capita approached 1000 U.S. dollars, PEC began production of high value-added consumer products, such as instant noodles, carbonated drinks, and other beverages. When GNP per capita surpassed 3000 U.S. dollars, the company further integrated into the distribution sector by entering the retail market of convenience stores and hypermarkets (supermarkets in larger scales). Finally, as GNP per capita reached 5000 U.S. dollars, the company diversified into service industries such as insurance and securities.

INTERNATIONALIZATION STRATEGY

The first phase of PEC's internationalization was exporting food products to Hong Kong in 1971. In comparison with Taiwan, Hong Kong presented an area with similar culture and language for PEC. On the other hand, PEC executives described the decision as more *reactive* than *proactive* since exporting began with unsolicited orders for instant noodles in Hong Kong. As one manager explained, "When PEC started exporting to Hong Kong in 1971, excess capacity in packaged noodles was the motivating factor. Executives of PEC, however, were first approached by their friends in that area." After the decision to sell noodles in Hong Kong, PEC began exporting other food products to Europe and North America, mostly to Chinatowns, where there were demands for its products.

Exporting, however, was not enough to achieve PEC's vision of being the largest food company in the world. Therefore, in the early 1990s, PEC began to form joint ventures and engage in foreign acquisition. PEC first acquired the Atlanta-based Wyndham Biscuits in 1990, and then purchased the Famous Amos cookie corporation in 1992. PEC also formed joint ventures in Indonesia and Thailand in 1991 and 1994, respectively. Both joint ventures manufactured instant noodles and beverages for their respective markets.

One executive explained the motive behind PEC's acquisition of Wyndham:

This was an important step towards being international. We decided to enter the U.S. market first because the company wanted a bigger market (Taiwan had become too small) and hoped to establish distribution channels in the U.S.

PEC considered the People's Republic of China as an alternative, but serious political hurdles were present in 1990. One executive commented on why PEC decided to invest in the United States instead of China:

The Taiwanese government did not allow PEC to invest in Mainland China because of problems associated with the Tienamen Square. Our Vice Chairman, Mr. Kao, had strong relationships with the government and therefore would not enter Mainland China at that time.

The lack of international brand names also led PEC to concentrate on foreign acquisition or joint ventures instead of exporting. The acquisitions of Wyndham and Famous Amos, for example, gave PEC instant brand names in the United States. PEC also used the name of its local partner (ABC Foods) in Indonesia.

The use of joint ventures allowed PEC to acquire local advantages that would otherwise have taken years to obtain. As one senior executive commented, "When we don't know the local market, a joint venture is more appropriate." For example, PEC's operations in Indonesia were managed by a joint venture with ABC Foods, a local Indonesian company. As explained by one PEC manager:

The decision to form joint ventures with ABC Foods is owing to its network with distributors in Indonesia. Distribution channels in Indonesia are very long and involve many middlemen.

The most recent of PEC's entries into overseas markets was foreign direct investment in China, where it built its own factories in a number of large cities. While China was the latest step in PEC's expansion process, it represented a geographical region to PEC with greater similarity in language, customs, food, and livelihood to Taiwan. Therefore, foreign direct investment was used instead of joint ventures. As one executive commented, "We own 100 percent of our subsidiaries in China because we have resources in managerial expertise, technology, capital, and know-how to do business." Because of these firm advantages, many executives inside PEC expressed confidence in investing in China.

PEC also saw China as an arena that offered both a cost-effective production base and a potentially vast retail market. Using Shanghai as a focal point, PEC invested approximately 150 million U.S. dollars in China and established manufacturing plants in cities along the coast line (Guangzhou, Beijing, Tianjin) and along the Yangtze River (Wuhan, Chengdu). These plants began manufacturing instant noodles, beverages, edible oils, and animal feeds. Among these, instant noodles were seen by PEC as the most important strategic product in China. In 1992, PEC was believed to hold a 30 percent market share in the highly competitive instant noodle market at Beijing. There were roadblocks, however, in China's market in terms of strict regulations on pricing and distribution. Although PEC had its own distributors in China, there were also physical barriers (roads, bridges) that blocked access to certain regions.

The largest challenge to PEC, however, was not geographical barriers. PEC encountered numerous managerial challenges when pursuing internationalization. As one executive described, the international effort remained troublesome for PEC after the acquisition in the United States and foreign direct investment in China. In the United States, PEC had to deal with "low market shares, establishing brand images, increased competition, advertising costs, gaining shelf space, and segmenting markets by tastes." In China, the problems were "government control of pricing, high costs of raw materials, and low living standards."

STRATEGIC CHOICES AND DILEMMAS

The first major hurdle during PEC's internationalization process was related to product decisions. In the food business, such decisions have tremendous impact on PEC's corporate performance in the global market. When PEC exported its products to the overseas market, the company made no deliberate changes to its content or labels. Because of the similarity between Taiwan and China, PEC also began with little modification to its Taiwanese products when marketing instant noodles in China. Although PEC was experienced in terms of the Chinese culture, subsequent experiences revealed that some product changes were necessary. One of the PEC's marketing managers remarked:

Depending upon demographics, products are tested in the local markets using key terms that are successful in Taiwan and tailoring product needs. Promotion procedures depends upon the local situation as well.

When making chili-based instant noodles in China, PEC also realized customers of different regions have different taste preferences:

Different areas require different tastes. West (China) is spicy, South is sweet, Mid-north is a bit sour, and the Central region has its own kind of spices.

This variation of local tastes has caused PEC to introduce more than thirty varieties of instant noodles in China. The lack of market knowledge in Indonesia also led PEC to delegate decisions on product designs to its local partners. During interviews, executives reiterated the importance of satisfying regional customers' tastes and preferences. For example, because "the Indonesian religion requires Indonesians to eat noodles manufactured by their own people," PEC decided to use the brand name of its local partners instead of its own in Indonesia.

In addition to product decision, PEC also encountered problems in terms of timing of entry. Historically, PEC has been a pioneer in the Taiwan market. The company was often the first to introduce many foreign food products (for example, Kentucky Fried Chicken) and distribution methods (for example, 7-Eleven) in Taiwan. PEC's acquisition of Wyndham was also the first in Taiwan's history in terms of the amount of foreign investment. But political factors caused the company to adopt a late entrant approach to some of its most important markets. For example, PEC considered itself a late entrant in Indonesia, owing to governmental restrictions and access to distribution channels. As a result, PEC held only 10 percent of the total noodle market there.

PEC's entry in China was also viewed by top management as a late entrant. After the Tienamen Square incident in 1989, the Taiwanese government imposed strict trade sanctions on China. These trade barriers could not be crossed by a company as large and reputable as PEC. However, a smaller Taiwanese company, Ding Xin, entered the market unnoticed. Its early entry allowed Ding Xin to enjoy a dominant position in China. Delayed by these governmental restrictions, PEC lost the opportunity to pioneer instant noodles in China. PEC executives of two different divisions expressed similar concerns:

Timing is very important. We entered China as a latecomer, due to political restrictions placed on Taiwan. Other smaller companies were allowed to enter the market before we were and gained considerable market share.

Ding Xin is a major competitor. It is smaller, more flexible, and more aggressive. A threat to PEC is if Ding Xin sets up a partnership with a large corporation. This will make it more difficult for PEC to catch up.

The missed opportunity caused PEC to leverage its vast financial resources and management skill to a market that had already been defined by Ding Xin. These experiences have caused PEC to seriously reconsider its future entry strategy in other Asian countries such as India, Vietnam, and the Philippines.

STRUCTURAL CHOICES AND DILEMMAS

The second hurdle PEC had to deal with was related to the influence of headquarters. Historically, PEC preferred to maintain a strong headquarters control over its foreign subsidiaries. Although products were often made in the host country, corporate headquarters at PEC provided guidance in terms of new business development, purchasing administration, and technical support. For example, the construction of new plants in China was coordinated by the New Business Development unit, which also conducted negotiations with government officials in China. Other headquarters units in Taiwan also managed accounting, finance, R&D, and purchasing decisions for manufacturing plants in China. The extensive headquarters influence is reflected in comments made by managers from two major product groups:

> *Take new product development as an example. [Our] division starts with the product development concept and must work closely with corporate until all the work is done.*

> *Ideally the SBU [Strategic Business Unit] prefers to do advertising and research themselves, however, we still need to keep marketing, advertisement, and research at the corporate [level] to some extent.*

> *About channel or advertising agents, sometimes they want control over that. SBU wants to choose the advertising agents and now that is done at the corporate [level].*

The influence of headquarters also extended to personnel decisions. As one human resource executive explained,

> *Corporate makes significant decisions and defines the process to follow with respect to any human resource activities. They provide different programs that employees are allowed to request.*

> *Local training must go through headquarters when the training needed exceeds SBU's training department's budget.*

As PEC continued to internationalize, however, top management recognized that there were certain limits to headquarters influence. Two senior executives from headquarters made the following remarks:

The communication between corporate and the SBU is not working efficiently because operational activities are not known very well at the corporate level and SBUs are expanding too fast and have too many departments to control.

The product management system was established in 1988 and at that time, product managers had no expertise in marketing. However it has been ten years so corporate level thinks that they [the SBUs] should be able to do certain marketing activities by themselves. In this way corporate will have more time to do research regarding potential markets.

At the corporate level, we want to spend more time in integration. Actually too much time is spent in marketing research for each SBU.

Similar remarks were echoed at the local level:

The SBU is in charge of the success and failure of the product so they need to have control, not to report to corporate. They need corporate as support, not to take power from them. Power for decision making, however, is ambiguous under the new structure.

Therefore, some delegation may be necessary to allow local subsidiaries to respond to host-country demands. As one local human resource manager explained,

For example, the [local] government just told us that if you hire a person that was laid off by another company you will be rewarded. In this particular case, the [local] human resource staff knew the information before corporate. The human resource staff informed corporate and then corporate passed the information to the SBUs.

The dilemma of headquarters influence also extended to the debate regarding how PEC's entire operation should be supervised. Before internationalization, PEC adopted a hybrid of the functional and divisional structure. The structure was made up of several functional departments (finance, administration, technology, planning) and four divisions that were responsible for each major product category (baking, beverages, aquatic feeds, foods). The structure, while effective for domestic operations, was not designed for multinational purposes. There were no designated units responsible for international operations except a small unit of the China Business Group. In 1996, PEC made extensive efforts to revisit its organizational structure. Top management considered consolidating the international operations under the product divisions of beverages and instant noodles since both were considered to be major international products. In this case, there would be area managers in charge of producing and marketing these products in China, Indonesia, and Taiwan. Executives of a major product division explained their control on international markets:

Currently, the SBUs all belong to a large product group and take care of sales. We are not sure if the international division will do the inte-

gration work. Now we have the power to handle operations overseas. The Assistant Vice President delegates decision making to each manager in the overseas factories unless they need help from headquarters.

Besides the structural option relying on products, there was also discussion that a geographical structure might be more appropriate. Under this proposal, each division would be responsible for manufacturing and marketing PEC products in its designated region. A senior marketing executive explained the importance of satisfying regional market, consumer, and channel needs from a geographical standpoint:

Previously, the SBUs sold products in their own way. Now we will try a new structure. The SBUs are product-oriented and we want to move them to marketing-oriented. We will go for a consumer-oriented approach and channel-oriented approach in the future to develop products.

Another executive from the planning division also hinted at similar changes:

In southeast Asia, regional centers will be set up in the long term, which will add a new dimension to the existing structure.

HUMAN RESOURCE CHOICES AND DILEMMAS

The third managerial choice PEC had to deal with was the management of its human resources (HR) during the internationalization process. PEC's human resource issues were handled by the Personnel Department, which was organized as part of the Administration Group. Basic systems for recordkeeping, employment and compensation, and finding the right people were the main concerns of the Personnel Department.

One major HR decision PEC had to confront was the staffing of its local subsidiaries. The selection of home-country nationals as overseas managers brought with it the advantage of using people with technical expertise and familiarity with company operations. As explained by a senior HR executive,

At the technical level such as marketing, production, and engineering, if we cannot find the people locally, we will import them from Taiwan.

We would like to train human resource managers in each SBU, assigning more powerful managers to this position.

One executive of a major food group also explained the practice of transferring Taiwanese managers to local subsidiaries:

Each SBU has product managers. After one to two years in corporate marketing, they will be transferred to the SBUs.

However, PEC was aware of racial and cultural issues that might not have favored the choice of Taiwanese managers. A marketing manager in PEC explained:

The reason we can train marketing people in China is that we have the same culture and language. But for other overseas operations, we cannot.

Even inside China, learning the local conditions is necessary for experienced Taiwanese managers. As one human resource executive commented,

We have a small-scale program in China where in a day or two, we talk about customs, laws, the factory situation, and the management experience.

During interviews, PEC's HR managers also suggested that it had become increasingly difficult to staff managerial positions in China because the company had yet to create a systematic expatriate program.

The type of manager needed in China was one who could accept more responsibility and work well in an autonomous environment with a high level of authority. There are many younger managers eager to go to China, but they do not have the experience the company wants. It was difficult staffing those positions.

Maybe there is a need for an international center in China for training managers from all countries. Returning managers can be used in the training programs. The expatriate system is set up so that less experienced managers are mentored by experienced managers. They do not immediately take responsibility of their duties but are allowed to adapt to the culture.

Moreover, because PEC's managers had expertise in only the Chinese culture, racial and cultural factors became evident when PEC created the Indonesian operations. In the case of Wyndham, PEC sent only a handful of Taiwanese executives to the United States. In other cases, host-country nationals were the only option for PEC due to laws. In this case, one senior human resource executive explained,

An evaluation team is sent abroad to enlist the support of consultant firms with local expertise in labor laws and regulations in different countries.

Compensation was another critical HR decision PEC had to make. PEC had to pay its expatriate managers more wages (20–60 percent higher, depending on the geographical region), additional bonuses, and offer time for family visits during their overseas assignments. PEC also had to consider how performance of foreign assignments should be evaluated. Compensation criteria considered by PEC included individual ability and business-unit performance. Managers from marketing and human resources discussed how compensation was done overseas:

In Taiwan, we have a rigid compensation system. But we know in foreign countries, employee compensation is based on their ability.

Appraisals are done at the SBU level and sent to the corporate [level]. Sixty percent of the pay is based on attainment of goals, and forty percent is based on subjective criteria.

But some PEC executives also expressed discomfort with the current system:

Unfortunately every division is burdened with a lot of work and that makes the evaluation process seem more like paperwork.

We are not satisfied with it and are trying to modify it. We need to change our performance management system in order to accomplish our goals.

THE FUTURE

Internationalization is a process of organizational change that evokes many hurdles and challenges that domestic companies must overcome before evolving to multinational status. Many of these changes challenge deeply held environmental, strategic, and organizational assumptions that companies institute as domestic growth occurs. PEC's managers from a major product group reflect on these internal hurdles due to changes:

The organization of the entire company is a top-down management. We are a bureaucratic company. Change is of course necessary, however we have a long history of corporate culture. You can't change it too fast.

The changing structure will cause a lot of sensitive problems. Some will get promoted and changes will be carried out at higher levels.

The success of PEC's internationalization will therefore depend on how the company resolves its strategic, structural, and human resource dilemmas in the future.

Source: Long W. Lam and Louis P. White, "Internationalization Process of the President Enterprise Corporation," (University of Houston, Clear Lake, TX, February 2000). A variation of this case, "An Adoptive Choice Model of the Internationalization Process," was published in the *International Journal of Organizational Analysis* 7, no. 2 (April 1999): 105–134. Printed with permission. The case was prepared as a basis for class discussion rather than to illustrate either effective or ineffective handling of an administrative or business situation. We would like to thank the many executives at President Enterprises Corporation for their most helpful assistance with this case. We also thank Diana Boyd, Tina Chien, Joseph Green, L. Carolina Hernandez, Wan-ting Huang, Catherine Phelps, Debbie Morrison, Lydia Ozuna, Jeffrey Ray, Nicholas Reigleman, Eric Stafford, and Wen-hua Su for their research assistance.

Providing Local Care on an International Scale

Companies making a foray into the global marketplace must talk the talk, and walk the walk, in order to succeed.

When the Prime Minister of a European nation recently suggested that "We live today in a global village," it appeared to usher in what could very well be the most profound oxymoron of the new millennium.

To suggest that our culture is at once part of the smallest community unit and the largest at the same time has significant implications for organizations that wish to join the growing trend to provide products or services on a multinational basis. Although people are people, they most certainly bring very different perspectives on how to do business.

Indeed, European reaction to the customs and culture of the United States represents a series of seemingly conflicting attitudes that can confuse the most seasoned international executive.

They respect, for example, American free enterprise. They resent, however, having American solutions forced on them. They admire American leadership in developing innovative healthcare programs and products, but they would not dream of implementing them without a thorough medical and technical review and a series of inevitable modifications. And when they appear completely disinterested in an American product or service, they might actually be quite interested, but careful not to acknowledge it.

With all the cultural and political differences between different regions of the world, what accounts for the increasing interdependence among them? Unlike periods in the United States' past when much of Europe was inaccessible due to war, trade barriers, and cultural isolation, U.S. companies today find that "going global" is facilitated by improvements in satellite, cellular, and fiber-optic technology, giving rise to an explosion in various forms of electronic commerce.

In addition, actually traveling to foreign destinations is easier and less costly, and more foreign cultures readily accept English as the governing language of business affairs. Changes in the political climate have promoted more international trade, with the formation of the European Union and a common currency, the fall of communism, and the introduction of economic reforms such as deregulation and privatization all bringing the world closer together.

MAKE A PLAN

Developing an international strategy makes sense for many healthcare companies because of the improved economic and political climate, and for practical reasons as well, because going global actually can be less risky than continuing to expand within the domestic market.

"Organic" growth in the domestic market will never offer sufficient momentum for a company to grow quickly enough to outpace globally-minded competitors, and entering new markets can be costly and time-consuming, with no guarantee that the new product or service will generate the desired return on investment.

Yet another growth strategy—acquisition—will be costly, and although it offers the potential for overnight growth, it carries with it the risk of enormous corporate distraction, emotionally bankrupt employees, and potential problems that led to its sale in the first place.

Finally, attitudes toward health vary widely, particularly within the countries of the European Union, and with such disparity in satisfaction, it will be increasingly hard for American companies to resist the temptation to enter foreign markets with American-style solutions.

A TAPESTRY OF PERSPECTIVES

Periodic surveys of satisfaction with various health systems in Europe reveal dramatic differences across the continent. Calls for healthcare reform are inversely related to consumer satisfaction, according to Robert G. Geursen, Ph.D., M.D., vice president of corporate public policy for Hoechst Marion Roussel in Frankfurt, Germany. Geursen reported his research during his presentation to the Annual International Summit on Managed Care, held last year in Miami, Florida.

According to Geursen's research, Europeans value rapid and uncompli-cated access to medical care, freedom of choice, no waiting lists, and equality of coverage without regard to the ability to pay. Those countries where access to care is subject to administrative bureaucracy, or where the basic infrastructure of a contemporary medical system is absent, also are subject to high levels of dissatisfaction and frustration.

Two of the largest corporations in U.S. healthcare already have made significant inroads in their attempt to build a global brand. Blue Cross/Blue Shield Association got its first global experience by attempting to prevent trade through the use of the Blue Cross brand overseas.

In the 1980s, they discovered uses of the brand overseas that consti-tuted a violation of their trademark and a threat to their plans for a future international strategy.

"By early 1991, we had won an important trademark lawsuit in Europe to protect our claim on the Blue Cross brand," says Diane Iorio, vice pres-ident of brand enhancement and extension for Blue Cross/Blue Shield Association, Chicago, Illinois. "After we won, we realized that with many valuable trademarks you use it or lose it, so we began a process of setting up international Blues Plans."

After experimenting with various organizational structures, Blue Cross realized the potential for synergy through alliances with local partners. Today, it has an ongoing presence in many parts of Central and South America based on the same franchising concept that the Blues plans pioneered in the United States healthcare market.

In 1997, it augmented these diverse programs with BlueCard Worldwide, a network of 130 hospitals in more than 40 countries where Blue Cross members frequently travel and require medical care.

"We recognized the opportunity to achieve a presence internationally while creating a competitive advantage within our domestic market for Americans that want security during their travels abroad," Iorio says. "We also recognize that this program would appeal to European travelers who, because of the nationalized medical programs in their own country, would have limited or no access to healthcare resources when they leave home."

Forming international alliances as a strategy to achieve international exposure is gaining favor rapidly among American corporations, though it already has been used widely among European companies operating in the United States.

According to a study of more than 5,000 corporations by the Dallas-based office of Horwath International, 20 percent of U.S. companies have used international alliances to support their international mission, whereas 50 percent of companies within the European Union have created them. On both sides of the Atlantic, these companies report much higher rates of return from well-conceived alliances than from domestic initiatives.

Minneapolis-based United Healthcare used a broader range of strategies when launching United Healthcare Global Consulting in 1993.

"Our projects range from straight consulting projects to management contracts with equity arrangements, with many variations in between," says Ed Griese, United's Managing Director of European Operations. Today, United has taken this approach to international ventures into Germany, Portugal, South Africa, and Asia.

"In the beginning, we attempted to replicate many of United's American-based managed care tools and techniques, with mixed success," Griese says. "Today we are better at detecting the nuances of each country's healthcare system, identifying techniques that will have a positive impact and customizing our approach based on cultural, regulatory, and individual client needs. Ideally, we end up with an equity relationship in an international market with a strong local partner."

United's activities in Germany exemplify the challenge and the opportunity to export American expertise in managed care and healthcare technology. The healthcare market in Germany is heavily regulated. Outpatient and inpatient services there are financed through separate mechanisms, and there is no incentive for physicians to move inpatient procedures to more economical settings. Various "sickness funds" provide coverage for most citizens, and German employers make contributions to the fund. United cooperated with one of these sickness funds to create a coordinated program of care that optimized use of inpatient and outpatient resources. In a pilot program among four Berlin hospitals, they demonstrated a 7 percent reduction in length of stay for targeted patients.

"In many parts of Europe, members stay within their sickness fund for life," Griese says. "Therefore American programs oriented around prevention, demand and disease management, clinical practice guidelines, and utilization management have great potential."

Iorio agrees, saying that the "length of hospital stays in Europe are often two to three times as long as they are in the United States. Also, the use of computers to aid in decision support is higher in U.S. hospitals. European markets appear very interested in adopting medical technology from the United States. They're looking at American know-how to maximize the efficiency of those systems for decision support purposes."

EUROPEAN VIEW OF AMERICAN TACTICS

With all the extraordinary opportunities available to American companies seeking expansion overseas, why do they continue to struggle in their international affairs?

The problems Americans face in conducting business overseas can be traced to their failure to recognize the many unique characteristics of their international target market, according to Mark Woodbridge, chief executive officer of Woodbridge Consulting, a German-based firm that specializes in promoting trade between companies in the United States and Europe.

"The most universal problem for American companies is that they fail to prepare for international expansion with the same level of planning and due diligence with which they would approach a domestic initiative," he says.

Woodbridge points to the fact that an international strategy requires a minimum three-year commitment.

"Unfortunately, upon deciding to support an international strategy, American companies will take their proven American products and proven American marketing model and will assume these will succeed equally well in another world altogether," he says. "When they find that they are rebuffed in their attempts to establish themselves overseas, they prematurely assume the venture has failed and they return to focus on domestic opportunities."

How does one begin to develop a global mentality so that common mistakes—because of the parochial historical perspectives of U.S. business—are avoided?

"This requires top management commitment and a statement by company leadership that your customers are no longer within American borders, and that wherever customers or prospects are located, they are entitled to the same level of high quality service as your most important domestic client," Woodbridge suggests.

Although the Pacific Rim and Latin America previously have been central targets for many American healthcare technology and service companies, economic instability and uncertainty in those parts of the world have turned recent attention to Europe. Today, 70 percent of exporting firms focus on Europe as their primary target, with an approximate annual volume of $150 billion. According to *Inc.* magazine, Western Europe represents the fastest-growing market for U.S. technology exports.

American corporations need to recognize that an international strategy will not always be compatible with the very short time frames and quarterly reviews with which publicly traded companies evaluate the profitability of new ventures. It might take several years to demonstrate the success of an international investment, and some U.S. corporations may find this discipline quite difficult to maintain. It could be of great value to these companies to spend some time examining the marketing philosophy and strategies of their European counterparts.

When an international venture fails, it can almost always be traced to problems in communication. American companies should realize that even where significant language barriers do not exist, significant cultural differences probably do.

An important paradigm shift, illustrated below, will help these companies adapt to the global market and will ensure that common mistakes in international marketing are avoided.

THE TRADITIONAL MODEL

In one scenario, which looks at the traditional perspective, companies approach an international initiative as an extension of the existing domestic marketing effort. The marketing director establishes a strategy and marketing plan to introduce the product overseas. A limited budget is allocated to allow for such things as market research, on-site visits, distributor recruitment, and promotional materials.

Projections for international penetration and corresponding revenues are developed and presented to the company's board.

A timeline is put in place so that expectations regarding return on investment are measured and evaluated.

While the approach reviewed above might appear to be well-conceived, it typically is viewed from the foreign perspective quite differently:

➤ Prices are quoted in American dollars, before shipping costs.

➤ The product is offered in an as-is condition, a poor fit for foreign end-users.

➤ The company is accessible only during U.S. business hours.

➤ No one in the company speaks the language of the foreign client.

➤ Reception personnel and client services departments are unaware that foreign users are attempting to contact the company.

➤ Materials provided in the local language are confusing and of little practical value.

➤ Initial customers begin to resent the American manufacturer.

➤ Distributors feel betrayed by a lack of thorough preparation and support.

Although it is not necessarily true that the traditional perspective will produce such disastrous results (which gives rise to the danger of generalization), it would benefit this theoretical organization to have introduced the following paradigm shift before making a decision to approach international expansion.

THE IDEAL PERSPECTIVE

Within an ideal perspective, management first must view its own domestic market as part of a larger universe, rather than viewing international markets as an extension of domestic markets. Having this global perspective will ensure that no one assumes that what is good for the domestic market will suit the international market.

Other important adjustments that come from this perspective:

➤ Marketing will ensure that communications take place in the language of the local market and will make it easier to understand product/ service benefits and ordering procedures.

➤ Pricing will be quoted in local currency, including freight and delivery charges.

➤ Marketing will ensure answers are available 24 hours a day, either through a local office, call center, or company Web site.

➤ Management will recognize the importance of hiring nationals as general managers from within the countries in which they have representation, not simply relying on American expatriates to maneuver through the complexities of government regulations and subcontracting relationships.

➤ Management will further acknowledge the potential need for product re-engineering and will empower the local general manager to guide this process, ultimately producing a product that fits well within the foreign market.

WORD OF ADVICE

"The best advice I can offer is to not approach international expansion based on what the competition is doing or on what tempting offer an international partner might make to satisfy their own needs," Iorio suggests.

"Instead, focus relentlessly on your customers. Know why you are going global.

"What are your current customers' global needs? What needs of international customers can you meet? What alliances will reduce the risk and increase the efficiency of your international venture? The answers to these questions will help you find 'true north,' your own international compass," she says.

Respecting the unique nature of foreign markets is the first step toward success in international marketing. But the rewards can be significant for the American company that is determined to learn and succeed in the global marketplace.

At the end of the day, there are times when being "less American" can mean all the difference in the world.

Source: Ian R. Lazaurus, "Providing Local Care on an International Scale," *Managed Health Care* 9, no. 6 (June 1999): 16–21. Copyright © 1999 Responsive Database Services. Inc., Business and Management Practices; Copyright © 1999 Advanstar Communications, Inc., Managed Healthcare.

INTEGRATIVE CASE 3

Steering Around Culture Clashes

It's 9 A.M. and the early shift at the Mercedes-Benz assembly plant is headed for its vesper, the first of the workday's ritual beer breaks.

Once back on the floor of the cavernous workshops, the newly refreshed employees, in their uniform blue coveralls and safety glasses, light up their cigarettes at the control panels and machining stations.

Robots do all the heavy lifting in this high-tech automotive heartland these days, but the workforce here remains overwhelmingly male.

Issues such as the risk of alcohol-related accidents, nonsmokers' rights, sexual harassment, and diversity in the workplace are sources of bemusement for those who turn out the cars whose name has become synonymous with perfection.

And one has only to glance at the official portrait of the new board of directors—18 members, all middle-aged, all white, all male—to be reassured that nothing has changed in Germany's hidebound automaking culture just because of the November [1998] merger of Daimler-Benz and Chrysler Corporation.

"We're not trying to bring two worlds together to create a new one. The ideal merged company will still have noticeable differences, like a choir that needs different voices to achieve the perfect sound," says Dirk V. Simmons, a corporate strategist from Daimler-Benz now serving on the Daimler-Chrysler integration team.

Those guiding history's biggest industrial marriage through its first daunting stages insist that the objective of uniting the two auto giants is to preserve each working environment's unique qualities.

But cultural frictions have been identified as the primary pitfalls in unsuccessful cross-border joint ventures, of which there have been many. More than 70 percent of such mergers are given up as failures within three years, according to Daimler's own extensive pre-merger research.

As a hedge against those discouraging statistics, DaimlerChrysler managers put together PMI. The initials may evoke images of a stress-induced affliction, but they stand for Post-Merger Integration, a 100-member team that has combed through the sorry details of 50 failed cross-border partnerships to identify the frictions before they can begin grating on this merger.

With trademark German efficiency, the integration specialists have produced lists of *do*'s and *don't*s for industrial partnerships, isolating 98 miserable marriage traps and consigning them to 12 hit lists to be tackled by a bicultural team. The themes targeted for scrutiny run from the broadly divergent packages of compensation and benefits accorded auto workers on opposite sides of the ocean to sensitivity training to help each side's executives understand the complexities of the other's industrial culture.

Late-night brainstorming sessions and videoconferences between the headquarters in nearby Stuttgart, Germany, and in Auburn Hills, Michigan, have themselves produced more issues for the strategists to ponder.

"We noticed right away that the American executives were more casually dressed," says corporate communications director Roland Klein, one of the younger German executives to whom the notion of casual Fridays has some appeal. "You would never see anyone here without a tie on, even if they came in on a Saturday."

The *lingua franca* of all management meetings now is English, which spares German executives the need to converse with each other using the informal *du* manner, as agreed by the PMI team. But Klein notes that the encouraged familiarity has not caught on: "As soon as two Germans are on their own again, they immediately revert to using *Sie*," he says, referring to the formal German word for "you."

German executives on the PMI team, which is supposed to finish its work and dissolve within two years, insist that the new cross-cultural partnership has the ideal qualities for a corporate marriage because Daimler-Benz had been evolving toward a more American style of corporate management since Juergen Schrempp took over as chairman in May 1995. His introduction of performance-related bonuses and streamlining of the industrial conglomerate to focus on its core products transformed Daimler-Benz into a profitable company that should adjust more easily to the U.S. strategies for doing business.

Under Schrempp's guidance, Daimler-Benz became one of the first German companies to switch to U.S. accounting methods. Initiatives launched in February 1997 to create a more globally competitive company included the German automaking world's first labor agreement allowing management to change production schedules to fulfill orders more efficiently. In exchange, Daimler-Benz workers were promised there would be no layoffs through the end of 2000.

Fear of job losses was the main theme of resistance to the $33 billion merger before it was approved by both companies and their unions last year, and employees recognize that the merger means eventual setbacks on the job market.

"People are worried, but that's not surprising in the current circumstances," says Gerhard Maier, a product manager whose extended family is dependent on the DaimlerChrysler empire for its livelihood. "The generation of my father expected to work for Mercedes-Benz until the end of their working lives, but those of us today can't be so sure."

Most workers shrug off the effects of the merger as imperceptible at the production level.

"I come through here 16 times a day, and I can't find one thing that is different now," says Herbert Spies, who conducts tours through the assembly facilities for visiting executives and new hires.

Finding a delicate balance between preserving a familiar working atmosphere and getting across to employees that their company has a new

TABLE 1	DaimlerChrysler at a Glance
A look at the assets of the combined DaimlerChrysler:	
Headquarters:	Stuttgart, Germany, and Auburn Hills, Michigan
Co-chairmen:	Juergen Schrempp and Robert Eaton
Employees:	434,000
1998 combined revenue:	$148 billion
1998 combined operating earnings:	$7.06 billion*
Group auto sales in 1998:	4.4 million units, with Chrysler, Dodge, Plymouth, and Jeep car and truck brands accounting for about 3 million units
Rank:	No. 5 in worldwide vehicle sales, behind General Motors, Ford, Toyota, and Volkswagen
Top sellers (U.S. market, 1998):	Plymouth Voyager and Dodge Caravan minivans, Dodge Durango sport-utility vehicle, Dodge Ram pickup series, Jeep Grand Cherokee sport-utility, Mercedes-Benz E300 sedan and E20 wagon, ML 320/430 sport-utility

*Estimate
Sources: Autodata Corp., company and wire service reports

identity is one of the most challenging tasks for the integration team, says Simmons, the corporate strategist.

Although cultural differences are said to be the downfall of most failed cross-border ventures, the merger's promoters cite production issues in arguing that their corporate marriage will be a success.

The most important factor in DaimlerChrysler's favor, Klein says, is that there is virtually no overlap in the combined product line spanning Plymouth subcompacts up to the Mercedes-Benz luxury S-Class. Even the few models that appear to compete for similar markets, such as the Jeep Grand Cherokee and Mercedes M-Class sport-utility vehicles, appeal to different types of consumers, he says.

"The Grand Cherokee driver is an adventurer, someone in cowboy boots, the Marlboro Man, while the Mercedes ML appeals to the traditional Mercedes driver, someone cautious, conservative, safety-conscious," Klein says.

The joined manufacturers expect to achieve $1.4 billion in cost-saving "synergies" in the first year alone by combining purchasing operations and some technology products, for example. The company says bigger economies may become possible later if the automakers produce future models together. And Daimler may not yet be done shopping for partners and new opportunities for growth; the company is among the rumored suitors for all or part of the troubled Nissan Motor Company of Japan.

But industry analysts are less sanguine about the very qualities that DaimlerChrysler strategists are promoting as keys to success.

"There is hardly any overlap in the product range of DaimlerChrysler, which means the potential for cost-savings in pretty limited," says Lothar Lubinetzki, automotive analyst for Enskilda Securities in London. "The real benefits of a merger come only with the implementation of a platform strategy, and there is no indication DaimlerChrysler is going to do this."

That strategy aims to cut costs by using common platforms—or the same basic underpinnings—for vehicles in more than one product line. Such a move would require redesign and departure from the new company's vehement insistence on preserving the individuality of each partner's output.

If DaimlerChrysler were to engage in joint manufacturing, it would be confronted by the cultural clashes of the American and German workforces and the intense pride autoworkers on both sides of the Atlantic take in their products, Lubinetzki says.

"The Mercedes guys think they're brilliant because their product is respected for its quality," the analyst says. "But Chrysler people feel the same way about their reputation for efficiency. You put the two together, and you are going to have clashes. The biggest challenge in a merger like this is on the production floor. The chairmen and boards of directors can be all for it, but it eventually comes down to the workforces."

One major difference between German and U.S. auto production is the relationship between management and labor. At DaimlerChrysler, as at all German automakers, representatives of the powerful IG Metall labor union sit on the board of directors.

The common German industrial practice of *mitbestimmung,* or co-determination, seeks to head off labor disputes by involving union leadership in decisions about production. The newly constituted supervisory board of DaimlerChrysler includes a representative of the United Auto Workers.

Mixing management and labor in the boardroom may help avert trouble on the production floor, but fluctuations between the wages and benefits of the two workforces could introduce new disputes at the executive level. U.S. assembly line workers earn more per hour than their German counterparts, but their benefits and insurance packages often pale against those of the Europeans, who enjoy a minimum of six weeks vacation each year, fully paid health care and education, and the right to a soul-soothing spa break every three years. When it comes to the boardroom, though, U.S. executives are usually far better compensated than their German equivalents.

German executives wave off concern about the two sides' wide variances in production costs as details unlikely to disrupt the venture. Where Daimler-Benz produces 850,000 passenger vehicles a year with about 120,000 employees, Chrysler makes 3 million with a workforce of about the same size.

Different spending priorities have become clear, even in the two months since the merger was completed, most obviously in corporate advertising for the new venture that has departed from Daimler's long-standing view that it had no need to invest in goodwill.

The multimillion-dollar promotion of the new company spread the diverse visages of executives, engineers, and assembly workers across the pages of the most influential European and U.S. publications, marking a clear preference for American image-marketing techniques.

One of the multipage advertisements depicts two crash-test dummies embracing as they selflessly plunge into the work of getting demolished. Although a fatal collision may be unlikely for the two automakers, the fact remains that most of those who have gone before them have crashed and burned.

Source: Carol J. Williams, "Steering Around Culture Clashes," *Los Angeles Times*, January 17, 1999, Part C, p. 1. Copyright © 1999 Times Mirror Company.

U.S. Fiber Industry Players Look Overseas

Fiber optics transmission companies generally focus on international expansion in order to seize a share of a global market totaling 600 million homes. However, the Asian financial crisis has weeded out all but the most dedicated to long-term success in some developing regions. Although the current situation is sobering for many companies, the general attitude toward the industry's international future is bright.

One reason corporations are looking overseas for expansion is illustrated by a recent study from Paul Kagan & Associates. The fiber market in the U.S., the report estimates, will fall from 860,000 fiber-miles in 1998 to under 550,000 but 2001, with steeper declines thereafter.

Antec (U.S.), for instance, points to China as a potentially lucrative market for fiber-optic line installations. The company will also enact operations in Latin American countries such as Argentina, Brazil, Chile, and Peru.

Corning, Inc. (U.S.), which produces glass for the fiber-optics companies, is looking abroad as well, having already acquired an interest in both BICC PLC (Wales) and Optical Waveguides (Australia).

Oriel Corporation (U.S.), a producer of laser-transmitters, is an exception. It has not made international growth a fixture of its corporate strategy.

The article elaborates on industry developments.

With glass, laser, and transmitter prices dropping by as much as 20 percent each year, many vendors and manufacturers of fiber products see the international market as an important component of their long-term revenues.

And with a global market of 600 million homes, it's no wonder that fiber-related businesses consider their international strategies vital for growth.

Yet international expansion can be exasperatingly slow. Inconsistent regulations, currency issues, lack of access to capital, and few quality infrastructures make it difficult to establish a beachhead internationally.

Mix in the current "Asian Flu" economic crisis, which has had a domino effect on once-fertile fiber markets such as Latin America and the Pacific Rim, and only patient companies with long-term visions and determined strategies are likely to succeed anytime soon. "I think we all got very ambitious and lost sight of the risks involved in the international markets, like the economy, government regulations, and so on," says Ron Coppock, president of Antec International, a producer of fiber-optic and radio-frequency transmission systems. "I think as an industry, we got ahead of ourselves."

Despite the odds, however, most cable and fiber industry executives agree that fiber's global future looks promising. "The international business will be very good," says John Dahlquist, vice president of broadband marketing for Harmonic Lightwaves, a designer and manufacturer of lightwave and digital hybrid fibercoaxial networks. "There's a tremendous amount of business out there [that will come to fruition] in three to five years. We're positioning ourselves on the head-end side, which we feel will see good growth."

Dahlquist and others see the international fiber market as a short-term hedge against a declining U.S. fiber market, which, according to a recent Paul Kagan & Associates study, will drop from 860,000 fiber-miles installed in 1998 to less than 550,000 in 2001, with dramatic decreases expected beyond that year.

And the international market's long-term payoff has the fiber industry salivating. "I think the international market has a good chance to [become] larger than the domestic market by next year," Dahlquist said.

Consequently, companies such as Antec are placing more emphasis on worldwide strategies. Coppock says the company is segmenting its international markets into five categories, all of which are expected to grow by about 10 percent annually over the next five years.

"Inherently, we have a different set of users internationally," he says. "So we have five different segments: China, Southeast Asia, Latin America, Canada, and Europe. And clearly, they're all growth markets."

Coppock points to China as an example. "There are three separate entities there who are all laying fiber: cable, telephony, and data. There are huge opportunities in China for us." He also cites Latin America as a fertile growth market "because of its huge growth in new-builds and telephony applications."

Antec, Coppock notes, is growing its business in Argentina, Chile, and Peru as well, with Brazil poised to become its most lucrative market, once the country gets beyond its current economic maladies. "It has a huge household and TV market, with segmented demographics. And they have the numbers," he explains. "But the government has yet to make the hard choices to fight their economic problems."

And, as companies like Antec migrate to international markets, an in-market presence becomes critical. This will create valuable local job opportunities for people with the proper skill-sets. "It's crucial," he adds. "We have to have full technical and support capabilities because our product is very technical in the system area. We need field engineers and maintenance people close by, not just marketing offices."

Setting up shop in international markets is paramount to companies seeking a competitive edge in the fiber business overseas. That strategy is prompting Corning, Inc., the leading producer of glass to the fiber industry, to expand its presence abroad as well. "We know MSOs won't [continue to] put in fiber at the rate they are now, so we are looking internationally," says Pat Brown, cable TV marketing manager for Corning.

Corning has experienced an annual 30 percent increase in the number of kilometers of fiber installed during the past eight years, an impressive figure the company aims to build upon. Says Brown: "We are being more aggressive internationally and want to address markets worldwide with partnerships. We have a rich history of partnering."

Corning recently acquired interests in BICC PLC, a Wales-based manufacturer of singlemode fiber, as well as Australia's Optical Waveguides.

For Oriel Corporation, however, developing a local presence overseas is not a critical part of its international strategy. The laser-transmitter producer is growing its international fiber business through domestic original equipment manufacturers (OEMs), so establishing itself locally is not an efficient business model, according to Bill Moore, the company's vice president and general manager.

Oriel's analysis of the international market, completed last year, crystallized the company's overseas fiber strategy, Moore adds. "We don't need a big sales force because we work with OEMs who sell overseas. It became really clear that in our business, working with OEMs is a much more economical way to go," he says.

Indeed the international fiber business will definitely gain importance as the North American market matures, Moore insists, regardless of its present state. "The international market is really growing in importance, despite the current economic crisis," he said.

Once the crisis passes, most fiber industry officials believe the international market will grow stronger, given the voracious appetite for fiber-rich plants, both in the United States and overseas. "If you look at what's driving network architecture—near video-on-demand, broadcast, HDTV, and more—they take up more bandwidth, and the optics segment of the business will allow greater capacity," says Bob Scott, director of marketing for optoelectronics at Scientific-Atlanta, Inc., a full-line cable-TV equipment manufacturer.

Members of the fiber industry are hopeful that this will translate into more sales worldwide. Turning those opportunities into actual sales is a speed bump for companies intent on driving deeper into international markets. For instance, developing and implementing a compatible billing system, which varies from country to country, can be one of the more daunting challenges to growing a fiber-rich plant and business overseas.

"Typically, our billing applications are universal, but each country has a unique layer of local requirements, like taxation," reports Curt Champion, director of marketing for cable and broadband solutions at Convergys Corporation.

A billing system, Champion says, must accommodate the myriad local nuances such as taxation, local database, and directory information, and requires distinct components in its billing nucleus. "Each market has a core interface. Then we create our solutions so that wherever they are deployed, there's another layer of applications that is unique to that market," he explains. "It's very important that we extend a portion of the applications to meet each country's different requirements."

To meet the increasing demands of its international business, Convergys routinely receives updates from its international customers regarding new tax laws, product launches, and market variables—all closely related to the expansion of fiber-rich plants overseas. "Our business will extend even further into the international market. As a result, we'll need to meet the increased demand by partnering with early-adopter companies in countries moving from regulated to unregulated markets," Champion notes.

The final challenge for the fiber industry as it expands into more international markets is to stay focused on advancing technologies and the new services they will ultimately bring to consumers worldwide. Concludes Champion: "The real challenge is to understand what capabilities 'rich-fiber networks' will be able to offer and what is the next wave of product offerings. We have to work closely with them."

Most of the fiber industry believes that the "next wave" of offerings is expected to reach high tide sometime in the next three to five years. Just which foreign soil it has the most impact on, and to what degree, will most likely depend on the fiber industry's patience and diligence

Source: Craig Kuhl, "U.S. Fiber Industry Players Look Overseas," *Business and Industry 5,* no. 3 (March 1999): 29. Copyright © 1999 Responsive Database Services, Inc.; Copyright © 1999 Capital Cities Media, Inc., Multichannel News International Supplement.

INTEGRATIVE CASE 5

Euro Disneyland

By the late 1980s, Europe was seen as the upcoming economic superpower of the twenty-first century. Trade restrictions were being methodically removed, and plans were being made to convert to one European currency unit. The "new Europe" was purported to be the next major area of growth and wealth accumulation.

The Disney company wanted to be part of Europe's future. In order to take full advantage of these changes, the management knew they had to get in early. In 1987, the decision was made to go ahead with a major development plan. With revenues springing to life from the parks in the United States and Tokyo Disneyland an unqualified success, Disney, under Michael D. Eisner, began to plan for its next major expansion—Euro Disneyland.

BACKGROUND

Euro Disneyland was not a new idea. It was simply the most recent manifestation of the Walt Disney Company's theme park strategy—the latest phase in Disney park evolution. Its predecessors can be directly traced back to Anaheim, California (1955), Orlando, Florida (1970), and Tokyo Disneyland in Japan (1982).

By the beginning of the 1950s, the Walt Disney Company was well established as a film studio. It had developed this success by utilizing a new film technology, animation, and developing an endearing cast of animated "stars"—Mickey Mouse, Goofy, Donald Duck, and Snow White to name a few. Starting with short film subjects in the 1920s (cartoons), the Disney organization was developing full-length animated films by the late 1930s. The broad acceptance of the Disney films by the American public, the strict adherence to high-quality production standards, the development of new film techniques, and the continuing creation of popular animated characters were key factors in establishing the success of the studio. Interestingly, the Disney animated cast would have a profound effect on the development of the theme parks.

The "Great Man"

The Disney studio was an entrepreneurial enterprise with its foundation in the arts. Founded by Walt Disney, it had his mark on every endeavor. There are few other such clear examples in American industry of the "Great Man" model. As a company, it developed as a patriarchal institution with Walt and his brother Roy controlling everything. With Walt Disney from the beginning, Roy Disney concentrated on the financial aspects of the burgeoning empire and allowed Walt, the creative sibling, to concentrate on the animation and marketing aspects. This partnership was extremely successful. The two Disneys built one of the most impressive design/marketing machines in the history of American business. Disney logos, shirts, animations, books, and films pervade our culture and are recognized throughout the world.

Walt Disney realized early on that his park would have a distinct advantage over every other amusement park in the world. He knew he could develop a strong relationship with the characters his studio had developed. No other park had universally recognized hosts like Mickey Mouse, Goofy, or Donald Duck, and its own one-hour TV show on Sunday nights with which to promote it. No other park could command the loyalty of thousands of children on the opening day. His cast of celluloid characters and their well-documented adventures became the park's most important marketing tool.

Management Orientation and Philosophy

Perhaps the most unique aspect of the Disney studio was its close adherence to the philosophy of its founder, Walt Disney. Unlike the other Hollywood studios at the time, Disney made sure that the studio maintained a strict moral environment. He was adamant that the studio and the products generated by the entire Disney corporation be closely associated with family values and a wholesome American image.

The Disney corporate attitude that evolved was a direct reflection of the personal beliefs of the founder. This legacy continued long after Walt Disney's death. During staff meetings, "executives clinched arguments by quoting Walt like Scripture or Marx." Taking a chapter from Chairman Mao of China, the Disney company eventually produced and distributed a little book with Walt's sayings.

A second important aspect of management philosophy developed by Walt Disney and maintained long after his death was the refusal to pay the enormous amounts demanded and received by movie talent at the time. Walt Disney believed that the studio should concentrate on wholesome family-oriented pictures that were produced within a relatively limited budget. It was this wholesomeness and tight financial control that became the hallmark of the Disney Company.

The success of Disneyland was immediate. Despite strenuous objections from Roy, who believed the company should remain focused on films, Disneyland generated record crowds from opening day. So successful was the park that all construction loans were retired within nine months.

Walt Disney never advertised his park in the media. The only communication used was through the television programs being generated for the ABC network. Despite this self-imposed (and frugal) limitation, the public media offered wide coverage because of the park's uniqueness and its devotion to cleanliness and family values. Within a short period, it became an American icon for family entertainment.

TABLE 1	Growth Rate in Los Angeles and California, 1950–1960		
	1950	1960	Percent Change in Population
Los Angeles	1,970,358	2,479,015	25.8%
California	10,586,223	15,717,204	48.5%

Source: Information Almanac, 1992.

The success of the park was directly attributable to the brilliant vision of Walt Disney. From the start, it was his devotion to the development of the idea of a theme park and the scrupulous way in which it was constructed and maintained that ensured its success.

Southern California—1950s

Another factor in its success was the location in which the Disney studios and subsequently Disneyland were built. The choice of Anaheim in Orange County as a site for the first Disney theme park had as much to do with the location of Disney Studios in Burbank, California, as it did with the rapid growth of the Los Angeles area in the 1950s and 1960s.

Even so, the choice and timing couldn't have been better. Not only was Southern California rapidly developing as an area of high technology and modern industry (electronics, aircraft, and military), but it had become a modern-day mecca for tourists seeking a vacation in the land of Hollywood and the home of the big-screen movie. It had become an important vacation destination. The construction of Disneyland was able to exploit these trends and reinforce the image of California as a vacation playland.

The "baby boom" was also of importance. Starting in 1946, the United States enjoyed a rapid increase in its number of children. By 1955, the first wave of this burgeoning group would be nine years old—the perfect age for Disney films, TV shows, and products, and for attending the new park. As this wave increased in number, Disneyland grew and prospered. The Disney planners were aware of this change and they took full advantage of it.

STRATEGIC DECISIONS IN EACH STAGE OF DEVELOPMENT

From Cartoons to the Theme Parks

The evolution of the Walt Disney Company can be clearly divided into various growth phases with each phase delineated by strategic decisions. The first phase was Walt Disney's commitment to films and animations.

Although he had intended originally to be a movie producer when he moved from Kansas City to Hollywood, he soon realized the advantages of concentrating his efforts in what he knew. The second phase began when the studio, now well financed, chose to enter the full-length movie market. Although the studio still made cartoons, it poured resources into the development of the full-length movies. The successes that followed (*Snow White*, 1937; *Pinocchio, Fantasia*, 1940; *Bambi*, 1942) illustrate the wisdom of this decision.

The third major strategic decision had the most direct impact on Euro Disneyland. In 1953, Walt Disney made the decision to build a theme park. It was his desire to combine the Disney Corporation's orientation toward family values and a wholesome environment with an amusement park that led to development of the first Disney theme park—Disneyland in California. The success of Disneyland (California) was directly responsible for the decision to build a second park in Florida, Walt Disney World. The idea of an East Coast park had been with Walt Disney from the beginning and he felt certain that it would have to be located somewhere in Florida.

The Magic Formula— EPCOT and MGM/Disney and Hotels

The fourth strategic decision was to develop an entire area, a cluster of Disney attractions, focused in one geographic area. The Florida location became the first test site. The Disney Company eventually developed three major theme parks surrounded by Disney theme hotels. The various theme parks would offer attractions to a much wider audience, and the hotels would offer Disney hospitality to a captive audience. This combination was to prove very successful.

The first ancillary park was EPCOT, the dream of the founder, Walt Disney. He had envisioned a city of the future where Americans could go to get a glimpse of the shape of things to come. EPCOT was to be a living social experiment that would embrace the latest technologies. Although he passionately believed that EPCOT would be even more significant than the Walt Disney theme park, he died before construction could begin.

In developing the Orlando region as a tourist center, Disney management was aware of how successful Universal Studios in California had been in attracting vacationing tourists. In Florida, Disney had both the land and the desire to create a theme park based on the movies. The result was a joint venture with MGM to develop a theme park similar to the one offered by Universal Studios in California.

Marketing Planning and Promotion

Both Disneyland and the Orlando Disney World/EPCOT/MGM complex had "struck a nerve" in American culture. Like EPCOT and MGM/Disney, they offered an escape to a contrived, safe, simpler time when the streets were clean and the inhabitants (Disney refers to them as "cast members"—a reference to their cinematic background) well-trained and polite. This combination was both profitable for the Disney Company and attractive to Americans as well as to a growing number of foreigners.

Walt Disney also believed that the park would never be "finished." As new advances in science or new artistic developments were achieved, they would be incorporated into the park. In an interview with the Hollywood *Citizen-News*, he explained, "the park means a lot to me. It's something that will never be finished, something I can keep developing, keep 'plussing', and adding to. It's alive. It will be a live, breathing thing that will need changes."

The marketing of Disney theme parks centered on the uniqueness of each park, the tie-in with Disney characters, and the constant change of attractions. Walt Disney had developed an attraction that was to become an American institution—a familiar place of wholesome fantasies. It would be a safe, clean, friendly environment where scenes were ever-changing and families could enjoy a day together. This was exactly how the parks were marketed—a place from the past to escape to and feel safe and secure.

The American Fit

The Disney theme parks were designed for Americans—from Davy Crockett's Frontierland right down to the Mississippi Riverboat Ride. Walt Disney wanted his parks to be closely aligned with America's past...and future. In order to achieve an American "feel," he chose a scene out of American folklore—a reproduction of a Midwestern town at the turn of the century (circa 1890–1910). Victorian buildings (undersized for additional warmth and sense of community), horse-drawn trams, and spotless walks populated by friendly guides became the standard. Disney's Main Street was the recreation of the ideal typical American town drawn from the movie maker's imagination.

The entire park was surrounded by a reduced-scale railroad based on a turn-of-the-century American model. The system would offer a powerful historical image and tie the park together with transportation services to various points along the park's perimeter. It would also serve as a barrier to the outside world.

Breaking off from the square were four American theme areas—Fantasyland, Adventureland, Frontierland, and Tomorrowland. Most of the attractions would be related to either the animated characters the studio had created and developed or geographic images of the fantasies the films had created. This intertwining of theme park attractions with Disney characters gave Disneyland a tremendous advantage over other park operators. America had grown up with the studio's cast of characters. This association allowed the park to be more than just a collection of amusement rides. It was an "American experience" where the visitor could actually enter into one of Disney's fantasies.

The importance of the movie-making experience was also important in the planning of the attractions. Drawing on his expertise in making movies, Walt Disney felt the park should be structured like a film with a strong sense of continuity. He wanted the visitor to move through the park much like a camera moves from scene to scene—another trait that sets it apart from the ordinary amusement park. Americans are comfortable with movies and accepted the park's structure as natural.

Driven by Walt Disney's creativity and marketing savvy and drawing heavily on the Disney Studios theatrical and animation design skills, Disneyland, Walt Disney World, EPCOT, and the Disney/MGM studios quickly developed a powerful identity of their own, unique to anything that had ever been developed. So phenomenal was the acceptance of the parks by the American public, they became a powerful symbol of both modern American entertainment and American culture.

GLOBAL EXPANSION

The success of the Disney theme parks in the United States encouraged management to consider expanding abroad. This was not a new idea. When Walt Disney was planning the Orlando complex, he commented to one of his aides that he could see a time when these (Disney World) parks would be scattered throughout the world.

The first foreign commitment came during the leadership of "Card" Walker. Walker had joined the Disney Studios as a messenger boy in 1938 and literally worked his way to the top. Following the deaths of Walt Disney and Roy Disney, E. Cardon Walker became the chief executive officer (1976–1983). He was a "flinty, strait-laced Idaho-born Mormon" who made studio decisions based on what he thought Walt would want. Quick to ridicule underlings in public and impervious to any point of view but his own, he is credited with losing touch with modern taste, resulting in the poor performance of the studio's offerings.

One of his successes, however, was entering into an agreement with the Oriental Land Company to build a Disney theme park in Japan. In keeping with the tight-fisted financial philosophy of the Disney Company, the agreement was structured as a franchise.

Competitive Advantage
The World Franchise—Disney Products

The greatest advantage enjoyed by the Disney Company is the worldwide public awareness of the products of the company. Children and their parents throughout the world know the images of Mickey Mouse and Goofy. The company has always maintained the highest quality in any of their offerings. As a result, the images and products of the Walt Disney Company are synonymous with quality and high-value entertainment.

The most important part of this worldwide Disney franchise is the cast of characters created by Walt Disney, carefully developed over the succeeding decades. Each character is an easily identified symbol that can be quickly associated with any Disney project. This instant identification capability gives Disney a deep-rooted competitive advantage.

This quality entertainment is not limited to the theme parks. Disney's movies, such as *Aladdin*, have enjoyed strong support in the theater and then strong sales as after-market videotapes. The Disney company extended the market for *Aladdin* products and the preceding *Beauty and the Beast* product line by developing Sega and Nintendo games.

Television has projected Walt Disney's animation throughout the world. The development of world communications has had a dramatic effect on developing the Disney mystique. "The company gospel is that entertainment delivery systems can become obsolete, but what is always in demand is the entertainment that travels throughout them." This philosophy has served them well in their expansion.

Deep Pockets—Cold Cash

The other important competitive advantage enjoyed by the Disney management is a healthy balance sheet. The Disney Company is not highly leveraged. Michael Eisner, the current CEO, "is fanatical about not overpaying. Armed with lots of cash and a balance sheet that would support billions in added debt, Disney has looked carefully at CBS Inc., Mattel Inc., a host of record companies, and many other businesses before backing off." The company's borrowing capability, that is, its access to capital, gives it market clout.

Consumer Needs and Wants

The success of the California park in 1955 and the Florida park in 1970 clearly indicates that the Disney Company very effectively filled an American desire. Both parks provide a pleasant escape from the realities of modern life. They take visitors back to another time when everything was clean and everybody pleasant, where simply by moving from one area to another, the visitor can enjoy singing mechanical bears or a spaceship ride to the planets. Fantasy is not only encouraged but cultivated.

EPCOT gives the visitor a chance to see the state of the art in science and a sense of things yet to come. It challenges as much as it entertains and educates. It is in every way a Disney experience. MGM/Disney brings the visitor face to face with the movie and television industries. It satisfies the fascination Americans have for two of the most creative industries. There is a question, however, as to whether American tastes can be extended throughout the world. The Disney management made the decision that "Yes, it can." Time will tell.

Competition

Walt Disney never felt that the traditional amusement park was competition for his planned Disneyland. He drew a sharp distinction between the usual "Great White Way" and his idea of a theme park. He was also adamant about not including the traditional ferris wheel in his park, despite all of the advice he received from park operators that you needed one to attract people. Although the traditional amusement park does not offer much competition to a theme park, that is not to say there are no other theme parks.

Besides the traditional amusement parks that dot the country, Disneyland and Walt Disney World are facing a growing list of competitors. Disneyland had Knotts Berry Farm, a well-established theme park, as a competitor for years. Both parks project a wholesome, family image. It is the development of Universal Studios theme parks, however, that has intensified the pressure on the Disney offerings.

Located in the Los Angeles area, Universal Studios offered the tourist an inside peek at the movies. As the technical sophistication of the movies increased, the exhibits developed by Universal became more like the Disney exhibits. The increasing success of the California park encouraged Universal to expand into new markets.

Tokyo Disneyland

In 1982, the Disney Company entered into an agreement with the Oriental Land Corporation (a joint venture between Mitsui Real Estate Development Company and Keisei Railway Company). Oriental Land felt that there was a need for a world-class theme park in Japan. Japan, which had worked so hard during the 1950s, 1960s, and 1970s, had reached economic superpower status. What was missing was recreational opportunity. Oriental Land wanted to fill it.

Franchise Agreement

The agreement with the Disney Company was simple. Disney would design the park and supply expertise in return for a royalty of 10 percent of the gate and 5 percent of concessions. Disney would also make sure that the Tokyo park was a close duplicate of the two American parks. Oriental Land wanted the genuine article—Disney Americana.

Oriental Land Company would carry the entire risk of constructing the park. Disney, on the other hand, would limit its risk to the cost of design and providing park expertise. Given the cost of the park (180 billion yen, approximately $1.5 billion), Disney had struck a shrewd bargain. The company believed it could determine whether or not a Disney theme park could be exported while at the same time assuming very little risk.

Disney's Concerns

It was obvious that Disney management was concerned about constructing a theme park, using Disney characters and Disney trademarks, in an Asian country and in a cold environment. They were uncertain as to how well the Disney images, so popular with American audiences for generations, would be accepted by a foreign culture.

With regard to the cultural challenge, Disney was able to prepare the Japanese market with a flood of cartoons, TV shows, movies, and cartoon characters. By the time the park was complete, Disney images were well known and growing in popularity in all segments of the Japanese population. The image of Mickey Mouse had become so popular that even Emperor Hirohito wore one on his wristwatch.

The location of the park was another matter. Walt Disney had expressed strong doubt as to ever building a theme park in a northern climate. He saw no way to keep the park open for fewer than twelve months a year and still generate a cash flow sufficient to meet park expenses. The California and Florida parks were able to remain open for twelve months of the year because they were in a warm climate. Would the Tokyo park be able to overcome this limitation?

Physical Adjustments

Because of the climatic differences, Tokyo being much father north than either Anaheim or Orlando, the park designers enclosed waiting areas to protect visitors from the elements. In addition, a number of the rides have covers over them to protect riders. These changes permitted the park to effectively operate twelve months out of the year.

Although similar to the two American parks in most important features, Tokyo Disneyland does make heavy use of bilingual signs. In addition, the park includes a number of Japanese food entrees on the menu (along with hamburgers, French fries, and hot dogs, of course).

Cultural Adjustments

In addition to the architectural changes to Tokyo Disneyland, there were also cultural and ethnic changes. "Melvin, Buff, and Max, the antlered commentators at the Country Bear Jamboree, speak in the grave basso profundos of Kurosawa samurais" rather than the country twang found in the American parks. Alice in Wonderland was given Asian features. Frontierland was changed into Westernland (the Japanese don't like frontiers). Finally, the center of the entire park, Main Street, was renamed the World Bazaar. These differences are relatively minor, however. The spirit and essence of the park are strictly Disney.

Financial Performance

After a slow start, the theme park was enthusiastically accepted by the Japanese. In 1987 over one million school children, who normally would

TABLE 2	Temperature and Precipitation				
	Average Temperature (F degrees)				Annual Precipitation
	January		July		
	Max.	Min.	Max.	Min.	(inches)
France	42	32	76	55	22.3
Japan	47	29	83	70	61.6

Source: The World Almanac & Book of Facts, 1992.

have been taken to the shrines of Japan, were brought to the park. Although financial numbers are not available, Oriental Land is pleased with its investment.

Impact on Company's Strategy

The success of Tokyo Disneyland had one important effect on the Disney company's plans for expansion. Just as the success of Disneyland had convinced Walt Disney to build a second park in Florida, the success of Tokyo Disneyland convinced Disney management to build a second park—a European park. Since there were certain similarities between the climates and the regions, management believed that if the Disney theme park idea worked in Japan, then surely it would work in Europe.

Euro Disneyland—The Second Venture

Michael D. Eisner was the driving force behind Euro Disneyland. Early in his career at Disney, Eisner had achieved great success by increasing the admission fare at the American Disney parks by 100 percent to generate much-needed capital. He reasoned correctly that an increase in the cost of admission would not discourage tourists from visiting the parks. He understood that Disney was one of the world's most powerful consumer franchises and was unique in the world of amusement parks and that people would pay to see it. This increase in park admission charges alone achieved a $450 million gain to pretax profits with no drop in attendance.

His second move was centered on the Walt Disney World complex in Florida. Sensing that the Orlando park area was not being properly exploited, he increased the number of hotel rooms on Disney property by 6,700 (4,400 owned directly by Disney). These strategies were successful. Disney reported earnings increased from $22 million in 1984 to $824 million in 1990.

In 1987, the decision was made to go ahead with a major development plan. The company envisioned a Disneyland-type theme park surrounded by theme hotels. This was the same formula used in Orlando. Once the hotel and park were firmly established, Disney would begin the second phase. This included the second and third theme parks and the office complex and housing project.

Euro Disneyland Goals

The goals for the new Euro Disneyland were fairly straightforward. Management wanted to:

1. Meet the goal of 11 million visitors at the end of one operational year.

2. Generate a profit from the theme park and the hotels by the end of the third operational quarter and continue to expand profits in each succeeding quarter.

3. Develop the financial foundation with the theme park and its supporting hotels so as to continue with the second phase (an American-like office park complex and another theme park—MGM/Disney) and the third phase (a housing project and a third theme park).

4. Have all of the elements of the project reinforce each other, thereby making the sum of the parts greater than the individual parts themselves and subsequently increasing tourist activity.

Key Concern 1—Site Location

The first strategic decision facing management was where to build it. If the Euro Disney theme park was to open in April of 1992, the choice of site had to be made. In 1987, during the early planning stages, the selection came down to a beet farm 20 miles east of Paris and two sites in southern Spain. David Lawday wrote in *U.S. News & World Report*, "at first, Disney was unsure whether to land in Spain or in France. Barcelona offered a sunnier climate—and cheerier populace—but Disney was ultimately swayed by France's superior infrastructure and quicker access to the 12-nation European Community's 320 million consumers. Paris not only boasts two international airports but a high-speed rail system that covers the country." Lawday adds, "in the future, this train will rush passengers from Britain via the Channel Tunnel and from the population heart of Germany."

The French government agreed to extend the suburban Paris subway directly to the park. Since Paris was a major vacation destination, it was believed that many tourists would be tempted to visit the park. Taken together—the location, the infrastructure, and the generous incentives offered by the French government—the Disney management was swayed. There was still a vexing problem, however: the weather.

Key Concern 2—Climate

Unlike the location of the two American parks, the Paris region was considered a temperate climate with cold winters. For the most part, many of

Disney's concerns were neutralized by the success of the Tokyo park, but there remained some anxiety as to whether the park would generate sufficient crowds during the winter months.

Since the Japanese park faced the same problem, Disney designers made similar adjustments in the Euro park design (extensive sheltered areas and numerous fireplaces). Management was now fairly certain the French would support the park in November, December, and January. The French government condemned the land used for growing sugar beets, and the project began.

Euro Disney Personnel

Robert Fitzpatrick, an American and a "tall bespectacled man of cosmopolitan bearing and enormous charm," was selected as the president of Euro Disney. His appointment was considered a masterstroke of personnel placement. Known as the former president of the California Institute of the Arts, director of the Olympic Arts Festival, and professor of French at the University of Maine, his charm and fluency in French (and his French wife) were seen as a means of demonstrating Disney's commitment to French culture.

The park, Euro Disneyland, came close to meeting its goal of 11 million visitors for the first year of operation. The park had not, however, been able to meet hotel occupancy and expenditures per visitor projections. These were far below expectations and were placing a strain on the theme park's finances. This poor showing also drew Disney's California-based senior management directly into the crisis in late 1993.

Exacerbating the financial shortfall is a heavy debt burden (approximately $3.7 billion) incurred by the Disney Company to build the Euro park. Denominated in French francs, it has become a victim of the French government's strategy of keeping interest rates high so as to protect the value of the franc.

The Disney management was desperately trying to determine the cause for the park's weak performance and develop a strategy to reverse it. The determination of a solution, however, would be neither simple nor easy because the nature of the problem was neither clear nor apparent. What is clear is that Disney management was facing an unexpected crisis situation—what should they do about Euro Disneyland?

Source: This case was prepared by Dr. Tung-lung Chang, College of Management, Long Island University—C.W. Post, with the assistance of his former graduate student, Mr. Edward Healy. The information came from various periodicals, books, and the company's financial reports. The case was developed for class discussion rather than to illustrate effective or ineffective management practices. Printed with permission. All rights reserved by Dr. Tung.

Sony in America

Akio Morita and a friend founded Tokyo Telecommunications Company (name translated) in Tokyo in 1945 and incorporated it in 1946. It manufactured communications equipment for Japanese telephone and telegraph companies and for the national railroad. From the beginning it stressed quality production and heavy investment in R&D. It started research on consumer goods in 1947 and brought out its first product, a tape recorder, in 1950. It brought out a transistor radio in 1955 and a pocket-sized version in 1957; the latter became its first export product and was quite successful in the United States and Europe. It introduced the world's first fully transistorized television set in 1959.

INTERNATIONAL EXPANSION

The company's early successes in exporting, combined with the Japanese government's drive to increase exports, stimulated its efforts to internationalize. It changed its name to Sony in 1958 because it wanted a shorter name that would be easier for foreign customers to remember. It began establishing overseas subsidiaries and joint ventures in 1960 and expanded rapidly. These were among the most important:

➤ Established Sony Corporation of America (originally a marketing company) in 1960 (U.S.A.)

➤ Incorporated Sony Overseas, S.A. in 1960 (Switzerland)

➤ Established Sony Tektronix Corporation in Japan as a joint venture with Tektronix Inc. to produce oscilloscopes in 1965 (U.S.A.)

➤ Set up Sony, Ltd. in 1968 (U.K.)

➤ Established CBS/Sony Group Inc., a 50/50 joint venture with Columbia Broadcasting System (CBS) in 1970 to manufacture and market musical equipment in Japan (U.S.A.)

➤ Set up Sony GmbH (1970) (which became Sony Deutschland GmbH in 1980) (West Germany)

➤ Established Sony Trading Company in 1972 to identify products manufactured in the U.S.A. and Europe and market them in Japan

➤ Established its first manufacturing facility outside Asia in San Diego, California, in 1972 to assemble television sets (U.S.A.)

➤ Set up Sony France, S.A. in 1973 (France)

➤ Established Sony Eveready, Inc. in Japan in 1975 as a joint venture with Union Carbide Corporation to import and sell Union Carbide's high-performance dry cells (U.S.A.)

➤ Acquired Wega Radio and Wega Hi-Fi, a highly reputed manufacturing group in 1975 (West Germany)

➤ Established Sony Prudential Life Insurance Company, Ltd. in 1979 as a joint venture (51 percent owned by Prudential Life Insurance Company of America) to sell life insurance in Japan

➤ Established Sony/Wilson, Inc. in 1979 as a joint venture with PepsiCo, Inc. (U.S.A.) to import and sell Wilson sporting goods in Japan

➤ Acquired hard disk technology and operations from Apple Computer Inc. (U.S.A.) in 1984 to produce hard disks in Japan and market them in the U.S.A.

➤ Sony Corporation of America acquired Digital Audio Disc Corporation from CBS/Sony Group Inc. in 1985 (U.S.A.)

➤ Entered joint venture agreement in 1985 with Vitelic Corp. (U.S.A.) to obtain Vitelic's proprietary CMOS memory technology in exchange for agreement to manufacture Vitelic products for sale by Vitelic

➤ Acquired CBS Records Inc. and CBS Inc.'s share of CBS/Sony Group Inc. for approximately $2 billion in 1988 (U.S.A.)

➤ Acquired (bought out) Materials Research Corporation in 1989 (U.S.A.)

➤ Purchased all the outstanding common stock of Columbia Pictures Entertainment, Inc. and of the Guber-Peters Entertainment Company (a Columbia affiliate that produced movies and TV fare) for approximately $3.6 billion and assumption of $1.5 billion of Columbia's debt (1989) (U.S.A.)

➤ Sony Music Entertainment Inc. (SMEI, formerly CBS Records) established Columbia House Company as a 50/50 joint venture with a subsidiary of Time-Warner Inc. (U.S.A.) to market music and home-video products in the U.S. and Canada (1991)

Over the years, Sony also set up 100 percent subsidiaries or joint ventures in Australia, Austria, Belgium, Brazil, Canada, Denmark, Hong Kong, Italy, Korea, Malaysia, Netherlands, Panama, Saudi Arabia, Singapore, Spain, Taiwan, and Thailand.

These companies show an evolution in Sony's strategy over the years. Its first overseas subsidiaries were marketing organizations to sell products manufactured in Japan. Its early joint ventures were for the purpose of obtaining technology for its home plants.

It set up its *sogo shosha* (Sony Trading Company) partly to diversify and partly because its overseas representatives found some good-quality foreign products it could sell back home. It could channel these products to its growing chain of retail outlets (which eventually reached 8,000) and eliminate the middleman's commission. This move also helped it deflect growing criticism of Japan's closed market.

Its first overseas manufacturing facilities were necessitated because upward revaluations of the yen, a reaction against the flood of Japanese goods, and the possibility of protectionism threatened to make exports from home uncompetitive. Later overseas manufacturing was to get closer to its markets and to find the lowest-cost production locations.

Many later acquisitions and joint ventures were for product diversification. Some later acquisitions of foreign companies were to gain additional returns on technology it had developed. Materials Research Corporation, for example, had been floundering until it obtained an infusion of capital, technology, R&D, and market credibility from Sony's buyout.

In 1991 Sony had a total of 16 manufacturing plants: nine in Japan, four in Europe, and three in the U.S.A. Its sales breakdown was 29 percent in the United States, 28 percent in Europe, 26 percent in Japan, and 17 percent in the rest of the world.

MARKETING PHILOSOPHY

Sony has always been product-driven and indeed has no market research facility. It allows its R&D and product people to follow their heads and develop the products they want to develop; it believes these are the products that will sell. One such product developed without any prior market research was the Sony Walkman, a small radio with earphones that could be carried in a person's pocket or belt and played in public places while doing other activities; it was a notable success. Morita once said, "We don't market products that have already been developed; rather, we develop markets for the products we make." The company is willing to sell off (or write off) investments in products that "don't work."

Sony has several times demonstrated its willingness to cut prices and profit margins in order to build market share. For example, in the fall of 1990 it cut prices on automobile compact disc players, which had been a major profit generator. An executive of an American competitor surmised that this was preparatory to pruning its line to make room for new products. Another said it should also help solidify Sony's brand name and image.

LONG-TERM PERSPECTIVE

Sony has been willing to take a long-term view of its investments in both R&D and production facilities. Sometimes its thoroughness and deliberate pace have worked to its disadvantage, however. For example, it started developing its betamax system for videocassette recorders (VCRs) in 1960, but didn't bring it to market until 1976. Then it hoped to reserve the market for itself and so failed to license the tape technology to other manufacturers. Soon thereafter, its archrival Matsushita Electric Company brought out VCRs using the VHS system, which it licensed widely and which eventually became the industry standard. Although many observers considered Sony's system superior, it never captured more than about a sixth of the market and ceased production in 1986. The company ended up having to write off a large portion of its R&D investment in the product.

THE QUESTION OF CHEAP LABOR

An ongoing question at Sony has been whether or not to open production facilities in less-developed countries (LDCs) in order to take advantage of cheap labor. Mexico was one of the countries that had approached the company to offer subsidized plant sites, tariff exemptions for components for products to be re-exported, and subsidies for training of labor. Such an offer would be especially attractive for products that had reached life cycle maturity, such as Sony's core of consumer electronics. But the company's top management was concerned about difficulties in rapidly imparting its product and technology innovations, maintaining its quality edge, and preserving its top-market image. It was especially concerned that products manufactured or assembled in less-developed countries might damage the reputation of the ones originating in Japan and other industrialized countries. Thus when it announced plans in 1990 to expand existing capacity and open new plants in Singapore, Malaysia, and Thailand, these were mainly to serve internal markets in Southeast Asia. Sony also wasn't convinced that assembly plants in less-developed countries would insulate it from the harmful effects of currency fluctuations, especially at times when the yen was strengthening. As a generalization, its Japanese managers were more reluctant than its foreign managers to entertain the possibility of production in less-developed countries.

MANAGEMENT PROBLEMS

Sony's overseas top management was all Japanese until 1972, when the company concluded it would have to internationalize its outlook and management practices. One of its first foreign top executives was an American, Harvey Schein, who became president of Sony Corporation of America. However, this and other non-Japanese appointments created some problems. The foreign executives had been accustomed to taking charge and making rapid, more or less unilateral decisions, and they chafed when they had to clear their major moves with Tokyo headquarters, especially since decisions there were made by the slow, collegial ringi process. There were also communications problems between headquarters and the foreign subsidiaries, due partly to difficulties of getting timely translations and partly to failures to understand what executives of the other nationality really *meant* by what they said. At any rate, Harvey Schein resigned in 1977. Akio Morita selected another American to replace him, a man considered to be more amenable to cooperating with Japanese executives.

A 1990 survey identified factors causing dissatisfaction among senior American executives in Sony and other Japanese and other foreign-based companies:

➤ Lower compensation than their counterparts in American-based companies

➤ Less upward mobility—the "bamboo curtain" keeping them out of the top ranks

➤ Less true decision-making power than their high public profiles would seem to signify, that is, a concern not to become mere tokens or figureheads

➤ The reluctance of Japanese top managers to allow their American middle managers to design and carry out statistically sound market assessments before committing large sums to the development and production of new products

➤ The feeling that there was always a Japanese in the shadows double-checking every move by the Americans

➤ Cultural barriers that seemed insurmountable, regardless of how much effort the American executive made to learn the language and customs of his corporate overlords

In the late 1980s, Sony began trying to create a hybrid Japanese-American structure based largely on personal rapport. It believed the new style could correct deficiencies typical of American managers such as a lack of communication with workers and poor management of pay scales. It also declared that its policy was to be "global localization," under which local companies were to obtain a global perspective on their operations while operating largely on their own and preserving their internal cultures. Materials Research Corporation, for example, retained most of its American top management after it was bought out. However, almost all the American executives of Columbia Pictures left their positions shortly after Sony purchased it in 1989. One who remained was the chairman of the television division, Gary Lieberthal, who signed a highly lucrative long-term contract and was appointed a Columbia director in 1990. However, he unexpectedly announced his retirement at the end of 1991 at age 46. Sony officials said the retirement was voluntary.

In 1991 all 18 of the parent company's senior, representative, and managing directors were still Japanese nationals. (These are different classes of directors under Japanese law.) Sixteen of its nineteen directors were Japanese, two were American, and one was Swiss. Its highest-ranking American executive was Michael P. Schulhof, vice chairman of Sony-USA and a director of Sony Corporation.

STOCKHOLDERS

Sony's stock is traded on the Tokyo Stock Exchange and also on the New York Stock Exchange (in the form of American depository receipts, or ADRs) and other foreign exchanges, and 37 percent of its shares were owned by foreigners. Its dividend payouts have been low by American standards, but American shareholders were willing to hold the stock as long as its growth prospects remained bright. However, American stockholders are quicker to react to the prospect of falling earnings than Japanese, and one disadvantage of having its ADRs traded on the NYSE is that it could come under heavier selling pressure in the face of a threat. In fact its stock fell from a high of 65 3/4 in 1989 to a low of 31 3/8 in 1991.

THE MOVE INTO THE ENTERTAINMENT INDUSTRY

Sony began diversifying into entertainment-related companies in the latter part of the 1980s for several reasons. Competition heated up in the consumer electronics business, making it harder for the company to maintain sales and profit growth in its core businesses. Morita noted the example of Kodak, which has made much more money on its film than on its cameras. Even after the market for VCRs and tape and disc players reached saturation, consumers would keep buying tapes and discs. Profit margins on those items could run up to 50 percent. The company believed it could find synergy by producing the tapes and compact discs to be played on its electronic hardware. It also believed it could create synergy between the Japanese and American entertainment industries by acquiring production companies in both countries, especially since American producers were acknowledged to be the world's leaders in entertainment. Finally, it viewed its move into Hollywood as an important test of American receptivity to an expanded Japanese role in U.S. culture.

At the same time Michael Schulhof was engineering the acquisitions of CBS and Columbia Pictures, rival Matsushita was similarly motivated to acquire MCA Corporation, owner of Universal Studios, for $6.1 billion in 1990. Some observers criticized both Sony's and Matsushita's acquisitions, saying the Japanese parent companies grossly overpaid for them. They also said the companies were spreading themselves too thin and going beyond their areas of special competence. Sony's core of developing and manufacturing leading-edge electronics and other up-market products was a very different business from recruiting and managing artists and selling music recordings.

At least Sony recognized that its American entertainment business would have to be managed in the American way. Hence Peter Guber, the driving force behind Guber-Peters, was made CEO of a new entity, Sony Pictures. His management style was much more tumultuous and free-spending than that of the buttoned-down engineers and accountants who ran the parent company and most of its subsidiaries. He spent over $1 billion on movie and TV production in his first two years, gambling that such movies as *Hook, Bugsy Siegel,* and *Prince of Tides* would take in hundreds of millions of dollars, enough to cover the multimillion-dollar compensation to stars like Dustin Hoffman, Madonna, Jack Nicholson, and Warren Beatty and still have something left over for the company to cover its costs and show a profit. He also started plans for a "Sonyland" theme park similar to Disneyland.

THE SITUATION IN LATE 1991

As shown above, Sony's major commitments from 1988 through 1991 were almost all in the United States, where it had invested almost $6 billion to acquire full ownership of CBS Records and Columbia Pictures and to set up its joint venture with Time-Warner. It took on more than $2 billion in debt to finance these acquisitions.

Unfortunately, much of the world entered a substantial recession just as these transactions were being completed. Demand for audiovisual equipment in Japan was sluggish, and the parent company's export competitiveness was damaged by the consistently high value of the yen, causing its revenues to decline at home. Consumer spending in the United States and Europe also fell off sharply, especially for discretionary items. The hoped-for synergy between Sony's Japanese and American entertainment businesses was very slow to materialize. Vigorous discounting by competitors in the United States and Europe drove down prices and profits. Sony was especially vulnerable to such declines because of its heavy debt service payments, and its net income falling 5 percent in the quarter ending June 1991. The company's financial officers imposed measures designed to cut costs by 10 percent, and they told Guber to shelve the plans for the Sonyland theme park.

Source: William A. Stoever, Professor of International Business at Seton Hall University. This case was prepared as a basis for class discussion rather than to illustrate effective or ineffective management practices. Printed with permission. All rights reserved.

INTEGRATIVE   CASE   7

Thai Chempest

In January 1991 Shep Susmar, President of Agricultural Chemicals International Corporation (ACIC), had to decide whether or not his company should set up manufacturing with a local partner in Thailand. He had received a letter in November 1990 from Kau Ah-Wong, President of Kau Teck-Meng & Company, in Bangkok, saying that rising tariffs might make it impossible for the Kau company to continue importing one of ACIC's profitable pesticides. Kau suggested that the two companies might begin a joint venture to do some of the processing in Thailand, a move that might be mutually profitable while also aiding the development of agriculture in his country. Susmar had to decide whether to enter into a joint venture, what problems might arise if they did enter it, and how to plan for and deal with such problems.

HISTORY OF ACIC

Agricultural Chemicals Corporation was founded in Rutherford, New Jersey, in 1960 by Tyrone Susmar, Shep Susmar's father. It specialized in developing and producing pesticides to meet the needs of individual purchasers. It kept in close contact with current and potential customers in order to learn about and supply their specialized needs. There was a steady demand since various insect species mutated rapidly and developed immunity to existing pesticides. Being a niche marketer, the company had to keep seeking new products that the large, resource-rich chemical manufacturers did not yet produce commercially. In the late 1970s Tyrone decided that the company could support a modest R&D program that went beyond the mere combining of previously known components. Agricultural Chemicals set up a small applications-oriented research laboratory to study new infestations that kept cropping up. The laboratory had a small, top-quality staff that was highly productive. It usually developed products to order for large customers, but sometimes it produced new compounds that were marketed under the company name. Some of these were innovative enough to qualify for patents. In order to protect the technology, the company established a small plant to manufacture some of these proprietary products.

Shep had started working full-time for the company in 1970 after completing a B.S. in chemical engineering. He earned an M.B.A. part-time during the next five years while working in a variety of functions and took over as president of the company in 1985.

OVERSEAS GROWTH

By the mid-1970s Tyrone had realized that the company had to go international if it wanted to maintain a steady rate of growth. To signify his commitment, Tyrone changed the company name to Agricultural Chemicals International Corporation (ACIC). The markets abroad, particularly in less-developed countries, were smaller, less mechanized, and less accustomed to the use of chemical aids than those in North America, and the giant chemical companies didn't find it worthwhile to devote a lot of effort to them. This meant that once ACIC established a market in a particular country, it could hope for several years of sales without strong international competition.

In 1978 Tyrone hired a young man named Bill Greene and gave him the title of "international manager." Greene had earned a B.S. in Chemical Engineering in 1970 and an M.B.A. in 1976. He had had eight years' experience in domestic and foreign sales for a large chemical manufacturer. His responsibilities in his new job were vaguely defined, but he seemed to have a good feeling for how to make his way.

Greene appointed area managers for Europe, the Middle East, and Asia. The area manager for Asia was Mike Mingas. They were all based in New Jersey but had to spend a lot of time traveling in order to stay close to their areas. ACIC began seeking distributors in southern Europe, the Middle East, and Asia. The initial contacts were made rather haphazardly, sometimes from approaches by local companies seeking a foreign supplier and sometimes on the recommendations of intermediaries. Some of the distributors had remained with the company, but a few had proven to be politically unastute, incompetent, lazy, or plain dishonest. Some arrangements failed to live up to expectations because of government restrictions, lack of foreign exchange, disappointing sales, or loss of interest by the local partner. In at least one case, ACIC believed the local distributor had deliberately hidden revenues and had failed to deliver ACIC's share of its profits.

Greene and the area managers had to rely on the parent company for technical assistance and staff functions. The responsibilities were not formalized; they just grew up over the years. In general, the international people had been able to get the support they needed, except on occasions when the staff and technical people's workloads were too heavy. Some of the parent company's personnel were becoming increasingly interested in the international aspect of the business; others paid little attention to the overseas operations.

In 1980 an Italian chemical company approached ACIC seeking a license to use its processes to manufacture finished products from basic raw materials purchased in Italy. The products were sold to distributors in Italy and other EU countries. ACIC received a healthy royalty, 2 percent of gross sales of the licensed products, but in exchange it gave up the right to export to the EU from its U.S. plants. ACIC received a royalty of almost $1 million in 1990.

In 1981, following a trip by Greene and Mingas to Australia, ACIC set up a processing plant, a wholly owned subsidiary, in that country. The plant contracted with local chemical companies for purchases of particular components, which it blended into finished products and packed for shipment. Its operations followed the processes specified by the parent company. The venture lost money for the first four years, finally turned a profit in 1987, and paid back the original investment in 1989. It contributed almost $1 million to the parent's profit before tax in 1990, and the prospects for further growth were promising.

By the mid-1980s the Susmars and Greene recognized that ACIC would have to begin producing in more overseas markets rather than simply exporting to them. Some distributor relationships were running into trouble because of import-substitution policies and shortages of hard currencies in many less-developed countries. Also, ACIC foresaw heightened competition from companies in Korea, Turkey, India, and other industrializing low-wage developing countries. However, ACIC wanted to evaluate any given country carefully before deciding whether to make an equity investment (100 percent or joint venture), to license its technology, to serve the market by exports (where allowed), or to give up the market. They hoped to start on a small scale, with a minimum commitment of capital and management time.

DEALINGS WITH KAU & COMPANY

In 1985 Kau Ah-Wong visited the United States. Among his goals was to find something to combat a wood-boring beetle that infested both hardwood and palm trees in Thailand and other countries of Southeast Asia and that had apparently developed resistance to the available insecticides. Kau heard about ACIC through professional contacts and called on the Susmars. Figuring there was nothing to lose, ACIC appointed Kau & Company as its distributor in Thailand and agreed to supply trial quantities of a newly developed pesticide called 3,5-D. (ACIC was waiting for a decision on its application for a U.S. patent on this compound.) The trials soon demonstrated that the new insecticide was effective in controlling the beetle. Kau didn't set up any formal marketing program, but his company began receiving commercial orders from the more progressive producers who had heard about the success of the trials. Volume was small at first, but enough to spark ACIC's interest.

Subsequently, Mingas made several trips to Bangkok to help promote the relationship. By 1989 ACIC was exporting about $1 million a year of the insecticide to Thailand, which Kau was reselling for about 50 million Thai baht. Even so, Mingas believed they had barely scratched the surface of the Thai market, and Kau had not yet promoted 3,5-D elsewhere in Southeast Asia.

KAU'S LETTER

Kau's letter of November 1990 came as something of a shock because it seemed to indicate that ACIC's exports to Thailand were threatened. The letter noted that the government was vigorously seeking to diversify Thailand's economy by developing manufacturing industries. It intended to restrict imports of selected products in order to promote manufacturing, and it especially favored products that promoted the country's agriculture. It intended to impose tariffs of 25 to 50 percent on imports of agricultural pesticides like 3,5-D although it would allow importation of components or ingredients at low or no duties for a while, provided that Thailand's portion of the value added was increased as quickly as possible. The Ministry of Industry wanted to restrict imports of 3,5-D immediately, but the Ministry of Agriculture and Cooperatives prevailed upon them to allow imports at a reduced level for at least one more year.

In view of this new development, Kau proposed that ACIC and Kau & Company set up a joint venture to use ACIC's technology and know-how to start production of 3,5-D and other pesticides in Thailand. He even suggested a name: Thai Chemical Pesticides Corporation. He offered to supply the buildings, local sales and administrative staff, and most of the working capital, and proposed that ACIC's contribution be imported equipment, technological knowledge, the necessary engineering, staff advice and support, and some of the working capital. Kau & Company wanted somewhere between 51 and 75 percent ownership since it was contributing the bulk of the capital, physical assets, and personnel. The new company would use ACIC's processes, which would be protected to the fullest extent possible under Thai law.

GREEN'S TRIP TO BANGKOK

Shep Susmar decided not to travel to Bangkok himself, both because of domestic business pressures and because he believed that Kau's business did not justify the investment of his time. Susmar telephoned Kau that ACIC's international manager would go in his place. When Greene arrived in early December, Kau expressed some displeasure at not seeing a counterpart of equally high rank from the American company, but he was quite gracious. He showered Greene with hospitality, including visits to some of Bangkok's notorious night spots. He also took him to call on officials at the Board of Investment, the Thai Development Bank, and in the Ministries of Industry,

Agriculture and Cooperatives, and Commerce. The Board of Investment officials assured Greene that it should be no problem to get approval of a Kau-ACIC joint venture, provided of course that Thailand's rules, regulations, and procedures were followed. Officials at the Development Bank seemed to be amenable to granting a long-term loan at a concessional interest rate,[1] again provided that the venture satisfied the bank's criteria. Greene had heard, however, that other ministries sometimes imposed roadblocks and that the approval process could be very corruption-prone, time-consuming, and frustrating.

After a week in Bangkok, Greene returned and reported on his findings. The Kaus were a wealthy family of Chinese origin who had been in Thailand for four or five generations. They had political connections built up partly by substantial contributions to General Prem Tinsulanonda's political party (see Appendix). Nonetheless, the Chinese were a somewhat distrusted minority in Thailand, and the government might discriminate against them or a company with which they were associated. Kau had made several trips abroad and was fairly fluent in English. Greene liked Kau personally and thought he was probably pretty reliable.

Kau Teck-Meng & Co. had been founded by Kau Ah-Wong's grandfather and his brothers. It was a trading company that imported and exported a variety of products. Among its imports were M.A.N. trucks, Massey-Ferguson tractors, some industrial chemicals from Monsanto Corporation, which it wholesaled to local plastics manufacturers, and some Japanese industrial control devices. It sold the bulk of its turnover in Thailand but exported rice and air-conditioning equipment to other nations of the Association of Southeast Asian Nations (ASEAN)[2] and Laos, Cambodia, and Burma. It also exported palm products and hand-carved teak furniture to the United States and to the EC. Greene could not be certain, but he had the impression that sales of ACIC's insecticide constituted 4 or 5 percent of its gross revenues.

Greene speculated that sales of the insecticide could increase markedly over the next five years if supplies were available; he estimated that sales might reach 250 million baht by 1995. He worked up a *pro forma* income statement, based mostly on figures from U.S. and Italian plants and following American accounting principles (Exhibit 1). At that time, the Thai government was requiring only that the final production stages be completed in Thailand; these were reasonably simple processes, and the necessary equipment was not too complicated or costly. Greene was aware that the government might demand that more production be moved to Thailand in the not too distant future. Nonetheless, the prospects looked good enough to suggest that ACIC consider a joint venture with as large an equity share as possible. He estimated that ACIC's initial capital expenditure need not exceed $800,000, of which about $400,000 would be for imported equipment and the rest for setup costs, expatriate expenses, and so on.

The Appendix contains information Greene collected on Thailand's economy and rules and policies on foreign investment.

ACIC'S RESPONSE

Shep Susmar held a meeting of his top domestic and international executives in mid-December 1990 to discuss the Kau proposal (which they'd already begun referring to as "Thai Chempest." He opened with these comments:

> *Our friend Mr. Kau seems eager to set up an alliance with us. It looks like a possibility to me, but there are some definite problem areas. Among them:*
>
> ➤   *Would it be more cost-effective or less risky to continue exporting as long as the government allows it, unless they raise the tariffs higher than Kau seems to anticipate?*
>
> ➤   *Should we license our processes to Kau's organization?*
>
> ➤   *If we go the joint venture route, what possible problems might there be with the Thai business climate and government?*
>
> ➤   *What terms might Kau want, and how should we respond?*
>
> ➤   *What kind of incentives, guarantees, and other terms could we get from the government?*
>
> *Kau might want to be managing director or president if we went into a joint venture. We'd have to decide whether that's a good idea, or how to handle it if we decide against him. We'd also have to figure out the financing and ownership structure. We want to be careful to avoid another situation where we get ripped off, like those so-and-so's in Asiatica did to us.*
>
> *If we do go ahead there, we'd need a plant manager, a chief financial officer, a chief technical officer, and maybe a sales manager to start in Bangkok. An immediate question is whether these should be Americans or Thais.*
>
> *I need you to draft some plans for what to do about Kau's proposal. Be as specific as you can; don't use phrases like "This problem will have to be planned for." We need concrete suggestions, nuts-and-bolts details.*

APPENDIX: POLITICAL AND ECONOMIC DATA ON THAILAND[3]

Political Structure

Thailand is a constitutional monarchy with a bicameral National Assembly. The Thai Senate includes members who are appointed and who represent constituencies ranging from labor to the military. The lower house consists of roughly 350 members who are elected for four-year terms. The Prime Minister is appointed by the king based on the recommendations of the National Assembly. The current king, Bhumibol Adulyadej, does not possess a great deal of legislative power but does exercise strong moral leadership.

1932–1980

The modern era is generally considered to have begun in 1932 with a *coup d'etat* that eliminated most true powers of the king. The absolute monarchy was replaced by a constitutional government, with the support of the king. The military has continued to exert strong influence over the government from the 1932 initial coup up to the present. The name of the country was changed from Siam to Thailand in 1939. The government's effectiveness was diminished during the country's reluctant involvement in World War II as an ally of Japan and during the wars in Vietnam, Laos, and Cambodia in the 1960s and 1970s. Between 1932 and 1980, there were 26 coups and countercoups and the adoption of 13 constitutions. There were a number of military governments mixed with several attempts at democracy.

1980–1990

General Prem Tinsulanonda took power in a coup in 1980 and held it into 1988 through a series of coalition governments. He never stood for election but was able to put down coup attempts in 1981 and 1985. His governments were noted for stability (itself something of an achievement in Thailand) rather than progressive policies. His government strove to improve the environment for foreign investment.

Prem's government resigned in 1988 rather than face a no-confidence vote called by Chatichai Choonhavan's Chat Thai party. Chatichai was elected President in the subsequent elections. He formed a coalition consisting largely of the same core as Prem's coalition. There were predictions that his government would not last long, due partly to intimations that his cabinet ministers were mainly interested in feathering their own nests—corruption has long been rife in Thai governments. However, Chatichai outlasted the initial expectations. He adopted a pro-business stance that bene-fitted his cabinet as well as foreign investors.

Currency

The Thai baht was tied to the U.S. dollar during the 1950s, but it became progressively overvalued and was eventually floated. In 1963 it was again fixed against the U.S. dollar. Up until 1978 there were a series of devalua-tions in the baht's gold backing in order to maintain a relatively stable cor-respondence to the U.S. dollar, which was gradually losing its value against gold. In 1978 the baht was detached from the dollar and its value pegged to a basket of currencies.

Foreign Investment

The government officially supports foreign investment. Multinational cor-porations should expect substantial delays in obtaining approvals of their investment applications although these should be no greater than for Thai businesses. Thai governments have long been known for being weighted with bureaucracy and for their slowness in making decisions. As of 1984, U.S. investment in Thailand was estimated at $4 billion, about 30 percent of all foreign investment in the country. By 1989, however, the United States accounted for only 8 percent of incoming investment, while Japan accounted for more than half.

The Thai Investment Law, which was passed in 1977, includes assur-ances against nationalization.

Foreign Equity Ownership

Industries approved for foreign investment are regulated by the Alien Business Law of 1972, which created three separate levels of foreign own-ership depending on the industry. The first level requires majority Thai shareholders for a public corporation. The second level requires majority Thai ownership for new investments but allows grandfathering of busi-nesses that existed prior to the passing of the law. The third level allows majority foreign ownership as long as an alien business license is approved. Despite these provisions, as a practical matter, 49 percent foreign owner-ship has been permitted even in the most restricted industries, although recent changes may reduce allowable foreign ownership levels.

Among the restrictions relating to specific industries are the require-ments for:

➤ 60 percent Thai equity in businesses involved in large-scale agriculture, livestock raising, and the production of fertilizers

➤ 100 percent Thai equity in businesses involved in agricultural product processing and rice milling

Land Ownership

Land ownership is restricted to Thai nationals except when special allowances are granted.

Local Content Requirements

There are strict requirements for local content in the automobile and motorcycle industries, but the proportion of local content in most other industries is generally controlled by high duties on nonlocal materials.

Remittability of Funds

Firms have little difficulty in repatriating funds as long as they can establish the foreign origination of those funds. Profits may be repatriated as long as proof of tax payment is presented.

Corporate Taxes

The nominal corporate tax rate is 30 percent for companies listed on the Securities Exchange and 35 percent otherwise. Tax evasion is common among Thai companies, however, either through the hiding of profits or through bribes to the tax authorities. In practice, the amount of many companies' tax payments is determined by negotiations with the government.

Incentives

The Investment Promotion Act of 1977 allows certain incentives to be offered for foreign investment. Industries eligible for incentives include agricultural products and commodities, minerals, chemicals and chemical products, general manufacturing, and others.

Because of the recent influx of foreign investment, the government is granting fewer incentives than before. It is trying to target incentives to ventures that make a strong contribution to national development. These are among the criteria to be considered:

➤ Location in up-country provinces
➤ Efficient use of natural resources
➤ Use of domestic labor and raw materials
➤ Share divestiture to Thai nationals and employee share ownership
➤ Advanced technology transfer
➤ Mobilization of offshore funds

Incentives include but are not limited to:

➤ Guarantees against nationalization

➤ Competitive protection

➤ Expatriate permission

➤ Land ownership permission

➤ Tax holidays and tax loss carry-forwards

The regulations establish a special category of Target Businesses, which includes those that develop natural resources or use agricultural raw materials for export manufacturing. An investment designated as a Target Business may be eligible for additional incentives such as:

➤ Exemption from machinery import tax

➤ 50 percent reduction of import duty on raw materials used in goods for local consumption

➤ Five-year exemption from import duties on raw materials used in export goods

➤ Five-year, 90 percent exemption from business tax

➤ 50 percent reduction in corporate income tax for 5 years after the tax holiday or from the first income-earning year

➤ Ten-year, 200 percent tax deduction for expenses for transport, electricity, and water

➤ Special depreciation rights for original installation

The regulations divide the country into three zones:

1. Bangkok and the five adjacent provinces
2. Ten provinces located near Bangkok, in the central region and on the eastern shore
3. The up-country provinces

The tax holidays, tariff exemptions, and other incentives are more generous for investments located in Zone 2 than for those in Zone 1, and the incentives for Zone 3 are substantially more generous than for Zone 2.

Labor

Thailand has a large supply of unskilled labor, but there is a shortage of skilled labor, particularly in newly introduced industries.

Patent Protection

Patents are governed by the Patent Act of 1979, which was adopted following strong pressure from the United States and other governments who objected to the flagrant copying in Thailand of products and processes that had been developed and patented in other countries. Patents may be regis-

TABLE 1	Thai Chempest *Pro Forma* Income Statement (in millions of baht)				
Year of operations	1st	2d	3d	4th	5th
Sales revenue	50	100	150	200	250
Cost of goods sold	35	70	105	140	175
Administrative costs	30	30	30	30	30
Depreciation and amortization*	004	004	004	004	004
PBIT	219	24	11	26	41
Interest*	002	002	002	002	002
PBT	221	26	9	24	39

*Depreciation (straight-line) @ 10% on $400,000 imported equipment and 10 million baht buildings, etc., 1 amortization of 40 million baht loan from government Development Bank at 5% interest, repayable in 20th year.

tered by Thai nationals and nationals of countries that have provided reciprocal patent rights to Thai nationals. Patents are granted for 15 years from the filing date with the possibility of cancellation after six years if no production is undertaken. Protection of trademarks and intellectual property has improved under this legislation, although strict enforcement still poses a problem.

Patents may be granted or recognized in Thailand only if the invention is new, involves an innovative step, and is capable of industrial application. Patents are not allowed in a variety of areas including agricultural equipment, pharmaceuticals, food, beverages, biological species, and computer programs.

One current issue is the protection of computer software and pharmaceuticals as mandated under the Uruguay round of the General Agreement on Tariffs and Trade in 1983. The United States is pushing for a quick resolution and is attempting to influence Thailand's decision through various international channels.

In late 1990 the U.S. government identified Thailand as a Priority Foreign Country that inadequately protects U.S. intellectual property under Section 301 of the Omnibus Trade and Competitiveness Act of 1988. As a result, the United States started investigating whether to institute or raise tariffs against selected imports from Thailand.

Notes

1. The interest rate on loans from Thai commercial banks was about 8.5 percent to 9.0 percent at the time. The Development Bank was offering loans to qualified borrowers at 3 to 4 percentage points lower.
2. The ASEAN countries consisted of Brunei, Indonesia, Malaysia, Philippines, Singapore, and Thailand. ASEAN was originally intended to be a customs union, but its members sometimes found it easier to cooperate on political matters than on economic.

3.The sources for the appendix material were: Business International Corporation, *Investing, Licensing and Trading Conditions Abroad* (July 1990): 3–5; International Trade Administration, U.S. Department of Commerce, "Thailand," *Guide to Doing Business in the ASEAN Region* (February 1990): 48–56; and current news reports.

INTEGRATIVE CASE 8

The Case of the Floundering Expatriate

At exactly 1:40 on a warm, sunny Friday afternoon in July 1995, Frank Waterhouse, CEO of Argos Diesel, Europe, leaves his office on the top floor of the Argos Tower, overlooking the Zürichsee. In the grip of a tension headache, he rides the glass elevator down the outside of the mirrored building.

To quiet his nerves, he studies his watch. In less than half an hour, Waterhouse must look on as Bert Donaldson faces the company's European managers—executives of the parts suppliers that Argos has acquired over the past two years. Donaldson is supposed to give the keynote address at this event, part of the second Argos Management Meeting organized by his training and education department. But late yesterday afternoon, he phoned Waterhouse to say he didn't think the address would be very good. Donaldson said he hadn't gotten enough feedback from the various division heads to put together the presentation he had planned. His summary of the company's progress wouldn't be what he had hoped.

It's his meeting! Waterhouse thinks, as the elevator moves silently down to the second floor. How could he not be prepared? Is this really the man who everyone at corporate headquarters in Detroit thinks is so fantastic?

Waterhouse remembers his introduction to Donaldson just over a year ago. Argos International's CEO and chairman, Bill Loun, had phoned Waterhouse himself to say he was sending the "pick of the litter." He said that Donaldson had a great international background—that he had been a professor of American studies in Cairo for five years. Then he had returned to the States and joined Argos. Donaldson had helped create the cross-divisional, cross-functional teams that had achieved considerable cost reductions and quality improvements.

Loun had said that Donaldson was just what Argos Europe needed to create a seamless European team—to facilitate communication among the different European parts suppliers that Waterhouse had worked so hard to acquire. Waterhouse had proved his own strategic skills, his own ability to close deals, by successfully building a network of companies in Europe under the Argos umbrella. All the pieces were in place. But for the newly expanded company to meet its financial goals, the units had to work together. The managers had to become an integrated team. Donaldson could help them. Together they would keep the company's share of the diesel engine and turbine market on the rise.

Waterhouse deserved to get the best help, the CEO had said. Bert Donaldson was the best. And later, when the numbers proved the plan successful, Waterhouse could return to the States a hero. (Waterhouse heard Loun's voice clearly in his head: "I've got my eye on you, Frank. You know you're in line.")

Waterhouse had been enthusiastic. Donaldson could help him reach the top. He had met the man several times in Detroit. Donaldson seemed to have a quick mind, and he was very charismatic.

But that wasn't the Donaldson who had arrived in Zürich in August 1994 with his wife and two daughters. This man didn't seem to be a team builder—not in this venue. Here his charisma seemed abrasive.

The elevator comes to a stop. Waterhouse steps into the interior of the building and heads toward the seminar room at the end of the hall.

Waterhouse keeps thinking of his own career. He has spent most of his time since Donaldson's appointment securing three major government contracts in Moscow, Ankara, and Warsaw. He has kept the ball rolling, kept his career on track. It isn't his fault that Donaldson can't handle this assignment. It isn't his fault that the Germans and the French still can't agree on a unified sales plan.

His thoughts turn back to Donaldson. It can't be all Bert's fault, either. Donaldson is a smart man, a good man. His successes in the States were genuine. And Donaldson is worried about this assignment; it isn't as though he's just being stubborn. He sounded worried on the phone. He cares. He knows his job is falling apart and he doesn't know what to do. What can he return to at Argos in the States if he doesn't excel here in Europe?

Let Donaldson run with the ball—that's what they said in Detroit. It isn't working.

Waterhouse reaches the doorway of the seminar room. Ursula Lindt, his executive assistant, spots him from the other side. Lindt is from a wealthy local family. Most of the local hires go to her to discuss their problems. Waterhouse recalls a few of her comments about Donaldson: Staff morale on the fifth floor is lower than ever; there seems to be a general malaise. Herr Direktor Donaldson must be having problems at home. Why else would he work until midnight?

Waterhouse takes a seat in the front row and tries to distract himself by studying the meeting schedule. "Managing Change and Creating Vision: Improving Argos with Teamwork" is the title. Donaldson's "vision" for Argos Europe. Waterhouse sighs. Lindt nears him and, catching his eye, begins to complain.

"A few of the managers have been making noises about poor organization," she says. "And Sauras, the Spanish director, called to complain that the meeting schedule was too tight." Her litany of problems continues: "Maurizio, the director in Rome, came up to me this morning and began to lobby for Donaldson's replacement. He feels that we need someone with a better understanding of the European environment." Seeing Waterhouse frown, Lindt backs off. "But he's always stirring up trouble," she says. "Otherwise, the conference appears to be a success." She sits down next to Waterhouse and studies her daily planner.

The room slowly fills with whispers and dark hand-tailored suits. Groups break up and re-form. "Grüss Gott, Heinz, wie geht's?" "Jacques, ça va bien?" "Bill, good to see you…Great." Waterhouse makes a perfunctory inspection of the crowd. Why isn't Donaldson in here schmoozing? He hears a German accent: "Two-ten. Ja ja. Amerikanische Pünktlichkeit." Punctuality. Unlike Donaldson, he knows enough German to get by.

A signal is given. The chitchat fades with the lights. Waterhouse turns his gaze to the front as Donaldson strides up to the podium.

Donaldson speaks. "As President Eisenhower once said, 'I have two kinds of problems, the urgent and the important. The urgent are not important, and the important are never urgent.'" He laughs, but the rest of the room is silent save for the sound of paper shuffling.

Donaldson pauses to straighten his notes and then delivers a flat ten-minute summary of the European companies' organizational structure. He reviews the basics of the team-building plan he has developed—something with which all the listeners are already familiar. He thanks his secretary for her efforts.

Then he turns the meeting over to Waterhouse, who apologizes for not having been able to give the managers any notice that this session would be shorter than planned. He assures them that the rest of the schedule is intact and asks them to take this time as a break before their 4 P.M. logistics meeting, which will be run by the French division head.

The managers exchange glances, and Waterhouse detects one or two undisguised smiles. Walking out of the seminar room, he hears someone say, "At least the meeting didn't run overtime." Waterhouse fumes. He has put in four years of hard work here in Europe. This is the first year of his second three-year contract. He is being groomed for a top management position back in the States. The last thing he needs is a distraction like this.

He remembers how Detroit reacted when, a little over a month ago, he raised the issue of Donaldson's failure to adjust. He had written a careful letter to Bill Loun suggesting that Donaldson's assignment might be over his head, that the timing wasn't right. The CEO had phoned him right away. "That's rubbish, Frank," his voice had boomed over the line. "You've been asking for someone to help make this plan work, and we've sent you the best we've got. You can't send him back. It's your call—you have the bottom-line responsibility. But I'm hoping he'll be part of your inner circle, Frank. I'd give him more time. Make it work. I'm counting on you."

More time is no longer an option, Waterhouse thinks. But if he fires Donaldson now or sends him back to Detroit, he loses whatever progress has been made toward a unified structure. Donaldson has begun to implement a team-building program; if he leaves, the effort will collapse. And how could he fire Donaldson, anyway? The guy isn't working out here, but firing him would destroy his career. Bert doesn't deserve that.

What's more, the European team program has been touted as a major initiative, and Waterhouse has allowed himself to be thought of as one of its drivers. Turning back would reflect badly on him as well.

On the other hand, the way things are going, if Donaldson stays, he may himself cause the plan to fail. One step forward, two steps back. "I don't have the time to walk Donaldson through remedial cultural adjustment," Waterhouse mumbles under his breath.

Donaldson approaches him in the hall. "I sent a multiple-choice survey to every manager. One of them sent back a rambling six-page essay," he says. "I sent them in April. I got back only 7 of 40 from the Germans. Every time I called, it was 'under review.' One of them told me his people wanted to discuss it—in German. The Portuguese would have responded if I'd brought it personally."

Waterhouse tells Donaldson he wants to meet with him later. "Five o'clock. In my office." He turns away abruptly.

Ursula Lindt follows him toward the elevator. "Herr Direktor, did you hear what Herr Donaldson called Frau Schweri?"

Bettina Schweri, who organizes Donaldson's programs, is essentially his manager. She speaks five languages fluently and writes three with style. Lindt and Schweri have known each other since childhood and eat lunch together every day.

"A secretary," Lindt says, exasperated. "Frau Schweri a secretary? Simply not to believe."

Back in his office, Waterhouse gets himself a glass of water and two aspirin. In his mind, he's sitting across from Donaldson ten months earlier.

"Once I reach a goal," Donaldson says, "I set another one and get to work. I like to have many things going at once—especially since I have only two years. I'm going for quick results, Frank. I've even got the first project lined up. We'll bring in a couple of trainers from the Consulting Consortium to run that team-skills workshop we talked about."

Waterhouse comes back to the present. That first workshop hadn't gone too badly—at least he hadn't heard of any problems. But he, Waterhouse, had not attended. He picks up the phone and places a call to Paul Janssen, vice president of human resources for Argos Europe. Paul is a good friend, a trusted colleague. The two men often cross paths at the health club.

A few seconds later, Janssen's voice booms over the line. "Frank? Why didn't you just walk down the hall to see me? I haven't seen you at the club in weeks."

Waterhouse doesn't want to chat. "Donaldson's first training weekend, in February," he says. "How'd it go? Really."

"Really. Well, overall, not too bad. A few glitches, but nothing too out of the ordinary for a first run. Bert had some problems with his assistant. Apparently, Frau Schweri had scheduled the two trainers to arrive in Zürich two days early to prepare everything, recover from jet lag, and have dinner at the Baur au Lac. They came the night before. You can imagine how that upset her. Bert knew about the change but didn't inform Frau Schweri."

Waterhouse has the distinct impression that Janssen has been waiting for a chance to talk about this. "Go on," Waterhouse says.

"Well, there were a few problems with the workshops."

"Problems?"

"Well, yes. One of the managers from Norway—Dr. Godal, I believe—asked many questions during Bert's presentation, and he became rather irascible."

"Bert?" Waterhouse asked.

"Yes. And one of the two trainers wore a Mickey Mouse sweater—"

"Mickey Mouse?" Waterhouse laughs without meaning to.

"A sweater with a depiction of Mickey Mouse on the front."

"What on earth does that have to do with Bert?"

"Well, Bert offered them a two-year contract after Frau Schweri advised him not to. He apparently told her he was satisfied with the trainers and, so far as he was concerned, questions about their personal habits and clothing weren't worth his time."

"Yes, and—"

"Well, there were complaints—"

"They all went to Frau Schweri?" He is beginning to see.

"One of the managers said the trainers provided too much information; he felt as though they were condescending to him. A bombardment of information, he called it. Other managers complained that Bert didn't provide enough background information. The French managers seemed to think the meeting was worthwhile. But Bert must think that because his style works with one group, the others will fall into place automatically. And everyone was unhappy with the schedule. The trainers always ran overtime, so everybody was displeased because there weren't any coffee breaks for people from various offices to network. Oh, and the last thing? All the name cards had first names and last names—no titles."

"No titles," Waterhouse says, and lets out a sigh. "Paul, I wish you'd told me all this earlier."

"I didn't think you needed to hear it, Frank. You've been busy with the new contracts." They agree to meet at the club later in the week, and they hang up. Waterhouse stares down at Donaldson's file.

His résumé looks perfect. He has a glowing review from the American University in Cairo, where he earned the highest ratings for his effectiveness, his ease among students from 40 countries, and his sense of humor. At Argos in the United States, he implemented the cross-divisional team approach in record time. Donaldson is nothing short of a miracle worker.

Waterhouse leans back in his swivel-tilter and lets the scuttlebutt on Donaldson run through his mind. Word is that he's an *Arbeitstier*. "Work animal" is the direct, unflattering translation. He never joins the staff for a leisurely lunch in the canteen, preferring a sandwich in his office. Word is he can speak some Arabic from his lecturing days in Cairo but still can't manage a decent "good morning" in Swiss German. Word is he walks around all day—he says it's management by walking around—asking for suggestions, ideas, plans, or solutions because he can't think of any himself.

Waterhouse remembers an early conversation with Donaldson in which he seemed frustrated. Should he have paid more attention?

"I met with Jakob Hassler, vice president of human resources at Schwyz Turbines," Donaldson had said, pacing the office. "I wanted some ideas for the training program. Schwyz is the first company we acquired here; I wanted to show Hassler that I don't bite. When I opened the door, he just stood there. I offered him a chair beside the coffee table, told him to call me Bert. He nodded, so I asked him about his family and the best place to buy ski boots, and he answered but he acted so aloof. I took a chair across from him, listened to ten minutes of one-word answers, and then I finally asked him how things were going in general, to which he said, 'Everything is normal.' Can you beat that, Frank? I told him I was interested in his ideas, so he pushed his chair back and said, 'Please let me know what you expect.' I reminded him that we're all on the same team, have only two years for major change, gave him a week to get back to me with a few ideas, and you know what he said? He said, 'Ja ja.'"

At the time, Donaldson's frustration seemed to stem from the normal adjustment problems that expatriates face. But he never did adjust. Why doesn't he just give Hassler what he needs to know and get out? Waterhouse knows this; why hasn't Donaldson figured it out?

His phone rings—the inside line. It's Ursula Lindt. "Frau Direktor Donaldson just called. She said Herr Direktor Donaldson was expected home at 4. I told her you had scheduled a meeting with him for 5." She waits. Waterhouse senses that there is more to her message. "What else did she say, Frau Lindt?"

"I inquired after her health, and she said she's near the end of her rope. Bored without her work. She said they thought Zürich would be a breeze after Cairo. Then she went into a tirade. She said that they're having serious problems with their eldest daughter. She'll be in grade 12 at the international school this fall. She's applying to college. Frau Donaldson said her daughter's recommendations from her British teachers are so understated that they'd keep her out of the top schools, and she keeps getting Cs because they're using the British grading scale. She reminded me that this is a girl with a combined SAT score of over 1350."

Lindt is done. Waterhouse thanks her for the information, then hangs up. Julie Ann is usually calm, collected. She has made some friends here. Something must have pushed her over the edge. And their daughter is engaging, bright. Why is this all coming to a head now?

Waterhouse recalls his most recent meeting with Donaldson, a couple of days before Donaldson's vacation in May.

"I've tried everything, Frank. I've delegated, I've let them lead, I've given them pep talks." Waterhouse remembers Donaldson sinking deep into his chair, his voice flat. "No matter what I do—if I change an agenda, if I ask them to have a sandwich with me at my desk—someone's always pissed off. We're talking about streamlining an entire European company and they're constantly looking at their watches. We run ten minutes overtime in a meeting and they're shuffling papers. I tell you, Frank, they're just going to have to join the rest of us in the postindustrial age, learn to do things the Argos way. I worked wonders in Detroit ... ."

The clock in Waterhouse's office reads 4:45. What can he do about Donaldson? Let him blunder along for another year? And take another 12 months of...he closes the door on that thought. Send him back and forget? Morale on the fifth floor will improve, the Europeans will be appeased, but with Donaldson will go the training program, such as it is. Corporate will just think that Waterhouse has forgotten how to play the American way. They'll think that he mistreated their star. Can he teach Donaldson cultural awareness? With the Ankara, Moscow, and Warsaw projects chewing up all his time? You can't teach cultural savvy. No way.

He hears Donaldson enter the outer office. A hanger clinks on the coat tree. How can he work this out?

Source: Gordon Adler, "The Case of the Floundering Expatriate," *Harvard Business Review* (July–August 1995): 24–30. Copyright 1995 by the President and Fellows of Harvard College. All rights reserved. Reprinted by permission.

INTEGRATIVE CASE 9

McDonald's Conquers the World

Sometime over the next 24 hours, while the rest of us merely work, eat, and sleep, McDonald's will open three more shiny-new restaurants. One may be out in a fast-growing suburb of Salt Lake City, another in the pristine downtown of Singapore, and the third in the smoggy bustle of Warsaw, where it will soon be flooded by smartly dressed young Poles hungry for a taste of America. Chances are good that within a year's time each of these stores will be grossing about $1.7 million a year and operating well in the black. And tomorrow? Same thing. Three more stores will open.

It wasn't long ago that many predicted McDonald's was doomed to become a lumbering cash cow in a mature industry. As events have turned out, the company has remained the nation's most profitable major retailer over the past ten years, even as the competition has become nimbler. Since 1983, McDonald's profits have more than tripled to almost $1.1 billion on revenues of $7.4 billion and systemwide sales of over $23 billion from over 14,000 stores.

Not that some of those predicted age marks aren't starting to show. Operating profits from the United States and same-store sales have climbed only slightly over the past several years, and the highly organized "McCulture" shows signs of becoming too rigid, too steeped in its own orthodoxy to cook up that all-important break-out-of-the-box, home run innovation. Most analysts believe a new "hitwich" on the order of the Big Mac or the Quarter Pounder will be required to solve McDonald's so-called "menu problem."

Whatever problems McDonald's may be having at home, however, are more than offset by its spectacular success abroad. Few of those skeptical about McDonald's in the 1980s were able to foresee that the fast-food giant—after stumbling in Holland in the 1970s—would take its act on the road and go global with a vengeance. In 1988 the company had 2,600 foreign stores and $1.8 billion in overseas revenue. Six years later it has 4,700 stores doing $3.4 billion a year. The result: McDonald's today is arguably the most awesome service machine on the planet and a virtual blueprint for taking a service organization global. While the seers and the management consultant crowd crow that service will become America's next great export, McDonald's is already doing it today, delivering world-standardized food, smiles, value, and cleanliness to every continent except Antarctica.

"We are seizing the global marketplace," says James Cantalupo, the raspy-voiced former accountant who heads McDonald's International.

McDonald's is in the rare and enviable position of possessing a truly global service brand, a name known to hundreds of millions around the world. "Only a few American brands are easy to export," says Caroline Levy of Lehman Brothers. "The recognition level must be very high, and the price point low. That means Coke, Marlboro, Wrigley, and McDonald's." Note: Of Levy's fab four, only McDonald's sells a service as opposed to a packaged good. And if the packaged-goods purveyors are any model, McDonald's untapped potential remains enormous. The company already sells its burgers in 73 countries and pulls in about 45 percent of its operating income from foreign operations. But global soft drink behemoth Coca-Cola, for instance, sells to 195 countries and brings home 80 percent of its income from abroad.

"It's hard for Americans to understand, but McDonald's is almost heaven-sent to these people," says Tim Fenton, the head of McDonald's Poland, as he gestures toward one of his 17 booming stores. "It's some of the best food around. The service is quick, and people smile. You don't have to pay to use the bathroom. There's air conditioning. The place isn't filled with smoke. We tell you what's in the food. And we want you to bring kids."

For all the strength of its brand, what McDonald's really has to export around the globe is that almost intangible, fragile concept—service. How does it do it? The answer: a collection of surprisingly simple strategies, mostly from the Lost Art School of Management. Here's what's on the syllabus:

➤ Gather your people often for face-to-face meetings to learn from each other.
➤ Put your employees through arduous and repetitive management training.
➤ Form paradigm-busting arrangements with suppliers.
➤ Know a country's culture before you hit the beach.
➤ Hire locals whenever possible.
➤ Maximize autonomy.
➤ Tweak the standard menu only slightly from place to place.
➤ Keep pricing low to build market share. Profits will follow when economies of scale kick in.

Of course McDonald's also lends incredible marketing support to its brand, blanketing the world with advertising and promotion. A $1.4 billion annual global budget makes McDonald's the most advertised single brand in the world. Kids, minorities, and the handicapped tug at emotional sleeves in dozens of languages, begging potential customers to "get up and get away." Ronald McDonald, according to some in the company, is more recognizable than Santa Claus.

McDonald's slavish devotion to regimentation is also key, and the company is constantly refining its organization, which is now so complex and far-reaching that one of those James Bond masterminds might envy it.

"Never have I seen a company more focused than McDonald's," says Don Keough, a McDonald's board member and retired president of Coca-

TABLE 1	How Many McDonald's Can He Build?

Cantalupo's Theorem: If nearly 15,000 McDonald's already sounds like plenty, just wait. James Cantalupo, president of McDonald's International, uses a formula to estimate how many stores he can build. He divides a country's population by the number of people per store in the United States and adjusts for differences in per capita income. Of course it doesn't account for factors like competition and eating habits. *Fortune* calculated the potential number of McDonald's that could be built worldwide. Answer: 42,000.

$$\frac{\text{Population of Country X}}{\substack{\text{No. of People per} \\ \text{McDonald's in U.S.} \\ (25,000)}} \times \frac{\text{Per Capita Income of Country X}}{\substack{\text{Per Capita Income} \\ \text{of U.S.} \\ (\$23,120)}} = \substack{\text{Potential} \\ \text{Penetration} \\ \text{of McDonald's} \\ \text{in Country X}}$$

McDonald's Biggest Markets			Some Underpenetrated Markets		
	Current number of restaurants	Minimum market potential		Current number of restaurants	Minimum market potential
Japan	1,070	6,100	China	23	784
Canada	694	1,023	Russia	3	685
Britain	550	1,794	Colombia	0	79
Germany	535	3,235	India	0	489
Australia	411	526	Pakistan	0	90
France	314	2,237	South Africa	0	190

Cola, a major supplier. "The company is an army with one objective that has never strayed."

Driving these zealous troops forward in the hamburger crusades is CEO Mike Quinlan, 49, or "Q," as he is called. (Hmm, maybe there is something to this James Bond thing.) Only the company's third CEO, the carrot-topped Quinlan, who started in the mailroom 31 years ago, wears a mantle passed down from patriarch Ray Kroc and current chairman Fred Turner. While Quinlan is proud of the company's record under his watch, he's more frustrated than anyone by its inability to develop that next big "hitwich." So Q has placed a bounty on innovation and is now scouring the globe for winners. "Want to know my definition of insanity?" asks Q. "It's doing the same thing over and over again and expecting different results. If there's anything I try to impart to our people, it's to never be satisfied. That means coming up with new ideas."

While many of the company's greatest successes, such as the Big Mac and the Egg McMuffin, came from rank-and-file U.S. franchisees, other brainstorms—mostly operational—have begun to filter in from overseas. The Dutch created a pre-fab modular store that can be moved over a weekend. The Swedes came up with an enhanced meat freezer. And satellite stores, or low-overhead mini-McDonald's, were invented in high-rent Singapore.

"There used to be resistance to ideas from abroad," says Ed Rensi, the portly chief of McDonald's USA. "No more."

And nowhere is the spirit of this global burgerpreneurism more evident than in Poland. Five years after the fall of communism, the Poles are busy scrubbing four decades of soot off buildings. New, brightly colored commercial signs, including those of Pizza Hut and Burger King, are cropping up like wild mushrooms. Fenton, McDonald's man in Poland, gazes out over Warsaw from a bar atop the new Marriott hotel and reflects on what he's seen. "When I first came here, two years ago, there were practically no lights. Now look," he says gesturing to the buddingly lit city. "I like this view because you can see all four of the city's McDonald's from here."

Nowadays Fenton can take time off to have a Johnnie Walker, a pleasant change from when he faced challenges not covered back home at Hamburger U. When he first arrived in Poland, one local official told him he would have to change "that silly logo with those arches." Say what? After a patient explanation on the power and value of trademarks, the apparatchik finally backed off.

And for all its brand recognition, McDonald's has to walk a fine line between being perceived as global or local and American. "People are more the same than they are different," says International chief Cantalupo, whose charge it is to sow the company's stores like seeds around the world. "I don't think our food is seen as American. It's seen as McDonald's." A lot of very intense preparation before entering a market, including the hiring of local managers, helps make this most American of brands seem pretty local too. Before Fenton came to Poland, the company planned for 18 months. Locations, real estate, construction, supply, personnel, legal, and government relations were all worked out in advance. Finally, in June 1992, Fenton charged in with a team of 50 from the United States, Russia, Germany, and Britain. Since then all except Fenton have been replaced by Poles in what McDonald's calls a sunset program.

Now Poles don't just want to eat at McDonald's; they want to work there too. With the average annual income in Poland around $2,000, counter jobs paying $1.70 an hour—or about 75 percent above that average—are snapped up. No wonder counter kids appear to hustle harder than in the United States. Managerial jobs at $900 a month, with a stint at Hamburger University in the United States, are especially coveted.

Doesn't this high profile rile the locals who don't get jobs? Isn't McDonald's in danger of being seen as some kind of U.S. culinary imperialist? "The only resistance comes from the same people who didn't want political change in the late 1980s," replies Fenton, as he sits in his Western-style open-architecture office in downtown Warsaw, fingering a brochure that teaches the Poles how to use a drive-in.

If the palpable excitement of Fenton's customers is any indication, the hard-liners had better find another capitalist stooge to pick on. It's the first day of school in Warsaw, and kids in new outfits stream into a McDonald's in the shadow of the Ministry of Culture building, a gift from Stalin and an ironic symbol of how quickly change has come to Poland. Fenton, a sturdy meat-and-potatoes guy from upstate New York, beams, frowning only when he uses his Polish to shoo away a ragged gypsy woman who is begging near the store entrance.

Fenton's Polish managers are taking to the McDonald's system with only a few small hitches. "The toughest concept to teach has been negotiation," he says, "because under communism there wasn't any. Also, the first year they came to a barbecue at my house in suits. This year I said, 'Anyone wearing a suit gets sent home.'" He also had to suggest, in Pollyanna-like McDonald's fashion, that customers not bring in vodka to drink with their Big Macs. By year-end, Fenton will be running 22 stores, and his operation should have positive operating income, even with prices 25 percent below those in the United States. By 1998, Fenton anticipates Poland will have 100 stores, but by then the sun will have set on him, and at his desk will sit a Pole.

Each country McDonald's enters presents its own problems—or opportunities. German law prohibits special promotions like "buy one, get one free" and advertised discounts. Labor unions in France recently accused the company of cheating workers out of overtime pay. Coping with foot-dragging officials sometimes requires McDonald's to take the offensive. In Germany a recent Chinese food promotion worked so well that the company ran out of spring rolls. "I tried to order more from our supplier in Denmark," explains Hans Griebler, the affable head of purchasing in Germany, "but he told us his company needed permission from the government to work on the weekends. I called the Danish labor minister and got it."

That kind of drive to provide service—which we almost take for granted in the United States—is at the core of what McDonald's offers its overseas customers. Listen to Rolf Kreiner, head of marketing at McDonald's 535-store German operation. "The world is becoming a service society. People are hungry for service, but in many countries they don't get any except at McDonald's. That's why our stores are so crowded. That's why we're ahead."

Supplying stores abroad can be a nightmarish exercise in logistics. When McDonald's first enters a country, it often has to import many of its supplies. Then the company tries to source locally as quickly as possible. "Transportation is cheaper when you stay in one country and you don't have to change currency," says vice chairman Jack Greenberg, an easygoing former CPA with Arthur Young and the rare outsider among McDonald's top management (he has only 12 years there). Sometimes the company contracts with local suppliers, with happy results for both parties. A German mustard and mayonnaise company that started with a $100 order some 20 years ago now sells McDonald's $40 million of condiments annually.

More frequently, though, McDonald's encourages its domestic suppliers to follow the company abroad. Chicago-based meat supplier OSI Industries has joint ventures in 17 countries, where it works with local companies making McDonald's hamburgers. One such site, a spotless meat plant in postcard-pretty Guenzburg, Bavaria, cranks out some 2.5 million patties a day. Computers mix ground beef to ensure that fat content meets the McDonald's world standard, 20 percent or less. Young second-generation Turkish women box patties quick-frozen by liquid nitrogen just as their counterparts would in the United States. The specs and production demands are exacting, and with monthly evaluations, the pressure for quality is constant. Says OSI International President Douglas Gullang: "Meeting McDonald's standards is a huge challenge. To some it seems insane what we do. But we realize our product isn't just meat; it's service. We've turned a meat plant into a service business."

For McDonald's, finding potential business partners around the globe isn't a problem—rather, the company is swamped with inquiries. Sorting through them is the real challenge. "McDonald's spent years going over dozens of applications before it picked its joint venture partner in Singapore," says Bob Kwan, managing director of the operation in that country. "Of course, I'm happy they chose me." The company prefers partners with connections. One of the heads of its Saudi Arabian operation is a member of the Saudi royal family.

The company also has more than one way of structuring its operations overseas, choosing from several options before it enters a new country. In the European theater, as Q calls it, the company usually runs wholly owned subsidiaries. The thinking is that since these markets resemble those in the United States, they can be run in roughly the same way as the domestic business, allowing for some adjustment. Take Holland. (In the early days of overseas expansion, the company would have said, "Please!") "We put stores in the suburbs like in the United States," says Michiel Hiemstra, a director of McDonald's Netherlands. "That didn't work because of different eating patterns. We learned to build downtown."

As in the U.S. market, these subsidiaries operate company-owned stores and also license out franchises—about 70 percent of the company's stores worldwide are franchised. Snagging one of these franchises ain't easy. Also as in the United States, potential franchisees slog through a two-year screening process. They must work at a store and go through training before gaining final approval, all for the right to plunk down $45,000 and sign a 20-year contract that guarantees McDonald's a royalty of 4 percent of sales, plus another 8.5 percent or more of sales for rent. Add to that 4 percent of sales for advertising, or over 16 cents of every dollar taken right off the top. But shed no tears for McDonald's operators, who organize themselves into webs of co-ops and service groups; they wind up taking home about $200,000 a year per store. High-volume stores in locales like Warsaw or Moscow can net three times as much.

In Asian markets, the company prefers joint ventures, such as the 1,000-plus store operation in Japan headed by eccentric billionaire Den Fujita. These usually 50/50 arrangements allow the company to tap into its partner's contacts and local expertise. The company lets such partners negotiate with cumbersome entities such as the Chinese government, which has already allowed McDonald's to open 23 restaurants, with dozens more on the way. McDonald's grabs the standard royalty off the top in these joint ventures, as well as 50 percent of the bottom line.

In its most exotic markets—Saudi Arabia, for example—the company reduces its risk by putting up no equity capital. It simply licenses the name with strict requirements as to standards, and takes an option to buy in later. Repatriating all these earnings and royalties from countries like Oman and New Caledonia is yet another challenge. McDonald's treasury department uses derivatives to hedge in 12 currencies, though in these derivative-phobic days, Greenberg insists it's never going to make a trading profit.

While other companies increasingly rely on technology to fill in gaps in communication, McDonald's still believes in the power of the good old face-to-face sit-down. The company that helped pioneer advanced point-of-sale computing has no e-mail system at headquarters, and Q doesn't even have a computer in his office. Ergo, no company gathers together more of its people from more places as often as McDonald's. "We constantly get together by region as well as by discipline, such as purchasing, construction, and accounting" says Kwan from Singapore. "We share successes and failures, and we work together to cut costs." A sampling of a typical month's meetings: an Asian store managers' conference in Sydney, the European purchasing board get-together in London, and a worldwide communications conference in Chicago.

McDonald's has also globalized its powerhouse real estate operation. For years a clique of managers saw McDonald's more as a real estate company than a fast-food chain, much to Ray Kroc's chagrin. It's easy to see why. The company owns about 9,000 properties, or about 60 percent of its store locations, making it the world's largest collector of land parcels, totaling some 36 million square feet of space. Book value: $10 billion. Market value: hard to say. One and a half times as much?

Today, though, real estate is pretty far down on the list of McDonald's priorities. No. 1 worry: that same old frustration at not finding a breakthrough at home—the double-digit-growth menu item. And there's no apparent solution in sight. Even Quinlan, a self-described "glass-is-half-full kind of a guy," calls new-product development "disappointing" and concedes that "new products are basically on the back burner." A longstanding, costly pizza project has been "like rolling a snowball uphill," says U.S. chief Rensi. A tableful of other dinner entrees, from pasta to corn on the cob, has also been coldly Sisyphean. "We're focusing on burgers, chicken, and breakfast. That's why people come to McDonald's," says Quinlan. But in the face of sluggish domestic growth, that focus has begun to look a bit like rationalization. To create a real winner, McDonald's may need to do something incredibly radical in its culture, like buying someone else's concept or hiring outsiders to come up with the next Quarter Pounder.

So far, the closest thing to a 90s hit has been the Extra Value Meal, a discounted package of burger, fries, and drink that offsets its lower margins with increased volume. But its success just shows what a tough game of nickel and dime the U.S. fast-food market has become. McDonald's now has one store per 25,000 people in the United States, and the company takes great pains not to cannibalize an existing store's volume when it opens another restaurant stateside, as it did 324 times last year. Grand Metropolitan's Burger King and PepsiCo's Taco Bell, KFC, and Pizza Hut are fierce, moneyed competitors that have all won battles against McDonald's.

So, Mike Quinlan, would you buy McDonald's stock if the company had only domestic operations? "Of course I would, you nut!" But why? Jim Adamson, CEO of Burger King, has an answer: "There are still so many new points of distribution out there—hospitals, sports arenas, and roadways. There's room for double-digit domestic growth in our business."

McDonald's is catching up, especially to Taco Bell, in the search for innovative locations. Examples: a train in Germany, an English Channel ferry, and an ice-skating rink in Wisconsin. It will also open over 500 smaller satellite stores in places like New York City and Brazil this year [1994]. Q is adamant: "I'm less concerned about saturation than at any point in my career. We only have a 21 percent share of the U.S. quick-serve restaurant business. Meanwhile we continue to lower costs, which allows us to penetrate smaller and smaller markets. We're vacuuming our P&L." Example: Standardizing kitchen equipment last year cut about $40,000 from the cost of equipping a restaurant.

One place McDonald's isn't cutting corners is employee training. Every geeky, pimply-faced burger flipper from Taipei to Topeka is put through the paces for two to three days. More than a few of us remember those lessons. The company claims the first job of one out of every 15 Americans was at a McDonald's.

For McDonald's managers the real business of training means matriculating at Hamburger University at company headquarters in Oak Brook, Illinois, just west of Chicago. Once mostly the butt of jokes, Hamburger U. today is—and hold the guffaws—akin to a crash executive MBA program. Procter & Gamble, Amoco, and the Red Cross all have visited recently looking for ways to improve their training. Fourteen times a year, 200 McDonald's managers with two to five years of experience arrive from 72 countries for the intensive two-week program. Simultaneous translation into 20 languages is provided for courses such as Building Market Share and Staffing and Retention II. Team building, just in time, close to your customer, TQM—called MQM here—it's been taught at HU for years. Some HU training borders on axiomatic: "Don't say: 'Juan! Clean up the parking lot!' Ask: 'Juan, would you please sweep up the parking lot?'" Other exercises are more challenging. Students are yanked out of classes and confronted in role-playing scenarios: "Hey, Jack, my hamburger tastes like it was made by Du Pont! What are you going to do about it?" Some 50,000 McDonald's employees, franchisees, and suppliers have received diplomas.

Whoa—suppliers you say? Yes, suppliers. In fact, many of today's cozy-up-to-your-supplier companies, such as Wal-Mart, learned from McDonald's. Why let the guys with the goods in on the system? Because "McDonaldizing" suppliers helps them meet company specs—though McDonald's suppliers are a unique animal to begin with. How about this for different? Many suppliers have open-book relationships in which McDonald's sets their profits. Some of them have McDonald's as their only customer, yet they have no contract with the company.

Though McDonald's does some business with companies like H.J. Heinz, Kraft General Foods, and Coca-Cola (see box), it buys a majority of its food from this shadow industry of formerly small companies whose collective annual sales now total around $3 billion. Meat supplier OSI Industries, distributor Martin Brower, and french-fry king J.R. Simplot Company have grown from mom and pop operations to $500 million dollar-plus companies mostly based on sales to McDonald's. Kroc didn't like buying from big food companies because they weren't responsive enough. According to John Love, author of *McDonald's: Behind the Arches*, Kraft once had McDonald's entire cheese business but lost three-quarters of it because it wouldn't make a sharper cheddar.

McDonald's gravitated in its earlier days toward small, hungry companies like J.S. Simplot's, then a mere sprout of an Idaho potato company. Simplot, today 85, remembers hooking up with Kroc back in 1967. "I went down to Santa Barbara and visited with Ray. He told me what he needed in a potato plant. I said, 'You got it.' We shook hands, and that was it—no price mentioned. McDonald's doesn't shop for the lowest price; they want service. They prize the relationship."

Don't kid yourself, though. With suppliers or anyone else, McDonald's knows how to throw its weight around. But in the past, McDonald's has learned all too well what it's like to play the bad guy and today works hard —more than any other large consumer company—to avoid wearing the black hat. The company took it on the chin as a symbol of the system in the 1960s when it was accused of racism, sexism, and anti-environmentalism. It reacted defensively, exacerbating the situation. No more.

"Now we try to be ahead of the curve," says the head of communications, Dick Starmann. Three years ago the company stopped using bleached white bags. "Half the scientific community said nay on white bags, the other half said yea, but customers didn't want them, so we got rid of them," says Starmann. A pilot program in Holland that recycles 100 percent of the waste at each store may be expanded to other countries.

This year the company banned smoking in company-owned U.S. stores and suggested that franchisees do the same. "There was no immediate pressure from customers, but we could see it coming," says Starmann. The tobacco companies were furious and demanded a sit-down. McDonald's

PRACTICAL PERSPECTIVE

Things Go Better with Coke—Just Ask McDonald's

Talk about corporate love affairs. Ask McDonald's CEO Mike Quinlan about his company's relationship with Coca-Cola Company, and his eyes light up. "Just wonderful," he gushes. "They are our partner." Echoes Don Keough, Coke's former No. 2 guy and now a McDonald's board member: "It's an enormously important strategic alliance. McDonald's is a hallmark customer."

No kidding. Not only is McDonald's the largest fountain-sales customer of Coke, but the two global giants also share a common No. 1 enemy: PepsiCo, which in addition to making Pepsi Cola owns fast-food rivals Pizza Hut, Taco Bell, and KFC.

Like any successful affair of the heart, the two companies enjoy getting together for those special occasions. Every 18 months or so, the top 100 executives from each company meet for a weekend at some locale like Palm Springs or Palm Beach, and they don't scrimp on the speaking fees. In past years, for example, they have given the podium over to Ronald Reagan, Margaret Thatcher, and Henry Kissinger.

The next gathering will be held this February in Phoenix, with an undisclosed heavy hitter scheduled to speak. "The focus of these meetings is on the future of the global marketplace," says Keough. "The companies have much common ground there." For example, the two companies worked together to open up the Russian market earlier last decade.

The relationship has a long history, going back some 40 years to McDonald's infancy. The payoff for Coke has been tremendous. Coca-Cola products are served in all 14,500 or so McDonald's stores and account for about 5 percent of its U.S. volume. Not a single restaurant serves Pepsi—although there is no actual company edict that prohibits it. The heresy of that act would be unthinkable to a McDonald's franchisee.

Those of us who aren't invited to these big powwows can certainly speculate that they're a great opportunity to get out on the links. Or plot the total destruction of PepsiCo? Not so, insists Keough. "We really don't get into that," he says, leaving the impression that McDonald's and Coke are too busy looking deeply into each other's eyes and swooning to bother with the competition. Not to mention carving up the world.

said no. The latest charge: using beef from cattle that grazed in pastures cleared from the rain forest. "We don't serve any," says Starmann, who eagerly pulls a policy statement out of his briefcase.

Even the staple McDonald's food is less unhealthy than it was ten years ago. "McDonald's has gotten better," says industry critic Michael Jacobson, executive director of the Center for Science in the Public Interest and co-author of *Fast-Food Guide*, "though much of the improvement is in the addition of healthier foods like cereal, a no-fat bran muffin, salads, carrots, and celery, and low-fat McLean burgers." According to Jacobson's work, McDonald's burgers generally contain fewer calories and less fat and sodium than comparable sandwiches from Burger King or Wendy's. But a steady diet of McDonald's Biscuit with Sausage & Egg might tie up traffic on the aortal highway in short order. Overseas, besides serving localized fast food—like black currant shakes in Poland—McDonald's offers more body-friendly items like salads with shrimp in Germany and veggie burgers in Holland. "Yes, people are interested in healthier food," says Quinlan, who is sensitive about his own double chin, "but they are most interested in taste, convenience, and value." And to those who say McDonald's is simply serving up junk to the world? "I say, 'Wake up, pal, you're not on the playing field.' We're giving customers what they want."

It's true that the more McDonald's globalizes, the more risks the company takes on. Still, it would take a mighty big log to make it stumble. Ultimately McDonald's isn't going to be hurt by a grandmother in Albuquerque suing over hot spilled coffee, nor Green protests in the Czech Republic, nor penny shortfalls in earnings, nor Burger King, nor PepsiCo. Probably only McDonald's could stop McDonald's.

But with all the focus that Don Keough talks about and an army of 840,000 system-wide employees fixated on its operations, McDonald's will in all likelihood still be teaching everyone else a thing or two about service into the new century. The best indication of this probably comes from talking to those throughout the McDonald's system—from Q on down. In those conversations you never get the feeling that there's any sense of victory within McDonald's. These folks are still at war—on all fronts.

Source: Andrew E. Serwer, "McDonald's Conquers the World," *Fortune* (October 17, 1994): 103–116. Copyright © 1994, *Time* Inc. All rights reserved. Reprinted with permission.

Glossary

A

Ad hoc groups Problem-specific teams or groups consisting of individuals who possess the relevant knowledge to address a particular organizational problem.

Adaptable management A firm's management is able to adapt managerial techniques to the unique needs of specific countries.

Adaptation Refers to the stage in the expatriation process in which the expatriate must learn to cope with cultures, laws, political systems, legal processes, and other subtleties that are different from his or her own.

Adaptation problems Difficulties that arise for expatriates during the adaptation process. They are especially common when the physical and sociocultural environments are at odds with the expatriate's own value system and living habits.

Adaptive transformative innovations Modify and adjust existing modern technologies (for example, in farming, a modern, more efficient tractor replaces an older, less efficient model).

Alliances Firms with unique strengths that join to be more effective and efficient than their competitors.

American-based leadership and motivation theories Traditionally, these theories advance the notion that participative leadership behavior is more effective than authoritative leadership behavior. Popular theories include McGregor's *Theory X and Theory Y Managers* and Likert's *System 4 Management*.

Antiplanning Belief that any attempt to lay out specific and "rational" plans is either foolish or dangerous and downright evil. Correct approach is to live in existing systems, react in terms of one's own experience, and not try to change them by means of some grandiose scheme or mathematical model.

Authoritative decision making Refers to a style of decision making in which the leader simply makes a decision and instructs followers what to do without consulting or involving them in the decision-making process.

B

Badwill What international corporations create when they exploit foreign markets without sharing benefits with locals.

Barriers Elements that inhibit the implementation and maintenance of various business programs and strategies

Body language Includes eye contact, physical distance and touching, hand movements, pointing, and facial expressions.

Business ethics gap Compared with other capitalistic societies, the approach to ethics is more individualistic, legalistic, and universalistic in the United States.

Business ethics visibility gap The people of the United States read and hear far more about business misconduct than people in other countries.

Bustarella Italian term for bribery/payoffs.

C

Cartels Groups of private businesses that agree to set prices, share markets, and control production.

Centralization Most of the important decisions relative to local matters are made by headquarters management rather than by managers in the local subsidiary.

Chief learning officer Responsible for developing on a worldwide scale the organization's human talent and for using the human knowledge present in the organization.

Circular cultures Believe that since individuals can see what has happened in the past, their past is ahead of them, and since they cannot see into the future, their future is behind them.

Clusters Geographic concentrations of interconnected companies and institutions in a particular field.

Collective In stage six of the social interaction paradigm, leaders look for opportunities that benefit the group as a whole.

Commitment An important reciprocal relationship in which the employee is committed to the organization and its goals and is matched by the employer's commitment to the employee's welfare.

Competitive environment This environment is affected by bribery and the existence of cartels.

Confiscation Occurs when a government seizes foreign-owned assets and does not make prompt, effective, and adequate compensation.

Confucianism A system of practical ethics based on a set of pragmatic rules for daily life derived from experience.

Consensus Employed in choice and implementation tactics within collectivist cultures to maintain harmony and unity.

Contingency decision making A style of decision making committed to recognizing the uniqueness of different situations and therefore using different approaches when confronting varying situations, cultures, and so on.

Contract enforcement Usually, a contract entered into by firms from different nations stipulates whose law is applied in the event of default. However, some countries' legal systems mandate that the laws of the nation where the contract was signed shall be applied. Other legal systems mandate that the laws of the country where the contract was executed shall be applied.

Contractual alliances Many enterprises enter foreign markets via non-equity-based joint ventures, often referred to as contractual alliances or strategic alliances.

Conversational principles Those principles governing verbal and nonverbal communication applicable in all aspects of cross-cultural communication.

Corporate culture Refers to an organization's practice, such as its symbols, heroes, and rituals, and its values, such as its employees' perception of good/evil, beautiful/ugly, normal/abnormal, and rational/irrational. The practice aspects differ from corporation to corporation within a national culture, and the value aspects vary from country to country.

Corporate social responsibility An objective to respond appropriately everywhere possible to societal expectations and environmental needs.

Countertrade A buyer of a product pays the seller with another product of the equivalent monetary value.

Country-related cultural factors framework Identifies certain national cultural dimensions and their impact on DMB (decision-making behavior).

Cross-cultural communication Effective communication across nations/cultures can only take place when the sender encodes the message using language, idioms, norms and values, and so on, that are familiar to the receiver or when the receiver is familiar with the language, idioms, and so on, used by the sender. Also, the sender and receiver must be aware of both his or her own and the other's environmental, cultural, sociocultural, and psychocultural contexts.

Cross-cultural message adjustment The process of adjusting and adapting incoming signifiers to the existing repository of signs, and of adapting and adjusting the repository of signifieds to create new signs.

Cross-cultural research Conducted by researchers from one culture to ascertain how people in one or more other cultures behave—usually to identify the similarities and differences existing among the cultures.

Cross-cultural social responsibility A firm's actions must take into account not only the well-being of stockholders, but also the well-being of the community, the employees, and the customers.

Cultural barriers Business behavior in one culture does not transfer well to another culture due to cultural differences. For example, Americans' "spirit of competitiveness" culture does not transfer well to "spirit of cooperation" cultures, such as Japan.

Cultural briefing Pre-depature education and orientation of the expatriate and his or her family about the foreign country. The briefing includes the country"s cultural traditions, history, government, economy, living conditions, and so on.

Cultural contexts See *Cross-cultural communication.*

Cultural environment To develop an effective international business strategy, the critical aspects of culture must be identified.

Cultural fluency A strong command of not only the language of a foreign country, but also its culture. This is required for effective cross-cultural communication.

Cultural imperialism Criticism by some that the United States is forcing its products and culture on other cultures through technological advances and the globalization of business.

Cultural relativism The belief that no culture's ethics are any better than any other's.

Cultural-toughness dimension Through a battery of tests, an assessor determines if an applicant for an expatriate assignment has the ability to adapt to the "toughness" of a specific culture.

Culture Comprises an entire set of social norms and responses that condition people's behavior; it is acquired and inculcated, a set of rules and behavior patterns that an individual learns but does not inherit at birth.

Culture-free A theory proposing that managerial behavior is affected by specific situations in all cultures.

Culture shock What expatriates experience after the novelty of living in a new culture wears out.

Culture shock phase The third phase in the expatriation process usually begins two months into the disillusionment phase. After two months of day-to-day confusion, the expatriate faces culture shock and wishes to go back to his or her old, familiar environment.

Culture-specific A theory proposing that managerial behavior is affected by a nation's culture.

Currency exchange rates Countries' currency exchange rates fluctuate. Fluctuations can be dirty or clean. Dirty fluctuations result when a government adjusts the exchange rate up or down. Clean fluctuations are the result of supply and demand.

Customer satisfaction An important measure of quality.

Customization Products are modified to fit the needs of specific markets.

Cybernetic system A system that enables corporations to monitor and coordinate the activities of its subsidiaries around the globe.

D

Decentralization Managers at the subsidiary are given the autonomy to make most of the important decisions relative to local matters.

Delay tactics Another form of leverage. A pause, or delay, by one party during a negotiation may make the other party overly anxious, causing them to make concessions. A delay tactic also allows a negotiator time to rest, recuperate, assess progress, obtain other information, and reformulate strategy.

Diffusion of innovation The process by which innovation is communicated through certain channels over time among members of a social system.

Direct exporting The firm produces at home and creates a division to export to foreign markets.

Disillusionment phase Beginning two months into the expatriation process, the novelty of the new culture wears out, and day-to-day inconveniences caused by different practices in the local culture along with the inability to communicate effectively create disillusionment for the expatriate.

Domestic enterprises Companies that derive all of their revenues from their home market.

Domestic environment Home country factors, including the political, competitive, economic, and legal and governmental climates, affect the enterprise.

Double taxation The situation in which an expatriate is taxed by both the home-country and host-country governments. In some cases the firm will pay for the over-taxation.

Dual translation Using an interpreter in a country to translate a sender's message into a foreign language and then using an interpreter in the foreign country to translate the message back into the sender's language.

Dumping The practice by an MNC of selling a product in a foreign market at a price lower than the price for which it sells the product in its own market and/or below production cost with the intent to eliminate its competition.

E

Economic environment The way in which people of a society manage their material wealth and the results of their management.

Emotions Even though behavior in business and negotiations is mainly intuitive, it should never be judgmental. To be able to listen to other negotiators, one should exclude his or her subjective opinions, preconceptions, or emotional filters. It is important to prevent emotions from controlling negotiations.

Empowerment Giving individuals or groups in the organization the decision-making power necessary to make effective and efficient decisions in their respective units.

Environmental contexts See *Cross-cultural communication.*

Ethical What members of a given society generally accept as being "right."

Ethnocentric staffing outlook The belief that key positions in foreign subsidiaries should be staffed by citizens from the parent company's home country.

Ethnocentric strategy Companies produce unique goods and services that they offer primarily to their domestic market, and when they export, they do not modify the product or service for foreign consumption.

Expatriate A home-country national, usually an employee of the firm, who is sent abroad to manage a foreign subsidiary.

Expatriation program Takes place while the expatriate is working in the foreign operations; certain delivery and communications programs are required.

Expropriation The seizure by a government of foreign-owned assets with prompt, adequate, and effective compensation.

External audit A company's management becoming familiar with the domestic, international, and foreign factors that affect its business activities.

External collaboration See *External cooperation.*

External cooperation To be more effective and efficient, a firm focuses on what it can do best, and forms an alliance with other firms to obtain the additional organizational capabilities needed to be more effective and efficient than their competitors.

Extortion An official in a foreign country in a position of power seeking payment from an individual or corporation for an action to which the individual or corporation may be lawfully entitled.

F

Fatalism A view that individuals cannot control their destiny, that God has predetermined the course of their life.

Five stages of national economic development A theory proposing that nations advance from an agricultural economy to an advanced industrial economy in five stages.

Flat structures Structures should be as flat as possible. That is, they should have fewer managerial layers than traditional hierarchical organizations.

The Foreign Corrupt Practices Act An established U.S. code of conduct making it illegal for United States businesses to bribe foreign government officials, political parties, and political candidates, even if it is an acceptable practice in the foreign country; requires appropriate accounting controls for full disclosure of firms' foreign transactions.

Foreign environment Refers to factors in a country that affect international business, including the country's cultural, legal, political, competitive, economic, and technological systems.

Foreign investment Many countries' laws dictate that foreign investments in their nation must be in the form of a joint venture with local partners and that the local partners must be majority owners.

Foreign subsidiary An international firm's operating unit established in foreign countries. It typically has its own management structure.

Formalization Represents decision making through bureaucratic mechanisms such as formal systems, established rules, and prescribed procedures.

Functional structure Product knowledge is centered in manufacturing, engineering, and marketing, and each is responsible for both domestic and international activities.

G

General Agreement on Tariffs and Trade, now called World Trade Organization A 124-nation organization that provides the conditions under which a nation can impose trade barriers such as tariffs. The new World Trade Organization was created to settle trade disputes.

Geocentric staffing outlook Holds that nationality should not make any difference in the assignment of key positions anywhere (local subsidiary, regional headquarters, or central headquarters); that competence should be the prime criterion for selecting managerial staff.

Global corporate culture Corporate core values that cut across all of a firm's subsidiaries located around the globe.

Global corporations International businesses that view the world as their marketplace.

Global manager An international executive with the ability to manage enterprises in diverse cultures.

Global mind-set In today's global environment, even for employees who may not go abroad, it is necessary to constantly sensitize everyone to the notion that the company is in a global business.

Global strategy A corporation using this strategy uses all of its resources against its competition in a very integrated fashion—all of its foreign subsidiaries and divisions are highly interdependent in both operations and strategy.

Globalization The notion that in the future more and more companies will have to conduct their business activities in a highly interconnected world, thus presenting their managements with the challenge of re-engineering their systems to cope with this new environment.

Goodwill What international corporations create when they share with locals the benefits derived from the markets they exploit.

Government policies Extreme social and economic conditions may sometimes force a political party into radical policy changes. Generally, however, governments change their policies gradually; they implement new policies to attract the foreign investments needed by the nation to attain its economic development objectives.

Guanxi A major dynamic of the Chinese society that refers to the special relationship two people have with each other. The two that share this relationship assume that each is committed to the other, and that they have agreed to exchange favors, even when official commands mandate that they act neutrally.

H

Hard currencies Money that is readily acceptable as payment in international business transactions—usually the currencies of industrially advanced countries.

High-context cultures In the course of business, participants establish social trust first, value personal relations and goodwill, make agreements on the basis of general trust, and like to conduct slow and ritualistic business negotiations.

Hinayana One of two main sects of Buddhism, *Hinayana* stresses the importance of self-restraint.

Horizontal promotions Instead of slowly climbing the organizational ladder, workers and managers make lateral movements, acquiring expertise in different functions such as marketing or manufacturing.

Host-country national A resident of the country where the firm's subsidiary is located, or will be located, employed to manage the operations.

I

I-Ching A Chinese philosophy that emphasizes that as social beings, people must deal with social responsibilities throughout their lives, and the greatest social welfare is achieved through the joint efforts of individuals creating better social and physical environments. In these environments others can actualize their capacities, and greater value is placed on the ability to lead individuals and groups to cooperative output than on the actualization of one's individual talent.

Implementor A type of leader who takes a newly initiated vision and systematically puts into operation the desired changes.

Indirect exporting The firm manufactures at home and employs a middle person to export its product(s) to foreign markets.

Individualism Refers to the degree to which people in a society look after primarily their own interests or belong to and depend on "in-groups."

Informal integration Allowing a foreign subsidiary to adopt the corporation's global vision, core values, and cultural principles in its own way. That is, the corporation's central management does not formally force these on the foreign subsidiaries; rather it listens to people at the local level and communicates with them.

Information-based services The provision of these services involves collecting, manipulating, interpreting, and transmitting data to create value. Examples include such services as accounting, banking, consulting, education, insurance, legal services, and news.

Inhwa Influences South Korean business behavior; stresses harmony; links people who are unequal in rank, prestige, and power; and stresses loyalty to hierarchical rankings and superiors' concern for the well-being of subordinates.

Initial phase The first phase in the expatriation process. When the expatriate transfers to the foreign assignment, the newness of the culture creates a great deal of excitement for him or her.

Innovator A type of leader who identifies new ideas and visions and "sells" them to the institution.

Internal audit A company's management becoming familiar with the firm's ability to implement a strategy aimed at coping with external demands.

Internal collaboration See *Internal cooperation.*

Internal cooperation The organization develops an internal environment where there is downward, upward, and horizontal communication, as well as a focal point to coordinate the communication, for the purpose of making effective and efficient decisions.

International corporations International businesses that produce products in their home country and export to other countries.

International division A unit established to supervise a firm's exports, foreign distribution agreements, foreign sales forces, foreign sales branches, and foreign subsidiaries.

International environment Refers to groupings of nations (such as the European Union), worldwide bodies (such as the World Bank), and organizations of nations by industry (such as the Organization of Petroleum Exporting Countries).

International human resource management function Consists of interplay among three dimensions: the broad function, country categories, and types of employees.

International labor relations The management of an MNC interacting with organized labor units in each country.

International organizational structures The firm's organizational structure is its "skeleton"; it provides support and ties together disparate functions.

International pricing A managerial decision about what to charge for goods produced in one nation and sold in another.

International product life cycle (IPLC) A theory that many products that are exported to foreign countries are eventually produced abroad, and that foreign producers subsequently obtain a competitive edge over the original producers, forcing them to either create a new product or go out of business.

International relocation and orientation The making of arrangements for predeparture training, immigration and travel details, and finalizing compensation details between the expatriate and the home country.

ISO 9000 Requires each enterprise to define and document its own quality process and provide evidence of their implementation. ISO stands for International Organization for Standardization.

J

Jidka A team orientation practiced in Japanese organizations referred to as total quality control (TQC).

Joint-ventures Two or more firms that band together to establish operations in foreign markets in order to capitalize on each other's resources and reduce risk.

K

Keiretsu Japanese giant industrial groups linked by cross-ownership.

L

Labor laws Laws in many countries provide extensive security for workers and make it extremely expensive to terminate an employee.

Language translator Fluent in both languages being used in a cross-cultural communication, translators help eliminate the verbal and nonverbal communication barriers.

Legal environment Includes rules of competition, packaging laws, patents, trademarks, copyright laws and practices, labor laws, and contract enforcement.

Less-developed country A country with a less diversified economy, a lower than average gross national product, and a lower than average per capita income.

Leverage Generally refers to the power you have in a negotiation. in negotiations, the more leverage (options) you have, the more concessions your opponent will have to make.

Linear cultures View the past as being behind them and the future in front of them; they view change as good and attempt to take advantage of business opportunities that they foresee.

Low-context cultures In the conduct of business, participants get down to business quickly, value expertise and performance, like agreement by specific, legalistic contract, and like to conduct business negotiations as efficiently as possible.

Lubrication bribes A payment made to an official to facilitate, expedite, and speed up routine government approvals or other actions to which the firm would be legally entitled.

M

Mahayana One of two main sects of Buddhism, *Mahayana* stresses selfless devotion to society.

Masculinity Refers to the degree to which people in a society stress material success and assertiveness and assign different roles to males and females.

Master of destiny A view that individuals can substantially influence their future, that they control their destiny, and through hard work they can make things happen.

Material possessions Individuals in some cultures equate success with material wealth. However, individuals in many cultures place relatively little importance on material possessions and view the flaunting of wealth as disrespectful.

Matrix structure This structure is strongly decentralized: it allows local subsidiaries to develop products that fit into local markets. And yet at its core, it is very centralized; it allows companies to coordinate activities across the globe and capitalize on synergies and economies of scale.

MBO In this approach, the manager and subordinate meet, and together set objectives for the subordinate.

Mechanistic organization Roles and objectives are clearly and rigidly outlined for employees—managers and subordinates are allowed little or no discretion. Historically, large organizations have tended to adopt the mechanistic form.

Mediators In some situations within cultures, it is not wise to send messages directly to the receiver(s); it is wise to use a mediator. The encoder sends the message to a mediator (a third party), who in turn conveys it to the receiver(s).

Monetary barriers Sometimes employed by governments to restrict trade, reduce competition, or encourage certain imports. Monetary barriers occur when governments sell foreign currencies needed to pay for undesired imports at a higher rate than the one charged for currencies needed to pay for desired imports.

Multicultural centers Some countries, such as the United States, are multicultural centers. These countries' residents came from many parts of the world and maintain much of their former country's culture.

Multicultural team Teams whose members represent diverse views and come from varied cultures.

Multidimensional development The ninth stage in the social interaction paradigm is characterized by "stepping aside," that is, leaving an important position and distributing political and economic power across private and public sectors.

Multidomestic strategy Unlike companies that apply an ethnocentric strategy, firms that apply a multidomestic strategy use a different strategy for each of their foreign markets.

Multinational corporations International businesses that establish subsidiaries in foreign markets.

N

National-culture scheme Proposes that HSRs are affected by national cultural dimensions.

Nationalization Occurs when a government takes over private property—reasonable compensation is usually paid by the government.

Nemawashi A Japanese term borrowed from gardening. In business terms, it means many private or semiprivate meetings in which true opinions are shared before a major decision-making meeting takes place.

Network A system in which everyone is linked and interconnected and where there is a free exchange of ideas and data.

Networks Similar to the contractual alliance arrangement, a corporation subcontracts its manufacturing functions to other companies.

Nonprogrammed decision making Entails analyzing current data and information, which was obtained through a systematic investigation of the current environment, for the purpose of identifying and solving a problem.

Nontariff barriers Sometimes employed by governments to restrict trade or reduce competition. Nontariff barriers occur when governments impose restrictive and costly administrative and legal requirements on imports.

Normative integration The headquarters-foreign subsidiary control relationship relies neither on direct headquarters involvement nor on impersonal rules but on the socialization of managers into a set of shared goals, values, and beliefs that then shape their perspectives and behavior.

O

Open criticism A style of Chinese management in which the practice of public scolding *(ma ren)* is used frequently. Represents the Chinese view that the practice of quiet, subtle criticism is sneaky and therefore all communication, including criticism, should take place in the open.

Organic organization Allows employees considerable discretion in defining their roles and the organization's objectives. Historically, small organizations have tended to adopt the organic form.

Organizational culture The pattern of basic assumptions that a given group has invented, discovered, or developed in learning to cope with its problems of external adaptation and internal integration; having worked well enough to be considered valid, the pattern may therefore be taught to new members as the correct way to perceive, think, and feel in relation to those problems.

Overcentralization Expatriates are unable to establish and maintain an effective relationship with local associates because their authority is constrained by headquarters management overcentralizing decision making.

P

Pacifier-oriented leader The type of leader needed in an organization that has achieved a certain level of stability and in which daily operations are running smoothly.

Participation Involving employees in the decision-making process.

Participative decision making Refers to making decisions after consulting others. This style of decision making is perceived negatively in many cultures and causes the decision maker to lose credibility in the eyes of subordinates.

Payoffs Illegal payments made abroad by MNCs to foreign government officials and politicians in the course of conducting business.

People-processing services In these services, customers become part of the production process. Such services include passenger transportation, health care, food services, and lodging services.

Performance-based pay Pay related to and directly derived from performance.

Personnel competencies The ability of a firm's personnel to implement its strategy to internationalize its operations.

Place/entry strategy Managers of business enterprises must determine how their products or services will reach the consumer. Distribution methods generally require variations from country to country as well as within each country.

PM theory of leadership A Japanese leadership theory; the P stands for showing a concern for subordinates and leadership that is oriented toward forming and reaching group goals; the M stands for leadership that is oriented toward preserving group stability.

Political environment A nation's political system, government policies, attitude toward the product, and management of scarce foreign exchange.

Political systems The types of political system—one-party, two-party, or multi-party—affects the level of stability and consistency in governmental policies as it relates to business.

Polycentric staffing outlook The belief that key positions in foreign subsidiaries should be staffed by host-country nationals (locals).

Positive adjustment phase Beginning at about month four of the expatriation phase, the expatriate begins to adapt, and by about month six of the assignment, the expatriate feels more positive about the foreign environment; in this phase, he or she will attain neither the "high" of the first phase nor the "low" of the second or third phases.

Possession-processing services Services of this nature involve tangible actions to tangible objects to enhance their value to customers. The customer may not be present. These services include transporting freight and installing and maintaining equipment.

Power distance Refers to the degree to which people in a society accept centralized power and depend on superiors for structure and direction.

Practices Cultural foundations of organizational behavior, including symbols, heroes, and rituals, and values.

Pre-expatriation program Once the expatriate has been selected for the foreign assignment, but before leaving the home country, he or she is involved in certain training to prepare for what will be encountered in the foreign country.

Presentation principles Those principles governing verbal and nonverbal communication that are applicable when making a presentation to a foreign audience.

Price strategy Some firms are influenced by the view that pricing is an active tool by which to accomplish their marketing objectives, while some are influenced by the belief that price is a static element in business decisions.

Primary audience In the communication process, those who receive a message directly.

Primary research To secure first-hand information about the environment.

Product division structure Each of the enterprise's product divisions is responsible for the sale and profits of its product.

Product/service strategy Managers are typically concerned with that the product or service should look like and what it should be able to do. In foreign markets, they must determine whether their product or service can be sold in standard form or be customized to fit differing foreign market needs.

Programmed decision making Making decisions based on precedent, custom, policies and procedures, and on training and development.

Promotion strategy Problems related to international promotion strategy include the legal aspects of the country, tax considerations, language complexities, cultural diversity, media limitations, credibility of advertising, and degree of illiteracy.

Psychocultural contexts See *Cross-cultural communication.*

Q

Quality Refers to products/services that meet or exceed consumers' expectations at the lowest cost possible.

R

Regiocentric staffing outlook The belief that key positions at the regional headquarters should be staffed by individuals from one of the region's countries.

Regional structure An international corporate structure wherein regional heads are made responsible for specific territories, usually consisting of multiple countries, such as Europe, East Asia, and South America.

Religion Different societies develop different religious systems, which are major causes of cultural differences in many societies. Religious systems provide motivation and meaning beyond the material aspects of life.

Repatriation Reassigning the expatriate to his or her home.

Repatriation program Programs that assist the returning expatriate in readjusting to the home country's environment. Attempts to alleviate the effects of reverse culture shock.

Respect-oriented leadership Prevalent in China, Japan, Korea, Singapore, and Turkey; characterized by avoiding confrontation, displaying patience, listening to others, and avoiding losing face.

Reverse culture shock What expatriates experience upon returning home after a long assignment in a foreign country.

Reverse engineering Learning to reproduce technology by taking it apart to determine how it works and then copying it.

Ringi A group-oriented participative decision-making technique used in many Japanese organizations.

Risk exposure Possible terrorism in a foreign country, especially in countries where some groups hold hostile feelings toward "capitalists," or where there is a high possibility of the expatriate being kidnapped for ransom.

S

Scanning system A system that enables corporations to monitor the activities taking place in markets around the globe for the purpose of responding to changing market needs.

Secondary audience In the communication process, those who do not receive a message directly, but who will hear about the message, need to participate in the decision-making, or are affected by the message.

Secondary research Uses information that was gathered through primary research by other organizations.

Self-reference criterion The unconscious reference to one's cultural values.

Sequential oral interpreters Used by clients involved in cross-language business negotiations and social functions. Unlike simultaneous oral interpreters, they translate both language and culture.

Settlement range A phase of strategic planning in which a negotiation range (all possible settlements that a negotiator would be willing to take) must be established. During this phase, the LAR (least acceptable result) and MSP (most supportable position) must be identified.

Sign A signal that is recognized, structured into a category, and assigned meaning.

Signal Transmitted by a sender to a receiver; the receiver must decode and try to understand the signal.

Signified The meaning attached to the signifier.

Signifier The sound or shape of the signal that is sensorially perceived without meaning yet attached to it.

Simultaneous oral interpreters Used by speakers in formal situations such as conferences, where the audience and the speaker communicate using different languages.

Situational scheme Proposes that certain situational factors influence the HSR in all countries.

Social altruism An individual's major concern is the functioning of society. He or she acts to generate vital long-term benefits for others without the want or need to acquire rewards for him or herself.

Social awareness Understanding human/societal needs outside one's own individual-based ends furnishes a base for interorganizational cooperative behavior and for molding effective strategies to merge human endeavors to solve difficult problems.

Social contribution Refers to the mixture of striving to fulfill other people's needs while simultaneously pursuing one's own growth and social power.

Social interaction paradigm Used to explain the inherent cooperative culture behind the economic success of the Pacific Rim economies; extends the hierarchy of needs beyond the self-actualization model.

Social responsibility The notion that corporations have an obligation to constituent groups in society other than stockholders and beyond that prescribed by law or union contract.

Socially unacceptable and unacceptable Standards or practices determined by each individual culture such that what is acceptable in one culture might be unacceptable in another.

Sociocultural contexts See *Cross-cultural communication.*

Soft currencies Refers to money that is not readily acceptable in international business transactions—usually the currencies of industrially less-advanced countries and of communist countries.

Southeast Asian management The basis of an opposing theory to Theory X and Y known as Theory T and T+,representing two styles and attitudes found to be prevalent in Southeast Asian countries.

Stage of subsidiary development Traditionally, MNCs have staffed foreign subsidiaries with expatriates in the early stages of establishing operations in the foreign country. In the later stages, at least at the lower levels, host-country nationals are employed.

Standardization Products sold unchanged or only slightly changed in all markets.

Stereotypes Generalizations about a particular culture and its members.Normally simple or brief, these are statements that characterize an entire group, culture, or its members. For example, "Americans are efficiency-oriented" or "The French are rude to non-French-speaking visitors."

Strategic alliance Two or more companies band together to attain efficiency (see *joint venture*).

Strategic objectives Guided by the enterprise's mission or purpose, they associate the enterprise with its external environment and provide management with a basis for comparing performance with that of its competitors, in relation to environmental demands.

Subsidiary A subunit of a business entity established in a foreign country for the purpose of serving that market or other markets, including the business entity's home-country market.

T

Tactical objectives Guided by the enterprise's strategic objectives, they identify the key result areas in which specific performance is essential for the success of the enterprise, and aim to attain internal efficiency.

Tariffs and quotas Often employed by governments to restrict trade or reduce competition. Tariffs are a form of tax imposed on incoming goods, and quotas specify the number of foreign units that can be imported.

Team culture See *culture*, as it pertains to teams.

Teams Many organizations manage themselves through empowered self-managed teams.

Theory T and Theory T+ Complementary theories based on Southeast Asian assumptions that work is a necessity but not a goal itself, people should find their rightful place in peace and harmony with their environment; absolute objectives exist only with God; in the world, persons in authority positions represent God, so their objectives should be followed; and people behave as members of a family and/or group, and those who do not are rejected by society.

Third-country national A resident of a country other than the home-country or host-country assigned to manage a firm's foreign subsidiary.

Time equals money The perception of people in some cultures that time is a commodity and an asset and high importance is placed on it.

Total quality management (TQM) A style of management with a long-term commitment to the ongoing improvement of quality throughout the whole system.

Trade barriers Imposed by nations to limit or restrict competition.

Transformative technological innovations Replace traditional technologies (in farming, a tractor replaces the plow).

Transnational strategy See *global strategy.*

U

Ubuntu An African thought system that stresses a high degree of harmony and emphasizes unity of the whole, rather than its distinct parts.

Uncertainty avoidance The extent to which people in a society tolerate uncertainty and ambiguity.

Unethical What members of the society generally accept as being "wrong."

United States Foreign Corrupt Practices Act (FCPA) Makes it illegal for U.S. citizens and businesses to practice bribery in the conduct of business not only in the U.S. but in other countries as well, even when it is an acceptable or expected business practice there.

Universal factors framework Identifies various universal situations and their impact on DMB (decision-making behavior).

Universalism A rigid global yardstick by which to measure all moral issues.

V

Value Refers to the usefulness, desirability, and worth of a product, object, or thing.

Values A company's vision, objective, and philosophy as communicated to employees and the public worldwide. National values include good/evil, beautiful/ugly, normal/abnormal, and rational/irrational. Values vary from corporation to corporation, and national values vary from country to country.

Virtual teams Groups of geographically and/or organizationally dispersed co-workers who are assembled using a combination of telecommunications and information technologies to accomplish an organizational task.

Visible pay inequity Visible pay inequity between the expatriates and their local peers could demoralize the foreign subsidiary's staff.

W

Wa A Japanese concept that necessitates that members of a group, be it in a work team, or a company, or a nation, cooperate with and trust each other.

Whitemail bribery Payments made to induce an official in a foreign country who is in a position of power to give favorable treatment where such treatment is either illegal or not warranted on an efficiency or economic benefit scale.

Wholly-owned subsidiary The firm establishes a subsidiary in a foreign country maintaining 100 percent ownership; unlike joint ventures, risks are not shared.

Written principles Those principles governing language and behavior that must be transmitted when sending a written message across cultures.

Index